Management Innov Healthcare Organizations

"This book executes on a remarkably good idea: reviewing the usefulness for healthcare delivery organizations of popular management techniques and innovations. By inviting leading organizational researchers to write chapters on individual topics, the editors have compiled a truly useful handbook of relevant research for healthcare leaders. Each chapter provides a clear and well-researched description of a particular management innovation before examining its fit with healthcare. The resulting volume is both thorough and useful".
—*Amy C. Edmondson, Harvard Business School*

"This is a text that effectively brings together current healthcare issues, leadership theories, strategies and concerns".
—*Leslie King, Franklin University*

"In today's complex and fast-paced healthcare environment, managers need a resource that helps to challenge and redefine current thinking and to encourage innovative solutions to some of health's wicked problems. *Management Innovations for Healthcare Organizations: Adopt, Abandon or Adapt?* is a timely text for all healthcare managers and leaders to encourage critical reflection on change and innovation. With recent major inquiries into health system failures pointing to healthcare organizations taking their focus off of the patient, it is indeed pleasing to see chapters emphasizing values-based healthcare, servant leadership, corporate social responsibility, decentralized healthcare and empowerment in healthcare organizations. Managers need constant challenges to improve practice and systems and this book provides that challenge. A must-have for every health managers library".
—*Gary E. Day, Griffith University*

Innovations in management are becoming more numerous and diverse, and are appearing in organizations that provide many different kinds of products and services. The purpose of this book is to examine whether some widely promoted examples of these management innovations—ranging from techniques such as *Kaizen* to styles of leadership and the management of learning—can usefully be applied to organizations that provide healthcare, and applied in different kinds of health systems. This book is distinctive in selecting a wide and diverse range and selection of managerial innovations to examine. No less distinctively, it makes an adaptive, critical scrutiny of these innovations. Neither evangelist nor nihilist, the book instead considers how these innovations might be adapted for the specific task of providing healthcare. Where evidence on these points is available, the book outlines that, too. Consequently, the book takes an international approach, with contributions from Europe, the Middle East, Australia and North America. Each contributor is an expert in the management innovation that he or she presents. This combination of features makes the book unique.

Anders Örtenblad is Professor of Organization and Leadership at the University of Nordland, Bodø, Norway.

Carina Abrahamson Löfström is a Researcher at the Gothenburg Region Association of Local Authorities, Sweden.

Rod Sheaff is Professor of Health Services Research at Plymouth University, UK.

Routledge Studies in the Management of Voluntary and Non-Profit Organizations

Series Editor: Stephen P. Osborne (University of Edinburgh, UK)

This series presents innovative work grounded in new realities, addressing issues crucial to an understanding of the contemporary world. This is the world of organized societies, where boundaries between formal and informal, public and private, local and global organizations have been displaced or have vanished, along with other nineteenth-century dichotomies and oppositions. Management, apart from becoming a specialized profession for a growing number of people, is an everyday activity for most members of modern societies.

Similarly, at the level of enquiry, culture and technology and literature and economics can no longer be conceived as isolated intellectual fields; the conventional canons and established mainstreams are being contested. Management, Organization and Society addresses these contemporary dynamics of transformation in a manner that transcends disciplinary boundaries, with books that will appeal to researchers, students and practitioners alike.

Management Innovations for Healthcare Organizations

Adopt, Abandon or Adapt?

Edited by Anders Örtenblad, Carina Abrahamson Löfström and Rod Sheaff

Routledge
Taylor & Francis Group

LONDON AND NEW YORK

First published 2016 by Routledge

2 Park Square, Milton Park, Abingdon, Oxfordshire OX14 4RN
711 Third Avenue, New York, NY 10017

Routledge is an imprint of the Taylor & Francis Group, an informa business

First issued in paperback 2018

Library of Congress Cataloging-in-Publication Data
Names: Ortenblad, Anders. | Lofstrom, Carina Abrahamson. | Sheaff, Rod.
Title: Management innovations for healthcare organizations : adopt, abandon
   or adapt? / edited by Anders Ortenblad, Carina Abrahamson Lofstrom, and
   Rod Sheaff.
Description: New York : Routledge, 2015. | Series: Routledge studies in the
   management of voluntary and non-profit organizations ; 18 | Includes
   bibliographical references and index.
Identifiers: LCCN 2015029502
Subjects: LCSH: Health services administration. | Medical informatics—
   Management. | Organizational change.
Classification: LCC RA971 .M3427 2015 | DDC 610.68—dc23 LC record
   available at http://lccn.loc.gov/2015029502

ISBN: 978-1-138-82569-7 (hbk)
ISBN: 978-1-138-61760-5 (pbk)

Typeset in Sabon
by Apex CoVantage, LLC

Contents

PART III
Conclusions and Future Research

Tables and Figures

TABLES

FIGURES

Contributor Presentations

Carina Abrahamson Löfström is a Researcher at the Gothenburg Region Association of Local Authorities and has a PhD in business administration from University of Gothenburg, Sweden. Her research interests are learning and change in public sector organizations, subjects on which she has published several books, reports and book chapters.

Nora Ahmad is currently an Assistant Professor on the Faculty of Health Studies at Brandon University, Canada. She holds a doctorate degree in nursing from the University of Sheffield, UK. She has over 22 years' experience in the nursing profession, and has published articles in several peer-reviewed journals.

Marie Carney, Associate Professor of Nursing, is currently Dean of the Faculty of Nursing and Midwifery at the Royal College of Surgeons in Ireland. She holds a doctorate degree in management from the Smurfit Business School at University College Dublin. She previously held the position of Head of the School of Nursing, Midwifery and Health Systems at UCD.

Mark Exworthy, Professor of Health Policy and Management at the Health Services Management Centre, University of Birmingham, has research interests in decentralization in healthcare, the impact of managerialism upon professionals in healthcare organizations and governance issues. He has published widely on all these topics.

Ewan Ferlie is Professor of Public Services Management at King's College London. He has published widely on restructuring and organizational change in healthcare. He is co-editor of *The Oxford Handbook of Public Management* and co-author of a monograph on business process reengineering in healthcare, also published by Oxford University Press.

Bettina Fiery, EdD, RN, ACC, presides over diverse organizational development initiatives at the American Public University System and works in concert with colleagues to ensure an active linkage between the organization's strategic plan, leadership development, talent management, employee engagement and change management.

Elin K. Funck is Associate Professor in Management Accounting at the School of Business and Economics, Linnaeus University, Sweden. Her research focuses on behavioral aspects of management accounting, primarily in the public healthcare sector. Her recent studies have focused on how instruments for control influence and are influenced by the context they are implemented in.

Thomas N. Garavan is Research Professor of Leadership at Edinburgh Napier Business School, Edinburgh Napier University. He is currently editor-in-chief of the *Journal of European and Industrial Training* and associate editor of *Personnel Review*. He is an editorial board member of the *Human Resource Development Review*, the *Human Resource Development Quarterly* and the *Human Resource Management Journal*.

Mark Graban, a consultant and speaker for health systems, is author of the book *Lean Hospitals* and is co-author of *Healthcare Kaizen*. Mark has a BS in industrial engineering from Northwestern University and an MS in mechanical engineering and an MBA from the Massachusetts Institute of Technology's Leaders for Global Operations Program.

Raj Gururajan is a Professor of Information Systems at the University of Southern Queensland, Australia. He focuses much of his research within the health informatics domain and has a very successful record of securing large grants as well as having many publications in this area.

Andreas Hellström is a Senior Lecturer in the Department of Technology Management and Economics at Chalmers University of Technology, Sweden and co-director of Centre for Healthcare Improvement—a center focusing on quality improvement, innovation and transformation in healthcare. In 2013, he was one of four selected in the first cohort of Vinnvård's Improvement Scientist Fellows.

Tony Huzzard is a Professor in Organization Theory in the Department of Business Administration at Lund University. He has researched and published widely on organizational learning, change and development, industrial relations and the sociology of work. He has been a visiting professor at the Centre for Health Care Improvement, Chalmers University of Technology in Gothenburg since 2011.

Michaela Kolbe leads Research and Development at the Simulation Center of the University Hospital of Zurich and holds a PhD in psychology. Her current research interests include the dynamics and promotion of "speaking up", after-action reviews in the clinical setting and advanced debriefing techniques for simulation-based team trainings.

Jacob Krive, PhD, is Clinical Assistant Professor at the University of Illinois at Chicago, Adjunct Assistant Professor at Nova Southeastern University and Project Manager at Valence Health. His research interests are in clinical decision support, project management, medical documentation and economics of health informatics. His healthcare industry experience includes leadership roles in provider and technology organizations.

Grigorios L. Kyriakopoulos completed 16 academic qualifications, ranging from CertsHE to postdoc, in business management, chemical engineering, education, energy, environment, Hellenic civilization, human resource management, psychology (counseling therapy). He is a reviewer at over 50 scientific journals and conferences. Dr. Kyriakopoulos is currently a Teaching and Research Associate at the School of Electrical and Computer Engineering (National Technical University of Athens).

Svante Lifvergren, MD, PhD, has worked as a senior physician since 1997 and is currently the quality director at the Skaraborg Hospital Group. He also serves as co-director for the Centre for Healthcare Improvement at Chalmers University of Technology. He is a member of the editorial board for the SAGE *Action Research* journal.

Gerri Matthews-Smith is a Senior Lecturer and Subject Group Leader for the Enduring Conditions and Community Care Team. Her research interests are in evidence-based practice. Her doctoral studies investigated the development of evidence-based practice in health. She has been published in a number of international healthcare journals and has participated in the development of the SIGN Guidelines.

Jack T. McCann, PhD, is an Associate Professor of Marketing and Management at Tusculum College in Greeneville, Tennessee and is the former dean of the School of Business at Lincoln Memorial University in Harrogate, TN. He is also an adjunct professor of business at Kaplan University. He teaches courses in management, marketing and strategy.

Joan F. Miller, PhD, RN, is Professor Emeritus in the Department of Nursing at Bloomsburg University, Bloomsburg, PA. Her research interests include the meaning of *good work* in healthcare settings and ways 360-degree evaluation can promote *good work*, or work that is excellent, ethical and engaging. She has spoken internationally and published on the subject of *good work* in peer- reviewed journals.

Ali M. Mosadeghrad is an Assistant Professor of Health Policy, Management and Economics at the School of Public Health at Tehran University of Medical Sciences. He received his PhD from the University of London. He is an author, speaker and a professional quality management consultant. His research interests include strategic quality management and organizational change in the health sector.

Nelson Ositadimma Oranye is currently an Assistant Professor at the College of Rehabilitation Sciences at the University of Manitoba, Canada. He holds a PhD in demography, and an MBA in management. He has taught at universities in Nigeria and Malaysia, and published articles in several peer-reviewed nursing and other journals.

Anders Örtenblad is Professor of Organization and Leadership at the University of Nordland, Bodø, Norway. He has edited volumes on the contextualization of fashionable management ideas in general, as well as of the following fashionable management ideas: The *Learning Organization*, *Knowledge Management* and *Corporate Social Responsibility*. All four volumes of his work are published by Edward Elgar Publishing.

Anjali Patwardhan (MD, MRCPCH, MRCPI, MSc in healthcare policy and quality, MBA, in information assurance from Harvard) is an Assistant Professor and Chief of Pediatric Rheumatology in the Department of Pediatrics at the University of Missouri School of Medicine. She is also the Director of Operational Quality at the University of Missouri, USA.

Drew Patwardhan (MEng MBA, Six Sigma Black Belt) is currently working as a Quality Manager at GE Healthcare, USA.

Prakash Patwardhan (BEng MBA) works as a Senior Quality Director at Medtronic, USA. Prakash believes that you can rent a person's back and hands, but that you must earn their head and heart to lead change or drive improvement.

D. David Persaud is a Professor in the School of Health Administration at Dalhousie University. He received his PhD from the Institute of Health Policy, Management and Evaluation at the University of Toronto. His research interests are in continuous organizational learning, innovation and sustainability, as well as the types of leadership necessary to enhance these outcomes.

Bozena Poksinska is Associate Professor at the Division of Logistics and Quality Management at Linköping University in Sweden. Her research focuses on quality management in the manufacturing and service industries. In recent years, she carried out research on the adoption of Lean in healthcare in Sweden. She also teaches quality management, Lean production and Six Sigma.

Marie-Pascale Pomey, MD, PhD, is a Professor in the School of Public of Health at the University of Montréal. She is the director of a master's program in quality and safety in healthcare. Her research interest focuses on the evaluation of quality and safety programs, on the impact of accreditation systems on health institutions and on patient involvement at the different levels of the healthcare system.

Martin Powell is Professor of Health and Social Policy at the Health Services Management Centre at the University of Birmingham. He has research interests in historical and contemporary perspectives on health policy, and has co-authored a number of pieces with Mark Exworthy on decentralization, implementation and health inequalities.

Jan Schmutz is a Researcher and Lecturer at the Swiss Federal Institute of Technology in Zurich, Switzerland (ETH Zurich) and has a PhD in industrial and organizational psychology. His research interests include human factors, and in particular, team processes in high-risk industries. He has published several articles in peer-reviewed journals in the fields of medicine and psychology.

Rod Sheaff is Professor of Health Services Research at Plymouth University, UK and a founding member of the South West Peninsula Collaboration for Leadership and Health Research in Care. His main research interest is in the relationship between organizational structures and the implementation of health policy, which he has studied in a number of countries. He is trained, and has worked, as a National Health Service manager.

Dawid Szescilo is a Doctor of Law and an Assistant Professor at the Public Administration Research Unit at the University of Warsaw. He was a visiting fellow at the Vienna University of Economics and Business (2014–2015). He is also an expert in OECD Sigma on public administration reform. His research interests focus on market-based mechanisms of public service delivery and the co-production of public services.

Sherif Adel Zaki Tehemar is an Associate Professor in the Oral and Maxillofacial Surgery Department and is a member of the faculty of dentistry at the Alexandria and Misr International Universities in Egypt. He is also the Chairman of the Development and Improvement Department at Misr International University, and is a CSR and Healthcare Management Consultant.

Annalena Welp is a Researcher and PhD student at the University of Fribourg, Switzerland. She holds a master's degree in work and organizational psychology from the University of Tilburg in the Netherlands. Her research focuses on the interplay between teamwork, employee well-being and patient safety in healthcare settings.

Nilmini Wickramasinghe (PhD, MBA, Grad DipMgtSt, BSc) is the Professor Director of Health Informatics Management at Epworth HealthCare and the Professor of Health Informatics Management at Deakin University. She researches and teaches within the information systems domain with particular focus on developing IS/IT solutions to effect superior, patient-centric healthcare delivery.

Foreword

Managing change in most organizations is problematic and difficult to initiate, but in healthcare organizations even more so, because it usually involves the state as well as private providers. As Machiavelli wrote in "The Prince", "It should be borne in mind that there is nothing more difficult to arrange, more doubtful of success, and more dangerous to carry through than initiating change . . . The innovator makes enemies of all those who prospered under the old order, and only lukewarm support is forthcoming from those who would prosper under the new". Yet, the need for change in healthcare providers, no matter which country they are in, is vital for the health of any nation, and without an effective national health strategy and system, you undermine the ability of the state to function economically, as we recently saw with the Ebola outbreak.

This edited volume provides not only the expert and innovative views of top scholars/practitioners about what needs to be done, but also covers topics that range from human resource management (e.g., *360-Degree Feedback*, the *Balanced Scorecard*) to organizational culture change to *Lean Management* to team building to *Shared Leadership* and to health providers as *Learning Organizations*. The range of topics covered by leading researchers in the field makes this book a must buy for anybody interested in effective healthcare management in a time of the increasing cost of health, of increasing government intervention and the unrelenting advance of technology. Dramatic and fast-moving change is required in healthcare: It is no longer an option to do nothing or to make minor changes at the fringes. As Mark Twain once wrote, "If you always do what you always did, you'll always get what you always got".

We need bold innovators in health to deal with the fast-changing world of health prevention and interventions. The upfront costs may be high, but the payoffs down the line will be great; we need to take calculated risks in management innovations because they will pay off in the long run. As James Bryant Conant once said, "Behold the turtle: he only makes progress when he sticks his neck out". This book has many bold suggestions of innovations for healthcare organizations; let's hope they take them up.

Professor Sir Cary L. Cooper
Manchester Business School,
University of Manchester, England

Foreword

A MUCH-NEEDED ANSWER TO AN IMPORTANT QUESTION

Healthcare is without a doubt the sector in society that will face the biggest challenges over the next few decades. With rapid technical development, healthcare plays an increasingly more important role in extending our life spans. At the same time, financing and equal distribution in a legitimate manner, nationally and globally, and innovative capacity must be upheld. A great deal of knowledge has been accumulated in relation to these well-known problems, yet viable political solutions are still lacking.

An equally urgent issue that has not attracted the attention it deserves concerns the management of healthcare services. A wide range of management concepts and management innovations have been, and are being, tested—despite the unfortunate truth that the managers who are spending enormous amounts of money and resources on implementing the new models know very little about what works well and what doesn't. Decision-makers often have to rely on a vast normative literature, all with an agenda to promote specific management models. They provide specific answers to the question of what works best; however, alongside a large number of relatively narrow evaluations, they provide little knowledge or experience that is applicable outside the respective objects of study. The bottom line is that we know remarkably little about what works in what context.

Thus, a book like *Management Innovations for Healthcare Organizations: Adopt, Abandon or Adapt?* is much appreciated. The editors show a clear ambition to answer the question of what constitutes good management for healthcare organizations in general. They carefully walk the reader through a large number of management innovations and discuss extensively how well they fit into the healthcare context.

All of the management concepts addressed in the book are relevant in the modern context. The question of which concepts should be considered relevant can be problematized, however. In practice, we can often sense a troubling ignorance of history in the adoption of new models. The implementers tend to lack the theoretical foundation that a critical approach requires. Since managers in healthcare organizations often lack the ability to recognize old concepts dressed in new clothes, they are doomed to repeat old mistakes.

It is also striking how often the concepts are structural in nature. A likely explanation is that it is easier to describe structural changes and measurable variables instead of the complex processes that are more likely to yield permanent changes in behavior. PowerPoint is perfect for presenting grandiose structural strategies, but useless in the tedious work to achieve seemingly mundane operational improvements. This does not mean that the latter is less common in practice, however.

Although the book discusses the issue of adopt or abandon, there is a clear focus on adapt—meaning how management innovations may need to be adapted to healthcare organizations specifically. This is a question that demands an answer. It is impossible to determine the exact costs in efficiency and quality losses of the widespread experimenting with poorly functioning management concepts. However, there is no reason to believe that the improvement potential with respect to management in healthcare organizations should be any smaller than for the service sector overall, where improvements in efficiency and quality have been much stronger over the past decades.

Even though *Management Innovations for Healthcare Organizations: Adopt, Abandon or Adapt?* takes a rather broad-based approach, it goes without saying that not all management innovations of relevance to modern healthcare organizations can be covered exhaustively in one book. Yet the editors have done a great job including many of the most important ones. There is a certain emphasis on Lean and adjacent concepts, which is well in line with the developments observed in Swedish practice. Michael E. Porter's value-based healthcare gets a chapter. This approach is probably the most dominating management trend in Sweden at the present time. But of course, something will be missing. As the line has to be drawn somewhere, some things have to be left out, unfortunately.

Value-based healthcare is a good example of a management concept with a high recognition factor. Lean, or a focus on flows, is a central aspect of this approach as well, as is team-based thinking. Other important features include learning organization, indicators à la the balanced scorecard and a tint of business process reengineering. As such, value-based healthcare is yet another package filled with assorted models and ideas that has been assigned a label as part of productifying it and making it suitable for marketing. Thus, the reader of the book finds elements that are relevant in relation to the most of the modern models used. In fact, most are likely also related to models that still have not been introduced.

An advantage of the book is, despite our reference to Sweden, its lack of local considerations. Medical research and practice rarely support the notion that the optimization of healthcare services depends on a patient's city or region of residence. The development of knowledge pertaining to healthcare is global in nature, and so is the development of knowledge pertaining to healthcare management. What works in one place generally works elsewhere as well, and a failed management model rarely becomes successful by merely implementing it in a new geographical location.

Nevertheless, some readers will probably question the conclusions by referring to structural differences in healthcare organizations. It should be remembered that this view of knowledge building is not supported by evidence. The fact remains, however, that a great variation in perceptions of what works and what doesn't work persists. The perceptions in this regard depend on factors such as location, time and previous experiences. All of this implies that the choice and evaluation of management concepts are not always rationally based. *Management Innovations for Healthcare Organizations: Adopt, Abandon or Adapt?* can be read as a critique of such instinctive and locally driven adjustments.

That said, however, organizations do differ in many respects. For example, location does matter. Those of us with a background in management training know how beneficial it can be to separate the world into different sectors, as it allows us to discuss similarities and differences along this dimension. Healthcare organizations can be thought of as comprising a sector with a universal set of characteristics and management needs. But since the editors of *Management Innovations for Healthcare Organizations: Adopt, Abandon or Adapt?* have opted for a more strict analysis, they have more carefully answered the question of which healthcare organizations they have in mind. Fair enough. We believe the book is of interest also to organizations belonging to the sector in a wider sense.

In the last chapter of the book, the editors present their answers in table form. This is a good but risky idea. The last thing our healthcare organizations need is an increased dose of relativistic discussions from management researchers. Instead, they need answers. Unless the researchers provide an answer that differs from the standard response—"it depends"—we are bound to send the managers straight into the open arms of model-oriented consultants who are ready to sell both a diagnosis and a convenient cure to anybody willing to put enough money on the table.

But although the editors provide us with an answer, we feel that this is not the primary contribution of *Management Innovations for Healthcare Organizations: Adopt, Abandon or Adapt?* What is even more important is the journey we embark on to arrive at the answer. An organization normally doesn't face the choice of replacing the entire gamut of previously implemented management concepts or of introducing a completely new management innovation. What is more common is that the organization adds another layer and that there is a shift in focus when a new innovation is adopted. By not rushing to present an answer, the reader is enabled to develop a thorough understanding of the complexity involved.

Thus, the book can serve as both a healthy history lesson and a theoretical introduction to various management innovations. When new concepts enter the scene, the respective marketing schemes often emphasize the dramatic differences compared with previous models. This enables the promoters to disregard all previous disappointments, shortcomings and ambiguities. The various ways in which different management models are connected and the fact that one model may be based on another may be good to know for managers, not least when purchasing consulting services.

The best method to accomplish a valuable edited volume is, of course, to assemble a team of competent authors. Anders Örtenblad, Carina Abrahamson Löfström and Rod Sheaff have done a great job, but it should be pointed out that the success of the book is a team effort. Many chapters are rather self-contained and together, they have a lot to offer readers who don't go straight from Chapter 2 to Chapter 21. We are confident this is something the managers who search for the answer by reading the whole book will appreciate.

Management Innovations for Healthcare Organizations: Adopt, Abandon or Adapt? offers a much-needed answer to an important question, and it does it in a way that increases the reader's ability to think critically. This is usually not accomplished by means of providing an answer. Those of you who have made it this far in the book can look forward to an enjoyable and educational reading experience.

Professor Björn Rombach
School of Public Administration,
University of Gothenburg, Sweden

and Hans Winberg
Secretary General, Leading Health
Care Foundation, Sweden

Preface

It has been a tough time for us getting this book together, and perhaps we could actually use some healthcare ourselves now—or at least a period of recovery followed by a return to normal life in the community. On the other hand, it has been a very stimulating project. Anders, who has edited several books on the need to adapt management innovations to make them relevant for organizations in particular generalized contexts, took the initiative in starting the book project a couple of years ago, and invited Carina and Rod, both of whom had much more professional experience of the healthcare sector than Anders. Thereafter, the three of us have met quite a lot of times via Skype and sent numerous emails to each other. So far, we have not met AFK (away from keyboard), but hope to do so as soon as possible. Nor have we met many of the contributors to the book AFK, but we sincerely hope also to meet them in the future. We believe that intercultural meetings are one way of making the world a better place, and hopefully the content of the book will also help in that ambition.

We would like to thank all the contributors, who have done a marvelous job getting together their chapters. Most of them have also offered comments on other chapters of the book, which means that the lion's share of the book has been "double-open peer reviewed", and in addition, each chapter received several rounds of comments from us, the editors.

Finally, we would like to dedicate this book to those of our beloved parents who are no longer with us:

Olle Örtenblad 1928–2012
Britt Lindberg (formerly Abrahamson) 1934–2003
Will Sheaff 1922–2010
Mary Sheaff 1925–2008

Anders Örtenblad,
Carina Abrahamson Löfström
and Rod Sheaff

Stockholm, Sweden,
Gothenburg, Sweden and
Liskeard, UK, June 2015

Part I
Background and Introduction

Now organizations in health
Keep management books on the shelf
The next panacea
Or verbal diarrhoea?
Read on and decide for yourself

Chris Blantern

1 The Relevance of Management Innovations for Healthcare Organizations

Anders Örtenblad, Carina Abrahamson Löfström and Rod Sheaff

Most people would think twice before wearing shorts at the Nobel Prize dinner. Wearing shorts, you would probably not be let in, unless, of course, you were the Swedish king or queen, or one of the Nobel Prize winners. On the other hand, such behavior would certainly be innovative and—who knows—something good might come out of it. Perhaps the arrangements for these dinners would loosen up and become more fruitful for the participants. What do you think, should the shorts-wearer reconsider, or do the Nobel Prize dinner arrangements need to learn how to loosen up a bit?

While this book is definitely not about the Nobel Prize event, it connects to the above reasoning. Every innovation fights a battle against the existing way of thinking and doing things. This is also true for the kind of innovations that we like to call "management innovations". Their relevance for healthcare organizations (see Chapter 2 of this volume for an extensive definition of "healthcare organization") will be examined in the present book. Healthcare is a sector struggling to find a balance between values such as cost minimizing and patient safety, and management innovations could possibly help in these efforts. Healthcare is also a sector that is known for quite far-reaching conflicts, both between the various professions that are involved in healthcare and between the professionals and the administration (see, e.g., Mintzberg, 1979). "Management" is a concept that lately has become something that is said to be relevant not only for private corporations, but also for organizations in the public sector, including healthcare organizations, although this idea has its critics (see, e.g., Beardwood et al., 1999). One sign of this increased space that "management" has received is the frequent occurrence of narratives on organizations that have succeeded through practicing certain management innovations and also the quite large market where more or less decontextualized versions of management innovations are bought and sold. Thus, this book examines whether the management innovations that have often been developed for managing private corporations better and that people working in the healthcare sector may be exposed to—or even actively search for—are also valid for healthcare organizations. Do these management innovations bring ideas on how to better manage healthcare organizations that are valuable enough for healthcare organizations to change in accordance with what the management innovations prescribe, or do these innovations not deserve to be "let in" into the world of healthcare? Is there reason for people working in the healthcare sector to start to practice any of these management innovations unchanged (cf. adoption), should they simply dismiss them (cf. abandonment), or should they take a closer look at them to see if there might be elements that could be useful (cf. adaptation)? Additionally, questions such as the following will be discussed: Is it a good idea to decentralize decision-making in healthcare organizations, as some of the management innovations taken up in the book prescribe? Is it a good idea to strive for increased quality in healthcare organizations in the same way as some of the management innovations suggest? How should leadership within healthcare organizations be performed? Should those management innovations that are quite business oriented be adopted by healthcare organizations, which take care of people rather than producing sellable products or services? Etcetera. Thus, the aim of this book is to test the relevance of quite an extensive set of management innovations for healthcare organizations and, should these tests show that any of these management innovations is partly relevant but not fully so, to suggest an adapted version of the management innovation, a version that fits healthcare organizations.

This book is a bit different from the existing literature where management innovations are put into the healthcare context. First, while major parts of the existing literature often tend to focus on one single management innovation (but see Hanson, 1995; Hanson & Finkler, 1995), in this book, quite a large number of various management innovations are put into the healthcare context. Second, the fact that so many management innovations are examined in the same book has offered the opportunity for all of the contributors to relate to the same definition of healthcare organization (see Chapter 2, this volume) when relevance testing and adapting management innovations in relation to healthcare organizations. Third, while much of the existing literature tends to suggest that ready-made versions of certain management innovations fit the healthcare sector simply as they are, without considering which elements of those management innovations are less relevant, or even totally irrelevant, in this book, each management innovation is first given a general definition and thereafter the contributor(s) discusses its relevance for healthcare organizations and how it may have to be adapted to fit these organizations. Such transparency gives the reader insight into the reasoning that lies behind the conclusions drawn, and, thus, an option to consider the reasoning itself instead of merely being presented with conclusions.

In the remainder of this chapter—which focuses on management innovations, while Chapter 2 focuses on healthcare organizations—the area and concept of "management innovation" will be discussed in more depth, and its relevance for healthcare organizations will be generally discussed. More specifically, the concept of "management innovation" will be defined, and some debates within the area of management innovations and their spread will be referred to, debates such as whether management innovations actually bring something useful or if they are to be regarded as useless frauds. All this is done in order to offer a more solid background for and an introduction to the book. At the end of the chapter, the remainder of the book is outlined.

ON MANAGEMENT INNOVATIONS AND HEALTHCARE ORGANIZATIONS

Management innovation can be defined as "the invention and implementation of a management practice, process, structure, or technique that is new to the state of the art and is intended to further organizational goals" (Birkinshaw et al., 2008, p. 825; see also Bort, forthcoming). Thus, management innovations represent some kind of ideal or normatively characterized prescription regarding how to better lead, structure, govern, control and organize organizations. They are "new" either in the sense that they are new to society in general or, at the least, to the organization that is implementing it (or is about to implement it). Examples of management innovations are *Business Process Reengineering, Knowledge Management, Servant Leadership* and *Total Quality Management*. These and quite a number of other management innovations will be examined in this book.

The image that is given of these management innovations in the literature about any certain management innovation (that is, literature presenting any certain management innovation in general, *not* specifically connected to healthcare organizations), as well as at business schools and by management gurus and consultants—and even by at least some scholars—is often one-sided. They are presented as quick-fix panaceas that bring various advantages to the organizations that adopt them, such as profitability, competitiveness and survival (Huczynski, 1993 [1996]; Kieser, 1997; Røvik, 2002). This supportive discourse rarely or never takes up any downsides that the management innovations might have. Occasionally, at the opposite pole, the management innovations are severely criticized. This discourse rarely or never mentions any gains that might occur from using the management innovations. For instance, the idea of the *Learning Organization*, which is one of the management innovations considered in this book, tends to be described either as "utopian sunshine" or as "Foucauldian gloom" (Driver, 2002), that is, either in terms of a one-sided recommendation to adopt the idea as is or, alternatively and much less often, a one-sided recommendation to all organizations to reject the idea.

The one-sidedness of this literature, and especially the dominating positive discourse, has, within the meta-literature on management innovations, given rise to an interpretation of organizational actors' approach to and use of management innovations as if it was controlled by fashion mechanisms (e.g.,

Abrahamson, 1991, 1996a,b; Abrahamson & Fairchild, 1999). "Fashion" implies, in our case, that a certain management innovation at a given point of time rapidly gains lots of attention and interest, but then, after a certain period of time,[1] its popularity vanishes as quickly as it emerged. The one-sided positive discourse that dominates during the major part of the management innovation's lifecycle tends to lead many organizational actors to "jump on the bandwagon" in a herd-like way (Sorge & van Witteloostuijn, 2004). But just as none of the many diets continuously appearing in the popular press, which those of us who need to lose some weight pin our hopes upon,[2] are probably capable of actually helping every single individual to lose weight, it cannot simply be assumed that management innovations are universally applicable panaceas. Thus, there is a risk that management innovations that appear attractive and are adopted by many other organizations but are fully or partly irrelevant are adopted (cf. Abrahamson, 1991). The reverse is, of course, also true. There is clearly a risk that management innovations that would be relevant and helpful for healthcare organizations are ignored because they are not fashionable enough or because they may not, from a quick glance, seem to fit healthcare organizations and their specific characteristics. Likewise, there is a risk that essential and even vital elements of a particular idea are not adopted or that elements that would be fatal for the organization are adopted (cf. Eccles & Nohria, 1992, p. 94). Thus, there is reason for researchers to "intervene" (Abrahamson, 1996a; Abrahamson & Eisenman, 2001; see also Birkinshaw et al., 2008) and engage in "researcher-assisted adaptation" (Örtenblad, 2013a, p. 9) of management innovations, to help organizational actors avoiding "maladaptive responses" such as dissociation or evangelicism (Whittle, forthcoming).

Even if it is impossible to escape the forces of fashion (e.g., Parker, forthcoming), and while it may not be possible to reach full rationality (Abrahamson Löfström, forthcoming), we want to believe that organizational actors as well as researchers have ambitions to actually improve organizations (Saxi, forthcoming) and are capable of becoming *more* rational regarding how they respond to and handle management innovations. Actually, one of the more recent perspectives of the use of management innovations proclaims that those traditionally seen as consumers—such as organizational actors—take part in the production of them, in terms of demanding them, while those traditionally regarded as producers—such as management gurus—also consume the management innovations (see, e.g., Alvarez, 1998; Clark & Salaman, 1998; Furusten, 1999; Thomas, 2003). Hence, unlike the literature that has tended to sketch management innovations in either white or black, this book is neither uncritically praising the management innovations, nor is it arguing that all management innovations are rubbish. Instead, this book takes a "critical-pragmatic approach" (see Örtenblad & Koris, 2014) and the book's keystone is that management innovations' relevance not should be taken for granted but, on the other hand, that they very well may add at least some value to the organizations in which they are used and, thus, that there are both pros and cons to any specific management innovation (Abrahamson, 1991; Collins, 2000; Gibson & Tesone, 2001; Kieser, 1997). The relevance of any specific management innovation for healthcare organizations must be critically examined, and if judged to be at all relevant for healthcare organizations, it might need to go through adaptation before it becomes fully relevant for such organizations. Hence, rather than suggesting that management innovations should be outright *adopted* (implying that healthcare organizations must change in accordance with what the management innovations prescribe) or outright *abandoned* (implying that the management innovations are totally irrelevant for healthcare organizations), this book suggests that adoption and abandonment are two possible outcomes of a process in which the relevance of a certain management innovation for healthcare organizations is explored, and where *adaptation* (implying that the management innovations are changed and that the healthcare organizations adopting them also go through changes as the management innovation is adopted) is perhaps not inevitable, as some argue (e.g., Mamman, 2002), but definitely another possible outcome. Thus, we have made efforts to encourage all contributors to the present book to approach management innovations in such a way that they are open both to a possible need to change healthcare organizations in order to make them more like what the particular management innovation requires, and to a possible need to modify the actual management innovation in order to make it fully relevant for healthcare organizations. Such an openness towards changes of both theory and practice, when researching the relevance of certain management innovations for organizations in certain contexts, has been called the "interactive approach" (Örtenblad, 2013b, Örtenblad, forthcoming).

The management innovations considered in this book may need to be adapted to fit healthcare organizations. By "adaptation" of management innovations, we mean that the given management innovation's content is modified so that it better fits healthcare organizations. There are various types of such modification. Borrowing mainly from Røvik (2011; see also Gond & Boxenbaum, 2013; Latour, 1986, p. 267; Mamman, 2002; Røvik, 1998), who has developed concepts for various types of *translation*[3] of management innovations (or "management ideas", as Røvik calls them), these may go through *adding*, meaning that some elements are added to the management innovation, *subtraction*, indicating that some elements are removed from the management innovation, or *alteration*, which means that the management innovation is radically changed.[4]

Management innovations can be used for different purposes. Borrowing from Pelz (1978), who wrote about the utilization of knowledge appearing in social science, management innovations can be used *instrumentally*—implying knowledge for action and knowledge being used for decision-making or problem-solving purposes, *conceptually*—indicating that knowledge influences thinking without putting information to any specific use, although the knowledge can enlighten the actors—and *symbolically* (or legitimatively)—which means that knowledge is used as a substitute for decision or to legitimize a policy. At least when discussing them on a meta-level, many scholars have acknowledged the symbolic function of management innovations (e.g., Abrahamson, 1991; Ansari et al., 2010; Kieser, 1997; Maassen & Stensaker, forthcoming). Just like fashionable clothes, the newest, most fashionable management innovations give the user legitimacy. It may even be, in some organizations, that the management innovation is merely a façade for legitimacy purposes and thus, managerial talk about how the organization has changed in accordance with the particular management innovation is totally decoupled from the actual practice, which remains unchanged (cf. Meyer & Rowan, 1977). This book focuses primarily on the instrumental use of management innovations, and to some extent also on conceptual use, rather than on symbolic use. Thus, of interest here is whether or not and to what extent the various management innovations are useful for healthcare organizations if they are put into practice—that is, what consequences there are from putting them into use—rather than whether healthcare organizations can gain legitimacy through appearing as if they had adopted the management innovations.

It must also be mentioned that the book discusses the relevance of various management innovations to healthcare organizations in general (as defined in Chapter 2, this volume), not to any particular individual healthcare organization. It is therefore of the utmost importance that each individual healthcare organization not employ the advice given in this book uncritically, but that organizational actors instead take the advice as a starting point for further consideration about the relevance of the certain management innovation for their particular organization with its particular characteristics and in its particular situation.

When talking about "management innovations" and, in addition, when each of them has a unique name, it may seem as if the management innovations are separate, unique and easily separable units. As the chapters in the book will show, at least some of the management innovations dealt with are not as separate as that. Some scholars even argue that management innovations are rather to be seen as "old wine in new bottles" (see, e.g., Kimberly, 1981, p. 100; Mazza & Alvarez, 2000, p. 576; Örtenblad, 2007; Spell, 2001), implying that there are major similarities between any "new" management innovation and at least one existing one. For instance, Spell (2001) shows that management fashions, as he calls them, are sometimes created by combining old, known and unthreatening beliefs with new labels. This has also been argued when it comes to particular management innovations; for instance, Baines (1997) argues that there is a big overlap between the *Learning Organization* and *Knowledge Management* concepts, Wilson (2002) claims that *Organizational Learning* work now comes under the heading of *Knowledge Management* and Castle (1996) suggests that *Business Process Reengineering* could be seen as a subsystem of *Total Quality Management*.

Consequently, it would make sense to argue that the origin of management innovations may simply be other management innovations (Spell, 2001). Furthermore, as quite a number of scholars have argued throughout the years, management innovations are often vague and/or ambiguous (e.g., Benders & van Veen, 2001; Benders & Verlaar, 2003; Giroux, 2006; Kieser, 1997; Mamman, 2002) and are thus not easily defined and, therefore, not easily distinguishable. They possess *interpretative viability* (Benders et al., 1998; Benders & van Veen, 2001), which means that they easily come to be interpreted differently by different actors. For instance, Kahn (1974) argued that *Organization Development* was a *convenience term*, i.e., a term denoting a conglomerate of things. Abrahamson (1996b) considered *Total Quality Management* to be an umbrella term that has come to mean almost everything—and therefore nothing.[5]

At least some of the management innovations considered in this book do have major similarities to each other (or to management innovations not taken up in this book). We have chosen, though, to take all of them up simply because they often appear to be new, separate entities, in that each of them is given a unique name and often is supported by a certain guru or group of management scholars/consultants, and the management innovations' names are what one often meets—in, for example, the business press, at business schools, or when meeting with management consultants. We have decided to consider also those management innovations that already have reached their popularity peak, because we refute the notion that management innovations are interesting only when they are fashionable. Just as those management innovations that presently are fashionable may be less relevant, those less-fashionable management innovations may be more relevant.

Finally, even if the main premise in the present book is that we believe in researchers intervening and suggesting reasonable adaptations of general management innovations to better fit healthcare organizations, there is, of course, also a need for people to think for themselves (see, e.g., Ohlsson & Rombach, forthcoming). The versions of the management innovations that are dealt with in this book are suggested to be fit for healthcare organizations on the basis of analyses made by individual authors (or small groups of authors) and are naturally based on these individuals' subjective worldviews and values. Furthermore, researchers, no less than others, follow fashion (Bort & Kieser, 2011; Örtenblad, 1999; Parker, forthcoming; Starbuck, 2009; Whittle, forthcoming). For these reasons, one cannot expect that researchers automatically would act purely in a rational and unbiased manner when contextualizing management innovations or when in other ways helping to determine the relevance of management innovations for certain organizations. The suggested versions of the management innovations should thus be seen as well-grounded suggestions rather than exact guidelines. Each healthcare organization still needs to consider whether the suggested model fits its particular unique characteristics and needs.

THE REMAINDER OF THE BOOK

The remainder of the book is structured as follows. Part I, entitled "Background and Introduction", offers a theoretical and conceptual background to the book. Chapter 2 complements the present chapter by offering a definition of "healthcare organization" and discusses healthcare organizations from an international perspective. It also outlines the empirical ground that the authors of the chapters in Part II base their contributions on, and elaborates in some more depth than the present chapter about the increased interest in management innovations in healthcare organizations.

Part II, "Examining Management Innovations", is the main part of the book. Here, the management innovations are considered in one chapter each. All chapters in this part of the book are authored by experts on each particular management innovation and its relevance for healthcare organizations, experts whom we have carefully selected. They are from various parts of the world and have also based their contributions on studies done in different parts of the world. The set of management innovations considered in this book is diverse, but yet unitary. All of them prescribe how organizations—or parts/aspects of them (such as their administration, certain operational units, etc.)—should be lead, structured, controlled or handled in any other way. These management innovations can be categorized in different ways. For instance, on a functional basis, some of the management innovations (such as *Consensus* and *Empowerment*) deal with decision-making, while some others (such as *Management by Objectives, Servant Leadership, Shared Leadership* and *Transformational Leadership*) deal with leadership. However, finding an accurate categorization that could group all the management innovations in a distinct way turned out to be more difficult than it first appeared. For instance, *Servant Leadership* could be said to not only deal with leadership but also with decision-making. Likewise, *Empowerment* could be said to deal with leadership in addition to decision-making. For this reason, we have in this book simply chosen to put the management innovations in alphabetical order (see Table 1.1).

Part III, "Conclusions and Future Research", contains one chapter only—Chapter 25—in which we, the book editors, draw conclusions from the chapters in Part II so that we can answer the main question put forth in this book; that is, whether and to what extent there is reason for people working in healthcare organizations to take a deeper interest in the various management innovations that circulate in time and space. We also suggest aspects that further studies of the relevance of management innovations for healthcare organizations should take into account, as well as which parts of the world such studies may want to focus on. The final section of Chapter 25 briefly outlines a few theoretical contributions from the book.

Table 1.1 The Management Innovations Considered in This Book

Chapter No.	Management Innovation	Author(s)
3.	*360-Degree Feedback*	Joan F. Miller
4.	*Accreditation*	Marie-Pascale Pomey
5.	*Balanced Scorecard*	Elin Funck
6.	*Business Process Reengineering*	Anjali Patwardhan, Dhruv Patwardhan and Prakash Patwardhan
7.	*Consensus*	Marie Carney
8.	*Corporate Social Responsibility*	Sherif Tehemar
9.	*Decentralization*	Mark Exworthy and Martin Powell
10.	*Empowerment*	Nelson Ositadimma Oranye and Nora Ahmad
11.	*Kaizen*	Mark Graban
12.	*Knowledge Management*	Nilmini Wickramasinghe and Raj Gururajan
13.	*Lean*	Bozena Poksinska
14.	*Learning Organization*	Rod Sheaff
15.	*Management by Objectives*	Grigorios L. Kyriakopoulos
16.	*New Public Management*	Dawid Sześciło
17.	*Servant Leadership*	Jack McCann
18.	*Shared Leadership*	D. David Persaud
19.	*Six Sigma*	Jacob Krive
20.	*Sustainability*	Tony Huzzard, Andreas Hellström and Svante Lifvergren
21.	*Teamwork*	Jan Schmutz, Annalena Welp and Michaela Kolbe
22.	*Total Quality Management*	Ali Mohammad Mosadeghrad and Ewan Ferlie
23.	*Transformational Leadership*	Bettina Fiery
24.	*Value-Based Healthcare*	Thomas Garavan and Gerri Matthews-Smith

ACKNOWLEDGEMENTS

The authors want to thank the members of the SOL-group at the Faculty of Social Sciences, University of Nordland, Norway, for valuable comments on a draft of this chapter, and Hilde Berit Moen, Faculty of Social Sciences, University of Nordland, Norway, for sharing her expertise on eating disorders.

NOTES

1 Between 20 and 40 years, depending on which scholar within the area you ask.
2 The low-carb, high-fat diet, for instance, may help many, but perhaps not those who suffer from eating disorders, who potentially may continue to eat no matter if they feel full or not. Thus, one of the advantages with this diet—that the high intake of fat makes the individual feel less hungry, so s/he consequently eats less—is ruined.
3 The concept of "translation" differs from "adaptation" in that the former rests on the theory of sociology of translation (see, e.g., Callon, 1986; Latour, 1986, 1987), implying that management innovations do not travel as such, but through continuously being interpreted and reinterpreted. For this reason, management innovations generally undergo modifications (that is, they are given a more or less different meaning) when being spread, but it may occasionally also happen that the content is left more or less intact as the management innovation spreads in time and space (that is, it may be reinterpreted similarly to how it was first being interpreted). But it must also be noted that there are those who consider all "translation" to imply "modification" of the translated item (e.g., Lervik et al., 2005).
4 The term "copying" is not included here, even if it is a form of *translation* according to Røvik (2011), since it is a term signifying that the management innovation is reinterpreted but that its meaning remains unchanged.
5 Also in this book, it happens that the same management innovation is given somewhat different definitions by different authors.

REFERENCES

Abrahamson, E. (1991). Managerial fads and fashions: The diffusion and rejection of innovations. *Academy of Management Review*, 16 (3), 586–612.
Abrahamson, E. (1996a). Management fashion. *Academy of Management Review*, 21 (1), 254–285.
Abrahamson, E. (1996b). Technical and aesthetic fashion. In B. Czarniawska & G. Sevón (Eds.), *Translating Organizational Change*. Berlin: de Gruyter, pp. 117–137.
Abrahamson, E., & Eisenman, M. (2001). Why management scholars must intervene strategically in the management knowledge market. *Human Relations*, 54 (1), 67–75.
Abrahamson, E., & Fairchild, G. (1999). Management fashion: Lifecycles, triggers, and collective learning processes. *Administrative Science Quarterly*, 44 (4), 708–740.
Abrahamson Löfström, C. (forthcoming). Corporatization as a managerial panacea: Rational adaptation in the context of a Swedish state-owned mail enterprise. In A. Örtenblad (Ed.), *Handbook of Research on Management Ideas and Panaceas: Adaptation and Context*. Cheltenham, England: Edward Elgar.
Alvarez, J.L. (1998). The sociological tradition and the spread and institutionalization of knowledge for action. In J.L. Alvarez (Ed.), *The Diffusion and Consumption of Business Knowledge*. London: Macmillan, pp. 13–57.
Ansari, S., Fiss, P., & Zajac, E. (2010). Made to fit: How practices vary as they diffuse. *Academy of Management Review*, 35 (1), 67–92.
Baines, A. (1997). Exploiting organizational knowledge in the learning organization. *Work Study*, 46 (6), 202–206.

Beardwood, B., Walters, V., Eyles, J., & French, S. (1999). Complaints against nurses: A reflection of "the new managerialism" and consumerism in health care? *Social Science & Medicine*, 48 (3), 363–374.

Benders, J., & van Veen, K. (2001). What's in a fashion? Interpretative viability and management fashions. *Organization*, 8 (1), 33–53.

Benders, J., van den Berg, R.-J., & van Bijsterveld, M. (1998). Hitch-hiking on a hype: Dutch consultants engineering re-engineering. *Journal of Organizational Change Management*, 11 (3), 201–215.

Benders, J., & Verlaar, S. (2003). Lifting parts: Putting conceptual insights into practice. *International Journal of Operations & Production Management*, 23 (7), 757–774.

Birkinshaw, J., Hamel, G., & Mol, M.J. (2008). Management innovation. *Academy of Management Review*, 33 (4), 825–845.

Bort, S. (forthcoming). Turning a management innovation into a management panacea: Management ideas, concepts, fashions, practices, and theoretical concepts. In A. Örtenblad (Ed.), *Handbook of Research on Management Ideas and Panaceas: Adaptation and Context*. Cheltenham, England: Edward Elgar.

Bort, S., & Kieser, A. (2011). Fashion in organization theory: An empirical analysis of the diffusion of theoretical concepts. *Organization Studies*, 32 (5), 655–681.

Callon, M. (1986). Some elements of a sociology of translation: Domestication of the scallops and the fishermen of St Brieuc Bay. In J. Law (Ed.), *Power, Action and Belief: A New Sociology of Knowledge*. London: Routledge & Kegan Paul, pp. 196–233.

Castle, J.A. (1996). An integrated model in quality management, positioning TQM, BPR and ISO 9000. *The TQM Magazine*, 8 (5), 7–13.

Clark, T., & Salaman, G. (1998). Telling tales: Management gurus' narratives and the construction of managerial identity. *Journal of Management Studies*, 35 (2), 137–161.

Collins, D. (2000). *Management Fads and Buzzwords: Critical-Practical Perspectives*. London: Routledge.

Driver, M. (2002). The learning organization: Foucauldian gloom or utopian sunshine? *Human Relations*, 55 (1), 33–53.

Eccles, R.G., & Nohria, N. (1992). *Beyond the Hype: Rediscovering the Essence of Management*. Cambridge, MA: Harvard Business School Press.

Fink, D. (2003). A life cycle approach to management fashion: An investigation of management concepts in the context of competitive strategy. *Schmalenbach Business Review*, 55 (1), 46–59.

Furusten, S. (1999). *Popular Management Books: How They Are Made and What They Mean for Organisations*. London: Routledge.

Gibson, J.W., & Tesone, D.V. (2001). Management fads: Emergence, evolution, and implications for managers. *Academy of Management Perspectives*, 15 (4), 122–133.

Giroux, H. (2006). "It was such a handy term": Management fashions and pragmatic ambiguity. *Journal of Management Studies*, 43 (6), 1227–1260.

Gond, J.-P., & Boxenbaum, E. (2013). The glocalization of responsible investment: Contextualization work in France and Québec. *Journal of Business Ethics*, 115 (4), 707–721.

Hanson, K.L. (1995). Implementation of management innovation at primary care health centers: Qualitative assessments. *Journal of Ambulatory Care Management*, 18 (2), 33–46.

Hanson, K.L., & Finkler, S.A. (1995). Case studies of management innovation at primary care health centers. *Journal of Ambulatory Care Management*, 18 (2), 54–65.

Huczynski, A.A. (1993 [1996]). *Management Gurus: What Makes Them and How to Become One*. London: Thomson.

Kahn, R.L. (1974). Organizational development: Some problems and proposals. *The Journal of Applied Behavioural Science*, 10 (4), 485–502.

Kieser, A. (1997). Rhetoric and myth in management fashion. *Organization*, 4 (1), 49–74.

Kimberly, J.R. (1981). Managerial innovation. In P.C. Nystrom & W.H. Starbuck (Eds.), *Handbook of Organizational Design*. London: Oxford University Press, pp. 84–104.

Latour, B. (1986). The powers of association. In J. Law (Ed.), *Power, Action and Belief: A New Sociology of Knowledge?* London: Routledge & Kegan Paul, pp. 264–280.

Latour, B. (1987). *Science in Action*. Cambridge, MA: Harvard University Press.

Lervik, J.E., Hennestad, B.W., Amdam, R.P., Lunnan, R., & Nilsen S.M. (2005). Implementing human resource development best practices: Replication or re-creation? *Human Resource Development International*, 8 (3), 345–360.

Maassen, P., & Stensaker, B. (forthcoming). Neutralizing managerial panaceas: How universities cope with management fads. In A. Örtenblad (Ed.), *Handbook of Research on Management Ideas and Panaceas: Adaptation and Context*. Cheltenham, England: Edward Elgar.

Mamman, A. (2002). The adoption and modification of management ideas in organizations: Towards an analytical framework. *Strategic Change*, 11 (7), 341–389.

Mazza, C., & Alvarez, J.L. (2000). Haute couture and prêt-à-porter: The popular press and the diffusion of management practices. *Organization Studies*, 21 (3), 567–588.

Meyer, J.W., & Rowan, B. (1977). Institutionalized organizations: Formal structure as myth and ceremony. *American Journal of Sociology*, 83 (2), 340–363.

Mintzberg, H. (1979). *The Structuring of Organizations*. Englewood Cliffs, NJ: Prentice-Hall.

Ohlsson, Ö., & Rombach, B. (forthcoming). The art of constructive criticism. In A. Örtenblad (Ed.), *Handbook of Research on Management Ideas and Panaceas: Adaptation and Context*. Cheltenham, England: Edward Elgar.

Örtenblad, A. (1999). *"The fashionable fashion concept" or "researchers have their fashions too"*. Paper presented at the EGOS 15th Colloquium, Warwick University, Coventry, England.

Örtenblad, A. (2007). The evolution of popular management ideas: An exploration and extension of the old wine in new bottles metaphor. *International Journal of Management Concepts and Philosophy*, 2 (4), 365–388.

Örtenblad, A. (2013a). Introduction. Putting the learning organization into context: An emerging research field. In A. Örtenblad (Ed.), *Handbook of Research on the Learning Organization: Adaptation and Context*. Cheltenham, England: Edward Elgar, pp. 3–21.

Örtenblad, A. (2013b). Contextualizing the learning organization: Approaches to research design. In A. Örtenblad (Ed.), *Handbook of Research on the Learning Organization: Adaptation and Context*, Cheltenham, England: Edward Elgar, pp. 51–67.

Örtenblad, A. (forthcoming). Researcher intervention in the process of contextualizing fashionable management ideas: Some previous experiences. In A. Örtenblad (Ed.), *Handbook of Research on Management Ideas and Panaceas: Adaptation and Context*. Cheltenham, England: Edward Elgar.

Örtenblad, A., & Koris, R. (2014). Is the learning organization idea relevant to higher educational institutions? A literature review and a "multi-stakeholder contingency approach". *International Journal of Educational Management*, 28 (2), 173–214.

Parker, M. (forthcoming). Theory as fashion: What are management ideas for? In A. Örtenblad (Ed.), *Handbook of Research on Management Ideas and Panaceas: Adaptation and Context*. Cheltenham, England: Edward Elgar.

Pelz, D.C. (1978). Some expanded perspectives on use of social science in public policy. In J.M. Yinger & S.J. Cutler (Eds.), *Major Social Issues: A Multidisciplinary View*. New York: Free Press, pp. 346–357.

Røvik, K.A. (1996). Deinstitutionalization and the logic of fashion. In B. Czarniawska & G. Sevón (Eds.), *Translating Organizational Change*. Berlin: de Gruyter, pp. 139–172.

Røvik, K.A. (1998). *The translation of popular management ideas: Towards a theory*. Paper presented at the EGOS 14th Colloquium, Maastricht, Netherlands.

Røvik, K.A. (2002). The secrets of the winners: Management ideas that flow. In K. Sahlin-Andersson & L. Engwall (Eds.), *The Expansion of Management Knowledge: Carriers, Flows and Sources*. Stanford, CA: Stanford University Press, pp. 113–144.

Røvik, K.A. (2011). From fashion to virus: An alternative theory of organizations' handling of management ideas. *Organization Studies, 32* (5), 631–653.

Saxi, H.P. (forthcoming). Management reforms as fashion? Critical remarks from a philosophy of science perspective. In A. Örtenblad (Ed.), *Handbook of Research on Management Ideas and Panaceas: Adaptation and Context*. Cheltenham, England: Edward Elgar.

Scarbrough, H., & Swan, J. (2001). Explaining the diffusion of knowledge management: The role of fashion. *British Journal of Management, 12* (1), 3–12.

Sorge, A., & van Witteloostuijn, A. (2004). The (non)sense of organizational change: An essay about universal management hypes, sick consultancy metaphors, and healthy organization theories. *Organization Studies, 25* (7), 1205–1231.

Spell, C.S. (2001). Management fashions: Where do they come from and are they old wine in new bottles? *Journal of Management Inquiry, 10* (4), 358–373.

Starbuck, W.H. (2009). The constant causes of never-ending faddishness in the behavioral and social sciences. *Scandinavian Journal of Management, 25* (1), 108–116.

Sturdy, A. (2004). The adoption of management ideas and practices: Theoretical perspectives and possibilities. *Management Learning, 35* (2), 155–180.

Thomas, P. (2003). The recontextualization of management: A discourse-based approach to analysing the development of management thinking. *Journal of Management Studies, 40* (4), 775–801.

Whittle, S.R. (forthcoming). Changing the story: Management panaceas as narrative interventions. In A. Örtenblad (Ed.), *Handbook of Research on Management Ideas and Panaceas: Adaptation and Context*. Cheltenham, England: Edward Elgar.

Wilson, T.D. (2002). The nonsense of "knowledge management". *Information Research, 8* (1). Retrieved from http://InformationR.net/ir/8–1/paper144.html (accessed 7 June 2015).

2 Healthcare Organizations and Managerial Innovations From an International Perspective

Rod Sheaff, Carina Abrahamson Löfström and Anders Örtenblad

While the focus in Chapter 1 was on management innovations, the focus in this chapter is on healthcare organizations. The primary aim in this chapter is to offer a definition of "healthcare organization" to help to make sense of the discussions on whether the various management innovations that will follow in subsequent chapters are relevant for healthcare organizations. The first section of the chapter delimits the area of study by clarifying exactly which healthcare organizations the book in general deals with. Thereafter, healthcare in general and healthcare organizations specifically are discussed from an international perspective—are they so similar across national borders that a claim regarding the relevance of a certain management innovation for hospitals in, say, Liberia is applicable also for hospitals in countries such as Nepal, Bolivia, Sweden and Iceland? Next, a table shows the specific kinds of healthcare organizations the individual contributions (hence, the management innovations) deal with, and in which part(s) of the world (hence in which kinds of health systems and social contexts) these healthcare organizations are located. This table also shows which data/material the individual chapters are based upon. The final section of the chapter gives a background to the relatively recent interest in management innovations in healthcare organizations.

WHICH HEALTHCARE ORGANIZATIONS?

A preliminary to analyzing management innovations is to delineate the field of study. At first sight, the concept of a "healthcare organization" appears unproblematic, but a comparison of health systems soon dispels that idea. Do healthcare organizations include, for example, pharmaceutical and medical equipment manufacturing (as they did in some of the pre-1991 communist countries), or the collection of blood and manufacture of blood products? Do university hospitals and other training establishments for clinicians count as healthcare organizations, part of the higher education system, or both? Because of their relevance to the spread of infectious disease and to human nutrition, veterinary services once counted as part of the health system in Italy. Another ambiguous category is the organizations, pressure groups and lobbies focused on public policy and legislation or promoting vested interests and particular health policies or decisions. Not only have we to decide whether the professional organizations of doctors, nurses and other occupations are included, but campaigning bodies such as (in the UK) the Family Planning Association or (in the USA) anti-abortion campaigners, and projects such as the WHO's Tobacco Free Europe campaign, or even the World Bank or International Monetary Fund, whose structural adjustment policies have often had severely adverse impacts on population health and healthcare in many health systems (Loewenson, 1993; Rowden, 2009; Sheaff, 2005). For which of these organizational settings shall we seek and study management innovations and their effects?

Our initial working definition of *healthcare organization* is that of an organization that produces healthcare, i.e., a healthcare provider organization. The most familiar examples are the organizations that run hospitals: The state (the National Health Service (NHS) foundation trusts, university hospitals in Germany, local government in many countries (e.g., Sweden); charities (for instance, the hospital ship MV Africa Mercy); religious organizations; corporations (e.g., Asklepios in Germany); and in the past, trade unions. Less obviously, they include co-operatives (e.g., Group Health in the USA) and mutual aid organizations (e.g., Medecins Sans Frontières); organizations that undertake just the management of hospitals under contract (as at Amadora Sintra in Portugal, or, until 2015, Hinchingbrooke Hospital in England); and the small groups of doctors or even individual doctors who own and manage clinics or hospitals (for instance, the physician-owned hospitals in America, France, Switzerland, Germany). All these types of organization can also be found providing community health services, i.e., care delivered in the patient's own home. Examples of all of them can also be found operating primary care services (general practices, family physicians or the equivalent). Another organizational form, common in primary care in the Anglophone world, but not only there, is the professional partnership, under which a group of doctors or dentists (and sometimes other professionals) jointly own a group practice. Among the partners, decisions are usually made on a more or less democratic and equal basis. Primary care is also the scene for networks of healthcare providers (e.g., some American HMOs, mental health networks), which are organized in a similar way or alternatively have a centralized network-coordinating body. For completeness, we also mention the "free" or "liberal" individual professional, although that provider only counts as an organization (and then usually a tiny one) when the professional employs other, non-professional staff. To complicate matters, hybrids are found. For instance, professional partnerships often employ support staff (receptionists, nurses, etc.). Another example is that of disaster relief services such as Medecins Sans Frontiéres, which combine service provision with fundraising. Similarly, some patient organizations (e.g., Mind in the UK) combine the provision of healthcare or support for self-care with fundraising and other activities.

All these obviously count as healthcare organizations: Providing health services is their main activity. However, specialized branches of certain large organizations also provide health services. Military forces in many countries (e.g., the Netherlands) and veterans (e.g., in the USA) have their own health services, as do large enterprises (e.g., BMW) and so, before 1991, did whole industries, such as the postal service in Poland or in the USSR, the railways. Retail pharmacies (e.g., Boots) in the UK have provided limited clinical services (e.g., flu vaccinations) alongside pharmaceutical sales. Many organizations, e.g., Virgin, have specialized divisions that provide healthcare (Virgin Care), although as one activity among many and not necessarily their largest. Prisons have their own health systems in many countries. Taken as a whole, these are not mainly healthcare organizations, but for the purposes of this book, we consider their specialized, healthcare-providing branches or departments separately, and would count them too as healthcare providers.

More activities than these are involved in maintaining the health of a population. We also count as health organizations those whose aims and activities are illness prevention and health promotion work, such as anti-smoking campaigns, occupational health measures, promoting family planning and sexual health, environmental quality and safety. Organizationally, these bodies are also diverse. They include international bodies (e.g., the WHO, regarding its smoking control and similar campaigns), national-level public environmental health and disease monitoring services (e.g., Sanitary-Epidemological Services [SESs] in Russia, the CDC in the USA, the Norwegian Institute of Public Health) and their equivalents in local government (e.g., the Labour Medical Inspectorate in France), occupational health services, some of which are industry-specific (e.g., the German Initiative Neue Qualität der Arbeit [New Quality of Work Initiative]). In the long term, these organizations have larger health impacts than primary or hospital care. To the extent that an organization undertakes these activities, our consideration of management innovations includes and applies to them also.

This range of organizations is very diverse, not only in their functions but in their size (a general practice might only have three or four staff, a large hospital above a thousand), their ownership (the state, a partnership, cooperative, corporate, charitable, a private individual), their case mix and their eventual health impacts. Even in the USA, the majority of healthcare organizations are publicly owned, "not-for-profit" or "third sector" (charitable, voluntary or self-help) bodies, or partnerships. Despite being so diverse, these organizations have some commonalities. All are healthcare providers, in the sense that their activities are intended to have a direct (if sometimes slow) impact upon individuals' physical and mental health, taken as the "complete physical, mental and social well-being and not merely the absence of disease or infirmity" (World Health Organization, 1946, p. 1). These organizations therefore apply a broadly common set of production processes and technologies based on the clinical sciences and epidemiology, and therefore tend to recruit a common set of occupations and occupational skills, of which nurses are the most numerous and, in most such organizations, doctors the most strongly professionalized and powerful. Consequently, healthcare organizations usually have a heavily professionalized workforce, with the result that their management has to constantly negotiate its actions with professional interests. Because both clinical error and the absence of healthcare can have radically harmful consequences, healthcare provision tends to be politically salient, and hence to be heavily legally and ethically regulated. Notwithstanding the scientifically sophisticated character of some healthcare interventions and the corresponding equipment, most healthcare activity is labor-intense service work.

One might trace the supply chain back from healthcare providers to the other organizations that supply their inputs, above all:

1) Knowledge, produced by the bodies that issue technical, including clinical, guidance (e.g., NICE [National Institute for Health and Care Excellence] (UK), IQWIG [Institute for Quality and Economy in Health Care] (Germany), the Joint Commission (USA)) and, beyond them, researchers (working in basic scientific research, clinical research, health services research and translational research). Not only the production of this knowledge, but its management, is of increasing importance;
2) Staff education and training;
3) Other "real-side" inputs: Pharmaceuticals, blood products, medical equipment and consumables;
4) Payers: Healthcare "commissioners" (e.g., clinical commissioning groups in England, local government in Italy and Sweden), social health insurers (e.g., the Netherlands's Siekenfonds, German Krankenkassen) and corporate health insurers (e.g., Aetna, UHG);
5) Regulatory bodies, both public agencies and professional bodies and networks.

Here, the health system boundary becomes ill defined. Management innovations that healthcare providers can use may not so obviously or so directly apply to the "supply chain" organizations listed above. This book therefore concentrates on the usefulness of management innovations to healthcare providers above all, considering the "supply chain" organizations only when a particular management innovation incidentally appears relevant to them too, on a case-by-case basis.

HEALTHCARE ORGANIZATIONS:
AN INTERNATIONAL OVERVIEW

Historically, many European countries legally protected a professional monopoly of clinical practice (i.e., medical, dental, nursing, physiotherapeutic and all the other kinds of diagnostic, curative and therapeutic interventions) in return for a tacit agreement that clinicians would practice conscientiously, in compliance with an ethical code, so as to make treatments as consistent, reliable, safe and error free as humanly possible. These requirements were enforced, in the first instance, by professional organizations themselves, although in the USA, litigation under civil law plays a larger role than elsewhere. Until 1991, the opposite applied in much of central and eastern Europe, with its very different legal systems, where heavy reliance was placed upon the conscientiousness of individual doctors. Evidence-based medicine is institutionalized in a more bureaucratic (Harrison & Wood, 2000), even "Fordist" way, involving, besides line management, specialist national bodies of the kinds mentioned above (NICE, IQWIG) and some international bodies (e.g., the WHO, the Cochrane Collaboration) that produce evidence-based guidelines and protocols, and conduct, collect and synthesize the research from which they derive. Many countries also have inter-organizational professional networks through which clinicians can share and learn current good practices. These may be centered upon medical schools or medical universities (examples exist in the Netherlands and the UK). They may be established by a payer ("commissioner", "insurer") to manage services' consistency and safety across all its provider organizations, or by individual clinicians (examples of both can be found among American HMOs (Robinson & Steiner, 1998)). They may also be established on a local or regional basis by a public authority (e.g., in Australia, Canada, Japan, the UK), with a remit ranging from a clinical audit only to the redesign of whole system-wide care pathways (Addicott et al., 2006), to occupational health and health promotion.

Health systems' clinical, diagnostic, information and pharmaceutical technology development has been institutionalized in many of the same ways, but especially and increasingly though evidence-based medicine. An important addition, though, is that pharmaceutical products especially also have to be licensed through what is, in many countries, a protracted and costly process requiring clinical trials. Because pharmaceutical production is dominated by multinational corporations, governments come under strong pressure to enforce through international trade agreements the intellectual property rights, brands and trademarks that these corporations generate in one health system (often, Germany, the UK or USA) across other health systems. A most important exception is India (and, in less systematic ways, Brazil, Malaysia and Thailand), whose government has only recognized patents from outside India since 2005 and which grants "compulsory licenses" for the local production of generic equivalents for many branded pharmaceuticals (Bird, 2009). The effect has been to make generic medicines, in particular those for treating HIV/AIDS, available at a fraction (sometimes below 10%) of the price of the branded alternatives, and therefore much more widely available. This is a dramatic example of the effects of a pro-generic medicines policy, one that many other health systems (e.g., Belgium, France, Italy, the UK) are also pursuing (while the pharmaceutical corporations, the WTO and the USA have attempted to weaken the effects of such policies—see Reichman, 2009). The actual procurement of new technologies is much more varied across health systems, sometimes being evaluated, controlled and even undertaken at national level (e.g., by the NHS, in part) or by individual provider organizations (the default arrangement in all health systems).

Independent general practitioners and non-hospital doctors based in "offices" or clinics (even if they have hospital admitting rights) are a substantial part of the medical workforce in many countries (e.g., in Australia, England, France, Germany, Ireland, the Netherlands, New Zealand, the USA; in some of these systems, about half of all doctors are independent). Ignoring individual clinicians who practice entirely alone, many of these are still small organizations, often with fewer than 20 members. While management innovations to, say, improve patient satisfaction or the safety of care remain obviously relevant to them, the question arises as to whether management innovations such as *Knowledge Management* or *Management by Objectives* are unnecessarily elaborate and complex for such small organizations.

A messy, complex picture results when we take an international view of the range of healthcare organizations and contexts, to which their advocates say the management innovations discussed in the following chapters are relevant. One therefore has to be critical, selective and inventive in deciding which management innovations are relevant to which healthcare contexts.

To illustrate the point, consider the aim of increasing consumer satisfaction. It is also obviously applicable to healthcare, but immediately with the caveat that most healthcare is a "distress good" which patients would prefer not to have to use at all. Furthermore, different health systems give a different balance of emphasis to three main methods of achieving this aim:

1) Patient choice of provider is one mechanism. It is used in primary care especially, but also in other services that can be provided by a single individual clinician or a range of provider organizations interchangeably. In theory, this mechanism exists wherever patient consent to treatment is required; the patient can simply withhold consent to being treated by any particular individual or organization except the one s/he prefers. In practice, it also depends on whether an alternative service is in fact available and upon how much weight the patient attaches to maintaining a good personal relationship with the clinician. (There is evidence that patients give it considerable weight, especially

for the treatment of chronic and non-trivial health problems—see
Guthrie et al., 2000; Mercer et al., 2007.);
2) Health systems with a strong element of state control have also attempted (in some countries) to include and involve patient representatives on the boards and other governance bodies of health
organizations; this occurs in patient cooperatives (e.g., Group Health,
USA), social insurers (e.g., Technische Krankenkasse, Germany) and
state funders (e.g., clinical commissioning groups, England). In Italy
and Germany, elected regional or *Land* governments play a large part
in regulating and planning their local health systems;
3) Consumer ("market") research methods are also routinely used on
a large scale, and not only in the corporate sector. In the UK, both
patient survey data (see Health and Social Care Information Centre
(2015) and qualitative data (see NHS Choices [2015]) on NHS-funded
provider organizations are published.

So even where the aim of a specific management innovation appears relevant to healthcare organizations, more than one management innovation
may be capable of achieving it.

Similarly, the relevance to healthcare of the aim of improving inter-
organizational coordination is immediately obvious from the burgeoning
literature about it ("integrated care") in, among other places, such publications as the *International Journal of Integrated Care* and the emergence
of bodies such as the International Foundation for Integrated Care. Speed
of treatment is also obviously relevant to healthcare, with the proviso that
access is even more important (without it, the question of speed of service
does not even arise). If it were feasible to adopt them, management innovations that claim to achieve better care coordination and faster access to care
would therefore offer important benefits to health systems.

THE CONTRIBUTORS' FOCI

Which kinds of healthcare organizations are the contributors referring to in
Chapters 3 to 24? Different chapters in the book vary as to which healthcare
setting they consider. As Table 2.1 shows, some authors focus on healthcare
organizations in general, but most of them consider hospitals specifically.
A few also discuss particular types of care, like nursing, acute care, hospital
pharmacies and mental health. In addition, some of them mention primary
care and social care. The chapters also span several countries and continents, but mainly, they concern North American, Australian, New Zealand
or European healthcare organizations. Moreover, as Table 2.1 also shows,
some chapters in the book are based on the authors' own previous empirical
studies, others upon secondary empirical sources (but mostly a combination) and one of them is based on a literature review.

Table 2.1 Overview of the Empirical Bases of Chapters 3 to 24

Chapter No., Management Innovation & Author(s)	Based on	Healthcare Setting
3. *360-Degree Feedback* Joan F. Miller	• Others' empirical studies	• Hospitals. Examples from UK, USA, Canada
4. *Accreditation* Marie-Pascale Pomey	• Others' empirical studies • Own previous empirical studies	• Healthcare organizations in Canada, USA and worldwide
5. *Balanced Scorecard* Elin Funck	• Own previous empirical study	• Three hospitals, one in Sweden and two in Canada
6. *Business Process Reengineering* Anjali Patwardhan, Dhruv Patwardhan and Prakash Patwardhan	• Own previous empirical study • Others' empirical studies	• Healthcare organizations • Hospitals
7. *Consensus* Marie Carney	• Own previous empirical studies • Others' empirical studies	• Nursing leadership in hospitals in Ireland • Other examples from Australia, Canada, New Zealand, USA, UK, Finland and the Netherlands, including hospitals and primary care
8. *Corporate Social Responsibility* Sherif Tehemar	• Others' empirical studies • Own previous empirical studies	• Healthcare organizations in general • Hospitals
9. *Decentralization* Mark Exworthy and Martin Powell	• Others' empirical studies • Own previous empirical studies	• Healthcare systems in various countries, especially the UK
10. *Empowerment* Nelson Ositadimma Oranye and Nora Ahmad	• Own previous empirical study • Others' empirical studies	• Nursing • Healthcare organizations
11. *Kaizen* Mark Graban	• Own professional experience • Others' empirical studies	• Hospitals in the USA

(*Continued*)

Table 2.1 (Continued)

Chapter No., Management Innovation & Author(s)	Based on	Healthcare Setting
12. *Knowledge Management* Nilmini Wickramasinghe and Raj Gururajan	• Own previous empirical studies	• Hospitals in Australia
13. *Lean* Bozena Poksinska	• Own previous empirical studies • Others' empirical studies	• Hospitals and primary care units in Sweden
14. *Learning Organization* Rod Sheaff	• Others' empirical studies • Own previous empirical studies	• Hospitals • Healthcare organizations in general
15. *Management by Objectives* Grigorios L. Kyriakopoulos	• Literature review	• Healthcare organizations in general • Hospital management, nursing, hospital pharmacy
16. *New Public Management* Dawid Sześciło	• Others' empirical studies • Own previous empirical studies	• Healthcare systems in several European countries
17. *Servant Leadership* Jack McCann	• Others' empirical studies • Own previous empirical study	• Hospitals in the USA, Canada
18. *Shared Leadership* D. David Persaud	• Others' empirical studies • Own previous empirical studies	• Different healthcare settings like acute care, mental health, primary care in different countries
19. *Six Sigma* Jacob Krive	• Others' empirical studies	• Hospitals, healthcare organizations in general, with examples from the USA, UK
20. *Sustainability* Tony Huzzard, Andreas Hellström and Svante Lifvergren	• Own previous empirical studies • Others' empirical studies	• Healthcare providers including primary care, hospitals, social care
21. *Teamwork* Jan Schmutz, Annalena Welp and Michaela Kolbe	• Own previous empirical studies. • Others' empirical studies	• Hospitals with focus on acute care

Chapter No., Management Innovation & Author(s)	Based on	Healthcare Setting
22. *Total Quality Management* Ali Mohammad Mosadeghrad and Ewan Ferlie	• Own previous empirical studies. • Others' empirical studies	• Healthcare organizations in general
23. *Transformational Leadership* Bettina Fiery	• Others' empirical studies	• Healthcare organizations in general • Hospital management
24. *Value-Based Healthcare* Thomas Garavan and Gerri Matthews-Smith	• Others' empirical studies	• Healthcare organizations worldwide

Between them, the settings for the studies in the following chapters thus range across many types of service (primary care, secondary care, social care and parts of the supply chains mentioned above). They cover Bismarck-ian systems, financed predominantly through social insurance and with a mixture of public, corporate and charitable service provider organizations; Beveridge systems, in which health services are predominantly financed and provided by public bodies; and the more mixed systems, where health ser-vices are both financed and provided by a mixture of public, corporate and charitable organizations. It is therefore a complex task that the following chapters attempt, to disentangle which management innovations are best suited to which of these settings and what adaptations would have to be made, even for a management innovation that has already been used suc-cessfully in one healthcare setting, to transfer it into another kind of health system or provider organization.

WHY SO MUCH MANAGEMENT INNOVATION?

As the following chapters also explain, many of the management innova-tions considered in this book originated in other economic sectors (e.g., manufacturing, especially engineering and car-building, aviation, education, land transport, etc.), and the main question put in this book is whether these management innovations are relevant to healthcare organizations. There has not really been any reason to ask such a question until quite recently. Sixty years ago, the pace of technological change in healthcare was already accelerating, but an exhaustive description of management innovations in the health sector would have been brief indeed. Many of the economic and policy factors subsequently stimulating the increasing quantity and variety of management innovations in healthcare are widely discussed, but many studies—especially management studies—leave the connections implicit.

There has since the 1970s been an increasing interest in the costs and effects of healthcare on the part of powerful economic interests, both think tanks and corporations (especially financial ones, in the Anglophone world), although the character of this corporate interest is complex. For many corporations, the availability of healthcare for their staff is a practical necessity, but also a considerable cost that it would be in their interests to minimize or shift to someone else. For the corporations involved, or potentially involved, in financing and providing healthcare, however, this money is not cost, but income and profit. Governments, especially those of a neo-liberal persuasion, are usually attentive to major corporations' interests, but in Europe especially, governments are still, even now, the inheritors of the post-1945 political settlement, whereby the provision of a welfare state was the price of political legitimacy at a time when the left (both the trade unions and, politically, communism and social democracy) was at its zenith, and most European states were exhausted and enfeebled by the war. Offe (1982) once remarked that such governments can neither live with the welfare state nor live without it. Not only does that remain true, but it also largely applies to corporations in most of the developed world. It applies to healthcare in particular, as the largest component of the welfare state in many countries. Healthcare reform since the 1980s has therefore had a paradoxical character. On the one hand, it has nearly everywhere been an essentially neo-liberal project, aiming to relieve the state (and indirectly, corporations) of the costs of and political responsibility for healthcare, and to open up the health sector (or keep it open) for commercial exploitation. On the other hand, governments have also increasingly wished to manage the healthcare system for these very reasons and because of its political salience.

The implementation of successive health "reforms" has in many countries (the UK since 1982 is not the only case in point) stimulated the emergence of a distinct, larger, more powerful and better-paid stratum of healthcare managers as the intermediaries between the government and the clinicians who actually deliver health services, and sometimes between the latter and corporate owners and financiers, too. One consequence has been to shift the balance of power between clinicians and managers in favor of the managers. Another has been an increasing exchange both of ideas and of managers themselves between healthcare and other sectors, encouraging the transfer and imitation (mimesis) of externally invented management innovations in the health sector. For their part, the managers have a natural interest in discovering, selecting, adopting or inventing instrumental innovations that will increase their control over the processes by which healthcare is produced, enabling them more readily to achieve (what they regard as) the proper objectives of healthcare. Equally, they have an interest in symbolic interventions to legitimate these activities and their own role as managers. A common rhetorical device is for governments and managers alike to justify themselves as those who introduce "new", "improved" structures and production processes, "change" (Courpasson, 1998) and consequently, "innovation".

Together, these developments have generated an accelerating pursuit of management innovations at team, organizational and inter-organizational levels within health systems, and a correspondingly burgeoning literature, both empirical and normative, some of whose characteristics Chapter 1 outlines.

This chapter's specification of what we mean by "healthcare organization" and its international overview return us to the overall aim of the book, which Chapter 1 expressed as being "to test the relevance of quite an extensive set of management innovations for healthcare organizations and, should these tests show that any of the management innovations is partly relevant but not fully so, to suggest an adapted version of the management innovation that fits healthcare organizations". We can now specify the aim somewhat more exactly by adding that the relevance testing means testing, above all, relevance to the organizations that actually provide healthcare, in the sense of activities having a direct impact upon individuals' physical and mental health, across a variety of health systems.

REFERENCES

Addicott, R., McGivern, G., & Ferlie, E. (2006). Networks, organizational learning and knowledge management: NHS cancer networks. *Public Money and Management*, 26 (2), 87–94.

Bird, R.C. (2009). Developing nations and the compulsory license: Maximizing access to essential medicines while minimizing investment side effects. *The Journal of Law, Medicine & Ethics*, 37 (2), 209–221.

Courpasson, D. (1998). Le changement est un outil politique. *Revue Francaise de Gestion*, 120 (5), 6–16.

Guthrie, B., Brampton, S., & Wyke, S. (2000). Does continuity in general practice really matter? Commentary: A patient's perspective of continuity. *BMJ: British Medical Journal*, 321 (7263), 734–736.

Harrison, S., & Wood, B. (2000). Scientific-bureaucratic medicine and UK health policy. *Policy Studies Review*, 17 (4), 25–42.

Health Social Care Information Centre. (2015). *Find data*. Retrieved from http://www.hscic.gov.uk/searchcatalogue?infotype=0%2FSurvey&sort=Relevance&size=10&page=1 (accessed 27 June 2015).

Loewenson, R. (1993). Structural adjustment and health policy in Africa. *International Journal of Health Services*, 23 (4), 717–730.

Mercer, S., Cawston, P., & Bikker, A. (2007). Quality in general practice consultations: A qualitative study of the views of patients living in an area of high socio-economic deprivation in Scotland. *BMC Family Practice*, 8 (1), 22.

NHS Choices. (2015). *Your health, your choices*. Retrieved from http://www.nhs.uk/Service-Search/Hospital/Location/7 (accessed 27 June 2015).

Offe, C. (1982). Some contradictions of the modern welfare state. *Critical Social Policy*, 2 (5), 7–16.

Reichman, J.H. (2009). Compulsory licensing of patented pharmaceutical inventions: Evaluating the options. *The Journal of Law, Medicine & Ethics : A Journal of the American Society of Law, Medicine & Ethics*, 37 (2), 247–263.

Robinson, R., & Steiner, A. (1998). *Managed Health Care.* Buckingham, England: Open University Press.

Rowden, R. (2009). *The Deadly Ideas of Neoliberalism: How the IMF Has Undermined Public Health and the Fight Against AIDS.* London: Zed Books.

Sheaff, R. (2005). Governance in gridlock in the Russian health system: The case of Sverdlovsk oblast. *Social Science & Medicine,* 60 (10), 2359–2369.

Sheaff, R., Child, S., Schofield, J., Pickard, S., & Mannion, R. (2012). *Understanding Professional Partnerships and Non-Hierarchical Organisations.* London: NIHR-SDO.

World Health Organization. (1946). *Preamble to the constitution of the World Health Organization as adopted by the International Health Conference* (official records of the World Health Organization No. 2). New York: WHO.

World Health Organization. (1985). *Health for All by the Year 2000.* Geneva: WHO.

Part II

Examining Management Innovations

3 360-Degree Feedback in Healthcare Organizations

Joan F. Miller

INTRODUCTION

During World War II, several developments occurred in the field of performance evaluation. Military leaders considered feedback from multiple sources a valuable resource for the evaluation, development and motivation of personnel (Hedge et al., 2001). They learned that feedback from multiple sources shifts the focus from superior to subordinate evaluation to one of multiple perspectives (Whiteside, 2004). A 360-degree evaluation system in the US Army continues to provide information for supervisors and subordinates as they learn about their respective strengths and areas for growth. Carefully crafted 360-Degree evaluations remain as a source for the promotion of leadership development in the military (Murphy, 2013).

During the 1990s, interest in feedback from multiple sources gained popularity in a variety of settings, including healthcare. Fleenor and Prince (1997) define *360-Degree Feedback*, or *Multisource Feedback (MSF)*, as, "An activity of gathering data about an employee from multiple sources in that person's circle of influence" (p. 71). Sources include co-workers, superiors, peers, subordinates, self and patients. The 360-Degree evaluation process has been viewed as a practical method for the assessment of professional development and competence in the workplace. Assessment techniques include the use of questionnaires, narratives and interviews. Methods of assessment may involve either electronic or paper and pencil completion of assessment tools. Assessment tools must meet certain criteria for validity. In other words, tools must demonstrate the potential for an accurate description of key aspects of the workplace behaviors of leaders, subordinates and co-workers. In addition, when applied to healthcare organizations, the process for evaluation must be consistent with the organization's strategic objectives. Plans for change and improvement of overall performance must be clear and embraced by all involved in the assessment process (Dubinsky et al., 2010).

Healthcare organizations utilizing multiple sources for feedback include private practices, physician-owned-and-managed healthcare systems and the governing bodies responsible for accreditation, licensure and leadership development (Garman & Lemak, 2011). Most evaluations in healthcare settings have focused primarily on clinical competence. However, more recently, evaluations have expanded to include professional development, medical team cohesion and leadership skills as well.

Research indicates that the process of 360-Degree evaluation is relevant for healthcare organizations in terms of leadership and professional development, teamwork, work satisfaction and quality of care for an organization. However, the process is not without its challenges. Lack of financial resources and support from senior management are two examples of challenges that impede the 360-Degree evaluation (McGill & Yessis, 2008).

This chapter will describe the benefits and challenges associated with implementation of 360-Degree evaluation in healthcare organizations, the criteria for effective 360-Degree evaluation and examples of the application of 360-Degree evaluation in various healthcare settings. The chapter will conclude with lessons learned and examples of steps healthcare institutions can take to ensure effective evaluation in a rapidly changing healthcare environment.

BENEFITS OF 360-DEGREE EVALUATION

In general, the benefits of 360-Degree evaluation in healthcare settings include professional development, improved work relationships and increased patient satisfaction with care (Garbett et al., 2007; Overeem et al., 2010; Sargeant et al., 2011). Fleenor and Prince (1997) cluster the benefits of 360-Degree evaluation into four categories: 1) Collection of perspectives with which a person's skills, behaviors and performance can be assessed; 2) Alleviation of limitations associated with top-down or single-source evaluations; 3) Creation of the opportunity to evaluate one's own performance; 4) Inclusion of a system for focusing on an institution's values and vision.

For example, when conducted in dermatology clinics in the United Kingdom, 360-Degree evaluation was associated with constructive criticism, reassurance and close observation (Cohen et al., 2009). Workplace assessment is mandatory in the National Health Service for most clinicians. Assessment includes direct observation of procedural skills, observation by an assessor during interaction with a patient and feedback from clerical, nursing and medical staff. After reflecting on the value of 360-Degree evaluation, one trainee stated that it is "[g]ood to know what your colleagues really think of you" (Cohen et al., 2009, p. 161.) The investigators stressed that validation during training is critical for continued success as an effective healthcare worker. Those evaluated have the opportunity to compare their self-evaluation against the evaluations of others within the scope of practice. The 360-Degree evaluation process provides an alternative to top-down or single-source evaluations, and professional development is the intended outcome.

Feedback from multiple sources also has the potential to improve patient satisfaction scores. Investigators in an orthopedic practice setting assessed the relationship between co-workers' ratings of physician performance and patient satisfaction with care, using retrospective data collected as part of a routine assessment within hospital operations (Hageman et al., 2014). Co-workers, including peers and clinical healthcare team members, used the *Physicians Universal Leadership-Teamwork Skills Education* (PULSE) tool to assess physician performance. *PULSE* addresses the core competencies endorsed by the Accreditation Council for Graduate Medical Education (ACGME), the American Board of Medical Specialties and the Joint Commission. Competencies include professionalism, leadership, teamwork quality, technical ability and interpersonal and communication skills. The mean age of the participating orthopedic surgeons was 50 years. The study focused on the correlation between patient satisfaction scores and coworker *PULSE* scores. Coworker ratings of a surgeon's ability to understand how his/her behavior translates in terms of respect and perception of the surgeon's leadership skill and capacity for teamwork, and predicted ratings addressing patient satisfaction with care. However, coworker ratings for technical competence did not correlate with patient satisfaction, raising the question that patients may not have the knowledge and necessary background to assess clinical competence. This example underscores the importance of addressing feedback from multiple sources when applying 360-Degree evaluation to a practice setting. Future studies should consider the matters that mean the most to patients: Technical skill, or the quality of physician-patient interaction?

The process of *360-Degree Feedback* has also been used to document the successful mastery of the core competencies established by *ACGME* among residents in training (Rodgers & Manifold, 2002). Faculty, fellow residents, medical students, nurses, support staff, patients, families and the resident's self-evaluation are all involved in the evaluation process. Evaluations generally use a rating scale to describe the frequency of a behavior, with one meaning "never" and five meaning "all the time". Verbal ratings are also used to describe the performance of skills, using terms such as "agree", "slightly agree", "neutral", "slightly disagree", "disagree". Computer-based assessment programs enhance the timeliness of the assessment process, a benefit for both the raters and ratees. Rodgers and Manifold (2002) suggest that professionalism, communication and interpersonal skills represent the most appropriate *ACGME* competencies to be evaluated by the 360-Degree evaluation.

Feedback for faculty-in-training settings also deserves attention. Faculty response to resident feedback varies. Some view feedback as an alert to perform better in some aspects of the faculty role, while others have limited intention to change. Faculty members state that reflection on feedback and the development of plans for change simply add a layer of responsibility and stress to an already demanding role. Nevertheless, Roermund et al. (2013)

underscore the need for feedback to promote positive role models in healthcare settings.

To realize the benefits of 360-Degree evaluation, preparation for the process is essential. Most organizations have been accustomed to top-down or single-source feedback during their evaluation of employees. Shifting to multiple-source feedback requires organizational commitment (Ewen & Edwards, 2001). Preparation includes determining that all stakeholders value the process in terms of added value. Methods for checking readiness include questioning employees regarding preference for evaluation from a single source or multiple sources, creating focus groups to discuss preference for a type of evaluation, conducting an employee survey for level of preference and assessing employee satisfaction with the process (Ewen & Edwards, 2001). Bracken and Timmreck (2001) stress *sustainability* as a prerequisite for successful 360-Degree evaluation in clinical settings. *Sustainability* requires elements of *MSF* that reinforce behavior change and skill development that will result in organizational effectiveness. Elements include relevancy of feedback and alignment of feedback in terms of the strategies, goals and values of the organization (Bracken et al., 2001). Feedback is more likely to enhance self-reflection and promote professional development when those assessed have the opportunity to engage in informed discussions with trusted colleagues (Lockyer et al., 2011).

A successful 360-Degree assessment requires a buy-in among all stakeholders in an organization, whether it is a practice or an educational setting. Informed discussions following evaluation and coaching have been associated with professional growth and leadership development. Efforts to achieve the benefits of 360-Degree evaluation must be weighed against the challenges and costs associated with the process.

CHALLENGES ASSOCIATED WITH 360-DEGREE EVALUATION

Several challenges associated with 360-Degree evaluation impact upon the successful enhancement of professional development and quality of care. Variation in feedback provided by doctors and patients has been noted in the process of 360-Degree evaluation or *MSF*. In attempts to learn whether patient feedback (PF) and 360-Degree evaluation identify sub-standard performance, Archer and McAvoy (2011) conducted a study to evaluate the utility of 360-Degree evaluation in healthcare settings. They found discrepancies between doctors' ratings of peer performance and patients' ratings of physicians. Physicians were rated using the *Sheffield Peer Rating Assessment Tool (SPRAT)*. SPRAT consists of 24 questions focusing on clinical and psychosocial attributes. Physicians selected their own assessors. Patients completed the *Sheffield Patient Assessment Tool*, which allows feedback on communication during an office visit. Patient ratings of physician performance were significantly higher than those of the colleagues selected to conduct a review. The validity of 360-Degree evaluation and PF as they are currently constructed must be examined. In addition, feedback bias may occur when physicians select their own assessors. Do physicians select subordinates who feel compelled to provide positive feedback? Do patients possess the knowledge required to identify the quality of performance in a given situation? Archer and McAvoy (2011) stress the need for continued research to determine the appropriate selection of peer evaluators and patient capacity for a quality evaluation of physician performance.

To advance understanding of peer and patient evaluations of physician performance, Campbell et al. (2010) studied the reliability and validity of two tools: The *Colleague Feedback Evaluation Tool (CFET)* and the *Doctor's Interpersonal Skills Questionnaire (DISQ)*. The CFET addresses colleagues' perceptions of a physician's clinical ability, teamwork and clinical knowledge. The *DISQ* addresses patients' perceptions of physician expertise, willingness to consider patient concerns and ability to listen. A statistical analysis of the responses from 2421 colleagues and 8474 patients revealed that both tools are reliable instruments for the evaluation of feedback from both colleagues and patients. Colleague assessment of a physician's clinical ability and knowledge and patient assessment of a physician's warmth, consideration and clinical ability were predictive of the likelihood for recommendation of the physician evaluated. These tools were designed for use in primary care and have the potential for use in other settings for assessment of patient satisfaction with care.

360-Degree evaluation is also useful for measuring leadership effectiveness in healthcare settings. Challenges associated with the effective assessment of a healthcare organization's leadership include full physician participation and the inclusion of all members of a leadership team. In addition, methods for measuring leadership capacity are complex. Assessment includes the ability of a leader to articulate a clear vision and build trust. Assessment also includes the ability of a leader to communicate a vision for growth based on effective communication, resilience and management. Additional competencies include professionalism and commitment to professional ethics, communication, self-management and a vision for organizational change (Garman & Scribner, 2011). All dimensions of effective leadership must be incorporated into the 360-Degree evaluation. In addition, a quality assessment must include full physician and leadership team participation in order to achieve an effective assessment.

Challenges associated with effective 360-Degree evaluation in healthcare settings include lack of time and resources. The development of assessment tools that address feasibility in terms of time commitment may enhance the potential for effective 360-Degree evaluation. Wilkinson et al. (2008) conducted a study to evaluate tools to reduce time commitment. The participants in their study continued to find the completion of tools time consuming. The participants included 230 medical specialist registrars in the United Kingdom. The tools used in their research included the mini-*Clinical*

Evaluation Exercise (mini-CEX), the *Directly Observed Procedural Skills* (*DOPS*), and *MSF*. The mean time to complete the mini-CEX was 25 minutes. Completion of the *DOPS* required the amount of time for the completion of the procedure plus additional time for feedback. The completion of the *MSF* form required six minutes. Although completion rates were lower than anticipated, Wilkinson et al. (2008) found the assessment methods to be feasible. To enhance participation in evaluation, the investigators recommend making feedback from several sources compulsory. In addition, the investigators suggest that gender issues be addressed. Receptivity to 360-Degree evaluation may be more acceptable if the evaluation includes a mix of genders, so that feedback is not relegated to male consultants only. The investigators conclude that, despite limitations, feedback is essential for formative evaluation and professional growth.

The limited availability of raters presents another challenge for the effective implementation of 360-Degree evaluation. The limited availability of qualified raters in cases where doctors are borderline in terms of performance is problematic. In such cases, more raters are needed to broaden the perspective of the evaluation and subsequent remediation. The use of abbreviated forms for assessment may mitigate time constraints and availability of raters (Davies & Archer, 2005). Abbreviated tools and the institution of action plans to support performance may enhance the effectiveness of 360-Degree evaluation. Of note, action plans agreed upon by both supervisor and trainee tend to improve performance associated with 360-Degree evaluation.

Cost also represents a challenge associated with 360-Degree evaluation (Tornow et al., 1998). Time and money are required to establish evaluation programs designed to advance the goals of healthcare organizations and educational programs. Despite cost and time commitments, the collection of information from different sources in a practice setting, including co-workers, patients and families, enhances the quality of organizational practice (Arah et al., 2011; Chandler et al., 2010). Acknowledging the effort required in conducting a 360-Degree evaluation in medical education, Shrank et al. (2004) underscore the value of evaluations from multiple sources to enhance student performance. Outcomes of 360-Degree evaluations often exceed the value of traditional individual evaluations from superiors in both organizational and educational settings.

The feasibility of conducting 360-Degree evaluations in healthcare organizations must be considered. Using guidelines derived from the *Assessment of Professional Behaviors* (*APB*) program, Richmond et al. (2011) assessed the feasibility of 360-Degree evaluation in residency and fellowship programs. The *APB* program is a multisource feedback program developed by the National Board of Medical Examiners in the USA that is responsible for assessing behaviors associated with safe, effective and ethical practice in medicine. Leadership orientation, participant orientation and feedback sessions are all part of the *APB* program. Of the 27 programs that indicated interest in participating in the assessment, only eight completed the full assessment. Program leaders cited time commitment and communication delays as major obstacles to completion. Following their analysis of the surveys, Richmond et al. (2011) found that despite time commitment, scheduling and communication delays, participants reported benefits, including a clear structure and a focus on professionalism that extended beyond existing procedural assessments. The authors recommend that future programs address efforts to reduce barriers to 360-Degree evaluation, including scheduling, technology and communication.

CRITERIA TO ENHANCE 360-DEGREE EVALUATION IN HEALTHCARE SETTINGS

Criteria for effective 360-Degree evaluation must be addressed in both educational and practice settings. In the field of medical education, the criteria for a quality assessment include validity or coherence, reproducibility, equivalence, feasibility, educational effect, catalytic effect and acceptability (Norcini et al., 2011). In terms of validity or coherence, the assessment process must serve a purpose for a particular discipline or organization. For example, the successful completion of the medical licensure examination serves as the basis for readiness to provide safe and effective medical care. "Reproducibility" means that assessment outcomes would be similar if conducted in different settings under similar circumstances. Assessments that meet the criterion of equivalence generally yield the same or similar results and decisions when administered in different institutions. Feasibility requires that the assessment process and resultant decisions are practical and applicable in terms of an organization's purpose and context. Educational benefit for both the person conducting the assessment and the person or group completing the assessment must be present. Educational follow-up is essential for evaluators and those being evaluated. Norcini et al. (2011) underscore the importance of the catalytic nature of good assessment. In other words, the assessment process must lead to the creation of efforts that will support growth and innovation within an organization. In all cases, key stakeholders must view the assessment process as acceptable and credible.

Instruments for 360-Degree evaluation for practicing physicians also require evaluation for quality, effectiveness and consistency with the criteria for good medical practice. Instruments in Canada include the *College of Alberta Physician Achievement Review (PAR)*, the *General Medicine Council (GMC)* questionnaire and a combination of the *CFET* and the *DISQ*, known as the *CFEP360 Tool*. Physicians in Canada must complete the *PAR* every five years in order to maintain licensure. The *PAR* instruments elicit feedback from patients, medical colleagues, co-workers and self in both family and specialty practices. The *GMC* questionnaire and the *CFEP360 Tool* are generic instruments designed for use in both general and specialty practices. Each instrument met at least five or six of the criteria for a quality assessment. None of the studies addressed the educational criterion for a good assessment. Lockyer (2013) notes that the applicability of instruments may vary according to setting, culture and particular need. Additional research is needed to determine the effectiveness of 360-Degree evaluation as well as the quality of instrumentation.

Responses to *MSF* or 360-Degree evaluation among evaluators and those being evaluated can vary. To enhance the effectiveness of evaluation, general practice trainers in the United Kingdom employed a model known as the *Emotion Content and Outcomes Model (ECO)* (Sargeant et al., 2011). This model was developed to facilitate discussion during feedback. The *ECO* aims to help trainees accept their feedback and plan steps for further development. To determine satisfaction among trainers and trainees, Sargeant et al. (2011) conducted semi-structured interviews using two open-ended questions addressing the acceptability and usefulness of the model and the potential for impact on individual outcomes. The results indicated that trainees valued the opportunity to reflect on the emotions associated with feedback. Trainers cited the positive influence reflection on emotions had on their role as coach or partner in the feedback process.

Wimer and Nowack (2006) discuss steps to take to ensure the successful implementation of the 360-Degree evaluation. Steps include defining a clear purpose of the evaluation, involving key stakeholders in the planning and execution of an evaluation process and ensuring that all stakeholders have the opportunity to discuss their concerns and goals. Confidentiality and resources to ensure timely feedback are essential. A systematic and rigorous evaluation of the assessment process is required to illuminate the steps required to achieve desired change and organizational growth. Despite attention to the criteria associated with the successful implementation of the 360-Degree evaluation, challenges still exist.

When properly implemented, the 360-Degree evaluation has the potential to promote effective management and growth among developing professionals. To achieve the catalytic effects that Norcini et al. (2011) addressed, it is anticipated that feedback will help employees and other professionals achieve their full potential (Robertson, 2008). When properly executed, the 360-Degree evaluation does promote professional growth if the process involves a clear understanding of the purpose of the feedback process, buy-in from the employees and leadership of the organization, accurate information related to the data collection process and coaching to support an employee's development. The lessons learned from the application of the 360-Degree evaluation in healthcare organizations provide additional insight into the effective implementation of this process.

LESSONS LEARNED FROM HEALTH PROFESSIONALS USING 360-DEGREE EVALUATION

Investigators from a variety of health professions maintain that instrument selection is key to a successful 360-Degree evaluation. The reliability and validity of the instruments are essential. Violato et al. (2008) assessed tools designed to assess competencies of psychiatrists in training in terms of communication skills, professionalism, collegiality and self-management. The instruments reviewed included those for patients, non-physician co-workers, medical colleagues and a self-assessment tool for the physician under review. The tools used in this study included those developed not only for use in psychiatry, but in pediatrics and internal medicine as well. The participants indicated they were unable to respond to certain items, indicating that the items on the tools were specific to pediatrics or internal medicine. The investigators learned that future investigations should include tools specific to a 360-Degree evaluation in a particular scope of practice.

In the field of nursing, Dyess et al. (2013) introduced the concept of caring into the matrix of the 360-Degree evaluation. The *Participatory Action Research (PAR)* project included concepts of caring, such as trust, patience, honesty and courage during evaluation. Healthcare personnel, faculty and students participated in the project via a one-on-one interview or focus group discussion. The aim of the study was to learn aspects of caring in a healthcare setting in order to transform a work environment. Dyess et al. (2013) admit that the process of evaluation with an emphasis on caring created a challenge in terms of separating emotion from mission in terms of the transformation of a workplace setting. However, the voices of nurses in this *PAR* project did contribute to change and commitment to caring values as a means of transforming commitment to quality in a practice environment.

Assessment among different members of a care team may also enhance the 360-Degree evaluation in a healthcare setting. To expand their knowledge of the value of the 360-Degree evaluation, nurses at Cedars-Sinai Medical Center in Los Angeles, California participated in a 360-Degree evaluation of residents in the department of obstetrics and gynecology (Ogunyemi et al., 2009). The nurses' evaluations of residents were compared with evaluations submitted by clinical faculty. Correlations, although not statistically significant, did exist between nurse and clinical faculty evaluations of interpersonal and communication skills and professionalism. Weaker correlations existed in the areas of medical knowledge and practice issues. Despite discrepancies in evaluations, particularly in terms of clinical skills, the authors learned that evaluations from different members of the healthcare team do provide perspectives that are useful for formative feedback and professional development.

In terms of leadership development, a 360-Degree evaluation requires time and must be consistent with a healthcare organization's values, vision and goals. Evaluation processes must be tailored "to local needs and adapted as the health system evolves" (Garman & Lemak, 2011, p. 4). The process of 360-Degree evaluation requires leadership commitment to development and culture change and growth.

A 360-Degree assessment is most effective when the process involves an objective rather than a biased approach. Questions to be addressed include the determination of whether the process reflects an assessment of the person being evaluated or a reflection of the evaluator's assessment of his/her own performance in a particular area (Buckingham, 2011). For example, when an evaluator assesses another's ability to listen during interactions, is the evaluation based more on the evaluator assessing his or her own ability to listen during interactions, or the ability of the person being evaluated to listen during interactions? To enhance objectivity in a 360-Degree evaluation, Buckingham (2011) suggests that leaders consider an evaluation of themselves in addition, including the creation of a 360-Degree evaluation tool that asks the rater to evaluate his or her ability to perform in areas of leadership as a first step to the evaluation of another's leadership performance. One lesson learned was that development of a tool for self-evaluation may help in the development of a tool for the evaluation of another's performance.

CONCLUSION

Military and industrial organizations have invested substantial resources in the 360-Degree evaluation. Healthcare organizations have adopted this form of evaluation to promote professional development and competence among healthcare workers and physicians in training, as well as satisfaction with care among patients. The basis of the 360-Degree evaluation is that every employee, regardless of position, receives feedback from all co-workers and leadership. Early emphasis on leadership skills and customer satisfaction has prompted efforts in healthcare organizations to seek feedback on multiple levels. The 360-Degree evaluation process has prompted interventions to promote professional development among healthcare workers. Interventions require training and support from leadership of healthcare organizations, including investment of time and finances. Benefits include professional development, worker satisfaction, teamwork, and patient satisfaction. The benefits of a 360-Degree evaluation in medical education include teaching excellence and enhanced professionalism among faculty and students. Implications for the future application of the 360-Degree assessment include modification of the methods of assessment to reduce time and communication concerns. The process of 360-Degree evaluation in a variety of healthcare settings affirms the process as a means of professional development, improved work relationships and patient satisfaction with quality of care. Future research should address the effectiveness of coaching in connection with the 360-Degree evaluation for supporting professional development. Leaders and accrediting bodies should continue to support the process of 360-Degree evaluation.

REFERENCES

Arah, O., Hoekstra, J., Bos, A., & Lombarts, J. (2011). New tools for systematic evaluation of teaching qualities of medical faculty: Results of an ongoing multi-center survey. *PLoS ONE, 6* (10), article no. e25983. Retrieved from http://

journals.plos.org/plosone/article?id=10.1371/journal.pone.0025983 (accessed 19 June 2015).

Archer, J.C., & McAvoy, P. (2011). Factors that may undermine the validity of patient and multi-source feedback. *Medical Education*, 45 (9), 886–893.

Bracken, D.W., & Timmreck, C.W. (2001). Success and sustainability: A systems view of multisource feedback. In D.W. Bracken, C.W. Timmreck, & A.H. Church (Eds.), *The Handbook of Multisource Feedback*, San Francisco, CA: Jossey-Bass, pp. 478–494.

Bracken, D.W., Timmreck, C.W., Fleenor, J.W., & Summers, L. (2001). 360 feedback from another angle. *Human Resources Management*, 40 (1), 3–20.

Buckingham, M. (2011). The fatal flaws with 360 surveys. *Harvard Business Review*. Retrieved from https://hbr.org/2011/10/the-fatal-flaw-with-360-survey (accessed 13 June 2015).

Campbell, J., Narayanan, A., Burford, B., & Greco, M. (2010). Validation of a multi-source feedback tool for use in general practice. *Education for Primary Care*, 21 (3), 165–179.

Chandler, N., Henderson, G., Park, B., Byerley, J., Brown, W., & Steiner, M. (2010). Use of a 360-degree evaluation in the outpatient setting: The usefulness of nurse, faculty, patient/family, and resident self-evaluation. *Journal of Graduate Medical Education*, 2 (3), 430–434.

Cohen, S.N., Farrant, P.B.J., & Taibjeet, S.M. (2009). Assessing the assessments: UK dermatology trainees' views of workplace assessment tools. *British Journal of Dermatology*, 161 (1), 34–39.

Davies, H., & Archer, J. (2005). Multi source feedback: Development and practical aspects. *The Clinical Teacher*, 2 (2), 77–81.

Dubinsky, I., Jennings, K., Greengarten, M., & Brans, A. (2010). 360-degree physician performance assessment. *Healthcare Quarterly*, 13 (2), 71–76.

Dyess, S., Boykin, A., & Bulfin, M.J. (2013). Hearing the voices of nurses in caring theory-based practice. *Nursing Science Quarterly*, 26 (2), 167–173.

Ewen, A.J., & Edwards, M.R. (2001). Readiness for multisource feedback. In D.W. Bracken, C.W. Timmreck & A.H. Church (Eds.), *The Handbook of Multisource Feedback*, San Francisco, CA: Jossey-Bass, pp. 33–47.

Fleenor, J.W., & Prince, J.M. (1997). *Using 360-Degree Feedback in Organizations: An Annotated Bibliography*. Greensboro, NC: Center for Creative Leadership.

Garbett, R., Hardy, S., Manley, K., Titchen, A., & McCormack, B. (2007). Developing a qualitative approach to 360-degree feedback to aid understanding and development of clinical expertise. *Journal of Nursing Management*, 15 (3), 342–347.

Garman, A., & Lemak, C. (2011). *NCHL white paper on developing healthcare leaders: What we have learned, and what is next*. Retrieved from http://www.nchl.org/Documents/NavLink/NCHL_Developing_Healthcare_Leaders__Nov_2011_uid11212011137292.pdf (accessed 30 May 2015).

Garman, A., & Scribner, L. (2011). Leading for quality in healthcare: Development and validation of a competency model. *Journal of Healthcare Management*, 56 (6), 373–384.

Hageman, M., Ring, D., Gregory, P., Rubash, H., & Harmon, L. (2014). Do 360-degree feedback survey results relate to patient satisfaction measures? *Clinical Orthopaedics and Related Research*, 473 (5), 1590–1597.

Hedge, J.W., Borman, W.C., & Birkeland, S.A. (2001). History and development of multisource feedback as a methodology. In D.W. Bracken, C.W. Timmreck, & A.H. Church (Eds.), *The Handbook of Multisource Feedback*, San Francisco, CA: Jossey-Bass, pp. 15–32.

Lockyer, J. (2013). Multisource feedback: Can it meet criteria for good assessment? *Journal of Continuing Education in the Health Professions*, 33 (2), 89–98.

Lockyer, J., Armson, H., Chesluk, B., Dornan, T., Holmboe, E., Loney, E., Mann, K., & Sargent, J. (2011). Feedback data sources that inform physician self-assessment. *Medical Teacher*, 33 (2), e113-e120.

McGill, A.R., & Yessis, J. (2008). Leadership development highly valued to drive organizational excellence, but not common practice. Retrieved from http://www.nrcpicker.com/PCC%20Institute/Member%20Resources/Research%20Library/Forms/Leadership.aspx (accessed 30 May 2015).

Murphy, J. (2013). From the deckplates: The good and bad of 360-degree feedback. *US Naval Institute Proceedings Magazine*, 139 (6), 324.

Norcini, J., Anderson, B., Bollela,V., Burch, V., Costa, M., Duvivier, R., Galbraith, R., Hays, R., Kent, A., Perrott, V., & Roberts, T. (2011). Criteria for good assessment: Consensus statement and recommendations from the Ottawa 2010 conference. *Medical Teacher*, 33 (3), 206–214.

Ogunyemi, D., Gonzalez, G., Fong, A., Alexander, C., Finke, D., Donnon,T., & Azziz, R. (2009). From the eye of the nurses: 360-degree evaluation of residents. *Journal of Continuing Education in the Health Professions*, 29 (2), 105–110.

Overeem, K., Lombarts, K., Arah, O., Klazinga, N., Grol, R., & Wollersheim, H. (2010). Three methods of multi-source feedback compared: A plea for narrative comments and coworkers' perspectives. *Medical Teacher*, 32 (2), 141–147.

Richmond, M., Canavan, C., Holtman, M., & Katsufrakis, P. (2011). Feasibility of implementing a standardized multisource feedback program in the graduate medical education environment. *Journal of Graduate Medical Education*, 3 (4), 511–516.

Robertson, C. (2008). Employee development: Getting the information you need through a 360° feedback report. *Chemical Engineering*, 115 (4), 63–66.

Rodgers, K.G., & Manifold, C. (2002). 360-degree feedback: Possibilities for assessment of the ACGME core competencies for emergency room residents. *Academic Emergency Medicine*, 9 (11), 1300–1304.

Roermund, T., Schreurs, M., Mokkink, H., Bottema, B., Scherpbier, A., & Weel, C. (2013). Qualitative study about the ways teachers react to feedback from resident evaluations. *BMC Medical Education*, 1 (98). Retrieved from http://www.biomedcentral.com/content/pdf/1472-6920-13-98.pdf (accessed 31 May 2015).

Sargeant, J., McNaughton, E., Mercer, S., Murphy, D., Sullivan, P., & Bruce, D. (2011). Providing feedback: Exploring a model (emotion, content, outcomes) for facilitating multisource feedback. *Medical Teacher*, 33 (9), 744–749.

Shrank, W., Reed, V., & Jernstedt, G. (2004). Fostering professionalism in medical education. *Journal of General Internal Medicine*, 19 (8), 887–892.

Tornow, W.W., London, M., & Center for Creative Leadership. (1998). *Maximizing the Value of 360-Degree Feedback: A Process for Successful Individual and Organizational Development*. San Francisco, CA: Jossey-Bass.

Violato, C., Lockyer, J.M., & Fidler, H. (2008). Assessment of psychiatrists in practice through multisource feedback. *Canadian Journal of Psychiatry*, 53 (8), 525–533.

Whiteside, C. (2004). From one to three sixty: Assessing leaders. *Military Review*, 84 (5), 86–88.

Wilkinson J.R., Crossley, J.G.M., Wragg, A., Mills, P., Cowan, G., & Wade, W. (2008). Implementing workplace-based assessment across the medical specialists in the United Kingdom. *Medical Education*, 42 (4), 363–373.

Wimer, S., & Nowack, K. (2006). *13 common mistakes using 360-degree feedback*. Retrieved from http://www.360degreefeedback.net/media/13commonmistakes.pdf (accessed 30 May 2015).

4 Accreditation and Other External Evaluations of Quality and Safety of Care and Services
Innovations for Improvement?[1]

Marie-Pascale Pomey

INTRODUCTION

Healthcare organizations (HCOs) across the world are searching for ways to improve quality of care and promote effective quality improvement strategies (Groene et al., 2009, 2010, Scrivens, 1997; Tricco et al., 2014). Some examples of these initiatives are reported by Funck (Chapter 5 in this volume), Graban (Chapter 11 in this volume), Poksinska (Chapter 13 in this volume), Krive (Chapter 19 in this volume) and Mosadeghrad and Ferlie (Chapter 22 in this volume). In addition, several countries have for years focused on external evaluation of quality and safety of care and services as a way to motivate HCOs to implement continuous quality improvement and integrated risk management programs. As the general public becomes more and more interested in the degree of quality and safety provided by HCOs, external evaluations meet the need for transparency and accountability. For this reason, governments have been tempted to make them mandatory, even though the links between them and the quality and safety of care are not easily proven.

These external evaluations can take different forms. They can cover entire establishments (e.g., *Accreditation*), specific processes (e.g., ISO standards) or specific areas (e.g. Managing Obstetrical Risk Efficiently (MORE)). They can also consist of individual evaluations, through visits by professional orders. Their common goal is to promote standards. Benezech (1996) describes them as a collective cognitive device helping HCOs to improve by capitalizing on their existing activities, practices and experiences (through transcription and formalization) to increase their knowledge (reflection on feedback). Since standards-based evaluation can lead HCOs to adopt new organizational structures, one can refer to them in terms of organizational innovation.

In this chapter, we will concentrate on external evaluations at the organizational level, providing a few examples. We will then discuss the limitations of *Accreditation* and conclude with a review of the future challenges facing external evaluation organizations.

ACCREDITATION

Accreditation is an internationally recognized evaluation process used to assess and improve the quality, efficiency and effectiveness of HCOs (Greenfield et al., 2012; Pomey et al., 2005; Shaw, 2000a). Simply put, *Accreditation* is based on the premise that adherence to evidence-based standards will produce higher-quality healthcare services in an increasingly safe environment. It is also a way to publicly recognize that an HCO has met national quality standards. *Accreditation* can be defined as "an internationally recognized evaluation process used to assess and improve the quality, efficiency, and effectiveness of healthcare organizations. Healthcare *Accreditation* programs consist of periodic or cyclical assessments of organizational and clinical practices and the measurement of an HCO's performance against pre-established, evidence-based standards. This is usually done through self-assessments, on-site visits and interviews by peer surveyors and careful study of administrative and clinical data as well as documentation. The process typically culminates in an *Accreditation* report and notification as to whether an organization is accredited (Greenfield et al., 2008).

Government regulations have increasingly relied on *Accreditation* as a means to ensure an acceptable level of quality among healthcare provider organizations (El-Jardali et al., 2008; Mays, 2004; Montagu, 2003; René et al., 2006). *Accreditation* is generally viewed as a formal process by which an authorized body, whether governmental or non-governmental, assesses and determines whether a healthcare organization meets applicable, predetermined and published standards. *Accreditation* standards are designed to be optimal and achievable, while encouraging continuous quality improvement efforts within accredited organizations (Rooney & van Ostenberg, 1999).

History

In the USA at the beginning of the 20th century, Drs. Ernest Codman and Edward Martin, concerned by the quality and inconsistency of hospital services and health professionals, began discussing plans to create a system for measuring the quality of care delivered to patients (Roberts et al., 1987). The objective was to promote efficient treatments and best medical practices. The proposal received support from hospital managers and health professionals in the USA and in Canada. Thus, in November 1912, at the 3rd Clinical Congress of the Surgeons of North America that followed, the founding of the American College of Surgeons (ACS), a resolution was adopted to implement a system for the standardization of work equipment in hospital settings, in order to improve its quality.

These founding principles and concepts led to the creation, on December 20th, 1917, of the Hospital Standardization Program and the development of five official minimum standards that would make up the first hospital *Accreditation* program. Two years later, the first evaluation of the application of these standards provided startling results: Only 89 of the 692 hospitals with more than 100 beds that were evaluated met the standards. To ensure that such damning results would not get into the hands of the press, the list of concerned establishments was promptly incinerated in the furnace of the Waldorf Astoria Hotel in New York (Lanteigne, 2009)!

As the need to improve the quality of services had been clearly demonstrated, the ACS took over management of the Hospital Standardization Program. In 1951, the American College of Physicians, the American Hospital Association, and the Canadian Medical Association joined the ACS to form the Joint Commission on Accreditation of Hospitals, an independent, non-profit organization known since 1988 as the Joint Commission on Accreditation of Healthcare Organizations (JCAHO). At the time, hospitals undertook the *Accreditation* on a voluntary basis.

Trends

Accreditation has spread across the world, becoming an integral part of healthcare systems in over 70 countries (Greenfield & Braithwaite, 2009). The International Society for Quality in Health Care (ISQua) (ISQua, 2013) is the largest associated international body accrediting national *Accreditation* bodies (ISQua, 2013). In some countries or regions, HCO *Accreditation* remains voluntary, while in others, it has become government mandated (Pomey et al., 2010). Its rapid growth over the last 40 years can be attributed partly to the media reporting on serious inadequacies in the quality and safety of healthcare services, and partly to an escalating focus on patient safety (IOM, 2000). ISQua was created to ensure a certain level of quality and consistency in *Accreditation*. There are currently 30 organizations recognized by ISQua for the purpose of setting up *Accreditation*, 59 programs meeting the requirements for an *Accreditation* program, and 16 surveyor training programs, together covering 33 countries (ISQua, 2015).

Impacts of Accreditation on HCOs

The actual impact of *Accreditation* on HCOs became a topic of interest to researchers beginning in the 1980s (Duckett, 1983). Since then, a number of studies have attempted to demonstrate links between *Accreditation* and an improvement in the quality and safety of care in establishments. A Cochrane review analyzed studies that had been conducted on the relationship between compliance with standards and external evaluations of quality. It highlighted one randomized controlled trial and one interrupted time series, both of which showed significant differences in the improvement of quality of care between establishments subject to intervention and those not (Salmon et al., 2003). However, as this kind of study is difficult to conduct, other research designs were developed to demonstrate specific changes. These changes fall under seven broad thematic categories (Accreditation Canada, 2008; Pomey & Fonseca, 2013).

Governance

Accreditation standards are beginning to include HCO governance. For example, in its latest program (Q-Mentum), Accreditation Canada introduced standards related to governance and more specifically, to board activities (Accreditation Canada, 2012). Although there is little literature to assess the impact of *Accreditation* on boards, boards have found that the standards are helpful as a reference in structuring their strategic plan (El-Jardali et al., 2013; JCAHO, 2002). For a long time, boards had neither the interest nor the resources to look at the quality and safety of healthcare. They are now aware that they play a crucial role in enhancing the quality of care and patient safety (Baker et al., 2010; IHI, 2013).

Operational and Frontline Staff

A review of professionals' attitudes towards *Accreditation* confirms that a large majority of health professionals agree that *Accreditation* programs bring improved communication, commitment to best practices, availability of information for evaluation and care quality activities, improved structures for quality, greater focus on patients and support for planned change, staff management and development (Gough & Reynolds, 2000; Kreig, 1996). For example, medical technologists preferred working in an accredited laboratory because *Accreditation* led to the improved traceability of their work and consequently improved their procedures (Greenfield et al., 2008). However, a number of professionals stated that *Accreditation* programs increased their workload and level of stress (Fairbrother & Gleeson, 2000; Grenade & Boldy, 2002; Verstraete et al., 1998). Hospital employees also perceived benefits when their opinions were valued, when their satisfaction was measured, when they were involved in quality initiatives and when there was improved employee safety and security, clearer lines of authority and accountability and promotion of teamwork (Joint Commission International (JCI), 2013; for more information about *Teamwork* and its relevance to healthcare organizations, see Schmutz et al., Chapter 21 in this volume). Another study showed that the self-assessment phase of *Accreditation* provided opportunities for the creation of social capital (Pomey et al., 2005) by enabling them to create a durable network of social relations or to develop membership in a stable group that individuals can mobilize as part of their action strategies. One study demonstrated this phenomenon in the context of mergers, where three HCOs used self-assessment activities to build relationships among individuals who had previously been in conflict or who had not been in contact due to the size of the territory and the number of sites involved (Pomey et al., 2010).

Patient Safety

Patient safety, defined as the avoidance, prevention and reduction of adverse outcomes or injuries stemming from healthcare processes (Cooper et al., 2000; IOM, 2000), is an integral component of *Accreditation* programs, the aim of which is to reduce the potential for adverse events occurring within healthcare and service organizations (Accreditation Canada, 2012; Greenfield et al., 2008). *Accreditation* enhances patient safety by effectively managing and mitigating clinical and safety-related risk (Mays, 2004; René et al., 2006; Salmon et al., 2003) and by fostering a culture of patient safety (Al-Awa et al., 2012).

A risk management program identifies problems or potential risk factors that can be eliminated or reduced to prevent accident or injury (Al-Awa et al., 2010), for example, in anesthesia (Riem et al., 2011). The *Accreditation* process for risk management and patient safety involves coordinating quality review activities for both inpatient and out-patient care (Al-Awa et al., 2010; Greenfield et al., 2008). It also addresses efforts to ensure the safe use of high-risk medications and reduce the risk of acquired infections as well as their impact across the continuum of care or service, while improving the effectiveness and coordination of communication among care or service workers and with the recipients of care or services across the continuum (Accreditation Canada, 2015; Haynes et al., 2009; Parisi, 2003).

Service Delivery

Accreditation focuses on the nature of the organization in which healthcare is delivered. Organizations are encouraged to enhance their understanding of the continuum of care by focusing on performance improvement and outcomes of care (JCAHO, 2002). *Accreditation* demands that management monitor its performance continually and institute quality improvement activities promptly if performance is deteriorating or fails to attain a standard associated with good practice. *Accreditation* advertises to consumers and regulators that a facility or a network has made a commitment to a quality culture and to voluntary external surveillance (Kern et al., 2002). It is essential to provide a framework that assists in the creation and implementation of systems and a process that improves operational effectiveness and enhances positive health outcomes (Alkhenizan & Shaw, 2011; Davis et al., 2007; Greenfield et al., 2008; Lanteigne, 2009; René et al., 2006; Salmon et al., 2003; The Conference Board of Canada (TCBC), 2011). Such a framework helps provider organizations create systems and processes to enhance positive outcomes and reduce clinical, financial and compliance-related risks (Al-Awa et al., 2011).

Financial Impact

Accreditation can be viewed as an essential long-term investment in patient safety and the quality of service (Mihalik et al., 2003). It also plays an important part in demonstrating credibility and commitment to quality and accountability (Beaumont, 2008; Sutherland & Leatherman,

2006). Although some studies judged that the cost of *Accreditation* was high for individual organizations (Fairbrother & Gleeson, 2000; Grenade & Boldy, 2002; Rockwell et al., 1993), the positive impact on safety and quality for patients and on the improvement of health services within HCOs could be considered more important in the long term. *Accreditation* also helps healthcare organizations identify areas in need of additional funding and build cases to request funding from regional or national decision-makers (Baskind et al., 2010; Gluck & Hassig, 2001; Mays, 2004; Pomey et al., 2010).

Ethics

Accreditation is sensitive to the rights and interests of patients and must be conducted in an ethically responsible manner (Jennings et al., 2007). *Accreditation* provides a framework of key concepts and practices that can ensure the responsible implementation of the activities and practical recommendations resulting from the *Accreditation* processes, while protecting the persons used as subjects of research (Al-Awa et al., 2011). Quality improvement initiatives and *Accreditation* must thus meet the same complex review and regulatory requirements that govern biomedical and other types of research related to human subjects (Jennings et al., 2007).

Relations With the Community

Accreditation also emphasizes the importance of maintaining good communication with the community, especially during the self-assessment period and during times of change, to identify weaknesses in service delivery. It provides an opportunity to involve patients and families in quality management, to solidify existing relationships, to bring new partners together and to create common ground and standards (Pomey et al., 2010). The benefits of *Accreditation* for the community include: Access to a quality- and safety-focused organization; rights that are respected and protected; comprehensive education and communication; evaluation of satisfaction; involvement in care decisions and care processes; and a focus on patient safety (JCI, 2013). Patients want to know that they are being referred to a good hospital that is recognized for high standards of care. Since consumers can choose which institution they go to for treatment, they may want information to help them make informed decisions (Scrivens, 1997).

OTHER EXAMPLES OF EXTERNAL EVALUATION OF QUALITY

There are many other methods for the external evaluation of the quality of care and services in HCOs. Just a few of them are ISO certification, the Health Promoting Hospital network, the Planetree model and the MORE program, which is specific to obstetrics.

International Organization for Standardization (ISO) Standards

The story of ISO began in 1946, when delegates from 25 countries met at the Institute of Civil Engineers in London and decided to create a new international organization "to facilitate the international coordination and unification of industrial standards" (ISO, 2015). Since beginning operations in February 1947, ISO has published over 19,500 International Standards covering almost all aspects of technology and manufacturing. It now has members from 163 countries and 3368 technical bodies to manage standards development. More than 150 people work full-time for the ISO's Central Secretariat in Geneva. ISO certification, the result of recognized work by an official organization following an international standard, leads to the implementation of an adapted organization in which internal "client–supplier" relations are formalized (Farges, 2015).

Some standards proposed by ISO are so general that they are applicable to the health sector, most often to establishments' financial and logistic services, as well as to technical facilities, particularly biomedical services or radiology laboratories. This is the case of the ISO 9000 quality management series, which covers eight quality management principles: 1) Customer focus; 2) Leadership; 3) Involvement of people; 4) A process approach; 5) System approach to management; 6) Continual improvement; 7) Factual approach to decision-making; 8) Mutually beneficial supplier relationships (ISO, 2008).

Other standards are specific to certain health fields, such as the ISO 15189:2012 (ISO, 2012) standard that applies to medical laboratories and their specific requirements for quality and competence (SCC, 2010). For this kind of biomedical service, ISO standards are a management and practice improvement tool. They may be made mandatory as part of *Accreditation*, as is the case in Canada (Cooper & Giroud, 2010; Lapointe, 2011; Pascale & Beyerle, 2006; SCC, 2010).

The audit tests compliance with ISO standards. During the visit, the auditor presents a list of problems to management. If the organization conforms to ISO standards, the certification body will issue a certificate. If major nonconformities are identified, the organization will present an improvement plan to the certification body and once the certification body is satisfied that the organization has carried out sufficient corrective action, it will issue a certificate. An ISO compliance certificate has to be renewed at regular intervals (Alkhenizan & Shaw, 2011; Croft, 2012; Shaw, 2000b).

The International Network of Health Promoting Hospitals and Health Services (HPH)

Another external evaluation is based on the principles of the Ottawa Charter, which defines health promotion as "the process of enabling people to increase control over, and to improve, their health" (WHO, 1986, p. 1). As part of a new vision based on these principles, a set of strategies was developed to help hospitals adapt to internal and external environmental changes so as to promote the health of their patients, their staff and the community (Lobnig et al., 1999). Thus, in 1988, the WHO laid the foundation for the HPH movement and, beginning in 1990, an International Network of Health Promoting Hospitals and Health Services was created. In 1992, the Budapest Charter set the objectives of the HPH network, and during 1993–1997, a European pilot project was carried out involving 20 hospitals in 11 countries. By 2011, more than 840 hospitals and health institutions in 40 countries had joined the HPH ranks.

The relatively lightweight HPH external evaluation mechanism is conducted every four years on a voluntary basis. CEOs sign a letter confirming participation, and the HCOs must implement five standards: 1) Endorsing health promotion; 2) Putting health promotion at the core of practitioner interventions; 3) Creating a healthy workplace; 4) Fostering close collaboration with the community; 5) Collaborating on an ongoing basis with other healthcare establishments in the community.

Although there is no deadline for implementing the standards, every two years, HCOs must self-evaluate their level of progress in achieving compliance. To be part of the HPH network, HCOs must pay a modest annual membership fee of 340 USD. In this case, there is no evaluation performed by visitors to ensure that establishments are properly complying with the standards (Dedobbeleer, 2010).

Planetree

The Planetree program was founded by Angelica Thieriot. Following a series of traumatic personal healthcare experiences, she conceived of a healthcare model that would not only treat patients, but also comfort, engage and empower them (Planetree, 2014). According to the Planetree care model, which describes itself as holistic and patient-centered, everything in an HCO's setting has to be evaluated from the perspective of the patient. Every element of the organization's culture has to be assessed based on whether it serves to personalize, demystify and humanize the patient experience. A premium is placed on making information available to patients, enabling them to be informed partners in their care. At the time the Planetree approach was developed, welcoming patients as partners in the care and healing process was a radical notion, challenging many existing ways of medical thinking (Charmel & Frampton, 2008).

All of the criteria focus on the patient experience, as well as the experiences of family members, frontline staff, leadership teams, the medical staff, patient and family advisors and board members. The purpose of the program is to create environments that foster well-being and revolve around people. It affects the work atmosphere, clientele and staff satisfaction, recruitment and retention of personnel, turnover rates and disability insurance.

An evaluation of the impact of the Planetree patient-centered model of care on inpatient quality outcomes, based on the evaluation of 869 hospitalized adults undergoing elective total-knee or total-hip joint replacement surgery, indicated that the Planetree patient-centered model of care positively affected patient satisfaction, length of stay and cost per case (Boulding et al., 2011; Frampton & Guastello, 2010; Isaac et al., 2010; Lepore, 2013; Stone, 2008). Other studies have also shown that HCOs involved in Planetree processes had managed to ensure that nights were quieter and premises cleaner, that communication concerning medication was clearer and pain management more effective, and finally, that health professionals and patients had a greater sense of shared responsibility (Planetree, 2010).

Managing Obstetrical Risk Efficiently (MORE)

Although the MORE program is not technically recognized as an external evaluation of quality, it is founded on several of the same criteria as the other innovations presented above, in that it represents an intervention built on evidence-based standards of best practices from an external organization that aims to improve the quality and safety of care. MORE is a program that was imported from the USA by Canada and that is led by the Society of Obstetricians and Gynaecologists of Canada in partnership with Healthcare Insurance Reciprocal of Canada, with the aim of reducing obstetric complications and related insurance costs (MORE, 2015). The program is based on the principles of high-reliability organizations, developed in the field of aviation, and centers on communication and inter-professional teamwork, with the aim of promoting collective learning in the workplace (Hines et al., 2008). MORE's objective is to develop an efficient teamwork culture; eliminate cultures of blame; build trust, respect and collaboration between team members; and encourage a team approach to knowledge-sharing and self-evaluation. It helps healthcare teams develop new models for practice in which practitioners in all disciplines work and learn together to build a practice community rich in knowledge and experience, by breaking down traditional reporting structures and establishing an environment marked by respect, trust and continuous learning (Chevalier, 2012; Chevalier & Mayault, 2009; Milne, 2010).

This project was launched in 2002 in three Canadian provinces. Currently, 211 Canadian establishments in nine provinces and territories are involved in the program (Canadian Patient Safety Institute (CPSI), 2010; Milne, 2010). The starting point of the program is a basic team that can include family physicians, obstetricians, nurses and midwives. Risk management personnel, along with members of senior management and of the board, commit to allocating time to the activities, while the team is tasked with training all staff. The program takes three years. In the first year, the team learns to work together through a two-day training session and distance learning assignments. In the second year, the team works through simulations to develop reflexive learning. The third year focuses on transforming the safety culture, on creating a community of practice and establishing institutional memory. The training is delivered using a web-based platform along with sessions directly in the workplace. Several other activities are carried out concurrently: A patient satisfaction monitoring exercise; a survey of the organizational culture among the entire team; and exercises on skills and emergency situation responses to build team reflexes. The team also learns to analyze undesirable outcomes together. The strengths of this program are recognized within the standards of Accreditation Canada, which encourages HCOs to participate in the program.

Studies on MORE's impact have highlighted a drop in lawsuits and in amounts paid out pursuant to harm or injury. Moreover, surveys on work culture have shown that the program positively affected empowerment (for more information about *Empowerment* and its relevance to healthcare organizations, see Oranye and Ahmad, Chapter 10 in this volume), learning, communication, patient safety, teamwork (for more information about *Teamwork* and its relevance to healthcare organizations, see Schmutz et al., Chapter 21 in this volume) and employee appreciation (Gagné et al., 2013; Thanh et al., 2010).

LIMITATIONS OF ACCREDITATION

We can point out a few limitations or criticisms of *Accreditation*. First, while it is relatively easy to monitor the impact of programs such as MORE on processes, outcomes and output, in the case of *Accreditation*, it is difficult to design experiments to measure cause-and-effect relationships, even though other qualitative and quantitative studies do show benefits in several areas.

A second criticism concerns the cost-benefit aspect. The financial investment in *Accreditation* is significant and difficult to quantify, especially when considering the number of hours spent preparing and conducting the visit, as compared to the actual returns.

A third criticism concerns the dichotomy between the philosophy of continuous quality improvement and the practice of one-time visits, which motivate establishments to comply with standards only during the evaluation. Thus, *Accreditation* organizations are increasingly revising their approach to build continuous improvement processes.

Moreover, given the abundance of methods on offer, HCOs may seek to distinguish themselves by undertaking several concurrently. In some cases, given the weight and redundancy of the methods, not to mention occasional contradictions in the recommendations, this duplication provides limited added value for the HCOs.

Another limitation of *Accreditation* organizations is their long-standing focus on hospitals. Although they try to be involved in the whole spectrum of care and services provided to the population, from regional health authorities to community care and services, long-term care facilities and primary care centers, they still mainly concentrate on hospitals. They also have difficulty in involving patients in their process, whether in developing standards or in getting patients to participate as experts during evaluation visits.

As with ISO, *Accreditation* is often seen as a program that mainly evaluates policies and procedures. *Accreditation* organizations have tried to change their approaches to cover care and management procedures, as well as the results assessed according to indicators and other performance measures (Mihalik et al., 2000). Thus, *Accreditation* organizations such as the JCAHO (2002), Accreditation Canada (2015), the *Haute autorité de santé* (2014a) and the National Committee for Quality Assurance (Romano, 1993) have now made the monitoring of results indicators mandatory.

Finally, *Accreditation*, which was originally conceived as voluntary, has increasingly been rendered mandatory by the state in healthcare systems where it is available (Pomey et al., 2010). In such contexts, *Accreditation* becomes a tool for control and accountability, as opposed to a voluntary process for organizational and professional development, which was the model that inspired the creation of the first agencies (Heidemann, 1999; Scrivens, 1997; Shaw, 2003; Touati & Pomey, 2009).

CONCLUSION

Since being introduced in HCOs at the end of the last century, external evaluations have gained in currency over the past thirty years, becoming key processes in many countries around the world during the early 2000s. They can be considered "management innovations", as they rely on evidence to re-examine the way organizations are managed. They help strengthen capacities related to *Learning Organization* (for more information about *Learning Organization* and its relevance to healthcare organizations, see Sheaff, Chapter 14 in this volume) and *Knowledge Management* (Wilson, 2002; for more information about *Knowledge Management* and its relevance to healthcare organizations, see Wickramasinghe and Gururajan, Chapter 12 in this volume), as well as *Business Process Reengineering* (Castle, 1996; for more information about *Business Process Reengineering* and its relevance to healthcare organizations, see Patwardhan et al., Chapter 6 in this volume). The main advantage of these approaches is that they help establishments structure their processes for quality of care and safety at the organizational level, while ensuring an impact at the individual practice level. External evaluation models can be specific to the health sector (*Accreditation*, HPM, MORE, Planetree) or applicable across sectors (ISO). Moreover, within the healthcare system, some may be focused on specific issues. Because of its potential and of the research that has been conducted to establish its contribution, *Accreditation* has increasingly become mandatory at the international level. However, its practical implementation may vary from one country to another (Touati & Pomey, 2009). One example of this is that the results of *Accreditation* visits are not always made public, even though it has been established that making performance reports public has a direct impact on encouraging HCOs to improve and adopt best practices (Contandriopoulos et al., 2014; Hafner et al., 2011).

For *Accreditation*, the challenge over the coming years will be to retain its added value with respect to other concurrent management innovations. The model implemented over years of evaluation, centering on a three- to five-year cycle, is currently being revisited. It has been repeatedly accused of being cumbersome, bureaucratic, expensive and document-heavy. In a context of decreasing resources and rapidly evolving establishments, *Accreditation* organizations are trying to ensure that HCOs incorporate continuous quality improvement and that they are more regularly accountable for the processes they undertake, for example, through the monitoring of results indicators, as has recently been implemented in France with the health account (HAS, 2014b).

NOTE

1 The author thanks Patrick Riley for his significant contribution in editing and translating, and his careful re-reading, which helped bring greater clarity and focus to the chapter, and Nathalie Clavel for her help in finalizing the references.

REFERENCES

Accreditation Canada. (2008). *The Value and Impact of Health Care Accreditation: A Literature Review*. Gloucester, Ontario: Accreditation Canada. Retrieved from https://www.accreditation.ca/sites/default/files/value-and-impact-en.pdf (accessed 15 June 2015).

Accreditation Canada. (2012). *Guide for Developing Qmentum Plans and Framework*. Ottawa, Ontario: Accreditation Canada. Retrieved from http://ontario.cmha.ca/files/2012/12/accreditation_canada_qmentum_plans_and_frameworks_guide.pdf (accessed 15 June 2015).

Accreditation Canada. (2015). *Required Organizational Practices*. Ottawa, Ontario: Accreditation Canada, Handbook. Retrieved from http://www.accreditation.ca/sites/default/files/rop-handbook-en.pdf (accessed 15 June 2015).

Al-Awa, B., Al Mazrooa, A., Habib, H.S., Rayes, O., Al Noury, K., Elhati, T., El Deek B., & Devreux, I. (2010). The impact of accreditation on patient safety and quality of care as perceived by nursing staff in a university hospital in Saudi Arabia. *Research Journal of Medical Sciences*, 4 (5), 319–323.

Al-Awa, B., De Wever, A., Melot, C., & Devreux, I. (2011). An overview of patient safety and accreditation: A literature review study. *Research Journal of Medical Sciences*, 5 (1), 200–223.

Al-Awa, B., Al Mazrooa, A., Rayes, O., El Hati, T., Devreux, I., Al-Noury, K., Habib, H., & El-Deek, B.S. (2012). Benchmarking the post-accreditation patient safety culture at King Abdulaziz University Hospital. *Annals of Saudi Medicine*, 32 (2), 143–150.

Alkhenizan, A., & Shaw, C. (2011). Impact of accreditation on the quality of health-care services: A systematic review of the literature. *Annals of Saudi Medicine*, **31** (4), 407–416.

Baker, R., Denis, J.L., Pomey, M.P., & MacIntosh-Murray, A. (2010). *Effective governance for quality and patient safety in Canadian healthcare organizations. A report to the Canadian Health Services Research Foundation and the Canadian Patient Safety Institute.* Retrieved from Canadian Health Services Research Foundation http://www.patientsafetyinstitute.ca/english/research/patientsafetypartner shipprojects/governanceforquality/documents/full%20report.pdf (accessed 15 June 2015).

Baskind, R., Kordowicz, M., & Chaplin, R. (2010). How does an accreditation programme drive improvement on acute inpatient mental health wards? An exploration of members' views. *Journal of Mental Health*, **19** (5), 405–411.

Beaumont, M. (2008). *L'agrément: Un agent moteur de développement des capacités, d'apprentissage collectif et de socialisation* (Doctoral Dissertation). Université de Montréal.

Benezech, D. (1996). La norme: une convention structurant les interrelations technologiques et industrielles. *Revue d'Économie Industrielle—Numéro spécial. Normalisation et organisation de l'industrie*, **75** (75), 27–43.

Boulding, W., Glickman, S.W., Manary, M.P., Schulman, K.A., & Staelin, R. (2011). Relationship between patient satisfaction with inpatient care and hospital readmission within 30 days. *The American Journal of Managed Care*, **17** (1), 41–48.

Canadian Patient Safety Institute (CPSI). (2010). *Rapport sur le sommaire des programmes de formation au travail d'équipe*. Ottawa, Ontario: CPSI. Retrieved from http://www.patientsafetyinstitute.ca/French/toolsresources/teamworkCommunication/Documents/Final%20Summary_of_training_programs-FR_2011_11_03.pdf (accessed 15 June 2015).

Castle, J.A. (1996). An integrated model in quality management, positioning TQM, BPR and ISO 9000. *The TQM Magazine*, **8** (5), 7–13.

Charmel, P.A., & Frampton, S.B. (2008). Building the business case for patient-centered care. *Healthcare Financial Management*, **62** (3):80–85.

Chevalier, P. (2012). *Approche multidisciplinaire en prévention des risques obstétricaux (MORE).* Trimestriel d'information aux établissements de santé, (7), octobre-décembre 2012. Retrieved from http://www.has-sante.fr/portail/upload/docs/application/pdf/2012–10/certification_actualites_7.pdf (accessed 15 June 2015).

Chevalier, P., & Mayault, C. (2009). Le programme canadien MORE (approche multidisciplinaire et prévention des risques obstétricaux). *Risques & Qualité en Milieu de Soins*, **6** (3), 134–135.

The Conference Board of Canada (TCBC). (2011). *Accreditation Canada: Leading the way toward improving quality in health care.* Retrieved from http://www.conferenceboard.ca/Libraries/NETWORK_PUBLIC/SHRMC_Accreditation-Canada.sflb (accessed 15 June 2015).

Contandriopoulos, D., Champagne, F., & Denis, J.L. (2014). The multiple causal pathways between performance measures' use and effects. *Medical Care Research and Review*, **71** (1), 3–20.

Cooper, G., & Giroud, C. (2010). Démarche d'accréditation des LBM selon l'ISO 15189. Exigences particulières pour la qualité et la compétence. Saint-Laurent, Québec: Bio-Rad Laboratories Inc. Retrieved from http://www.qcnet.com/Portals/53/PDFs/ISO%2015189%202010pdf (accessed 15 June 2015).

Cooper, J.B., Gaba, D.M., Liang, B., Woods, D., & Blum, L.N. (2000). The National Patient Safety Foundation agenda for research and development in patient safety. *Medscape General Medicine*, **2** (3), E38.

Croft, N.H. (2012). ISO 9001:2015 and beyond—Preparing for the next 25 years of quality management standards. *ISO.* Retrieved from http://www.iso.org

/iso/home/news_index/news_archive/news.htm?refid=Ref1633 (accessed 10 June 2015).

Davis, M.V., Reed, J., Devlin, L.M., Michalak, C.L, Stevens R., & Baker, E. (2007). The NC accreditation learning collaborative: Partners enhancing local health department accreditation. *Journal of Public Health Management and Practice*, **13** (4), 422–426.

Dedobbeleer, N. (November 2010). La performance et le concept « hôpital promoteur de santé » Paper presented at COLUFRAS, Campo Grande, Brésil. Retrieved from http://www3.servicos.ms.gov.br/colufras/fr/Colufras_Apresentacoes/COLUFRAS%2030–11–2010/Bloco%206/Nicole%20Dedobbeleer%20%20Colufras 2010A.pptx (accessed 15 June 2015).

Duckett, S.J. (1983). Changing hospitals: The role of hospital accreditation. *Social Science and Medicine*, **17** (20), 1573–1579.

El-Jardali, F., Ammar, W., Hemadeh, R., Jamal, D., & Jaafar, M. (2013). Improving primary healthcare through accreditation: Baseline assessment of readiness and challenges in Lebanese context. *The International Journal of Health Planning and Management*, **28** (4), e256–e279.

El-Jardali, F., Jamal, D., Dimassi, H., Ammar, W., & Tchaghchaghian, V. (2008). The impact of hospital accreditation on quality of care: Perception of Lebanese nurses. *International Journal for Quality in Health Care*, **20** (5), 363–371.

Fairbrother, G., & Gleeson, M. (2000). EQuIP accreditation: Feedback from a Sydney teaching hospital. *Australian Health Review*, **23** (1), 153–162.

Farges, G. (2015). *Biomedical Website*. Retrieved from http://www.utc.fr/~farges/dess_tbh/99–00/Stages/Mignardot/partieII.htm (accessed 15 June 2015).

Frampton, S.B., & Guastello, S. (2010). Patient-centred care: more than the sum of its parts—Planetree's patient-centred hospital designation programme. *World Hospital and Health Services*, **46** (4), 13–16.

Gagné, G.B., Goubayon, A., & Dupont, C. (2013). La sécurité des soins obstétricaux, une affaire de travail d'équipe; l'expérience canadienne du programme MOREOB/MOREOB. *Revue de médecine périnatale*, **5** (1), 3–11.

Gluck, J.C., & Hassig, R.Z. (2001). Raising the bar: The importance of hospital library standards in the continuing medical education accreditation process. *Bull Medical Library Association*, **89** (3), 272–276.

Gough, L., & Reynolds, T. (2000). Is clinical pathology accreditation worth it? A survey of CPA-accredited laboratories. *Clinical Performance and Quality Health Care*, **8** (4), 195–201.

Greenfield, D., & Braithwaite, J. (2009). Developing the evidence base for accreditation of health care organisations: A call for transparency and innovation. *Quality and Safety in Health Care*, **18** (3), 162–163.

Greenfield, D., Braithwaite, J., & Pawsey, M. (2008). Health care accreditation surveyor styles typology. *International Journal of Health Care Quality Assurance*, **21** (5), 435–443.

Greenfield, D., Pawsey, M., Hinchcliff, R., Moldovan, M., & Braithwaite, J. (2012). The standard of healthcare accreditation standards: A review of empirical research underpinning their development and impact. *BMC Health Service Research*, **12**, 329.

Grenade, L., & Boldy, D. (2002). The accreditation experience: Views of residential aged care providers. *Geriaction*, **20** (1), 5–9.

Groene, O., Klazinga, N., Wagner, C., Arah, O.A., Thompson, A., Bruneau, C., Suñol R., & DUQuE Research Project. (2010). Investigating organizational quality improvement systems, patient empowerment, organizational culture, professional involvement and the quality of care in European hospitals: The 'Deepening our Understanding of Quality Improvement in Europe (DUQuE)' project. *BMC Health Services Research*, **10**, 281.

Groene, O., Klazinga, N., Walshe, K., Cucic C., Shaw, C.D., & Suñol, R. (2009). Learning from MARQuIS: Future direction of quality and safety in hospital care in the European Union. *Quality and Safety in Health Care*, **18** (Suppl 1): i69–i74.

Hafner, J.M., Williams, S.C., Koss, R.G., Tschurtz, B.A., Schmaltz, S.P., & Loeb. J.M. (2011). The perceived impact of public reporting hospital performance data: Interviews with hospital staff. *International Journal for Quality in Health Care*, **23** (6), 697–704.

Haute Autorité de Santé (HAS). (2014a). Le Compte Qualité. *HAS*. Retrieved from http://www.has-sante.fr/portail/upload/docs/application/pdf/2015–01/20150113_brochure_cq_v2014_2015–01–15_12–23–17_976.pdf (accessed 15 June 2015).

Haute Autorité de Santé (HAS). (2014b). Manuel de certification des établissements de santé. V2010. Saint-Denis La Plaine: HAS, direction de l'amélioration de la qualité et de la sécurité des soins. Retrieved from http://www.has-sante.fr/portail/upload/docs/application/pdf/2008–12/20081217_manuel_v2010_nouvelle_maquette.pdf (accessed 15 June 2015).

Haynes, A.B., Weiser, T.G., Berry, W.R., Lipsitz, S.R., Breizat, A.H., Dellinger, E.P., & Gawande, A.A. (2009). A surgical safety checklist to reduce morbidity and mortality in a global population. *New England Journal of Medicine*, **360** (5), 491–499.

Heidemann, E.G. (1999).The ALPHA program. Agenda for leadership in programs for healthcare accreditation. *International Journal for Quality in Health Care*, **11** (4), 275–277.

Hines, S., Luna, K., & Lofthus, J. (2008). *Becoming a high reliability organization: Operational advice for hospital leaders* (AHRQ Publication No. 08–0022). Agency for Healthcare Research and Quality (AHRQ). Retrieved from http://archive.ahrq.gov/professionals/quality-patient-safety/quality-resources/tools/hroadvice/hroadvice.pdf (accessed 15 June 2015).

Institute for Healthcare Improvement (IHI). (2013). The role of the board in quality & safety. Leadership development program. Chicago, IL: IHI. Retrieved from http://app.ihi.org/marketing/program_documents/Prof_Dev/2013_IHI_Role_of_the_Board_in_Quality_Safety_brochure.pdf (accessed 15 June 2015).

Institute of Medicine (IOM). (2000). *To Err Is Human: Building a Safer Health System*. Institute of Medicine, Committee on Quality of Health Care in America. Washington, DC: National Academy of Sciences. Retrieved from http://www.nap.edu/catalog/9728/to-err-is-human-building-a-safer-health-system (accessed 15 June 2015).

International Organization for Standardization (ISO). (2008). *ISO 9001:2008. Quality management requirements*. Retrieved from https://www.iso.org/obp/ui/#iso:std:iso:9001:ed-4:v2:en (accessed 15 June 2015).

International Organization for Standardization (ISO). (2012). *ISO 15189:2012. Medical laboratories requirements for quality and competence*. Retrieved from http://www.iso.org/iso/home/store/catalogue_tc/catalogue_detail.htm?csnumber=56115 (accessed 15 June 2015).

International Organization for Standardization (ISO). (2015). *About ISO*. Retrieved from http://www.iso.org/iso/home/about.htm (accessed 10 June 2015).

International Society for Quality in Healthcare (ISQua). (2013). Retrieved from http://www.isqua.org/accreditation/accreditation (accessed 17 April 2015).

International Society for Quality in Healthcare (ISQua). (2015). Retrieved from http://www.isqua.org/accreditation/accreditation (accessed 15 June 2015).

Isaac, T., Zaslavsky, A.M., Cleary, P.D., & Landon, B.E. (2010). The relationship between patients' perception of care and measures of hospital quality and safety. *Health Services Research*, **45** (4), 1024–1040.

Jennings, B., Baily, M.A., Bottrell, M., & Lynn, J. (2007). *Health care quality improvement: ethical and regulatory issues*. New York, NY: Hastings Centers. Retrieved from

http://www.thehastingscenter.org/uploadedFiles/Publications/Special_Reports/
Health%20Care%20Quality%20Improvement.pdf (accessed 15 June 2015).
Joint Commission on Accreditation of Healthcare Organizations (JCAHO). (2002).
Board approves JCAHO corporate priorities and updated strategic plan. *Joint
Commission Perspectives*, **22** (1), 4.
Joint Commission International (JCI). (2013). *Joint Commission International
Accreditation Standards for hospitals*. Retrieved from the Joint Commis-
sion International: http://www.jointcommissioninternational.org/assets/3/7/
Hospital-5E-Standards-Only-Mar2014.pdf (accessed 15 June 2015).
Kern, M., Saraiva L.M., & Dos Santos Pacheco, R.C. (2002). Peer review in educa-
tion: Promoting collaboration, written expression, critical thinking, and profes-
sional responsibility. *Education and Information Technologies*, 8 (1), 37–46.
Kreig, T. (1996). *An Evaluation of the ACHS Accreditation Program: Its Effects on
the Achievement of Best Practice*. Sydney: University of Technology.
Lanteigne, G. (2009). *Case Studies on the Integration of Accreditation Canada's Program in Relation to Organizational Change and Learning: The Health Authority of Anguilla and the Ca'Focella Ospetale di Treviso*. (Doctoral dissertation),
Université de Montréal.
Lapointe, S. (2011). Le contrôle de qualité dans les laboratoires de biologie médicale: les conditions gagnantes. *Le Labexpert*, 1 (4), 8–20.
Lepore, M. (2008). *Patient-centered strategies for HCAHPS improvement*. Retrieved
from http://www.engagingpatients.org/wp-content/themes/magazine-basic/library/
documents/npsf_Lepore_slides.pdf (accessed 15 June 2015).
Lobnig, H., Krajic, K., & Pelikan, J.M. (1999). The international WHO-network of
health promoting hospitals: State of development of concepts and projects—1998.
Conference paper. In H. Berger, K. Krajic, & R. Paul (Eds.), *Health Promoting
Hospitals in Practice: Developing Projects and Networks. Proceedings of the
6th International Conference on Health Promoting Hospitals, Darmstadt, 29
April–2 May, 1998*. Gamburg: G. Conrad, pp. 15–20.
Managing Obstetrical Risk Efficiently. (2015). Retrieved from http://www.moreob.
com/news/20-MORE-launches (accessed 15 June 2015).
Mays, G.P. (2004). *Can accreditation work in public health? Lessons from other ser-
vice industries*. Working paper prepared for the Robert Wood Johnson Founda-
tion. Arkansas: Department of Health Policy and Management, College of Public
Health, University of Arkansas for Medical Sciences. Retrieved from http://www.
cdc.gov/nceh/ehs/ephli/resources/can_accreditation_work_in_public_health.pdf
(accessed 15 June 2015).
Mihalik, G.J., Scherer, M.R., & Schreter, R.K. (2003). The high price of quality:
A cost analysis of NCQA accreditation. *Journal of Health Care Finance*, 29 (3),
38–47.
Milne, J.K. (2010). *Amélioration des performances en matière de sécurité des patients
et de réduction des risques grâce à la participation au programme MOREOB*.
Études des données nationales des hôpitaux participant au programme Salus
MOREOB sur la sécurité des patients en obstétrique. London, Ontario, Salus
Global Corporation. Retrieved from http://www.MOREob.com/assets/Annexe4.
pdf (accessed 15 June 2015).
Montagu, D. (2003). *Accreditation and other external quality assessment systems for
health care: Review of experience and lessons learned*. London, England: DFID
Health Systems Resource Centre. Retrieved from https://www.wbginvestment
climate.org/toolkits/public-policy-toolkit/upload/Accreditation-Review-
Montagu-2003.pdf (accessed 15 June 2015).
Nicklin, W. (2013). *The value and impact of health care accreditation: A literature
review*. Accreditation Canada. Retrieved from http://dispatchhealthcare.co.uk/

dump/Value%20of%20Accreditation_EN%20May%202013%20Report.pdf (accessed 15 June 2015).

Parisi, L.L. (2003). Patient identification: The foundation for a culture of patient safety. *Journal of Nursing Care Quality*, **18** (1), 73–79.

Pascale, P., & Beyerle, F. (2006). Les référentiels qualité applicables dans les laboratoires d'analyses de biologie médicale. *Pathologie Biologie*, **54** (6), 317–324.

Planetree. (2010). *Planetree annual report 2010*. Derby, CT: Planetree. Retrieved from http://dev.planetree.org/wp-content/uploads/2012/01/2010Planetree.pdf (accessed 15 June 2015).

Planetree. (2014). *Reputation*. Retrieved from http://planetree.org/reputation/ (accessed 15 June 2015).

Pomey, M.P., Champagne F., Contandriopoulos A.P, Tosh, A., & Bertrand, D. (2005). Paradoxes of French accreditation. *Quality and Safety in Health Care*, **14** (1), 51–55.

Pomey, M., & Fonseca, A. (2013). *Creating value through hospital accreditation*. Ottawa: Accreditation Canada International.

Pomey, M.P., Lemieux-Charles, L., Champagne, F., Angus, D., Shabah, A., & Contandriopoulos, A.P. (2010). Does accreditation stimulate change? A study of the impact of the accreditation process on Canadian health care organizations. *Implementation Science*, **5**, 31.

René, A., Bruneau, C., Abdelmoumene, N., Maguerez, G., Mounic, V., & Gremion, C. (2006). *Improving patient safety through external auditing: The SIMPATIE (Safety Improvement for Patients in Europe) project*. Saint-Denis La Plaine: Haute Autorité de Santé.

Riem, N., Boet, S., & Chandra, D. (2011). Setting standards for simulation in anesthesia: The role of safety criteria in accreditation standards. *Canadian Journal of Anaesthesia*, **58** (9): 846–852.

Roberts, J.S., Coale, J.G., & Redman, R.R. (1987). A history of the joint commission on accreditation of hospitals. *JAMA: The Journal of the American Medical Association, Journal of American Medical Association*, **258** (7), 936–940.

Rockwell, D.A., Pelletier, L.R., & Donnelly, W. (1993). The cost of accreditation: One hospital's experience. *Hospital and Community Psychiatry*, **44** (2), 151–155.

Romano, P.M. (1993). Managed care accreditation: The process and early findings. *Journal for Healthcare Quality*, **15** (6), 12–16.

Rooney, A.L., & van Ostenberg, P.R. (1999). *Licensure, accreditation, and certification: Approaches to health services quality*. Bethesda, MD: USAID Quality Assurance Project, Center for Human Services. Retrieved from http://pdf.usaid.gov/pdf_docs/PNACF510.pdf (accessed 15 June 2015).

Salmon, J.W., Heavens, J., Lombard, C., & Tavrow, P. (2003). *The impact of accreditation on the quality of hospital care: KwaZulu-Natal Province, Republic of South Africa*. Operations Research Results. Bethesda: U.S. Agency for International Development (USAID). Retrieved from http://www.hadassah-med.com/media/2021788/theimpactofaccreditationonqofhospitalcare.pdf (accessed 15 June 2015).

Scrivens, E. (1997). Putting continuous quality improvement into accreditation: Improving approaches to quality assessment. *Quality in Health Care*, **6** (4), 212–218.

Shaw, C.D. (2000a). The role of external assessment in improving health care. *International Journal for Quality in Health Care*, **12** (3), 167.

Shaw, C.D. (2000b). External quality mechanisms for health care: Summary of the ExPeRT project on visitatie, accreditation, EFQM and ISO assessment in European Union countries. External peer review techniques. European foundation for quality management. International organization for standardization. *International Journal for Quality in Health Care*, **12** (3), 169–175.

Shaw, C.D. (2003). Evaluating accreditation. *International Journal for Quality in Health Care*, **15** (6), 455–456.

Standards Council of Canada (SCC). (2010). *Program for the accreditation of laboratories—Canada (PALCAN)—PALCAN Handbook* (Program Requirements for Applicant and Accredited Laboratories. CAN- P- 1570). Ottawa, Ontario:SCC.

Stone, S. (2008). Retrospective evaluation of the impact of the Planetree patient-centered model of care on inpatient quality outcomes. *HERD*, **1** (4), 55–69.

Sutherland, K., & Leatherman, S. (2006). *Regulation and Quality Improvement: A Review of the Evidence*. London: Health Foundation. Retrieved from http://www.health.org.uk/public/cms/75/76/313/531/Regulation%20and%20quality%20improvement%20full%20report.pdf?realName=IclYbv.pdf (accessed 15 June 2015).

Thanh, N.X., Jacobs, P., Wanke, M.I., Hense, A., & Sauve, R. (2010). Outcomes of the introduction of the MOREOB continuing education program in Alberta. *Journal of Obstetrical and Gynaecology Canadian*, **32** (8):749–755.

Touati, N., & Pomey, M.P. (2009). Accreditation at a crossroads: Are we on the right track? *Health Policy*, **90** (2–3), 156–165.

Tricco, A.C., Antony J., Ivers, N.M., Ashoor, H.M., Khan, P.A., Blondal, E., & Straus, S.E. (2014). Effectiveness of quality improvement strategies for coordination of care to reduce use of health care services: A systematic review and meta-analysis. *Canadian Medical Association Journal*, **186** (15), E568–E578.

Verstraete, A., van Boeckel, E., Thys, M., & Engelen, F. (1998). Attitude of laboratory personnel towards accreditation. *International Journal of Health Care Quality Assurance Incorporating Leadership in Health Services*, **11** (1), 27–30.

Wilson, T.D. (2002). The nonsense of knowledge management. *Information Research*, **8** (1), 144.

World Health Organization (WHO). (1986). *Ottawa Charter for Health Promotion. An International Conference on Health Promotion*. Ottawa, Ontario: WHO. Retrieved from http://www.phac-aspc.gc.ca/ph-sp/docs/charter-chartre/pdf/charter.pdf (accessed 15 June 2015).

5 The Balanced Scorecard in Healthcare Organizations

Elin Funck

INTRODUCTION

In recent decades, healthcare organizations have undergone several attempts to introduce more "rational" management by implementing new forms of "businesslike" management innovations (Hood, 1995; Power, 1997). This chapter focuses on one such innovation: The *Balanced Scorecard* (BSC).

The *BSC* was proposed in 1992 as a new management control instrument based on measurements in several dimensions (Kaplan & Norton, 1992). The idea that measurements from a financial perspective needed to be balanced by measurements from additional perspectives was argued as providing stakeholders with a more holistic representation of the organization and would ultimately result in better decision-making. It is also claimed that it ensures long-term profitability and is an "excellent" instrument for managing the implementation of a company's strategy (Kaplan & Norton, 1992, 1993, 1996). Since its introduction, the *BSC* has become one of the most popular and widely adopted performance measurement models (Lipe & Salterio, 2002; Marr & Neely, 2003). However, interest in the *BSC* has not been limited to companies in different sectors and countries. Instead, the numerous reforms over the last few decades within the public sector in the Organisation for Economic Co-Operation and Development (OECD) countries have contributed to the growth in popularity of management control instruments there, as well as their diffusion among public organizations. The interest in the *BSC* among healthcare organizations can be exemplified by the vast number of scientific articles discussing the *BSC* and healthcare. Studies have, among other things, discussed how many and which perspectives should be included (Bevan, 2006; Santiago, 1999), the weight between different perspectives (Heberer, 1998) and the meaning of the concept of balance (Chambers, 2002). It has also been described how the *BSC* can be used for quality improvement (Moullin, 2004), for benchmarking (Cheng & Thompson, 2006) and for communication strategies (Pieper, 2005).

Management control models such as the *BSC* are designed and implemented to facilitate managers' decision-making and control behavior (Anthony & Govindarajan, 2001; Simon et al., 1954). However, several studies have discussed the challenge of managing healthcare organizations with formal administrative structures (Abernethy & Stoelwinder, 1995; Kouzes & Mico, 1979; Ouchi, 1980). In healthcare organizations, a number of features pose challenges for the implementation and use of management control instruments (Abernethy et al., 2007). First, healthcare organizations have complex core production processes. This means that it is not easy to decide which measures to use, how to set targets or how to analyze results. Second, these core production processes have traditionally been controlled by professionals. Since a profession claims specialized knowledge that is authoritative in a functional sense, professionals state that their work can only be understood, controlled and regulated by professionals like themselves. Consequently, the label "profession" signifies self-regulation and self-control (Wilensky, 1964), terms dissimilar to administrative control and external supervision.

From the discussion above, one may ask if a management control model based on performance measurement can at all be relevant for healthcare organizations. By following and comparing two healthcare systems in Sweden and Canada, where the *BSC* was introduced, this chapter discusses whether or not healthcare organizations should adopt the *BSC* and what may be important to consider if the model is supposed to be relevant in this context. I will argue that the extent of knowledge of the cause and effect relations among those who decide on performance measures will affect what will be measured and how the organization will use these measures.

This chapter is organized as follows. In the next section, I outline a theoretical framework for understanding the complexity of decision-making in healthcare organizations. Then, the research design is described. After a presentation of the empirical findings, the relationship between how the *BSC* is designed and used in healthcare organizations is analyzed. A tentative model of different effects is presented, followed by some concluding comments of the relevance of the *BSC* in healthcare organizations.

THEORETICAL FRAMEWORK

In 1992, Kaplan and Norton introduced the *BSC* as an alternative to traditional management control. The authors declared that in order to create value for the increasingly demanding stakeholders, management control needed to become multidimensional. Managers should no longer have to choose between financial or operational information. Instead, financial information needed to be combined with non-financial measures focusing on the future (Kaplan & Norton, 1992, 1996). This multidimensionality became explicit in the *BSC's* four perspectives: A financial perspective, an externally oriented customer perspective, an internally oriented process perspective and a future-oriented learning and growth perspective. The combination, it is claimed, should result in better decision-making and ultimately help companies stay competitive in a competitive market. Measurement matters, and with the *BSC*, performance became more salient, leading to more deliberate and active attempts to manage it.

In the first articles by Kaplan and Norton (1992, 1993), the *BSC* was described as a management instrument combining new performance measurements. However, over the course of time, the model has developed into a strategic management instrument with the aim of executing and implementing strategies and driving organizational changes (Kaplan & Norton, 2000, 2001, 2004, 2006, 2008). In 1997, the *BSC* was designated one of the last 75 years' most influential business ideas by the *Harvard Business Review* (Ho & Chan, 2002). However, the use of performance measurements for decision-making in healthcare organizations is a challenge. By focusing on two dimensions—the complexity of decision-making and different responsibilities in healthcare organizations—I will now describe the elements that hamper the use of the *BSC* in healthcare organizations.

The Complexity of Decision-Making

Ouchi (1980) stated that when the ability to measure outputs is low and the knowledge of the transformation (i.e., production) process (the means-ends relationships involved in the basic service activities) is imperfect, collegial controls are more suitable than hierarchical ones. In contrast to behavioral or output control, collegial control is marked by a social agreement among the members of an organization. He thus implies that when communal values and norms can be generated among the members of an organization, the need for formal control of individual performance decreases. In healthcare organizations, medical professionals have undergone prolonged training not only in practical skills, but also in values and norms. Consequently, the behavior of medical professionals is already given in the rituals, history and ceremonies of the organization, meaning that performance models with the aim of managing behavior become irrelevant. The same can be said of output control. Since the work of medical professionals often is performed in teams and the patient is sent between different units, it is difficult to evaluate individual performance and measure output. Hence, in healthcare organizations, a control system based on mutual codes, norms and agreements among the organization's members is preferable to output control.

Using performance measurements in healthcare organizations may lead to gaming, i.e., to maladaptive or dysfunctional behaviors (Bevan, 2006; Mellemvik et al., 1988; Weick, 1976). Studies have also demonstrated how management control models may not include information about patients and treatments. As a consequence, they become unsuitable for managing and monitoring professional activities (Pettersen, 2001), and the situation may result in loose coupling between healthcare activities and formal administrative structures like the *BSC* (Weick, 1976).

Managerial and Professional Responsibility

A second characteristic of healthcare organizations is the ambiguity of objectives that exists as a consequence of actors with different goals, interests and priorities (Kouzes & Mico, 1979). Due to the politicized environment, preferences for healthcare are debated within and across professional groups as well as between hospital administrators and professionals. Hence, when implementing performance measurements, a dilemma appears between managers' focus on administrative control and individual responsibility for performance and the medical professionals' concentration on professional values and norms, communal responsibility and quality of medical care (Lindkvist & Llewellyn, 2003). This implies that the information derived from performance measurements that may be relevant for hospital managers may not be relevant for the day-to-day medical activities. For different actors, different kinds of information become essential for decision-making. This ambiguity most likely affects the way different actors look at performance measures, how they should be designed and what they should report on.

The function of the *BSC* is to support key decision-makers with relevant and essential information. Key decision-makers can be described as "those who exercise the power to decide on the use of resources and the performance of services" (Pettersen & Solstad, 2007, p. 135). However, in healthcare organizations, the classification of key decision-makers becomes complicated. On the one hand, managers are responsible for the organization's performance and would strive for tight control of the employees' actions. On the other hand, the performance of services is related to the medical professionals' autonomy to judge each case and decide on treatment. Medical professionals are thus ultimately responsible to the patients and (they argue) without some professional autonomy in treatment and research, service will suffer. A control system within a healthcare organization can therefore not be too tight since it has to leave a great deal of autonomy to the professionals.

The complexity of decision-making in healthcare organizations and the differences in perspectives on performances will most likely be visible in the way the *BSC* is implemented and used. From the two dimensions, one may ask if the information derived from the measures is relevant both for managers and medical professionals in their decision-making. Is the *BSC* used for reducing uncertainty, to problematize different questions, or is it just loosely coupled to activities? These questions are pertinent to the analysis of whether or not healthcare organizations should adopt the *BSC* and what may be important to consider if the model is supposed to be relevant in this context.

THE RESEARCH DESIGN

This study is based on three case studies in Swedish and Canadian health-care, also reported in Funck (2009). In both contexts, the *BSC* was introduced in the end of the 1990s and, at the time of the study, was used both at the hospital and department levels of the organizations. However, the implementation processes were different in the two countries. In Sweden, the *BSC* was introduced by a medical professional and tested in smaller project groups before being implemented organization-wide. In Canada, the initiative to use the *BSC* came from the Hospital Association and the Ministry of Health.

For several reasons, it is fruitful to compare the implementation of the *BSC* in Swedish and Canadian healthcare. First, healthcare in both countries is financed and managed by the regional government. Second, since the mid-1980s, *New Public Management* has had a great impact on the organization and control of healthcare in the two countries. Third, in both Sweden and Canada, the *BSC* was spread among healthcare organizations. In Canada, the instrument has been used to report on and compare performances among hospitals since 1997, and the Swedish hospital studied was the first in Sweden to implement the *BSC*. Hence, similarities between the two countries made it possible to discuss if the *BSC* is suitable for healthcare organizations.

The empirical material was primarily collected through semi-structured interviews focusing on how the *BSC* was designed and used. In 2004 and 2006, thirty-six interviews were conducted with actors at the clinical and the central management in a hospital in southern Sweden and two hospitals in Canada. The choice of hospitals was based on the idea of as small a variance as possible. Therefore, all three hospitals are public emergency hospitals with approximately 1500 employees. The one variable that differs is how the *BSC* was implemented.

The interviews, which ranged from one to two hours in duration, were tape-recorded and fully transcribed. In addition, a comprehensive amount of secondary material was collected to complement the interview material. The empirical descriptions were structured and organized according to key themes (Miles & Huberman, 1994) and analyzed by comparing the findings from the two healthcare systems. Since the findings demonstrate the importance of the way the *BSC* is implemented and designed for answering the research questions, I will start the empirical description by describing how it all started.

EMPIRICAL FINDINGS

How It All Started

The work with the *BSC* started at about the same time in both the Swedish and the Canadian healthcare organizations. However, the *BSC* was developed in different ways. In the Swedish case, the performance measurement model was introduced by a medical professional, the head of the medical clinic, and tested in smaller project groups before it was required in the entire organization. An important motive for the implementation of the *BSC* was the need to create new ways of describing and evaluating the performance of medical work. The introduction of the *BSC* can therefore be seen as an attempt to replace or at least complement the one-sided financial description of the performance with other information that was pertinent for key decision-makers within the organization.

With the support of the council director, nine clinics adopted an experimental work in 1997. The mission was for each clinic to develop its own the *BSC* and report on the experiences. At the beginning of 1998, the experiences were summarized and analyzed at a meeting with all the employees involved in the test project. At this meeting, it was stated that the advantages of the *BSC* were that it captured more dimensions than just the financial performance, it was multidimensional and it encouraged a dialogue about activities and costs in a new way. The disadvantages stated were that the *BSC* was time consuming, that it might encourage top-down control instead of dialogue and that performance measurements might direct attention towards the wrong activities. Even though some weaknesses and risks with using the *BSC* were stressed, the message was still that the *BSC* could and should be used in healthcare. As a consequence, the hospital management decided that the *BSC* would be the basis for budget reports, annual financial reports and all monitoring within the hospital.

The Swedish case emphasizes that the *BSC* developed over the years. Starting as an experiment at a few clinics, the *BSC* spread to other departments in the hospital. The case also illustrates that the model developed from the bottom up. The *BSC* was initially designed within the clinics and with little direction from the hospital management. Instead of forcing the departments to implement a ready-made model, the clinics were encouraged to develop a *BSC* that was best suited to their department:

> The medical professionals would never have bought it if the *BSC* had been implemented top-down. We had never got the same commitment to the instrument that we have now. (Financial manager, Swedish hospital, author's translation)

The close link between the *BSC* and the operational work in the organization can be seen in several documents. For example, the directives for the annual planning for 1999 described the *BSC* as a way of illustrating and communicating the performance targets of the clinics and wards and as an instrument that should support improvements in the organization. According to the 1998 planning document,

> Quality improvements are an absolute condition for being able to carry on efficiency work. It is therefore essential that the already begun

work with improvements continues and is reflected in different document of planning and monitoring such as annual planning documents, annual budgets, financial report for part of the year and annual reports. (County councils multi-annual plan 1998–2000)

From the above extract, it seems as if the *BSC* was not originally intended as a management control model. Instead, performance measurements were used to emphasize the quality of improvements taking place at the medical professional level of the organization.

In contrast to the Swedish case, the work with the *BSC* in the Canadian healthcare context started at the principal level. Increased healthcare costs led to a growing debate that healthcare organizations needed to transform and become more efficient. To avoid the hospitals in the province being forced to start using a performance measurement model they did not want, in 1997, the Hospital Association, in collaboration with a research team, developed a *BSC* called the Hospital Report. The purpose was to measure and report on hospitals' performances. Although participation was voluntary, several interviewees pointed out that participation seemed mandatory. The situation can be interpreted as if the participation in the Hospital Report offered some legitimacy to the hospital (Meyer & Rowan, 1977). When participating in the Hospital Report, an image was created of the single hospital as being a modern organization that reported on its performance and that was accountable to the Ministry of Health and the citizens. At the same time, participation in the reporting came to create isomorphic tendencies among the hospitals (DiMaggio & Powell, 1983). In other words, the drive to meet the expectations of society and to receive legitimacy resulted in almost all hospitals joining the reporting.

At first, the Ministry of Health had no part in the Hospital Report. However, in 2001, it joined the project and became a co-financier. In 2005, the Ministry issued a second *BSC* report, the Hospital Accountability Agreement, as an obligatory contract between the Ministry and each individual hospital. With the second *BSC* report, results from the measures became more essential. The Hospital Report had always attracted much attention, since the results were published in the newspapers. However, a poor result had no consequences. The new agreement changed this situation. Since the Hospital Accountability Agreement was a contract between a single hospital and the Ministry of Health, a poor result had consequences for hospital management, the worst of which was the dismissal of the CEO of the hospital. Hence, fulfilling the obligations in the contract became of special importance.

If the *BSC* model in the Swedish case was built from the bottom up, the Canadian model was built from the top down. Here, the initiative to implement the *BSC* in the healthcare organizations came from the Hospital Association, and later on, the Ministry was involved. Hence, the use of the

BSC was never the decision of a single healthcare organization. Instead, a ready-made model consisting of perspectives and performance measures was "forced on" the healthcare organizations.

Although the two performance measurement models in the Canadian case were mainly intended for hospital managers, the aim of the Hospital Report was to help managers ensure the maintenance of the high quality of care enjoyed by residents. Quality improvements instead of management control were thus the ambition. However, the aim with performance measurements changed somewhat with the introduction of the Hospital Accountability Agreement. Suddenly, more emphasis was placed on accountability. It also became evident that hospital managers were to be held personally responsible for the performance of the hospital, and that incentives and penalties would be distributed depending on the result of the hospital. But it was not only the aims and implementation processes that differed between Sweden and Canada. The way the *BSC* was implemented also affected the way measures were designed.

Heterogeneous or Standardized Performance Measurements?

Although a central decision was taken in the Swedish case that the *BSC* should be the basis for budget reports, annual financial reports and all monitoring within the entire hospital, nothing was said about what should or should not be measured. Instead, the hospital management decided that content of the *BSC* was a question for each clinic. To start on a small scale and use simple measures was considered important if the *BSC* model was not to be abandoned. As the hospital manager declared, simplicity was important for creating participation and interest in the new performance measurement model. As a consequence, the hospital management decided that the *BSC* should be interpreted as a model to illustrate, capture and scrutinize complex questions from multiple points of view. The most important thing was not for the managers to control behavior, but instead to convince members of the organization to begin measuring performance and think in terms of quality improvement. Aspects that needed to be measured were, on the contrary, left to each clinic.

The freedom to decide what should be measured at each clinic resulted in the design of the *BSC* and the number of measures that the *BSC* contained varying dramatically among clinics and wards. Some clinics had as many as fifty items to measure. At other clinics, the number of measures was much more restricted. Most of the measures included in the operational units' *BSCs* concentrated on quality and on procedures relevant for the process perspective. These results were collected mainly from national quality registers and profession-specific reports. Hence, the access to potential parameters for measuring professional work had an impact on how many and what performance measurements were to be included in the *BSC* of each clinic. It was also common with self-produced measures as an expression of a quality ambition.

> There are some output figures that we have collected from the national quality registers. It's important that we keep up with the standards and not fall behind when it comes to knowledge or quality. We need to treat our patients in accordance to the guiding principles that exist in Sweden today. (Clinical manager, Swedish hospital, author's translation)

> Some of this is a bit "homemade." Some of the indicators are national indicators that we have found in different medical registers. For example, we know that the number of ultrasound examinations per delivered woman should not exceed 2.2 if we want to be cost efficient. Other indicators, for example that we should discover 75 percent of underweight children before delivery, that's an indicator that we have come up with within the hospital. (Clinical manager, Swedish hospital, author's translation)

A question that the interviewees came back to several times during the interviews were for whom the information from the performance measurements were intended. Was the *BSC* an instrument that should be used to inform the hospital management of each clinic's performance or should the *BSC* be used to improve the quality of care at the medical professional level of the organization?

> For some indicators the result is always 100 percent. In these cases perhaps we should abandon the measure. A good example is that we have as a goal that each ambulance should be driven by a person who is educated in emergency driving. We measure this in our *BSC* since we think it is extremely important. At the same time this outcome is expected of us. The difficulty is to know for whom the information in the *BSC* is. We might need to inform our politicians and the hospital management that we demand a specific education in emergency driving, and this we can do with such a measure. But if the aim with the *BSC* is to improve our operations the same measure is not important. At present we have decided to remove this measure from our *BSC*, which probably means that we think the *BSC* is intended for the operational level of our organization. (Ward manager, Swedish hospital, author's translation)

In the Canadian case, a ready-to-use *BSC* was imposed on the hospitals. Consequently, there was no opening for local adjustments and reinterpretation at the medical professional level of the organization. The systematic procedure for deciding what measures to include in the two Canadian reports can be described as an effect of the aim of the reports. The measures within the Hospital Report and the Hospital Accountability Agreement were used not only for stressing accountability; it was equally important to be able to make comparisons among the performances of the hospitals. As a result, the measures had to be identical, standardized and not replaced too often.

> That [Hospital Accountability Agreement] will be part of the corporate *BSC*. Based on what the Ministry has picked as indicators we picked modifications of that and what fits us, so yes it all drills down to or drills back to that level. (Director of Patient Services, Canadian case)

While the free approach for deciding what to measure in the Swedish case resulted in heterogeneous measures, the Canadian case reveals the story of a more systematic approach. Simplicity and homemade measures were thus contrasted with precision, validity and standardization. However, to standardize or more freely choose measures created different dilemmas. In the Swedish case, several interviewees stressed the difficulty of comparing results both within and between hospitals and the difficulty of finding useful objectives for homemade measures. Nevertheless, the interviewees claimed that it was possible to use trial and error and replace measures once they were attained. As a hospital manager claimed:

> It is not merely about measuring. It is also about keeping a process alive. Planning is not something we should do once a year, but all the year around. What the organization needs is to develop a culture in which everyone is responsible for finding improvement within the strategic framework of the organization. (Hospital manager, Swedish hospital, author's translation)

In the Canadian case, comparisons were easier, since all of the hospitals measured the same things. However, several medical professionals claimed that the aggregated and standardized measures could be problematic. Since the standardized measures were complex and only showed the overall performance of the hospital, it became difficult to isolate the result for a specific clinic or trace the causes for a specific result at the operational level. Therefore, the results from the *BSC* indicators were rarely used for improving medical professional work. Instead, the *BSC* was decoupled from the operational units (Meyer & Rowan, 1977) at the same time as measures from national healthcare programs (measures outside of the *BSC*) and information found in professional journals served as input when medical professionals tried to improve their work.

> They [performance indicators] are very time consuming. I mean to actually measure and analyze and then do something about it is very, very time consuming. And some of the clinical indicators are really resource-intensive. . . . I think we have to choose what indicators we

should monitor because we could monitor ourselves to death. If we monitor everything we will end up making no improvements. So there needs to be a balance. . . . You can't just measure for the sake of measuring, you need to be doing something with it or you are wasting your time. And I think that's where the challenge is, to find that balance and making sure that you are actually doing something with the data. Otherwise there is no sense of measuring it from the beginning. (Director of Professional Practice, Canadian case)

Some directors are very good at using the information and understanding it and perhaps make decisions about how to change their operations, others are not as good at that. We have to understand that in hospitals many of the directors are clinical. They have clinical backgrounds. They haven't been taught in terms of a business background so looking at finances or performance measurements are not their primary skill. Their primary skill is patient care. What we have learned is that one of the roles of Decision Support [department] is really to educate our staff and directors. They need to become more comfortable with budgets and the indicators that are presented to them since this is part of their work. (Vice President, Diagnostic and Support Services, and Chief Financial/ Information Officer, Canadian case)

What the empirical findings indicate is that the way the *BSC* was introduced for the healthcare organization affects both the design of the model and the performance measurements included. In the Swedish case, the emphasis on quality improvement resulted in a bottom-up approach and heterogeneous performance measurements in different departments. In the Canadian case, the highlighting of accountability and comparisons among hospitals resulted in a top-down approach and the establishment of standardized performance measurements.

The BSC and Action

While medical professionals in the Swedish case were involved in the development of the *BSC*, the opposite was the case in the Canadian healthcare organizations. Hence, different approaches, different aims and performance measurements providing key decision-makers with different information all had an impact on the ways in which the *BSC* was used. Studies have found that information generated from performance measurements can be a powerful language (Aidemark, 2001; Burchell et al., 1980; Mellemvik et al., 1988; Pettersen & Solstad, 2007). What the Canadian case indicates is that the language was not considered relevant where operational decisions were made. At the medical professional level, the focus was on the details. This was not to be found in the standardized and aggregated measures included in the *BSC*. As a consequence, medical professionals used other performance measurements, found outside of the *BSC*, when making decisions on the improvement of the quality of care. However, performance measurements can be a basis of power in other situations.

> It [the *BSC*] is a self-reporting, self-directed tool, that you really can make look as good as you want it to be. If I want to highlight something we are really doing well and broadcast it to the province, I use *BSC*. You can broadcast all your successes. If you want to use it as a working tool you have to be a little more self-critical. And sometimes you want to be self-critical and sometimes you don't. (Chief of Staff, Canadian case)

The statement indicates that even though medical professionals did not consider the *BSC* as relevant for decisions made in medical work, the model could still be used to highlight or legitimize already performed actions both for the management within the organization and for citizens (Mellemvik et al., 1988).

In the Swedish case, the same pattern of using the *BSC* for highlighting and legitimizing specific actions taken by medical professionals to the management was found. However, since the *BSC* had been developed by medical professionals at different clinics with great knowledge of the production processes, the principal role of the *BSC* was to provide medical professionals with relevant information in order to improve the quality of care. Hence, the findings indicate that the *BSC* was used differently depending on who was involved in the design of the measures and what kind of information was generated from the measures and for what purposes.

DISCUSSION

Inventors' Knowledge of the Production Process

Ouchi (1980) maintains that measurements of behavior or output are inappropriate in a professional organization like healthcare organizations. A professional organization is characterized by imperfect knowledge of the production process and uncertainty about what to measure. Studies focusing on healthcare organizations have given examples of how the problem of measuring and monitoring performance has resulted in loose coupling between measurement techniques and the medical professional operations (Kragh Jespersen, 1999). The empirical findings of how the Hospital Report and the Hospital Accountability Agreement were used in the Canadian case support this argument. The *BSC* was rarely, if ever, used for professional work. Instead, the results were discussed and analyzed at the hospital management level, indicating a separation between how performance was judged at the administrative and the operational levels. In contrast to the Canadian case, the Swedish case illustrates how the *BSC* was used not just at the managerial level of the organization, but also at the medical professional level.

Here, the *BSC* had a more active role, and the interviewees pointed out an ambition among medical professionals to measure, monitor and constantly search for more suitable performance measurements (Burchell et al., 1980). But how does this fit with Ouchi's statement?

Ouchi claims that when organizational members have imperfect knowledge of the production process, it will be difficult to formulate relevant output measures. When looking at the problem from the hospital management viewpoint, I am inclined to agree with Ouchi. Since hospital management usually consists of people who are not medical professionals, their knowledge of the production process will probably be impaired by their lack of detailed insights into operating conditions (Brignall & Modell, 2000, p. 293). As a consequence, it would be difficult to decide what performance measures to use.

However, in the Swedish case, it was not the hospital management who decided what measures to use. Instead, the questions of the design of the *BSC* and of what to measure were referred to the medical professionals in different clinics and wards with better knowledge of and insight into the production processes of healthcare. Since the medical professionals in the Swedish case determined what measures to use, Ouchi's assertion that key decision-makers in healthcare organizations always possess imperfect knowledge of the production process becomes questionable. At the same time, the eagerness of medical professionals to measure and the large number of performance measurements included in the process perspectives in different departments in the Swedish case indicate that it was possible to find measures that reflected the production processes of healthcare. Hence, the findings indicate that Ouchi's discussion needs to be modified. It is not possible to assume that a complex production process per se will imply that performance measurements are impossible to use. If anything, the relevance of performance measurements will depend on who is responsible for constructing the system and on how much insight this person has in the production process taking place in the organization. This is not to say that Ouchi is wrong. What I challenge is the assumption that the knowledge of the production process will always be uncertain in a professional organization.

. . . will Have an Impact on Performance Measurements and Information Need

In this chapter, I argue that the extent of knowledge of cause and effect relations among those who decide on performance measures will affect what will be measured and how the organization will use these measures. One can expect that the weaker an individual's knowledge of the production process is, the more general and composite the performance measurements he will suggest should be used. In the same way, an individual with good knowledge of the production process is capable of developing more specific and detailed performance measurements relevant for the day-to-day activities in the organization. General and composite performance measurements are described here as aggregated performance measurements. A general and composite performance measure is thus a measure that consolidates several elements, for example, patient satisfaction. Patient satisfaction is an issue that is affected by several underlying factors. Which factor will be of the most importance for the outcome is hard to grasp from the aggregated performance measurement.

Several researchers have commented on the dilemma of aggregating financial data in accounting (Harvey et al., 1979; Merchant & Shields, 1993; Otley & Dias, 1982). However, while the aggregation of financial data into more condensed performance measurements might result in the information from the measures losing some of its detail. Overly detailed information might be confusing and frustrating to the recipient due to his or her lack of detailed insight into the operations (Harvey et al., 1979; Otley & Dias, 1982). Whether to strive for detailed information or not depends on the situation and on the intended recipient (Merchant & Shields, 1993). Even though Harvey et al. (1979), Otley and Dias (1982) and Merchant and Shields (1993) discuss financial performance measurements, I would claim that the same argument could be used here. As the findings indicate, medical professionals created the *BSC* in the Swedish case. The result was that the performance measurements used were specific to the single department's specialty at the same time as the information generated from the measurements was detailed and considered relevant for that department. Hence, the performance measurements implemented in the healthcare organization were suitable for managing and monitoring professional activities.

In contrast to the Swedish case, the *BSCs* developed in the Canadian case were used to make comparisons among hospitals. As a consequence, measures were built on tight control (Merchant, 1998) and standardization, which unfortunately resulted in medical professionals finding the information generated from the measurements irrelevant for their day-to-day activities. These findings can be compared to the results from a study of the use of accounting information in higher education institutions in Norway (Pettersen & Solstad, 2007). The authors observed that accounting figures presented at the aggregated level of the organization lacked relevance in the conduct of day-to-day activities. Since the accounting reports were too standardized, they failed to offer useful information on planning and teaching activities and instead of integrating the administrative world with the professional one, the two remained separated.

Merchant and Shields (1993) state that aggregated performance measurements can be of relevance in complex situations. Referring to how a person learns to play chess, they explain that a novice could become overwhelmed by a teacher who assumes that the novice should have the repertoire of moves that an expert does. When several specific performance measurements are used, this will generate too many signals for a novice. In these situations, it might be better to use general and aggregated performance measurements that generate a clear and distinct signal. Hence, from the perspective of hospital management or the citizens, the main recipients in the Canadian case, it might not be surprising that aggregated performance measurements were considered more relevant. Too much detailed information would just make the *BSC* hard to understand. However, the opposite was the case at the medical professional level. The use of aggregated performance measurements resulted in the *BSC* losing relevance as the basis for decision-making on the quality of care at the medical professional level. The situation is not surprising. Just as the experienced chess player has learned the rules and the moves of the game, the medical professional can handle specific and detailed information. This is information that s/he cannot just handle, but that s/he needs to make good and rational decisions. What the findings indicate is that the use of the *BSC* in a healthcare organization does not depend just on who will develop and decide which performance measurements to use. The use of the *BSC* is also dependent on the recipient of the information generated by the measurements. As Otley and Dias (1982) express it, the content of a report must be matched against the type of task that is to be performed. Consequently, when the hospital management or the citizens are supposed to make decisions as to whether or not a hospital is performing in accordance with its objectives, aggregated performance measurements may be more relevant. In a situation where the medical professionals are supposed to react to the results from performance measurements in order to change and improve working methods and the quality of care, specific and detailed measures may be more relevant. In the first case, the *BSC* may be decoupled from the medical professional activities of the organization and the effect may only be gained legitimacy (Mellemvik et al., 1988). In the second case, the *BSC* may be tied to the medical professional activities and instead used to improve the quality of care. The discussion of inventors, recipients and relevance of the *BSC* is summarized in Figure 5.1.

		Inventors of BSC	
		Good knowledge of the production process	Weaker knowledge of the production process
Recipients of BSC information	**Good knowledge of the production process**	Specific/aggregated measurements Detailed information *For improving operational activities*	Aggregated measurements General information *Can result in loose coupling*
	Weaker knowledge of the production process	Specific/aggregated measurements Detailed information *The information can become overwhelming*	Aggregated measurements General information *For external comparison and to inform the general public*

Figure 5.1　Inventors, Recipients and Relevance of *BSC* in Healthcare Organizations

CONCLUSION

The focus of this chapter has been on the relevance of using the *BSC* in healthcare organizations. In order to investigate this, two healthcare systems where the *BSC* was introduced were presented. The results indicate that a recommendation to healthcare organizations on whether or not to adopt the *BSC* is not dependent on what or how many perspectives an organization chooses to use. To present performance measurements in one, two, four or five perspectives does not imply that the decision-making in an organization will improve. Instead, the relevance of the *BSC* depends on the relation between the purpose of the *BSC*, who is involved in the implementation process and the information needs of the key decision-makers. In other words, if medical professionals are supposed to use the *BSC* for quality improvement, the information generated from performance measurements needs to be detailed in order to track causes from a specific output. If the information generated from the measurements is general, it becomes irrelevant for medical professionals and there is a risk that loose coupling will arise between management intentions and medical professional actions. In contrast, if performance measurements are supposed to be used for comparisons and to inform the public of different hospitals' performances, the information needs to be general and more aggregated. In such a situation, excessively detailed information may cause confusion among the users in their decision-making.

Further, the findings indicate that medical professionals and managers' different information needs to influence who needs be involved in the decision of what to measure. Since quality improvement work demands specific information of activities at the operational level, medical professionals with good knowledge of the production process are more suitable to participate in the design of the *BSC*. In contrast, when the performance measurements are to be used for comparisons, managers with a composite knowledge of healthcare are more appropriate to participate in the design of the *BSC*.

To conclude, the *BSC* may very well be relevant for healthcare organizations. Jones and Filip (2000, p. 50) claim that "to connect clinical and organizational practices, outcomes, quality, value, and cost, the use of a BSC is essential". Studies have also described how healthcare organizations using the *BSC* have been able to reduce costs (Berger, 2004), turn financial crises (Meliones, 2001), gather healthcare units round a common strategy and increase the interest in performance measurements among managers and physicians (Junttila et al., 2007). Consequently, the *BSC* is not just an attractive relabeling of a normal good management practice, it helps managers focus on and manage important issues, but also to change organizational behavior. What this study adds to the discussion of whether the *BSC* is relevant or not for healthcare organizations is that every organization needs to reflect on how the *BSC* is supposed to be used before designing and implementing it. There is more than one way to interpret and implement a *BSC*, and it is important that the design and the level of details in the data collection fit the purposes and the key decision-makers' information needs. If not, there is the risk that the BSC will end up as just another management fad.

REFERENCES

Abernethy, M.A., Chua, W.F., Grafton, J., & Mahama, H. (2007). Accounting and control in health care: Behavioural, organisational, sociological and critical perspectives. In C.S. Chapman, A.G. Hopwood, & M.D. Shields (Eds.), *Handbook of Management Accounting Research* (Vol. 2), Oxford, England: Elsevier, pp. 805–829.

Abernethy, M.A., & Stoelwinder, J.U. (1995). The role of professional control in the management of complex organizations. *Accounting, Organizations and Society,* 20 (1), 1–17.

Aidemark, L.G. (2001). The meaning of balanced scorecards in health care organisations. *Financial Accountability and Management,* 17 (1), 23–40.

Anthony, R.N., & Govindarajan, V. (2001). *Management Control Systems* (10th ed.). Boston, MA: Irwin/McGraw-Hill.

Berger, S.H. (2004). 10 ways to improve healthcare cost management. *Healthcare Financial Management,* 58 (8), 76–80.

Bevan, G. (2006). Setting targets for health care performance: Lessons from a case study of the English NHS. *National Institute Economic Review,* 197 (1), 67–79.

Brignall, S., & Modell, S. (2000). An institutional perspective on performance measurement and management in the "new public sector". *Management Accounting Research,* 11 (3), 281–306.

Burchell, S., Clubb, C., Hopwood, A., & Hughes, J. (1980). The roles of accounting in organizations and society. *Accounting, Organizations and Society,* 5 (1), 5–27.

Chambers, D.W. (2002). Measured success. *The Journal of the American College of Dentists,* 69 (3), 61–67.

Cheng, S.M., & Thompson, L J. (2006). Cancer care Ontario and integrated cancer programs: Portrait of a performance management system and lessons learned. *Journal of Health, Organization and Management,* 20 (4), 335–343.

DiMaggio, P.J., & Powell, W.W. (1983). The iron cage revisited: Institutional isomorphism and collective rationality in organizational fields. *American Sociological Review,* 48 (2), 147–160.

Funck, E.K. (2009). *Ordination Balanced Scorecard—Översättning av ett Styrinstrument Inom Hälso-och Sjukvården.* Växjö, Sweden: Växjö University Press.

Harvey, D.W., Grant Rhode, J., & Merchant, K.A. (1979). Accounting aggregation: User preferences and decision making. *Accounting, Organizations and Society,* 4 (3), 187–210.

Heberer, M. (1998). Erfolgsfaktoren der Krankenhausführung. *Der Chirurg,* 69 (12), 1305–1312.

Ho, S-J.K., & Chan, Y-C.L. (2002). Performance measurement and the implementation of Balanced Scorecards in municipal governments. *Journal of Government Financial Management,* 51 (4), 8–16.

Hood, C. (1995). The "new public management" in the 1980s: Variations on a theme. *Accounting, Organizations and Society,* 20 (2–3), 93–109.

Jones, M.L., & Filip, S.J. (2000). Implementation and outcomes of a balanced scorecard model in women's services in an academic health care institution. *Quality Management in Health Care,* 8 (4), 40–51.

Junttila, K., Meretoja, R., Seppälä, A., Tolppanen, E.-M., Ala-Nikkola, T., & Silvennoinen, L. (2007). Data warehouse approach to nursing management. *Journal of Nursing Management,* 15 (2), 155–161.

Kaplan, R., & Norton, D. (1992). The Balanced Scorecard: Measures that drive performance. *Harvard Business Review*, 70 (1), 71–79.

Kaplan, R., & Norton, D. (1993). Putting the balanced scorecard to work. *Harvard Business Review*, 71 (5), 134–141.

Kaplan, R., & Norton, D. (1996). *The Balanced Scorecard*. Boston, MA: Harvard Business School Press.

Kaplan, R., & Norton, D. (2000). Having trouble with your strategy? Then map it. *Harvard Business Review*, 78 (5), 167–177.

Kaplan, R., & Norton, D. (2001). *The Strategy-Focused Organization*. Boston, MA: Harvard Business School Press.

Kaplan, R., & Norton, D. (2004). *Strategy Maps*. Boston, MA: Harvard Business School Press.

Kaplan, R., & Norton, D. (2006). *Alignment*. Boston, MA: Harvard Business School Press.

Kaplan, R., & Norton, D. (2008). *The Execution Premium*. Boston, MA: Harvard Business School Press.

Kouzes, J., & Mico, P. (1979). Domain theory: An introduction to organisational behavior in human service organisations. *Applied Behavioral Science*, 15 (4), 449–469.

Kragh Jespersen, P. (1999). New public management reformers betydning for den adminstrative og laegefaglige profession i sygehusorganisationen professionalisering. In E. Zeuthen Bentsen, F. Borum, G. Erlingsdóttir, & K. Sahlin-Andersson (Eds.), *Når Styringsambitioner Møder Praksis*, Copenhagen, Denmark: Handelshøjskolens Forlag, pp. 143–169.

Lindkvist, L., & Llewellyn, S. (2003). Accountability, responsibility and organizations. *Scandinavian Journal of Management*, 19 (2), 251–273.

Lipe, M.G., & Salterio, S. (2002). A note on the judgmental effects of the balanced scorecard's information organization. *Accounting, Organization and Society*, 27 (6), 531–540.

Marr, B., & Neely, A. (2003). Automating the balanced scorecard: Selection criteria to identify appropriate software applications. *Measuring Business Excellence*, 7 (3), 29–36.

Meliones, J.N. (2001). Get connected, get results and get smarter. *The Physician Executive*, 27 (1), 20–25.

Mellemvik, F., Monsen, N., & Olson, O. (1988). Functions of accounting: A discussion. *Scandinavian Journal of Management*, 4 (3–4), 101–119.

Merchant, K.A. (1998). *Modern Management Control Systems*. Upper Saddle River, NJ: Prentice Hall.

Merchant, K.A., & Shields, M.D. (1993). Commentary on when and why to measure costs less accurately to improve decision making. *Accounting Horizons*, 7 (2), 76–81.

Meyer, J.W., & Rowan, B. (1977). Institutionalized organizations: Formal structure as myth and ceremony. *The American Journal of Sociology*, 83 (2), 340–363.

Miles, M.B., & Huberman, A.M. (1994). *Qualitative Data Analysis*. Thousand Oaks, CA: Sage.

Moullin, M. (2004). Evaluating a health service taskforce. *International Journal of Health Care Quality Assurance*, 17 (5), 248–257.

Otley, D.T., & Dias, F.J.B. (1982). Accounting aggregation and decision-making performance: An experimental investigation. *Journal of Accounting Research*, 20 (1), 171–188.

Ouchi, W. (1980). Markets, bureaucracies and clans. *Administrative Science Quarterly*, 25 (1), 129–141.

Pettersen, I.-J. (2001). Implementing management accounting reforms in the public sector: The difficult journey from intention to effects. *The European Accounting Review*, 10 (3), 561–581.

Pettersen, I.-J., & Solstad, E. (2007). The role of accounting information in a reforming area: A study of higher education institutions. *Financial Accountability and Management*, **23** (2), 133–154.

Pieper, S.K. (2005). Reading the right signals: How to strategically manage with scorecards. *Healthcare Executive*, **20** (3), 8–14.

Power, M. (1997). *The Audit Society*. Oxford, England: Oxford University Press.

Santiago, J.M. (1999). Use of the balanced scorecard to improve the quality of behavioral health care. *Psychiatric Services*, **50** (12), 1571–1576.

Simon, H.A., Kozmetsky, G., Guetzkow, H., & Tyndall, G. (1954). *Centralization vs. Cecentralization in Organizing the Controller's Department*. New York: Controllership Foundation.

Weick, K. (1976). Educational organizations as loosely coupled systems. *Administrative Science Quarterly*, **21** (1), 1–19.

Wilensky, H.L. (1964). The professionalization of everyone? *The American Journal of Sociology*, **70** (2), 137–158.

6 Business Process Reengineering in Healthcare Organizations

Anjali Patwardhan, Dhruv Patwardhan and Prakash Patwardhan

THE CONCEPT OF BUSINESS PROCESS REENGINEERING

Business Process Reengineering (BPR) was mostly used initially by the engineering and manufacturing industries as a quality improvement tool that aimed for quantum leaps in productivity and performance. The use of *BPR* in healthcare settings is relatively new but not scarce. Although not everyone agrees with its use, it has been experimented with and used in healthcare worldwide. The emerging concept of *Patient-Centered Care* requires a drastic change in the conventional clinician-centered service organizations. Their processes and structures now need to be focused on how to best and effectively combine and provide multi-level, interdisciplinary and multi-specialty services as an integrated healthcare experience to the individual patients. Clearly, using a traditional, continuous quality management process on these conventional infrastructures and processes may not yield the desired results in the era of fast-growing competition. The aim of *BPR* is to reduce waste, remove redundancies to improve efficiency and gain competitiveness to achieve goals.

The concept of *BPR* was first introduced in the late 1990s by Michael Hammer in his article (1990) and his book, which he wrote together with James Champy (2006). Davenport and Short defined *BPR* as "the analysis and design of workflows and processes within and between organizations", and then Teng et al. (1994, p. 25) defined *BPR* as "the critical analysis and radical redesign of existing business processes to achieve breakthrough improvements in performance measures". As the name suggests, *Business Process Reengineering* is the investigation and radical restructuring of the workflow within and between organizations aiming to improve cost, quality, service, speed and value, or reduce waste. Just as *Continuous Quality Improvement (CQI)* and *Total Quality Management (TQM)* (for more information about *Total Quality Management* and its relevance to healthcare organizations, see Mosadeghrad and Ferlie, Chapter 22 in this volume) do, *BPR* also focuses on the production process, the key difference being the drastic nature of the change in *BPR* compared with the small and cautious changes in *TQM/CQI*. Davenport (1992) has detailed the differences between *BPR* and *TQM/CQI*. *BPR* is a radical, high-risk structural as well as cultural change in a process, beginning with a clean-slate start, which is a top-down approach and requires a long time to complete. *TQM* involves several small, incremental, ongoing, moderate-risk cultural changes in already existing processes, which requires a bottom-up approach and can be completed in less time. The primary enabling technology in *BPR* is information technology, while that of *TQM* is statistical process control. The use of IT changes the approach and speed of the processes involved, and old processes cannot be used due to this changed approach. Shewhart in the 1920s developed *Statistical Process Control (SPC)*, which was revised later by Deming and used to monitor and control the process of change. *SPC* is based on the presumption that in any process, there are two types of variation: The first is chance variation, also called *Common Cause Variation (CCV)*. CCV is inherent in a production process; it always exists and remains stable over time. The second type of variation is assignable to a cause and called *Special Cause Variation (SCV)*, which is unstable over time but can be managed. The process is monitored over time, and the data collected is plotted in control charts. When a small change is made in a process, its effect can be visualized through *SPC* charges to confirm that the change is an improvement. *SPC* is applied to reduce waste in a process, reduce variability, objectively improve productivity, reduce costs, identify hidden process shortcomings, react to process changes promptly and finally, to be able to make real-time decisions to improve and predict outcomes. The limitations of *SPC* are that its performance is dependent on the skill with which it is applied and the suitability or amenability of the process to which it is applied. Therefore, as illustrated in Figure 6.1, the selection of the right tool for a specific production process is at heart of both *TQM* and *BPR*. In non-manufacturing industries, such as research and development or healthcare, where the processes are non-repetitive and knowledge-intense, the use of *SPC* is still controversial (Binder, 1997; Brooks, 1987; Raczynski & Curtis, 2008).

In summary, the characteristics of *BPR* are as follows:

1) Reengineering cannot be implemented in small steps that address one small issue at a time. It is an all-or-none approach;
2) Its results cannot be guaranteed or accurately predicted. It is an exercise involving huge efforts with uncertain results;
3) It is a top-down approach;
4) It is a high-risk strategy;
5) It is all about discontinuous thinking, i.e., identifying and replacing outdated rules and processes, on the assumption that organizational goals cannot be achieved through the old system;
6) Starting from a clean slate and building a system that is generated on the basis of a new philosophy, working techniques and rules;

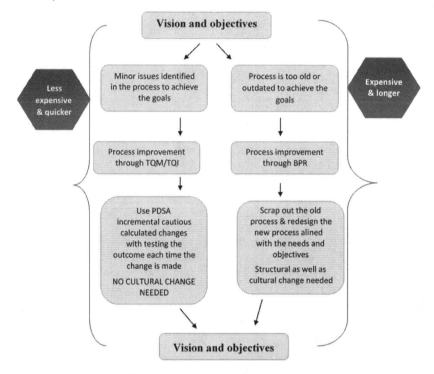

Figure 6.1   Selection of *BPR* as a Process Improvement Tool

7) Its goal is to systemize production processes around outcomes, not tasks;
8) The change includes structural, functional, cultural and holistic change.

Business Process Reengineering has been defined as being based on three dimensions. In the context of manufacturing, engineering industries and service industries, they are that *BPR*:

1) Is **based on organizational units:** The production process runs between organizational units (inter-organizational, inter-functional or interpersonal);
2) Has a **material basis:** The processes involve influencing and transforming objects (both physical and informational);
3) Is **based on undertakings:** It involves managerial operational activities.

A popular myth attached to *BPR* that it is mostly used for downsizing organizations (Leatt et al., 1997; Veninga, 1997; Weil, 2003). The concept of starting the *BPR* with a clean slate may not be true in the real world, and most productive processes, if redesigned, for the most part qualify as examples of *BPR*. *BPR* is mostly accepted in order to reduce the cost of change. Some researchers, such as Stoddard and Jarvenpaa (1995), argue that although reengineering can deliver radical designs, it does not necessarily promise a revolutionary approach to change. Moreover, a revolutionary change process might not be feasible given the risk and cost of revolutionary tactics. This statement is contrary to Hammer's (1990) and Hammer and Champy's (2006) thinking on starting the process from zero to avoid the environmental influence of past processes and on all-or-none approach in the implementation of *BPR*. Although most organizations use several process improvement tools depending on their needs, such as *BPR*, *TQM*, etc., the term "*BPR*" is occasionally also used (incorrectly) interchangeably with "*Organizational Transformation*" (*OT*). In reality, *BPR* is one of several instruments that can be used during *OT*, and as a standalone technique, it is not equivalent to *OT*.

For Hammer (1990, p. 104), the concept of *BPR* was all about "discontinuous thinking, recognizing and breaking away from the outdated rules and fundamental assumptions underlying operations that no longer hold". He strongly believed that Information Services (IS), also called Information Technology (IT), is a key facilitator in the use of *BPR*. He defined seven principles for the implementation of *BPR*:

1) Organize around outcomes, not tasks;
2) Have those who use the output of *BPR* perform it;
3) Subsume information processing work into the real work that produces the information;
4) Treat geographically dispersed resources as though they were centralized;
5) Link parallel activities instead of just integrating their results;
6) Put the decision point where the work is performed, and build control into the process;
7) Capture information once and at the source.

Some researchers even believe that *BPR* is the only tool that, if applied correctly, is able to deliver improved efficiency and a reduction in waste, and therefore, effectiveness and a reduced cost in better-quality products or services in a fast and timely manner. According to Hammer (1990), most organizations' planning and decisions about improvements are still based on orthodox values, assumptions and beliefs about technology, clinicians, patients and healthcare organizational goals that no longer hold true. Transparency, collaborative effectiveness and quality of care at a reduced cost have become necessary to attract "customers" who are well informed and enjoy their autonomy. The management and administration have moved out of clinicians' hands to business managers, and healthcare organizations have become more commercialized and diverse, but also more compartmentalized industries. The traditional assumptions about healthcare have been so ingrained in the minds of policy makers that they fail to identify alternatives to fit the needs of the modern world. When a conventional production process is used to achieve the goals of the contemporary world, the integration fails to achieve the desired outcomes and then the need for *BPR* becomes apparent.

BPR AND INFORMATION TECHNOLOGY AND SYSTEMS

BPR utilizes Information Technology/Systems (IT/IS), and its friendliness to new technology makes it flexible to adapt to different systems. *IT/IS* is the key to *BPR's* success. *IT/IS* and *BPR* have a co-promoting relationship in that *IT/IS* competencies facilitate successful *BPR* implementation by reducing the expenses of coordination, and at the same time, *BPR* improves the performance and capabilities of *IT/IS*. Most healthcare organizations aim for reducing lead time and improving access, return of customers, comprehensiveness, capabilities and responsiveness, leading to advantages over other business competitors. All these require collaboration- and coordination-centered production processes. To achieve this, they need to reduce the costs of coordination in terms of money and time, which is only possible through efficient *IT/IS* systems. On the other hand, redesigning the production processes and structures will be necessary to make them *IT/IS*-friendly. Several researchers have argued that "IT is an enabler of BPR" and "IT-enabled BPR ensures achieving higher targets, reducing risk and providing measures for sustaining results over a long time". The most commonly used *IT* resources for reengineering are Enterprise Resource Planning (ERP) systems, outsourcing, consulting firms, Enterprise Application Software (EAS) and Electronic Data Interchange (EDI) between various partner organizations or sites. *EDI* replaces the faxing and mailing of paper documents and therefore reduces cost and lead time, and replaces legacy systems so data can be moved to a new database, etc. *ERP* in a healthcare organization setting can provide enterprise intelligence and help achieve lean hospital supply chain management, rigorous fiscal control and reorganized human capital management in vision-critical areas (Botta-Genoulaza & Milletb, 2006; Motwania et al., 2005; Stefanou & Andreas, 2006). Recently, *ERP* has been used successfully in service industries, including healthcare systems worldwide, in risk management (Akiyama, 2007), developing database systems (Begg & Connolly, 2005), inventory management (Kontio et al., 2014), and in scheduling and operation room management (Epstein & Dexter, 2000). Telehealth initiatives are very useful for reducing the cost of consultations as well as improving access in remote areas. It has been successfully used in behavioral health (Stamm, 1998), veterans hospitals (Darkins et al., 2008), with elderly, high-resource users with complex comorbidities (Noel et al., 2004) and in several other programs in the USA (Brennan, 1999). It saves patients and clinicians both the travel time and the expense (Chaudhry et al., 2006; Goldzweig et al., 2009; Shekelle et al., 2006). Healthcare organizations using automated translation services are greatly benefited by being able to serve multi-language and multicultural consumers.

It can be argued that not all organizations, including small and maybe medium-sized organizations, will require or benefit from these tools, since their implementation may not be cost effective. In the past, this point would have applied to many health organizations.

EVOLUTION FROM HEALTHCARE SYSTEM TO AN INDUSTRY

In the early 19th century, the healthcare services in the United Kingdom and western European countries were predominantly custodial and predominantly nursing care that cared for poor, disadvantaged and sick people till they met their ultimate destiny. Hospital practice was limited to only the few who could afford it. Even these rich people wanted to be treated at home or in private clinics when they needed inpatient care. Healthcare organizations were service organizations in a real sense and were for the most part run by charities and churches. Men, as the breadwinners, took precedence over women and children when resources for treatment were limited. Around and after World War II, greater social and financial stability allowed greater attention to be given to preventive health and hospital services. The role of physicians evolved over time as the need for better services and the economic advantages of a positive health status were recognized. Healthcare started enjoying economic gains and as a result, healthcare turned into a mixed business and service industry. Competition grew between the healthcare organizations as well as various clinicians to do a better job at a lower cost, which occurs in any engineering industry. The concepts of access, equity, quality and comprehensiveness are apparent in consumers' and policy makers' minds. History endorses the fact that better healthcare rewarded populations with longevity and a higher quality of life, over time. As the competition between healthcare provider organizations grew, customer satisfaction was recognized to be the game changer. The methods for survival and winning in the market included providing better services in the most cost-effective way. In the contemporary ecosphere, healthcare is facing almost similar challenges worldwide. The list includes increasing healthcare costs, increasing demand due to aging populations, increasing consumer awareness due to the Internet, the availability of novel treatment options, competitive provider markets and finally, strict quality and safety regulations. Increasing customer awareness about their rights and responsibilities along with knowledge through World Wide Web about the latest research and technology has given customers the capacity to choose their providers. These circumstances have made the competition for survival and supremacy fierce for the healthcare providers. The ongoing challenges for healthcare organizations including long wait times, poor access, the inability to achieve comprehensiveness, the inability to achieve equality/equity and medical errors leading to risks of litigation.

The speed of change in the healthcare industry environment was faster than the ongoing modifications in the health system could keep pace with. The necessity for such a change was not even recognized up until the early to mid-20th century. It is not an exaggeration to say that the industrial structure and several functional aspects of health organizations are still in the early stages of developing *BPR*, but this is stated with the expectation that they will in time deliver a better performance. In the current scenario, it is recognized that saving money and time is equal to productivity. The best way to be efficient is to reduce waste in terms of money and lead time, to streamline production processes to remove redundancies and to improve communication. Finding ways to reduce the errors was the key to reducing litigation and improving patient satisfaction. With the arrival of the computer age, the concepts of confidentiality and privacy were more overtly recognized.

Paper records and documentation are still one of the major contributors to medical errors due to several factors, including illegibility, incompleteness, the inability to secure and preserve them and access issues in a multidisciplinary system (Chaudhry et al., 2006; Shekelle et al., 2006). They also come with a huge time expense. All of these issues could be addressed by Electronic Medical Record Systems (EMRS), which are progressively becoming more popular (Hunt et al., 2009; Tang et al., 1999). Not only the wait time, but processing time, administrative delays, lead times, and intercommunication time can be controlled with the ability to use audio-visual, multi-team communication in an *IT*-friendly environment. Both the efficiency and effectiveness of the system will improve. *IT* is not necessarily the same as *BPR*, but *BPR* is almost always necessary to make the health system completely exploit the available *IT*. It is unimaginable to use *TQM* to change the environment from paper-based systems to *EMRS*.

EXPERIENCE OF BPR IN HEALTHCARE

In some circles, the perception is still that the primary mission of healthcare organizations is first care and then business, which is not realistic (Goeppinger, 1996). Healthcare organizations have moved on from their original functions of nursing and care. Nowadays, healthcare organizations have to be as business oriented as any manufacturing industry to survive, because that is what is expected of them by their current customers, who want efficiency, efficacy, effectiveness, comprehensive care and customer satisfaction. Many clinicians are neither equipped for nor trained in business strategies. The concept of introducing business strategies in healthcare started in the 1980s. Medical managers and administrators became more empowered to manage business stratagems to make services suited to the needs of contemporary customers. *BPR* has been used in healthcare across Europe and North America for the past two decades, with mixed results. People have identified the barriers to excellence, and some have used *TQM* initially as a cost-cutting approach, but failed and then turned to *BPR*. At other times, *BPR* was the initial choice for process improvement. There are some generic differences between the healthcare service industry and manufacturing or engineering industries. When quality improvement processes designed for manufacturing industries are applied to the service industries, changes in approach need to be made. Some researchers believe that *BPR* and other process improvement tools that are designed for the business industry are not usable in service industries such as healthcare, because there is a basic difference between their attitudes and philosophies. Typically, service industries were notorious for lengthy protocols and bureaucratic principles, a less transparent environment, poorly defined commitments and accountabilities, poor communication channels in a multi-layered system and time delays. The public sector was mostly considered not to be profit oriented and more liberal towards employees and stakeholders than profit earning. Around the 1980s, when industrialization was reaching its peak, managers in service industries started their struggle with rising expectations and monetary problems (Jurisch et al., 2012; Parys, 2003). At this point, they were drawn towards business policies and management styles.

Even today, private industries have relatively easy, independent and quick decision-making policies with flexible and autonomic hierarchies compared with the public sector and service industries. In service industries and the public sector, the typical organization's culture and structure necessitates higher participation and consensus between major stakeholders to drive *BPR*. There are complex legal, statutory and regulatory requirements in public service industries to protect the rights of other stakeholders and of patients. This may make *BPR* implementation lengthier in the public sector. It has been pointed out by several researchers and leaned from some past experiences that the success rate in the private sector has been higher than in the public sector (Marlen et al., 2012; Scholl, 2004). Some researchers believed that less-than- radical changes would work better in public service industries. They also recommended an extra end step, an "institutionalization phase" for *BPR* implementation in the public sector and service industries. The institutionalization phase may include a short period of *TQM* implementation to drive the culture of change, training and development of frontline staff and/or to bridge the gap between planning and expectations before *BPR* is implemented.

The public sector and service industries have to adhere to several multi-level internal and external precepts imposed by laws and political interests. Service organizations are also indirectly restricted by public pressure, social image and political agendas (Fountain, 2003). Due to these restrictions, service industries and the public sector are less likely to achieve more radical change and will be less willing to take risks, in spite of financial struggles (Corby, 2005; Hughes, 1994).

Inherent to their cultural makeup, the public sector and service industries have poor control over their production processes, making radical change more difficult (Dennis et al., 2003). Apart from structural and cultural differences, consumer expectations are also different for these two domains, which makes the change a far more risky, unpopular venture for service industries. Consumers not only expect quality, value for their money and speed from service industries, but empathy and compassion as well, which puts these industries in a unique position. Assuming these divergent physiognomies and diverging expectations exist, in some researchers' view, the public sector should rather adapt than adopt the *BPR* method to suit the structure and goals of the public sectors, although it has been shown that the factors for successful implementation are the same in both domains (Jurisch et al., 2012). Despite the similarities in the factors responsible for success, different approaches are required to fully achieve them due to fundamental differences in the concept and mission of these two domains. The evidence from experience has shown that whether they adapt or adopt, the service industries and public sector need to familiarize themselves with the new, cost-effective technologies and time-saving approaches to be able to deliver what is expected by their consumers. Out of several others, *IT* is the most important modality, and the healthcare system cannot afford to ignore it if it wants to meet the increasing demand that is accompanied by finite resources in the contemporary world.

The opponents of *BPR* in service industries believe that the public sector and service industries should not be aiming for profits and cost effectiveness, but instead focusing on quality of care and empathy and should be ethical, non-profit organizations. This goes with the old portrait of healthcare, and it can be argued that in the current consumer-clinician relationship, the business aspect has become meaningful so as to make healthcare organizations able to deliver the care that is needed. The argument that the service and business industries cannot be compared because they have fundamental differences in their values also seems invalid. The healthcare system has two clear elements: Its business element, and its ethical, medical and humanitarian elements. The industries are very similar in their business aspects, which are the marketing, competition and the financial métier of the organization. As a way to maintain quality of care with expanding needs and shrinking resources, *Quality Improvement (QI)* tools could be saviors for the service industries. When applying business industry *QI* tools, it is important to look at differences that may affect the implementation of these tools in a healthcare setting. These differences do not necessarily make *QI* tools less meaningful for healthcare, but they do require healthcare organizations to use them with the necessary modifications. There are several differences between these two industry types that need attention. The following differences are important to consider and may have contributed to an unsatisfactory success rate with *BPR* in healthcare in the past:

1) The healthcare industry is highly compartmentalized;
2) It is multisystem, complex, ad hoc, dynamic and multidisciplinary;
3) The system has multiple and varied process that are specialty dependent. For example, the admission process in pediatric units will be different from that in adult units, and will differ from surgical units to medical units to emergency rooms. However, similar rules apply for similar processes found in all parts of healthcare organizations, such as outpatient flow, no show rates, quality measures, etc.;
4) Production processes in the healthcare setting need individualization on almost a daily basis. They differ from manufacturing industries' fixed processes, which are designed to produce a part of a machine with the least variation;
5) Usually, errors and delays are reflected in patient outcomes and the increasing cost of services. The safety margin for any new intervention or change is narrow. Effectiveness and safety are more important in healthcare, against efficiency and cost in manufacturing industries;
6) Healthcare organizations' working practices are implemented by clinical professionals but managed by administrators, and both struggle to understand each other's requirements, difficulties and perspectives;
7) The frontline workers do not necessarily understand process improvement tools and culture, and resist change, leading to poor compliance and poor sustainability of *BPR*;
8) When process improvement efforts are undertaken by outside consulting teams, it can lead to poor acceptance and active disengagement from change by the teams inside the organizations (Barkaoui et al., 2002; Becker & Janiesch, 2008);
9) Business process managers sometimes fail to understand the real "needs" of the process and the inbuilt human components in it. Greater ethical awareness and sensitivity is needed in healthcare; working with patients is poles apart from working in manufacturing industry.

In old times, the single family physician was treating everyone in the family and every single disease of the family members. In the modern world, sub-specialization and more sophisticated care have made healthcare multidisciplinary. Not only do sub-specialists treat different organ systems and different age groups of patients, but allied professionals are required to support physicians in their work. These allied specialists, such as physical therapists, occupational therapists, chiropractors, pain management teams, phlebotomists, etc. also become the part of healthcare processes. This makes healthcare processes very distinct, indeed unique, in themselves.

The dynamic character of healthcare processes is due to continuous research, improved technology, fast new therapies and new discoveries in drugs and about diseases. It is almost impossible to catch up with the day-to-day advances in the medical field. The changing technical structure of healthcare necessitates fast changes in healthcare production processes.

Clinicians exercise their judgment and discretion in the matters that clinical guidelines and protocols leave undefined, or where there are no evidence-based guidelines. Sometimes, the decisions that fall between the broad headings in evidence-based guidelines are made on ad hoc basis, since they are based on the individual patient's specific and dynamic health status. They are taken "On Site" rather than predicated in their plan. The autonomy to deviate from standard work protocols in special circumstances also lies in the hands of the professionals. It is a "judgment call". This character makes healthcare system processes wide open to unpredictable, capricious, inconsistent and non-repeating scenarios, which frequently demand changes in plans. Opinions and approaches differ amongst various healthcare teams. The medical decisions are often complex and involve various subspecialties and disciplines. This makes healthcare processes very specific and multi-leveled. The patients do not always read the book, and therefore their presentation and response to therapy are varied, subjecting healthcare processes to unpredictable situations. The data that may be generated are difficult to standardize into a single norm because they are disease- and process-specific. This is different to a single, standard process in manufacturing industries that runs best without variations. A closer and more sensitive and open approach is needed when developing a production process in healthcare, considering the involvement of a human as the subject part that is managed—and treated (worked upon)—in healthcare.

Nevertheless, *BPR* has been used widely in healthcare (Bendavid et al., 2010; Dumas et al., 2013; Kumar & Ozdamar, 2004).

CAUSES OF FAILURE OF BPR IN HEALTHCARE

The healthcare industry also shares all the factors with the manufacturing industry that can lead to implementation failure (see Figure 6.2). The failure rate of *BPR* recorded in the published literature so far is at or above 70 percent (Patwardhan & Patwardhan, 2008). Sometimes, the cause of the published poor performance results of *BPR* is the inappropriate selection of *BPR* as a tool in the given scenario. Most of the time, multiple process improvement tools are employed in addition to *BPR* for cost-saving purposes, which adulterates the impact of *BPR*. Frontline employee engagement is easier to achieve in *TQM/CQI* than in *BPR* because of *BPR*'s more drastic nature. This adversely affects its acceptance rate and the sustainability of change. The concept of a "clean slate" transformation that is at the heart of *BPR* is generally restricted to structural and process parts of the old system. The continuation of old cultural values, attitudes, individual interests and organizational policies defeat the change. Organizational politics controls

Figure 6.2 Causes of Failure of BPR (Holistic approach involves organizational structure, process/policies/procedure/humans (employees)/culture, and part of organization or the whole organization)

the possibilities of collaboration and integration in the newly transformed system. More often than not, internal factors, such as values, dependencies, power and organizational dynamics, regulate the progress and impact of the new system. It is imperative to bring about appropriate changes in macro-, meso- and micromanagement and protocols alongside structural and process changes for *BPR* to be successful. Commitment from the top leadership and willingness to change, in the event of power struggles, is an essential ingredient for the recipe for success. The disadvantages of *BPR* are that if not used wisely and correctly, it can not only fail, but it can cause massive losses to the organization attempting to use it. It is the great "maker or breaker". It takes lots of time and resources and can therefore obstruct the regular running of the production system for a long time. It is not a quick fix. It is a holistic change from scratch and therefore far more expensive than any other *QI* process. It brings a fear of losing jobs into the organization because it has been used as cost-cutting tool. It needs to be used with the right teams, in the right environment and to solve the right type of problem to be successful. If *BPR* is associated with downsizing, subtle changes in the workforce affect the long-term outcomes, which may get ignored in the rush of a big change. The employees' behavior and loyalties change along with the changing team, which affects the immediate outcomes after the event (Lahner et al., 2014; Mohle, 2014; Tuazon, 2008). The employees' morale is shaken, and these uncertainties make for poor predictability of employee behavior in the future. Employee engagement is not at its best during and immediately after the event (Campbell & Pepper, 2006).

ADVANTAGES OF BPR IN HEALTHCARE INDUSTRIES

As illustrated in Figure 6.3, *BPR* clearly brings several benefits to organizations (Al-Shaqha & Zairi, 2000; Elkhuizen et al., 2006; Ivey, 1995; Newman, 1997). The implementation of *BPR* has been shown to facilitate the reduction of bureaucracy. If implemented as intended, it should deliver less expensive, quicker, better quality and customized services to patients (Chaudhry et al., 2006). Above all, it will lead to greater transparency and the appropriate use of resources. The *BPR* process may give administrators and policy makers the chance to review the use and rationality of the procedures, guidelines and safety measures of the old system. It may also provide opportunities to identify new redundancy and waste, and opportunities for *TQM* implementation at a later date.

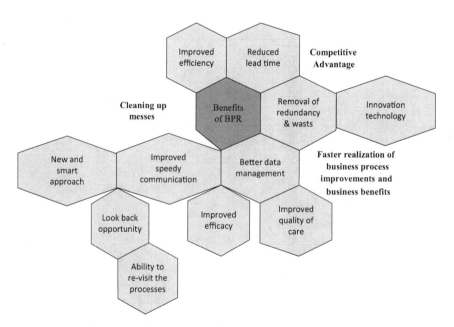

Figure 6.3 Advantages of *BPR* Implementation

Potential advantages due to the information technology aspect of *BPR* implementation include (Davenport, 1992; Goldzweig, et al., 2009; Panda, 2013):

1) Quick, accurate and easy access to patient and system information with comprehensive archives across multiple systems;
2) Easy-to-coordinate care, effective communication and improved outcomes, due to the ability to hold staff accountable for errors and to continually be optimizing processes, business rules, and routing. The decentralization of data and information reduces the "red tape";
3) *IT*-enabled *BPR* implementation allows for the sharing of knowledge/experience with an interphase that is secure, intuitive within intranet and also with the social interphase;
4) Visibility and accountability, which are further improved by real-time reports;
5) Easy-to-develop standard production processes, leading to a patient-centered approach with easy handovers, case management, consult, chart reviews and accessibility due to the creation of patient-based *IT* portals;
6) An amalgamated view of up-to-date information across multiple systems, like *Electronic Medical Records* (EMRs), insurance information, meaningful use, medication reconciliation and billing, etc.;
7) Improved and easy referrals and consultations due to *EMRs*;
8) Easy accessibility of data on any electronic device so that clinicians are more approachable for patients;
9) Improved patient satisfaction;
10) Increased openness and transparency in the system, behaviors, patient-clinician relationships, easy auditing and helping research;
11) Patient portals generate more trust and confidence in patients due to transparency and accountability;
12) Improved monitoring: Automated special milestones and risk-alert systems can be developed in the patient chart, based on clinical activities and events. This can avoid missed opportunities and help in risk management. These activities all have great potential to improve outcomes;
13) The clinicians' response to prescriptions, refills, parent or patient health-related concerns and other non-emergent issues can be improved through *EMRs*. The records are archives to prevent litigation.

HUMAN FACTORS IN BPR

Most often during a change, the focus is on the measure of the changes, and neglects the human factor. That is, managers fail to recognize that all of these changes have to be brought about by and delivered through people.

Resistance to change by the users of BPR is a major reason for BPR failing to achieve its objectives. Another is the communication gap between the managers and frontline staff, and between the policy-making leadership and the end users of BPR. For example, if at the beginning of BPR implementation, the employees (end users) were brought into the concept and goals, the leaders and end users would all agree with the proposed changes and be aware of the vision and mission. In some cases, the expected changes in individuals' working styles and obligations were determined by senior management, but unfortunately, this was not communicated to the employees. At the same time, it was presumed that they knew their roles and responsibilities. This is a perfect example of poor "hoshin planning" and failure to "walk the talk", which will lead to failure without a shred of doubt. (The Japanese in the 1960s developed a system/process called hoshin kanri/hoshin process/hoshin planning, whose aim was to work towards key strategic initiatives ("hoshin" in Japanese) in a focused way (Akao, 2004).)

More often than not, BPR is professed as a job-cutting exercise and it threatens the employees in terms of job loss, job contents, opportunity for progression and their hierarchical position. It lowers employee morale and confidence in management. Some organizations try to perform TQM to start with, but change to BPR if TQM fails. It is believed that TQM exercises develop the right environment for BPR to accommodate drastic changes. For example, Stewart (1993, p. 45) created the slogan, "You cannot do reengineering without an environment of continuous improvement or TQM".

Training and skill development are essential when implementing BPR. Training in computing, data management, IT skills, specific software training and troubleshooting skills is paramount for frontline employees (Yeo, 2002). BPR includes the redesign of jobs, the restructuring of accountabilities and job responsibilities and finally, the redesign of the hierarchical structure (Hutchins, 1996).

In practice, changing an organizational culture takes years, if not decades. Consultants engaged in BPR may aim to improve timelines, lead time and dollars' worth of savings, but the old cultural constraints can make the whole effort fail. For the speed of cultural change and the speed of BPR implementation cannot be the same unless the organization already has a CQI culture.

The challenging issues that will be at the heart of the success are:

1) Is the current culture appropriate for the change, or is there huge organizational inertia? How will the change be perceived by the users of BPR? The culture of "we have always done it this way successfully for years" has to be let go of;
2) The change will bring IT and other new technologies into the production process and questions will arise as to whether IT users have the required skills, or of training and development will be needed;

3) Process lines where users will need training, what specific training and how that will be monitored;

4) Change always comes with stress, which may be stress due to uncertainty, poor understanding, new skill requirements and new expectations. An infrastructure needs to be in place to manage stress at all the levels of staff well before *BPR* is implemented;

5) Communication between the policy makers, frontline staff and the change team should be frequent enough to translate every structural change into functional change. Leadership should "walk the talk", using every single opportunity for communication;

6) The impact of the change on the organization and individuals should be communicated well in advance so that educated decisions may be taken by the users as to whether they want to take part or not;

7) An unrecognized aspect of performance improvement is emotion and the bonding of the project teams. This aspect can make or break a project. Managing the buildup of frustration and fretfulness over time will reduce resistance and facilitate acceptance of the change.

CHANGE MANAGEMENT: AN ESSENTIAL STEP IN BPR

Structural and process changes are not enough. Cultural change, as mentioned above, is an essential step for the success of *BPR* (Al-Mashari & Zairi, 1999). *BPR* encompasses holistic and drastic changes in the structures, technology and functions of the process transformed, departmental and individual behaviors, training, the leadership's attitudes and motivation and reward systems: In a nutshell, in the culture of the organization. There could be several lost opportunities if the implementation is not carefully carried out. *BPR* should be followed by *CQI* to continuously build on the right infrastructure. If *TQM* is used in place of *BPR* where *BPR* is needed, all that happens is that the defective process is made to produce defective pieces or to cause errors more efficiently. It is important that correct, committed individuals are selected and trained to turn them into high-performing, functional teams. The emotional intelligence of the leadership can play a tremendous role in connecting with the teams, bonding and with motivating them to obtain a distinctive team effort. Techniques and focused efforts will be needed to modify the culture to be more accepting of the change.

The most engaging style of some leaders is to tell the story of a vision of the organization and emotionally connect with the employees, as they are the essential people to achieve this. These leaders make the task a joint mission, with employees and the leadership owning *BPR* together. These leaders connect with the employees at emotional levels that generate mutual trust and ownership of the task. The need for the change has to be communicated by managers at every possible opportunity so that employees can be brought into the concept and start realizing the need for change. The resistance to change is best tackled by establishing the need and urgency for the change. Most projects in which the importance of change management is not realized succumb in their infancy or do not reach their maximum potential. It is easy to manage a change in the equipment, structure or production process, but not in the humans, who cannot be programmed like machines to work differently. It is generally observed that the resistance comes most from those who use the new production process the most.

A culture develops over several years in an organization, reflecting its traditional, cumulative practices, behaviors, beliefs, attitudes and responses. Apart from evolving over time, it is governed by the organization's policies, recognition-reward systems, employees' learned behavior and the leaders' and role models' own manners of behavior. Not only does it take years, but it is extremely difficult to change the culture of an organization. It may be less difficult to create a culture in a new organization than to change that of an established one.

CONCLUSION

Business Process Reengineering is a manufacturing process improvement tool that has been widely used in the public sector and healthcare. It differs from all other process improvement tools in its approach and the magnitude of change. It is a holistic approach, starting from a clean slate, and involves all parts of the organization that it is applied to. It is a drastic change involving the structure, function and culture of the organization (or part of the organization). The appropriate selection of the process improvement method, which may be *TQM* or *BPR*, is the essential first step for success and for achieving desired outcomes. It is a top-down approach, and a correct balance among leadership techniques and management and the use of power, rewards and a recognition system in an appropriate mix and delivered in a timely manner, delivers the best results. As in manufacturing or the engineering industry, *BPR* can be successfully used in healthcare, provided a customized approach focusing on the fundamentals of the mission of healthcare that can take care of the business as well as the humane aspect is used. Greater ethical awareness and sensitivity is needed when implementing *BPR* in healthcare because healthcare teams deal with humans in their production processes and not with machine parts, as in the engineering industries.

REFERENCES

Akao, Y. (Ed.) (2004). *Hoshin Kanri: Policy Deployment for Successful TQM* (1st ed.). New York: Productivity Press.

Akiyama, M. (2007). Risk management and measuring productivity with POAS—Point of act system—a medical information system as ERP (Enterprise Resource Planning) for hospital management. *Methods of Information in Medicine*, **46** (6), 686–693.

Al-Mashari, M., & Zairi, M. (1999). BPR implementation process: An analysis of key success and failure factors. *Business Process Management Journal*, 5 (1), 87–112.

Al-Shaqha, M., & Zairi, M. (2000). Re-engineering pharmaceutical care: Towards a patient-focused care approach. *International Journal of Health Care Quality Assurance Incorporating Leadership in Health Services*, 13 (4–5), 208–217.

Becker, J., & Janiesch, C. (2008). Restrictions in process design: A case study on workflows in healthcare. Hutchison, D., Kanade, T., Kittler, J., Kleinberg, J.M., Mattern, F., Mitchell, J.C., Naor, M., Pandu Rangan, C., Steffen, B., Terzopoulos, D., Tygar, D., Weikum, G. (Ed.), *Business Process Management Workshops, Lecture Notes in Computer Science*, Vol. 4928, Berlin Heidelberg: Springer, pp. 323–334.

Begg, C., & Connolly, T. (2005). *Database Systems: A Practical Approach to Design, Implementation, and Management* (4th ed.). Boston, MA: Addison-Wesley.

Bendavid, Y., Boeck, H., & Philippe, R. (2010). Redesigning the replenishment process of medical supplies in hospitals. *Business Process Management Journal*, 16 (6), 991–1013.

Binder, R.V. (1997). Can a manufacturing quality model work for software? *IEEE Software*, 14 (5), 101–105.

Blumenthal, B.H. (1994). Towards a definition of corporate transformation. *Sloan Management Review*, 35 (3), 101–106.

Botta-Genoulaza, V., & Milletb, P. (2006). An investigation into the use of ERP systems in the service sector. *International Journal of Production Economics*, 99 (1–2), 202–221.

Brennan, P. (1999). Telehealth: Bringing health care to the point of living. *Medical Care*, 37 (2), 115–116.

Brooks, F.P. (1987). No silver bullet essence and accidents of software engineering. *Computer*, 20 (4), 10–19.

Campbell, R., & Pepper, L. (2006). Downsizing and social cohesion: The case of downsizing survivors. *New Solutions*, 16 (4), 373–393.

Caudron, S. (1997). The human side of a technology launch. *Training and Development*, 51 (2), 21–24.

Chaudhry, B., Wang, J., Wu, S., Maglione, M., Mojica, W., & Roth, E. (2006). Systematic review: Impact of health information technology on quality, efficiency, and costs of medical care. *Annals of Internal Medicine*, 144 (10), 742–752.

Chevreul, K., Durand-Zaleski, I., Bahrami, S.B., Hernandez-Quevedo, C., & Mladovsky, P. (2010). France: Health system review. *Health Systems in Transition*, 12 (6), 1–291.

Corby, S. (2005). Spot the difference between the public and private sectors: Disputes and third-party intervention in Britain. *Public Money and Management*, 25 (2), 107–114.

Corrigan, S. (1997). *Human and organizational aspects of Business Process Reengineering, Research Report*. Sheffield, England: Institute of Work Psychology, University of Sheffield. Retrieved from http://bprc.warwick.ac.uk:80/shef-summ.html (accessed 30 November 2014).

Darkins, A., Ryan, P., Kobb, R., Foster, L., Edmonson, E., Wakefield, B., & Lancaster, A.E. (2008). Care coordination/home telehealth: The systematic implementation of health informatics, home telehealth, and disease management to support the care of veteran patients with chronic conditions. *Telemedicine and e-Health*, 14 (10), 1118–1126.

Davenport, T.H. (1992). *Process Innovation: Reengineering Work through Information Technology* (1st ed.). Harvard, MA: Harvard Business Review Press.

Davenport, T.H., & Short, J.E. (1990). The new industrial engineering: Information technology and business process redesign. *Sloan Management Review*, 34 (4), 11–27.

Dean, E.B. (1996). *Business process reengineering from the perspective of competitive advantage* [Online article]. Retrieved from http://spartan.ac.brocku.ca/~pscarbrough/dfca1stmods/dfc/bpre.html (accessed 10 February 2015).

Dean, J.W., & Bowen, D.E. (1994). Management theory and total quality: Improving research and practice through theory development. *Academy of Management Review*, 19 (3), 392–418.

Dennis, A.R., Carte, T.A., & Kelly, G.G. (2003). Breaking the rules: Success and failure in groupware-supported business process reengineering. *Decision Support Systems*, 36 (1), 31–43.

Dumas, M., La Rosa, M., Mendling, J., & Reijers, H. (2013). *Fundamentals of Business Process Management*. Berlin: Springer.

Elkhuizen, S.G., Limburg, M., Bakker, P.J., & Klazinga, N.S. (2006). Evidence-based re-engineering: Re-engineering the evidence—a systematic review of the literature on business process redesign (BPR) in hospital care. *International Journal of Health Care Quality Assurance Incorporating Leadership in Health Services*, 19 (6–7), 477–499.

Epstein, R.H., & Dexter, F. (2000). Economic analysis of linking operating room scheduling and hospital material management information systems for just-in-time inventory control. *Anesthesia and Analgesia*, 91 (2), 337–343.

Fountain, J.E. (2003). Information, institutions and governance: Advancing a basic social science research program for digital government. *Social Science Research*, 1 (1), 1–123.

Goeppinger, S. (1996). Old financial systems do not match the new world process or need. *Seminars for Nurse Managers*, 4 (1), 72–77.

Goldzweig, C.L., Towfigh, A., Maglione, M., & Shekelle, P.G. (2009). Costs and benefits of health information technology: New trends from the literature. *Health Affairs*, 28 (2), 282–293.

Greenwood, R., & Hinings, C.R. (1996). Understanding radical organizational change: Bringing together the old and new institutionalism. *Academy of Management Review*, 21 (4), 1022–1054.

Gunasekaran, A., & Kobu, B. (2002). Modelling and analysis of business process reengineering. *International Journal of Production Research*, 40 (11), 2521–2546.

Gupta, G. (2007). *Workflow and process mining in healthcare*. Master thesis, Technische Universiteit Eindhoven.

Halachmi, A., & Bovaird, T. (1997). Process reengineering in the public sector: Learning some private sector lessons. *Technovation*, 17 (5), 227–235.

Halley, A. (1995). *Downsizing*. The Meridian International Institute, April 5, 1995 Report, McLean, VA, USA.

Hammer, M. (1990). Reengineering work: Don't automate, obliterate. *Harvard Business Review*, 68 (July–August), 104–112. Retrieved from https://hbr.org/1990/07/reengineering-work-dont-automate-obliterate/ar/1 (accessed 27 October 2015).

Hammer, M., & Champy, J. (2006). *Reengineering the Corporation: A Manifesto for Business Revolution*. New York: HarperCollins.

Horak, B.J. (2001). Dealing with human factors and managing change in knowledge management: A phased approach. *Topics in Health Information Management*, 21 (3), 8–17.

Hughes, O.E. (1994). *Public Management and Administration*. New York: Palgrave MacMillan.

Hunt, J.S., Siemienczuk, J., Gillanders, W., LeBlanc, B.H., Rozenfeld, Y., Bonin, K., & Pape, G. (2009). The impact of a physician-directed health information technology system on diabetes outcomes in primary care: A pre- and post-implementation study. *Informatics in Primary Care*, 17 (3), 165–174.

Hutchins, N.L. (1996). *Thriving on change—BPR has one big problem: People*. Retrieved from http://www.reengineering.com/articles/mar96/mngchnge.html (accessed 30 January 2015).

Ivey, M.F. (1995). Re-engineering for dramatic improvement in the medication-use process. *American Journal of Health-System Pharmacy*, 52 (23), 2681–2685.

Jurisch, M.C., Ikas, C., Palka, W., Wolf, P., & Krcmar, H. (2012). *A review of success factors and challenges of public sector BPR implementations.* Paper presented at the 45th Hawaii International Conference on Systems Science (HICSS 2012), Maui, Hawaii.

Jurisch, M.C., Palka, W., Wolf, P., & Krcmar, H. (2014). Which capabilities matter for successful business process change? *Business Process Management Journal*, 20 (1), 47–67.

Kaboolian, L. (1999). Quality comes to the public sector. In R. Cole & W.R. Scott (Eds.), *The Quality Movement and Organization Theory* (1st ed.), London: Sage, pp. 26–27.

Kassahun, A.E., & Alemayehu, M. (2011). *BPR complementary competence for developing economy public sector: A construct and measurement instrument.* Conference paper. Pacific Asia Conference on Information Systems, PACIS 2011: Quality Research in Pacific Asia, Brisbane, Queensland, Australia, 7–11 July 2011.

Kontio, E., Lundgrén-Laine, H., Kontio, J., Korvenranta, H., & Salanterä, S. (2014). Enterprise resource planning systems in healthcare: A qualitative review. *International Journal of Information Systems in the Service Sector archive*, 6 (2), 36–50.

Kumar, A., & Ozdamar, L. (2004). *Business process reengineering at the hospitals: A case study at Singapore hospital.* Paper presented at the 18th European Simulation Multiconference, Magdeburg, Germany, June 13–16.

Lahner, J.M., Hayslip, B., McKelvy, T.N., & Caballero, D.M. (2014). Employee age and reactions to downsizing. *The International Journal of Aging and Human Development*, 79 (3), 225–255.

Lavy, A. (1986). Secondary planned change: Definition & conceptualization. *Organizational Dynamics*, 38 (7), 583–586.

Leatt, P., Baker, G.R., Halverson, P.K., & Aird, C. (1997). Downsizing, reengineering, and restructuring: Long-term implications for healthcare organizations. *Frontiers of Health Service Management*, 13 (4), 3–37.

Lenz, R., & Kuhn, K.A. (2004). Towards a continuous evolution and adaptation of information systems in healthcare. *International Journal of Medical Informatics*, 73 (1), 75–89.

Lenz, R., & Reichert, M. (2007). IT support for healthcare processes: Premises, challenges, perspectives. *Data & Knowledge Engineering*, 61 (1), 39–58.

MacIntosh, R. (2003). BPR: Alive and well in the public sector. *International Journal of Operations & Production Management*, 23 (3), 327–344.

Malhotra, Y. (1998). Business process redesign: An overview. *IEEE Engineering Management Review*, 26 (3), 27–31. Retrieved from http://www.kmbook.com/bpr.htm (accessed 6 February 2015).

Mans, R., Schonenberg, H., Leonardi, G., Panzarasa, S., Cavallini, A., Quaglini, S., & van der Aalst, W. (2008). Process mining techniques: An application to stroke care. *Studies in Health Technology and Informatics*, 136 (1), 573–578.

Mans, R., Schonenberg, M., Song, M., van der Aalst, W., & Bakker, P. (2009). Application of process mining in healthcare: A case study in a Dutch hospital. In A. Fred, J. Filipe, & H. Gamboa (Eds.), *Biomedical Engineering Systems and Technologies*, International Joint Conference, BIOSTEC 2008 Funchal, Madeira, Portugal, January 28–31, pp. 425–438.

Marlen, C.J., Palka, W., Wolf, P., & Krcmar, H. (2012). *A review of success factors and challenges of public sector BPR implementations.* HICSS paper presented at the 45th Hawaii International Conference on System Sciences, Hawaii, 4–7 January.

McNulty, T., & Ferlie, E. (2004). *Reengineering Healthcare: The Complexities of Organizational Transformation.* Oxford, England: Oxford University Press.

Mohle, B. (2014). Freedom from fear. *Old Nurse*, 33 (5), 3.

Motwania, J., Subramaniana, R., & Gopala Krishna, P. (2005). Critical factors for successful ERP implementation: Exploratory findings from four case studies. *Computers in Industry*, 56 (6), 529–544.

Newman, K. (1997). Towards a new health care paradigm. Patient-focused care. The case of Kingston Hospital Trust. *Journal of Management in Medicine*, 11 (5–6), 357–371.

Noel, H.C., Vogel, D.C., Erdos, J., Cornwall, D., & Levin, F. (2004). Home tele-health reduces healthcare costs. *Telemedicine Journal and e-Health*, 10 (2), 170–183.

Nwabueze, U., Morris, D.S., & Haigh, R.H. (1995). Organizational diagnosis: A healthcare experience of BPR. *Annual Quality Congress, Cincinnati OH*, 49 (1), 833–839. Retrieved from http://asq.org/qic/display-item/?item=10335 (accessed 28 October 2014).

Oberoi, R. (2013). Applying business process re-engineering to public sector as a new public management strategy: Understanding the contra views and limits. *Journal of Government and Politics*, 4 (2), 245–270.

Panda, M. (2013). IT enabled business process reengineering. *International Journal of Information Technology & Management Information System*, 4 (3), 85–95.

Parys, M. (2003). *Business process reengineering: Or how to enable bottom-up participation in a top down reform program.* Paper presented at the Annual meeting of the European Group of Public Administration, Oeiras, Portugal, 3–6 September.

Pateli, A., & Philippidou, S. (2011). Applying business process change (BPC) to implement multi-agency collaboration: The case of the Greek public administration. *Journal of Theoretical and Applied Electronic Commerce Research*, 6 (1), 127–142.

Patwardhan, A., & Patwardhan, D. (2008). Business process re-engineering: Savior or just another fad? One UK health care perspective. *International Journal of Health Care Quality Assurance*, 21 (3), 289–296.

Pettigrew, A., & Whipp, R. (1991). *Managing for Competitive Success.* Oxford, England: Basil Blackwell.

Poulymenopoulou, M., Malamateniou, F., & Vassilacopoulos, G. (2003). Specifying workflow process requirements for an emergency medical service. *Journal of Medical Systems*, 27 (4), 325–335.

Raczynski, B., & Curtis, B. (2008). Software Data Violate SPC's Underlying Assumptions. *IEEE Software*, 25 (3), 49–51.

Scholl, H.J. (2004). *Current practices in e- government-induced business process change (BPC).* Paper presented at the Proceedings of the 2004 annual national conference on Digital government research, Seattle, Washington, USA, 24–26 May.

Scholl, H.J. (2014). *E-Government: Information, Technology, and Transformation* (3rd ed.). Stuttgart, Germany: Routledge.

Schrage, C.R. (1997). The Human Factors of Reengineering: Organizations with Information Technology. Retrieved from https://www.uni.edu/~schragec/tphuman.htm (accessed 15 January 2015).

Shekelle, P.G., Morton, S.C., & Keeler, E.B. (2006). *Costs and Benefits of Health Information Technology.* Rockville MD: United States Agency for Health Care Policy and Research.

Stamm, B.H. (1998). Clinical applications of telehealth in mental health care. *Professional Psychology: Research and Practice*, 29 (6), 536–542.

Stanton, S., Hammer, M., & Power B. (1992). From resistance to results: Mastering the organizational issues of re-engineering. *Insights Quarterly: The Executive Journal of Business Reengineering*, 4 (2), 6–16.

Stefanou, C.J., & Andreas, R. (2006). ERP integration in a healthcare environment: A Case Study. *Journal of Enterprise Information Management*, **19** (1), 115–130.

Stewart, T. (1993). Reengineering: The hot new management tool. *Fortune*, August 23, 41–48.

Stoddard, D., & Jarvenpaa, S. (1995). Business process redesign: Tactics for managing radical change. *Journal of Management Information Systems*, **12** (1), 81–107.

Tang, P.C., LaRosa, M.P., & Gorden, S.M. (1999). Use of computer-based records, completeness of documentation, and appropriateness of documented clinical decisions. *Journal of the American Medical Informatics Association*, **6** (3), 245–251.

Teng, J.T.C., Grover, V., & Fiedler, K.D. (1994). Business process re-engineering: Charting a strategic path for the information age. *California Management Review*, **37** (7), 9–31.

Tuazon, N. (2008). Survivor guilt after downsizing. *Nursing Management*, **39** (5), 19–23.

Veninga, R.L. (1997). After the downsizing. How to build loyalty and productivity in the wake of restructuring. *Health Progress*, **78** (5), 14–17.

Weerakkody, V., Janssen, M., & Dwivedi, Y.K. (2011). Transformational change and business process reengineering (BPR): Lessons from the British and Dutch public sector. *Government Information Quarterly*, **28** (3), 320–328.

Weil, T.P. (2003). Hospital downsizing and workforce reduction strategies: Some inner workings. *Health Services Management Research*, **16** (1), 13–23.

Wilson, J.Q. (1991). *Bureaucracies: What Government Agencies Do and Why They Do It* (2nd ed.). New York: Basic Books.

Yeo, K.T. (2002). Critical failure factors in information system projects. *International Journal of Project Management*, **20** (1), 241–246. Retrieved from http://www.elsevier.com/locate/ijproman (accessed 23 March 2015).

7 Consensus as a Management Strategy for Healthcare Organizations
Culture, Involvement and Commitment

Marie Carney

INTRODUCTION

The purpose of this chapter is to present *Consensus* as a concept that is relevant in management, and particularly in healthcare management. *Consensus* is viewed differently in organizations. *Consensus Management* was once explicitly defined by the National Health Service in the United Kingdom as the requirement for all decisions being made by a decision-making body to be fully consensual. There is no agreement on a definition or on the value of *Consensus* in organizations or on the concepts and dimensions making up *Consensus Management*. In this chapter, the notion of *Consensus Management* is explored. The question considered is whether *Consensus Management* is appropriate in healthcare organizations, the focus of this chapter, and if so, in what way is it appropriate. This narrative will be presented through the *Consensus Management Model of Healthcare*. This model integrates into the concept of *Consensus* the management concepts of involvement, commitment and culture, and some of their dimensions, such as the values utilized in professional approaches to healthcare delivery, in this context. So it is pertinent to ask if each of those management concepts alone contributes to the *Consensus* of healthcare strategy or if a combined approach is more effective to gaining an understanding of *Consensus Management*. The model resulted from quantitative and qualitative research carried out amongst middle-manager healthcare professionals in the Republic of Ireland. Most of the conclusions presented in this chapter are based on studies from healthcare organizations and hospitals based in Australia, Ireland, Canada, the United Kingdom, the USA and New Zealand. The *Consensus Management* approaches used in Australia, Ireland, the United Kingdom, the USA and New Zealand are outlined from the perspectives of strategic management as a means to achieve goals, organizational objectives and decision-making. The advantages and disadvantages to using *Consensus Management* in healthcare organizations are presented.

In this chapter, culture is presented as being a factor that influences *Consensus*. Culture has been identified as an important component of organizational consensus that serves to underpin professional values. Culture may be defined as observed behavioral regularities that occur during interactions between individuals, and is multifaceted and multidimensional. Managers working in organizations where a strong culture exists demonstrate higher levels of strategic consensus than those working in organizations where the culture is weak. Two further concepts presented in the chapter are involvement and commitment. Involvement in planning is an ongoing decision-making process that is designed to specify the ideals, goals and objectives needed by the organization in the future. Involvement influences how *Consensus* evolves within the organization. Commitment to the organization influences strategic involvement. If managers are initially involved in the development of a strategy, they will direct their efforts and exercise a higher level of commitment to a consensus on the strategy being developed. The next section explores the concept of *Consensus*.

CONCEPT OF CONSENSUS

The concept of *Consensual Decision-Making* is one approach whereby consensus decision-making is viewed as a group decision-making process that seeks the consent of all participants and is concerned with a process that includes the assessment, implementation and evaluation of a decision made by the group (Carney, 2006c). A further concept of *Consensus* is put forward by Black and Gregersen (1997), who explore participative decision-making as an integration of multiple dimensions when examining the integration of participation and decision-making processes and their relationship with satisfaction and performance, and they suggest the concept of involvement is important when generating alternatives, planning and evaluating results. The concept of *Consensus* is viewed by Tjosvold and Field (1983), in their simulated study of 114 students arranged in four groups, as an agreement on the means for innovative activities amongst group decision-makers. These authors found that competitive or cooperative conditions exist in groups where mandatory consensus or majority decision-making is required, resulting in enhanced organizational performance, but also conversely that coalition influences strategic consensus negatively by making goal attainment difficult to achieve, particularly when the consensus process is forced on participants, resulting in a lack of agreement on strategic decisions. *Consensus Decision-Making* may be viewed as an alternative to adversarial decision-making processes. Hartnett (2011) says *Consensus Decision-Making* may come about in a negative way due to difficulty in reaching unanimity, whereby consent may be the result of coercion. Carmelli et al. (2009) question whether participatory decision-making in top management teams enhances decision effectiveness.

Concepts of *Consensus* as management strategies can thus be viewed differently. In this section, three dimensions have been presented: Involvement, competition and agreement. The next section explores the *Consensus Management* approaches used in organizations.

CONSENSUS MANAGEMENT APPROACHES IN ORGANIZATIONS

One of the first authors to study the concept of *Consensus* in organizations was Stagner (1969), in his study of 109 responses from Fortune 500 organizations, in which he found that a link existed between managerial cohesiveness and decision-making. However, the first empirical study, which was undertaken by Bourgeois (1980) and involved a sample of 67 managers in 12 organizations, identified that a consensus on goals and the means to achieve goals did not indicate high performance. These studies were undertaken in not-for-profit organizations. Later, Dess (1987) explored the environment and strategy consensus in 19 for-profit hospitals in the USA in a study that involved 86 strategic decision-making teams and found a positive relationship between *Consensus Management* and the achievement of organizational objectives. Floyd and Wooldridge (1992b), in a study of middle managers working in manufacturing and financial environments, found that in turbulent environments, the integration of organizational environment, structure and strategic consensus is needed for the formulation of strategy. They defined four levels of strategic consensus amongst middle managers. Level 1 identified managers as having a common understanding and shared commitment to a strategy, Level 2 is described as "blind devotion" with poorly informed managers, even when well intentioned, Level 3 depicts "informed skepticism", where managers are informed but unwilling to act on a strategy, and Level 4 is described as managers having a low level of shared understanding and commitment to organizational goals and strategy. These levels may be apparent in different organizations.

Carney (2003) developed the *Consensus Model*, which incorporates strategic involvement, commitment to the organization and the culture of the organization from findings from 860 clinician and non-clinician managers in head-of-department roles in 60 of the 65 acute care public hospitals in the Republic of Ireland that are managed by the Health Service Executive. She identified a multidisciplinary approach to healthcare management as incorporating dimensions of managerial, behavioral, professional and organizational dimensions, and she identified the importance of professionals being committed to delivering excellent healthcare in the most effective and efficient way possible. *Consensus Management* approaches used in organizations thus include the integration of the organizational environment as well as the need for structure and strategic consensus in formulating strategy. The next section explores the advantages and disadvantages of *Consensus Management* in healthcare.

ADVANTAGES AND DISADVANTAGES OF CONSENSUS MANAGEMENT IN HEALTHCARE

Organizations in different countries determine the importance of strategic consensus differently. The National Health Service (NHS) in Britain used

Consensus Management as a mandatory, standard practice during the period from 1972–1982. Then, *Consensus Management* was explicitly defined as the requirement for all decisions of a decision-making body (e.g., the board, management team, executive group) to be fully consensual. This form of management was termed "consensus" and "diplomatic management" and came about following a Department of Health and Social Security (DHSS) document known as the "Grey Book" (DHSS, 1972), which set out the NHS philosophy for reorganization and was influenced by Brunel University's Health Services Organization Research Unit and McKinsey Management Consultancy Group recommendations. *Consensus Management*, in this context, was based on teams of equals who would make decisions by consensus, that in effect gave every single board, district, area, region, group or committee member a right of veto, and where decisions were made collectively following a group discussion of alternatives (Morgan, 1994).

The advantage to this approach was that *Consensus Management* encouraged multidisciplinary cooperation and collaboration. However, disadvantages were quickly identified. One *alleged* consequence was slow and lowest-common-denominator decision-making, with managers avoiding controversial or "hard" decisions due to the powers of veto being held by just one or a few members of the team and because of a lack of accountability, thus leading to poor resolution of difficult decisions. In an effort to address some of these difficulties, a new NHS structure was set out that placed emphasis on management training and the development of local plans that were more in keeping with a modern health service. In 1982, following further NHS reorganization, *Consensus Decision-Making* remained at the district level, and below this level, management units were set up with clear reporting structures.

The Griffiths Report (1983), which made a significant contribution to NHS management, recommended the adoption of the concept of "general management" to replace "consensus management". Harrison (1988), in summarizing research findings prior to the introduction of the Griffiths Report, found that the main problems were "pluralism", where no single person was in charge, resulting in no accountability; reactiveness, whereby problems arising were dealt with on an ad hoc basis; incrementalism, where managers were slow to propose major changes or to question existing patterns of work; and introversion, where managers adopted an inward approach to managing that served other managers and their peers rather than looking outward to their consumers or patients/clients. The Griffiths Report put general managers in charge of the NHS and made them accountable at all three levels: Regional, district and unit. However, this structure was criticized also. Strong and Robinson (1994) argued that Griffiths was only a partial break with the past and led to a long management chain of command, and that local managers remained constrained by supervisors, politicians and civil servants. The era of consumerism from 1998 to the present has placed greater emphasis on quality controls, measurement audits and cost effectiveness, leading to the decentralization of services (Morgan, 1994).

Hence, both advantages and disadvantages to *Consensus Management* in healthcare organizations can be identified. *Consensus Management* based on teams of equals who make decisions by consensus encourages multi-disciplinary cooperation and collaboration. But the disadvantages to this approach can be that the lowest common denominator in decision-making generates managers who avoid controversial or "hard" decisions. The next section presents a specific *Consensus Management* approach used by nursing organizations in the USA.

CONSENSUS MANAGEMENT APPROACH IN A NURSING ORGANIZATION

The Advanced Practice Registered Nurse Advisory Committee (APRN) (2012) in the USA is utilizing the *LACE Consensus Model* to regulate advanced practice nurses. Despite the lack of definitive knowledge of their numbers, APRNs represent a significant resource for meeting the country's growing healthcare needs in the most effective way possible. The Institute of Medicine (2012) report entitled, "Future of Nursing: Leading Change, Advancing Health", recognizes that nurses should practice to the full extent of their education and training and become full partners, with physicians and other health professionals, in redesigning healthcare in the USA, as this will result in effective workforce planning and policy making and improved information infrastructure. Stanley (2012) states that the advanced practice nursing community, through the development of the *Consensus Model* for APRN regulation, *Licensure, Accreditation, Certification and Education (LACE)*, positioned itself to assume a leadership role within the healthcare system and participate as an equal partner in redesigning healthcare in the USA. The *LACE Consensus Model* has been recognized by policy makers and others outside of nursing as foundational to the future of APRN practice implementation. Transparent communication among all *LACE* entities is recognized as being the most critical component in achieving and maintaining consensus as advanced practice nursing moves toward the goal of full implementation of this new regulatory model by 2015 (Stanley, 2012).

In the next section, some *Consensus Management* strategies used in other segments of healthcare delivery are presented.

CONSENSUS MANAGEMENT STRATEGIES IN OTHER SEGMENTS OF HEALTHCARE

In more recent times, medical organizations in Australia and New Zealand have introduced a consensus approach to formulating health policy through consensus statements. The Australasian Faculty of Occupational and Environmental Medicine (AFOEM) and the Faculty of the Royal Australasian

College of Physicians (RACP) launched the *Australian and New Zealand Consensus Statement on the Health Benefits of Work*, on March 30th, 2011 (Kolbe et al., 2011). The purpose of the consensus statement was to bring together a wide range of stakeholder signatories, who each affirm the importance of work as a determinant of health and who would commit to promoting awareness of the health benefits of work through offering support and encouragement to those attempting to access the health benefits of work. The consensus statement also advocates for continuous improvement in public policy around work and health, in line with the principles articulated in the consensus statement. It is intended that the statement will act as a facilitator for further discussion regarding the detail of what is required to achieve positive change.

Consensus amongst diverse stakeholders is a powerful and empowering tool. The RACP says that the *Consensus Statement* demonstrates that medical, nursing and allied professionals, unions, government authorities, business groups and other stakeholders are willing to work together, but that a comprehensive shift in thinking and practice is needed. They also acknowledge that this shift will not occur if stakeholders continue to speak only as individuals and individual organizations and do not speak with one voice and a shared purpose. The need for a cooperative enterprise between employers, those who represent the best interests of employees, the government and its agencies is necessary for the successful implementation of strategy (Kolbe et al., 2011). To facilitate this consensus approach education, training and professional leadership, drawing on a sound academic base and good research, is needed (Black, 2008).

Canadian research has also influenced thinking on *Consensus Management*. In 2004, Haggerty et al. undertook a consultation with 20 Canadian primary healthcare experts via a telectronic Delphi process to define the attributes that should be evaluated in a proposed model of primary healthcare. In four iterative rounds, the participants were asked to propose and modify operational definitions. Consensus was achieved on most attributes, with each round incorporating feedback from the previous round. Consensus was achieved on the importance of having multidisciplinary team engagement and on communication, coordination, relationship continuity, cultural sensitivity and the quality improvement processes needed.

Consensus on strategy is dependent upon the creation by management of an organizational culture that serves to promote involvement and excellence in care delivery through a management coterie that are seen as capable of managing the tensions existing between quality of care and cost effectiveness (Carney, 2006c). Viewing the role of department head as pivotal to healthcare management is critical to consensus building in healthcare planning and delivery, and in improving efficiency and effectiveness in organizations (Carney, 2006c). This view is supported by Dooley and Fryxell (1999) in their study of 86 strategic decision-making teams in American hospitals. They found that consensus building was an important factor in the strategic decision-making process. Carney (2003) identified the prevailing culture within the organization as influencing the level of consensus occurring amongst heads of department.

Consensus Management strategies have thus been used for healthcare organizations in many countries. In Australia and New Zealand, a consensus statement issued by the AFOEM advocates continuous improvement in public policy around work and health, in line with the principles articulated in this statement. Canadian primary healthcare experts also defined the attributes that should be evaluated in a proposed model of primary healthcare through a consensus approach. In Ireland, viewing the role of department head as pivotal to healthcare management was found to be critical to consensus in effective healthcare planning and delivery, and in American hospitals, consensus building was found to be an important factor in the strategic decision-making process undertaken by strategic decision-making teams. The next section explores organizational culture and questions if culture is a precondition for a strategic consensus to occur.

ORGANIZATIONAL CULTURE

The culture of the organization is a critical driver of norms and the "way we do things around here" (Deal & Kennedy, 1988). It plays a powerful and pervasive role in shaping the life of the organization (Saffold, 1988). Shared cultural values have been associated with commitment, self-confidence and ethical behavior (Carney, 2006c; Schein, 1992). Culture is constantly being reinforced through employees behaving in a similar manner to their colleagues (Wickens, 1995), while conversely, divergent cultures work alongside each other (Fasting, 2004; Thorne, 2000). A unified culture is therefore a precondition for a strategic consensus to occur (Carney, 2003). As Bally (2007) reports in relation to strategic nursing leadership, an organizational culture that fosters mentoring is required in a rapidly changing healthcare environment in order to ensure that overall organizational stability and performance is maintained. Daymon (2000) explored cultural influences in media organizations and found that culture forms through a continuous sequence of interactions between relevant parties, indicating that consensus is difficult to achieve where there are multiple perspectives, as is the case to some extent in nearly all organizations, but especially in healthcare organizations, with their multiple professions. Carney (2003) found that where the views and knowledge of these particular groups are not accepted, acknowledged or appreciated by senior managers, consensus about organizational strategy does not occur. Carney also found that strategic consensus is present when high levels of strategic involvement are combined with high commitment to the organization's strategy and where a strong organizational culture exists. A strong organizational culture promotes involvement, collaboration and participation amongst managers in organizational strategy.

Organizational culture is thus a precondition for a strategic consensus to occur. Shared cultural norms shape the life of the organization and are associated with commitment, self-confidence and ethical behavior. In the next section, the effects of cultural influences on *Consensus* are explored.

CULTURAL INFLUENCES ON CONSENSUS

Certain influences work together to form an organization's culture. The cultural influences found to be key determinants of strategic consensus, affecting healthcare delivery, are ethical values, excellence in care delivery, cost effectiveness, organizational choices, involvement in strategy development, professionalism, commitment to managing care in an efficient and effective manner and thinking strategically when planning care (Carney, 2003, 2006c; Morris et al., 2007). Values determine the individual's action system. Emphasis is placed on the ethical dimensions of multi-professional healthcare delivery that encompass such concepts as accountability, responsibility, trust and professional standards of care. These dimensions are presented in a code of ethical conduct for each nurse and midwife (Nursing and Midwifery Board of Ireland, 2014). Hewison (1999), in his study of NHS values, writes that "the values of an organization are key factors which influence the way it is managed" (p. 253), but acknowledges that there is not a single moral model or set of guidelines to assist in healthcare management. Watley and May (2004), in their study of 314 professional managers, found that it was individual managers and not the organization that determined the organization's ethical direction, and that healthcare organizations require a moral or ethical code of practice. Fasting (2004) argues that organizations should build on the moral fabric of the health professions and stimulate the ethical values that reside within them. Rights are important factors in providing professional guidance for moral conduct. Values underpin professional practice rights (NMBI, 2014; Valvira, 2014).

Brooten et al. (2012) acknowledge that international considerations need to be considered when measuring and costing the effectiveness of advanced practice nurses. A report from the Institute of Medicine (2011) in the USA, explored the role of nurses in leading change and advancing health amongst diverse populations in the most efficient manner possible. It is likely that some clinicians misunderstand the ethical tension between cost efficiencies and quality of care. A study undertaken in Finland amongst managers in university hospitals found that concepts for efficiency and cost effectiveness had been adopted, but also that first-line nurse managers were captive to their own professional culture in this regard also (Viitanen et al., 2007). Carney (2004), in a study of the management roles of 50 directors of nursing in the Republic of Ireland, found that the conflict existing between value for money and excellence in care delivery was a barrier to clinical effectiveness and as such, value for money needs to be viewed as an ethical means of delivering healthcare, and not as a conflict between quality and cost. Findings from this study indicate that excellence is perceived as resulting in patient safety, high standards and commitment to quality-focused care, findings that contrast with two studies undertaken in 2002 by Cooper, Frank, Hansen and Gouty on 2000 members of the American Nurses Association and the American Organization of Nurse Executives. These authors identified "quality of service", or "failure to provide service of the highest quality owing to economic constraints determined by the organization", and "failure to provide service of the highest quality consistent with the standards of the nursing profession" as the two most important ethical issues encountered during the course of their work (Cooper et al., 2004, p. 149). They argue that healthcare organizations have become more accountable to the expectations of stakeholders such as Trust Managers in Britain and the Health Service Executive in Ireland. Carney (2006c) argues that this perception of accountability raises ethical issues for health professionals, resulting in the collision of "clinical ethics and organizational ethics" (p. 121). Hemingway and Maclagan (2004) argue that there are difficulties in establishing if the values held by managers are personal or organizational, and they question whether both merge in time through rational choice or in order to achieve compromise or consensus.

It can thus be concluded that cultural influences affecting healthcare delivery include ethical values, excellence in care delivery and commitment to managing care in an efficient and effective manner. Care delivered through multidisciplinary team is an important organizational, cultural influence on *Consensus Management*. It can also be recognized that it is the individual managers and not the organization that determine the organization's ethical direction. In the next section, involvement as a concept in the strategic process is discussed.

INVOLVEMENT AS A CONCEPT IN THE STRATEGIC PROCESS

A further influence on how culture evolves within the health service is involvement in the planning of care delivery. Strategic involvement involves the dimensions of strategic integration, strategic thinking, planning and agreement. Strategic planning is an ongoing decision-making process designed to specify the ideals, goals and objectives needed by the organization in the future (Floyd & Wooldridge, 1996). Senior managers need to invest time and effort in ensuring that strategic thinking amongst middle managers and department heads is developed and that the organization's strategy is known, understood and accepted by them, thus ensuring that strategic planning and consensus occurs at all levels (Ferlie & Pettigrew, 1996). This process requires involvement in, and commitment to, implementing the goals of the organization. A study by Floyd and Wooldridge (1992b) of 259 managers in 25 mainly for-profit organizations found that middle managers were involved in strategy development. Carney (2003) found that strategy development involved strategic thinking by the heads of departments. Multi-level professional collaboration in health services delivery places emphasis on strategic involvement and consensus on strategy (Ashmos et al., 1998; Carney, 2006a; Harrison et al., 1994).

When exploring management concepts, Powell Davies et al. (2008) systematically reviewed the evidence from Australia, Netherlands, New Zealand, the USA and the UK on the impact of a range of strategies designed to coordinate primary healthcare around the needs of the patient and with other parts of the healthcare system. These authors identified management strategies that were mainly focused on chronic disease, including case management, multidisciplinary teamwork, joint consultations, shared patient assessments, improving communication, better information systems to support coordination, such as care planning, and support for service users, such as patient reminders. These studies showed improved health outcomes and improved patient experience and satisfaction. They also identified that better quality is generally associated with lower total costs of care and associated patient education, often combined with structured clinical follow-up and case management, multidisciplinary care teams, multidisciplinary clinical pathways, including care protocols, and feedback, reminders and education for professionals. These care coordination activities are enhanced and promoted by staff involvement in strategy development and in *Consensus Management*.

Carney (2004) asked, in her study with directors of nursing, if non-involvement in the strategic process is deliberate. She found that these healthcare managers recognized the need to avoid making excuses for non-involvement in the strategic process. They talked about the need to cease the learned helplessness that some professional clinicians adopt as an excuse for non-involvement in strategy development. They recognized that access to strategic meetings was the most important facilitating factor in seeking strategic involvement, as it was often perceived that they were being deliberately excluded, but acknowledged that this may be due to always being busy and seeing their professional role as being the most important role and not making the effort to attend strategic meetings.

A further dimension is added to the strategy dilemma. In her review of 1063 scholarly international nursing and management titles published between 1997 and 2007, which aimed to determine the profile of "strategy" in the titles, Carney (2007) found that fewer than 10% contained the word "strategy". A further review of the abstracts of 250 of those articles and the full text of 100 identified that what was presented as "strategy" was in the majority of cases either policy, administration or management with little strategy theory presented, leading her to conclude that the health services and the nursing profession do not appear to have adopted the terms "strategy" or "strategic management" to any great extent. As a result, the management roles of nurse managers, particularly decision-making and critical analysis, which are strategic in nature, are undervalued by health-care managers and by nurses themselves. She argues that if managers are given more organizational support and provided with enhanced education in the areas of strategy development and strategic management, they could play a much greater role in enhancing healthcare delivery. This is not a new phenomenon. Terminology with the word "strategy" has been used, albeit infrequently, in nursing journals. A study undertaken in Queensland, Australia refers to "strategic planning" in the context of retention of nurses. Eley et al. (2007) use the word "strategy" in the context of developing a career ladder in the professional development of nursing, and Tørstad and Bjørk (2007) state that most nurse managers do not think strategically in promoting clinical ladders at the organizational level, mainly because they have not been involved in the development of strategic consensus in their organizations.

It can thus be concluded that involvement as a concept in the process of strategy formation includes dimensions of strategic integration, strategic thinking, planning and agreement. Multi-level professional collaboration in health services delivery places emphasis on strategic involvement and consensus on strategy, but some managers avoid involvement in strategy development. The benefits demonstrated from involvement in management strategy development include improved health outcomes, patient experience and satisfaction: Outcomes negated by non-involvement. In the next section, commitment influences on strategic involvement are discussed.

COMMITMENT INFLUENCES ON STRATEGIC INVOLVEMENT

Commitment to the organization influences, and is influenced by, strategic involvement (Carney, 2003). If professionals are initially involved in the development of a strategy, they will direct their efforts and exercise a higher level of commitment to the strategy (Carney, 2004; Floyd & Wooldridge, 1992a,b). This commitment allied with a strong organizational culture leads to an understanding and acceptance of that strategy, and to more effective and efficient delivery of services to consumers (Carney, 2003; Dutton et al., 1997). Carney (2003) found a positive relationship between a culture of excellence and a high level of commitment to the strategic aims of the organization, leading to managers being willing to take greater responsibility for ensuring that a strategic consensus is fostered and maintained. Carney (2006c) identified professionalism and the recognition of expertise as two determinants of culture, but also that there is a requirement to identify expertise and to appreciate that expertise is a critical asset in seeking strategic involvement from senior and middle managers. Commitment to the role and to the organization is a determinant of professionalism (Bally, 2007). Cooper et al. (2004) concur in identifying the key ethical dimensions encountered in healthcare organizations. However, professionals frequently express the view that clinician expertise and professional approach to service delivery are not appreciated, understood or accepted by senior managers or by non-clinicians, causing distress amongst clinicians and often leading to a sense of disempowerment. A contrary view is that in general, respect for professionals' ideas and well-being are accepted by top managers, but professional expertise is not always appreciated, valued or even recognized, leading to clinicians not seeking involvement in strategic decision-making (Carney, 2004). Corbally et al. (2007) agrees when discussing health professionals' understanding of and experiences of *Empowerment* in healthcare delivery, as Kuokkanen et al. (2007) do when discussing work-related empowerment.

British, American and Australian authors have discussed the importance of professional networks, preferably of a multidisciplinary nature, in assisting in disseminating information regarding strategic thinking, professional expertise and regulation of nursing within various healthcare organizations and that serve to validate the professionalism and expertise of healthcare professionals amongst their peers (Ferlie & Pettigrew, 1996; Kolbe et al., 2011; Thomas, 2008). Wade-Benzoni et al. (2002) acknowledge that there are frequently barriers to resolution in ideologically based negotiations, such as those discussed here, that question the role of values and institutions in the resolution process. Watley and May (2004) discuss moral intensity and the roles of personal and consequential information in ethical decision-making, leading to inherent difficulties in resolving ethical and moral dilemmas in healthcare management.

Hence, managerial commitment to the strategic involvement of clinical professionals in the management of healthcare organizations means that benefits accrue to patients as a consequence. If professionals are initially involved in the development of a strategy, they will direct their efforts and exercise a higher level of commitment to it. Commitment allied to a strong organizational culture that is based on professional values leads to understanding of and acceptance of a strategy and to more effective and efficient delivery of services to consumers (see Table 7.1: Summary of the Consensus Model).

CONCLUSION

Individual, group, team and organizational research suggests that various factors contribute to *Consensus Management* in healthcare organizations, and to consensus about organizational strategy. These factors, which are found to be significant through an extensive literature search, are strategic involvement, commitment to the strategy adopted and the prevailing culture in the healthcare organization. The cultural dimensions found to be key determinants of strategic consensus are ethical values, excellence in care

Table 7.1   Consensus Management Model: Concepts and Dimensions

Concepts	Dimensions
COMMITMENT TO ORGANIZATION	Multidisciplinary approach to include dimensions of managerial, behavioral, professional and organizational
ORGANIZATIONAL CULTURE	Cultural sensitivity
	Continuous sequence of actions Managing tensions (costs vs. quality)
	Values
	Ethical behaviors and dimensions
	Excellence in care delivery
	Professionalism
	Leadership
STRATEGIC INVOLVEMENT	Transparent communication
	Multidisciplinary collaboration in strategic involvement
	Participative decision-making
CONSENSUS MANAGEMENT	Innovative relationships
	Coalition influences multidisciplinary teams
	Positive relationship between consensus and organizational objectives
	Agreement on strategy formulation

delivery, professionalism, a perception of being involved and strategic thinking (Carney, 2006b). The *Consensus Management Model of Healthcare* (see Figure 7.1) incorporates the concepts of strategic involvement, organizational commitment and a strong organizational culture. This model, if adopted, would enhance consensus and understanding of the concept of *Consensus* across healthcare organizations.

To be effective, the *Consensus Management Model of Healthcare* requires the presence of other cultural dimensions, such as a positive value system and commitment to deliver excellence in managing and delivering care. Care delivered through a multidisciplinary team approach was found to be the most important organizational cultural influence on *Consensus Management*. An integrated, multidisciplinary approach underscores a strong organizational culture, thus ensuring the maintenance of ethical cultural norms such as caring, professionalism and quality focus. Networking, professional groupings and multi- and interdisciplinary discussions on innovative approaches to healthcare delivery may prove to be effective learning pathways. Those cultural influences require strategic thinking, strategic planning and strategic involvement for optimum effectiveness. The cultural change that results from increased levels of commitment by professionals to their role and to their organization leads to greater levels of strategic consensus. An understanding of cultural influences will enhance greater consensus on

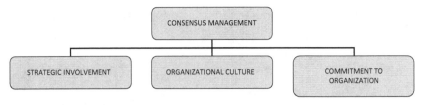

Figure 7.1   Consensus Management Model for Healthcare

strategy amongst health professionals. The *Consensus Management Model of Healthcare* is equally pertinent to the broader constituency, who need to possess a familiarity with management theories and techniques and an understanding of health service cultures.

REFERENCES

Ashmos, D.P., Duchon, D., & McDaniel, R.R., Jr. (1998). Participation in strategic decision-making: The role of organizational predisposition and issue interpretation. *Decision Sciences*, **29** (1), 25–51.

Bally, J.M.G. (2007). The role of nursing leadership in creating a mentoring culture in acute care environments. *Nursing Economics*, **25** (3), 143–157.

Black, D.C. (2008). *Working for a healthier tomorrow: Dame Carol Black's review of the health of Britain's working age population.* Norwich, England: Stationery Office. Retrieved from https://www.gov.uk/government/uploads/system/uploads/attachment_data/file/209782/hwwb-working-for-a-healthier-tomorrow.pdf (accessed 31 May 2015).

Black, J.S., & Gregersen, H.B. (1997). Participative decision-making: An integration of multiple dimensions. *Human Relations*, **50** (7), 859–878.

Bourgeois, L.J., III. (1980). Performance and consensus. *Strategic Management Journal*, **1** (3), 227–248.

Brooten, D., Youngblut, J.M., Deosires, W., Singhala, K., & Guido-Sanz, F. (2012). Global considerations in measuring effectiveness of advanced practice nurse. *International Journal of Nursing Studies*, **49** (7), 906–912.

Carmelli, A., Sheaffer, Z., & Halevi, M.Y. (2009). Does participatory decision-making in top management teams enhance decision effectiveness and firm performance? *Personnel Review*, **38** (6), 696–714.

Carney, M. (2003). *A strategic consensus model for not-for-profit organizations.* Unpublished PhD thesis, Smurfit Graduate School, University College Dublin, Ireland.

Carney, M. (2004). Middle manager involvement in strategy development in not-for-profit organizations: The director of nursing perspective—how organizational structure impacts on the role. *Journal of Nursing Management*, **12** (1), 13–21.

Carney, M. (2006a). Understanding organizational culture: The key to successful middle manager strategic involvement in health care delivery? *Journal of Nursing Management*, **14** (1), 23–33.

Carney, M. (2006b). Positive and negative outcomes from values and beliefs held by health care clinician and non-clinician managers. *Journal of Advanced Nursing*, **54** (1), 1–9.

Carney, M. (2006c). *Health Service Management: Culture, Consensus and the Middle Manager*. Cork, Ireland: Oak Tree Press.

Carney, M. (2007). How commitment and involvement influence the development of strategic consensus in healthcare organizations. *Journal of Nursing Management*, 15 (6), 649–658

Carney, M. (2014). *Principles needed to support advanced practice. Working group advanced nurse and midwife practice.* Nursing and Midwifery Board of Ireland. Retrieved from www.nursingandmidwiferyboard.ie (accessed 31 May 2014).

Cooper, R.W., Frank, G.L., Hansen, M.M., & Gouty, C.A. (2004). Key ethical issues encountered in healthcare organizations, *Journal of Nursing Administration, JONA*, 34 (3), 149.

Corbally, M.A., Scott, A.P., Matthews, A., Mac Gabhann, L., & Murphy, C. (2007). Irish nurses' and midwives understanding and experiences of empowerment. *Journal of Nursing Management*, 15 (2), 169–179.

Daymon, C. (2000). Culture formation in a new television station: A multi-perspective analysis. *British Journal of Management*, 11 (2), 121–135.

Deal, T.E., & Kennedy, A.A. (1988). *Corporate Cultures: The Rites and Rituals of Corporate Life*. Harmondsworth, England: Penguin.

Dess, G.G. (1987). Consensus on strategy formulation and organizational performance: Competitors in a fragmented industry. *Strategic Management Journal*, 8 (3), 259–277.

Dooley, R.S., & Fryxell, G.E. (1999). Attaining decision quality and commitment from dissent: The moderating effects of loyalty and competence in strategic decision-making teams. *Academy of Management Journal*, 42 (4), 389–402.

Dutton, J.E., Ashford, S.J., O'Neil, R., Hayes, E., & Wierba, E. (1997). Reading the wind: How middle managers assess the context for selling issues to top managers. *Strategic Management Journal*, 18 (5), 407–425.

Eley, R., Buikstra, E., Plank, A., Hegney, D., & Parker, V. (2007). Tenure, mobility and retention of nurses in Queensland, Australia: 2001 and 2004. *Journal of Nursing Management*, 15 (3), 285–293.

Fasting, U. (2004). Editorial comment. *Nursing Ethics*, 11 (1), 4.

Ferlie, E., & Pettigrew, A. (1996). Managing through networks: Some issues and implications for the NHS. *British Journal of Management*, 7 (S1), s81–s99.

Floyd, S.W., & Wooldridge, B. (1992a). Managing strategic consensus: The foundation of effective implementation. *Academy of Management Executive*, 6 (4), 27–39.

Floyd, S.W., & Wooldridge, B. (1992b). Middle management involvement in strategy and its association with strategic type: A research note. *Strategic Management Journal*, 13 (S1), 153–167.

Floyd, S.W., & Wooldridge, B. (1996). *The Strategic Middle Manager: How to Create and Sustain Competitive Advantage*. San Francisco, CA: Jossey-Bass.

Griffiths, R., Bett, M., Blyth, J., & Bailey, B. (Griffiths report) (1983). *National Health Service management inquiry*. Letter to the Secretary of State and recommendations for action. Department of Health and Social Security, London, England: DHSS.

Haggerty, H., Burge, F., Lévesque, J-F., Gass, D., Pineault, R., Beaulieu, M-D., & Santor, D. (2007). Operational definitions of attributes of primary health care: Consensus among Canadian experts. *Annals of Family Medicine*, 5 (4), 336–344.

Harrison, S. (1988). *Managing the National Health Service: Shifting the Frontier?* London: Chapman & Hall.

Harrison, S., & Pollitt, C. (1994). *Controlling Health Professionals: The Future of Work and Organization in the National Health Service*. Buckingham, England: Open University Press.

Hartnett T. (2011). *Consensus-Oriented Decision Making*. Gabriola Island, BC, Canada: New Society.

Hewison, A. (1999). The new public management and the new nursing: Related by rhetoric. *Journal of Advanced Nursing*, 29 (6), 1377–1384.

Hemingway, C.A., & Maclagan, P.W. (2004). Managers' personal values as drivers of corporate social responsibility. *Journal of Business Ethics*, 50 (1), 33–44.

Institute of Medicine (IOM). (2011). *The Future of Nursing Leading Change: Advancing Health*. Washington, DC: National Academic Press.

Kolbe J., Chase R., & Beaumont D. (2011). *Consensus Statement: Realising the Health Benefits of Work*. Australasian Faculty of Occupational & Environmental Medicine (AFOEM), Royal Australasian College of Physicians, Australia. Retrieved from http://www.racp.edu.au/page/afoem-health-benefits-of-work (accessed 8 June 2015).

Kuokkanen, L., Suominen, T., Rankinen, S., Kukkurainen, M.-L., Savikko, N., & Doran, D. (2007). Organizational change and work-related empowerment. *Journal of Nursing Management*, 15 (5), 500–507.

Morgan, P.I. (1994). Development of the National Health Service. In E.L. La Monica (Ed.), *Management in Health Care: A Theoretical and Experimental Approach*. Hampshire: MacMillan.

Morris, S., Delvin, N., & Parkin, D. (2007). *Economic Analysis in Health Care*. Chichester, England: John Wiley and Sons.

Powell Davies, G., Williams, A.M., Larsen, K., Perkins, D., Roland, M., & Harris, M.F. (2008). Coordinating primary health care: An analysis of the outcomes of a systematic review. *Medical Journal of Australia*, 188 (8), s65–s68.

Quinn, J.B. (1995). The strategy concept. In H. Mintzberg, J.B. Quinn, & S. Ghoshal (Ed.), *The Strategy Process* (European ed.), London: Prentice Hall, pp. 3–12.

Saffold, G.S., III. (1988). Culture traits, strengths and organizational performance: Moving beyond "strong" culture. *Academy of Management Review*, 13 (4), 546–558.

Schein, E.H. (1992). (Ed.) *Organizational Culture and Leadership* (2nd ed.). San Francisco, CA: Jossey-Bass.

Stagner, R. (1969). Corporate decision-making: An empirical study. *Journal of Applied Psychology*, 53 (1), 1–13.

Stanley, J.M. (2012). Impact of new regulatory standards on advanced practice registered nursing: The APRN consensus model and LACE. *Nursing Clinics of North America*, 47 (2), 241–250.

Strong, P., & Robinson J. (1990). *The NHS under New Management*. Milton Keynes, England: Open University Press.

Thomas, K. (2008). *Advanced practice nursing advisory committee report*. Washington, DC. Retrieved from https://www.bon.texas.gov/pdfs/board_meetings_pdfs/2008/April/6-3.pdf (accessed 8 June 2015).

Thorne, M.L. (2000). Cultural chameleons. *British Journal of Management*, 11 (4), 325–339.

Tjosvold, D., & Field, R.H.G. (1983). Effects of social context on consensus and majority vote decision-making. *Academy of Management Journal*, 26 (3), 500–506.

Valvira (2014). *National supervisory authority for welfare and health: Professional practice rights*. Retrieved from http://valvira.fi/en//professionalpracticerights/nurses (accessed 21 September 2014).

Viitanen, E., Wiili-Peltola, E., Tampsi-Jarvala, T., & Lehto, J. (2007). First-line nurse managers in university hospitals-captive to their own professional culture? *Journal of Nursing Management*, 15 (1), 114–122.

Wade-Benzoni, K.A., Hoffman, A.J., Thompson, L.L., Moore, D.A., Gillespie, J.J., & Bazerman, M.H. (2002). Barriers to resolution in ideologically based negotiations: The role of values and institutions. *Academy of Management Review*, 27 (1), 41–57.

Wickens, P.D. (1995). *The Ascendant Organization: Combining Commitment and Control for Long Term, Sustainable Business Success.* Basingstoke, England: McMillan Business.

Watley, L.D., & May, D.R. (2004). Enhancing moral intensity: The roles of personal and consequential information in ethical decision-making. *Journal of Business Ethics,* 50 (2), 105–126.

8 Corporate Social Responsibility for Healthcare Organizations

Sherif Tehemar

INTRODUCTION

Corporate Social Responsibility (CSR) is the term used to describe the way that a business takes into account the financial, environmental and social impacts of the decisions and actions it is involved in. It is an increasingly important issue in business, as managers, consumers, investors and employees have begun to understand how economic growth is linked to social and environmental well-being. While *CSR* is a mostly voluntary activity, there is increasing pressure on organizations to make a positive contribution to society, or to at least reduce their negative impact. Internationally, governments are also moving towards the enforcement of certain elements of *Corporate Social Responsibility*, particularly in regards to the protection of the environment. Responsible businesses may not necessarily be able to measure the positive impact their behavior has on their performance. However, irresponsible businesses are likely to notice the negative impact their decisions have on their bottom line. Business sustainability now and in the future depends on organizations taking into account the social and environmental consequences of their decisions and actions.

In the past, many businesses and managers were primarily concerned with increasing shareholder value. For a small business, this may be a single business owner. In a large corporation, this could include thousands of people who hold shares in the company and receive dividends. Traditionally, managers were focused on short- to medium-term profits and driving the share price up. However, there has been a developing trend that goes away from simply increasing the return for shareholders and instead focuses on increasing the value of the business in terms of the stakeholders. Stakeholders are the people who are affected by the actions and performance of the business, and include both internal and external parties. Business stakeholders include people such as consumers, shareholders, associates, employees and business owners. Businesses that are socially responsible aim to make decisions that are in the best interests of their various stakeholders (Ackerman, 1973; Carroll, 1979; Drucker, 1984).

Clearly, organizations that want to be socially responsible must face many challenges and overcome a number of barriers and criticisms. One needs to weigh all of the advantages and disadvantages that are associated with *Corporate Social Responsibility* and determine what is best for the sustainability of the business.

The following sections will highlight some of the fundamentals of the *CSR* concept, its evolution, its advantages and drawbacks and the different terminologies in relation to healthcare management. The implementation of the *CSR* strategy will be discussed, as well as its relation to the concept of *Total Quality Management (TQM)*.

CSR: THE FUNDAMENTALS

The publication of Howard R. Bowen's *Social Responsibilities of the Businessman* (1953) can be considered the first to highlight the concept of *CSR*. He defined *CSR* as the obligations of businessmen to pursue those policies, to make those decisions, or to follow those lines of action that are desirable in terms of the objectives and values of our society.

The Definition

A landmark contribution to the concept of *CSR* came from the Committee for Economic Development (CED) in its 1971 publication "Social Responsibilities of Business Corporations". The CED declared that a "business functions by public consent and its basic purpose are to serve constructively the needs of society—to the satisfaction of society" (Committee for Economic Development, 1971, p. 21). Another major contribution came from Carroll (1998), who suggested that corporations are expected to fulfill certain responsibilities, just as private citizens are. She categorized these responsibilities as four "pillars": economic, legal, ethical and philanthropic. In the late 1990s, one of the most comprehensive definitions of *CSR* appeared when the World Business Council for Sustainable Development (WBCSD) defined *CSR* as "the continuing commitment by business to behave ethically and contribute to economic development while improving the quality of life of the workforce and their families as well as of the local community and society at large" (WBCSD, 2000). In 2010, the International Standards Organization (ISO) introduced ISO 26000, which defines social responsibility as the responsibility of an organization for the impacts of its decisions and activities on society and the environment, through transparent and ethical behavior that:

1) Contributes to sustainable development, including health and the welfare of society;
2) Takes into account the expectations of stakeholders;

3) Is in compliance with applicable law and consistent with international norms of behavior; and

4) Is integrated throughout the organization and practiced in its relationships.

In general, the author believes that the broad concept of CSR and the best definition of it is that of Hopkins (2007, p. 9), who wrote, "CSR is the role that a company takes to integrate responsible business practices and policies into its business model to promote higher standards of living in society, for employees, and the environment while preserving profitability".

The Benefits

More companies have begun to realize the importance and the benefits of embracing CSR programs. The financial crisis, damage to nuclear power stations and the Thailand floods have shown the increasing importance of CSR. Several studies and surveys concluded that consumers are ready to buy from companies that have a CSR agenda. A 2002 study by Hill and Knowlton found that 79% of Americans take CSR practices into consideration when deciding on a product purchase (Hill & Knowlton, 2002). Moreover, research done by the Chartered Institute of Marketing shows that the number of customers who felt guilty about unethical purchases has increased from 17% to 35% (CIM, 2007). The same applies to employees, who are more motivated, productive and loyal to companies that adopt CSR programs.

There are at least six reasons for encouraging companies to adopt CSR practices: Innovation, cost reduction, brand differentiation, long-term thinking and customer and employee engagement (Epstein-Reeves, 2012). Other benefits include increased sales and revenue, expanded market share, better work environment, improved relationships with local authorities and improved crisis management.

However, for companies to benefit from CSR, they have to adopt a CSR strategy, link CSR programs to their core business and competencies and engage with their stakeholders.

The Downsides

One of the common criticisms of *Corporate Social Responsibility* is that there is a conflict between the purpose of business and the concept of social responsibility. It is argued by many businesspeople and economists that the true purpose of business is to make a profit for the benefit of shareholders. Doing anything outside of this purpose undermines this fundamental business principle.

Another criticism of *Corporate Social Responsibility* is that the actual benefit received by the community is negligible or nonexistent. Social responsibility should result in positive outcomes for both the business and the community. However, often, the results fall heavily in favor of the business involved. Businesses invest a comparatively small amount into the challenges of socially responsible business community projects and then use their efforts to promote their brand and gain access to markets all around the world. The public relations and brand building they receive far outweighs their investment in socially responsible projects.

One of the serious challenges that businesses face when becoming involved in *Corporate Social Responsibility* is growing consumer cynicism. Consumers now recognize that for many organizations, social responsibility is simply a public relations campaign in disguise. They are skeptical about the true motivation behind *Corporate Social Responsibility* and are not easily convinced that a business is acting in the best interests of the community and environment.

Even businesses that are genuine in their commitment to social responsibility face the challenge of winning over customers. Businesses need to be careful to not be seen boasting about their socially responsible endeavors. Basically, consumers view this as a marketing ploy and often disregard what is being said as the business simply trying to drum up good public relations. This is especially apparent when businesses have made profits from irresponsible behavior for many years and then expect praise from consumers when they suddenly start to make small changes to their practices.

The Strategy

One of the challenges that companies need to overcome when developing a *CSR* strategy is to consider all the factors relevant to their short- and long-term futures. The adoption of a sustainable approach requires a much longer time frame and perspective than the short- to medium-term planning horizon that most business leaders use. Successful *CSR* requires a store of important elements including clearly articulated business drivers and prioritizing the issues and the objectives to be achieved. In general, the following elements and objectives have to be included in any *CSR* strategy:

1) Minimize the environmental impact of the company's operations;
2) Ensure that employees are motivated and engaged in business operations and contribute effectively and efficiently to achieving the company's objectives;
3) Engage heavily in the community and invest in the well-being of society;
4) Improve the quality of the service or products delivered and provide measures to continuously develop, or at least maintain, customer satisfaction;
5) Develop a comprehensive communication plan that encourages interaction with different stakeholders;
6) Foster a culture of transparency and innovation;

7) Invest in the health and safety of the workplace;
8) Introduce and maintain responsible practices within its supply chain;
9) Provide tools to measure and control.

McElhaney (2009) proposed a five-step model for creating a *CSR* strategy:

1) Senior leadership and management of the company, including the board, must make an authentic, firm and public commitment to *CSR* and engage in it;
2) Determine the top three business objectives and priorities for the company and develop a *CSR* strategy that contributes to the achievement of those business objectives;
3) Align *CSR* strategy with the core competencies of the company;
4) Fully integrate *CSR* into the culture, governance and strategy development efforts of the company and into existing management and performance systems;
5) Develop clear performance metrics or key performance indicators to measure the impact of the *CSR* strategy.

One of the key elements of the *CSR* strategy and its communication framework is to understand the different concepts and how they can be implemented in a healthcare setting. The following section will shed light on these matters.

CSR CONCEPTS AND THEIR APPLICATIONS IN HEALTHCARE

The main concepts of CSR are normative: They specify the ethical requirements that the activities of a business would have to satisfy for that business to be regarded as showing *Corporate Social Responsibility*.

Sustainability

Sustainability (for more information about *Sustainability* and its relevance to healthcare organizations, see Huzzard et al., Chapter 20 in this volume) means that a company performs its operations in a manner that meets the needs of the present without compromising the ability of future generations to meet their own needs. Sustainable development involves devising a social and economic system that ensures that these goals are sustained, i.e., that real incomes rise, that educational standards increase, that the health of the nation improves and that the general quality of life is advanced. *Sustainability* refers to a comprehensive way of doing business that delivers economic value and opens up new opportunities in terms of its social, economic and environmental impacts. Companies can generate substantial business value through *Sustainability* while also improving quality of life and protecting the environment.

Healthcare improves quality of life through preventive and therapeutic approaches and by improving the community's well-being. This is inherently a sustainable business and with some improvements, can be made to be more holistic.

The Triple Bottom Line

The *Triple Bottom Line* (abbreviated as *TBL* or *3BL*, and also known as *People, Planet, Profit* (or, not to be confused with the four different pillars mentioned above, *The Three Pillars*) captures an expanded spectrum of values and criteria for measuring organizational (and societal) success: Economic, ecological and social. *Triple Bottom Line* accounting means expanding the traditional company-reporting framework to take into account not just financial outcomes, but also environmental and social performance. The *Triple Bottom Line* concept is based on the principle that for a company to truly prosper, it needs to worry about the three elements in its bottom line (People, Planet and Profit) instead of the conventional focus on profits only. The concept draws attention to the fact that company *Sustainability* is in fact dependent on elements beyond profitability. Some companies use *TBL* as the basis of their *CSR/Sustainability* strategy, such that their *CSR* objectives are concerned with the issues of *People, Planet and Profit*.

It is imperative that hospitals focus on the triple bottom line *rather than just the financial bottom line because of the nature of their services. Initiatives directed to employees, customers (patients) and the environment (waste management, renewable energy) will be an added value to the organization and will have a positive impact on its TBL.*

The Governance System

An organization's governance system is the framework of rules and practices by which board of directors ensures accountability, fairness and transparency in a company's relationship with its stakeholders (financiers, customers, management, employees, the government and the community). The presence of an effective *Governance System* within an individual company and across an economy as a whole helps to provide a degree of confidence that is necessary for the proper functioning of a market economy. *Corporate Governance* is the set of mechanisms that ensures that an organization's management is running the organization (whether private, public or "third sector") to the best of its ability and to the maximum benefit of the stakeholders. It is not only relevant for publicly traded companies, but also for public and non-profit organizations, and includes elements such as procedures for reporting, supervision and internal controls. The purpose of a strong *Corporate Governance* structure is to ensure that the rights of the stakeholders are safeguarded and also to ensure that all organizations are subject to the same standard of transparency and disclosure so as to assist stakeholders in decision-making.

Effective Corporate Governance *and leadership are crucial for the healthcare sector to identify its mission and vision and to provide a clear direction to achieve its goals. This process is clearly identified in every healthcare accreditation standards set and is a must when managing* CSR *initiatives. The presence of solid* Corporate Governance *system and a committed leadership are the most essential prerequisites for* CSR *to succeed.*

Cause Marketing

Cause Marketing, or *Cause-Related Marketing*, refers to a type of marketing involving the cooperative efforts of a "for-profit" business and a non-profit organization for mutual benefit. *Cause-Related Marketing* can be any type of marketing effort by a company that makes use of its association with a social or charitable cause. *Cause Marketing* differs from *CSR* in that the latter comprises a set of activities in line with the company strategy and meant to address issues specific to the company stakeholders, while *Cause Marketing* is only a marketing effort that makes use of a social cause to gain free publicity and also raise money for the cause.

A very popular and well-received example of a *Cause Marketing* effort is the Pepsi Refresh Project. The campaign invites people to post proposals for change in their communities and others to vote on their ideas. Funds are awarded to the most popular proposals. In 2010, 7,000 projects garnered 51 million votes; 287 ideas from 203 cities and 42 states won $11.7 million. The campaign resulted in huge media exposure for Pepsi at multiple forums and locations that would not have been possible with a stand-alone advertising campaign.

In a healthcare setting, management should be aware of the difference between CSR *and* Cause Marketing. CSR *should be embedded in the hospital's strategic plan, with a clear defined strategy with* SMART *(specific, measurable, achievable, realistic and time-bound) objectives and goals. On the other hand,* Cause Marketing, *if undertaken, should be carefully used with defined objectives and for a specific cause, so as not to crowd out the* CSR *initiatives from being seen by the public.*

Transparency

Transparency can be defined as the lack of hidden agendas and conditions, accompanied by the full availability of the information required for collaboration, cooperation, and collective decision-making. *"Transparency"* can also refer to the practice of being open about company issues and proceedings and providing full information about any negative or scandalous news related to the company as well as about regular business operations. *Transparency* does not mean that a company has to make all information public, but that enough information is made available to everyone so as to enable the open exchange of opinions and facilitate decision-making.

Mining and extractive industries are among the most notorious when it comes to the availability of information about their business operations. The Extractive Industries Transparency Initiative (EITI) is a non-profit, multi-stakeholder organization meant to help mining companies improve their image and contribute to the sustainable development of mining communities by being transparent and responsive to local needs. Some 20 countries across the world subscribe to EITI, ranging from Peru to Trinidad and Tobago, Azerbaijan and Nigeria.

> *For the healthcare sector,* Transparency *is a must have. With the increase in medical errors and with reports of healthcare provider organizations trying to hide these instances, more and more people are losing trust in hospitals. By being more open about their operations and owning up to mistakes, hospitals can build trust among the community. On the other hand, it is important to differentiate between transparency and the confidentiality of patient data. Consequently, although transparency is important in terms of sharing problems and outcomes, it is also ethically important not to breach the confidentiality of patient data (which is considered the basis of trust in the clinical-patient relationship).*

Carbon Footprint

The carbon footprint is the total amount of greenhouse gases produced to directly and indirectly support human activities, usually expressed in equivalent tons of carbon dioxide (CO^2). The *Carbon Footprint* is the sum of all emissions of CO^2 (carbon dioxide) that were produced by a company's activities in a given time frame. When companies use oil, gas, electricity or coal in their factories or offices, they generate CO^2. The fuel used by delivery trucks, pool cars or any form of transportation also has a carbon emission element. Other greenhouse gases that might be emitted as a result of company activities include methane and ozone. These greenhouse gases are normally also taken into account for the *Carbon Footprint*. The purpose of calculating a company's *Carbon Footprint* is two-fold: To monitor and control the footprint, and to minimize the footprint by planting trees and other "carbon offset activities".

Google, for example, has released its *Carbon Footprint* numbers. Google's 2010 electricity consumption was 2,259,998 MWh, which results in 1,457,982 metric tons of carbon dioxide. This is enough electricity to power about 41 Empire State Buildings, and is more than the carbon footprint of the country of Togo.

> *Electrical generators using fuel, Freon and incinerators are usually considered the source of Green House Gas (GHG) emissions in a hospital setting. Efforts to reduce GHG emissions should be considered and highlighted as environmental initiatives while being monitored on a yearly basis.*

Environment, Health and Safety

Environment, Health and Safety (EHS) refers primarily to programs that promote employees' health and protect their safety; environmental protection programs were traditionally included in the same management category. The inclusion of elements such as employee safety and well-being, environmental conditions and occupational health concerns in the overall management of a company is referred to as *EHS*. Effective management of *EHS* issues entails the inclusion of *EHS* considerations in corporate- and facility-level business processes in an organized manner. The International Finance Cooperation's "Environmental, Health, and Safety Guidelines" (International Finance Corporation, 2007) are technical reference documents that provide examples of international best practices in *EHS*. The guidelines can be used as a general resource as well as an industry-specific resource. In many countries, some *EHS* requirements, and often others too, are legally enforced, but *CSR* is likely to require an organization to do more than the legally required bare minimum in its *EHS* activities.

> *Every hospital should have a holistic* EHS *program in place. Issues like the health and safety of the workforce waste management and environmental conservation should all be a part of* EHS, *and hospitals may also consider getting certifications for their* EHS, *such as* ISO14001, *and the Occupational Health and Safety Management System* (OHSAS-18001).

Corruption

There are several definitions in the literature for "corruption". However, the one that is the most widely accepted is, "Corruption is the abuse of power by an official for private gain". Economic corruption (i.e., company managers offering or taking bribes or kickbacks) is an important form of corruption.

However, it is not the only form of corruption. There are non-economic forms of corruption, including many types of police corruption, judicial corruption, political corruption, academic corruption and so on. Indeed, there are at least as many forms of corruption as there are human institutions that might become corrupted. Further, economic gain is not the only motivation for corruption. Different kinds of attractions motivate it. These include status, power, addiction to drugs or gambling, and sexual gratification as well as economic gain.

> *Every organization, including those in healthcare, should closely address issues of corruption. Corruption in a healthcare organization might have an effect on patients' lives (e.g., using medical supplies of lesser quality); thus, this issue is more important than in other sectors and should be closely monitored. This can be managed through an anti-corruption policy, a strategic framework for controlling corruption, prevention programs and education. A particular form of corruption in some health systems is for health workers to expect "gifts" or supplementary personal ("under-the-table") payments for care that is already paid for by the state or the patient's health insurer.*

Risk Management

Risk Management is the identification, assessment and prioritization of risks followed by the coordinated and economical application of resources to minimize, monitor and control the probability and/or impact of unfortunate events or to maximize the realization of opportunities. The strategies to manage risk typically include transferring the risk to another party (although this is ethically questionable), avoiding the risk, reducing the negative effect or probability of the risk or even accepting some or all of the potential or actual consequences of a particular risk. Certain aspects of many of the *Risk Management* standards have come under criticism for having no measurable improvement on risk, even though the confidence in estimates and decisions seems to increase.

> *It is the responsibility of the governance bodies in a hospital to identify and prioritize the risks through a risk matrix and to formulate policies and procedures for managing the risks accordingly.*

Waste Management

Waste Management is the collection, transport, processing or disposal, managing and monitoring of waste materials. The term usually relates to materials produced by human activity, and the process is generally undertaken to reduce their effect on health, the environment or aesthetics. *Waste Management* is a distinct practice from resource recovery, which focuses on delaying the rate of consumption of natural resources. The management of wastes treats all materials as a single class, whether solid, liquid, gaseous or radioactive substances, and tries to reduce the harmful environmental impacts of each through different methods. The management of waste is a key component in a business's ability to maintain its *ISO14001* accreditation. Companies are encouraged to improve their environmental efficiencies each year by eliminating waste and by shifting away from *Waste Management* to *Sustainability*-related resource recovery practices like recycling. Materials such as glass, food scraps, paper and cardboard, plastic bottles and metal can be recycled.

In hospitals, waste is categorized into three types: General, infected and pathological waste. The existence of an efficient and effective Waste Management *system is crucial in any hospital, not only from a* CSR *perspective, but also for the health of the community. Hospitals should comply with national and international laws and regulations for waste disposal.*

Supply Chain Management

Supply Chain Management (SCM) is the management of a network of interconnected businesses involved in the provision of product and service packages required by the end customers in a supply chain. *Supply Chain Management* spans all movement and storage of raw materials, work-in-process inventory and finished goods from point of origin to point of consumption. The term "supply chain management" entered the public domain when Keith Oliver, a consultant at Booz Allen Hamilton, used it in an interview with the *Financial Times* in 1982. The term was slow to take hold, and the lexicon was slow to change. It gained currency in the mid-1990s, when a flurry of articles and books came out on the subject. In the late 1990s, it rose to prominence as a management buzzword, and operations managers began to use it in their titles with increasing regularity.

As the supply chain costs as much as 40 percent of the typical hospital's budget, it is imperative that hospitals should effectively and efficiently manage their supply chains. A hospital practicing CSR *has to take steps to ensure that its vision of* CSR *is shared by its suppliers, and to encourage them to also engage in responsible actions.*

Stakeholder Engagement

Stakeholder Engagement is a means of describing a broad, inclusive, and continuous relationship between a company and those potentially impacted by the organization's full range of activities and approaches over the entire life of a project. It means involving the stakeholders in the decisions impacting them, i.e., the people who may be affected by the decisions it makes or who can influence the implementation of its decisions. It is two-way communication that is meant to give stakeholders the chance to influence decision-making. This differentiates it from regular forms of communication, which seek to issue a message or influence groups to agree with a decision that is already made. Like any other business function, *Stakeholder Engagement* needs to be managed. It should be driven by a well-defined strategy and have a clear set of objectives, timetable, budget and allocation of responsibilities. All staff should be made aware of the program, and understand why it's being undertaken and what implications it might have for project outcomes.

THE BENEFITS OF CSR FOR HEALTHCARE

There are many reasons why it pays for companies, both big business and small and medium enterprises, to be socially responsible and be conscious about the interests of all of their key stakeholders. Healthcare has a variety of challenges that the average person may not fully understand; issues such as stringent regulatory compliance, intense labor shortages in nursing, increased and costly technological advances, implementation of international quality standards and substantial community dependence make healthcare one of the most operationally difficult sectors. Hospitals have to work harder than other organizations to win and retain trust while coping with operational challenges. *CSR* could play a major role in this context by highlighting the performance of a hospital in a transparent and sincere way and result in better understanding from the community about the above-mentioned challenges that this sector faces. Moreover, *CSR* will help the healthcare sector to engage with social issues that could serve to improve its image and enhance stakeholder engagement by making its performance indicators available to the public.

Getting a License to Operate From Key Stakeholders, Not Just Shareholders

The private sector is gaining a much bigger role and more responsibility for economic development globally. This responsibility is not limited to economic issues, but must also include a social and environmental contribution. Hospitals that fail to recognize this responsibility are at risk of being denied the social acceptance that comes from the community. Without this acceptance, hospitals can never function in a profitable and sustainable manner.

Reputation Management

Reputational risk is considered one of the most crucial threats facing an organization and is even more critical for a hospital. This includes risks not only of the loss of patients, but goes beyond to hospital itself, and may even impact healthcare as a whole. After a reputational crisis involving a hospital, the consequences could be huge in terms of lost trust, legal costs and patient loyalty. A damaged reputation might require years to rebuild and cost a large sum of money. A hospital that has a sound *CSR* mechanism and a history of exceptional service to society and the environment often does not suffer as much as a hospital with no *CSR* plans, should a reputation crisis occur.

More Efficient Use of Resources

Utilization of a holistic *CSR* framework in hospitals can result in greater efficiency in operations. For instance, improved efficiency in the use of energy and natural resources can result in substantial cost savings. A better waste management system will not only reduce the amount of waste, but will also ensure its safe disposal.

Enhanced Patient Loyalty

Patients need to be able to trust a hospital in order to recommend it to someone. Trust is probably the most valuable currency in healthcare, and it doesn't come easy. In order for hospitals to earn patient trust and loyalty, they need to go beyond healthcare services and create an emotional bond with the patient through ethical business practices. Patient loyalty goes a long way in contributing towards sustainable business growth for a hospital.

Increased Ability to Attract and Retain Quality Employees

There is clear evidence (Bauman & Skitka, 2012) linking employee morale and loyalty to the social performance of a company. This is especially vital in the case of a hospital. If a hospital employee continually witnesses violations of ethical norms in the hospital, he or she would not want to be involved with that hospital.

Responsible Competeiveness

When competitors adopt less costly but not socially responsible and ethically sound healthcare solutions, a hospital should take advantage of this challenge and explore new innovative and green solutions. This raises the barriers to entry and will make *CSR* the industry norm.

Attracting Investors and Business Partners

Investors no longer only rely on financial data, but also look at how a healthcare organization deals with relevant social and environmental issues. If the management is not prudent enough to pay any attention to these issues, with time, it will lose credibility. For a healthcare service provider to attract investors who can fund their expansion, they need to focus on social, environmental and economic performance in addition to financial performance.

Governmental Support

A *CSR* program developed in accordance with the overall government direction can help the company win favor from the government. Many governments give financial incentives for sound *CSR* initiatives, including environmentally friendly innovations. Hospitals that demonstrate that they are engaging in practices that go beyond regulatory compliance are being given massive support from governments in the forms of waivers and less scrutiny.

Improved Bottom Line

All of the above factors inevitably translate into better financial performance over the years.

THE DRAWBACKS OF CSR FOR HEALTHCARE

If an organization has a responsibility to its shareholders to make as much profit as possible, how can it justify spending some of those profits on socially responsible projects or making decisions that will negatively affect the bottom line? This argument against social responsibility remains valid until patients and shareholders begin to expect a hospital's management to act in a responsible way. In healthcare, this issue might become worse, as part of the annual budget of a hospital practicing *CSR* might be directed to initiatives that have no direct impact on the health of the patient.

Another significant challenge that results from socially responsible behavior is that it can negatively affect business profit margins. How can a hospital's management justify spending on activities that provide no measurable returns? Of course, the solution is to find socially responsible projects that do offer some tangible benefits. However, many consider this to corrupt the motivation behind responsible business practices. It is debatable as to how much profit a hospital's management should sacrifice in its pursuit of social responsibility.

Corporate Social Responsibility also comes under criticism because it is disposable or reversible. Many healthcare organizations get involved in sustainable projects when economic conditions are excellent and they have plenty of disposable resources. However, as soon as conditions worsen, their community projects are the first thing to go. This can be detrimental to groups who were reliant on the assistance they were receiving from the organization.

CORPORATE SOCIAL RESPONSIBILITY VERSUS TOTAL QUALITY MANAGEMENT

Ghobadian and Gallear in 1996 defined *Total Quality Management* (for more information about *TQM* and its relevance to healthcare organizations, see Mosadeghrad and Ferlie, Chapter 22 in this volume) as a structured attempt to refocus the organization's behavior, planning and working practices towards a culture that is employee driven, problem solving and stakeholder oriented. Furthermore, the organization's business practices are based on seeking continuous improvement, the devolution of decision-making, the removal of functional barriers, the eradication of sources of error, *Teamwork* (for more information about *Teamwork* and its relevance to healthcare organizations, see Schmutz et al., Chapter 21 in this volume), honesty and fact-based decision-making. *TQM* is one of the most durable management innovations of the past three decades, and it has been implemented worldwide in service, manufacturing, private, public, large and small organizations. *Corporate Social Responsibility*, on the other hand, is a more recent phenomenon, and dates back to the 1980s. However, *CSR*, like *TQM*, impinges on all facets of organizations.

In the field of *TQM* and *CSR*, concerns were raised about the degree of overlap between these two powerful and all-embracing concepts. Clearly, if the two concepts have a great deal in common, then *TQM*, with its greater penetration in organizations of all shapes and size, can act as a key catalyst for developing *CSR* within the organization. *TQM* successfully strikes a balance between the goals of an organization and doing the right thing in terms of respecting the interest of wider stakeholders. Similarly, *CSR* accepts the legitimacy of profits as a goal, but it considers value-based behavior—for example, valuing people and the environment—as the root of a sustainable performance. Hence, *TQM* can play an important part in facilitating a deeper penetration of *CSR* in a broad range of organizations (Ghobadian et al., 2007). *TQM* officers in the organization have the responsibility of ensuring that the ethical basis of quality is not overlooked and that quality management takes a leadership role in promoting ethical practices. Therefore, *CSR* will not simply happen because an organization has *TQM*. To make it happen, it is necessary to have a *CSR* team/department capable of addressing the issue explicitly. Moreover, the *CSR* team will adjust the elements of *TQM* so that they consciously address facets of *CSR*.

Both *TQM* and *CSR* are accepted management concepts that are based on ethical, economic and legal principles. Shared values or a common culture between different stakeholders are required for the success of both approaches. Due to a growing social awareness on the part of healthcare organizations, they develop new values, strategies and policies to support their functioning in areas (people and planet) that were once left to others. More and more healthcare organizations accept this new position in society and strive to be proficient and transparent in these issues. In this way, *CSR* is about redefining the role of healthcare organizations in society. This development has led to a wide range of approaches that all address social responsibilities and also to a growing interest in indicators for managing social performances.

CONCLUSIONS

In this chapter, we have adopted the definition of *CSR* as being the continuing commitment by a business to behave ethically and contribute to economic development while improving the quality of life of the workforce and their families as well as of the local community and society at large. We think that this definition by the WBCSD is the most comprehensive definition and is practical for healthcare organizations.

The healthcare sector can be considered a social investment. If seen and realized as such, there will be no problems with implementing *CSR* initiatives, and they will be highly accepted by shareholders and stakeholders alike. Previously we argued that *Total Quality Management* (which is a core of healthcare management) can be considered as a catalyst for proper *CSR* implementation. Additionally, a proper and effective *CSR* initiative that takes into consideration the four pillars of *CSR* (patient, employee, environment and community) will definitely focus on improving *TQM* and health promotion for the patient as core activities for both business and *CSR* purposes. That is how *CSR* will positively affect the triple bottom line of the hospital.

A common misconception about socially responsible investment is that it almost always results in lower returns and higher costs. Generally, this isn't the case: Many sustainable investments return comparatively similar results to regular investment portfolios. If healthcare organizations take into consideration the triple bottom line (economic, social and environmental), then it could be argued that socially responsible investments actually perform better in many cases. This can be considered a drawback, as not every social investment behaves as such. Consequently, healthcare organizations should focus on promoting the full concept of the triple bottom line and not just part of it.

Healthcare organizations should consider developing a set of policies or guidelines that outline the expectations of the business in regards to social responsibility. They should define their standpoint on issues such as ethics and moral standards so that their teams are able to gain a clear understanding of how they are expected to behave when working for the organization. The challenge remains on how to choose the right initiative and most importantly, how to communicate it to the public (Tehemar, 2014).

REFERENCES

Ackerman, R.W. (1973). How companies respond to social demands. *Harvard Business Review*, **51** (4), 88–98.

Bauman, C., & Skitka, L. (2012). Corporate social responsibility as a source of employee satisfaction. *Research in Organizational Behavior*, **32**, 63–86.

Bowen, H.R. (1953). *Social Responsibilities of the Businessman*. New York: Harper & Brothers.

Carroll, A.B. (1979). A three-dimensional conceptual model of corporate social performance. *Academy of Management Review*, **4** (4), 497–505.

Carroll, A.B. (1998). The four faces of corporate citizenship. *Business and Society Review*, **100–101** (1), 1–7.

CIM. (2007). *Shape the agenda: The good, bad and indifferent—Marketing and the triple bottom line*. Retrieved from http://www.researchforresults.co.uk/downloads/Triple_Bottom_Line_Booklet_web.pdf (accessed 20 April 2013).

Committee for Economic Development. (1971). *Social responsibilities of business corporations*. New York: Committee for Economic Development (CED).

Drucker, P.F. (1984). The new meaning of corporate social responsibility. *California Management Review*, **26** (2), 53–63.

Epstein-Reeves, J. (2012). Six reasons companies should embrace CSR. *Forbes*, February 21. Retrieved from http://www.forbes.com/sites/csr/2012/02/21/six-reasons-companies-should-embrace-csr/ (accessed 26 December 2013).

Ghobadian, A., & Gallear, D. (1996). Total quality management in SMEs. *Omega*, **24** (1), 83–106.

Ghobadian A., Gallear D., & Hopkins, M. (2007). TQM and CSR nexus. *International Journal of Quality and Reliability Management*, **24** (2), 704–721.

Hill, B., & Knowlton, S. (2002). Scandals turn spotlight on company reputation. London, England: Corporate Reputation Watch.

Hopkins, M. (2007). *Corporate Social Responsibility and International Development: Is Business the Solution?* London, England: Earthscan.

International Finance Corporation. (2007). *Environmental, health, and safety (EHS) guidelines*. Washington DC, USA: World Bank Group.

International Standards Organization (ISO). (2010). *ISO 26000 project overview*. Retrieved from http://www.iso.org/iso/iso_26000_project_overview.pdf (accessed March 12 2011).

McElhaney, K. (2009). A strategic approach to corporate social responsibility. *Executive Forum*, **2009** (52), 30–36. Retrieved from http://responsiblebusiness.haas.berkeley.edu/documents/Strategic%20CSR%20(Leader%20to%20Leader,%20McElhaney).pdf (accessed 10 June 2015).

Tehemar, S. (2014). *Communication in the CSR Context*. London: Bookboon.

World Business Council for Sustainable Development (WBCSD). (2000). *Corporate Social Responsibility: Making Good Business Sense*. Geneva, Switzerland: World Business Council for Sustainable Development.

FURTHER READING

Detert, J.R., Schroder, R.G., & Maureil, J.J. (2000). A framework for linking culture and improvement initiatives in organizations. *Academy of Management Review*, **25** (4), 850–863.

9 Decentralizing Healthcare

Mark Exworthy and Martin Powell

INTRODUCTION

Decentralization enjoys a special status as a panacea in healthcare organizations and health systems across the globe. It has been claimed, at various times and in differing contexts, to solve or improve organizational efficiency, democratic accountability and equity, among many other policy and organizational problems; it is thus often "regarded as essential to good management" (Aucoin, 1990, p. 122). Pollitt et al. (1998, p. 1) observed that it has been seen as a miracle cure for a host of bureaucratic and political ills. According to Greener et al. (2009), the *Decentralization* of public sector services has become something of an organizational solution for all seasons. Yet it has also been claimed that it has been the cause of dysfunctional vices as well as virtues, which is partly linked to the appeal of *Decentralization* being linked to definitional imprecision. This chapter explores the salient characteristics of *Decentralization* (and centralization) that make it so appealing to healthcare organizations, primarily in high-income countries (but these features might also apply to low- and middle-income countries).

From one point of view, *Decentralization* is an excellent example of a management innovation, regarded as a panacea by many supporters in many countries and over time. However, from another point of view, this makes it difficult to see it as a passing fad or fashion. Indeed, *Decentralization* may be seen as the hardy perennial "flower" in the public administration "garden". *Decentralization*, or localism, has a long history, from the Greek polis through the European city-states and Edmund Burke's "little platoons" to *New Public Management* (NPM) (see, e.g., Jenkins, 1995; for more information about *NPM* and its relevance to healthcare organizations, see Sześciło, Chapter 16 in this volume). It also has elements of a symbolic management innovation (see Chapter 1 in this volume), as it can be argued that the discursive element of *Decentralization* outweighs (or even counterbalances) its practical implementation (see Greener et al., 2009; Klein, 2010).

This chapter is organized into three main sections. First, we explore definitions of *Decentralization*, drawing on literatures primarily from the disciplinary traditions of organization studies, political science and public administration. Second, we place these definitions in terms of the wider socio-political developments of neo-liberalism, including *NPM* in the latter parts of the twentieth and the start of the twenty-first centuries. Third, we elaborate on a number of theoretical perspectives to illustrate the ways in which the ambiguity of *Decentralization* can be exercised to portray it as a panacea but also as part of the problem. These issues are illustrated through a prime focus on the English health system, the National Health Service (NHS).

DEFINITIONS OF DECENTRALIZATION

All health systems are faced with the same challenge of reconciling the seemingly contradictory objectives of improving access to services, raising the quality of those services and controlling healthcare expenditure. Yet the ways in which this "triple aim" is tackled vary between countries, largely on the basis of how the health system is financed (according to general taxation, social insurance, private insurance or a combination of these) and organized (centralized or decentralized). In the case of the UK's NHS, for example, Klein (2010) explores the "eternal triangle" of the tension between three policy goals—equity, efficiency and democracy. Given the predominant roles of national governments in the financing of health systems, it is almost inevitable that questions of how that funding is disbursed, and to whom, are central questions in the organization of health systems across the world. However, the nature and extent of *Decentralization* is also critical, since it shapes the ways in which questions of equity, efficiency and effectiveness are prioritized and enacted.

The term *Decentralization* (and its derivatives) has been widely used in health systems, which, in turn, has created a significant degree of confusion for understanding such policy developments. Many have argued that there are problems with defining *Decentralization* (e.g., Atkinson, 1995; Exworthy, 1994; Gershberg, 1998; Hales, 1999; Levaggi & Smith, 2004; Saltman et al., 2003, 2007); so, clarity is required.

At its simplest, *Decentralization* can be defined as:

> . . . the transfer of authority and power from higher to lower levels of government or from national to sub-national levels. (Saltman et al., 2007, p. 10)

A similar definition is offered by Smith (1985):

> Decentralization entails the subdivision of a state's territory into smaller areas and the creation of political and administrative institutions in those areas. (p. 1)

The typology of Pollitt et al. (1998) presents three aspects of *Decentralization*, each with a binary option, leading to specific configurations of (decentralized) powers:

1) Politics: Authority decentralized to elected representatives versus authority to managers or appointed bodies;
2) Competitive: Competitive tendering versus non-competitive (involving an agency being given greater authority to manage its own budget);
3) Internal: *Decentralization* within an organization (devolution) versus *Decentralization* to a legally separate organization.

Drawing mainly on development studies, perhaps the most commonly used typology is Rondinelli's (1983), which distinguished between scale, autonomy, decision-making and ownership:

1) Deconcentration: A shift in authority to regional or district offices within the structure of government ministry;
2) Delegation: Semi-autonomous agencies are granted new powers;
3) Devolution: A shift in authority to state, provincial or municipal governments;
4) Privatization: ownership is granted to private entities.

It is debatable whether the fourth element is critical, since privatization could occur (and has) without *Decentralization*.

It is axiomatic that these frameworks are contingent upon the settings they are describing (e.g., local government, healthcare, education, etc.) and the temporal context. Empirical generalization is therefore limited (Peckham et al., 2005). Moreover, the use of these definitions in policy and practice thus reflects their socio-political context, making a universal approach unlikely. The constant oscillation of power between the center (or centers) and periphery (or peripheries) (cf. Klein, 2010) make the analysis of *Decentralization* problematic in determining its value as a panacea and as an ephemeral phenomenon. We seek therefore to reveal here how different definitions have been deployed, often with contradictory meanings.

Assuming that centralization is integral to thinking about *Decentralization*, it is important to understand the implications of centralization. A priori, a form of centralization must occur in order for *Decentralization* to take place; powers must have been held centrally if they are to be disbursed to the periphery. Moreover, it cannot be assumed that the "center" remains unaffected by the *Decentralization* of "its" powers. Indeed, the hollowing of the state to supra-national bodies, to market-like institutions and to local organizations, has fundamentally changed the nature of the state (Jessop, 1994). For example, in the UK, *Decentralization* (with related reforms discussed below) has also entailed the implementation of new regulatory bodies (such as quality and performance inspectors) at the national (central) level and new discourses of surveillance (Power, 1997). Thus, centralization does not simply imply that powers are "returned" to *l'ancien regime*, but increasingly, to multiple *centers*. This shifts the balance of power between the center and the periphery, and between the center(s). That is, it leads as much to new forms of centralization as to central power being dispersed locally.

Thus, the predominant *Decentralization* narrative has often masked an undercurrent of centralization; indeed, some healthcare systems have seen forms of re-centralization (Saltman, 2008; Saltman et al., 2007). Centralization might also enable an "enhancement of the power of executive authority" to chief executive and government ministers (Aucoin, 1990, p. 120), although it would be unlikely to be presented by them as such. The process of (re-)centralization (to the state) has been studied less in terms of the converse of *Decentralization*, but increasingly in terms of neo-bureaucracy (Farrell & Morris, 2003), post-bureaucracy (Pollitt, 2009), new forms of governance (Newman, 2005) and surveillance (Gabe et al., 2012).

THEORETICAL PERSPECTIVES ON DECENTRALIZATION

To make sense of these perspectives on *Decentralization*, it is useful also to review the conceptualizations of *Decentralization*. We offer a selection of conceptualizations here to illustrate our subsequent arguments about *Decentralization* as a panacea.

Ambiguity by Design

Much of the appeal of *Decentralization* lies in its conceptual ambiguity (Vancil, 1979). Exworthy et al. (2010) argue that:

> There is a high degree of ambiguity in definitions used, with some frameworks not defining their terms in sufficient detail, while others use the same terms with different meanings. (p.14)

They conclude that "while decentralisation and devolution tend to be the dominant terms, they are rarely defined or measured, or linked to the conceptual literature" (p. 15). In particular, Peckham et al. (2005) noted that *Decentralization* was rarely operationalized in terms of the "where" and "what". In other words, the models and frameworks of *Decentralization* did not offer a clear explanation of where powers were being relocated from and to. Equally, they did not often specify which aspects or dimensions or instruments of power were being transferred. Framed in this way, it is possible to see that *Decentralization* is more nuanced. It implies, for example, the flow of powers in *both* directions, between central bodies and the periphery. Vancil (1979) argued that organizational autonomy can only be achieved when the authority of a given organization is matched by its responsibility.

The latter without the former creates a sense of powerlessness, while the former without the latter can lead to corruption.

The Arrows Framework

To address this conceptual ambiguity, Peckham et al. (2005) developed the "Arrows Framework", which portrayed *Decentralization* in terms of the flow of power from and to specific sites in the organizational and/or political hierarchy (see Figure 9.1). *Decentralization* from the national government to a regional body might, for example, be very different from *Decentralization* from a city authority to a neighborhood. Equally, using an input-process-outcome schema as a categorization of the powers that might be relocated, the *Decentralization* of control over inputs (such as expenditure decisions) would be different to control over outcome measures (such as performance).

The Arrows Framework assumes that powers can flow in both directions simultaneously (see also Aucoin, 1990, p. 129). For example, control over staffing (inputs) might be decentralized to local organizations, while control over performance (outcome) measures might be relocated to a regional body. Aucoin (1990) argues that this simultaneous *Decentralization*/centralization relies on:

> [t]he capacity and willingness of the strategic apex of the government to single out those functions which require centralisation on the one hand and decentralisation on the other, and, at the same time, to maintain some continuity in these regards. (p.129)

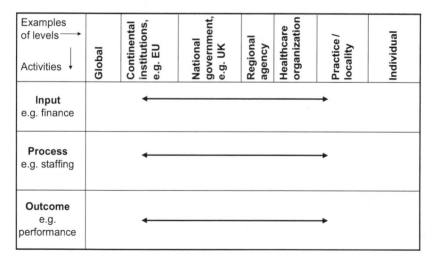

Figure 9.1 "Arrows Framework" (adapted from Peckham et al., 2005, p. 43). Arrows to right indicate decentralization; those to the left indicate centralization

In others words, *Decentralization* and centralization coexist; this makes the perennial appeal of *Decentralization* even more significant, since certain powers can be decentralized even when the dominant paradigm extols the virtues of centralization, and vice versa. Moreover, this framework indicates that the source and destination of powers need not necessarily be the same. It is also a reminder that the rhetoric or discourse of *Decentralization* at a central level might differ, sometimes substantially, from local practice.

Decision Space

Another conceptual elaboration of *Decentralization* is Bossert's (1998) notion of "decision space", which considers the range of choices that are transferred from central institutions to local institutions, and the nature of that local autonomy. Exworthy and Frosini (2008) conceptualize this decision space in terms of vertical autonomy (central-local) and horizontal autonomy (among local institutions). Local organizations may, for example, thus enjoy significant vertical autonomy from (say) the government, but limited horizontal autonomy among their local network of organizations with whom they share governance arrangements. This helps explain why *Decentralization* may be implemented, but the decentralized powers are not actually exercised because of local constraints (Exworthy et al., 2011).

THE RATIONALE FOR DECENTRALIZATION

The ascendancy of *Decentralization* in recent decades has been in response to a dominant narrative that posits that *Decentralization* is an effective solvent for improving efficiency, empowering local agents, increasing innovation, increasing accountability, improving the quality of service delivery (e.g., user experience and responsiveness) and increasing equity. Osborne and Gaebler (1993) made a number of claims about the importance of devolved units in the delivery of improved public services:

> They are far more flexible and can respond quickly to changing circumstances and customers' needs; They are far more effective than centralized institutions . . . they know what actually happens; They are far more innovative . . . innovation happens because good ideas bubble up from employees, who actually do the work and deal with the customers; Decentralized institutions generate higher morale, more commitment and greater productivity . . . especially in organizations with knowledge workers.
>
> (Osborne & Gaebler, 1993, p. 253)

Saltman et al. (2007) claim that:

> It thus appears that decentralisation covers the full range of possible judgements, with what seem to be broadly positive outcomes to some

authors or in certain contexts, becoming broadly negative to other authors or in other contexts. (p. 9)

Decentralization could thus raise the responsiveness of the healthcare system to local needs, stimulate competition across jurisdictions and promote experimentation. On the other hand, *Decentralization* might also result in undue institutional complexity, waste through duplication, lax control over spending when responsibilities overlap and insufficient exploitation of economies of scale.

These claims and judgments are set out in Table 9.1.

Table 9.1   Claims for *Decentralization* and Associated Controversies (adapted from Saltman et al., 2007)

Putative objective	Rationale	Controversies
To improve technical efficiency	1. Through fewer levels of bureaucracy and greater cost consciousness at the local level. 2. Through organizational disaggregation and introduction of market-type relations	1. Incentives required for managers. 2. Market-type relations may lead to negative outcomes.
To improve allocative efficiency	1. Through better matching of public services to local preferences. 2. Through improved patient responsiveness.	1. Increased inequalities among admin units. 2. Tension between center and periphery.
To empower local agents	Through more active local participation	Lack of clarity about participation and contested by local agents
To increase innovation	1. Through experimentation and adaptation to local conditions. 2. Through increased autonomy of local government and institutions.	1. and 2. Rise of inequalities between local areas.
To increase accountability	1. Through public participation. 2. Transformation of role of central government	1. and 2. Complex web makes accountability problematic.

Putative objective	Rationale	Controversies
To improve service delivery	1. Through decisions being taken closer to users. 2. Through better local integration between services (e.g., information) systems. 3. Through improved access to services for vulnerable groups.	1. Local organizations can be unresponsive (without appropriate incentives). 2. Integration is not a guarantee of service improvement. 3. See "allocative efficiency" above.
To increase equity	Through better allocation of resources to local needs.	Inter-area/group equity may decrease, but intra-area/group equity may improve.

LOCATING DECENTRALIZATION AS A PANACEA

The shift in emphasis (back) towards *Decentralization* in healthcare systems and organization has been global over the past 30 years (Klein, 2003, 2010; Marmor, 2004; Saltman et al., 2007). Significantly, a less visible but nonetheless powerful process of centralization has also been apparent during this time. This renewed emphasis in most health systems has come from three directions: Top-down, bottom-up and abroad. These are heuristic distinctions, since the empirical evidence would point to a combination of impulses for *Decentralization* rather than a single one.

Top-Down Structural Pressures

The primary source of interest in *Decentralization* has arguably been the growing distrust of hierarchical bureaucracies, the erosion of the post-war consensus about the welfare state and the introduction of the tenets of *NPM* (Ferlie et al., 2005; for more information about *NPM* and its relevance to healthcare organizations, see Szeéciło, Chapter 16 in this volume). Inter alia, these tenets advocated the disaggregation of former monolithic bureaucracies into separate, more autonomous organizations, financial responsibility being allocated to these organizations, competition between them (and private companies) and an emphasis on entrepreneurial behavior (implying innovation and risk-taking). *Decentralization* was, therefore, an essential ingredient for the widespread reform of public services (including healthcare) in many countries. Indeed, Marmor (2004) posits a broader claim about such managerialism facilitating an ephemeral ("fad") interest in apparent organizational panaceas (see also Aucoin, 1990), an interest encouraged by management consultancies and business schools (Saint-Martin, 2004).

The impulse for this top-down perspective is the isolation of "failure". Deficiencies or shortcomings with the system can be re-framed as individual problems, the solution to which, the *Decentralization* narrative argues, lies in local agents responding to market and/or user signals, rather than being directed by the "center". Yet the center is instrumental in the design of that system, and indeed, its functioning. While the center may wish to decentralize blame and centralize credit, it cannot absolve itself of complete responsibility. As Klein (2003) argues, the center has a "gravitational pull" (p. 196), especially in tax-funded health systems like that in the UK.

Bottom-Up Pressures

By contrast, the narrative that sees *Decentralization* as emanating from bottom-up, local pressures is based around notions of localism and community or public engagement. This perspective places emphasis on the role of local agency rather than structural imperatives.

While the problem is seen to have similar origins as the top-down perspective (namely, a sclerotic and unresponsive bureaucracy), the solution points to control being placed in the hands of local officials and/or the public (collectively or individually) (Lowndes & Stoker, 1992; Seabrook, 1984). It thus promotes a view of "small government". This model of *Decentralization* can be found in examples of municipal socialism in inner-London local government in the 1980s (Burns et al., 1994) and in GP fundholding in the 1990s (the scheme giving primary care doctors more control over their budgets for services) (Weiner & Ferris, 1990). The former retains democratic elements, whereas the latter is founded on "public choice" principles.

A related impulse for this bottom-up perspective comes from the notion of subsidiarity. This involves "the delegation of functions to smallest, lowest or least centralized competent authority" (Exworthy et al., 2010, p. 173; see also Aucoin, 1990). It is a default position in that powers should only be centralized when they cannot be exercised or fulfilled locally. Subsidiarity might imply, for example, that organizations should not be the destination of decentralized powers. Thus, it might be that individual patients could receive decentralized powers to "purchase" their own care, as has been implemented in some cases in England. Equally, Enthoven (1985) proposed that the NHS quasi-market should devise contracts with individual senior hospital doctors (consultants) (rather than with the hospitals and other provider organizations, which is what has in fact been implemented since 1991).

International Policy Transfer and Diffusion

Decentralization has not been immune to the tendency for international policy transfer and diffusion. Policy transfer refers to the process by which ideas, policies and practices from one jurisdiction are adopted by another (Dolowitz, 2000). Notwithstanding the different types of transfer (e.g., copying, emulation, combination, inspiration—see Dolowitz & Marsh, 2000) and the motivation (e.g., voluntary or coercive—see Dolowitz, 2000), the policy transfer of *Decentralization* has become increasingly common in many jurisdictions. This has been aided by information technology, management consultancies, international travel and cross-national networks, among other factors.

A notable example of policy transfer was the way in which international institutions such as the World Bank and International Monetary Fund, sought to make their loans subject to the requirement of reform. Such coercive mechanisms involved the *Decentralization* of state decision-making and the privatization of (many) public services (Common, 2001). These loans were also linked to the introduction of user fees for such services (Gilson, 1997). *Decentralization* was also touted as a panacea by the Organization for Economic Co-operation and Development (OECD) (Charbit, 2011) and the WHO (WHO, 2000). Over time, the pendulum in low- and middle-income countries has swung away from user fees towards universal health coverage, implying a more central role of the national government (McPake et al., 2011).

A second example of policy transfer relating to healthcare *Decentralization* relates to the English experience. Noting the limits of the previous centralist regime, the then-Health Minister Alan Milburn sought to decentralize through the granting of autonomy to high-performing organizations (Klein, 2003). This model of earned autonomy was heavily influenced by the experience of the Spanish hospitals that the minister had visited (Exworthy & Greener, 2008). Milburn (2002) stated that, on his visit to Alcorcon hospital in Madrid, he was struck by the fact that the greater independence it enjoyed from the rest of the state-run health system had given patients there faster waiting times and improved outcomes despite dealing with a more complex case mix than comparable state-run hospitals. He added that greater independence has improved performance in hospitals across Europe.

Policy Pendulum

Drawing on these top-down, bottom-up and international forces, many commentators have claimed these as objectives for and virtues of *Decentralization* (see Table 9.1). Previously, there might have been stronger claims made for *centralization* on the basis of economics of scale, social solidarity and equity, among others. For example, one of the main arguments for the centralized or nationalized nature of the British NHS made by Minister of Health Aneurin Bevan in the 1940s was that localism would necessarily be associated with inequity (Jenkins, 1995; Klein, 2010). It was thus in response to the perceived shortcomings of the centralization paradigm of the welfare state in the UK (and elsewhere) that purveyors of *Decentralization* were able to gain more traction in public debates (Marmor, 2004). Alternative scenarios were (made) more appealing. In this sense, the policy pendulum swung away from centralization towards *Decentralization* in the late 20th century (Aucoin, 1990). This account of the pendulum is redolent of Kingdon's (1995) "windows" model of policy adoption, which argues that a "problem" needs to be identified as being amenable to policy action if it is to become the focus of a policy that a government actually adopts (see also Stone, 1989). Significantly, in Kingdon's model, the "windows" can open and close, denoting the waxing and waning of a policy's appeal.

It seems that the perennial policy tensions and organizational dilemmas in each round of *Decentralization* (or centralization) need to be "revealed" or made apparent to multiple agents (politicians, policy-makes, practitioners, the public, etc.) (Exworthy et al., 2010, p. 12). Over time, the swings of the policy pendulum (or the "revolving door"; Klein, 2003, 2010) reveal the inadequacies of the former regime and, therefore, the attractiveness of the alternative.

The pendulum perspective assumes that that the alternatives are indeed different and distinct. Yet de Vries (2000) claims that their respective proponents often make the *same* arguments for *Decentralization* and for centralization. Thus, there is less a swing of *the* (one) pendulum than two pendulums operating simultaneously. Understanding this oscillation in the context of national health systems is vital to explaining why *Decentralization* and centralization might be observed at the same time within the same country and between different countries.

Can we claim, therefore, that *Decentralization* is a panacea for healthcare organizations? It is misleading to claim the *Decentralization* alone can be a solution, since it is often accompanied by equal and opposite trends in centralization (albeit for different powers or competencies). This conclusion is significant in the case of the UK (see below).

UNDERSTANDING DECENTRALIZATION IN HEALTHCARE SETTINGS

The nature of healthcare and its associated organizations raises the need to qualify the "standard" definitions and conceptualizations of *Decentralization* for its application to healthcare. This needs to be done to recognize three defining features of modern health systems: The centrality of the central government in financing healthcare, the professionalized nature of health services and the nature of the "center" in health systems.

First, the role of the central government in almost all health systems is significant. This is because health expenditure accounts for over 10% of the national income in many countries, and more than 50% of the expenditure of health in all OECD countries is accounted for by the government (OECD, 2014). This proportion is noticeably higher in tax-based health systems, but even in the USA (with its supposedly "private" health system), just over 50%

of all health is funded by the federal, state or local government through programs such as Medicare, Medicaid and the Veterans Health Administration. Governments are, therefore, rightly concerned about ensuring accountability for such state spending. Thus, whether the political regime is devolved (e.g., Spain), federal (e.g., Germany) or centralized (e.g., traditionally, the UK), national health systems inevitably have a primary concern with health expenditure—the allocation of resources, the accountability for them and the consequences. Arguably, tax-based health systems (such as those in the UK, many of the Mediterranean countries, Australia and New Zealand) are most concerned with accountability for that spending. By contrast, it would appear that in social insurance systems, the regulation and ownership aspects of the government's oversight of the health system are less salient (Bankauskaite & Saltman, 2007). It is in this context of centralization that recent reforms, including *Decentralization*, need to be understood.

Possibly because of the scale of health systems, the multi-tiered hierarchy of health systems means that *Decentralization* can take place between many different sites. Indeed, the traditional model of *Decentralization* has, in terms of the Arrows Framework, involved the transfer of powers between national health ministries and local organizations (such as hospitals). Just as many health competencies are now supra-national, so there are different local levels, including intra-organizational levels and individual users. Regarding the former, the introduction of the Resource Management Initiative, introduced in the 1980s and 1990s in the UK, sought to devolve power within organizations to clinical directorates (Packwood et al., 1991). This initiative also had the effect of increasing the surveillance of local managers and clinicians in these organizations (Bloomfield, 1991). More recently, in England, *Decentralization* to hospitals (in the NHS foundation trust program) has been conditional upon their performance (Allen et al., 2012).

Second, the professionalized nature of healthcare services implies that "street-level" practitioners enjoy significant degrees of discretion in diagnosing, treating or prescribing medicines (Lipsky, 1980). "Street-level bureaucracy" rests upon the notion that the daily discretionary decisions of professional staff become the de facto policy of the organization. However, professions enjoy differing levels of autonomy, with some (e.g., nurses) being more constrained than, say, doctors. It is therefore significant that initiatives such as the Resource Management Initiative (mentioned above) have devolved powers primarily to the business managers and medical managers responsible for clinical divisions (Lega, 2008). Nurses have often been absent from such initiatives. With such localized power, the implementation of *Decentralization* can become tokenistic and/or make local decision-making dysfunctional (Exworthy, 1994). Yet, local organizations (and the agents within them) are subject to ever more stringent controls on accountability and performance, through inspection, audits and monitoring.

Moreover, in many healthcare settings, the notion of patient autonomy has become more significant in recent years, as consumerism and expert patient programs have been prevalent. In this sense, local professional power has become contested. Health policy in some countries has acknowledged this with the introduction of personal budgets whereby some patients (especially those with long-term chronic conditions) can purchase their own care, given their accumulated knowledge and experience of their own needs (Alakeson, 2014). Such a policy is an extension of *Decentralization* beyond the professional. The Arrows Framework accommodates this. However, it is possible that such "individual *Decentralization*" creates a sense of "responsibilization" (Scourfield, 2007) whereby if patients spend their budget on (say) frivolous or ineffective items, it is "their" fault. This radical decentralization would potentially see a much-reduced state, as some of its functions become the users' own responsibility.

Third, the "center" in a healthcare system is not simply a hierarchical bureaucracy located in a government ministry, though it is often seen in this way. Beyond the diversification of centers (involving quality and performance inspectors) and largely unrelated to the rise of the *NPM*, there has been the emergence of evidence-based medicine, which represents "a new (and countervailing) paradigm of central knowledge to which normative and cognitive behaviors of medical professionals are increasingly expected to conform" (Exworthy, 2015, p. 3). Moreover, health professionals have become increasingly subject to financial incentives, which aim to align their practice with centrally determined protocols (Harrison & Dowswell, 2002; McDonald et al., 2007). These alternative forms of central authority have become significant in a context where trust in healthcare professionals has been waning, since they seemingly reduce the autonomy of individual practitioners, contrary to Lipsky's theory. Combined, the centralizing effect of evidence-based medicine and performance measures have challenged notions of the professional or clinical autonomy of individual practitioners (Exworthy et al., 2003; Harrison, 1998).

EVIDENCE OF DECENTRALIZATION IN HEALTHCARE

Given the multitude of definitions and conceptual approaches, and the "terminological obfuscation and analytical confusion" surrounding the term, it is difficult to establish the level and direction of *Decentralization* in healthcare systems (Greener et al., 2009; Klein, 2010). Its meaning and salience are equally hard to decipher. In this section, we begin a brief cross-national summary before focusing on the UK in a little more detail.

Cross-National Comparisons

Numerous countries have recently transferred some responsibilities from the national to sub-national governments (e.g., Italy and Spain). However, many others (including Denmark, Ireland, Norway and Poland) have re-centralized healthcare responsibilities (Saltman, 2008; Saltman et al., 2012). *Decentralization* reforms have taken place in many healthcare systems over recent years, such as the federal states of Canada, Australia and Switzerland, Spain and Italy, and in terms of national devolution, as in the UK. For example, in Spain, with regions being responsible for health financing, there is a weak coordinating role for the health ministry. Differences in regional expenditure are apparent as a result (Lopez-Casasnovas et al., 2005). Lehto et al. (2015) point to broad operational (managerial) *Decentralization* to municipalities (in Finland) and regions and municipalities (in Denmark and Sweden) in the 1970s, and this trend continued in Finland and Sweden throughout the 1990s.

Bidgood (2013) notes the long-standing Swedish commitment to subsidiarity, and localist rather than centralist approach to the delivery of healthcare, as both financing and provision responsibilities lie with the regional and municipal levels of government. The 21 county councils and regions and 290 municipalities are in charge of the day-to-day management of the health system and its facilities, raise over 70% of the financing for the system through local taxation and make decisions locally about how services are organized and provided in their areas, in line with the will of their local electorates. While the county councils tend to manage medical services, under the principle of subsidiarity, the smaller municipalities tend to handle social care. Although he notes a process of "creeping centralisation", he claims that Sweden has so far largely rejected "re-centralisation" reforms on the scale now being pursued in neighboring Denmark and Norway. He points out that the Nordic model means that service differences arise as a result of deliberate and open decisions made by elected local office holders accountable to their local electorates (Fredriksson et al., 2014; Saltman, 2015), in contrast to the inadvertent and opaque ways in which they arise in the UK's NHS. Although there may be service differences by "postcode" in both models, unlike the UK, the Nordic model does not have an unpredictable "postcode lottery". As Jenkins (1995) puts it, divergent standards are the price of localism (even though centralism has not delivered consistent ones either).

Journmard et al. (2010) claim that the highest degree of *Decentralization*/delegation in decision-making over key health policy issues occurs in Canada, Finland, Spain, Sweden and Switzerland. They argue that most decentralized countries tend to regulate healthcare resources and/or prices more than the OECD average. A high degree of *Decentralization* is often associated with a relatively weak consistency of responsibility assignments across levels of governments, suggesting that overlap in responsibilities for healthcare management tends to be present in decentralized systems. Alves et al. (2013), drawing on the Journmard et al. (2010) measure of *Decentralization*, claim that *Decentralization* has broadly positive impacts in terms of health outcomes, but ambiguous results for equity.

The NHS in the UK

Within England, *Decentralization* is largely administrative rather than political *Decentralization*, as local NHS organizations do not have devolved political power or the ability to raise funding. (Currently, 75% of the NHS budget is spent by local commissioning groups—see Klein, 2010.) However, in 2015, there were proposals (by the central government) to devolve powers to major cities, and further devolution is planned to city regions. In addition, there has been political *Decentralization* or devolution to the nations of Northern Ireland, Scotland and Wales (Greer, 2005; Peckham et al., 2012).

In the case of the UK's NHS, Klein (2010) points to the contradiction of successive governments over the past thirty years or so proclaiming their belief in devolving power to the periphery, while gradually but inexorably strengthening their grip on the service, transforming an exhort-and-hope system of governance into a command-and-control model. Arguably, these contradictions are inevitable by-products from the forms of governance that have been implemented in recent decades. Klein (2010, p. 285) explains that one interpretation of this contrast between the reality of centralization and the rhetoric of devolution could be that the rhetoric of devolution is simply the "tribute that the vice of centralisation pays to the virtues of localism". However, he points to another explanation involving tensions built into the very design of the NHS, incorporating competing, possibly irreconcilable, goals (see below).

The policy of "earned autonomy" for local English NHS organizations (Department of Health, 2000; Milburn, 2002) and the associated idea of "foundation trusts" again illustrates the simultaneous centralization and *Decentralization* of policy. Earned autonomy, as the name implies, led to organizations that had demonstrated the ability to excel at meeting the specific criteria and targets of the performance regime (outcome centralization) being granted greater freedoms from inspection and additional rights, including, for example, the ability to borrow from the private sector and set up joint ventures with it (Mannion et al., 2007). Outcome centralization led to process *Decentralization*, but still with a remaining element of outcome centralization in place.

More recently, following the 2012 reforms that sought to end the "micro-management" of the NHS (Department of Health, 2010), about 75% of the NHS budget is now devolved to local commissioning organizations. However, it is difficult to judge the extent to which power and resources can be equated, within an increasingly complex web of local and central accountability (Checkland et al., 2013). Likewise, the devolution of autonomy to the NHS foundation trusts was supposed to liberate their decision-making. Yet such "freedom" has not always been exercised, due to centralizing tendencies elsewhere in the current policy landscape, including the role of regulators (Exworthy et al., 2011).

In summary, therefore, the noticeable feature of recent English health policy has been the dominance of the *Decentralization* narrative, while less attention has been paid to centralizing tendencies. Not only has there been the (rhetorical) ebb and flow of *Decentralization* (and centralization), but also the content and scope of these initiatives have varied over time. As a consequence, assessing the level of *Decentralization* in the NHS is highly problematic (Peckham et al., 2005). Nonetheless, Bevan's much quoted formulation that "when a bedpan is dropped on a hospital floor, its noise should resound in the corridors of the Palace of Westminster" (in Klein, 2010) appears as relevant today as at the inception of the NHS.

CONCLUSIONS

Decentralization (and necessarily, centralization) illustrates well the notion of a managerial panacea, its appeal ebbing and flowing over time in accordance with the wider socio-political fads and policy imperatives. This chapter has described and explained the nature of *Decentralization* and why it has become such a useful tactical and rhetorical device for politicians and policy-makers; it has been deployed for different purposes in different contexts. We have outlined evidence that the proponents *and* critics of *Decentralization* can point to specific objectives. Perhaps more importantly, it is the oscillation of powers (decentralizing and centralizing) that implies that both can occur at same time and in the same place. Given the influence of exogenous and endogenous factors and its malleability as a concept, the (temporal and spatial) context is vital to understanding the implementation and impact of *Decentralization and* centralization in a health system.

Tactically, *Decentralization* has been used to reform and restructure the organization and delivery of health services in the UK and many other countries over the last 30 years. It has been a key component of *NPM* in fostering market-style approaches, but also in facilitating centrally direct performance regimes. This disaggregation of former large-scale state bureaucracies does, however, mask centralization in terms of quality and performance regimes, which arguably constrains local autonomy (Hoque et al., 2004).

Moreover, the symbolism of *Decentralization* is worth further investigation, given the process of centralization that invariably accompanies its actual implementation. In the context of managerial fads, rhetorical *Decentralization* (or centralization) calls for widespread adoption (or outright abandonment). We argue that adoption and abandonment are possible outcomes of a process in which the relevance of a certain management innovation for healthcare organizations ebbs and flows. Given the multiple perspectives on and types of *Decentralization*, there is no universal design. *Decentralization* reflects the different types of healthcare systems and so, different types of *Decentralization* may fit better with different systems and policy goals. Klein (2010) argues that explicit recognition of the compromises between policy goals (such as access, costs and quality) is often absent. This symbolic role of *Decentralization* does, however, also need to be viewed in terms of the instrumental role within the restructuring of the modern state. Indeed, some forms of *Decentralization* go even further and bypass organizations, offering devolved powers to individual service users (through personalized budgets, for example).

Policy makers may therefore need to be more explicit about the aims and objectives of *Decentralization* (in relation to inputs, processes and outcomes and based on a clear awareness of the limited evidence base), to be more aware of the importance of context in transferring mechanisms from one context (e.g., one country's health system or one economic sector) to another, to recognize that *Decentralization* is a process and not a single event and to address the changing central context as responsibility over outcomes shifts between central organizations (Peckham et al., 2005). This agenda will remain both ambitious and challenging, whether health systems seek to decentralize or centralize.

REFERENCES

Alakeson, V. (2014). *Delivering Personal Health Budgets: A Guide to Policy and Practice*. Bristol, England: Policy Press.
Allen, P., Keen, J., Wright, J., Dempster, P., Townsend, J., Street, A., & Verzulli, R. (2012). Investigating the governance of autonomous public hospitals: Multi-site case-study of Foundation Trusts. *Journal of Health Services Research and Policy*, 17 (2), 94–100.
Alves, J., Peralta, S., & Perelman, J. (2013). Efficiency and equity consequences of decentralization in health: An economic perspective. *Revista Portuguesa de Saude Publica*, 31 (1), 74–83.
Atkinson, S. (1995). Restructuring health care: Tracking the decentralisation debate. *Progress in Human Geography*, 19 (4), 486–503.
Aucoin, P. (1990). Administrative reform in public management: Paradigms, principles, paradoxes and pendulums. *Governance*, 3 (2), 115–137.
Bankauskaite, V., & Saltman, R. (2007). Central issues in the decentralization debate. In R. Saltman, V. Bankauskaite, & K. Vrangbaek (Eds.), *Decentralisation in Health Care*, Maidenhead, England: Open University Press, pp. 9–21.
Bidgood, E. (2013). *Healthcare Systems: Sweden and Localism—An Example for the UK?* London: Civitas.
Bloomfield, B. (1991). The role of information systems in the UK NHS: Action at a distance the fetish of calculation. *Social Studies of Science*, 21 (4), 701–734.
Bossert, T.J. (1998). Analyzing the decentralisation of health systems in developing countries: Decision space, innovation, and performance. *Social Science and Medicine*, 47 (10), 1513–1527.
Burns, D., Hambleton, R., & Hoggett, P. (1994). *The Politics of Decentralisation*. Basingstoke, England: Macmillan.
Charbit, C. (2011). *Governance of public policies in decentralised contexts: The multi-level approach* (OECD Regional Development Working Papers, 2011/04). Paris: OECD.
Checkland, K., Allen, P., Coleman, A., Segar, J., McDermott, I., Harrison, S., Petsoulas, C., & Peckham, S. (2013). Accountable to whom, for what? An exploration of the early development of Clinical Commissioning Groups in the English

NHS.' *BMJ Open*, **3** (12). Retrieved from http://bmjopen.bmj.com/content/3/12/e003769.full (accessed 30 June 2015).

Common, R. (2001). *Public Management and Policy Transfer in South-East Asia*. Aldershot, England: Ashgate.

De Vries, M.S. (2000). The rise and fall of decentralization: A comparative analysis of arguments and practices in European countries. *European Journal of Political Research*, **38** (2), 193–224.

Department of Health. (2000). *The NHS: A plan for investment, a plan for reform* (Cmd. 4818). London: Stationery Office.

Department of Health. (2010). *Equity and excellence: Liberating the NHS* (Cmd. 7881). London: Stationery Office.

Dolowitz, P. (2000). *Policy Transfer and British Social Policy: Learning from the USA?* Buckingham, England: Open University Press.

Dolowitz, P., & Marsh, D. (2000). Learning from abroad: The role of policy transfer in contemporary policy-making. *Governance*, **13** (1), 5–24.

Enthoven, A. (1985). *Reflections on the management of the NHS: An American looks at incentives to efficiency in health services management in the UK*. London: Nuffield Trust.

Exworthy, M. (1994). The contest for control in community health services: General managers and professionals dispute decentralisation. *Policy and Politics*, **22** (1), 17–29.

Exworthy, M. (2015). The cage and the gaze: Interpreting physician control in the English health system. *Professions and Professionalism*, **5** (1). Retrieved from https://journals.hioa.no/index.php/pp/article/view/944/1242 (accessed 25 June 2015).

Exworthy, M., & Frosini, F. (2008). Room to manoeuvre? Explaining local autonomy in the English National Health Service. *Health Policy*, **81** (2–3), 204–212.

Exworthy, M., Frosini, F., & Jones, L. (2011). NHS Foundation Trusts: "you can take a horse to water. . .". *Journal of Health Services Research and Policy*, **16** (4), 232–237.

Exworthy, M., Frosini, F., Jones, L., Peckham,S., Powell, M., Greener, I., Anand, P., & Holloway, J.A. (2010). *Decentralisation and performance: Autonomy and incentives in local health economies* (Final report to the NHS NCC-SDO research and development programme). Retrieved from http://www.nets.nihr.ac.uk/__data/assets/pdf_file/0005/64292/FR-08-1618-125.pdf (accessed 30 June 2015).

Exworthy, M., & Greener, I. (2008). Decentralisation as a means to re-organise health-care in England: From theory to practice. In L. McKee, E. Ferlie, & P. Hyde (Eds.), *Organising and Re-Organising: Power and Change in Health-Care Organisations*, Basingstoke, England: Palgrave, pp. 46–58.

Exworthy, M., Wilkinson, E.K., McColl, A., Roderick, P., Smith, H., Moore, M., & Gabbay, J. (2003). The role of performance indicators in changing the autonomy of the general practice profession in the UK. *Social Science and Medicine*, **56** (7), 1493–1504.

Farrell, C.M., & Morris, J. (2003). The neo-bureaucratic state: Professionals and managers and professional managers in schools, general practices and social work. *Organization*, **10** (1), 129–157.

Ferlie, E., Lynn, L., & Pollitt, C. (Eds.). (2005). *The Oxford Handbook of Public Management*. Oxford, England: Oxford University Press.

Fredriksson, M., Blomqvist, P., & Winblad, U. (2014). Recentralizing healthcare through evidence-based guidelines: Striving for national equity in Sweden. *BMC Health Services Research*, **14** (11), article no. 509. Retrieved from http://www.biomedcentral.com/1472–6963/14/509 (accessed 30 June 2015).

Gabe, J., Exworthy, M., Jones, I.R., & Smith, G. (2012). Towards a sociology of disclosure: The case of surgical performance. *Sociology Compass*, **6** (11), 908–922.

Gershberg, A.I. (1998). Decentralisation, re-centralisation and performance accountability: Building an operationally useful framework for analysis. *Development Policy Review*, 16 (4), 405–430.

Gilson, L. (1997). The lessons of user fee experience in Africa. *Health Policy and Planning*, 12 (3), 273–285.

Greener, I., Exworthy, M., Peckham, S., & Powell, M. (2009). Has labour decentralised the NHS? Terminological obfuscation and analytical confusion. *Policy Studies*, 30 (4), 439–454.

Greer, S.L. (2005). The territorial bases of health policy-making in the UK after devolution. *Regional and Federal Studies*, 15 (4), 501–518.

Hales, C. (1999). Leading horses to water? The impact of decentralisation on managerial behaviour. *Journal of Management Studies*, 36 (6), 831–851.

Harrison, S. (1998). The politics of evidence based medicine in the United Kingdom. *Policy and Politics*, 26 (1), 15–31.

Harrison, S., & Dowswell, G. (2002). Autonomy and bureaucratic accountability in primary care: What English General Practitioners say. Sociology of Health and Illness, 24 (2), 208–226.

Hoque, K., Davies, S., & Humphreys, S. (2004). Freedom to do what you are told: Senior management autonomy in an NHS acute Trust. *Public Administration*, 82 (2), 355–375.

Jenkins, S. (1995). *Accountable to None: The Tory Nationalization of Britain*. London: Hamish Hamilton.

Jessop, B. (1994). The transition to post-Fordism and the Schumpeterian workfare state. In R. Burrows & B. Loader (Eds.), *Towards a Post-Fordist Welfare State?* London: Routledge, pp. 13–37.

Jourmard, I., André, C., & Nicq, C. (2010). *Health care systems: Efficiency and institutions* (Economics Department Working Paper 769). Paris: OECD.

Kingdon, J.W. (1995). *Agendas, Alternatives and Public Policy*. New York: Harper Collins.

Klein, R. (2003). The new localism: Once more through the revolving door? *Journal of Health Services research and Policy*, 8 (4), 195–196.

Klein, R. (2010). The eternal triangle: Sixty years of the centre-periphery relationship in the National Health Service. *Social Policy and Administration*, 44 (3), 285–304.

Lega, F. (2008). The rise and fall(acy) of clinical directorates in Italy. *Health Policy*, 85 (2), 252–262.

Lehto, J., Vrangbaek, K., & Winblad, U. (2015). The reactions to macro-economic crises in Nordic health system policies: Denmark, Finland and Sweden 1980–2013. *Health Economics, Policy and Law*, 10 (1), 61–81.

Levaggi, R., & Smith, P. (2004). *Decentralisation in health care: Lessons from public economics*. Unpublished paper, Centre for Health Economics, York University, Toronto, Canada.

Lipsky, M. (1980). *Street-Level Bureaucracy: Dilemmas of the Individual in Public Services*. New York: Russell Sage Foundation.

Lopez-Casasnovas, G., Costa-Font, J., & Plana, I. (2005). Diversity and regional inequalities in the Spanish system of health care services. *Health Economics*, 14 (S1), s221–s235.

Lowndes, V., & Stoker, G. (1992). An evaluation of neighbourhood decentralization, Part 1: Customer and citizen perspectives. *Policy and Politics*, 20 (1), 47–61.

Mannion, R., Goddard, M., & Bate, A. (2007). Aligning incentives and motivations in health care: the case of earned autonomy. *Financial Accountability and Management*, 23 (4), 401–420.

Marmor, T. (2004). *Fads in Medical Care Management and Policy*. London: Nuffield Trust.

McDonald, R., Harrison, S., Checkland, K., Campbell, S., & Roland, M. (2007). Impact of financial incentives on clinical autonomy and internal motivation in primary care: Ethnographic study. *BMJ: British Medical Journal*, 334 (7608), article no. 1357. Retrieved from http://www.bmj.com/content/bmj/334/7608/1357.full.pdf (accessed 30 June 2015).

McPake, B., Brikci, N., Commetto, G., Schmidt, A., & Araujo, E. (2011). Removing user fees: Learning from international experience to support the process. *Health Policy and Planning*, 26 (S2), 104–117.

Milburn, A. (2002). Speech by the Rt Hon Alan Milburn MP, Secretary of State, on NHS Foundation Hospitals, May 22. Retrieved from http://webarchive.national archives.gov.uk/+/www.dh.gov.uk/en/MediaCentre/Speeches/Speecheslist/DH_4000768 (accessed 16 June 2015).

Newman, J. (Ed.). (2005). *Remaking Governance: Policy, Politics and the Public Sphere*. Bristol, England: Policy Press.

OECD. (2014). *Health at a Glance: Europe 2014*. Paris: OECD and European Commission.

Osborne, D., & Gaebler, T. (1993). *Reinventing Government*. New York: Addison Wesley.

Packwood, T., Keen, J., & Buxton, M. (1991). *Hospitals in Transition: The Resource Management Experiment*. Buckingham, England: Open University Press.

Peckham, S., Exworthy, M., Powell, M., & Greener, I. (2005). *Decentralisation, centralisation and devolution in publicly funded health services: Decentralisation as an organisational model for health-care in England*. Report to the NHS NCC-SDO research and development programme. Southampton, UK: National Institute for Health Research.

Peckham, S., Mays, N., Hughes, D., Sanderson, M., Allen P., Prior, L., Entwistle, V., Thompson, A., & Davies, H. (2012). Devolution and patient choice: Policy rhetoric versus experience in practice. *Social Policy and Administration*, 46 (2), 199–218.

Pollitt, C. (2009). Bureaucracies remember, post-bureaucratic organizations forget. *Public Administration*, 87 (2), 198–218.

Pollitt, C., Brichall, J., & Putnam, K. (1998). *Decentralising Public Service Management*. London: Macmillan.

Power, M. (1997). *The Audit Society: Rituals of Verification*. Oxford, England: Oxford University Press.

Rondinelli, D.A. (1983). Implementing decentralisation programmes in Asia: A comparative analysis. *Public Administration and Development*, 3 (3), 181–207.

Saint-Martin, D. (2004). *Building the New Managerialist State: Consultants and the Politics of Public Sector Reform in Britain, Canada and France* (2nd ed.). Oxford, England: Oxford University Press.

Saltman, R.B. (2008). Decentralization, re-centralization and future European health policy. *European Journal of Public Health*, 18 (2), 104–106.

Saltman, R. (2015). Structural patterns in Swedish health policy: A 30-year perspective. *Health Economics, Policy and Law*, 10 (1), 195–215.

Saltman, R., Bankauskaite, V., & Vrangbaek, K. (2003). *Decentralisation in Health Care: Strategies and Outcomes*. Madrid: EOHCS.

Saltman, R., Bankauskaite, V., & Vrangbaek, K. (Eds.). (2007). *Decentralisation in Health Care*. Maidenhead, England: Open University Press.

Saltman, R., Vrangbaek, K., Lehto, J., & Winblad, U. (2012). Consolidating national authority in Nordic health systems. *Eurohealth*, 18 (3), 21–24.

Scourfield, P. (2007). Social care and the modern citizen: Client, consumer, service user, manager and entrepreneur. *British Journal of Social Work*, 37 (1), 107–122.

Seabrook, J. (1984). *The Idea of Neighbourhood: What Local Politics Should Be About*. London: Pluto Press.

Smith, B.C. (1985). *Decentralization: The Territorial Dimension of the State.* London: Allen and Unwin.

Stone, D. (1989). Causal stories and the formation of policy agendas. *Political Science Quarterly,* **104** (2), 281–300.

Vancil, R. (1979). *Decentralisation: Management Ambiguity by Design.* Chicago, IL: Dow Jones-Irwin.

Weiner, J., & Ferris, T. (1990). *GP budget holding in the UK: Lessons from America* (Research report no.7). London: King's Fund Institute.

World Health Organization. (2000). *The world health report, 2000.* Geneva, Switzerland: WHO.

10 Empowerment in Healthcare Organizations

Nelson Ositadimma Oranye and Nora Ahmad

INTRODUCTION

The purpose of this chapter is to determine whether *Empowerment* is an appropriate management model for healthcare organizations, and if so, in what way? A second purpose is to understand whether there are aspects of empowerment practices that are more strongly associated with positive work outcomes in healthcare than others. This chapter will also explore how the model of work empowerment in healthcare organizations is comparable to practices in other organizations, and will suggest a model of *Empowerment* based on research evidence that healthcare organizations might follow in the healthcare environment.

There is no doubt that the healthcare system today is still beset by numerous challenges posed by the changing environment of health service delivery. Most countries have continued to experience a smaller healthcare workforce than is desired, resulting in increased workload, high work stress and burnout among health workers (Ahmad & Oranye, 2010). It has become imperative that nurses and other healthcare workers have sufficient power and work in an environment that enables them to exercise reasonable control over their area of professional practice in order to function at an optimal level.

Empowerment as a process of achieving social justice and access to economic resources was popularized in the 1960s by the Civil Rights Movement (McCarthy & Freeman, 2008); it has flourished since then and been widely applied in disciplines such as social work and nursing within the last three decades. The origin of the concept of *Empowerment* dates back to organizational theories in sociology and psychology. Also, the concept of power, which is central to empowerment, has been integral to the discipline of political science. However, the concept of *Employee Empowerment*, especially in organizational and management literature, flourished in the 1990s, deriving from the principles of industrial democracy (Appelbaum et al., 1999). The long history of the application of *Empowerment* in these disciplines with very diverse epistemological positions has made it difficult to develop a consensus definition of *Empowerment*. Nonetheless, two dominant theoretical frameworks—of *Empowerment* as structural and *Empowerment* as psychological—have emerged within the fields of healthcare and nursing.

The importance of staff empowerment in healthcare management and the benefits associated with it are well documented in the literature. The empowerment of healthcare workers, especially nurses and other frontline healthcare workers, has become an important strategy for organizational success, effectiveness and enhancing organizational competitiveness (Ahmad & Oranye, 2010; Eo et al., 2014). As Eo et al. (2014, p. 42) pointed out, "[A] hospital's work-related efficiency is directly linked to the efficiency of its nurses". This type of perspective where organizations begin to see their staff empowerment and efficacy as linked to organizational efficacy has projected the *Empowerment* model as a key component of organizational strategies. Manojlovich (2007) underscored the importance of empowerment among nurses by highlighting the negative consequences of powerlessness among nurses, which include ineffectiveness, less satisfaction with the job and greater susceptibility to burnout and depersonalization.

Creating a work environment that is conducive to staff empowerment therefore remains a major priority for the healthcare sector. If the numbers of health workers are fewer and the atmosphere of work has become extremely challenging, it makes the most sense that the workers are enabled to function at an efficient and optimal level. Evidence from the literature continues to point to the positive work outcomes of an empowered healthcare workforce and the need for organizations to create work environments that support staff empowerment.

DEFINING EMPOWERMENT

The concept of *Empowerment* is logically rooted in the concept of power, which has a long history in philosophy and social science. However, our discussion will be restricted to workplace empowerment. Ahmad and Oranye (2010) outlined how the meaning of *Empowerment* within the organizational literature has changed since the 1980s. For instance, in the early 1980s, *Empowerment* was used to refer to job enrichment through participation (Hackman & Oldham, 1980) and managerial practices, such as the transfer of organizational power (Kanter, 1977, 1983). Later, *Empowerment* was seen as energizing followers through leadership (Block, 1987), enhancing self-efficacy by reducing powerlessness (Conger & Kanungo, 1988) and increasing intrinsic task motivation (Thomas & Velthouse, 1990). From 1990 until recently, many researchers have further enlarged the concept of *Empowerment* as a psychological process of perceived control, competence and energizing towards achieving goals (Menon, 2001).

The above definitions of *Empowerment* align closely with Hokanson Hawks's (1992, p. 609) definition of *Empowerment* as "the interpersonal process of providing the proper tools, resources and environment to build, develop and increase the ability and effectiveness of others to set and reach goals for individual and social ends". In the healthcare literature, empowerment is commonly described as either a psychological process or a work outcome. As a work outcome, empowerment is characterized by the presence of self-efficacy, competency, autonomy and finding meaning in one's work (McCarthy & Freeman, 2008; Shanta & Eliason, 2014). Johnson (2011, p. 265) has defined *Healthcare Empowerment* as "the process and state of being engaged, informed, collaborative, committed, and tolerant of uncertainty regarding healthcare". Gibson (1991, p. 359) recognized *Empowerment* as "a social process of recognizing, promoting and enhancing people's abilities to meet their own needs, solve their own problems and mobilize the necessary resources in order to feel in control of their own lives", but the significance of his definition is the recognition that *Empowerment* is "the process of helping people to assert control over the factors which affect their health".

The increased interest in *Empowerment* among healthcare researchers has resulted in the inclusion of many new variables as researchers strive to grapple with the meaning and how to effectively measure empowerment. Scholars have sought to expand the sphere of the discussion on *Empowerment* by examining it from new and interesting perspectives, such as being valued, respected and so on. Bradbury-Jones et al. (2011) noted that the feeling of being valued as a learner, or as a team member and as a person were critical elements of *Empowerment* among nursing students in clinical practice. The sense of being valued is a psychological element of *Empowerment*.

Thus far, we have seen that *Empowerment* is essentially about enabling people to access those resources that would help them exert some degree of control over their own affairs, health, work or other responsibilities and to engender a feeling of confidence and self-efficacy in their work performance. These definitions speak both to a structural dimension, which is about resources, and to psychological *empowerment*, which relates to a person's internal motivation. Worker empowerment is basically a product of the interactions among individual level factors and organizational and sociocultural factors (Johnson, 2011; Rao, 2012). The model of *Empowerment* proposed by Johnson (2011) points to the complexity of factors related to *Empowerment*, and the challenges for measuring and understanding empowerment in healthcare.

THEORETICAL MODELS OF EMPOWERMENT

As we have noted, there are multiple concepts of *Empowerment*, which makes it difficult to have a uniform definition. In spite of the plethora of definitions and perspectives on *Empowerment*, we can decipher that all the perspectives can be brought under one or two of the principal theoretical perspectives: The structural and psychological *Empowerment* theories.

Structural Empowerment Theory

Kanter (1983) recognized the central role of power in facilitating or hindering access to the resources, support and opportunities that people require to function within an organization. Thus, it seems quite natural that Kanter's theory of structural empowerment may have been inspired by the social philosophy of the Civil Rights Movement, which was critical of power imbalances and their influence on access to resources. The concept of structural empowerment (Kanter, 1977, 1983) derives from organizational or management theory. Structural empowerment has been defined as the ability to get things done, to mobilize resources, to get and use whatever it is that a person needs for the goals he or she is attempting to meet (Kanter, 1983). In a sense, structural empowerment has been perceived as the actual, not just the perceived, ability to make autonomous decisions (Chaudhuri et al., 2013). It has primarily focused on organizational characteristics and management as the core of employees' empowerment.

The theory of structural empowerment suggests that employees who have access to empowerment structures in their work environment, which include access to information, resources, support and the opportunity to learn and develop, are more likely to be effective at work than others. In other words, a worker's attitude and behavior in the workplace, especially with respect to efficiency and productivity, can best be understood by looking at the worker's position and situation within her work environment. Stated succinctly, workers who are in a position where they exercise sufficient autonomy in their job are likely to have positive outcomes for themselves, their clients and the organization (Koberg et al., 1999; Laschinger et al., 2001). The structural empowerment theory has spurred much interest in empowerment research, especially in the field of nursing, among those investigating the impact of an empowered work environment on nurses and patient outcomes. They suggest that:

1) The key components of structural empowerment can be identified as "opportunity structures", which can be categorized as the opportunities for learning, growth and personal advancement within the organization;
2) Power structures include information, resources and support. Formal and informal powers are necessary to access these structures (Laschinger et al., 2010, p. 6).

According to the theory, members of an organization who experience increased autonomy, decreased job stress, lower burnout, increased job satisfaction and higher commitment to the organization will be more successful than others. Generally, structural theory has argued that these structural factors within the work environment have a greater influence on employee work attitudes and behaviors than do personality or socialization experiences. However, Spreitzer's (1995, 1996) model of psychological empowerment focuses on the underlying psychological meaning of "empowerment" and how it provides the motivational force for action.

Psychological Empowerment Theory

According to Laschinger et al. (2001), the structural empowerment model describes the conditions of the work environment but does not describe the employees' reactions to these conditions. The psychological empowerment theory (Spreitzer, 1995), which is derived from social psychology models, looks at the interaction between these individual factors and the individual's environment. From this perspective, "empowerment" is seen as an individual's psychological experience, arising from the interaction of personal traits and environmental factors. So the mere presence of structural factors is insufficient to explain the dynamics of empowerment and workers' experiences. Conger and Kanungo (1988) have viewed psychological empowerment as a motivational construct whose locus lies within the individual. Building on that model, Thomas and Velthouse's (1990) cognitive empowerment model also describes psychological empowerment as an intrinsic task motivation. Psychological empowerment plays a critical role in workers' commitment to organizational goals. It represents a set of congruent, cognitive elements that come together to define individuals' perceptions or attitudes towards their work and contribution to the workplace. These elements typically include the four domains of the meaningfulness of the work, self-determination, perceived competency or self-efficacy in work performance and perceived impact on work outcomes (Spreitzer, 1996; Thomas & Velthouse, 1990). Meaning refers to the intrinsic value people have in their work goals, competence is an individual's belief in his/her capacity to perform a specific job, self-determination is the degree of autonomy or control one has over work behavior/processes and impact is the extent to which an individual believes he/she can influence the outcomes at work (Spreitzer, 1995).

Ahmad and Oranye (2010) reviewed the motivational construct of empowerment in the psychological literature, where power, control and empowerment are treated as motivations, expectancies, beliefs or psychological states that are internal to individuals. "Power" in this motivational sense refers to an intrinsic need for self-determination (Deci, 1975) or a belief in personal self-efficacy (Bandura, 1986). Any management strategy or technique that strengthens this need for self-determination or the self-efficacy belief among employees will make the workers feel more powerful. According to McClelland (1975), individuals' power needs are met when they perceive that they have power or when they believe that they can adequately cope with the events, situations and people they confront. On the other hand, individuals are frustrated when they believe they are unable to cope with the physical and social demands of the environment. Thus, to empower is to enable, and implies motivating through enhancing the sense of personal efficacy and creating intrinsic motivation.

The psychological theory of empowerment represents the subjective reality of power and the meaning of work to the worker. From a phenomenological viewpoint, it is the world of meaning that people assign to things around them which defines the realities more than the "objective" phenomena do. The theory of psychological empowerment brings us to the realm of the meaning of empowerment to the individual, and can help us understand the whys of perceived or lack of perceived empowerment among workers within the same organization. The key element of psychological empowerment is the intrinsic motivation of the worker, such as the meaningfulness of the work, self-determination or autonomy, perceived self-efficacy in work performance and perceived impact on work outcomes rather than on managerial practices.

The importance of psychological empowerment was highlighted in the recent study by Brewer et al. (2006) in New York. The researchers reported a feeling of a lack of power among nurses to influence their working conditions; the existence of power structures within organizations does not often translate into a psychological feeling of empowerment. In our view, the effectiveness of structural empowerment can be better determined not just by the existence of the structures of empowerment, but whether, when and where the presence of these structures is able to engender intrinsic motivation in the worker.

Other studies have tried to integrate the structural and psychological perspectives of empowerment (Ahmad & Oranye, 2010; Baker et al., 2011), which endorses the utility of both frameworks in providing a comprehensive and balanced understanding of the dynamics of workers' empowerment.

Empowerment as a Relational Construct

The relational construct, which is located within the structural empowerment framework, focuses on behaviors within the organizational structure, and as such de-emphasizes individual psychological factors, such as a sense of competence and self-efficacy (Conger & Kanungo, 1988). From this perspective, "power" is primarily a relational concept used to describe the perceived power or control that an individual actor or organizational subunit has over others. According to Pfeffer (1981), power arises when individuals' or subunits' performance outcomes are contingent not simply on their own behavior, but on what others do or how others respond.

Hokanson Hawks (1992, p. 609) underlined the fact that empowerment is an interpersonal process that "occurs between two or more people, the person who empowers and the person(s) who is (are) empowered". Some scholars have looked at the relational construct of empowerment from the perspective of feminist theory, especially socialist feminism, which is in some ways akin to the civil rights philosophy of the 1960s. Manojlovich (2007) has argued that the relational theory of empowerment might be more suitable for understanding the empowerment experience of nurses in the contemporary healthcare system than either workplace or motivational views of empowerment, as nurses work in a multidisciplinary healthcare system, where role responsibilities intermesh and are often shared with other healthcare workers. Moreover, the current patriarchal healthcare system has been dominated by the medical profession, which remains mostly male, while nursing remains predominantly a female profession.

Levels of Empowerment

Different levels of empowerment among nursing staff, educators and managers, ranging from moderate (Wang et al., 2013) to high levels of empowerment (Suominen et al., 2005), have been reported in health studies. The level of empowerment varies by the status of the study subjects. Most of the research indicates moderate empowerment among nursing staff (Barden et al., 2011; DeVivo et al., 2013), while a high level of empowerment was reported among nurse managers (Trus et al., 2012). However, there are a few deviations from this pattern. An Australian study by Bish et al. (2014) reported moderate level of empowerment among rural nurse managers. Piazza et al. (2006) found a significant difference in the levels of empowerment between certified and non-certified nurses. Also, the survey by Baker et al. (2011) of clinical and academic nursing faculty members in America reported moderate empowerment. Another American study (Fitzpatrick et al., 2010) reported higher empowerment among nurses who were Asians, followed by whites, African Americans, Hispanics and other nurses. Ahmad and Oranye (2010) reported higher empowerment among Malaysian as compared to British nurses, although the British nurses were more satisfied than their Malaysian counterparts. So it seems that different factors, such as ethnic or racial group membership, country, job status and being certified or non-certified, influence the level of empowerment among healthcare workers within the same organization. This makes it important that researchers and managers pay attention to the meaning of empowerment to each individual worker and that they try to understand the differential access to empowerment among different groups of healthcare workers.

EXAMINING THE RELEVANCE FOR HEALTHCARE ORGANIZATIONS

What are the benefits of *Empowerment* to healthcare organizations? What strategies can healthcare organizations and management use to empower their healthcare workers? As we have seen thus far, the empowerment of healthcare workers will lead to positive work outcomes that are beneficial to the healthcare worker and healthcare organizations and can lead to improved quality of care for patients.

Empowerment and Work Outcomes

Empowerment among healthcare workers has been linked to several positive work outcomes for the health worker, clients and their families. Some of the outcomes of an empowered healthcare workforce include increased job satisfaction, work productivity and increased work value for the staff (Koberg et al., 1999; Spreitzer, 1995). Shipper and Manz (1992) have argued that *Empowerment* is a major weapon against the challenges faced by the nursing profession. Burnout among nurses has remained one of the major concerns for nurse management. *Empowerment* in the workplace can have mediating effects on the association between work environment and burnout (Wang et al., 2013); nurses who feel empowered report less burnout than others.

Many studies (DeVivo et al., 2013; Laschinger et al., 2009) suggest a strong relationship between perceived empowerment and patient outcomes. Nurses who feel empowered are likely to have the positive work outcomes of effectiveness, high quality care, job satisfaction and satisfied clients. Khammarnia et al. (2014) reported on the relationship between psychological empowerment and workers' readiness to accept organizational changes among primary health workers in western Iran. Armellino et al. (2010) observed an increased patient safety culture among registered nurses who had high structural empowerment. They equally noted that the association between structural empowerment and patient safety culture was essential for delivering efficient, competent, quality care.

Other studies have reported an association between medical errors in healthcare systems and structural empowerment. Armellino et al. (2010) identified that medical errors are related to the structural environment of a healthcare organization, and that they are more likely to occur in organizations that have poorly designed processes of care and lack support systems for decision-making. Several other studies have revealed the relationship between structural issues in the healthcare environment and specific employee attitudes and behaviors, including the intent to stay on the job, burnout, job satisfaction and organizational commitment (Ahmad & Oranye, 2010; Fitzpatrick et al., 2010).

A relationship between empowerment and feelings of being respected has equally been reported. Faulkner and Laschinger (2008) observed that nurses who perceive themselves to be structurally and psychologically empowered felt more respected in the workplace than their counterparts. Another study speaks of the relationship between empowerment and innovative behavior among nurses. Knol and Van Linge (2009) have argued that both structural and psychological empowerment can promote innovative behavior in nurses, but that psychological empowerment plays a crucial role in this relationship because of its mediating effect between structural empowerment and nurses' innovative decision-making.

A study of 39 "magnet" hospitals, which are hospitals designated as having good nursing care in the USA, found that features of empowerment, such as greater status, increased autonomy, control and nurse-physician collaboration, led to lower patient mortality rates in the "magnet" hospitals compared to the matched control "non-magnet" hospitals (Aiken et al., 1994).

Some studies have emphasized the relationship between a healthy work environment and empowerment. A healthy work environment is one that promotes staff empowerment. The common outcomes of a healthy work environment include autonomy, self-efficacy, job satisfaction, commitment to the organization, patient satisfaction and good-quality patient care. The role of empowerment in promoting a healthy work environment, productivity and innovativeness among nurses has also been highlighted (Eo et al., 2014; Knol & Van Linge, 2009). Studies have shown that creating an empowering work environment can create a healthy work environment and improve work outcomes for the healthcare worker, the client and healthcare organization (DeVivo et al., 2013; Menon, 2001).

Although the research findings on the work outcomes of *Empowerment* for healthcare workers, clients and the organizations are quite diverse, there are common patterns. These include a healthy work environment, autonomy, job satisfaction, work efficiency, organizational and work commitment, reduced labor turnover, increased productivity, reduced costs and wait times, improved quality of care, client satisfaction with care and the attainment of the organizational goals (DeVivo et al., 2013; Faulkner & Laschinger, 2008). Overall, the evidence shows that employees who are structurally and psychologically empowered tend to be innovative, effective decision-makers, act as change agents in their organizations and produce positive outcomes for themselves, their clients and the organization.

What Work Environment Factors Enhance Empowerment?

Research evidence has consistently shown that empowerment among healthcare workers is a function of the type of work environment. The work environment plays an important role in creating autonomy and self-efficacy in the workers (DeVivo et al., 2013; Schmalenberg & Kramer, 2008), which bring out positive energy in the worker. Thomas and Velthouse (1990) have argued that the four elements of psychological empowerment are determined by the work context. Put succinctly, the way workers perceive their work environment would have significant implications for their psychological empowerment. Manojlovich and DeCicco (2007) have identified that work environment factors, particularly poor nurse-physician communication, were probably the most important predictor of adverse patient outcomes, such as excess hospital mortality in critical care settings. Aiken et al. (1994) reported that work environment factors related to organizational characteristics, such as hospital ownership, size, autonomy and the degree of control accorded to nurses were significant predictors of patient mortality. Management behavior is another important work environment characteristic that affects workers' empowerment status. Macphee et al. (2012, p. 159) argued, "When nurse leaders use structural and psychological empowerment strategies, the results are safer work environments and better nurse outcomes".

Besides leadership and management style, a professional practice model that involves the shared governance model (Barden et al., 2011; Hess, 2004) has been projected as an effective strategy for achieving nurses' empowerment, improved quality of care, improved recruitment and retention of nurses and cost containment. It is believed that professional practice models empower the nurses by placing the control of professional practice into the hands of staff nurses. The model of shared governance, which seeks to transfer more authority to healthcare workers in areas of their professional practice, derives from modern management philosophies of participative management or democratic management, which emphasizes job enrichment, less bureaucracy and greater involvement of staff in decision-making.

Creating a healthy work environment is probably the most effective way to achieve workers' empowerment in the healthcare sector (Huddleston, 2014). Healthcare organizations that engage the employees in the pursuit of common goals, such as patient safety, quality outcomes, employee productivity and employee retention, ultimately forge the culture of a healthy work environment (Huddleston, 2014; Wooten & Carne, 2003). Some of the core characteristics that identify a healthy work environment are the existence of organizational policies and practices that:

1) Value the workers, treating them with respect and equitably. Equity does not mean equality, but a sense of justice underlined by transparency;
2) Recognize the individual worker as an asset and not just a cost;
3) Promote a strong sense of trust among all employees;
4) Empower employees to be effective decision-makers and risk takers by giving them greater autonomy and power to act in areas of professional competence and performance;
5) Provide the employees with opportunities for personal and professional growth;
6) Promote the existence of an organizational culture that supports effective communication and interprofessional collaboration;
7) Promote a physically and culturally safe work environment.

Organizational justice, as already noted, is a feature of a healthy work environment. Kuokkanen et al. (2014) conceptualized organizational justice as the extent to which employees perceive themselves as being treated fairly in their workplace. The importance of perceived fair treatment was highlighted in Eo et al. (2014), where workers who perceived a fair compensation system in the organization felt empowered and actively participated in organizational tasks. Kuokkanen et al. (2014) observed that the level of empowerment, commitment and work motivation among workers increases in organizations that promote organizational justice and where workers perceive opportunities to use their individual professional skills.

Strategies for Work Empowerment in Healthcare Organizations

Having identified the work outcomes of empowerment in healthcare and the types of environments that promote empowerment among healthcare staff, management and educators, it seems reasonable to suggest that any effective strategy for *Healthcare Empowerment* should derive from the empirical knowledge of effective and best practices outlined above. Different studies have suggested diverse strategies for empowering healthcare workers. The challenge of choosing the best practice model has become daunting, given that the evidence is diffuse. What is effective in one country or group may not be effective in another.

There is no one best way of managing, because "management practices are complex, contested, emergent, locally enacted and context specific" (Jenkins & Delbridge, 2013, p. 2670). According to Psychogios et al. (2009, p. 448), "employee autonomy and its application are considered to be culture-bound and highly responsive to the nature of society". Some countries have more flexible work planning and task organization than others, which affects the level of autonomy granted to employees (Dimitriades, 2001; Psychogios et al., 2009). Also, evidence from cross-cultural and cross-country studies (Ahmad & Oranye, 2010; Fitzpatrick et al., 2010) points to the fact that empowerment does not produce the same result in all countries. This means that we have to pay attention to the combination of factors that produce empowerment in different work environments, rather than to a specific empowerment factor. Also, it is known that the perception of empowerment could be a function of cultural beliefs, values, socio-political environment, etc. So, the choice of strategy for empowerment should be based on contingency and a dynamic application of models.

The implication of this scenario is that *Empowerment* models or practices may not be easily transferable from one culture or country to another. If *Empowerment* is deeply rooted in the values and social expectations of a people, which are culture specific, then the question is: Can there be a universal model of *Empowerment*? In view of this underlying question, this chapter will present some of the best strategies, without suggesting the superiority of one over the other.

Within the healthcare literature, especially in nursing research, there has been a huge emphasis on the role of the manager in promoting *Empowerment* by creating an empowering work environment for the staff (Faulkner & Laschinger, 2008; Feltner et al., 2008). Some of the practical ways through which nurse managers can achieve nurse empowerment include creating opportunities for skill variety, task identity and task significance, and the recognition of work outcomes through feedback (Lim et al., 2008), promoting inter- and intraprofessional collaboration (Faulkner & Laschinger, 2008) and using evidence-based practice to promote innovative behavior (Belden et al., 2012).

The role of healthcare managers in promoting *Empowerment* is obviously dependent on the type of managerial or leadership style (Kuokkanen et al., 2014; MacPhee et al., 2012). A *Transformational Leadership* style (for more information about *Transformational Leadership* and its relevance to healthcare organizations, see Fiery, Chapter 23 in this volume) has particularly been recognized as promoting nursing staff empowerment (Avolio et al., 2004). Closely related to management/leadership style is the quality of the leader-member relationship. The leader-member exchange theory has been widely used to examine how the type and quality of the relationship between the nurse leader and the nursing staff can affect nurses' perception of *Empowerment*. A study by Farr-Wharton et al. (2012) supports the view that "in-group" members who experience a strong positive relationship with their nurse manager would experience a higher level of empowerment than the "out-group" members, who have poor leader-member relationships. Laschinger et al. (2009) equally concluded that the quality of the unit-level leader-member exchange relationship positively influences staff nurses' feelings of psychological empowerment and organizational commitment.

PROPOSED MODEL OF EMPOWERMENT IN HEALTHCARE ORGANIZATIONS

There are four basic drivers of *Empowerment*: The healthcare manager, the healthcare practitioner, the internal environment of practice and the external environment.

Healthcare managers have the requisite skills, knowledge, influence, authority and resource control to champion *Empowerment*. Their leadership style and commitment to *Empowerment* principles are important determinants of *Empowerment* outcomes, and it is important that they create a practice environment that promotes *Empowerment*. The internal environment of healthcare practice is a product of management-staff interaction. Managers who adopt shared governance encourage shared decision-making that would create a conducive internal work environment. The external environment, which includes the social, cultural and political economy, influences the dynamics of healthcare, but ultimately, the responsibility to champion staff empowerment lies with management. The model in Figure 10.1 shows what the work outcomes of an empowering healthcare system could be.

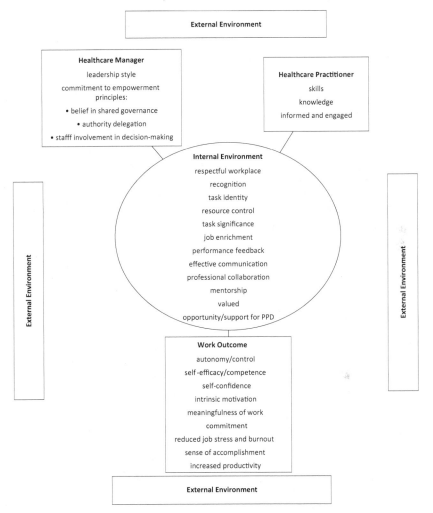

Figure 10.1   Collaborative Model of *Empowerment*

CONCLUSION

A substantial amount of research supports the notion that staff empowerment is crucial for achieving positive work outcomes, such as self-efficacy, competency, autonomy, job satisfaction and organizational commitment among healthcare workers. These work outcomes are mutually beneficial to the organization, healthcare practitioner, clients and their families, as well as the society at large. Empowering healthcare staff would create a healthy work environment and reinforce quality nurse-leader relationships. Armellino et al. (2010) pointed to this fact when they said,

> [F]eelings of empowerment augment access to individuals within the organization, assist with dissemination of information and enhance feelings of support to allow decision making, which affects processes of care, increases quality patient care and potentially improves patient outcomes. (p. 797)

We did not find any study that reported a negative work outcome of empowerment among nurses or other healthcare practitioners. However, in the 1990s, during the early period of industrial democracy and the struggle to dismantle the apparatus of the bureaucratic systems, some scholars viewed employee empowerment with pessimism. Kaler (1999) argued that:

> [E]mpowerment would seem to be a somewhat one-sided deal. Management gains from being partly relieved of its responsibilities while losing none of its power. Employees gain responsibilities while acquiring nothing by way of power within the organization . . . employees do more without getting anything from empowerment except the rather dubious privilege of having more to do. (p. 110)

Other studies have identified challenges to the practice of staff autonomy, which include a lack of resources and time and healthcare practitioners not being trained in *Empowerment* techniques (Corbally et al., 2007; Scambler et al., 2012).

Experts in organizational theory have called for caution in applying *Empowerment* models. There are a number of guiding principles that healthcare managers should consider when adopting employee empowerment. They include:

1) Recognition that staff autonomy comes with sense of responsibility and commitment to the organization. This will help to avoid misuse of the freedom and power to act;
2) Healthcare practitioners who desire autonomy should be cautious of the power they wield and be prepared to be independent, innovative risk takers;
3) Managers should not abdicate their responsibility to manage, and should maintain an oversight of the system through effective and open communication with the staff;
4) Managers should have a reasonable understanding of their staff and the conviction that staff members possess characteristics that support autonomy, such as self-regulation, a sense of responsibility and personal liability, organizational loyalty and commitment. (Psychogios et al., 2009, p. 448).

It is particularly difficult to prescribe specific work environments or conditions under which employee empowerment must be practiced. However, a growing volume of evidence suggests that a shared management system would be appropriate, as it is able to promote staff autonomy and place responsibility for professional practice in the hands of the healthcare workers. This practice should include a strong program that supports continuous professional development and skill improvement for the practitioners.

Although there has been a blossoming of empowerment research since the 1990s, we believe that "healthcare empowerment" will benefit from more cross-cultural and multi-country comparative studies that explore the aspects of empowerment that work in specific cultures, work contexts and possibly in specific populations. Empirical studies that utilize randomized controlled trial designs would provide high-level evidence on empowerment work outcomes that could guide healthcare organizations and managers.

SUMMARY

The evidence suggests that *Empowerment* has positive work outcomes for healthcare practice and is therefore an appropriate management model for healthcare organizations. A collaborative model of work empowerment is proposed. The principles of *Empowerment* are much the same for all workplaces, although the work environments may differ. Nurses and other healthcare practitioners possess specialized skills and high levels of competence in their areas of clinical practice. *Empowerment* would enable them to apply these special skills more effectively and efficiently.

REFERENCES

Ahmad, N., & Oranye, N.O. (2010). Empowerment, job satisfaction and organizational commitment: A comparative analysis of nurses working in Malaysia and England. *Journal of Nursing Management*, 18 (5), 582–591.

Aiken, L.H., Smith, A., & Lake, E.T. (1994). Lower medicare mortality among a set of hospitals known for good nursing care. *Medical Care*, 32 (8), 771–787.

Appelbaum, S.H., Hébert, D., & Leroux, S. (1999). Empowerment: Power, culture and leadership—A strategy or fad for the millennium? *Journal of Workplace Learning: Employee Counselling Today*, 11 (7), 233–254.

Armellino, D., Quinn Griffin, M.T., & Fitzpatrick, J.J. (2010). Structural empowerment and patient safety culture among registered nurses working in adult critical care units. *Journal of Nursing Management*, 18 (7), 796–803.

Avolio, B.J., Zhu1, W., Koh, W., & Bhatia, P. (2004). Transformational leadership and organizational commitment: Mediating role of psychological empowerment and moderating role of structural distance. *Journal of Organizational Behavior*, 25 (8), 951–968.

Baker, S.L., Fitzpatrick, J.J., & Griffin, M.Q. (2011). Empowerment and job satisfaction in associate degree nurse educators. *Nursing Education Perspectives*, 32 (4), 234–239.

Bandura, A. (1986). *Social Foundations of Thought and Action: A Social Cognitive View*. Englewood Cliffs, NJ: Prentice Hall.

Barden, A.M., Griffin, M.T.Q., Donahue, M., & Fitzpatrick, J.J. (2011). Shared governance and empowerment in registered nurses working in a hospital setting. *Nursing Administration Quarterly*, 35 (3), 212–218.

Belden, C.V., Leafman, J., Nehrenz, G., & Miller, P. (2012). The effect of evidence-based practice on workplace empowerment of rural registered nurses. *Journal of Rural Nursing and Health Care*, 12 (2), 64–76.

Bish, M., Kenny, A., & Nay, R. (2014). Perceptions of structural empowerment: Nurse leaders in rural health services. *Journal of Nursing Management*, 22 (1), 29–37.

Block, P. (1987). *The Empowered Manager*. San Francisco, CA: Jossey-Bass.

Bradbury-Jones, C., Sambrook, S., & Irvine, F. (2011). Empowerment and being valued: A phenomenological study of nursing students' experiences of clinical practice. *Nurse Education Today*, 31 (4), 368–372.

Brewer, C.S., Zayas, L.E., Kahn, L.S., & Sienkiewicz, M.J. (2006). Nursing recruitment and retention in New York State: A qualitative workforce needs assessment. *Policy, Politics, & Nursing Practice*, 7 (1), 54–63.

Chaudhuri, T., Yeatts, D.E., & Cready, C.M. (2013). Nurse aide decision making in nursing homes: factors affecting empowerment. *Journal of Clinical Nursing*, 22 (17–18), 2572–2585.

Conger, J.A., & Kanungo, R.N. (1988). The empowerment process: Integrating theory and practice. *Academy of Management Review*, 13 (3), 471–482.

Corbally, M.A., Scott, P.A., Matthews, A., Gabhann, L.M., & Murphy, C. (2007). Irish nurses' and midwives' understanding and experiences of empowerment. *Journal of Nursing Management*, 15 (2), 169–179.

Deci, E. (1975). *Intrinsic Motivation*. New York: Plenum Press.

DeVivo, D., Griffin, M.T.Q., Donahue, M., Fitzpatrick, J.J., Commack, N.Y., Cleveland, O.H., & Danbury, C.T. (2013). Perceptions of empowerment among ED nurses. *Journal of Emergency Nursing*, 39 (6), 529–533.

Dimitriades, S.Z. (2001). Employee in total quality: Designing and implementing effective employee decision-making strategies. *Quality Management Journal*, 8 (2), 19–28.

Eo, Y., Kim, Y., & Lee, N. (2014). Path analysis of empowerment and work effectiveness among staff nurses. *Asian Nursing Research*, 8 (1), 42–48.

Farr-Wharton, R., Brunetto, Y., & Shacklock, K. (2012). The impact of intuition and supervisor—nurse relationships on empowerment and affective commitment by generation. *Journal of Advanced Nursing*, 68 (6), 1391–1401.

Faulkner, J., & Laschinger, H. (2008). The effects of structural and psychological empowerment on perceived respect in acute care nurses. *Journal of Nursing Management*, 16 (2), 214–221.

Feltner, A., Mitchell, B., Norris, E., & Wolfle, C. (2008). Nurses views on the characteristics of an effective leader. *AORN Journal (Association of periOperative Registered Nurses)*, 87 (2), 363–372.

Fitzpatrick, J.J., Campo, T.M., Graham, G., & Lavandero, R. (2010). Certification, empowerment, and intent to leave current position and the profession among critical care nurses. *American Association of Critical Care*, 19 (3), 218–229.

Gibson, C.H. (1991). A concept analysis of empowerment. *Journal of Advanced Nursing*, 16 (3), 354–361.

Hackman, J.R., & Oldham, G.R. (1980). *Work Redesign*. Reading, MA: Addison-Wesley.

Hess, R.G., Jr. (2004). From bedside to boardroom—Nursing shared governance. *Online Journal of Issues in Nursing*, 9 (1). Retrieved from http://web.a.ebscohost.com.proxy2.lib.umanitoba.ca/ehost/ (accessed 10 March 2015).

Hokanson Hawks, J. (1992). Empowerment in nursing education: Concept analysis and application to philosophy, learning and instruction. *Journal of Advanced Nursing*, **17** (5), 609–618.

Huddleston, P. (2014). Healthy work environment framework within an acute care setting. *Journal of Theory Construction & Testing*, **18** (2), 50–54.

Jenkins, S., & Delbridge, R. (2013). Context matters: Examining "soft" and "hard" approaches to employee engagement in two workplaces. *The International Journal of Human Resource Management*, **24** (14), 2670–2691.

Johnson, M.O. (2011). The shifting landscape of health care: Toward a model of health care empowerment. *American Journal of Public Health*, **101** (2), 265–270.

Kaler, J. (1999). Does empowerment empower? In J.J. Quinn & P.W.F. Davies (Eds.), *Ethics and Empowerment*. London: Macmillan, pp. 90–114.

Kanter, R.M. (1977). *Men and Women of the Corporation*. New York: Basic Books.

Kanter, R.M. (1983). *The Change Masters: Innovations for Productivity in the American Corporation*. New York: Simon Schuster.

Khammarnia, M., Ravangard, R., & Asadi, H. (2014). The relationship of psychological empowerment and readiness for organizational changes in health workers, Lorestan, Iran. *Journal of Pakistan Medical Association*, **64** (5), 537–541.

Knol, J., & Van Linge, R. (2009). Innovative behavior: The effect of structural and psychological empowerment on nurses. *Journal of Advanced Nursing*, **65** (2), 359–370.

Koberg, C.S., Boss, R.W., Senjem, J.C., & Goodman, E.A. (1999). Antecedents and outcomes of empowerment. *Group and Organisation Management*, **24** (1), 71–91.

Kuokkanen, L., Leino-Kilpi, H., Katajisto, J., Heponiemi, T., Sinervo, T., & Elovainio, M. (2014). Does organizational justice predict empowerment? Nurses assess their work environment. *Journal of Nursing Scholarship*, **46** (5), 349–356.

Laschinger, H.K.S., Finegan, J., Shamian, J., & Wilk, P. (2001). Impact of structural and psychological empowerment on job strain in nursing work settings. *Journal of Nursing Administration*, **31** (5), 260–272.

Laschinger, H.K.S., Finegan, J., & Wilk, P. (2009). Context matters: The impact of unit leadership and empowerment on nurses' organizational commitment. *Journal of Nursing Administration*, **39** (5), 228–235.

Laschinger, H.K.S., Gilbert, S., Smith, L.M. & Leslie, K. (2010). Towards a comprehensive theory of nurse/patient empowerment: Applying Kanter's empowerment theory to patient care. *Journal of Nursing Management*, **18** (1), 4–13.

Lim, J.Y., Kim, M.S., & Kim, Y.H. (2008). The effects of job characteristics on the nursing organizational effectiveness. *Journal of Korean Academy Nursing Administration*, **14** (2), 107–117.

Macphee, M., Skelton-Green, J., Bouthillette, F., & Suryaprakash, N. (2012). An empowerment framework for nursing leadership development: Supporting evidence. *Journal of Advanced Nursing*, **68** (1), 159–169.

Manojlovich, M. (2007). Power and empowerment in nursing: Looking backward to inform the future. *The Online Journal of Issues in Nursing*, **12** (1). Retrieved from http://www.nursingworld.org/MainMenuCategories/ANAMarketplace/ANAPeriodicals/OJIN/TableofContents/Volume122007/No1Jan07/Looking-BackwardtoInformtheFuture.html (accessed 31 May 2015).

Manojlovich, M., & DeCicco, B. (2007). Healthy work environments, nurse-physician communication, and patients' outcomes. *American Journal of Critical Care*, **16** (9), 536–543.

McCarthy, V., & Freeman, L.H. (2008). A multidisciplinary concept analysis of empowerment: Implications for nursing. *Journal of Theory Construction & Testing*, **12** (2), 68–74.

McClelland, D.C. (1975). *Power: The Inner Experience*. New York: Irvington Press.

Menon, S. (2001). Employee empowerment: An integrative psychological approach. *International Association for Applied Psychology*, **50** (1), 153–180.

Pfeffer, J. (1981). *Power in Organizations*. Marshfield, MA: Pitman.

Piazza, I.M, Donahue, M., Dykes, P., Quinn Griffin, M., & Fitzpatrick, J.J. (2006). Differences in perceptions of empowerment among nationally certified and non-certified nurses. *Journal of Nursing Administration*, 36 (5), 277–283.

Psychogios, A.G., Wilkinson, A., & Szamosi, L.T. (2009). Getting to the heart of the debate: TQM and middle manager autonomy. *Total Quality Management & Business Excellence*, 20 (4), 445–466.

Rao, A. (2012). The contemporary construction of nurse empowerment. *Journal of Nursing Scholarship*, 44 (4), 396–402.

Scambler, S., Newton, P., Sinclair, A.J., & Asimakopoulou, K. (2012). Barriers and opportunities of empowerment as applied in diabetes settings: A focus on health care professionals' experiences. *Diabetes Research and Clinical Practice*, 97 (1), e18–e22.

Schmalenberg, C., & Kramer, M. (2008). Essentials of a productive nurse environment. *Nursing Research*, 57 (1), 2–13.

Shanta, L.L., & Eliason, A.R.M. (2014). Application of an empowerment model to improve civility in nursing education. *Nurse Education in Practice*, 14 (1), 82–86.

Shipper, F., & Manz, C.C. (1992). Employee self-management without formally designated teams: An alternative road to empowerment. *Organizational Dynamics*, 4 (3), 48–61.

Spreitzer, G.M. (1995). Psychological empowerment in the workplace: Dimensions, measurement, and validation. *Academy of Management Journal*, 38 (5), 1442–1465.

Spreitzer, G.M. (1996). Social structural characteristics of psychological empowerment. *Academy of Management Journal*, 39 (2), 483–504.

Suominen, T., Savikko, N., Puukka, P., Irvine Doran, D., & Leino-Kilpi, H. (2005). Work empowerment as experienced by head nurses. *Journal of Nursing Management*, 13 (2), 147–153.

Thomas, K.W., & Velthouse, B.A. (1990). Cognitive elements of empowerment: An "interpretive" model of intrinsic task motivation. *Academy of Management Review*, 15 (4), 666–681.

Trus, M., Razbadauskas, A., Doran, D., & Suominen, T. (2012). Work-related empowerment of nurse managers: A systematic review. *Nursing and Health Sciences*, 14 (3), 412–420.

Wang, X., Kunaviktikul, W., & Wichaikhum, O. (2013). Work empowerment and burnout among registered nurses in two tertiary general hospitals. *Journal of Clinical Nursing*, 22 (19–20), 2896–2903.

Wooten, L.P., & Carne, P. (2003). Nurses as implementers of organizational culture. *Nursing Economics*, 21 (6), 275–279.

11 Kaizen in Healthcare Organizations

Mark Graban

In too many workplaces, people are asked to "check their brains in at the door", meaning that they should just do their jobs without speaking up, complaining or suggesting new ways of doing things. There is a long-standing bias in business that people who are higher up in the chain of command, or those of a higher educational or social standing, should do most of the thinking, including determining how work is done, while the people doing the work should just do their jobs as specified by others.

This dynamic was common in the author's experience in the manufacturing sector, with the exception being companies that followed a new approach with roots in the work of Dr. W. Edwards Deming and the example set by Toyota and other organizations that practice *Lean* or the *Toyota Production System*. In this approach, employees are expected to be fully engaged in the design of work and the improvement of work. People are encouraged to seek "pride" and "joy" in their work, seeking higher levels of fulfillment than just a paycheck, as they are invited to be creative and to have a full voice in how to improve the workplace and best meet customer needs.

The author has observed similar opportunities in healthcare organizations. Highly educated healthcare professionals, such as nurses and laboratory medical technologists, report that they are expected to "not make waves" and that speaking up about problems and opportunities for improvement gets them labeled as "troublemakers" or worse. Hospitals, as did factories, have an opportunity to also fully engage the intelligence and creativity of every participant in the healthcare organization. Many organizations are doing this through the practice of a method and philosophy called *Kaizen*.

WHAT IS KAIZEN?

Masaaki Imai (1986), author of the seminal book *Kaizen*, defines *Kaizen* as "continuous improvement by everybody, every day, everywhere" (p. 3).

Donald Berwick (1989), a pre-eminent voice in the global healthcare quality and patient safety movements, published an article in the *New England Journal of Medicine* entitled, "Continuous Improvement as an Ideal in Health Care". He defined *Kaizen* as "the continuous search for opportunities for all processes to get better". Berwick wrote that continuous improvement "holds some badly needed answers for American health care" (p. 1424).

Kaizen is a Japanese word that means "good change" and can also be translated as "change for the better" (Kato & Smalley, 2011, p. 102). The *Kaizen* approach provides an approach that can help address our healthcare challenges, not just in the USA, but also around the world. These challenges include a shocking number of preventable errors resulting in harm to patients, increasing costs (Institute of Medicine (IOM), 2012), long wait times (Siciliani et al., 2014) and unhappy medical professionals (Lu et al., 2012). *Kaizen*, as practiced by a growing number of health systems, is not just the search for opportunities: It's a method and a mindset that implements improvements in a structured, but non-bureaucratic way.

When Imai introduced the term *Kaizen* to the West in the 1980s, it was in the context of what was described at the time as "just-in-time manufacturing" or "Japanese management practices". Automakers and manufacturers were scurrying to copy Japanese manufacturers, namely Toyota, in an attempt to close large gaps in quality and cost. Driven by the increasingly global competition in the 1970s and 80s, manufacturers around the world have adopted practices and mindsets from the *Toyota Production System* and what we would now call *Lean Management* or *Lean Thinking*. The first American healthcare organizations started adopting *Lean* methods in the late 1990s, and it started becoming more widely adopted around 2005.

As a relatively early adopter of *Kaizen* methods in healthcare, Greg Jacobson and others (2009) at Vanderbilt University Medical Center summarized Imai's key *Kaizen* principles, which include:

1) Continually improve;
2) No idea is too small;
3) Focus change on common sense, low-cost and low-risk improvements, not major innovations;
4) Collect, verify and analyze data to enact change;
5) Empower the worker to enact change;
6) All ideas are addressed and responded to in some way. (p. 1341)

The employees at Franciscan St. Francis Health, a three-hospital system in Indianapolis, Indiana, have implemented and documented almost 25,000 improvements since 2007. In a given year, approximately 40 percent of their employees participate (and, in some departments, it is nearly 100 percent). These *Kaizen* improvements have generated millions of dollars in hard cost savings (Graban & Swartz, 2012, p. 25). But, more importantly, the *Kaizen* method has engaged healthcare professionals and managers in a process that:

1) Improves patient and staff satisfaction levels;
2) Reduces safety risks to patients and staff;
3) Improves quality;
4) Reduces wait times;
5) Creates a better experience for patients and their families;
6) Creates a better workplace for healthcare professionals.

The *Kaizen* method has been a major part of Franciscan's *Lean Six Sigma* program, as *Kaizen* is one of the two main pillars of the "Toyota Way" management system (Liker, 2004, p. xi). While *Kaizen* is associated strongly with Toyota and manufacturing companies, its principles and methods fit very well into healthcare. ThedaCare, a health system in Wisconsin, also aims to engage every employee in a process they call "continuous daily improvement", implementing 20,000 improvements in the year 2012 alone as part of their *Lean* improvement and management system (John Toussaint, personal communication, 2013). Compared to manufacturing, *Kaizen* might be easier to embrace in healthcare because of the intrinsic motivation that clinicians and other staff have, along with their very strong sense of mission and purpose.

Franciscan, ThedaCare and organizations like them are still the exception rather than the norm in healthcare. Too many organizations still have environments where staff members are not encouraged to speak up, or where they are actively discouraged from doing so. Low employee engagement scores and high turnover rates are a symptom of dysfunctional cultures that get in the way of improvement. The Institute of Medicine (2012) declared that patients would be "better served by a more nimble health care system that is consistently reliable and that constantly, systematically, and seamlessly improves". The IOM (2012) endorsed methods such as *Lean* as a way to create "continuously learning" and continuously improving organizations.

Let's say an organization decides that it's time to engage its employees and physicians in continuous improvement. It is easy for an organization to list "creating a culture of continuous improvement" as a goal on its website or in its mission statements (Graban, 2014). It seems that most healthcare organizations say they want a culture of continuous improvement, or that they already have one, but first-hand evidence often proves otherwise. The author has met nurses, medical technologists and other healthcare professionals who have said things like, "They don't listen to our ideas... they just want us to do our jobs and not make waves".

Many healthcare organizations would say they are "implementing *Lean*", but they rely heavily on weeklong *Rapid Improvement Events* (or

Kaizen Events) that could be considered episodic improvement, not continuous. Most healthcare organizations, even before adopting *Lean*, take on large-scale improvements, such as implementing a new electronic medical records system. These complex improvements could be referred to as "strategic *Kaizen*". Some organizations, like ThedaCare and Virginia Mason Medical Center in Seattle, effectively combine large-scale *Kaizen* and formal team-based events with ongoing continuous improvement efforts.

There are many problems, large and small, to be solved in healthcare. Berwick's (1989) assessment and the IOM's (2012) recommendations are still correct: Healthcare needs to do more to engage everybody in a culture of continuous improvement. These methods can work and the concepts seem simple, but they are not guaranteed to work in a healthcare organization where leadership is lacking and the culture is not changed to allow people to speak up and take action to solve the thousands of small opportunities for improvement that exist in every hospital. In the author's experience, many healthcare organizations have said that they "tried to implement *Kaizen*", but it "didn't work". As with any failed initiative or program, it might be more likely true that management did not know how to change or how to utilize the methods, more so than saying a method failed.

WHY WERE SUGGESTION BOXES INEFFECTIVE?

Some organizations have hoped that the traditional suggestion box systems would lead to a culture of continuous improvement. The author has yet to see a healthcare organization where that is actually the case. When visiting hospitals or giving talks at conferences, I often ask people if their suggestion box has been effective. People shake their heads "no" and people rarely defend or celebrate their suggestion box. So, we need to improve the way we improve.

Suggestion boxes are well intended, but the physical nature of the box, along with the managerial mindsets that accompany the box, have some fatal flaws that doom the suggestion box to gather dust. These include:

1) Suggestion boxes are opaque and locked, preventing any visibility or collaboration;
2) Employees are encouraged to submit "suggestions" that do not first identify a problem or opportunity for improvement;
3) Employees usually expect a manager or others to evaluate and implement their idea, instead of maintaining ownership and participation;
4) The box is opened rarely, usually only for a monthly or even quarterly review meeting;
5) Suggestions are evaluated by a committee and are merely accepted or rejected without any discussion with the employees who submitted them;

6) A very low percentage of suggestions, usually one to three percent, are accepted;
7) Employees and management argue with each other over who gets credit for a suggestion and who gets any promised incentive payments or rewards.

With or without a suggestion box, many managers and senior leaders fall into a trap of thinking that they have to be the ones who come up with the solutions to every problem. Sometimes, leaders don't trust their employees to have good ideas, but other times, the leaders just think it isn't their employees' job to have ideas or to implement them. With an effective *Kaizen* approach, that all changes for the better.

A healthcare organization could engage any number of methodologies, such as *Total Quality Management* (for more information about *Total Quality Management* and its relevance to healthcare organizations, see Mosadeghrad and Ferlie, Chapter 22 in this volume), *Six Sigma* (for more information about *Six Sigma* and its relevance to healthcare organizations, see Krive, Chapter 19 in this volume), or *Lean* (for more information about *Lean Healthcare* and its relevance to healthcare organizations, see Poksinska, Chapter 13 in this volume) and *Rapid Improvement Events*. Many of these approaches have, unfortunately, been focused on experts or a small number of people dictating changes to the rest of the organization. It's easy for leaders to label employees as being "resistant to change" when the problem is leaders not engaging employees in developing changes and improvements from the start. The *Kaizen* framework provides a more effective method—if leaders believe that employee ideas can be worthwhile and if leaders put in the effort to engage people consistently over time.

A FIVE-STEP KAIZEN METHOD

At Franciscan, and at many other healthcare organizations, *Kaizen* is a practical five-step process that is followed by employees and managers (Graban & Swartz, 2012). These five steps are:

1) *Find* problems, opportunities, or ideas;
2) *Discuss* these with colleagues and/or a manager;
3) *Implement* the idea and evaluate its effectiveness;
4) *Document* the *Kaizen*;
5) *Share* the *Kaizen* with others. (p. 100)

The rest of this chapter will cover these steps in more detail and will also explain common pitfalls or challenges.

Find and Discuss

While we utilize a five-step *Kaizen* process, the first two steps are very intertwined—finding and discussing *Kaizen* opportunities. Unlike a suggestion box system, where ideas might sit for weeks or months before being addressed, *Kaizen* ideas are discussed within days and often get implemented immediately.

Again, the first step in the *Kaizen* process is to encourage staff to find problems and opportunities for improvement. Problems could be anything that isn't working well and opportunities could be anything that could be better than it is today. Healthcare professionals can usually tell you what needs to be improved, but they often don't speak up. Managers play a key role in asking staff to participate in the *Kaizen* process on a regular basis.

Leaders can keep things simple and start by asking employees questions such as:

1) What bothers you or frustrates you at work?
2) What interferes with providing the best patient care?
3) What opportunities do you see?
4) What do patients or their families complain about?

In some organizations, employees might be afraid of speaking up due to a lack of trust in their leaders or a fear of being blamed for the problems and opportunities that are discussed. While the *Kaizen* method, in the author's experience, can work in large academic medical centers, community hospitals and small, critical access hospitals, *Kaizen* would likely not be effective in an environment that does not have a minimal level of trust and collaboration. Rather than blaming employees for being fearful, leaders should focus on building trust and creating an environment that makes it safe to speak up.

It's critically important that leaders emphasize small ideas, especially at first. Many healthcare professionals are accustomed to being asked for big ideas that might result in major cost savings. Big ideas are scary, time consuming and risky, which means big ideas usually don't get implemented. So, employees and leaders get discouraged and stop talking about improvement. When we start with small ideas and small problems, often the smallest problems possible, it's faster, easier and less risky to test new process changes.

Solving small problems with small ideas helps staff build confidence in their improvement capabilities. It also helps leaders become more comfortable with their employees solving problems on their own or with minimal input from leaders. It's better to "get the ball rolling" with small ideas, as experience in multiple healthcare organizations shows that staff eventually start identifying and solving larger problems over time, but only if they get started at all.

Kaizen Cards and Boards

When a staff member identifies a problem or has an idea, it is very helpful to immediately write it down on a *"Kaizen* card", which generally contains the following information:

1) Problem or opportunity;
2) Idea;
3) Date;
4) Originator's name;
5) Expected benefits of the idea;
6) Who do we need to get input from?

Or, some organizations will have staff enter that same information into a web-based software system.

It should become a new daily routine to ask employees about problems they have faced or ideas they might have. This can take place at team huddles, in the hallway or during any moment during the day. If a leader or co-worker sees an employee struggling with something or sees a frustrated look on their face, they are likely observing a *Kaizen* opportunity. If an employee complains to them in the hallway, a good practice is for the leader to immediately hand the employee a *Kaizen* card and to ask them, with an appreciative smile, to fill it out to the best of their ability. Unlike a suggestion box, filling out the card is the first step in that person's involvement, not the last.

Ideally, an employee would fill out as much of the front side of the card as possible. Leaders should encourage people, through verbal coaching and other forms of feedback, to not just write down an idea; they should also write down a problem. One reason old suggestion box systems failed is that employees were encouraged just to write down their suggestion. Weeks or months later, a distant committee or group of managers would look at the suggestion and either accept it or reject it. Often, an initial suggestion or idea might not be practical for some reason. So, in a *Kaizen* process, it's the responsibility of the manager to collaborate with the employee to find a different idea that does solve the identified problem.

Examples of problems that might be written down on the cards include:

1) Patients ask for ginger ale when they are nauseous and it's not available on this floor;
2) Hand sanitizer dispensers are empty too often;
3) Have to climb on hands and knees under desk to plug in rolling computers;
4) Mothers do not have privacy in NICU bays for nursing;
5) Patients get lost trying to find the chemotherapy department;
6) Spend too much time searching for the clinic's thermometer.

Sometimes, managers say, "Don't bring me problems, bring me solutions". In a *Kaizen* culture, we want employees to point out problems. In fact, we'll celebrate it. Leaders should thank employees for speaking up and making a problem visible to the manager and team. If a manager sees a card that only has an idea written down, the first question should be, "How do you think we could solve that problem?"

An employee might bring the card to the manager for some initial discussion, or they might present the card at a daily team huddle. Eventually, team members might discuss an idea amongst themselves before bringing the card to a manager. Either way, instead of hiding the card in a locked suggestion box, we put the card on a board, as shown in Figure 11.1—maintaining visibility and transparency in the ideas and the process (Graban & Swartz, 2013, p. 90).

In some organizations, web-based databases or software systems are used to submit ideas, providing digital visibility. This can be especially helpful for organizations that want to share ideas across distributed teams, different departments or different physical locations.

In using the *Kaizen* board, an employee might find an opportunity, discuss it with their team or supervisor and then put it on the board under the "Idea" header (which sometimes might say "New Ideas"). Or, an employee might first put the idea on the board, where the card sits until a team huddle

Figure 11.1 Board for Identifying and Tracking Problems and Improvements (image source and copyright: Mark Graban)

or a moment when a manager sees the card and finds the employee to discuss it. The card should be discussed and evaluated as soon as possible, ideally within a day or two.

Some problems have obvious solutions that are easy to test, such as asking dietary services to start bringing ginger ale to the unit. In those cases, we would move quickly to implement and test the idea. Other problems require more discussion and analysis. But not every problem requires a root cause analysis. Leaders help their team strike the right balance in not rushing to solutions but, likewise, not overanalyzing each *Kaizen* opportunity.

Coaching Kaizen

As part of a collaborative improvement process, it's important that leaders not react negatively to something they think is a bad idea. Managers should avoid saying negative things like:

1) That's not what I would do;
2) That will never work;
3) That's not an important problem to solve.

As author Norman Bodek says (personal communication, 2008), we should treat each idea, even a so-called bad idea, "like a gift". Leaders should honor the person who proposed the bad idea by thanking them for pointing out the problem or opportunity. Even if the idea seems impractical or too costly, the manager should thank the person for speaking up, especially if doing so might have been seen as risky in the old, pre-*Kaizen* culture. Instead of just rejecting an idea, leaders have an obligation to work together with employees to improve the idea as a way of more effectively solving the problem. If people are jumping to solutions, we have an obligation to help them to be better problem solvers.

If an employee suggests building a new parking garage, leaders should ask why. What is the underlying problem? If employees say they often get wet when it rains unexpectedly and they have to walk to their car at the end of the day, a leader could ask what other ideas they have that might be easier and less expensive to implement. An employee might suggest a way of signing out umbrellas from the front desk and returning them the next day. That's a more creative and clever way to keep dry for the trip home.

If the employee has written an idea on a card, such as, "Add a second blanket warmer to the unit", the manager might ask the employee to write down a problem statement. Managers should ask questions in a constructive way, in the spirit of helping the employee find something to implement that solves the underlying problem. They should not be negative or overly critical. The manager might ask, "Why do you want a second blanket warmer?" to which the employee might reply, "Because ours is empty far too often and we have to go searching for blankets, which wastes our time and delays bringing warmth to the patient". Before rushing to get a second blanket warmer, which would take up space and have some cost, the manager and employee or a group of employees might want to further discuss the problem.

"Why are the blanket warmers empty? Would adding a second blanket warmer mean that we now have two empty blanket warmers?" Those are questions a manager might ask. The manager might ask the employee to go research the issue further, looking into how many blankets are used on a daily basis and what is the process for replenishing them. The blanket restocking process might be too slow or happen too infrequently. Or, it's possible that nurses and assistants are using blankets unnecessarily or in inappropriate ways (as a workaround to some other problem, perhaps). In this collaboration and discussion, everybody is focused on solving the problem and making sure warm blankets are always available when needed. The goal is not to prove or disprove the initially proposed solution of the second blanket warmer—the goal is to solve the problem and to meet the needs of the patients.

Once the *Kaizen* cards have been initially discussed, they get moved to the "To Do" column. Note there are no columns for "approved" and "rejected". People in a *Kaizen* culture implement roughly 90 percent of their ideas, or at least they eventually find something that helps to solve the problem they have identified. Having a "To Do" column shows our bias for action and our bias for approving ideas as often as possible, or adjusting the idea until it is one that seems like will likely work.

What Are the Challenges Related to Finding and Discussing Kaizen Opportunities?

It might seem simple for leaders to encourage their employees to point out problems and to suggest improvements in processes and daily work. However, there are many challenges, all of which can be overcome with persistence and the right leadership behaviors.

In many existing healthcare cultures, staff members are afraid to speak up. This often happens because the organization has encouraged them, explicitly or more subtly, to keep quiet or not make waves. One nurse I worked with at a hospital said that she had been reviewed negatively in her personnel file as "creating a negative work environment" for speaking up, identifying problems and proposing solutions.

By comparison, Toyota leaders say, "Problems are treasure", meaning they are to be valued rather than hidden (Liker, 2013). If we don't identify problems, we can't improve. Managers need to encourage people to step forward, even if they would have normally been perceived as just merely complaining. A complaint often leads to the development of an improvement idea that can solve or alleviate the problem. When people point out problems, leaders need to thank them instead of being upset or labeling the employees as being negative. Changing this culture won't happen overnight, but it's important for managers and leaders to behave differently in this *Kaizen* process and culture.

The most frequently raised concern is leaders saying they don't have time to even talk with employees about *Kaizen*, yet alone implement anything. Employees often don't have time or they are not allowed to take advantage of "free time" to identify and discuss problems. Instead of letting "lack of time" be an excuse, it is often the first problem we need to solve. Is it true that we do not have the time, or do we choose not to make the time?

How do we create time for *Kaizen*? When patient volume or census is low, hospitals can choose to let staff work on *Kaizen* instead of sending them home early. The hospital knows how much money they "save" by sending people home early, but it's much more difficult to estimate how much money they lose over time because improvements are not being made on a daily and weekly basis. Success with *Kaizen* is primarily based upon how much time leaders spend working on *Kaizen*. Just hanging a board and expecting to *Kaizen* to magically happen is not a realistic strategy.

Many leaders have discovered that creating a *Kaizen* culture in their department actually frees up some of their time. Ronda Freije, a pharmacy director at Franciscan St. Francis Health says,

> If you would have told me that when I began the Kaizen process that I would have more free time, I would have not believed that. I can say that my team is very self-sufficient now taking care of issues. I can focus more on the future, on where we need to be and work on the bigger issues in the department and strategically plan versus working on those day-to-day fires that were coming up.
>
> (Personal communication, 2014)

Even with education about *Kaizen* and examples of success from other healthcare organizations, some leaders are tentative or afraid to get started with this approach to improvement because they think they might not do it well. In the spirit of the *Plan-Do-Study-Adjust (PDSA)* cycle, it is helpful to spend some time planning for a *Kaizen* process, which can include reading books or articles or taking classes and workshops. But, at some point, the only way to start creating a culture of continuous improvement is to start. Mistakes will be made along the way, and no manager (or staff member) should be expected to be perfect. As we start to practice *Kaizen*, we can study and adjust, as needed. If the wrong thing is said in a team huddle, such as "that will never work", leaders can acknowledge the bad behavior, pledge to do better, and move on. We can continuously improve the way we continuously improve.

The barriers to *Kaizen* are not insurmountable, but *Kaizen* programs often fade, with participation among staff and managers falling to zero. In the author's experience, some *Kaizen* programs have been formally canceled, with boards and other artifacts being removed from the workplace. In other instances, it is a de facto decision where it is apparent that new ideas are not being submitted and ideas are not being implemented. In these situations, it is most often a lack of manager or supervisor participation that leads to the death of a *Kaizen* program rather than a lack of ideas from the staff.

Implement

In the *Kaizen* process, we are, of course, not happy with just collecting ideas about how our healthcare organization can perform better. We have to actually implement those ideas. More accurately, we test those ideas to see if they actually lead to improvement.

As *Kaizen* cards reach the "To Do" column, there is usually an individual assigned to "own" the card and its progress. That ownership means, of course, involving others in the further discussion and testing of the idea. *Kaizen* is rarely an individual effort, as all but the smallest changes will affect other staff. As mentioned earlier, *Kaizen* is not a process where a supervisor or manager owns all of the ideas, makes all of the decisions or does all of the work. More often than not, *Kaizen* cards are assigned back to the person who had the idea—as who is more motivated to see the idea through and to solve the problem?

Nurses in the endoscopy unit at Franciscan St. Francis say, happily, that the culture in their department expects and encourages "staff input into everything". The nurses are happy that leaders ask them to think about what they can "do to make our job easier and quicker" or better for the patients. Better yet, they report that their manager "allows us to implement things". As they explain, "You can submit *Kaizen* ideas [all day long], but if your managers don't allow you to implement it and see if it will work, then there's no point in it. But she allows us to do that" (Rhonda Roseman and Julie Pickett, personal communication, 2014).

When we share the workload for improvement, we're able to test and implement more ideas than if a single person has that responsibility. When we spread out the work, we don't need to spend as much time prioritizing which improvements we work on next. On any given week, a department with a *Kaizen* culture will be testing and evaluating many changes at the same time. This requires a lot of communication, both in team huddles and on an ad hoc basis.

A key *Kaizen* principle is that we utilize small tests of change as part of the *PDSA* cycle. If there is a proposed change, for example, about the way discharge instructions are communicated to patients (including confirming that the patient has understood them), it would be risky for every nurse to try the new method all at once. Small tests of change minimize the risk that we might incur when a proposed change turns out to not really be an improvement. We can learn from small tests of change and use those lessons to adjust the idea. Or, we might abandon the original idea, leading us to then try something else that might solve the identified problem. If the new process turns out to be better, we can then teach it to others and make it the new standardized practice (until we improve again!).

Before *Kaizen* cards are moved from "To Do" to "Doing" status, we need to make sure that there has been the right amount of "Plan" before we "Do" in *PDSA*. There are some changes that are easy to test, introduce no risk and can be changed back easily. These *Kaizens* should be tested as soon as possible. For example, if a team wants to move the location of a phone on a nurses station desk, we should have a bias for action. We can move the phone and let team members evaluate if it's better. If it's not better, what's the worst that can happen? We can move the phone back, thereby studying and adjusting.

There are other changes that might be riskier, more expensive or more difficult to undo. For example, if a nurse proposes knocking down a wall on the side of the nurses station, the team probably needs to spend more time discussing and planning the change. Leaders might ask not only what the cost would be for the demolition, but also what the expected benefits would be. Would there be any side effects caused by taking down the wall? The last thing we want to do is to rush into knocking down a wall to then, two days later, coming back to senior management and the facilities department, asking for a new wall to be put back up. A way of testing the change before actually knocking down the wall might be to create some paper or cardboard models or simulations, showing staff walking patterns and how things would work after the wall was taken down.

At Franciscan St. Francis, leaders celebrated a time when they implemented a change and realized that in practice, it wasn't really an improvement. The facilities department had been installing hands-free paper towel dispensers throughout the hospital as an infection control measure, something generally seen as an improvement that was worth the expense. However, in the NICU, the new paper towel dispenser created a new problem. It was much noisier than the old dispenser and the babies who slept nearby were often awakened by it, which affects their ability to develop and go home healthy. Shown the effect of the dispenser, the hospital quickly agreed to change back to the old dispensers. They planned, they did, they studied and they adjusted (by removing the dispenser). The hospital used this example to demonstrate that no change should be considered fully implemented unless it has been proven to be beneficial. Being willing to change back helps others accept changes they are uncertain about.

As in other cases, this is the type of change that requires us to get input from the entire team (and possibly from other departments) before we take action. There are other times where we can make the change, and then inform everybody after the fact (leaving open, of course, the possibility that we make additional tweaks or go back to the old process).

As we implement ideas, managers are very often evaluating tradeoffs in different ways. Managers might ask, "When do I delegate the improvement to an employee and when do I need to help?" or "When do we Plan and discuss more and when do we go ahead and Do?" Leaders get better at finding this balance over time through practice and reflection.

The role of leaders changes in a *Kaizen* culture. Leaders no longer get to make all of the decisions, but they also don't have the entire burden on their shoulders, either. At the same time, leaders don't dump responsibility on employees without remaining involved in a collaborative way. A manager might challenge an employee to take on the implementation of an idea, showing trust in them and giving them space, while also making it clear that the employee can come to them for help, if needed.

As we are implementing our changes, different steps can be listed on the back of the *Kaizen* card. Some *Kaizens* are a "just do it" with a single step ("move the phone"), while more complex problems may require multiple steps, such as phone calls, data collection, discussion and small tests. After our initial test, the team, along with the manager, will evaluate the impact of the *Kaizen*. Did things really improve? If so, how? What did we learn along the way? The final question might be to ask if our policies and procedures need to be updated to reflect our *Kaizen*.

What Are the Challenges Related to Finding and Discussing Kaizen Opportunities?

Some organizations find it's easier to generate ideas than it is to test, implement and evaluate them. It might be a bit risky, at first, to point out problems or to volunteer ideas for improvement. There is a fear of being questioned or even mocked. The risk might seem even higher when it comes to taking action in the early stages of creating a *Kaizen* culture.

Many organizations have a strong fear of failure, which makes people cautious about taking action unless there is complete 100% certainty that a change will actually be an improvement. Of course, we hardly ever have situations with such certainty. Organizations that have a culture of continuous improvement often say that they've made it acceptable to fail, albeit it in small ways. Let's say we have a small test of change, adding a second blanket warmer, but it doesn't solve the problem (the missing blankets).

In a *Kaizen* culture, leaders won't make anybody feel bad for their best efforts and especially won't punish somebody for a small "failure". We can view the poor result, or unexpected result, as a learning opportunity. It's nobody's fault if the bad outcome wasn't anticipated during the team's discussion of an idea. If we punish people for bad outcomes, they are unlikely to try to improve again in the future.

Another concern that is raised about both larger *Kaizen Events* and smaller *Kaizen* improvements is sustainability. When we have implemented a change, do we still see that new process being followed a week, a month or a year later? If so, we have sustained the improvement. Better yet, has the team continued improving rather than just sustaining a static change? In my experience, staff members will more readily accept and adopt a change that is truly beneficial to them or their patients (or both). When a change isn't really an improvement, perhaps it shouldn't be forcibly sustained. We should go back and try something new in an attempt to solve the problem.

What's sometimes described as "lack of sustainment" is oftentimes a "lack of adoption", where team members did not embrace or adopt the change to begin with. Causes of this can include poor communication or poor training on the new process. If we see sustainment challenges, as with anything, we should ask why they are occurring and try to solve the problem.

One final concern, usually expressed by non-clinical managers, is that it will be difficult to engage physicians in the *Kaizen* process. As the Jacobson et al.(2009) article shows, physicians willingly participate in *Kaizen* when asked, especially when their physician leaders are asking them for ideas and are supportive throughout the process. In a *Kaizen* culture, physicians will point out problems that matter to them, such as preventing delays in the start of surgical procedures. Some of these problems will need to be fixed by others in the organization, working to provide a better work environment for the physician. Some situations find the physicians actively working on the *Kaizen* improvement cycle, such as emergency physicians noticing that department clinical protocols are outdated and working together to update and consistently adopt newer, more effective protocols.

Document and Share

In our blanket warmer example, the team decided to implement two improvements to the process:

1) Stamping the hospital's name on the blankets to reduce loss due to theft or patients accidentally taking them home;
2) Restocking the blanket warmer daily instead of every other day.

In the first case, blankets still disappeared, even with the hospital's name on them. So, the team went back and tried to find another solution to that problem. But increasing the frequency of blanket restocking was considered a success, even though it slightly increased the labor cost from the time spent delivering blankets more often. Reducing the time nurses and assistants spend searching for blankets offset the slightly higher cost for the materials department. The hospital could not necessarily calculate a specific "return on investment", but it's still important to document the *Kaizen* for a number of reasons.

In the *Kaizen* process, it is important to document each of our improvements in a simple and easily understandable way (see an example in Figure 11.2).

People often ask, "Why should I take the time to document our *Kaizens* instead of using that time to find and solve more problems?" Or, nurses might prefer to not take time away from patient care. It is important to note that documenting a *Kaizen* should take just a few minutes, whether using a PowerPoint template or entering the improvement into a database. In successful implementations of this approach, the person who owned the

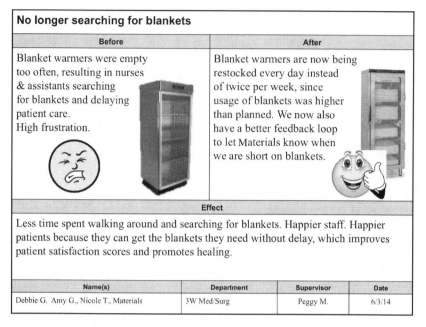

No longer searching for blankets	
Before	**After**
Blanket warmers were empty too often, resulting in nurses & assistants searching for blankets and delaying patient care. High frustration.	Blanket warmers are now being restocked every day instead of twice per week, since usage of blankets was higher than planned. We now also have a better feedback loop to let Materials know when we are short on blankets.
Effect	
Less time spent walking around and searching for blankets. Happier staff. Happier patients because they can get the blankets they need without delay, which improves patient satisfaction scores and promotes healing.	

Name(s)	Department	Supervisor	Date
Debbie G. Amy G., Nicole T., Materials	3W Med/Surg	Peggy M.	6/3/14

Figure 11.2   An Example of a *"Kaizen* Report"

(image source and copyright: Mark Graban)

Kaizen generally writes up the reports, rather than the reports being written up by a manager or a specialist. But, there are instances when a supervisor or *Kaizen* specialist will take a verbal report from the staff member, to then write it up formally.

One reason we document *Kaizens* is to take time to reflect on what we have done. What was our original problem? What did we accomplish and what were the benefits? What did we learn along the way? These are powerful questions that further develop our employees and their ability to practice *Kaizen*.

A second reason is to provide recognition to the people who were involved in the *Kaizen* process. Most *Kaizen* reports have more than one name on them, as different people may have been involved in one or more of the stages of the process (identifying the problem or brainstorming possible solutions). Putting people's names on the reports can be a way for them to feel appreciated for their efforts, especially when *Kaizen* reports are shared and celebrated at team huddles, or are posted on bulletin boards or online databases. People often talk about the need for "rewards and recognition", but with *Kaizen*, it's important to realize that recognition—including a sincere thank you from a leader—can be very meaningful.

Some organizations use formal rewards for *Kaizen* participation—rewards given for actually implementing an improvement. Suggestion box systems generally promised a large payout to the employee who had the idea, offering a percentage of the recognized cost savings. This might seem like a fair or reasonable approach, but suggestion box payouts quickly get dysfunctional when people fight over who gets the credit for the idea (since only one person gets paid) or when the employee and management argue over the value of the suggestion.

For this reason, successful *Kaizen* programs either rely on recognition (which builds on existing intrinsic motivation) or small, token rewards that are shared broadly with everybody who participated in a *Kaizen*. At Franciscan St. Francis Health, employees earn "VIP points" for each *Kaizen*, regardless of any cost savings, or lack thereof (Graban & Swartz, 2013, p. 143). The points can be used to receive apparel with the hospital logo or gift cards. Some organizations also use *Kaizen* participation as a basis for annual employee reviews and determining salary adjustments, rewarding high levels of *Kaizen* participation in less direct ways.

A third reason for taking the time to document completed *Kaizens* is to share improvements with other departments and other hospitals or clinic sites within a larger healthcare organization or country. If one nursing unit highlighted a problem, such as not having warm blankets available at all times, different units in a hospital and throughout a system should be able to share ideas with each other. That one unit is likely not the only one with that particular problem; thus, it is useful to make *Kaizens* more widely visible and searchable by staff in different departments or sites.

While we want each healthcare organization, each department and each individual to develop the ability to see problems, to speak up and to solve problems, there is nothing wrong with leveraging and borrowing ideas from others. In larger organizations, web-based or intranet software solutions have been helpful. Franciscan St. Francis Health has an intranet database that allows people to search for phrases in documented *Kaizens* like "blanket", "IV bag" or "falls" (Graban & Swartz, 2013, p. 94). Some healthcare organizations have systems that allow the organization to keep track of ideas that did *not* work, which is a different form of organizational learning beyond having a repository of improvements.

As we aim to share and spread ideas, a *Kaizen* mindset is different from what some healthcare organizations describe as the "roll out" of an improvement or a new process. In many healthcare organizations, a new process is essentially forced on others as a new "best practice". This can be very demoralizing to people, even if the new process is better, as they might question why they aren't able to participate in furthering the improvement.

A better practice is to share *Kaizens* with the following mindsets and questions in mind:

1) Does our department have the same problem that other people solved?
2) Can we use that *Kaizen* as a starting point to build upon, creating an additional improvement that can be shared with those who improved before us?

3) Are we adopting the new practice because it is truly better, because there is some other reason to standardize across departments or both?

With *Kaizen*, we can learn from each other and spread changes in a way that builds pride and intrinsic motivation rather than stifling people. If people are forced to change, that most likely reduces their willingness to participate voluntarily in *Kaizen*.

What Are the Challenges Related to Documenting and Sharing Kaizens?

The argument for documenting and sharing *Kaizens* is compelling. Taking the time to do this builds enthusiasm for more improvement, which further develops people and provides greater benefits to the organization. However, some challenges do come up that need to be addressed.

Some staff members in healthcare organizations do not have the computer skills required to feel comfortable working with a PowerPoint template as a way of documenting their *Kaizens*. Although it has become very easy to take a digital picture with a smartphone, email it to oneself and paste it into PowerPoint, some have never done this. So, leaders and peers can help and coach these individuals and teach them the required skills, helping them as they practice. If people feel like photographs are more of a burden than a benefit, people could be encouraged to write up the *Kaizen* with just text. That is probably better for the organization than not writing it up at all.

Some organizations do not have a good infrastructure for the sharing of ideas in an electronic format. Solutions that can be pursued include shared drives, databases built behind intranet pages, Microsoft SharePoint and more specific commercial software solutions. As with any *Kaizen* situation, if we identify a problem ("it's difficult for people at different sites to see our *Kaizen* board"), then we can consider technology as a solution to that problem. That being said, technology alone will not create a culture of continuous improvement—we also need consistent methodologies (like *Kaizen*) and active and engaged leadership.

CREATING A KAIZEN CULTURE—IT'S ALL ABOUT LEADERSHIP

It's not easy to create a culture of continuous improvement. But, it's not the most difficult challenge, either. *Kaizen* requires consistent effort and behaviors from leaders over time, as it might take a year or more for *Kaizen* to become the new way of thinking in a department and it might take years for an entire organization to catch on.

Franciscan St. Francis Health has had the benefit of highly engaged senior executives who have consistently promoted and reinforced the importance of *Kaizen* each year since 2007. In the past few years (2012 through 2014), about 40 percent of their staff members have been formally involved in implementing and documenting at least one *Kaizen* improvement (and some implement and document dozens per year). They would like that percentage to be higher, of course. They do not blame the 60 percent of employees who choose not to participate. They challenge themselves to be better leaders in a way that will engage others.

Almost every healthcare professional I have met can identify problems and things they want to improve. Most of them can come up with ideas for improvement. This is a vast untapped resource, unfortunately, in most healthcare organizations. Leaders need to ask employees to point out problems and generate ideas. They need to ask not just once, but on a continuing basis. Leaders need to create an environment where it's safe to speak up and to take the small risks that are usually involved in the *Kaizen* process.

Leaders also need to be collaborative, working with employees, giving up control and not being the all-knowing, infallible "boss" that they once thought they could be. It's important to work together, empowering staff without abandoning them, delegating while continuing to help as needed. Leaders at all levels play an important role in recognizing and celebrating people's efforts in *Kaizen*.

There is a great risk that an organization might make a superficial attempt at initiating a *Kaizen* program. In some organizations, leaders give one presentation, hang boards on the wall and post cheerful signs announcing the program, only to follow that up by rejecting most of the ideas that are submitted. Many organizations have one or more months of active *Kaizen* activity, but participation declines when ideas are not implemented or leaders stop asking staff to point out problems or bring forward ideas. The principles of *Kaizen* are simple and powerful, yet changing a culture and adopting new leadership mindsets is difficult and not guaranteed to succeed.

Healthcare professionals want to improve. They care deeply for their patients and for their co-workers. Leaders need to do more than say they want a culture of continuous improvement. They need to take action to create an environment that allows people to thrive and improvement to happen. That's what *Kaizen* is all about and why it's so powerful in addressing our important healthcare challenges.

REFERENCES

Berwick, D.M. (1989). Continuous improvement as an ideal in health care. *New England Journal of Medicine*, 320 (1), 1424–1425.

Graban, M. (2014). *Continuous improvement in healthcare: Are we walking the walk?* Retrieved from http://www.slideshare.net/mgraban/continuous-improvement-in-healthcare-are-we-walking-the-walk-37881340 (accessed 31 May 2015).

Graban, M., & Swartz, J.E. (2012). *Healthcare Kaizen: Engaging Front-Line Staff in Sustainable Continuous Improvements*. New York: Productivity Press.

Graban, M., & Swartz, J.E. (2013). *The Executive Guide to Healthcare Kaizen: Leadership for a Continuously Learning and Improving Organization*. New York: Productivity Press.

Imai, M. (1986). *Kaizen: The Key to Japan's Competitive Success.* New York: McGraw-Hill.

Institute of Medicine. (2012). *Best care at lower cost: The path to continuously learning health care in America.* IOM Report, September. Retrieved from http://www.iom.edu/~/media/Files/Report%20Files/2012/Best-Care/BestCareReport-Brief.pdf (accessed 2 June 2015).

Jacobson, G.H., Streiff McCoin, N., Lescallette, R., Russ, S., & Slovis, C.M. (2009). Kaizen: A method of process improvement in the emergency department. *Academic Emergency Medicine,* **16** (12), 1341–1349.

Kato, I., & Smalley, A. (2011). *Toyota Kaizen Methods: Six Steps to Improvement.* New York: Productivity Press.

Liker, J. (2004). *The Toyota Way: 14 Management Principles from the World's Greatest Manufacturer.* New York: McGraw-Hill.

Liker, J. (2013). *A problem can be a treasure if leaders make efforts to eliminate fear of failure.* Retrieved from http://theleanedge.org/?p=255359 (accessed 31 May 2015).

Lu, H., Barriball, K.L., Zhang, X., & While, A.E. (2012). Job satisfaction among hospital nurses revisited: A systematic review. *International Journal of Nursing Studies,* **49** (8), 1017–1038.

Siciliani, L., Moran, V., & Borowitz, M. (2014). Measuring and comparing health care waiting times in OECD countries. *Health Policy,* **118** (3), 292–303.

12 Knowledge Management in Healthcare Organizations

Nilmini Wickramasinghe and Raj Gururajan

INTRODUCTION

Knowledge Management (*KM*) is a contemporary management technique that is aimed at solving the current challenges to increase the efficiency and efficacy of the core production of care processes while simultaneously incorporating continuous innovation. The premise for the need for *Knowledge Management* is based on a paradigm shift in the environment where knowledge is now central to organizational performance (Dalkir, 2013; Drucker, 1993, 1999). Specifically, *KM* offers organizations many tools, techniques and strategies to apply to their existing production or care processes. Healthcare is information rich, with extremely large and complex data sets that need to be analyzed. The collection of data permeates all areas of healthcare, and when coupled with the new trends in evidence-based medicine and electronic medical records systems, it is imperative that healthcare embraces the tools, technologies, strategies and processes of *Knowledge Management* if it is to fully realize the benefits from all these data assets (Wickramasinghe & Schaffer, 2010).

The successful application of *Knowledge Management* hinges on the development of a sound knowledge management infrastructure and the systematic and continuous application of specific steps supported by various technologies. This serves to underscore the dynamic nature of knowledge management where the extant knowledge base is always being updated. The *Knowledge Management Infrastructure* (*KMI*) framework not only helps organizations to structure their knowledge assets, but also makes explicit the numerous implicit knowledge assets currently evident in healthcare (Wickramasinghe & Davidson, 2004), while the *Intelligence Continuum* (*IC*) provides the key tools and technologies needed to facilitate superior healthcare delivery (Wickramasinghe & Schaffer, 2005). Taken together, the *KMI* and *IC* can enable healthcare to realize its value proposition of delivering effective and efficient value-added healthcare services.

KNOWLEDGE MANAGEMENT

> Land, labor, and capital now pale in comparison to knowledge as the
> critical asset to be managed in today's knowledge economy.
>
> Drucker (1999, p. 47)

The nations that lead the world into the next century will be those who can shift from being industrial economies, based upon the production of manufactured goods, to those that possess the capacity to produce and utilize knowledge successfully. The focus of the many nations' economies shifted first to information-intensive industries, such as financial services and logistics, and now is shifting toward innovation-driven industries, such as computer software and biotechnology, where the competitive advantage lies mostly in the innovative use of human resources. This represents a move from an era of standardization to an era of innovation, where knowledge and its creation and management hold the key to success (Bukowitz & Williams, 1997; Drucker, 1993, 1999).

Knowledge management is a key approach to help solve current business problems, such as competitiveness and the need to innovate, that are faced by organizations today. The premise for *Knowledge Management* is based on a paradigm shift in the business environment where knowledge is central to organizational performance (Newell et al., 2002; Swan et al., 1999). In essence, *Knowledge Management* not only involves the production of information but also the capture of data at the source, and the transmission and analysis of these data as well as the communication of information based on or derived from the data to those who can act on it (Davenport & Prusak, 1998). Thus, data and information represent critical raw assets in the generation of knowledge, while successful knowledge management initiatives require a tripartite view; namely, the incorporation of people, production processes and technologies (Wickramasinghe, 2003).

Broadly speaking, *Knowledge Management* involves four key steps:

1) Creating/generating knowledge;
2) Representing/storing knowledge;
3) Accessing/using/re-using knowledge;
4) Disseminating/transferring knowledge (Alavi & Leidner, 2001; Davenport & Prusak, 1998; Markus, 2001; Wickramasinghe, 2006).

Knowledge creation, generally accepted as the first step for any knowledge management endeavor, requires an understanding of the knowledge construct as well as its people and technology dimensions. Given that knowledge creation is the first step in any knowledge management initiative, it naturally has a significant impact on the other consequent *KM* steps, thus making the identification of and facilitating of knowledge creation a key focal point for any organization wanting to fully leverage its knowledge potential.

Knowledge, however is not a simple construct. Specifically, knowledge can exist in essentially two forms: Explicit or factual knowledge, and tacit knowledge, or "know how" (Polanyi, 1958, 1966). It is well established that while both types of knowledge are important, tacit knowledge is more difficult to identify and thus manage (Nonaka, 1994; Nonaka & Nishiguchi, 2001). Of equal importance, though perhaps less well defined, knowledge also has a subjective component and can be viewed as an ongoing phenomenon being shaped by the social practices of communities (Boland & Tenkasi, 1995). The objective elements of knowledge can be thought of as primarily having an impact on the production process, while the subjective elements typically impact innovation (Wickramasinghe, 2003). Enabling and enhancing both effective and efficient production processes as well as the functions of supporting and fostering innovation are key concerns of *Knowledge Management.*

Organizational knowledge is not static; rather, it changes and evolves during the lifetime of an organization. What is more, it is possible to transform one form of knowledge into another, i.e., to transform tacit knowledge into explicit and vice versa (Wickramasinghe, 2006). This process of transforming one form of knowledge into another is known as the knowledge spiral (Nonaka, 1994). Naturally, this does not imply that one form of knowledge is necessarily transformed 100% into another form of knowledge. According to Nonaka (1994):

1) Socialization or tacit-to-tacit knowledge transformation usually occurs through apprenticeship-type relations, where the teacher or master passes on the skill to the apprentice;
2) Combination or explicit-to-explicit knowledge transformation usually occurs via the formal learning of facts;
3) Externalization or tacit-to-explicit knowledge transformation usually occurs when there is an articulation of nuances; for example, if an expert surgeon is questioned as to why he performs a particular surgical procedure in a certain manner, his articulation of the steps makes the tacit knowledge become explicit;
4) Internalization or explicit-to-tacit knowledge transformation usually occurs when explicit knowledge is internalized and can then be used to broaden, reframe and extend one's tacit knowledge.

Integral to these transformations of knowledge through the knowledge spiral is that new knowledge is being continuously created (Nonaka, 1994), and this can potentially bring many benefits to organizations. What becomes important then, for any organization in today's knowledge economy, is to maximize the full potential of all its knowledge assets and successfully make all germane knowledge explicit so it can be used effectively and efficiently by all people within the organization as required (Wickramasinghe & Davison, 2004; Wickramasinghe et al., 2004). This is done by enhancing all four stages in the knowledge spiral.

Healthcare is currently facing major challenges at a global level (Wickramasinghe & Schaffer, 2005, 2010; Wickramasinghe & Silvers, 2003). It has yet to embrace *Knowledge Management*. Yet, *KM* appears to provide several viable possibilities to address the current crisis faced by global healthcare in the areas of access, quality and value (Wickramasinghe & Schaffer, 2005). In healthcare, one of the most critical knowledge transformations to effect is that of tacit to explicit, i.e., externalization, so that the healthcare organization can best leverage its knowledge potential to realize the healthcare value proposition (Wickramasinghe et al., 2004). Integral to such a process is the establishment of a robust knowledge management infrastructure and the adoption of key tools and techniques. This is achieved by the application of the *KMI* and *IC* models.

ESTABLISHING A KNOWLEDGE MANAGEMENT INFRASTRUCTURE

The most valuable resources available to any organization are human skills, expertise and relationships. *Knowledge Management* is about capitalizing on these precious assets (Duffy, 2001). Most companies do not capitalize on the wealth of expertise in the form of the knowledge scattered across them (Hansen et al., 2001). Information centers, market intelligence and learning are converging to form knowledge management functions. Knowledge management offers organizations many strategies, techniques and tools to apply to their existing production processes so that they are able to grow and effectively utilize their knowledge assets. The *KM* infrastructure not only forms the foundation for enabling and fostering knowledge management, continuous learning and sustaining an organizational memory (Drucker, 1999), but it also provides the foundations for actualizing the four key steps of *Knowledge Management*, namely, creating/generating knowledge, representing/storing knowledge, accessing/using/reusing knowledge, and disseminating/transferring knowledge (discussed above). An organization's entire "know-how", including new knowledge, can only be created for optimization if an effective *KM* infrastructure is established. Specifically, the *KM* infrastructure consists of social and technical tools and techniques, including hardware and software, that are established so that knowledge can be created from any new events or activities on a continual basis. In addition, the *KM* infrastructure will have a repository of knowledge, systems to distribute the knowledge to the members of the organization and a facilitator system for the creation of new knowledge. Thus, a knowledge-based infrastructure will foster the creation of knowledge, and provide an integrated system to share and diffuse the knowledge within the organization (Srikantaiah, 2000), as well as provide support for the continual creation and generation of new knowledge (Wickramasinghe, 2003). The *Knowledge Management Infrastructure* contains the five essential elements that together must be present for any *KM* initiative to succeed (Table 12.1 summarizes this normative model):

1) Infrastructure for collaboration;
2) Organizational memory;
3) Human asset infrastructure;
4) Knowledge transfer network;
5) Business intelligence infrastructure.

Table 12.1 Elements of the *Knowledge Management* Infrastructure (adapted from Wickramasinghe, 2006)

Element of the Knowledge Management Infrastructure	Description
Infrastructure for Collaboration	The key to competitive advantage and improving customer satisfaction lies in the ability of organizations to form learning alliances, these being strategic partnerships based on a business environment that encourages mutual (and reflective) learning between partners (Holt et al., 2000). Organizations can utilize their strategy framework to identify partners and collaborators for enhancing their value chain.
Organizational Memory	Organizational memory is concerned with the storing and subsequent accessing and replenishing of an organization's "know-how", which is recorded in documents or in its people (Maier & Lehner, 2000). However, a key component of knowledge management not addressed in the construct of organizational memory is the subjective aspect (Wickramasinghe, 2003). Knowledge as a subjective component primarily refers to an ongoing phenomenon of exchange where knowledge is being shaped by the social practices of communities (Boland and Tenkasi, 1995) in the tradition of a Hegelian/Kantian perspective, where the importance of the divergence of meaning is essential to support the "sense-making" processes of knowledge creation (Wickramasinghe and Mills, 2001). Organizational memory keeps a record of knowledge resources and locations. Recorded information, whether in human readable or

(Continued)

Table 12.1   (Continued)

Element of the Knowledge Management Infrastructure	Description
	electronic form or in the memories of staff, is an important embodiment of an organization's knowledge and intellectual capital. Thus, strong organizational memory systems ensure the access of information or knowledge throughout the company to everyone at any time (Croasdell, 2001).
Human Asset Infrastructure	This deals with the participation and willingness of people. Today, organizations have to attract and motivate the best people, and reward, recognize, train, educate and improve them (Ellinger et al., 1999) so that the highly skilled and more independent workers can exploit technologies to create knowledge in learning organizations (Thorne and Smith, 2000). The human asset infrastructure, then, helps to identify and utilize the special skills of people who can create greater business value if they and their inherent skills and experiences are managed to make explicit use of their knowledge.
Knowledge Transfer Network	This element is concerned with the dissemination of knowledge and information. Unless there is a strong communication infrastructure in place, people are not able to communicate effectively and thus are unable to effectively transfer knowledge. An appropriate communication infrastructure includes, but is not limited to, the internet and intranets for creating the knowledge transfer network, as well as discussion rooms and bulletin boards for meetings and for displaying information.
Business Intelligence Infrastructure	In an intelligent enterprise, various information systems are integrated with knowledge-gathering and analyzing tools for data analysis, and dynamic end user querying of a variety of enterprise data sources (Hammond, 2001). Business intelligence infrastructures have customers, suppliers and other partners embedded into a single, integrated system. Customers will view their own purchasing habits, and suppliers will see the demand pattern, which may help them to offer volume discounts, etc. This information can help all customers, suppliers and enterprises to analyze

Element of the Knowledge Management Infrastructure	Description
	data and provide them with a competitive advantage. The intelligence of a company is not only available to internal users, but can even be leveraged by selling it to others, such as consumers, who may be interested in this type of information intelligence.

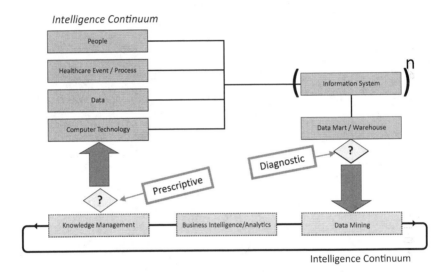

Figure 12.1   Application of the Intelligence Continuum to the Generic Healthcare System

(adapted from Wickramasinghe & Schaffer, 2005)

THE INTELLIGENCE CONTINUUM

The *Intelligence Continuum* consists of a collection of key tools, techniques and processes of the knowledge economy, including data mining, business intelligence/analytics and knowledge management, which are applied to a generic system of people, production processes and technology in a systematic and orderly fashion (Wickramasinghe & Fadlalla, 2004; Wickramasinghe & Lichtenstein, 2006; Wickramasinghe & Schaffer, 2005, 2010; Wickramasinghe & Silvers, 2003; Wickramasinghe et al., 2005). Taken together, they represent a very powerful system for refining the raw data material stored in data marts and/or data warehouses and thereby maximizing the value and utility of these data assets for any organization (Geisler, 1999, 2000, 2001, 2002; Geisler & Wickramasinghe, 2006; Kostoff & Geisler, 1999). As depicted in Figure 12.1, the *IC* can be applied to the output of the generic healthcare information system. Once applied, the results become part of the data sets that are reintroduced into the health information system and combined with the other inputs of people, production processes and technology to develop an improvement continuum. Thus, the intelligence continuum includes the generation of data, the analysis of these data to provide a "diagnosis" and their reintroduction into the health information cycle as a "prescriptive" solution. In this way, the next iteration, or "future state", always represents the enhancement of the extant knowledge base of the previous iteration. For the *IC* to be truly effective, however, the *KMI* must already be in place so that all data, information and knowledge assets are explicit and the technologies of the *IC* can be applied to them in a systematic and methodical fashion.

A CASE STUDY

This case study focuses on the design, development and implementation of an intelligent clinical support tool for acute healthcare contexts in Australia. It serves to represent how the key elements from this environment pertain to *Knowledge Management* in healthcare, and its benefits and applications in this setting. Exploratory case study research was adopted to enable the generation of rich data in a non-restrictive manner. Information was gathered from several sources, including semi-structured interviews, the collecting of germane documents and memos, numerous site visits and the direct observation of various procedures, thus enabling triangulation among the different data sources (Eisenhardt, 1989). Rigorous coding and an extensive thematic analysis were conducted to analyze the qualitative data gathered (Boyatzis, 1998; Kvale, 1996). Each of the points listed was confirmed by multiple interviews, written documentation and passive observation, thus ensuring the highest level of reliability possible for qualitative research (Boyatzis, 1998).

Introduction

Nurses are pivotal in coordinating and communicating patient-care information. Despite nurses' central role in healthcare delivery, the relevant information systems have historically rarely been designed around nurses' operational needs. This could explain the poor integration of technologies into nursing work processes and consequent rejection of these technologies by nursing professionals. The complex nature of acute care delivery in hospitals and the frequently interrupted patterns of nursing work suggest that nurses require flexible, intelligent systems that can support and adapt to their variable workflow patterns. This study explored nurses' initial reactions to a new *Intelligent Clinical Support Tool* (*ICST*) for acute healthcare. We worked together with an Australian small- to medium-sized enterprise to evaluate key issues in design, development and deployment.

Methods

Four focus group interviews involving 60 nurses purposefully selected from medical and surgical wards at two hospitals in Melbourne, Victoria, one private and one public, were conducted. The interviews were audio recorded and transcribed verbatim. Further, they were subject to content and thematic analyses in order to understand the nature of the nurses' reactions to the *ICST* as well as any/all facilitating or hindering aspects.

Results and Findings

The nurses' initial responses to the technology were generally positive, and rich qualitative data were gathered on barriers, facilitators and enhancements. The analysis of these data using well-established techniques such as thematic analysis informed recommendations regarding enhancing the required *ICST* as well as developing a suitable theory for integrating technology into acute healthcare settings. Succinctly, the technology solution automated, recorded and managed nursing workflow while improving quality of care. In addition, it provided decision support for doctors, nurses and other medical staff by automatically creating a chart of all clinical measurements and activities and then cross-referencing these. The *ICST* also deployed smart sensors to validate and track medication, which has a significant, positive impact on patient safety.

Key insights included the nurses' initial reactions to the new technology, the feasibility of the proposed *ICST* and their concerns about the potential for its impact on clinical skills and decision-making. A unique aspect of the project has been the incorporation of user-centered design principles and thus a theoretical contribution of how to conduct such studies in healthcare contexts.

Knowledge Management and the ICST

To illustrate the full potential of the *ICST*, Table 12.2 maps it onto the above outline of *KMI*. This mapping illustrates the potential of this enterprise-wide solution to facilitate superior healthcare delivery in a systematic and

Table 12.2   Mapping of *ICST* to *KMI*

Element of the *Knowledge Management Infrastructure*	Mapping with ICST
Infrastructure for Collaboration	The *ICST* is a cloud-based portal entry system. Thus, collaboration is enabled through easy access into the portal and depending on the clinician's designation, e.g., specialist, nurse, allied health, etc., the appropriate view and access are enabled.

(*Continued*)

Table 12.2   (Continued)

Element of the Knowledge Management Infrastructure	Mapping with ICST
Organizational Memory	Given that the technology solution serves as an online repository for all medical interventions for the patient along the patient's journey in the hospital, an essentially complete record is thus collated, which in turn serves to preserve organizational memory at an optimal level as well as assist with searching and sorting key aspects.
Human Asset Infrastructure	Treating and managing patients in the ward is too often hectic and chaotic. This means that nurses are continually under pressure to multitask and be flexible and agile. Nurses are paramount to the success of patient recovery and care in the ward and the technology solution provides decision support and records all interventions and interactions. This frees up nurses' time and thus enables the human infrastructure to be deployed most beneficially to where it can add the most value, i.e., at the patient's bedside, attending to and addressing all critical patient needs.
Knowledge Transfer Network	By enabling the seamless transfer, storing and updating of data and information, the technology solution provides an effective and efficient knowledge transfer network. This in turn is critical to achieving quality care outcomes.
Business Intelligence Infrastructure	The potential for the data and information to be analyzed in a systematic and strategic fashion exists in the *ICST* solution. To date, however, this capability has not been fully utilized, as attention has been focused on near-term needs, such as immediate care of the patient. Once the analytics possibilities are realized, the solution will indeed have a robust business intelligence infrastructure.

consistent fashion. Further, it is possible to conceptualize the *ICST* as a generic healthcare information system and then analyze it using the *IC* model (Figure 12.1). This will in turn ensure that continuous improvement takes place in the ward so that optimal health outcomes ensue.

DISCUSSION AND CONCLUSION

Healthcare globally is facing many challenges, including escalating costs and more pressures to deliver high-quality, effective and efficient care. Moreover, it has been continually noted that a critical imperative for healthcare today is to define value (Porter & Teisburg, 2010). By nurturing knowledge management and making their knowledge assets explicit, healthcare organizations will be more suitably equipped to meet these challenges, since knowledge holds the key to developing better practice management techniques, while data and information are necessary in disease management and evidence-based medicine.

The case study data presented depicted the complexity of the service delivery process, driven by the complexity of the issues being dealt with by various clinicians, which in turn requires that many disciplines create and share knowledge to enable the delivery of a high quality of care. Thus, the need for shared knowledge is a fundamental requirement, while the access to relevant healthcare data, pertinent information and germane knowledge increases value for healthcare delivery. The *KMI* described above was presented and used to structure these disparate knowledge assets as explicit and integrated within a larger system, the generic healthcare information system. This allowed for the analysis of the extent of the knowledge management infrastructure for the *ICST* in the ward context. Further, such a framework in particular supports in a systematic and structured fashion all four key knowledge transformations identified by Nonaka (1994), in particular that of externalization (tacit to explicit). To this generic healthcare information system, the application of the *IC* ensures that the maximization of appropriate and germane knowledge assets occurs and a superior future state will always be realized.

Healthcare continues to struggle to realize the promised benefits from the myriad of technology solutions currently being implemented. One of the reasons for this is that the full benefits of these technology solutions have yet to be realized. We believe that by incorporating a *KM* perspective, mapping the specific solution with the *KMI* and in addition, conceptualizing the system in such a fashion so that the *IC* can then be applied, it will then be possible to realize the full potential of such solutions. To illustrate, we presented the case study of a nursing informatics solutions.

In closing, we do, however, note that in conjunction with an appropriate *KM* strategy, it behooves any healthcare organization when trying to implement technology solutions into healthcare contexts also to focus on the following non-technical critical success factors (Wickramasinghe & Schaffer, 2010; Wickramasinghe et al., 2015):

1) Examine existing production processes, policies and protocols and determine if there are possibilities to streamline and improve, standardize across all locations and perhaps even embrace *Lean* and *Six Sigma* principles;
2) Engage all clinicians and develop appropriate strategies to foster sponsorship. Further, this must be addressed early to ensure optimal clinical support;
3) Ensure smooth assimilation of solution, which includes ensuring that the appropriate level of support, training and assistance is available to all users.

REFERENCES

Alavi, M., & Leidner, D.E. (2001). Review: Knowledge management and knowledge management systems: Conceptual foundations and research issues. *MIS quarterly*, **25** (1), 107–136.

Boland, R.J., Jr., & Tenkasi, R.V. (1995). Perspective making and perspective taking in communities of knowing. *Organization science*, **6** (4), 350–372.

Boyatzis, R.E. (1998). *Transforming Qualitative Information: Thematic Analysis and Code Development*. London: Sage.

Bukowitz, W., & Williams, R. (1997). New metrics for hidden assets. *Journal of Strategic Performance Measurement*, **1** (1), 12–18.

Croasdell, D.C. (2001). IT's role in organizational memory and learning. *Information Systems Management*, **18** (1), 8–11.

Dalkir, K. (2013). *Knowledge Management in Theory and Practice*. Burlington, VT: Elsevier Butterworth-Heinemann.

Davenport, T., & Prusak L. (1998). *Working Knowledge*. Boston, MA: Harvard Business School Press.

Drucker, P.F. (1993). *Post-capitalist society*. New York: HarperCollins Publishers.

Drucker, P.F. (1994). *Post-Capitalist Society*. London: Routledge.

Drucker, P.F. (1999). Beyond the information revolution. *The Atlantic Monthly*, **284** (4), 47–53. Retrieved from http://pqasb.pqarchiver.com/theatlantic/results.html?st=advanced&QryTxt=&type=current&sortby=REVERSE_CHRON&datetype=6&frommonth=01&fromday=1&fromyear=1999&tomonth=12&today=28&toyear=1999&By=Drucker&Title= (accessed 23 June 2015).

Duffy, J. (2001). The tools and technologies needed for knowledge management. *Information Management Journal*, **35** (1), 64–67.

Eisenhardt, K.M. (1989). Building theories from case study research. *Academy of management review*, **14** (4), 532–550.

Ellinger, A.D., Watkins, K.E., & Bostrom, R.P. (1999). Managers as facilitators of learning in learning organizations. *Human Resource Development Quarterly*, **10** (2), 105–125.

Enthoven, A.C. (1993). The history and principles of managed competition. *Health affairs*, **12** (S1), 24–48.

Geisler, E. (1999). Mapping the knowledge-base of management of medical technology. *International Journal of Healthcare Technology and Management*, **1** (1), 3–10.

Geisler, E. (2000). *The Metrics of Science and Technology*. Westport, CT: Greenwood.

Geisler, E. (2001). *Creating Value with Science and Technology*. Westport, CT: Greenwood.

Geisler, E. (2002). The metrics of technology evaluation: Where we stand and where we should go from here. *International Journal of Technology Management*, **24** (4), 341–374.

Geisler, E., & Wickramasinghe, N. (2006). *Knowledge Management: Concepts and Cases*. Armonk, NY: M.E. Sharpe.

Hammond, C. (2001). The intelligent enterprise. *InfoWorld*, **23** (6), 45–46.

Hansen, M.T., & Oetinger, B.V. (2001). Introducing T-shaped managers: Knowledge management's next generation. Harvard Business Review, **79** (3), 106–116.

Holt, G.D., Love, P.E.D., & Li, H. (2000). The learning organization: Toward a paradigm for mutually beneficial strategic construction alliances. *International Journal of Project Management*, **18** (6), 415–421.

Kostoff, R., & Geisler, E. (1999). Strategic management and implementation of textual data mining. *Government Organizations, Technology Analysis & Strategic Management*, **11** (4), 493–525.

Kvale, S. (1996). *Interviews: An Introduction to Qualitative Research Interviewing.* Thousand Oaks, CA: Sage.

Maier, R., & Lehner, F. (2000). *Perspectives on knowledge management systems theoretical framework and design of an empirical study.* Proceedings of 8th European Conference on Information Systems (ECIS), Vienna.

Markus, L.M. (2001). Toward a theory of knowledge reuse: Types of knowledge reuse situations and factors in reuse success. *Journal of Management Information Systems,* **18** (1), 57–93.

Newell, S., Robertson, M., Scarbrough, H. & Swan, J. (2002) Managing Knowledge Work, Palgrave, Basingstoke, Hampshire.

Newell, S., Robertson, M., Scarbrough, H., & Swan, J. (2009). *Managing Knowledge Work and Innovation.* Basingstoke, England: Palgrave Macmillan.

Nonaka, I. (1994). A dynamic theory of organizational knowledge creation. *Organizational Science,* **5** (1), 14–37.

Nonaka, I., & Nishiguchi, T. (2001). *Knowledge Emergence.* Oxford, England: Oxford University Press.

Polanyi, M. (1958). *Personal Knowledge: Towards a Post-critical Philosophy.* Chicago, IL: University Press Chicago.

Polanyi, M. (1966). *The Tacit Dimension.* London: Routledge & Kegan Paul.

Porter, M.E., & Teisberg, E.O. (2005). *Redefining Healthcare.* Boston, MA: Harvard Business School Press.

Sharma, S.K., Wickramasinghe, N., & Gupta, J.N.D. (2011). Knowledge management in healthcare. In N. Wickramasinghe, J.N.D. Gupta, & S.K. Sharma (Eds.), *Creating Knowledge-Based Healthcare Organizations.* Hershey, PA: Idea Group, pp. 1–13.

Srikantaiah, T.K. (2000). Knowledge Management for Information Professional. ASIS Monograph Series, Maryland, USA: Information Today, Inc.

Swan, J., Scarbrough H., & Preston J. (1999). *Knowledge management: The next fad to forget people?* Proceedings of the 7th European Conference in Information Systems, Vienna 2009. Retrieved from http://www.researchgate.net/profile/Harry_Scarbrough/publication/221408661_Knowledge_Management_-_The_Next_Fad_to_Forget_People/links/00b49519a6a56e98be000000.pdf (accessed 23 June 2015).

Thorne, K., & Smith, M. (2000). Competitive advantage in world class organizations. *Management Accounting,* **78** (3), 22–26.

Wickramasinghe, N. (2003). Do we practice what we preach: Are knowledge management systems in practice truly reflective of knowledge management systems in theory? *Business Process Management Journal,* **9** (3), 295–316.

Wickramasinghe, N. (2006). Knowledge creation: A meta-framework. *International Journal of Innovation and Learning,* **3** (5), 558–573.

Wickramasinghe, N., & Davison, G. (2004). Making explicit the implicit knowledge assets in healthcare: The case of multidisciplinary teams in care and cure environments. *Health Care Management Science,* **7** (3), 185–195.

Wickramasinghe, N., & Fadlalla, A. (2004). An integrative framework for HIPAA-Compliant I*IQ Healthcare information systems. International Journal of Health Care Quality   Assurance, 17 (2), 65–74.

Wickramasinghe, N.S., Fadlalla, A.M.A., Geisler, E., & Schaffer, J.L. (2005). A framework for assessing e-health preparedness. *International Journal of Electronic Healthcare,* **1** (3), 316–334.Wickramasinghe, N., Haddad, P., Han-Lin, C., Delimtros, H., & Vaughn, S. (2015). *Varian white paper.* Unpublished internal project report Epworth HealthCare.

Wickramasinghe, N., & Lichtenstein, S. (2006). Supporting knowledge creation with e-mail. *International Journal of Innovation and Learning,* **3** (4), 416–426.

Wickramasinghe, N., & Mills, G. (2001). Integrating e-commerce and knowledge management: What does the Kaiser experience really tell us? *International Journal of Accounting Information Systems*, 3 (2), 83–98.

Wickramasinghe, N., & Schaffer, J. (2005). Creating knowledge-driven healthcare process with the IC. International conference on the management of healthcare & medical technology, Aalborg, Denmark 16–18 August 2005.

Wickramasinghe, N., & Schaffer, J.L. (2006). Creating knowledge-driven healthcare processes with the intelligence continuum. *International Journal of Electronic Healthcare*, 2 (2), 164–174.

Wickramasinghe, N., & Schaffer, J. (2010). Realizing value driven patient centric healthcare through technology. Washington, DC: IBM Center for the Business of Government.

Wickramasinghe, N., Schaffer, J., & Fadlalla, A. (2004). *Actualizing the knowledge spiral through data mining: A clinical example.* MedInfo Conference, San Francisco, CA, November 2004.

Wickramasinghe, N., & Silvers, J. (2003). IS/IT the prescription to enable medical group practices attain their goals. *Health Care Management Science*, 6 (2), 75–86.

13 Lean Healthcare
What Is the Contribution to Quality of Care?

Bozena Poksinska

INTRODUCTION

Improving the quality of healthcare systems has become an important priority for the Swedish government as well as other welfare state governments (Pillinger, 2001). Newspaper headlines regularly inform us of the challenges facing healthcare systems. For example:

"Cost Crisis may Deepen"
"Demand for Healthcare Services Increases"
"Bad Accessibility is a Continuing Problem"
"Patients Want More Involvement and Engagement on Care Decisions"
"Aging Population Puts Strain on Hospital Care"
"The Availability of Competent Staff is a Concern"
"Patient Safety is a Serious Issue"

Although advances in medicine and technology have actually improved medical outcomes and the overall performance of healthcare systems, healthcare organizations are currently facing great pressure to change. Among the main reasons for this pressure are the increasing complexity of healthcare systems, the focus on efficiency and effectiveness and the move towards more individualized, patient-centered care (SKL, 2007). The aging of society is being accompanied by an increasing demand for healthcare services, but not by increasing financial resources (Feldstein, 2011). Patients want to have confidence that healthcare services are safe and provide consistent, high-quality care. Unfortunately, there is strong evidence that healthcare routinely fails to deliver its potential benefits and too frequently harms patients (for example, see Soop et al., 2009). The debate over how to manage and improve quality and safety is more relevant than ever (Groene et al., 2013). In addition, the patient role has changed from one of a passive recipient to a more autonomous, active or collaborative participant (Elg et al., 2012). The needs, wants and opinions of patients, their representatives and society are expected to have a legitimate role in defining, measuring and assuring the quality of care.

In other words, there are several—often conflicting—requirements for the improvement of quality of care that need to be met. According to the US Institute of Medicine (2001), the quality of care can be defined by six dimensions: That is, by being patient-centered, safe, effective, efficient, timely and equitable. These dimensions have been accepted internationally and appear in policy contexts worldwide (Beattie et al., 2013) and have also been recognized by the Swedish National Board of Health and Welfare (Socialstyrelsen, 2006). The current challenge is that healthcare cannot afford to meet all the dimensions unless it changes the way it operates.

In the search for management innovations, many healthcare organizations have adopted *Lean* to tackle the challenges. *Lean* grew of the *Toyota Production System*. The term "Lean" was coined by Krafcik (1988) and popularized by Womack et al. in their book *The Machine that Changed the World* (1990). Those authors aimed to explain the productivity and quality differences between Japanese and Western automakers and used the term "lean" to describe the superiority of the Toyota Production System, which requires fewer resources to make a greater and growing variety of products with fewer defects (Womack et al., 1990). The underlying idea of *Lean* is to create a continuous flow that delivers the right products in the right quantity at the right time (just-in-time principle) with the ability to detect quality problems early in the flow and prevent costly rework (*jidoka*). The strategic goals include achieving the best quality, lowest cost, shortest lead time, best safety and high morale, and are rooted in two key principles—"continuous improvement" and "respect for people" (Liker, 2004). The "continuous improvement" principle implies an ongoing effort to improve products, services or processes with employee involvement. The "respect for people" principle is about developing and challenging employees, and creating an environment of mutual trust and cooperation (Toyota, 2001).

Womack and Jones (1996) were among the first authors to suggest that *Lean* could be adopted in healthcare. They argued that the first step in the adoption of *Lean* in healthcare is developing care processes based on the patient's perspective, with a focus on shortening lead times and increasing the value for the patient (Womack & Jones, 1996). Could *Lean* be the management innovation that helps healthcare organizations tackle their current challenges? How is *Lean* adopted in healthcare? What are the opportunities and limitations of adopting a production-based system to an advanced service system such as healthcare? This chapter aims to present how *Lean* has been adopted by healthcare provider organizations in hospital and primary care settings, and to discuss the implications for quality of care.

The findings and conclusions presented in this chapter are based on six years of research on the practices and outcomes of adopting *Lean* in hospital units and primary care centers in Sweden. The starting point of the research was the Swedish national development program *Lean Healthcare*, which was assigned to and coordinated by the author of this chapter in 2008 and 2009. The purpose of the program was to share experience with *Lean*

Healthcare adoptions in Sweden, and to critically review and discuss the possibilities and limitations of adopting *Lean* in healthcare organizations. Sixty people participated in the program, representing 20 county councils responsible for healthcare provision at the county level. The ongoing *Lean* initiatives in Swedish healthcare were mapped, reviewed and discussed (Poksinska, 2009). The development program triggered a research project on the prerequisites, methods and processes for establishing and leading a *Lean* management system in healthcare organizations, financed by the Swedish Governmental Agency for Innovation Systems. Within this project, the research group, led by the present author, performed three in-depth case studies of healthcare organizations that were regarded as successful examples of *Lean* adoptions in healthcare. Two primary care centers and one hospital unit were studied (e.g., Drotz & Poksinska, 2014; Poksinska et al., 2013). We also performed a quantitative survey on the adoption of *Lean* practices in 58 primary care units from the perspective of managers (Fialkowska & Poksinska, 2014). Finally, we analyzed the data from the Swedish National Patient Survey. In this study, we compared results on patient-perceived quality of care for 23 primary care centers working with *Lean* (n = 2550 patients), with a control group of 23 randomly selected care centers that did not work with *Lean* (n = 2731 patients). We also analyzed changes in patient-perceived quality of care over time (Poksinska et al., 2014).

APPLYING FIVE LEAN PRINCIPLES IN HEALTHCARE

Lean is often described by the five principles defined by Womack and Jones (1996). These principles are:

1) Specify value: See value as defined by the end-use customer;
2) Identify the value stream: Understand all the activities required to produce a product, and then optimize the whole process from the view of the end-use customer;
3) Create flow: Get the activities that add value to flow without interruption;
4) Establish pull: Respond to the demand of the customer;
5) Strive for perfection: Systematically identify and eliminate waste in production. (pp. 16–26)

The strength of these principles is that they are general and can be quite easily translated into different contexts. All organizations have "customers" (although, as explained below, this is a somewhat problematic concept for healthcare) and have value streams; the challenge is to identify them. The next section presents and discusses how the five principles are adopted and the extent to which they are practiced by healthcare organizations.

Specify Value From the Customer's Perspective

The foundation of *Lean* is to understand value from the customer's point of view. According to Ohno (1988), who is often referred to as the father of the Toyota Production System, activities performed in value streams can be divided into value adding and waste. Waste is any step or action in a value stream that is not required to meet a customer's needs. There are seven types of waste: Overproduction, waiting, transportation, inventory, motion, overprocessing and defective units (Ohno, 1988). Specifying value correctly is the starting point for improving value streams. Womack and Jones (1996) stated that "[. . .] failure to specify value correctly before applying *Lean* techniques can easily result in providing the wrong product or service in a highly efficient way—pure *muda* (waste)" (p. 141).

Our research and several other studies (e.g., Radnor et al., 2012) have shown that healthcare organizations pay little attention to defining customer value when adopting this principle. None of the studied organizations involved patients in defining value. The focus is on identifying waste and it is healthcare staff who decides what is waste and what adds value. A simple assumption is made: "What is not waste must be value".

Why is value not defined from the patient's perspective? The most frequently mentioned explanation is the notion of the term "customer" in the healthcare context and the lack of appropriate methods to define value from the patient's perspective (see also Radnor et al., 2012; Young & McClean, 2008). In healthcare, the primary "customer" is the patient. Traditionally, patients have been perceived as passive recipients of care who accept the advice of doctors without inquiry into their own special needs. It was commonly assumed that healthcare professionals are better at judging what the patients really need than the patients themselves (Berwick et al., 1992). The staff frequently believes that they already know what adds value for patients, because they meet patients every day. Another problem is that patients are not customers in a market economic sense. In healthcare, the customers are people who are often fragile, vulnerable and scared, and they are unable to define the product or service they need, or explain how this would help them get better. In most cases, patients do not directly pay for their care, and there are also other "customers" that need to be considered, including family members, healthcare workers and policy makers. The various and incompatible notions of the "customer" in healthcare make it difficult to determine what constitutes "value" in the healthcare delivery process. Joosten et al. (2009) summarized this with the following statement:

> In health care, value consists of a 'bewildering array of value-concepts, reflected in a plethora of quality measures and frameworks', where different actors have different views of value. Oftentimes, improving value for one actor leads to deterioration of value for another actor. (p. 343)

The Swedish healthcare system is financed by public funds with a limited budget and aims to provide the best possible care while also providing all citizens with equal access to healthcare services. One of the biggest challenges in healthcare is finding the right balance between achieving the best clinical outcomes for patients and keeping costs reasonable. An important question in this respect is whether the value should be defined "by individual patients passing through the service, those who commission services on behalf of their patients to ensure quality and appropriate service or indeed political representatives in government" (Radnor et al., 2012, p. 370). The answer to that question and the patients' role in healthcare are further discussed in the sections "*Lean* Contributions to Patient-Centered Care" and "Limitations of *Lean* From the Service Perspective" (see below).

Identify the Value Stream

In a manufacturing context, a product goes through production steps that increase the value of the product by adding work or material. In healthcare, the "product" is patients who flow through the healthcare system. The patient flow frequently comprises several healthcare organizations, where value is created for the patient through diagnosis, testing and treatment. Compared to manufacturing, the value streams in healthcare are complex and not easy to see. *Value Stream Mapping* (VSM) is one of the first activities that many healthcare organizations undertake on their *Lean* journey. VSM provides a high-level view of a process that has been targeted for improvement. The usual practice is to identify patient groups that have similar needs and require similar care services. In the next step, a cross-profession team maps all the steps through which a patient passes in a value stream. In many cases, the mapping of patient flows is complemented with the mapping of the staff activities required to perform a task for a patient. VSM is a way of visualizing processes and creating a common view of patient flows or activities flow for all employees. The VSM is a starting point for identifying waste and finding opportunities for improvement. In the manufacturing context, an important part of VSM is the analysis of Takt time (the term comes from German *Taktzeit*, which means the rate of time at which a product or service is being ordered), cycle times and lead time. This is not the case for healthcare organizations. In the healthcare setting, Takt time varies due to variations in demand, and stable cycle times are difficult to achieve. Lead time is usually estimated, but the focus instead lies on identifying problems in the value stream, especially in the referrals between different healthcare units. The usual questions asked in the healthcare context are: Where does the patient have to wait? Does the value stream contain any duplicated work? Where are the problems for patients? Where are the delays, interruptions and problems for staff?

Although many patient flows cross several healthcare units, the majority of value stream mappings are done only within one organizational unit that is part of a larger healthcare organization. Most of the *Lean* adoptions in healthcare start locally at a single primary care or hospital unit, and a common problem is that other healthcare units involved in the value stream are not ready to change and become involved in *Lean* improvement activities. Another difficulty is that the current financial system and the management structure frequently do not comply with the value stream orientation. In some cases, it is difficult to say which healthcare organization is the owner of the value stream. This is because single units contribute small parts, but none wants to or can take responsibility, challenge and allocate resources for improving the whole value stream. In these situations, there is a need to establish a cross-organizational team that has the responsibility and resources to work jointly to improve the entire value stream. An example of such initiatives is the value streams of stroke patients. Integrated care pathways and inter-organizational care coordination is an important research area and development trend in healthcare (e.g., Campbell et al., 1998; Strandberg-Larsen & Krasnik, 2009).

Create Flow

Creating flow implies linking operations together and making the activities flow smoothly without interruption. The current healthcare systems are often designed with a focus on the doctors, nurses and other clinical staff to optimize their work performance. Care services are often "batch and queue", with patients waiting between different activities. *Lean* healthcare, on the other hand, focuses on better patient flow. Looking at value streams from the patient perspective brings problems to the surface and creates opportunities for improvement. The most common methods used to create flow in healthcare are linking activities and performing them in parallel, visual management, 5S and standardized work.

Linking Activities and Performing Them in Parallel

Many activities in healthcare are performed in sequence, with patients waiting between the different process steps. The adoption of *Lean* inspires healthcare staff to redesign their way of working and to link activities together. One example is the diagnostic process, in which many healthcare professionals need to be involved. Instead of meeting the patient separately, often at different times and places, a team consisting of all the necessary healthcare professionals is created. The team meets the patient just once and makes a diagnosis and treatment decision jointly.

Many activities that are done in sequence can actually be done in parallel. An obvious example is when many tests and investigations need to be performed in order to make a diagnosis and treatment plan. By adopting *Lean*, organizations often look how they can better synchronize and coordinate the necessary tests and investigations.

Visual Management

Visual management is a method for creating a work environment that is rich in instant and visually stimulating information. Simple visual tools are used to clarify goals and metrics and provide timely feedback on process performance. The idea is to give healthcare staff more control over value streams so they can quickly identify when something is going wrong or not happening at all. One example is visual control of patient flow, where metrics and indicators such as patient status, discharge times, necessary checks, handoffs and wait times are visualized. In this way, doctors can reduce delays between the moment that information becomes available and the moment at which decisions are carried out, or nurses can see how they can best leverage resources and coordinate work.

5S: Sorting, Setting in Order, Systematic Cleaning, Standardizing and Sustaining

5S is a method for organizing the workplace so that everything necessary to perform the work is well organized and easily accessible. 5S is frequently adopted in healthcare organizations. For example, one of the studied care centers introduced 5S to treatment trolleys in doctors' rooms. The primary care physicians agreed on the items that are necessary to perform the daily work with patients and set a standard for how the items should be organized. The benefit was that doctors could meet and examine patients in different rooms, did not spend time on unnecessary searching, and could pass on the responsibility for organizing and refilling the treatment trolleys to others.

Standardized Work

This *Lean* method is about standardizing individual tasks by defining a single best way of doing an activity. Standardized work is the foundation for continuous improvement, since work that has not been standardized cannot be improved (Imai, 1986). Healthcare has its own method for standardizing clinical processes—*Evidence-Based Medicine (EBM)*—which involves using the best current evidence to make decisions about what care is right for each individual patient.

Standardization has a negative connotation in healthcare and has received mixed reactions from healthcare staff and patients. Critics claim that patients' individual needs can go unmet or can be inappropriately addressed when work is standardized. Further, doctors are highly trained individuals who are used to acting with autonomy. Standardization implies their role changing from being highly skilled individuals who act on their own decisions to members of a collective who follow a set of procedures to treat patients. There is also difficulty and resistance to the overly far-reaching standardization of tasks that include contact with the patient.

Our experience is that clinical practice and patient-doctor meetings are not a subject of discussion and target for improvement when healthcare organizations adopt *Lean*. Instead, the focus of standardization lies on administrative routines and processes, which do not imply direct patient contact and have the primary objective of creating more efficient patient flows, in which waste, such as wait time, is reduced. The standardized work is usually introduced at a more general level in value streams and not at the level of treating individual patients. This is understandable, since *EBM* plays an important role in clinical practice and is an established method to standardize best care practices. *Lean* and *EBM* complement each other in respect to standardization: The former influences decision-making and practice at the value stream or organizational level, the latter at the clinical level.

Establish Pull

Essentially, pull means doing work in response to actual customer demand in order to avoid overproduction and the buildup of inventory. Since patients cannot be treated for stock, healthcare does not really involve overproduction and inventory in the sense defined in manufacturing. It could be said that healthcare is a pull system by its nature, since nothing can be done until a need arises in the patient. But this is not true, since pull needs to be established in the complete value stream. The consecutive steps in the value stream must be ready to take care of patients in order to avoid the buildup of waiting lists and wait times for patients.

In manufacturing, the value stream is optimized, which means that every process step follows a standardized cycle time (the time it takes for an operator to go through all the activities before repeating them) to meet the Takt time (the time required to complete a product to meet customer demand). In healthcare, pull is difficult to implement because demand for care services may vary considerably, as do patient needs. It is often difficult to achieve a standardized cycle time since every patient has specific needs that require customized care. Further, unexpected events may occur and influence the time required for a visit or treatment. Therefore, healthcare rarely involves discussions about cycle and Takt times. Instead of implementing pull in its original form, healthcare organizations attempt to better match staff capacity with patient demand for care. They try to understand the variation in patient demand for care during the day, week and month, and adjust their capacity to meet the varying demands. This requires significant flexibility in staffing patterns and that value streams be designed with room for variability in patient numbers and acuteness.

Strive for Perfection

This principle is about continuous problem solving and improvement efforts at all levels. The basic assumption is that employees have knowledge, creativity and problem-solving skills and that this potential can be used to the benefit of patients, the organization and its employees. In *Lean* organizations, employees are more empowered and receive more responsibility for managing and improving daily activities (Poksinska et al., 2013). Through everyday work, employees learn and gain valuable knowledge about the prevailing conditions and opportunities; this knowledge can then be translated into concrete ideas for improvement. However, nothing happens until an enabling culture and supporting structure for involving employees in improvement work is established. Continuous improvement should be systematic, integrated in the daily work and realized by employees (Bessant, 2003).

There is evidence that employee-driven problem solving and continuous improvement are not widely practiced in healthcare organizations (Graban & Swartz, 2012; Tucker & Edmondson, 2003). When healthcare staff members experience an interruption, problem or other distraction in their daily routine, they work around the problem instead of solving it. The physical presence of patients when performing the work diverts attention away from the problem itself, and instead places the focus on the current patient's comfort and safety. Dedicated and highly skilled professional staff members are supposed to compensate for any operational failures that might occur during the care delivery process (Tucker & Edmondson, 2003). In fact, this leads to a system in which problems are hidden rather than seen as a possibility for improvement. Adopting *Lean* has the potential to change this situation. The employee-driven improvement work is frequently one of the first *Lean* principles implemented by healthcare organizations. Our research shows that many *Lean* initiatives in healthcare start by involving healthcare staff in daily improvement activities. The usual practice is to turn attention to daily problems and establish routines to solve them. The healthcare organizations frequently create whiteboards for stand-up meetings, where healthcare staff can systematically discuss improvement opportunities. The improvements are then put into action with the active participation of those who propose improvements or others who work in the affected work area. Taking care of the daily problems is a good way to engage employees in the improvement work and create motivation for the continued adoption of *Lean*.

THE CONTRIBUTION OF LEAN TO THE QUALITY OF CARE

The contribution of *Lean* to the improvement of quality of care is discussed in the following sections.

Lean Contribution to Patient-Centered Care

According to the definition of "quality of care" provided by the Institute of Medicine (2001, p. 40), patient-centered care means "providing care that is respectful of and responsive to individual patient preferences, needs, and values, and ensuring that patient values guide all clinical decisions". *Lean*, as it is adopted in healthcare organizations today, does not make a great contribution to patient-centered care. As described in the previous section, a central concept of *Lean* is to understand value from the customer's perspective, but healthcare organizations adopting *Lean* tend to take the organization's perspective in defining value and improving the value streams rather than the patient's perspective. It is healthcare staff members who define patient value and implement improvements that they feel should benefit the patient.

In one of our studies, we used the data from the Swedish National Patient Survey to investigate whether there were significant differences in patient-perceived quality of care between primary care units working with *Lean* and a control group (primary care units not working with *Lean*). We also investigated how the *Lean* primary care units improved over time (Poksinska et al., 2014). The survey measured patients' perceived quality of care based on a set of indicators such as staff responsiveness, patient involvement in care, information sharing, accessibility, trust, patient value, recommendation and overall impression. Patients in the *Lean* primary care units did not perceive a better quality of care on any of the investigated indicators. Instead, our results show that patients perceived a deterioration of information quality in the patient-doctor meeting. The differences were very small but statistically significant, and indicated that the *Lean* group was worse than the control group in terms of listening to what the patients had to say and paying sufficient attention regarding patient skills and experience; in other words, in involving patients in decision-making and care. The results were surprising, but could indicate that healthcare organizations do not pay sufficient attention to incorporating the patient's perspective in the current adoptions of *Lean*.

Lean Contribution to Safe Care

The expected contribution of *Lean* to safe care was not confirmed by our studies. None of the studied healthcare organizations explicitly focused on patient safety and measured the improvements in this respect. The interviewed healthcare staff stated that although improvements in patient safety were achieved, they were only subjectively perceived effects. Can patient safety improvements be expected from the *Lean* adoptions? From the theoretical perspective, there are several *Lean* tools and methods that can make a contribution in this respect. For example, better workplace organization through 5S can minimize several risks when locations for supplies and equipment are made obvious and easily accessible. Problems and waste in values stream can lead to dangerous mistakes and errors. By identifying the problems, applying root cause analysis and putting solutions into place, both the value stream and patient safety can be improved. Furthermore, standardizing value streams can help to achieve more consistent and predictable care outcomes. *Lean* certainly has the potential to contribute to patient safety. A few studies have reported measured results, such as the reduced rate of incidents per patient (Ballé & Regnier, 2007), improved Papanicolaou test quality (Raab et al., 2006), increased number of patient safety alerts (Kaplan & Patterson, 2008) and reduced surgical instrument processing errors (Blackmore et al., 2013).

Lean Contribution to Timely Care

The most commonly stated effects from *Lean* adoption in healthcare were decreased overall time that patients spent on care and reduced wait times (Poksinska, 2010). As the lead time can be reduced by eliminating waste in a manufacturing company, the same effect can be achieved in healthcare. The mapping of patient flows highlights the time that the different activities take and the wait times between the activities. All seven types of waste—overproduction, waiting, transportation, inventory, motion, overprocessing and defective units (Ohno, 1988)—can be translated and found in healthcare. Patients are unnecessarily transported for testing and treatment. Equipment is moved from centralized storage. Healthcare staff members waste time by walking and looking for items, searching for patients or gathering supplies and instruments. There is overprocessing by capturing redundant information, multiple testing and recording and logging of data. By looking for waste and connecting activities, healthcare organizations are able to eliminate wait times for doctors or nurses, for patients being assigned a bed or being discharged and for test results to arrive. In Sweden, hospitals that adopted *Lean* include Skåne University's hospital and Saint Göran Hospital in Stockholm. These hospitals report results such as shortening the time of investigation for cervical cancer from four weeks to nine days (Lövtrup, 2008a), decreasing the time to see a doctor in the emergency department by half and reducing the total processing time of patients by 40 percent (Lövtrup, 2008b).

Sometimes, simply rearranging work activities or using more staff at bottlenecks can lead to a radical reduction in wait times. One example is the reduction of telephone queues in one of the studied care centers. By analyzing the problem of telephone availability, it was discovered that telephone lines were particularly long on Mondays. Further investigation revealed that patient demand for care was higher at the beginning of the week, but there was less healthcare staff availability since doctors used to plan their "appointment-free days" on Mondays. Understanding this fact revealed several changes that improved the telephone availability and decreased the wait time for doctor visits at the care center (over 90 percent of patients received contact with the care center within one day and could visit the doctor within seven days).

Lean Contribution to Efficient Care

Efficient care means using available resources in the best possible way to achieve the goals set (Institute of Medicine, 2001). The available resources are the healthcare staff as well as the equipment, supplies, ideas and energy needed to perform the value-adding care activities. For nurses and doctors, the most important aspect is spending as much time as possible on the direct care of patients. In order to achieve that, healthcare organizations need to minimize the time that nurses and doctors spend dealing with things other than patients, such as doing paperwork or searching for equipment. Many *Lean* adoptions in healthcare have focused explicitly on this aspect. The primary goal of *Lean* adoption in the UK's National Health Service (NHS) is releasing time to care. The NHS's *Lean* initiative, called "The Productive Ward", focuses on improving care processes and environments to help nurses and therapists spend more time on patient care and thereby improve safety and efficiency (Morrow et al., 2010).

One example from our research is the diagnostic process for heart patients at the physiology clinic. The primary activity of the physiology clinic is to perform different types of diagnoses and tests ordered by other clinics in the hospital. Therefore, the clinic considers both patients and other healthcare workers as the most important customers. To improve the diagnostic process for heart patients, a joint improvement project, including staff from both clinics, was completed. The result of this joint initiative was that the activities of the physiology and heart clinics were coordinated and integrated into one process. This allowed achieving savings on paperwork since it was no longer necessary to write and circulate medical records and reports. The outcomes for patients included shortened wait times and a quicker diagnosis.

The *Lean* principles and tools adopted into healthcare have the potential to contribute to more efficient care. The efficiency gains are in addition to reduced wait times, which is one of the most cited and acknowledged effects of adopting *Lean* in healthcare (Dickson et al., 2008; Kim et al., 2006; Radnor et al., 2012).

Lean Contribution to Effective Care

Effectiveness can be defined as "care that is based on the use of systematically acquired evidence to determine whether an intervention, produces better outcomes than alternatives—including the alternative of doing nothing" (Institute of Medicine, 2001, p. 49). This definition is the foundation of *EBM*, which implies the integration of clinical expertise, patients' values and the best available evidence in making patient care decisions (Sackett et al., 1996). As mentioned above, clinical practice is usually excluded from *Lean* interventions. Medical procedures and treating patients are seldom subject to discussion and improvements when *Lean* is adopted in healthcare. This is understandable, since it would be somewhat surprising if a production system designed for car manufacturing impacted such critical care aspects as clinical decision-making and practice. On several occasions, interviewed healthcare staff raised the following argument against *Lean*: "We work with evidence-based medicine, but where is the evidence that *Lean* is the right approach for improving healthcare?" *Lean* makes a contribution to effective care at the value stream level. Treating patients according to the best available evidence (contribution from *EBM*) is a crucial aspect of care, but the care must also be coordinated and integrated with ease of access to services (contribution from *Lean*). By focusing on patients' flows, *Lean* contributes to timely, predictable and controlled value streams.

Lean Contribution to Equitable Care

The equity dimension means providing care that does not vary in quality because of personal characteristics, but is equal for the whole society. Our empirical evidence, as well the case studies available in the literature, do not indicate either that *Lean* is adopted to the purpose of providing more equitable care or that any results in this area are reported. However, this does not mean that *Lean* does not contribute to equitable care. First, equity is not a prime target for improvements in healthcare. Second, the equitable provision of care services is more difficult to measure than efficiency and accessibility. However, it can be expected that improvements in the efficiency and accessibility of healthcare might enhance the equity of healthcare; for example, by creating better conditions for healthcare organizations to balance the desire to give current patients the best possible care with the need to provide care to people who are waiting to access services.

LIMITATIONS OF LEAN FROM THE SERVICE PERSPECTIVE

The adoption of *Lean* in healthcare can certainly contribute to several dimensions of quality care. Having said that, we must acknowledge that adopting a production system designed for car manufacturing to an advanced service system such as healthcare cannot meet all the development needs of healthcare. Although healthcare and the manufacturing sector bear many similarities, there remain significant areas of difference, which must be considered when adopting an industry approach into the healthcare context. The main limitation of *Lean* is that it supports a view of the "customer" that is in contrast to the current developments in service research. According to Grönroos and Ojasalo (2004), both internal efficiency (cost control without decreasing quality) and external efficiency (experienced quality of the customer) are crucial to achieve service productivity. In the service field, the perception of the customer role has undergone a change. The customer is seen as a "co-creator of value" instead of a passive consumer, and should play an active role in the service creation and delivery processes (Grönroos, 2008; Vargo & Lusch, 2004). From the service perspective, *Lean* represents a traditional view of the customer, whereby the value is solely created by producers and not co-created with customers.

In healthcare, a paradigm shift has occurred in the relationship with patients, and concepts such as patient-centered care, patient involvement, patient participation and patient empowerment have attracted a great deal of attention in recent years. It is now increasingly acceptable to perceive a patient as a "customer" who "acquires information, seeks alternatives, is movable, makes choices, and gets involved in producing value" (Nordgren, 2009, p. 118). We discern a trend, whereby healthcare politicians, commissioners and healthcare professionals are increasingly striving to find ways to organize for greater patient involvement. *Lean* does not seem to support this trend in Sweden. Improvements are being undertaken to achieve more patient-centered care, but there is little focus on an active involvement of patients in planning and delivering healthcare services in the current adoptions of *Lean* in healthcare.

Healthcare can be developed from either an inside-out or an outside-in perspective (Day, 1994). The former stresses the efficiency of services and improvements based on the lens of the organization. The latter views the service through the lens of the patient and focuses on providing value for the patient. According to our experience, *Lean* is adopted in healthcare using an inside-out perspective and focuses on internal efficiency. In service research, emphasis is placed on co-creating value with the customer (Grönroos, 2008) and using the "lens of the customer" to achieve customer satisfaction (Gustafsson & Johnson, 2003). Patients have unique knowledge of their own healthcare problems and their treatment, and have their own views on what creates value in the healthcare delivery process. In a service context, it is important to pay attention to *how* the service is delivered (functional quality) rather than just *what* is delivered (technical quality) (Grönroos, 2001). Healthcare organizations frequently focus on delivering the technical quality, but do not pay sufficient attention to functional quality, that is, how the patient receives and experiences the service (Kenagy et al., 1999). *EBM* focuses primarily on technical quality rather than on functional quality. The current adoptions of *Lean* in healthcare are no better in this respect.

Therefore, an important strategy is to develop systematic approaches to defining patient value that integrate both the organization's and the patient's perspectives in the adoption of *Lean* in healthcare. Value is a more complex construct in healthcare than in other settings. Whereas customers in other contexts may have the ability to determine the value of the services received, this is far from the case in the healthcare context. It is not always feasible for the patient, who suffers from some combination of illness, pain, uncertainty and fear, to take on the role of a customer. The crucial point is not to approach a patient as a "customer", but rather to understand the process of value creation from the patient's perspective and use the knowledge to make healthcare more responsive to individual patient preferences, needs and values.

Greater improvements can be achieved when *Lean* is combined with methods for patient involvement and participation. The doctor-patient meeting is a foundation of care. It is in these meetings that value is primarily created in the eyes of the patients. Doctors need to have time for these meetings, and that time that is often not available. *Lean* can help release more time for these meetings, but this time needs to be used to meet the current expectations on patient-centered care.

CONCLUSIONS

Improving the quality of care—in terms of providing care that is patient-centered, safe, effective, efficient, timely and equitable—has become an important priority of many welfare state governments. *Lean* undoubtedly has the potential to contribute to the improved quality of care. Several key tools and principles have proved to be effective in improving healthcare processes, especially in terms of providing more timely and efficient care. However, it is important to acknowledge that *Lean* was originally designed for car manufacturing and cannot meet all the development needs of healthcare. Healthcare is an advanced service system in which patients have a different role and position than the customers of manufacturing companies. The current adoptions of *Lean* in healthcare pay too little attention to incorporating the patient's perspective in the improvements being implemented. It is healthcare staff members who decide what creates value for the patient, and patients are seldom involved in defining value.

In order to achieve care that is not only more timely and efficient, but also more patient-centered, we suggest the following interpretation of the original five *Lean* principles (Womack & Jones, 1996):

1) Specify value: Incorporate both the expertise of healthcare staff and the patients' preferences and experiences in defining value;
2) Identify the patient flow: Understand all the activities required to provide care for patients. Focus not only on finding waste, but also how patient experience can be improved;
3) Create flow: Remove waste to make the activities flow without wait times and implement improvements that make care more responsive to individual patient preferences and needs;
4) Establish pull: Understand the variation in patient demand and match the capacity and resources in line with this demand;
5) Strive for perfection: Systematically identify and eliminate waste in patient flows and implement activities that improve patient experience.

REFERENCES

Ballé, M., & Regnier, A. (2007). Lean as a learning system in a hospital ward. *Leadership in Health Services*, 20 (1), 33–41.

Beattie, M., Shepherd, A., & Howieson, B. (2013). Do the Institute of Medicine's (IOM's) dimensions of quality capture the current meaning of quality in health care? An integrative review. *Journal of Research in Nursing*, 18 (4), 288–304.

Berwick, D.M., Enthoven, A., & Bunker, J.P. (1992). Quality management in the NHS: The doctor's role—II. *BMJ: British Medical Journal*, 304 (6822), 304–308. Retrieved from http://www.bmj.com/content/bmj/304/6822/304.full.pdf (accessed 31 May 2015).

Bessant, J.R. (2003). *High-involvement Innovation: Building and Sustaining Competitive Advantage through Continuous Change*. Chichester, England: Wiley.

Blackmore, C.C., Bishop, R., Luker, S., & Williams, B.L. (2013). Applying lean methods to improve quality and safety in surgical sterile instrument processing. *Joint Commission Journal on Quality and Patient Safety*, 39 (3), 99–105.

Campbell, H., Hotchkiss, R., Bradshaw, N., & Porteous, M. (1998). Integrated care pathways. *BMJ: British Medical Journal*, 316 (7125), 133–137. Retrieved from http://www.bmj.com/content/316/7125/133 (accessed 31 May 2015).

Day, G.S. (1994). The capabilities of market-driven organizations. *The Journal of Marketing*, 58 (4), 37–52.

Dickson, E.W., Singh, S., Cheung, D.S., Wyatt, C.C., & Nugent, A.S. (2008). Application of lean manufacturing techniques in the emergency department. *Journal of Emergency Medicine*, 37 (2), 177–182.

Drotz, E., & Poksinska, B. (2014). Lean in healthcare from employees' perspective. *Journal of Health Organization and Management*, 28 (2), 177–195.

Elg, M., Engström, J., Witell, L., & Poksinska, B. (2012). Co-creation and learning in health-care service development. *Journal of Service Management*, 23 (3), 328–343.

Feldstein, P.J. (2011). *Health Care Economics*. Clifton Park, NY: Delmar.

Fialkowska, M., & Poksinska, B. (2014). *Lean in primary care: A critical appraisal from the service perspective*. Paper presented at the 17th QMOD conference on Quality and Service Sciences ICQSS 2014, Prague, Czech Republic.

Graban, M., & Swartz, J.E. (2012). *Healthcare Kaizen: Engaging Front-Line Staff in Sustainable Continuous Improvements*. Boca Raton, FL: CRC Press.

Groene, O., Botje, D., Suñol, R., Lopez, M.A., & Wagner, C. (2013). A systematic review of instruments that assess the implementation of hospital quality management systems. *International Journal for Quality in Health Care*, 25 (5), 525–541.

Grönroos, C. (2001). The perceived service quality concept: A mistake? *Managing Service Quality*, 11 (3), 150–152.

Grönroos, C. (2008). Service logic revisited: Who creates value? And who co-creates? *European Business Review*, 20 (4), 298–314.

Grönroos, C., & Ojasalo, K. (2004). Service productivity: Towards a conceptualization of the transformation of inputs into economic results in services. *Journal of Business Research*, 57 (4), 414–423.

Gustafsson, A., & Johnson, M. (2003). *Competing in a Service Economy: How to Create a Competitive Advantage through Service Development and Innovation*. San Francisco, CA: Jossey-Bass.

Imai, M. (1986). *Kaizen: The Key to Japan's Competitive Success*. New York: McGraw-Hill.

Institute of Medicine (IOM). (2001). *Crossing the Quality Chasm: A New Health System for the 21st Century*. Washington, DC: National Academy Press.

Joosten, T., Bongers, I., & Janssen, R. (2009). Application of lean thinking to health care: Issues and observations. *International Journal for Quality in Health Care*, 21 (5), 341–347.

Kaplan, G., & Patterson, S. (2008). Seeking perfection in healthcare. A case study in adopting Toyota Production System methods. *Healthcare Executive*, 23 (3), 16–21.

Kenagy, J.W., Berwick, D.M., & Shore, M.F. (1999). Service quality in health care. *JAMA: The Journal of the American Medical Association*, 281 (7), 661–665.

Kim, C., Spahlinger, D., Kin, J., & Billi, J. (2006). Lean health care: What can hospitals learn from a world-class automaker? *Journal of Hospital Medicine*, 1 (3), 191–199.

Krafcik, J. (1988). Triumph of the lean production system. *Sloan Management Review*, 30 (1), 41–52.

Liker, J. (2004). *The Toyota Way: 14 Management Principles from the World's Greatest Manufacturer*. New York: McGraw-Hill.

Lövtrup, M. (2008a). Den nya modellen har fått fäste på Lunds universitetssjukhus. *Läkartidningen*, 105 (47), 3398–3399. Retrieved from http://www.lakartidningen .se/OldWebArticlePdf/1/10791/3398_3399.pdf (accessed 31 May 2015).

Lövtrup, M. (2008b). Modell från bilindustri ska rädda sjukvården. *Läkartidningen*, 105 (47), 3396–3399. Retrieved from http://ww2.lakartidningen.se/pdf/ LKT0847s3396_3399.pdf (accessed 31 May 2015).

Morrow, E., Griffiths, P., Maben, J., Jones, S., & Robert, G. (2010). *The Productive Ward: Releasing Time to Care-learning and Impact Review*. London: NHS Institute for Innovation and Improvement/ King's College. Retrieved from http:// www.institute.nhs.uk/images/ResearchAndEvaluationReports/PW_review_full_ report.pdf (accessed 31 May 2015).

Nordgren, L. (2009). Value creation in health care services—developing service productivity: Experiences from Sweden. *International Journal of Public Sector Management*, 22 (2), 114–127.

Ohno, T. (1988). *Toyota Production System: Beyond Large-Scale Production*. Portland, OR: Productivity Press.

Pillinger, J. (2001). *Quality in Social Public Services*. Dublin: Office for Official Publications of the European Communities. Retrieved from http://www. uni-mannheim.de/edz/pdf/ef/00/ef00127en.pdf (accessed 31 May 2015).

Poksinska, B. (2009). Lean i Vården—Rapport från Sveriges Kommuner och Landstings Utvecklingsprogram. Report from Swedish Association of Local Authorities and Regions. Stockholm: Sveriges Kommuner och Landsting.

Poksinska, B. (2010). The current state of lean implementation in healthcare: Literature review. *Quality Management in Health Care*, 19 (4), 319–329.

Poksinska, B., Fialkowska, M., & Engström, J. (2014). *Does lean healthcare lead to improvement of patient-perceived quality of care?* Paper presented at the 17th QMOD conference on Quality and Service Sciences ICQSS 2014, Prague, Czech Republic.

Poksinska, B., Swartling, D., & Drotz, E. (2013). The daily work of lean leaders: Lessons from manufacturing and healthcare. *Total Quality Management & Business Excellence*, 24 (7–8), 886–898.

Raab, S.S., Andrew-JaJa, C., Condel, J.L., & Dabbs, D.J. (2006). Improving Papanicolaou test quality and reducing medical errors by using Toyota production system methods. *American Journal of Obstetrics and Gynecology*, 194 (1), 57–64.

Radnor, Z.J., Holweg, M., & Waring, J. (2012). Lean in healthcare: The unfilled promise? *Social Science & Medicine*, 74 (3), 364–371.

Sackett, D.L., Rosenberg, W., Gray, J., Haynes, R.B., & Richardson, W.S. (1996). Evidence based medicine: What it is and what it isn't. *BMJ: British Medical Journal*,

312 (7023), 71–72. Retrieved from http://www.bmj.com/content/312/7023/71?hwoa sp=authn:1364839783:4058629:3580401867:0:0:akttKuV0ELm5ctUF/uivwA% 3D%3D (accessed 31 May 2015).

SKL. (2007). *En fråga om demokrati: Inriktningen av Sveriges Kommuner och Landstings verksamhet för kongressperioden 2007–2011.* Inriktningsdokument 3. Stockholm: Sveriges Kommuner och Landsting.

Socialstyrelsen. (2006). God vård: Om ledningssystem för kvalitet och patientsäkerhet i hälso- och sjukvården. Stockholm: Socialstyrelsen. Retrieved from http://www.skane.se/upload/Webbplatser/Utvecklingscentrum/dokument/SoS_handbok_God_vard_sosfs200512.pdf (accessed 31 May 2015).

Soop, M., Fryksmark, U., Köster, M., & Haglund, B. (2009). The incidence of adverse events in Swedish hospitals: A retrospective medical record review study. *International Journal for Quality in Health Care,* 21 (4), 285–291.

Strandberg-Larsen, M., & Krasnik, A. (2009). Measurement of integrated healthcare delivery: A systematic review of methods and future research directions. *International Journal of Integrated Care,* 9 (January–March). Retrieved from https://www.ijic.org/index.php/ijic/article/view/305/609 (accessed 31 May 2015).

Toyota. (2001). *The Toyota Way, Internal Document.* Nagoya, Japan: Toyota City.

Tucker, A.L., & Edmondson, A.C. (2003). Why hospitals don't learn from failures: Organizational and psychological dynamics that inhibit system change. *California Management Review,* 45 (2), 55–72.

Vargo, S.L., & Lusch, R.F. (2004). Evolving to a new dominant logic for marketing. *Journal of Marketing,* 68 (1), 1–17.

Womack, J., & Jones, D. (1996). *Lean Thinking: Banish Waste and Create Wealth in Your Corporation.* New York: Simon & Schuster.

Womack, J., Jones, D., & Roos, D. (1990). *The Machine That Changed the World: The Story of Lean Production.* New York: Rawson.

Young, T., & McClean, S. (2008). A critical look at lean thinking in healthcare. *Quality and Safety in Health Care,* 17 (5), 382–386.

14 Learning Organizations
Panacea or Irrelevance?

Rod Sheaff

WHAT IS A LEARNING ORGANIZATION?

Advocates of the *"Learning Organization"* (*LO*) offer a set of prescriptions for improving an organization's performance by means of transforming it into a "learning" organization, not just an "understanding", "knowing" or "thinking" one (Giesecke & McNeil, 2004). The *LO* is thus regarded as a specific, ideal form of organization (Örtenblad, 2001). This chapter considers how the *LO* ideal would have to be interpreted or altered to maximize its relevance to healthcare organizations.

There is some evidence that, at least in commercial settings mostly outside of healthcare, certain characteristics of the *LO* are associated with faster organizational change, product or service introduction, better "organizational performance" (Kontoghiorghes et al., 2005) (sometimes equated with financial performance, see Davis & Daley, 2008; Ellinger et al., 2002) and "competitive advantage" (Barringer & Harrison, 1991; Kontoghiorghes et al., 2005; Mowery et al., 1996). Accordingly, the *LO* has joined the list of managerial innovations. Mostly, the literature on *LOs* is not scientific but normative; indeed, it is often uncritical of the *LO* (Tsang, 1997). The wide range of applications, organizations and contexts to which the *LO* has been applied justify calling the *LO* a "panacea". A plethora of consultancies and others offer it for sale to managers.

Various definitions of the *LO* exist (Crites et al., 2009 categorize them), but certain common characteristics recur. Örtenblad and Koris (2014) define an *LO* as an organization that contains (or ought to contain) all four of the following:

1) Learning at work;
2) Organizational learning;
3) Learning structures;
4) A climate for learning.

Of course, an organization might not adopt all of these, but only some, or just one. Below, the term "*LO* approach" is used for a more partial, selective adoption of one, two or three of the above four components. Phrases such as "the *LO* requires . . . " are a shorthand for saying, "Managers and others who wish to establish a *Learning Organization* will have to . . . " Having elaborated on the four main characteristics in terms of who learns, how, what they learn and why, this chapter uses mainly secondary empirical evidence about the *LO* approach in healthcare to assess which of these characteristics are relevant or applicable to healthcare organizations, which are not, and therefore, how the *LO* has to be adjusted for application to healthcare.

Learning at Work

LO advocates assert that every member of an *LO* should learn continuously through their daily work. This learning, however, occurs simultaneously at three main levels: Individual, work team and whole organization (Ferlie & Shortell, 2001). What is learned varies accordingly.

Individual Learning

All the individual members of an *LO* should, Senge (1992) argued, acquire a "personal mastery" of work-related knowledge, with this education being continuously refreshed ("lifelong learning", see Nevis et al., 1997). Its production workers (in healthcare, clinicians, see Mohr, 2005) are key learners and *LO* implementers for any organization because they perform the core productive processes that literally produce whatever outcomes the organization achieves. The *LO* approach requires that workers work in a conscious, reflective way that is constructively critical of existing work practices (Bess et al., 2011) This is practical learning at work and through work (Dymock & McCarthy, 2006), often in an experimental, trial-and-error way. Indeed, early models of organizational learning (Dixon, 1999) were homologous with certain accounts of individual learning, especially Kolb's (2014). Kolb posited that when someone learns a new skill, she does so through a cycle of concrete experience, reflective observation, abstract conceptualization and active experimentation. The cycle combines cognitive and practical moments, and implicitly the affective and relational, even moral, aspects of learning (Tsasis, 2009). A concomitant of learning new working practices is "unlearning" obsolete or counter-productive mental models (de Holan, 2004).

The individuals who so learn do so "on behalf of teams/organizations" (Crites et al., 2009, p. 7). If everyone is to be a learner, learning activity and its management must also, advocates of the *LO* say, be dispersed throughout an organization, so that its individual members can be (co-)learners, coaches, mentors or teachers. That requires managers to be open to such experiences and opportunities for learning, and that this expertise is distributed across many members of the organization (Collins et al., 1989).

Team Level

One sign of an *LO* is that it reengineers whole work processes in response to problems rather than changing them in more superficial ways (Fiol & Lyles, 1985; Klunk, 1997). Many organizations' core productive work is undertaken by a complex of work teams (Ferlie & Shortell, 2001). At the level of production processes, an *LO* is recommended (Nevis et al., 1997) to focus on what its products are used for and "design and make" activities, adapting production to accommodate changes in scientific knowledge, resources and external constraints (legislation, competitors, etc.). That requires both the internal invention of new working practices and the ability to copy best practices from other organizations, and "ambidexterity" (see also Chapter 20 in this volume), i.e., both be innovative and make efficient use of knowledge that already exists.

Team learning is therefore required; an *LO* formalizes the tacit knowledge that production teams apply (Giunipero, 1996), in particular how to coordinate and standardize work both within teams—which often means across professions—and across multiple teams. That requires each person understanding the mental models they hold themselves, while understanding and appreciating those that others hold (Bess et al., 2011; Senge, 1992). Team-based learning may also be expected to promote divergent and plural modes of thinking. The systematic review by (Crites et al., 2009) suggests that teams who make decisions collaboratively use research findings and adapt to innovations more quickly. It has therefore been argued that organizations should create "communities of practice" to stimulate innovation and learning (Li et al., 2009; Wenger et al., 2002) and to promote goodwill, solidarity and collaboration, hence the sharing of learning, across all ranks and professions (Dovey, 1997).

Whole-Organizational Level

In practice, all of the above activities require top management support, or at least its permission, to be implemented (Garvin et al., 2008). *LO* managers initiate the above kinds of learning deliberately (Giesecke & McNeil, 2004), not just updating working practices in response to external stimuli or internal problems after they occur. In particular, these managers need, say the advocates of *LOs*, learning from "beyond the walls" (Cepetelli, 1995) to understand how their work fits into the wider organization and its environment (the presence of any competitors, new production technologies, etc.). Given that simple coercion is not an option, managers in any organization also need to learn how to persuade others to undertake, or at least assist, the work. In managerial idiom, they have to formulate a "cohesive vision" expressing the organization's unifying purpose (Senge, 1992) and "guiding ideas" for strategies to attain it (Hassouneh, 2001).

Organizational Learning

An essential feature of an *LO* is that individuals' and team learning is appropriated, synthesized, distributed and applied in a collective, organization-wide way: The whole organization learns (Örtenblad, 2005). The predominant explanation (Dixon, 1999) of how an *LO* learns regards organizational learning as a similar but larger-scale process to that of individual learning (Carroll & Edmondson, 2002; Senge, 1990; Tsang, 1997); that is, as a four-stage cycle of:

1) Reflection upon the causes of the problems that have been observed in the organization's work;
2) "Connecting", i.e., devising a range of possible practical solutions;
3) Deciding which practical solution to adopt, and formulating the reason(s) for that choice;
4) "Doing", i.e., implementing the chosen solution in an experimental frame of mind.

By reflecting upon what then occurred as a result of the "Doing" stage, the learners launch a second cycle. (*Total Quality Management*—see Mosadeghrad and Ferlie, Chapter 22 in this volume—can be regarded as a special case of this cycle.)

An *LO* then elaborates on this cycle with additional "loops". First, repetitions of the cycle result in a gradual accumulation of knowledge, in which learning is not only a present activity but the long-term accretion of a body of knowledge (Mowery et al., 1996). It is path dependent, because subsequent learning builds upon earlier learning. Second, besides learning the solution to whatever immediate problem an *LO* approach is used to address, wider lessons are drawn about how successfully the organization's performance is pursuing its objectives, resulting in larger adjustments at the level of organizational structures, of routine working practices and even of strategy, as Argyris' (1976) double-loop model of learning describes. This mode of learning is supposedly well-adapted to dealing with non-programmable, complex issues (Contu et al., 2003). Then, the cycle of learning itself becomes something that the participants can reflect upon, creating triple (third-order) learning (Davies & Nutley, 2000).

Learning Structure

Once acquired, the above learning has then to be "shared" among the rest of the organization and utilized (Nevis et al., 1997). Multiple structures can be used simultaneously to implement and sustain the organizational learning cycles, and so develop an *LO's* learning capability (DiBella, 1995): Collaborative enquiry, formal training, management information systems, coaching, audits, investigations and others (Carroll & Edmondson, 2002;

Garvin et al., 2008). Different writers prioritize them differently, but learning structures typically include:

1) *Knowledge Management* (Koeck, 1998) (for more information about *Knowledge Management* and its relevance to healthcare organizations, see Wickramasinghe and Gururajan, Chapter 12 in this volume), i.e., systematically managing knowledge diffusion and use within organizations;
2) Knowledge transfer into the organization from outside sources and building absorptive capacity, trust, alliances and "relational capital" (Kale et al., 2000);
3) Formalization (documentation) of and dissemination of workers' knowledge (Nevis et al., 1997) across the organization;
4) Routine analysis of errors or accidents so as to reveal any systemic causes arising from the organization's structure or working practices;
5) Creating flatter managerial hierarchies with decentralized control (van Wijk et al., 2008), which supposedly encourage the spread of knowledge, especially a "whole-picture" understanding, of an organization (Morgan, 2007);
6) A focus on measuring key activities and outputs, with discussions of these metrics serving in themselves as a learning activity (Nevis et al., 1997);
7) Using a specialized quality or research and development department to enable work teams to improve their work; this raises a firm's performance more than relying on audits (Koeck, 1998).

Nevis et al. (1997) argue that *LOs* have a preference for generating knowledge internally, but also do much environmental scanning. Then, the focus of the learning cycle shifts to include activities aimed at reducing environmental uncertainty, for instance, by learning what other organizations are doing, how they work (including their capabilities as *LOs*) (Garvin et al., 2008) and what their discourses and interests are (van Bueren et al., 2003). By establishing relationships with other organizations, an organization can create wider opportunities for learning, i.e., generating and sharing knowledge (van Raak et al., 2005). It has even been argued that internal learning is becoming complementary or ancillary to inter-organizational learning, even obsolete (Li et al., 2009).

A Climate for Learning

Repeatedly, the foregoing is summed up as creating a "culture" of learning and development. An *LO* would place a premium on the validity of information and knowledge (Lipshitz et al., 1996). But what knowledge? At the level of the production process, the knowledge will largely be technical. As for how to undertake the social organization of work, it is often assumed that an organization is a collection of individuals jointly acting as one collective actor pursuing a set of objectives (Argyris, 1992; Dixon, 1999). Hence, the requisite knowledge would appear to be: How to achieve the organization's objectives more fully (Argyris & Schön, 1978; Fiol & Lyles, 1985; Lipshitz et al., 1996). The learning that an *LO* undertakes is performative. Individuals learn how to pursue their organization's objectives, and the organization learns how to pursue its owners' objectives; in for-profit corporations, typically, this is the "bottom-line performance" or "added value".

The trial-and-error character of the aforementioned learning cycles is usually assumed to require an organizational culture that tolerates open dialogue about multiple perspectives, uncertainty, contested viewpoints, the expression of doubts or criticism, the exposure of mistakes and openness to acquiring knowledge from outside the organization (Snell & Chak, 1998; Vassalou, 2001). For that, the workplace environment must provide the "psychological safety" to do such things (Garvin et al., 2008); hence, it must adopt a "no-blame" culture that tolerates *bona fide* errors (i.e., those arising from bad luck, unforeseen circumstances, human error) provided that practical lessons are drawn from them. As with technical "ambidexterity", an organization's culture also requires updating when its existing rhetoric becomes "debunked" or contested. Managerial innovations, including that of the *LO* itself, can partly be understood as rhetorical rejuvenation of that kind (Driver, 2002).

HOW RELEVANT IS THE LEARNING ORGANIZATION TO HEALTHCARE?

Healthcare Applications (Often Under Other Names)

Since they are complex, adaptive systems (Anderson & McDaniel, 2000; Tsasis, 2009), the idea of becoming an *LO* appears attractive to health organizations. Elements of the *LO* ("*LO* approaches") can and have been applied in practice in healthcare organizations, sometimes but not always under the "*LO*" label. Like healthcare improvement activities generally (Ferlie & Shortell, 2001), *LO* has to be applied simultaneously at individual, team, organization and inter-organizational levels.

Individual Level
Much clinical work applies both theoretical knowledge and practical, often manual and tacit, skills (Anderson & McDaniel, 2000). The maintenance and development of clinicians' personal competences makes a huge contribution to healthcare, something that becomes most obvious when these competences are lacking. The recently abolished UK National Patient Safety Agency estimated that medical errors harm around 300,000 people a year in the UK, ultimately killing 30,000 of them: To put this in perspective, this

is a greater annual mortality rate than that of breast, prostate and colorectal cancers combined. Classen et al. (2011) suggest that up to a third of inpatients experience an adverse event, which for 6% of them means a prolonged hospital stay and being discharged home with a permanent or temporary disability.

What might establishing an *LO* contribute to reducing these numbers? At the level of individual learning, the "learning at work" and learning cycle elements of the *LO* are (under other names) already applied in healthcare, not least as a means of clinicians' professional self-development (Davies et al., 2007). The widely used *Plan-Do-Study-Act* cycle (Berwick, 1996), which is implicitly what structures the medical audit and clinical audit generally, is an instance of the learning cycles outlined above. *Total Quality Management* is another instance of such double-loop learning. Clinical work often requires considerable discretion, even with simple technologies, for example, because of the unforeseen complexity of patients' care needs or circumstances (Abrahamson Löfström, 2013). Crites et al. (2009) and Wenger and Snyder (2000) argue that the application of *LO* methods can be used to bring even tacit knowledge into the organizational learning of healthcare providers (individuals, teams and organizations). So, paradoxically, *LO* models for individual learning can be used to standardize clinical care processes so as to improve reliability (Resar, 2006) and safety. However, *LO* activities at the individual level require protected time and reflective practice (Rushmer et al., 2004).

Secondly, healthcare depends heavily on the application of scientific knowledge, whose development continues to accelerate. Healthcare innovations are time limited (knowledge changes), for which cyclical, *LO*-like review methods are required (Rushmer et al., 2004). The assumption that clinicians' learning therefore needs to be lifelong is an obvious way to assist the timely unlearning of ineffective or wasteful working practices and assist their replacement with evidence-based alternatives (e.g., by requiring doctors to justify their decisions to override prescribing protocols). *LO* emphasizes the translation of external knowledge into working practice, and the *LO* learning cycle readily accommodates, legitimates, structures and guides the ways in which practitioners adapt and apply external knowledge and guidance in their own practices. Consequently, the *LO* can also be represented (Crites et al., 2009) as a way of reducing the translation gap between evidence-based medicine and clinical practice.

Thus, an *LO* is one way to focus and harness clinicians' tendency to value education, learning, science and personal development, and thereby also increase their work satisfaction and organizational commitment (Jeong et al., 2007). The anti-bureaucratic tone of *LO* rhetoric may also appeal to independent-minded professionals (Giesecke & McNeil, 2004). However, the *LO* also suggests the value and feasibility of using less formal learning activities, such as study circles and coaching for the less skilled staff involved in the care of the elderly (Abrahamson Löfström, 2013).

Team Level

In healthcare, an *LO* would at the team level focus on learning "design and make" activities. The individual learning methods described above have been extended across whole professions. Thus, the clinical audit originated in the UK, and parts of the USA in the 1990s as a medical audit, with analogous uni-professional audits (nursing audit, physiotherapy audit, etc.) developing in parallel. Communities of practice were originally conceived as networks, often uni-professional (Lave & Wenger, 1991; Li et al., 2009), through which practitioners validate, combine, revise and apply in their own practice guidance or knowledge generated by other organizations (Crites et al., 2009). These communities of practice thus combine two elements of the *LO*: Cyclical learning "in work", and seeking knowledge from external sources to apply locally.

Of growing relevance, given the growing proportion of patients with multiple chronic conditions (now around half the number of hospital bed days used in many health systems), are multi-professional care teams. An important application for the *LO* in healthcare is therefore learning how to combine separate clinical or therapeutic techniques into a coherent sequence of activities across different settings (the patient's home or workplace, the clinic, the hospital ward, etc.), i.e., as a coherent, "integrated" care pathway and model of care. Applying the *LO* approach to team learning, especially that of inter-organizational care teams, has therefore been represented (Tsasis et al., 2013) as a way of promoting the "integration" of disparate health services. Another important example of this approach, again not usually badged as an *LO* activity, is case management, whose basic principle is that a multi-professional team be responsible for the care of a patient with ongoing, complex care needs. One member of the team coordinates care, but when the patient enters case management, the team as a whole assesses the patient's health, other circumstances and needs, agrees what action has to be taken (care plan, treatment plan), then reviews the patient's condition either periodically or when it changes substantially (e.g., following an event such as a fall or reaching a new stage in the progression of the disease). These reviews can also be used to analyze what the team's work processes contributed to the eventual patient outcome (Crites et al., 2009). At need, it is possible not only to review what inputs the patient receives, but who will now manage the case and how, another example of how complex, non-programmable clinical tasks can, through an *LO*-like approach, become sources of "double-loop" learning.

Organizational Level

Hospitals and other health organizations already have a large repertoire of individual learning, team learning and evidence-translation methods. Their learning structures often already include active *Knowledge Management* (for more information about *Knowledge Management* and its relevance to healthcare organizations, see Wickramasinghe and Gururajan, Chapter 12 in this volume), in particular, actively gathering new scientific and epidemiological knowledge and models of care from outside the provider organization for feedback into the hospital's or clinic's internal learning (Crites et al., 2009) and service development at the individual and team levels (Tsasis et al., 2013). The *LO* provides a framework through which to assemble a *bricolage* of such learning structures and combine then into a system for producing coherent, innovative models of care (Anderson & McDaniel, 2000). Constant reiteration though several channels makes individual and team learning prominent among the large amounts of information and guidance that clinicians have to digest. It also reduces the risk that *LO* activities remain dependent on one or a few individuals (Abrahamson Löfström, 2013), and hence, fragile.

At the individual, team and whole-organizational levels, the use of outcome measurement as a basis and stimulus for learning already comes naturally to health organizations. Management information systems to harvest routine data for this purpose from medical records and payment systems is in some healthcare organizations well-established (Tsasis et al., 2013). In particular, many health organizations have routinized the analysis of accidents, errors, near-misses, reliability failures and "untoward incidents". Resar (2006) argues that the secret of success in doing so is to focus on just a few key clinical processes at once. Many hospitals have a specialized quality management or R&D department for these purposes, although it is often internally focused on audit, quality and safety monitoring rather than gathering knowledge externally.

Insofar as an organization's culture is the product of management activity (Marshall et al., 2003; Scott et al., 2003) rather than a reflection of existing work practices, an important part of organizational-level activity for sustaining the hospital or clinic as an *LO* model is to promote a culture or climate for learning that above all supports learning at the team level (Ferlie & Shortell, 2001). Part of this culture is a culture of openness (Rushmer et al., 2004), that healthcare staff will share information, especially between professions, which cannot be taken for granted (Ferlie et al., 2005), and therefore requires managerial and senior clinician intervention to sustain it. It also requires a culture of psychological safety (Carmeli & Gittell, 2009), i.e., confidence that exposing the need to learn how to improve existing work practices will not bring punishment down upon the informant or "whistleblower". A manager's style of work, and above all, inclusiveness, appears to help create such a climate (Nembhard & Edmondson, 2006). The importance of this part of the *LO* has, unfortunately, been confirmed by its absence in some National Health Service (NHS) hospitals, where highly centralized management and a bullying culture of "targets and terror" severely compromised patient care (The Mid Staffordshire NHS Foundation Trust Inquiry, 2010).

Inter-Organizational Level

It has even been suggested that whole health systems can become like *LOs* in many respects. Health organizations' learning-about-learning is often accomplished by informal communications, exchanging work placements across other organizations (Davies & Nutley, 2000) and participating in inter-organizational networks. Care networks undertake the cross-organizational management of patients who need services from many organizations at once (e.g., stroke patients, see Tsasis et al., 2013). Program networks promote and help implement a particular model of care, e.g., the health-promoting hospital (Pelikan et al., 2001). In the NHS, for example, such networks were established after 1995 with a heavy practical emphasis on hospitals, primary care trusts and other organizations collaboratively using *LO*-style methods to help implement updated standards of care (Sheaff et al., 2011).

Learning Organizations: Limitations for Healthcare

Against all this, simply copying some of the assumptions and applications of the *LO* model from other sectors (e.g., manufacturing, finance) into healthcare is problematic, either because of the obstacles to implementation, or because some of these assumptions, aims and methods are irrelevant, misconceived or beyond a single healthcare organization's power to influence.

One obstacle concerns clinical "learning at work". The links between a healthcare process (including a newly learned one) and its outcomes are often tenuous (Resar, 2006). Hence, the connections can only be learned through large-scale, formal research rather than informal learning-at-work.

In healthcare, vested professional interests can often inhibit innovation and (Anderson & McDaniel, 2000; Ferlie et al., 2005) and make knowledge transfer "sticky" (professionals are at times reluctant to share their specialized knowledge with other occupations) (Ferlie et al., 2000). Vested professional interests are also a source of resistance to management initiatives generally (Ferlie & Shortell, 2001). These vested interests include trade secrets: For example, by not training ophthalmology technicians to do simple cataract extractions under supervision, this relatively simple, and in private practice, well-paid, procedure could be reserved for senior ophthalmologists. The same factors tend to protect variation in clinical practice (Resar, 2006). It may also be counter-cultural for professionals—especially doctors—who are trained and view themselves as experts to view themselves as learners (Anderson & McDaniel, 2000). Clinicians often find difficulty in accommodating and tolerating mistakes, as the price of learning, in activities where (as noted above) the consequences of mistakes can be fatal. Managers' power paradoxically increases as organizations become more informally structured (Örtenblad & Koris, 2014), and insofar as doctors perceive that, it may lessen the attraction of partly informal managerial methods such as the *LO*.

The path dependency of the organizational learning on which the *LO* relies can be a mixed blessing insofar as it involves the persistence of professional silos, jurisdictional disputes and petty wars of professional status. Health organizations are "multicultural" (Ferlie & Shortell, 2001); professional cultures persist alongside managerially-promoted ones; indeed, multiple professional cultures whose education, learning methods and jurisdictional assumptions are often misaligned (Wilkinson et al., 2004). In healthcare (Davies & Nutley, 2000), as elsewhere, trust among the internal "stakeholders" is a requirement for an *LO*, but when managers have to persuade diverse, rival constituencies to implement the same policy, it becomes useful, indeed rational, for them to keep policy or managerial objectives ambiguous or obscure (Sheaff et al., 2009). This is an obstacle to learning, evidence basing and knowledge transfer (Coff et al., 2006). Since the construction of an *LO* is only a means to the organization's wider ends, the prioritization of other targets or the pursuit of narrow, over-stable aims and centralized control may practically "crowd out" concerns about becoming a *Learning Organization* (hence, of course, not all changes in work practices result from "*Learning Organization*" activities—see Gherardi, 2001).

Primary care, especially in USA but also in Britain and Germany, is largely a "cottage industry" of fragmented, scattered, small-scale partnerships (Davies et al., 2007), and (still) many single-handed doctors. This small scale limits the scope for learning within a single practice, and maybe also from nearby ones if they are seen as competitors. The same problem of small scale applies to the fragmented, casual workforce in residential care homes, especially in care for the elderly in many health systems, although there is evidence (Abrahamson Löfström, 2013) that *LO* approaches are feasible even there. Independent GPs' role as the proprietors of small businesses may also inhibit an egalitarian learning culture (Rushmer et al., 2004).

Similar obstacles confront most management initiatives in healthcare organizations, but these practical obstacles do not amount to objections in principle to the *LO*. More radical objections arise from *LO* assumptions that are either irrelevant to healthcare, incoherent or just wrong.

One such assumption is that *LOs*, for instance in primary care (Rushmer et al., 2004), either require or actually develop "flatter hierarchies". The foregoing arguments suggest that this is a red herring for health organizations; flatter hierarchies are neither obviously necessary nor obviously unnecessary for an *LO* in healthcare. However, the above arguments about the increasing importance of coordinated care for people with multiple long-term morbidities implies that team learning in healthcare does require not professional "silos", but multi-professional organizational structures, not so much "flatter" as "wider" structures (which in an inter-organizational setting will not be hierarchies anyway, but networks). Similarly, the community of practice model can certainly be implemented in healthcare—one of the first to be described in those terms was a learning community of midwives (Lave & Wenger, 1991)—and often is seen as a variation on the *LO*

(Li et al., 2009). The same argument suggests that a "flat" structure is less important for implementing *LO* approaches at the team level than a "wide" structure that applies to the community of practice.

Of rare or doubtful relevance to healthcare too is the original rationale for the *LO*. *LO* ideas were initially justified and gained managerial popularity partly as a putative means of restoring US, and to lesser extent, western European, firms' declining market shares in the face of increasingly competitive far-eastern manufacturing in the 1980s (Contu et al., 2003). In many health systems, competitive advantage is almost irrelevant to the care provider organizations (and also to the payers, in the Beveridge systems found in Scandinavia, around the Mediterranean, in the UK, and in Australia and New Zealand). Many provider organizations have either a legal or a de facto geographical monopoly, and when they do not, the demand or (differently) need for their services often exceeds the supply. Few health organizations have international competitors.

LO writers often assume that learning or organizational culture or both are independent variables that affect organizational performance (Gherardi, 2001), and can therefore be managed so as to improve it. However, the relationship is more complex than that. An organization's culture also, perhaps primarily, reflects its existing work practices and power relations (Schein, 1998). If so, the main locus for interventions to produce an *LO* has to be individuals', and above all, teams', work practices, with culture change as a consequence. Furthermore, as noted above, in healthcare organizations, multiple different cultures usually coexist: Managerial culture, a distinct culture for each profession, perhaps also a trade union culture, etc. Since these stakeholders' interests are correspondingly diverse, the purpose and desired character of *LO* activities may be contested (Contu et al., 2003). Li et al. (2009) document the development of the "*Learning Community*" from a means of personal growth into a corporate management tool, and one would expect the same to apply to the *LO*.

In healthcare, some conditions that *LO* models assume lie partly or wholly beyond a provider organization's power to influence. Healthcare provider organizations can actively initiate learning and internal knowledge generation about local working practices and models of care, but for the basic science underlying health, most learning occurs perforce in research centers, pharmaceutical and equipment firms and, to a lesser extent, university hospitals. Furthermore, this external environment is often hostile to learning. Business imperatives have been alleged to motivate the non-publication of randomized controlled trials or other research whose findings might debunk pharmaceutical or other firms' (Gold & Studdert, 2005) marketing claims, and motivate the selective publication of "positive" findings. Thus, business-sponsored trials of vaccines were more than four times less likely to report mixed or negative findings about the product under test than were other published trials (Manzoli et al., 2014). "Sponsor-dependent" differences in non-publication rates are reported for numerous trials of diverse types of therapeutic agents for various diseases. Other, more subtle distortions of research findings are not rare (Altman & Moher, 2013; Ioannidis et al., 2013).

As it is for the market environment, so it is for the policy environment, at least for highly politicized health systems such as the NHS. Over-centralized management appears to inhibit organizational learning and the production of new knowledge (Crites et al., 2009), both essential ingredients of the *LO*. At the whole health-system level, the NHS managerial regime has been described as one of "targets and terror" (senior managers are dismissed for failing to achieve centrally defined targets, such as reducing hospital wait times) (Bevan, 2006). Strong external monitoring appears to inhibit organizational learning (Davies & Nutley, 2000). The Francis inquiry (The Mid Staffordshire NHS Foundation Trust Inquiry, 2010) revealed the lengths some NHS managers went to to ensure that their own superiors, the government and the public should *not* learn the reasons for what occurred in their hospital. Managers in politicized health systems also face incentives, at times, to adopt symbolic policies whose main purpose is demonstrate to policy makers or the public that something has been done to address an ongoing problem, or to demonstrate adherence to a policy, for instance by implementing some favored managerial panacea such as the *LO*. There is a paradox, if not a self-contradiction, in the ideas of "controlled empowerment" or an "imposed *LO*" (Rushmer et al., 2004; Wilkinson et al., 2004).

Contu et al. (2003) ask: Who could be against learning? Yet, one might still ask whether certain things are worth learning at all. Learning how to provide safer healthcare is one thing; learning how to sell, say, unnecessary cosmetic surgery is arguably less worthwhile, for the patient if not the clinician or organization that provides it.

Adapting LO to Healthcare

These difficulties pose the question of how to adapt the *LO* model for application to healthcare, and suggest the following revisions.

In a healthcare organization, a particularly important application for the "learning at work" component of the *LO* is to those care pathways that extend across professions and/or organizations. One way to do so is to exploit patient transfers and hand overs (e.g., those between nursing shifts), which probably already are occasions for informal information exchange, and for informal learning at work, and to share knowledge generated by the *PDSA* cycle and other *LO* activities (Rushmer et al., 2004). Doctors' seniority and privileged position places an onus particularly upon them to lead by example (otherwise, they become an influential obstacle to the *LO*). For this purpose, negotiative ("soft") approaches to problem solving are generally more useful than directive ("hard") styles of management that rely heavily on formal organizational structures (Tsasis et al., 2013). Nevertheless, it is also necessary, in healthcare, to distinguish clearly between the areas of work where discretion and experimentation (an *LO* approach) are permissible and those where they are not, for example, in regard to obtaining informed consent to treatment and maintaining patient safety (which often involves strict protocolization of care). Where discretion is not permitted, an *LO* approach is limited to methods for implementing a protocol, not revising the protocol itself or the law. Where discretion is permitted, a healthcare *LO* will still have to be so designed as to distinguish mistakes due to learning or the individual variation of patients from those due to systemic errors, criminality, professional incompetence or negligence.

For the mutual reinforcement of the different elements of the *LO*, it is not only necessary to synchronize *LO* activities across all four of the above levels (individual, team, organization, inter-organizational network) (Alexander et al., 2001). Health systems contain strong professional networks for learning purposes, networks that coexist with managerial structures but function largely independently of them (Noordegraaf, 2011). *Learning Organization* activities in healthcare therefore also have to contain ways of aligning these different types of learning structures. A final adaptation is that for most health organizations, the main use of the *LO* in adjusting to the hospital's or clinic's external environment is not so much for competitive advantage as to adapt health services more successfully to the constantly shifting demographic, epidemiological and social factors causing—or preventing—ill health, all of which continue to change (Pelikan et al., 2001).

PANACEA OR IRRELEVANCE?

What an organization needs to learn depends upon its objectives, even for technically similar organizations under different ownership; this is a warning against overly general prescriptions for constructing an *LO* (Tsang, 1997). The number and complexity of the conditions for, and constraints upon, creating an *LO* in healthcare suggests that a contingency theory is required (Örtenblad, 2013). The foregoing chapter suggests some hypotheses. First, *LO* approaches appear more straightforwardly applicable to clinical than managerial work, especially when goal alignment and compatibility of interests among a health organization's different "stakeholders" are weak. Public and third sector organizations appear to face weaker competitive incentives than corporations to withhold learning from other organizations, but a highly politicized and internally professionalized health system also appears unfavorable for transparency and learning. Nevertheless, the *LO* does appear applicable in many respects to many kinds of health organizations. What is so far scarce is comparative empirical research into the feasibility and consequences of trying to implement such managerial innovation for different kinds of care groups and in different kinds of organizational settings.

REFERENCES

Abrahamson Löfström, C. (2013). The learning organization in elderly care—can it fit? In A. Örtenblad (Ed.), *Handbook of Research on the Learning Organization: Adaptation and Context*. Cheltenham, England: Edward Elgar, pp. 196–202.

Alexander, J.A., Waters, T.M., Burns L.R., Shortell, S.M., Gillies, R.R., Budetti, P.P., & Zuckerman, H.S. (2001). The ties that bind: Interorganizational linkages and physician-system alignment. *Medical Care*, **39** (7), i30–i45.

Altman, D.G., & Moher, D. (2013). Declaration of transparency for each research article. *BMJ: British Medical Journal*, **347** (7920), article no. f4796.

Anderson, R.A., & McDaniel, R.R., Jr. (2000). Managing health care organizations: Where professionalism meets complexity science. *Health Care Management Review*, **25** (1), 83–92.

Argyris, C. (1976). Single-loop and double-loop models in research on decision making. *Administrative Science Quarterly*, **21** (3), 363–375.

Argyris, C. (1992). *On Organisational Learning*. Oxford, England: Blackwell.

Argyris, C., & Schön, D. (1978). *Organizational Learning: A Theory of Action Approach*. Reading, MA: Addison-Wesley.

Barringer, B., & Harrison, J. (1991). Walking a tightrope: Creating value through inter-organizational relationships. *Journal of Management*, **26** (3), 367–403.

Berwick, D.M. (1996). A primer on leading the improvement of systems. *BMJ: British Medical Journal*, **312** (7031), 619–622.

Bess, K., Perkins, D., & McCown, D. (2011). Testing a measure of organizational learning capacity and readiness for transformational change in human services. *Journal of Prevention & Intervention in the Community*, **39** (1), 35–49.

Bevan, G. (2006). Setting targets for health care performance: Lessons from a case study of the English NHS. *National Institute Economic Review*, **197** (1), 67–79.

Carmeli, A., & Gittell, J.H. (2009). High-quality relationships, psychological safety, and learning from failures in work organizations. *Journal of Organizational Behavior*, **30** (6), 709–729.

Carroll, J.S., & Edmondson, A.C. (2002). Leading organisational learning in health care. *Quality & Safety in Health Care*, **11** (1), 51–56.

Cepetelli, E. (1995). Building a learning organization beyond the walls. *Journal of Nursing Administration*, **25** (10), 56–60.

Classen, D.C., Resar, R., Griffin, F., Federico, F., Frankel, T., Kimmel, N., Whitting, N., Frankel, R., Seger, A., & James, B.C. (2011). "Global trigger" tool shows that adverse events in hospitals may be ten times greater than previously measured. *Health Affairs*, **30** (4), 581–589.

Coff, R.W., Coff, D.C., & Eastvold, R. (2006). The knowledge-leveraging paradox: How to achieve scale without making knowledge imitable. *Academy of Management Review*, **31** (2), 452–465.

Collins, A., Brown, J., & Newman, S. (1989). Cognitive apprenticeship: Teaching the crafts of reading, writing and mathematics. In L.B. Resnick (Ed.), *Knowing, Learning and Induction*. Hillside, NJ: Erlbaum, pp. 435–490.

Contu, A., Grey, C., & Örtenblad, A. (2003). Against learning. *Human Relations*, **56** (8), 931–952.

Crites, G.E., McNamara, M.C., Akl, E.A., Richardson, W.S., Umscheid, C.A., & Nishikawa, J. (2009). Evidence in the learning organization. *Health Research Policy and Systems*, **7** (4), 1478–1505.

Davies, H., Powell, A., & Rushmer, R. (2007). *Healthcare Professionals' Views on Clinician Engagement in Quality Improvement: A Literature Review*. London: Health Foundation.

Davies, H.T.O., & Nutley, S.M. (2000). Developing learning organisations in the new NHS. *BMJ: British Medical Journal*, **320** (7240), 998–1001.

Davis, D., & Daley, B.J. (2008). The learning organization and its dimensions as key factors in firms' performance. *Human Resource Development International*, **11** (1), 51–66.

De Holan, P.M. (2004). Managing organizational forgetting. *MIT Sloan Management Review*, **45** (2), 45–51.

DiBella, A.J. (1995). Developing learning organizations: A matter of perspective. *Academy of Management Proceedings*, 287–290.

Dixon, N. (1999). *The Organizational Learning Cycle. How We Can Learn Collectively*. Aldershot, England: Gower.

Dovey, K. (1997). The learning organization and the organization of learning. *Management Learning*, **28** (3), 331–349.

Driver, M. (2002). The learning organization: Foucauldian gloom or Utopian sunshine? *Human Relations*, **55** (2), 33–53.

Dymock, D., & McCarthy, C. (2006). Towards a learning organization? Employee perceptions. *The Learning Organization*, **13** (5), 525–537.

Ellinger, A.D., Ellinger, A.E., Yang, B., & Howton, S.W. (2002). The relationship between the learning organization concept and firms' financial performance: An empirical assessment. *Human Resource Development Quarterly*, **13** (1), 5–22.

Ferlie, E., Fitzgerald, L., & Wood, M. (2000). Getting evidence into clinical practice: An organisational behaviour perspective. *Journal of Health Services & Research Policy*, **5** (2), 96–102.

Ferlie, E., Fitzgerald, L., Wood, M., & Hawkins, C. (2005). The nonspread of innovations: The mediating role of professionals. *Academy of Management Journal*, **48** (1), 117–134.

Ferlie, E.B., & Shortell, S.M. (2001). Improving the quality of health care in the United Kingdom and the United States: A framework for change. *Milbank Quarterly*, **79** (2), 281–315.

Fiol, C., & Lyles, M. (1985). Organizational learning. *Academy of Management Review*, **10** (4), 803–813.

Garvin, D.A., Edmondson, A.C., & Gino, F. (2008). Is yours a learning organization? *Harvard Business Review*, **86** (3), 109–116.

Gherardi, S. (2001). From organizational learning to practice-based knowing. *Human Relations*, **54** (1), 131–139.

Giesecke, J., & McNeil, B. (2004). Transitioning to the learning organization. *Library Trends*, **52** (1), 54–67.

Giunipero, L.C. (1996). Organizational change and survival skills for materiel managers. *Hospital Materiel Management Quarterly*, **18** (3), 36–44.

Gold, J.L., & Studdert, D.M. (2005). Clinical trials registries: A reform that is past due. *The Journal of Law, Medicine & Ethics*, **33** (4), 811–820.

Hassouneh, J. (2001). Developing a learning organization in the public sector. *Quality Progress*, **43** (1), 106–108.

Ioannidis, J.P., Karassa, F.B., Druyts, E., Thorlund, K., & Mills, E.J. (2013). Biologic agents in rheumatology: Unmet issues after 200 trials and [dollar] 200 billion sales. *Nature Reviews Rheumatology*, **9** (11), 665–673.

Jeong, S.H., Lee, T., Kim, I.S., Lee, M.H., & Kim, M.J. (2007). The effect of nurses' use of the principles of learning organization on organizational effectiveness. *Journal of Advanced Nursing*, **58** (1), 53–62.

Kale, P., Singh, H., & Perlmutter, H. (2000). Learning and protection of proprietary assets in strategic alliances: Building relational capital. *Strategic Management Journal*, **21** (3), 217–237.

Klunk, S.W. (1997). Conflict and the dynamic organization. *Hospital Materiel Management Quarterly*, **19** (2), 37–44.

Koeck, C. (1998). Time for organisational development in healthcare organisations. *BMJ: British Medical Journal*, 317 (7168), 1267–1268.

Kolb, D.A. (2014). *Experiential Learning: Experience as the Source of Learning and Development*. Upper Saddle River, NJ: FT Press.

Kontoghiorghes, C., Awbre, S.M., & Feurig, P.L. (2005). Examining the relationship between learning organization characteristics and change adaptation, innovation, and organizational performance. *Human Resource Development Quarterly*, 16 (2), 185–212.

Lave, J., & Wenger, E. (1991). *Situated Learning: Legitimate Peripheral Participation*. Cambridge, England: Cambridge University Press.

Li, L., Grimshaw, J., Nielsen, C., Judd, M., Coyte, P., & Graham, I. (2009). Evolution of Wenger's concept of community of practice. *Implementation Science*, 4 (1), article no. 11. Retrieved from http://www.implementationscience.com/content/4/1/11 (accessed 30 June 2015).

Lipshitz, R., Popper, M., & Oz, S. (1996). The design and implementation of organisational learning mechanisms. *Journal of Applied Behavioural Science*, 32 (3), 292–305.

Manzoli, L., Flacco, M.E., D'Addario, M., Capasso, L., De Vito, C., Marzuillo, C., Villari, P., & Ioannidis, J. (2014). Non-publication and delayed publication of randomized trials on vaccines: Survey. *BMJ: British Medical Journal*, 348 (7959), article no. g3058.

Marshall, M.N., Mannion, R., Nelson, E., & Davies, H.T. (2003). Managing change in the culture of general practice: Qualitative case studies in primary care trusts. *BMJ: British Medical Journal*, 327 (7415), 599–602.

The Mid Staffordshire NHS Foundation Trust Inquiry. (2010). *Independent enquiry into the care provided by Mid Staffordshire NHS Foundation Trust 2005–2009*. London: HMSO.

Mohr, J.J. (2005). Creating a safe learning organization. *Frontiers of Health Services Management*, 22 (1), 41–44.

Morgan, G. (2007). *Images of Organization*. Thousand Oaks, CA: Sage.

Mowery, D., Oxley, J., & Silverman, D. (1996). Strategic alliances and interfirm knowledge transfer. *Strategic Management Journal*, 17 (S2), 77–91.

Nembhard, I.M., & Edmondson, A.C. (2006). Making it safe: The effects of leader inclusiveness and professional status on psychological safety and improvement efforts in health care teams. *Journal of Organizational Behavior*, 27 (7), 941–966.

Nevis, E.C., DiBella, A.J., & Gould, J.M. (1997). Understanding organizations as learning systems. *Sloan Management Review*, 36 (2), 73–85. Retrieved from http://sloanreview.mit.edu/article/understanding-organizations-as-learning-systems/ (accessed 15 June 2015).

Noordegraaf, M. (2011). Remaking professionals? How associations and professional education connect professionalism and organizations. *Current Sociology*, 59 (4), 465–488.

Örtenblad, A. (2001). On differences between organizational learning and learning organization. *The Learning Organization*, 8 (3), 125–133.

Örtenblad, A. (2005). Of course organizations can learn! *The Learning Organization*, 12 (2), 213–218.

Örtenblad, A. (Ed.). (2013). *Handbook of Research on the Learning Organization: Adaptation and Context*. Cheltenham, England: Edward Elgar.

Örtenblad, A., & Koris, R. (2014). Is the learning organization idea relevant to higher educational institutions? A literature review and a "multi-stakeholder contingency approach". *International Journal of Educational Management*, 28 (2), 173–214.

Pelikan, J.M., Krajic, K., & Dietscher, C. (2001). The health promoting hospital (HPH): Concept and development. *Patient Education and Counseling*, 45 (4), 239–243.

Resar, R.K. (2006). Making noncatastrophic health care processes reliable: Learning to walk before running in creating high-reliability organizations. *Health Services Research*, 41 (4 Pt. 2), 1677–1689.

Rushmer, R., Kelly, D., Lough, M., Wilkinson, J.E., & Davies, H.T.O. (2004). Introducing the learning practice—I: The characteristics of learning organizations in primary care. *Journal of Evaluation in Clinical Practice*, 10 (3), 375–386.

Schein, E.H. (1998). Culture: The missing concept in organization studies. *Administrative Science Quarterly*, 41 (2), 229–240.

Scott, T., Mannion, R., Davies, H.T., & Marshall, M. (2003). Implementing culture change in health care: Theory and practice. *International Journal for Quality in Health Care*, 15 (2), 111–118.

Senge, P.M. (1990). *The Fifth Discipline: The Art and Practice of the Learning Organization*. New York: Random House.

Senge, P.M. (1992). Mental models. *Planning Review*, 20 (2), 4–11.

Sheaff, R., Pickard, S., & Dowling, B. (2009). Is evidence-based organizational innovation in the NHS a chimaera—Or just elusive? *Social Policy and Administration*, 43 (3), 290–310.

Sheaff, R., Schofield, J., Charles, N., Benson, L., Mannion, R., & Reeves, D. (2011). *The management and effectiveness of professional and clinical networks*. London: SDO.

Snell, R., & Chak, A.-K. (1998). The learning organization: Learning and empowerment for whom? *Management Learning*, 29 (3), 337–364.

Tsang, E.W.K. (1997). Organizational learning and the learning organization: A dichotomy between descriptive and prescriptive research. *Human Relations*, 50 (1), 73–89.

Tsasis, P. (2009). The social processes of interorganizational collaboration and conflict in nonprofit organizations. *Nonprofit Management and Leadership*, 20 (1), 5–21.

Tsasis, P., Evans, J.M., Rush, L., & Diamond, J. (2013). Learning to learn: Towards a relational and transformational model of learning for improved integrated care delivery. *Administrative Sciences*, 3 (2), 9–31.

Van Bueren, E.M., Klijn, E., & Koppenjan, J.F.M. (2003). Dealing with wicked problems in networks: Analyzing an environmental debate from a network perspective. *Journal of Public Administration Research and Theory*, 13 (2), 193–212.

Van Raak, A., Paulus, A., & Mur-Veeman, I. (2005). Why do health and social care providers co-operate? *Health Policy*, 74 (1), 13–23.

Van Wijk, R., Jansen, J.J.P., & Lyles, M.A. (2008). Inter- and intra-organizational knowledge transfer: A meta-analytic review and assessment of its antecedents and consequences. *Journal of Management Studies*, 45 (4), 830–853.

Vassalou, L. (2001). The learning organization in health-care services: Theory and practice. *Journal of European Industrial Training*, 25 (7), 354–365.

Wenger, E., McDermott, R.A., & Snyder, W. (2002). *Cultivating Communities of Practice: A Guide to Managing Knowledge*. Boston, MA: Harvard Business Press.

Wenger, E., & Snyder, W. (2000). Communities of practice: The organizational frontier. *Harvard Business Review*, 84 (1), 139–145.

Wilkinson, J.E., Rushmer, R.K., & Davies, H.T.O. (2004). Clinical governance and the learning organization. *Journal of Nursing Management*, 12 (2), 105–113.

15 Management by Objectives in Healthcare Organizations Then and Now

A Literature Overview of MBO Limitations and Perspectives in the Healthcare Sector

Grigorios L. Kyriakopoulos

INTRODUCTION TO THE MBO SYSTEM

Management by Objectives (*MBO*) can be described as a process whereby the superior and subordinate managers of an organization jointly identify the organization's common goals, define each individual's major area of responsibility in terms of the results expected of him/her and use these measures as guides for operating the unit and assessing the contribution of each of its members. Under the *MBO* system, both employees and managers jointly identify goals and define responsibilities in light of the expected results, assessing each employee's contribution in accordance to the set objectives. Subsequently, the results of the *MBO* system are evaluated against the established and specific goals, rather than against common goals for all managers. As a result, the *MBO* system signifies more the role of managerial behavior, rather than the managerial personality, as an essential feature. In effect, *MBO* perspectives mainly reflect an organization's social and political values, rather than quantified details of its production processes (Maguire, 1987).

During the mid-20th century, the main management styles in businesses were "scientific" methods that emphasized efficiency under harsh discipline. *MBO* was introduced in 1954 by the theorist Peter Drucker, who stressed out that managers should direct the organizations towards the accomplishment of measurable results rather than merely human relationships, which writers of the human relations school of management had emphasized. The introduction of *MBO* was a response to the imperative that theories should be revised continuously in light of their practical applications (Maguire, 1987).

Under the *MBO* system, managers can oversee workers of any educational level or competence, provided that their employees have the appropriate knowledge both of their own working performance and of the relevant goals and measurable outcomes. In parallel, the *MBO* system enhances communication paths among the departments of each organization, encouraging subordinate input and active participation in decision-making (Maguire, 1987). Moreover, the *MBO* system is oriented towards effort and resources, since each manager identifies a particular goal that has to be accomplished in a finite time frame. In particular, the manager allocates the time and sets the pace for his/her employees towards the completion of their sub-goals/ objectives, while the overall *MBO* system provides an assessment of the overall progress achieved. Moreover, the objectives are tangible and measurable against standards or prior expectations (Maguire, 1987). However, despite the aforementioned positive features, the *MBO* system has been criticized as a doubtful method that has been frequently applied in an authoritarian way, regardless of the intentions of the managerial hierarchy (Haines, 1977).

The rest of this chapter holistically reviews the *MBO* system. In particular, the value of *MBO* is analyzed in relation to the planning and modeling of managerial roles. Therefore, the success of *MBO* is specifically considered across a wide spectrum of *MBO* models, but all of them rely on the dominant role of objective setting in a successful implementation of the *MBO* system. Subsequently, the chapter outlines a literature overview covering the applicability of *MBO* to four healthcare organization contexts, namely, healthcare organizations in general, hospital management, nursing and hospital pharmacy. The chapter concludes by reassessing the *MBO* philosophy in the light of *MBO* perspectives and their adaptation to the ongoing dynamic pace of change that many organizations face in an epoch of economic illiquidity and social reform.

THE ROLE OF PLANNING IN MBO

Nowadays, planning is considered one of the most significant and essential contributions of the *MBO* process to management. Planning has shown a strong structural affiliation with a plethora of *MBO* applications. Elvik (2008) investigated the attractive characteristics and the weak points of a comprehensive *MBO* system of road safety in light of the Norwegian Transport Plan for 2010–2019. Wibeck et al. (2006) assessed the ecological concerns and environmental objectives within the Swedish environmental quality standards as an integrated *MBO* system, structured into national, political and administrative norms. In an earlier study, Dirsmith and Jablonsky (1979) evaluated the *MBO* system as a management technique for political strategies in which planning was considered a fundamental component.

Odiorne (1975) described the pronounced roles of *MBO* in long-range planning and the five-year plan. Specifically, long-range plans are most valuable when they are revised, adjusted and reset anew at shorter intervals; for example, when a five-year plan is reconstructed annually in turn for each of the following five years. The determining parameter of this *MBO*-based planning is the accurate measurement of the results of the first year's experience with the plan against the target of the plan (Migliore, 1976). As Edward C. Schleh expressed it: "Whenever a man has a responsibility for a result, he should also have the responsibility for planning ahead to prevent crises that may prevent the accomplishment of that result" (Migliore, 1976, p. 59).

In Richard Johanson's *Systematic Approach to Corporation Planning*, the *MBO* process is positioned as a subset in a greater management system that requires a total organizational view. *MBO* is an ongoing cybernetic system that should be characterized as a "way of life". *MBO* features are built into the dynamic planning process. At the same time, such a five-year plan is based upon environmental factors, as well as the strengths and weaknesses of the company. The five-year plan features outline the framework to meet those goals (Migliore, 1976). As the foundation of *MBO*, these broad objectives are defined and measurable goals are set to meet them.

Subsequently, the annual operating plan is then just the first year of the five-year plan. Besides, the five-year plan is annually updated. This dynamic planning process is characterized as cybernetic due to its flexibility for recycling and changes where needed. Such *MBO*-based planning is thus tolerant of any factor that affects the company during the planning cycle, including changes in the environment, its relative strengths to the company, and its assumptions, criteria, objectives and goals (Migliore, 1976).

THE RELEVANCE OF MBO FOR HEALTHCARE ORGANIZATIONS

A plethora of studies—which were mainly published in the 1970s and 1980s—addressed the applicability of *MBO* to:

1) Nursing services (Banasik, 1979; Bromet et al., 1971; Cain & Luchsinger, 1978; Chapman, 1975; Cornillon & Trazzini, 1981; Gillott et al., 1978; Hempson, 1981; Lopp, 1970; Maillard, 1976; Mills, 1983; Odiorne, 1975; Palmer, 1971, 1973; Smith, 1971; Skarupa, 1969, 1971);
2) Health professions (Bean, 2002; Bruton & Berkowitz, 1978; Cuming, 1972);
3) Medicine, throughout the second half of the 20th century (indicatively) (Essakalli et al., 2013; Elvik, 2008; Ekblom & Oxhammar, 1995; Jeffers, 1988; Johnson & McMurry, 1982);
4) *MBO* approaches have also been promoted by managers of mental healthcare services, services for hypertension patients and occupational health protection among health professionals.

A literature review by Kyriakopoulos (2012) examined the applicability of the *MBO* method in the healthcare sector. This review was done during the first quarter of 2011. It identified studies through three search strategies.

First, computerized database searches from 1970 to 2010, using the key words "management by objective" and "*MBO*" were conducted. Second, manual searches of those journals that were featured in both the databases of the ISI Web of Knowledge and Scopus were also conducted. Finally, the reference lists in several meta-analyses were examined. An expanded and updated literature review of the applicability of the *MBO* method to healthcare organizations—based on the aforementioned review of Kyriakopoulos (2012), and focusing on four healthcare-oriented services—covered the studies presented in Table 15.1.

Table 15.1 Literature Overview: *MBO* Applicability to the Healthcare Sector During the Second Half of the 20th Century

Reference item #	Reference
Healthcare (general context)	
1	Pavlova and Afanasieva (2009)
2	Ricci, Bonomolo, and Marconcini (1999)
3	Migliore and Gunn (1995)
4	Braithwaite, Westbrook, and Lansbury (1991)
5	Racz and Simon (1990)
6	Adorian, Silverberg, Wamoscher and Tomer (1986)
7	Bozis (1986)
8	Kost (1986)
9	Deegan 2nd and O'Donovan (1984)
10	Brumback and McFee (1982)
11	Kenneth and Lampi (1982)
12	Martin, Spratt, Hoye and Polk (1982)
13	Garrison and Raynes (1980)
14	Taylor (1980)
Hospital Management	
15	Buj Fernández, Córdoba García, and Rodríguez Gómez (1991)
16	Hatfield (1982)
17	Cornillon and Trazzini (1981)
18	Covaleski and Dirsmith (1981)
19	Deegan 2nd (1981)
20	Hand and Hollingsworth (1975)
Nursing	
21	Lee and Ahn (2010)
22	Tan, Liu, and Ma (1997)
23	Maguire (1987)
24	Fain and Sheathelm (1984)
25	Pollok (1983)

Reference item #	Reference
26	Bell (1980)
27	Mills (1983)
28	Hempson (1981)
29	Cain and Luchsinger (1978)
30	Gillott, Qazi, and Quigley (1978)
31	Maillard (1976)
32	Bromet, Caudrelier, and Clairac (1971)
Hospital Pharmacy	
33	Cai and Hu (2005)
34	Lively (1987)
35	Noble (1983)

Table 15.1 shows that studies of *MBO* in healthcare are concentrated on general healthcare and nursing-based studies (almost 40% each). On balance, the studies suggest that *MBO* is a managerial tool that could be appropriate to healthcare organizations, since it balances out human and non-human attributes in the establishment and implementation of organizational objectives.

Together, the studies listed under the "general context" heading revealed that this managerial approach is a method of strategic planning for primary medical care, hospitals and clinics that enhances their organizational effectiveness and the goal-oriented behavior of healthcare managers. *MBO* is commonly developed from the guidelines of senior healthcare managers, and it is structured by the functions of objective setting, objective using and employee involvement, with recognition of the pronounced role of human sources in implementing the healthcare organization's objectives. *MBO* is a goal-directed performance management system that has been positioned as a key factor in introducing national health programs, and it should be effectively adapted to undergoing rapid changes in healthcare services. *MBO* has also been introduced in clinical laboratory divisions and in other academic medical center laboratories, under the preconditions that the healthcare manager commits the necessary time and resources to install the *MBO* system carefully, and that it is a relatively loose, locally administered form of management, rather than a rigid one. *MBO* should also meet the prerequisites of, and fit organizational systems to, the local management environment. Thus implemented, it should prove beneficial in improving communication, organizational clarity, planning for deadlines, motivation of participants, workload distribution and productivity. *MBO*'s effectiveness depends upon the individual performance planning among the *MBO* participants. It is of further value in terms of minimizing the waste of time, money and effort towards agreed-upon standards of successful organizational performance.

Another specific healthcare application of the *MBO* system is in hospital management. The need and the appropriateness of applying *MBO* in hospital management reside in the fact that in public hospitals, there is often no concentration of power in the hands of one person. Therefore, the *MBO* approach attempts to identify who are the real prime movers—"those persons who get things done"—both internally and externally and who, therefore, set the hospital's objectives in practice. Subsequently, the autonomy of the public hospital itself would be negotiated via the adoption of an *MBO*-based, decentralized management plan for its work. Moreover, reformulating hospital objectives is an enormous and risky task that involves an evolution of the administrative environment, as well as an improvement in organizational planning and control across the whole healthcare sector. As a goal-directed managerial approach, *MBO* may, however, also lead to dysfunctional decision-making at the institutional level within organizations, especially those facing complex and dynamic environments. Nevertheless, whenever *MBO* is valued as a philosophy of management administered at the sub-unit level, it may serve as a catalytic agent for encouraging decentralized decision-making and performance evaluation. *MBO* approaches in hospital management are appropriate for managing high employee turnover rates in hospitals, which detract from the quality of patient care and sub-optimize financial resources.

The studies of nursing services listed in Table 15.1 also revealed that *MBO* is an appropriate tool in the activities of planning, communication, administration, formulation of goals and objectives, development of action plans and implementation, in order both to increase the accountability of staff and to utilize clients' input through problem-solving processes. This *MBO* functionality in nursing is also shown to support increasing the measurability of objectives in mental health facilities. Indeed, *MBO* is not a mechanical or dehumanizing approach, but one that recognizes the importance of human relations to effective administration. The role of nursing leadership is to minimize frustration among staff, and to optimize nursing effectiveness and job satisfaction. A healthcare manager is called upon time and time again to increase the productivity of staff by handling potential conflicts between the organization's goals and the individual staff member's needs. Motives for introducing *MBO* include democratic procedures, involvement and motivational techniques for promoting involvement. The prerequisites of *MBO* are a considerable amount of time and energy, in addition to organizational support.

Finally, the applicability of *MBO* as a hospital pharmacy managerial tool is less investigated in the relevant literature. In such healthcare applications, *MBO* had been focused on drug administration processes in order to strengthen hospital pharmacy management and the professional quality of staff. The objectives of such an *MBO* system were built into out-patient and inpatient departments, as well as in emergency pharmacies. Specifically, *MBO* was evaluated in terms of the accuracy of prescribing, drug quantities and error rates of checking drug costs. Nevertheless, it is noteworthy that *MBO* deserves a wider (than today) development in the future of drug administration in hospital pharmacies.

The aforementioned literature review summed up the limitations and the advantages of *MBO* planning and modeling, especially noting that in the healthcare organizations, there is commonly no single objective-setting power, but the healthcare managers have to adopt the most appropriate *MBO* system and subsequently be flexible in adapting this generalized *MBO* process within the specific healthcare organization of their responsibility. The rest of this section addresses the complications and the perspectives of the *MBO* system in an organizational overview.

According to Haines (1977), an objective is a definable and measurable entity that has to be clearly understood by both the person formulating the objective and by the person for whom it is specifically intended. *MBO* should start at the "top" organizational hierarchy and has to sustain a clear statement of the overall objectives of the business. Potential *MBO* assignments that are operating only with middle management often lead to failure as the gap between their objectives and those at the higher levels becomes apparent. The main limitations of *MBO* are the practical difficulties of establishing the overall objectives of the organization, as well as the fact that managers have sometimes operated corporate planning and *MBO* as two separate tasks or "techniques", even though these are inseparable components of an integrated *MBO* system.

A manager responsible for introducing and operating an *MBO* system should be clear that its success is not merely an issue of quantitative targets, but it is also driven by human traits, such as the personality of the stakeholders, their behavior and persistence in teamwork, the appropriate timing of when to establish an *MBO* system, as well as the appropriate planning and allocation of roles as departmental, sectional and individual objectives. Managers setting wrong or improper objectives would result in a waste of time and effort. On the other hand, a "bottom-up" approach in *MBO* is not always effective, since the objectives formulated at the lower level may conflict with the views at the top, leading to fruitless meetings, blank refusals, destructive criticism and the discouragement of proposers to amend the objectives and to submit them again. Subsequently, aroused expectations from managers are followed by frustration, disillusionment and skepticism with the motives for the *MBO* exercise, on behalf of the team members involved in the *MBO* system (Haines, 1977).

Another crucial parameter of the success of an *MBO* system is the decisive role of the board of directors, who must be committed to the whole process, both as board members and as the heads of their departments. This top-down commitment is imperative, since without it, the attempt to introduce *MBO* should not be made, because it can easily do more harm than good, considering the management team as a whole (Haines, 1977). On the other hand, a negotiative aspect could emerge while implementing an *MBO* system in healthcare organizations, due to the fact that in some hospitals, there is no single controlling authority, such as in cases where medical staff are rather autonomous. Therefore, there should be a negotiation about determining "a good service" and whether such a good service to the public ought to come first, before the (other) interests of an organization. For this reason, the ways in which these relative duties are to be defined are in practice often left to the individual, as the problem is what s/he should do when s/he finds the interests of the public conflict with those of his/her work and, incidentally, of his/her livelihood (Haines, 1977). This statement is of the utmost importance in the healthcare sector, since healthcare personnel commonly confront bioethics-based dilemmas, such as dilemmas about euthanasia, abortion and genetically modified human genomes.

The board of directors in healthcare organizations should play the role of *MBO* policy makers who have to confront the following two-fold problem, since—as it is faced with a barrage of exhortation, pressures and choices—the board's job is much more difficult than at the time when *MBO* was first introduced into organizational practice (about half a century ago). This problem can be outlined in the following questions (Haines, 1977):

1) How should healthcare organizations determine the requirements of the various stakeholders?
2) How should these requirements be translated into tangible and measurable objectives for the healthcare organization and for its management at all levels? (p. 15)

In response to these questions, it is of the utmost importance that someone identify the most important pressure groups within the healthcare organization. One such impersonal criterion for identifying them might be how much noise a particular group makes. Nevertheless, this criterion might be misleading, since the less vocal stakeholders may prove in time to be more influential on the fortunes of the organization. Besides, in privately owned organizations, the shareholders can be commonly undemonstrative, but react swiftly and violently when their interests are threatened. The board of directors must still exercise its judgment to identify the most significant stakeholder group, while the board itself has to be involved and committed throughout (Haines, 1977).

Especially in for-profit healthcare organizations, there is commonly a conflict of objectives between the maximization of profit and the protection of the well-being of all patients, including the less underprivileged and socially marginalized ones. This conflict arises due to the difficulty of explicitly defining, setting and balancing between human interests (such as health protection) and non-human (such as revenue-driven) interests. Specifically, which should be the "safeguard policy" for sustaining the viability of *MBO* in a private healthcare organization whenever there arises an unexpected need to treat an uninsured, poor or unemployed patient at its specialized healthcare center? In response to such a question, *MBO* objectives might fail either to reconcile profits with non-profit imperatives, or to adopt a procedure that would enable the effective tracking and control of the overall *MBO* system (Haines, 1977). Additionally, an appropriate *MBO*-driven system in a healthcare organization should enable the board of directors to balance the views and expectations of the various stakeholders within it, for example, to evaluate in precise terms the demands of the environmental lobby versus the demands of a trade union for a shorter work week, when the financial outlay may be the same for anti-pollution precautions and a higher wage bill. Prior to each *MBO*-objective setting process, the key factor in deciding between mutually conflicting issues is a discussion between the individuals concerned and the board of directors about the positive and negative aspects of all the issues involved. In cases when the objective is not easily quantified, a thorough discussion between the board of directors and the team members must be held in order to ensure that everyone involved understands the issue. Additionally, the verbal expression—describing the objective—has to be chosen with even more precision than usual (Haines, 1977).

Thus, the introduction of *MBO* can prove beneficial in understanding and establishing common ground among the stakeholders of a healthcare organization. In particular, the responsible manager can draft objectives and encourage the directors, the other groups and the lower echelons to go through the essential stages of the *MBO* model. The responsible manager will have succeeded when the healthcare managers are confident that the *MBO* system is their system and that the *MBO* objectives are their objectives (Haines, 1977). Under these conditions, *MBO* should be one of the most effective management approaches for healthcare organizations.

A MODEL FOR IMPLEMENTING MBO SUCCESSFULLY

Setting Organizational Objectives

Normative models for the successful implementation of the *MBO* system were developed during the 1970s. In particular, Haines (1977) introduced a 12-stage model that formulates company objectives. Haines assumed that an external consultant would carry out this work, but here, this study is adapted to reflect the situation when a senior manager within an organization takes on that task. Haines's (1977) model has been further adapted to suit the construction of an *MBO* system in the contemporary healthcare sector. Therefore, in the following 11-stage adapted model, the first and the second stages of the original 12-stage model of Haines were unified into one stage (the first stage), while the remaining 10 stages of Haines's 12-stage model were adjusted accordingly, as presented below:

1) The board chair arranges for the whole board to formulate the objectives that will guide the *MBO* system in their organization. The board selects a manager to be responsible for implementing the *MBO* system.

This step is the hardest for the healthcare manager to accomplish, and without commitment from all who are involved in the *MBO* planning, the chances of success are prejudiced from the beginning. A complication arises whenever part-time members of the board are reluctant to spend the time required. Thus, the manager is responsible for identifying the most determined team members at the beginning of the *MBO* system, since late refusals of participants who are burdened with sensitive and responsible healthcare activities—such as the opposition of a surgeon or a hospital technician—would endanger the overall success of the *MBO* system.

2) The responsible manager draws up a questionnaire in discussion with them, covering the main headings that might influence the formulation of the objectives.

The step is significant, since it assists the healthcare manager in analyzing the views and attributes under suitable headings and it highlights those that are most important. Besides, the questionnaire step ensures that the participants cover all the important components of the *MBO* system. The healthcare manager should construct the questionnaire with the board, reflecting precisely their views and preserving their approval of the *MBO* goals.

3) The board selects the recipients of the questionnaire (other than the board members themselves, all of whom will also receive it).

The decision on selecting the recipients of the questionnaire plays a dominant role in the overall success of the *MBO* system in the healthcare sector, since once an individual is involved in the process, s/he should stay in it throughout. Accordingly, this step should be treated with care and sensitivity by the healthcare manager, in order to avoid frustration or offending the non-participants in the questionnaire process.

4) The chairman sends the questionnaire to everyone selected in stage three. The chairman's cover letter states that the replies are confidential to the responsible manager alone, to encourage frankness. The letter stresses that the replies should cover any subject that appears significant to the future of the organization, even if the ideas have little supporting data at this stage.

"Everyone selected to participate in the questionnaire process" does not mean "everyone who works at the healthcare organization". Besides, this step aims at keeping the replies confidential to the healthcare manager.

5) The responsible manager discusses each reply fully with the individual.

This step is especially applicable in the healthcare sector, since there are participants who, because of their profession, cannot be made to commit their objectives to paper, or are simply reluctant to fill in the questionnaire, though their contribution to the *MBO* system remains valuable. Therefore, the discussion focuses on the importance of the individual's contribution, which is what is most needed.

6) The responsible manager summarizes the replies to the questionnaire.

Even though every response might be unbiased, open and frank, some editing is usually unavoidable in order that the board of the *MBO* system can easily group and rank all replies in order of importance.

7) The chairman and board review the progress to date in the light of the summarized replies to the questionnaire and in the light of the informal views of the board members.

In this step of MBO modeling, the formation of the setting objectives becomes rigorous. Thus, this feedback step offers a chance to participants to review the proposed objectives, to check if there is consensus among the other team members on the emerging changes in the organization's objectives.

8) The chairman sets up working groups to deal with any objectives that are still not definite from the progress review in stage seven. Each working group should be led by a board member to ensure sufficient political weight.

External bodies of investigation, inspection and auditing of the activities of healthcare organizations are welcome, especially when, as in some hospitals, there is no single controlling authority (e.g., because medical staff are rather autonomous).

9) The working groups report back to the board group, which discusses their reports against the objectives previously agreed upon.

By this stage, the healthcare manager responsible for formulating the *MBO* objectives has largely withdrawn, since his/her role is more that of a catalyst who encourages the board to hold meetings and to keep active all the processes involved in the *MBO* system. This healthcare manager should also give assurance that any contributor should be ready to stand up and to be counted.

10) The board puts the final touch on the objectives. The chairman issues them to whichever groups inside and outside the company have been selected to receive them.

It is noteworthy that what is right for one healthcare organization simply would not work for another. Therefore, the healthcare manager should be careful and prudent to ensure the success of the *MBO* of the healthcare organization that s/he manages occurs without pushing the organization towards a course of action that is against its management style.

11) The organization's objectives are split into departmental, sectional and individual ones, using the discussion aspects of this model as the basis for doing so. A member of the board oversees the implementation in each department.

Regular meetings for monitoring the *MBO* objectives are needed in line with the changes to the key factors that influenced the initial setting of the *MBO* goals and that may impact upon the achievement of those goals. Internal and external changes should be both included at this final step.

Setting Individual Objectives

The disciplines and the mission of a healthcare organization lead to the development of job descriptions that specify what the healthcare organization expects of each employee. The expectations should be measurable and directed to the behavior, rather than to the personality (Maguire, 1987). For setting individuals' objectives within the above organization-wide objectives, Migliore (1976) described the following six-stage model, adopted by the US company Alcoa:

1) An individual writes down his/her major performance objectives for the coming year, and his/her specific plans, including target dates for achieving these objectives;
2) S/he submits them to his/her boss for review. Out of the discussion comes an agreed-upon set of objectives;
3) On a quarterly basis, s/he verbally reviews progress toward these objectives with his/her boss. Objectives and plans are revised and updated as needed;
4) At the end of the year, the individual prepares a brief "accomplishment report", which lists all major accomplishments with comments on the variances between results actually achieved and results expected;

5) This self-appraisal is discussed with the boss. Reasons for goals not being met are explored;

6) A new set of objectives is established for the next year.

In this six-stage model, the specific *MBO* elements are planning, objectives and goals, negotiation, performance review and evaluation (Migliore, 1976). To illustrate more concretely the character of these elements, Lee and Ahn (2010) developed *MBO* key performance evaluation indicators, which were categorized into 10 domains in order to estimate their weights for hospital nurses (in general wards, intensive care units, emergency medical centers hemato-oncology, obstetrics and pediatrics and other hospital services).

Lee and Ahn's informants gave the highest weight of the 10 domains to customer satisfaction, which was followed by (in descending order): Patient education, direct nursing care, profit increase, safety management, improvement of nursing quality, completeness of nursing records, enhancing competence of nurses, indirect nursing care and cost reduction. Lee and Ahn (2010) pointed out that such performance evaluation key indicators and their weights enable the impartial evaluation of *MBO* for hospital nurses, while there is still room for future research in verifying indicators that would lead to the successful implementation of *MBO*.

An *MBO* system in, say, nursing, is driven towards performance evaluation; the charge nurse first determines if the clinical nurse is familiar with the job description and both together identify needs and objectives focused on the subordinate's job description and areas of interest. Within the *MBO* system, the main goals are grouped as routine duties, problem-solving goals, creative goals and personal goals. Other key factors that determine the *MBO*'s success are encouragement for staff, additional training and teaching and assistance in setting realistic time frames for accomplishment (Maguire, 1987). *MBO* planning is structured when the charge nurse and the clinical nurse are capable of stating the objectives, the measures of acceptable results and the length of the performance period. Upon agreement on the objectives, their accomplishment becomes the responsibility of the clinical nurse, who can use his/her creativity and flexibility to make a continuous informal evaluation of his/her progress, prior to the final formal evaluation of it.

CONCLUSIONS

General Conclusions

Management by Objectives is applicable on a plethora of administrative levels in a managerial hierarchy, to both planning and operation. *MBO* is an organized, efficient, flexible and easily adaptive management method that supports managers in accomplishing their goals. *MBO* evaluation of their work focuses on their professional behavior rather than on personal characteristics (Maguire, 1987). This focus on professional behavior implies that a manager should compare an employee's actual behavior with their expected behavior in order to make his/her employees feel more cooperative rather than defensive or vaguely criticized for poor attitudes. The literature review about the applicability of *MBO* to the healthcare sector revealed that the *MBO* system readily fits into the nursing profession, since it is consistent with the nursing process (Maguire, 1987). On the other hand, "openness" and "participation"—or feeling obliged to follow the *MBO* approach—are not panaceas for all healthcare organizations because what is right for one organization would not work for another (Haines, 1977). On this basis, the best managerial approach is for a manager to be cautious, not putting into practice a course of actions that are against his/her management style or that of his/her organization, but to adopt a management style that could, under favorable conditions, cope with the assets and the philosophy of his/her organization, so as to set goals for it and contribute to its overall prosperity.

The future orientation of an *MBO* system in the healthcare sector should, particularly, encourage innovations and promote good practice in hospital care for people with mental health issues and learning difficulties (Gillott et.al., 1978). Besides, *MBO* is appropriate for managing the human relationships within public hospitals under the two pillars of Organization and Staff (Bromet et.al., 1971), as well as the specifications of these pillars, leading to the optimum coordination among the staff, the clients and the patients (Maillard, 1976).

Future Orientations of MBO in the Healthcare Sector

This chapter concludes by addressing a future perspective on *MBO* in nursing services, since *MBO* has proved to be a mature managerial tool (Cain & Luchsinger, 1978) for the organization and administration of nursing. That is, it is useful for:

1) Supporting the task of structuring nursing work;
2) Encouraging greater involvement among nurses and managers;
3) Emphasizing employees' participation in planning their jobs;
4) Increasing employees' effectiveness;
5) Maximizing job satisfaction within a reasonable cost framework.

In a typical decentralized institution such as a public hospital, the administrative structure starts with the managing director at the top, followed by a coordinating director and a head nurse, while a staff of general charge nurses would follow at levels below the head nurse. The management team consists of the management and the coordinating directors who manage human resources, fiscal resources, facilities and materials (supplies). This team has a 24-hour responsibility for the operating room and for smooth cooperation with other healthcare disciplines to develop policies that are consistent with the mission of the organization.

Table 15.2   A Three-Step Management Process in Nursing (adapted from Maguire, 1987, p. 758)

Phase sequence	Perioperative nursing	Nursing process	Management by Objectives (MBO)
1	Preoperative	Assess Plan	Plan
2	Intraoperative	Implement	Do
3	Postoperative	Evaluate	Check

The implementation of an *MBO* system necessitates overcoming potential conflict, misunderstanding or confusion, and adopting a nonthreatening and objective manner of confronting any issues that arise. The ultimate goals of such an *MBO* system should be, on the one hand, the solution of problems and the maintenance or enhancement of good working relationships while prioritizing departmental goals and, on the other hand, the assurance that the healthcare manager will compare actual behaviors with expected behaviors, ensuring that the employees feel cooperative rather than defensive (Maguire, 1987).

The healthcare manager should master skills in written communication and develop fluency in understanding the organization's goals and objectives. Finally, the *MBO* system in nursing would be successful when initiated by top-level management and implemented by the charge nurse to manage his/her area of responsibility. Such an *MBO* process is executed in three phases, like those of perioperative care (preoperative-intraoperative-postoperative), a process of moving from assessing and planning to implementation and evaluation, which is analogous to the "plan-do-check" of the *MBO* system (Table 15.2).

At the end of the *MBO* planning phase, the charge nurse evaluates who should accomplish the objectives that have been set, for example, by considering inputs from the participants regarding the necessary duration of teaching and seminars, and the level of practical experience needed to accomplish the objectives set by the *MBO* method. In this way, changes to the initial action plan produced by the *MBO* system can be made for subsequent participants, while the charge nurse ascertains that all nurses have received the instruction and experience described in the *MBO* objectives (Maguire, 1987).

REFERENCES

Adorian, D., Silverberg, D.S., Wamoscher, Z., & Tomer, D. (1986). Use of management-by-objective for the case finding and treatment of hypertension. *The British Journal of General Practice*, 36 (282), 17–18.

Banasik, R.C. (1979). Materiel management by objectives. *Hospital Materiel Management Quarterly*, 1 (1), 9–16.

Bean, J. (2002). The implementation of the incident control system in NSW: Span of control and management by objectives. *Australian Journal of Emergency Management*, 17 (3), 8–16.

Bell, M.L. (1980). Management by objectives. *Journal of Nursing Administration*, 10 (5), 19–26.

Bozis, D.E. (1986). Management by objectives in medical group practice. *College Review (Denver, CO)*, 3 (2), 3–13.

Braithwaite, J., Westbrook, J.I., & Lansbury, R.D. (1991). Beyond management by objectives: The implementation of a goal-directed performance management system in Australian teaching hospital. *Australian Health Review*, 14 (2), 110–126.

Bromet, E.J., Caudrelier, J.M., & Clairac, B. (1971). Management by objectives. *Revue Hospitaliere de France*, 4, 59–75.

Brumback, G.B., & McFee, T.S. (1982). From MBO to MBR. *Public Administration Review*, 42 (4), 363–371.

Bruton, P.W., & Berkowitz, S.A. (1978). Financial management by objectives in hospitals. *Health Care Management Review*, 3 (3), 25–32.

Buj Fernández, A., Córdoba García, J.F., & Rodríguez Gómez, D. (1991). Management by objectives in hospital units. *Revista de Enfermeria (Barcelona, Spain)*, 14 (158), 23–26.

Cai, Z., & Hu, J.H. (2005). Application of management by objective to drug administration. *Pharmaceutical care and Research*, 5 (4), 345–348.

Cain, C., & Luchsinger, V. (1978). Management by objectives: Applications to nursing. *Journal of Nursing Administration*, 8 (1), 35–38.

Chapman, A. (1975). Management by objectives for mental health executives. *Journal of Mental Health Administration*, 4 (1), 58–67.

Cornillon, G., & Trazzini, J.X.A. (1981). Hospitals and participation in management by objectives. *Newspaper Federal Hospital of France*, 45 (346 I), 993–1060.

Covaleski, M.A., & Dirsmith, M.W. (1981). MBO and goal directedness in a hospital context. *Academy of Management Review*, 6 (3), 409–418.

Cuming, M.W. (1972). Management by objectives. *Physiotherapy*, 58 (5), 161–163.

Deegan, A.X., II (1981). Management by objectives: Does it work for hospitals? *Michigan Hospitals*, 17 (8), 16–19.

Deegan A.X., II, & O'Donovan, T.R. (1984). Budgeting and management by objectives. *Health Care Management Review*, 9 (1), 51–59.

Dirsmith, M.W., & Jablonsky, S.F. (1979). MBO, political rationality and information inductance. *Accounting, Organizations and Society*, 4 (1–2), 39–52.

Ekblom, B., & Oxhammar, S. (1995). Quality assurance through management by objectives. *Nordic Journal of Psychiatry*, 49 (S35), 25–28.

Elvik, R. (2008). Road safety management by objectives: A critical analysis of the Norwegian approach. *Accident Analysis and Prevention*, 40 (3), 1115–1122.

Essakalli, M., Atouf, O., Ouadghiri, S., Bouayad, A., Drissi, A., Sbain, K., Sakri, L., Benseffaj, N., & Brick, C. (2013). Management by objectives: An experience by transfusion and immunology service in Rabat. *Transfusion Clinique et Biologique*, 20 (4), 440–447.

Fain, J.A., & Sheathelm, H.H. (1984). Management by objectives (MBO) (as applied to nursing service). Nursing *Forum*, 21 (2), 68–71.

Garrison, J.E., & Raynes, A.E. (1980). Results of a pilot management-by-objectives program for a community mental health outpatient service. *Community Mental Health Journal*, 16 (2), 121–129.

Gillott, J.S., Qazi, H.S., & Quigley, J. (1978). The use of management by objectives in developing services for the mentally handicapped at Darenth Park Hospital. *Hospital Health Services Review*, 74 (12), 425–427.

Haines, R.W. (1977). Corporate planning and management by objectives. *Long Range Planning*, 10 (4), 13–20.

Hand, H.H., & Hollingsworth, A.T. (1975). Tailoring MBO to hospitals. *Business Horizons*, 18 (1), 45–52.

Hatfield, B.P. (1982). MBO: Management by objectives (or objections). *Hospital Topics*, 60 (1), 42.

Hempson, D.A. (1981). Management by objectives. *Medical Group Management*, 28 (2), 38–44.

Jeffers, M. (1988). Management by objectives: Use in the radiation oncology center. *Administrative Radiology*, 7 (7), 88–94.

Johnson, J.B., & McMurry, P.V., Jr. (1982). Drucker's management by objective concept. *Hospital Management Quarterly*, 23–24.

Kenneth, R.J., & Lampi, G.L. (1982). Management by objective: How to make it work in the business office. *Journal of Patient Account Management*, August–September, 16–19.

Kost, G.J. (1986). Management by objectives for the academic medical center. *American Journal of Clinical Pathology*, 86 (6), 738–744.

Kyriakopoulos, G. (2012). Half a century of management by objectives (MBO): A review. *African Journal of Business Management*, 6 (5), 1772–1786.

Lee, E.H., & Ahn, S.H. (2010). Development of key indicators for nurses performance evaluation and estimation of their weights for management by objectives. *Journal of Korean Academy of Nursing*, 40 (1), 69–77.

Lively, B.T. (1987). Management by objectives: Getting back to basics. *Topics in hospital pharmacy management/Aspen Systems Corporation*, 7 (3), 1–11.

Lopp, D.W. (1970). Management by objectives. *Hospitals*, 44 (16), 136–141.

Maguire, M.C. (1987). Management by objectives: Applications for OR nursing. *AORN Journal, Association of perioperative Registered Nurses*, 45 (3), 752–760.

Maillard, C. (1976). The management by objectives in public hospital: The delegation of power. *Techniques Hospitalieres—Medico-Sociales et Sanitaires*, 32 (375), 41–57.

Martin, L.F., Spratt, J.S., Jr., Hoye, R.E., & Polk, H.C. Jr. (1982). Application of "management by objectives" to a surgical residency. *Archives of Surgery*, 117 (9), 1203–1205.

Migliore, R.H. (1976). Planning and management by objectives. *Long Range Planning*, 9 (4), 58–65.

Migliore, R.H., & Gunn, B.J. (1995). Strategic planning/management by objectives. A boon for healthcare administrators. Hospital *Topics*, 73 (3), 26–32.

Mills, M.M. (1983). The social service model of management by objectives: Wedding MBO and the task-centered system. *Journal of Mental Health Administration*, 10 (2), 19–21.

Noble, S. (1983). Management by objectives. *Aspen Systems Corporation*, 2 (4), 56–61.

Odiorne, G.S. (1975). Management by objectives: Antidote to future shock. *Journal of Nursing Administration*, 5 (2), 27–30.

Palmer, J. (1971). Management by objectives. *Journal of Nursing Administration*, 1 (1), 17–23.

Palmer, J. (1973). Management by objectives. *Journal of Nursing Administration*, 3 (5), 55–60.

Pavlova, J., & Afanasieva, L. (2009). Decision tree and management by objectives: Effective methods in the practice of general practitioners in Bulgaria. *Archives of the Balkan Medical Union*, 44 (4), 311–314.

Pollok, C.S. (1983). Adapting management by objectives to nursing. *Nursing Clinics of North America*, 18 (3), 481–490.

Racz, L., & Simon, G. (1990). Application of "management by objectives" in the Szabadsaghegy Children's Sanatorium (Budapest). *Health Economics Review*, 28 (5–6), 343–348.

Ricci, N., Bonomolo, M., & Marconcini, M. (1999). Application of the C.C.N.L. in the management if National Health Service: Experience of the USL 2 Pentria

Agency in the introduction of the MBO (management by objectives) System. *Annali di Igiene: Medicina Preventiva e di Comunita*, **11** (3), 237–244.

Skarupa, J.A. (1969). Management by objectives: A systematic way to manage change. *Hospitals*, **43** (18), 49–52.

Skarupa, J.A. (1971). Management by objectives: A systematic way to manage change. *Journal of Nursing Administration*, **1** (2), 52–56.

Smith, W.E. (1971). Clinical pharmacy services: Management by objectives. *American Journal of Hospital Pharmacy*, **28** (9), 692–696.

Tan, Y.Z., Liu, X.Q., & Ma, X.J. (1997). Application of management-by-objective principles in training all-round nurses. Chinese Journal of Nursing, **32** (4), 217–218.

Taylor, H.M. (1980). Occupational health management—by objectives. *Personnel*, **57** (1), 58–64.

Wibeck, V., Johansson, M., Larsson, A., & Öberg, G. (2006). Communicative aspects of environmental management by objectives: Examples from the Swedish context. *Environmental Management*, **37** (4), 461–469.

16 New Public Management in Healthcare Organizations[1]

Dawid Sześciło

NEW PUBLIC MANAGEMENT: MARKET REVOLUTION IN PUBLIC SERVICES DELIVERY

In the first half of twentieth century, the healthcare system was focused primarily on quarantining patients (isolation) rather than treatment (Dodds, 2013). The explosion of welfare states after World War II reoriented and significantly expanded the scope of health services (as well as other human services) and the responsibilities of the state for managing the health conditions of the society. The welfare state of post-war times emerged from the lessons of the war and the economic depression years that preceded global military conflict. For at least two decades (1950s and 1960s), it provided in Western countries an effective combination of free market economy with extensive social protection and mitigation of the market's failures. The economic crisis of the 1970s that affected all Western economies invoked, however, the welfare state's demise and fostered the transformation of public healthcare systems (Hemerijck, 2012).

The most influential policy response to the welfare state's crisis emerged from the neo-liberal theory of economy, state and society. The foundations of this doctrine reflects Margaret Thatcher's slogan about "rolling back the state", i.e., reducing public spending (especially for human services), contracting out public services, privatization and deregulation. In public administration theory, this new version of laissez-faire classical liberalism has been conceptualized as the *New Public Management* (*NPM*). The *NPM* is a hybrid of a neo-liberal vision of the state and managerialism, i.e., the doctrine promoting the transfer of business-like management methods and techniques to public sector organizations (König, 1997). The neo-liberal foundations of the *New Public Management* are reflected by the idea of the marketization and privatization of public services provision. As Savas noted, "The purpose of government is to steer the boat, not row. Direct provision of services to citizens is rowing, and the government is not very good at rowing" (Savas, 1982, p. 136). According to this approach, the state should not be involved in the direct provision of public services and should focus on policy making and strategic planning of the system of public services.

Who should take on the role of direct service provider? Private entities, mostly commercial, competing in competitive markets for public services. The consequence of the acquisition by the private sector of a leading role in the direct provision of public services must be the extensive privatization of public enterprises and other public service providers, or at least the introduction in public providers of a management model that would enable them to compete effectively with, or mimic, business. Hence, the pressure on cost-effectiveness and performance management.

The application of *New Public Management* into the area of public services leads not only to institutional and managerial redesign, but also triggers revolution in the values of the public services system. The traditional, statist paradigm of public services placed strong emphasis on ensuring the fair and equal access of all citizens to public services. The *NPM* favors tailoring services to individual needs and the customer's choice of service provider from those in the competitive market (Pierre, 2009). The role of state is reduced to that of a supermarket that should ensure access to good-quality products in the most efficient way (Christensen & Laegreid, 2002). This approach clearly leads to diminishing the role of the state in organizing the citizens' lives and also illustrates the triumph of individualism over collectivist thinking. If public services are to be tailored to individual needs, and the state is to act like a business, it is hard to expect it to realize objectives other than narrowly defined efficiency. As Denhardt and Denhardt (2011) surmise, the *NPM* is not limited to the implementation of new management techniques, but it also brings to the public sector a new set of values taken from the market and business.

The *New Public Management* had the faces of Margaret Thatcher and Ronald Reagan (Kjaer, 2004), although the theoretical assumptions of the *NPM* were conceptualized later, mainly by Osborne and Gaebler (1992) and Hood (1991). Thatcherism brought the flagship project of compulsory competitive tendering of public services, which forced the local administration to contract out technical services such as construction, facilities management, waste collection and school catering (Cutler & Waine, 1997; Wilson, 1999). The most advanced and comprehensive version of *NPM* reforms was implemented in New Zealand. As Kamarck reports, the so-called New Zealand experiment was based on rejecting the idea that there is a core of public tasks that should be performed by state institutions. As a result, all the public functions of the state should be subject to competitive contracting. The philosophy penetrated also into the internal management of the government itself, e.g., the government had to "buy" services from its own bureaucracy and other public and private entities, including policy advice (Kamarck, 2012). A natural consequence of this approach was also the massive privatization of public enterprises and their transformation into joint stock companies. In the UK, the shift towards the *New Public Management* was continued by Tony Blair's cabinet, which placed strong emphasis on the expansion of public-private partnership, which made UK the leading public-private partnerships (PPP) market in the world (Greve, 2010).

The *New Public Management* as an important part of the neo-liberal agenda was largely promoted by international economic and financial institutions—the World Bank, the International Monetary Fund (IMF) and the Organisation for Economic Co-operation and Development (OECD) (Hood & Peters, 2004; Jones & Thompson, 2007). The economic crisis of the 1970s increased the level of dependence of many states of these institutions, and thus opened the way for the reforms imposed by them. The *NPM* has also become a key element of the reform package proposed or imposed by these institutions in the post-socialist countries of central and eastern Europe. It had fertile ground in those countries as a natural response to the need for far-reaching destatization of the economy and marketization of public services.

The overall impact of the *NPM* on public service delivery, including healthcare, might be illustrated with reference to the public services provision cycle.

Table 16.1 Public Service Delivery in the Statist and Market Model

Component of the public service provision process	Classic service-providing administration	Market model of public service provision (*NPM*)
Strategic stewardship: Setting institutional and legal framework for services delivery, long-term, strategic planning, identifying and predicting global and domestic trends and developments and citizens' needs	State responsibility	State responsibility
Financing: Collection and distribution of funds for service delivery	Responsibility of public administration (partial payments in exceptional cases)	Primary responsibility of public administration, but fees or co-payment are applied on a larger scale; gradual reduction of public spending and tighter control over how they are used

(Continued)

Table 16.1 (Continued)

Component of the public service provision process	Classic service-providing administration	Market model of public service provision (NPM)
Delivery (direct provision): Providing the services directly to citizens and managing institutions responsible for service delivery	Provided by organizational forms established pursuant to public law operating in a hierarchical public administration structure (mainly administrative establishments)	Marketization and privatization based on civil law contracts concluded with service providers participating in competitive tender procedures
Monitoring and evaluation: Continuous supervision over the quality of services, accountability mechanisms and developing ideas for improvements	Responsibility of administration; executed by public-law-based acts of internal management with respect to organizational entities providing services	Responsibility of administration; mainly carried out by means of contractual liabilities

(*source:* Sześciło, 2014a, p. 50)

KEY ELEMENTS OF THE NPM PROGRAM: MARKETIZATION, DECENTRALIZATION, DEPUBLICIZATION

The *New Public Management* as an umbrella concept does not contain a fixed list of ideas for public services reengineering. However, there are three major streams of reforms powered by the *NPM* doctrine: The marketization of public services and service providers, the decentralization of public services management and the "depublicization" (privatization in legal sense) of public services and their providers.

Marketization

A cornerstone of the *New Public Management* is the transformation of public services through their marketization. According to this concept, the system of public services should be organized as competitive markets of private and public providers operating mainly under contracts from the state authorities, with wide scope for customers' choice (Hood, 1991; Sześciło, 2014a). Marketization leads to a fundamental change in the role of public administration in the area of public services—a shift from rowing to steering. Public administration commissions, coordinates and controls the provision of services by autonomous or external providers selected through competitive tendering procedures.

Marketization is carried out according to three major types of organizational and financial arrangement:

1) Classical outsourcing of public services, i.e., contracting for public services by the process of an open and competitive tender, resulting in a contract with the entity that offered the best conditions. The contract stipulates the quantity of services, the standards of their provision and the compensation due from the state. Outsourcing has been applied in administration for a long time (one distinct form was the provision of "services" by mercenary armies), but thanks to marketization, it expanded to include new public service sectors, becoming particularly widespread in social services;

2) Public-private partnership, which is a more advanced formula of execution of "turnkey" infrastructure projects, where the private entity is responsible not only for project execution but also for providing funds to finance the project, and in some cases for operating the services that use the infrastructure, at least for an initial period;

3) Vouchers for public services—people entitled to a given service or benefit receive the right to choose their supplier. Unlike the classic outsourcing formula, it is the citizen, not a public authority, that decides who will provide the service in question. No charges, however, apply to the payer—it is still the state that is responsible for funding service delivery (OECD, 2005).

Marketization usually goes hand in hand with functional privatization, i.e., the broad inclusion of private actors in the process of performing public tasks (Fabian, 2010). Private entities contracted by the public authorities responsible for the provision of certain public services are gaining a larger market share of public services, thereby limiting the scope of services provided by public institutions or state-owned enterprises. Public entities are not formally excluded from the market, and they may compete for contracts for services provision (Pallessen, 2010). However, the competitive pressure from private providers is expected to stimulate revolutionary changes in the business models of public providers, especially placing greater emphasis on cost control and customer satisfaction. Lack of a performance-oriented adaption strategy results in the dramatic loss of market position.

As a result, public institutions were forced to implement business-like management models. This included a wide variety of performance management tools, e.g., management by results based on predefined targets and indicators of success, performance budgeting, quality management, pay-for-performance schemes, cutting costs of operation (particularly labor costs) and acquiring regular feedback from the customers (Ashburner et al., 1996; Barzelay & Armajani, 1992; Dunleavy & Hood, 1994; Hood, 1991; OECD, 2010; Pollitt & Dan, 2011).

Decentralization

Although there is a consensus among *NPM's* advocates on the benefits of decentralization, the concept itself seems to be vague and heterogeneous. A classic definition of decentralization developed by Rondinelli and Nellis (1986) refers to:

> [the] transfer of responsibility for planning, management, and the raising and allocation of resources from the central government and its agencies to field units of government agencies, subordinate units or levels of government, semi-autonomous public authorities or corporations, area-wide, regional or functional authorities, or non-governmental private or voluntary organizations. (p. 5)

This definition represents an extremely broad concept of decentralization, including four different processes:

1) Deconcentration—dispersing some tasks to territorial branches of central government. It is a clearly technical operation aimed at improving the performance of the central government without empowering local or regional communities;
2) Delegation—transferring some responsibilities to local or regional government units that enjoy some scope of autonomy, yet are ultimately accountable to the central government;
3) Devolution—form of extensive decentralization based on transferring responsibilities and authority from the central level to an autonomous unit of local/regional government;
4) Privatization—engaging private entities (commercial or not-for-profit organizations) in public services delivery, mainly on a contractual basis (Rondinelli et al., 1983).

This extensive approach to defining decentralization is not shared by all scholars. Pollitt and Bouckaert focus on "political decentralization", described as transferring powers and responsibilities from the central government to autonomous public law bodies, primarily regional/local self-government units (Pollitt & Bouckaert, 2004). Polidano distinguishes also management decentralization, defined as "giving line managers in government departments and agencies greater managerial authority and responsibility" (Polidano, 1999, p. 19).

The most general argument for decentralization is based on the theory of organization. It is believed that greater specialization of work, enhanced by decentralization, fosters efficiency (Bouckaert et al., 2010). In the context of healthcare, the following objectives and rationale for this process are also indicated in the literature (Bankauskaite & Saltman, 2007, p. 16):

1) Improving technical and allocative efficiency thanks to reducing levels of bureaucracy, greater cost consciousness and better matching of public services to local preferences;

2) Empowering local governments through enabling more active local participation in policy making and services delivery;
3) Enhancing the innovation of service delivery thanks to creating conditions for local policy experiments;
4) Increasing accountability through public participation in policy making and implementation and the transformed role of the central government;
5) Increasing quality of health services and equity to be enhanced by allocating resources according to local needs and enabling local organizations to better meet the needs of particular groups.

Depublicization (Privatization)

The classic paradigm of public administration, especially in the continental, bureaucratic administrative culture, is primarily legalistic. The principle of legality is the cornerstone of public administration. *New Public Management* policies do not openly undermine this principle, yet they aim at reducing the role of administrative (public) law regulation and induce a shift towards a model of regulation, steering and control based on private law (i.e., the law regulating private organizations). This includes in particular organizing public services by contracting them under civil law contracts instead of administering them under hierarchical relations based on public law, as well as transforming public institutions enjoying the special status of public law entities into companies and other institutional forms of private sector organizations. The latter process is usually described as the corporatization of state institutions (Lane, 2005).

In other words, as the doctrine of managerialism requires, public institutions and their rules of operation should not differ from those applied in the private sector, namely business. It reflects Lipsey and Lancaster's (1956) theory of second best applied into public administration reform—if it is not possible to privatize some public services, the aim should be to mimic the private sector in terms of managing services. There should be only a very limited field of regulation applicable solely to public organizations. The process of performing public tasks should be as far as possible subject to the regime of private law, which is governed by contracts concluded on the basis of the autonomy and equality of the parties and that are subject to the jurisdiction of the general courts. In addition, public organizations should operate according to the same legal model as private entities, in particular, in the form of commercial companies. A level playing field needs to be ensured both for public and private providers of public services. Public providers must not enjoy a privileged position in the market game, based on their special legal status guaranteeing, e.g., safeguards against bankruptcy, preferential access to state aid or other special rights.

"Depublicization" also applies to the legal relationship between the citizen and public service providers. The citizen, now perceived as a customer or consumer of public services, receives services under the civil law contract.

Citizens may therefore use, as a rule, the same instruments to protect their rights as when buying any other services or goods on the market. As a result, potential disputes between customers and service providers should be resolved according to consumer laws.

RECEPTION OF NEW PUBLIC MANAGEMENT IN HEALTHCARE ORGANIZATIONS

The *New Public Management* has had a profound impact on administrative systems on a global scale. Although it was associated primarily with the Anglo-Saxon countries, it has also transformed the traditional western European bureaucracies, and through policy transfer programs pursued by international organizations, it also affected the transition of post-socialist administrative systems in eastern Europe. To some extent, a convergence of administrative systems has been achieved as a result of *NPM* reforms (Toonen, 2007).

Healthcare systems, as a crucial element of the welfare state, have been targeted by *NPM* reforms too. All key elements of the *New Public Management* agenda have been reflected in healthcare reforms, though to diverse extents. As Saltman et al. (2011, p. 20) noted, the *NPM*-driven reforms in healthcare organizations "have sought to stimulate entrepreneurial hospital management by relying on quasi-market forces rather than planning, and by introducing strong performance measurement and monitoring mechanisms". In addition,

> public hospital governance structures in some countries have been reconfigured, by creating quasi-independent Supervisory Boards that could make a range of operating and financial decisions without obtaining direct political approval [. . .] Public hospital managers were hired, with professional skills as managers that politicians, civil servants and public administrators often lacked.
>
> (Saltman et al., 2011, p. 20)

For Blank and Burau, the most significant outcome of *NPM* reforms in healthcare systems is the transformation of patients into customers within a market of regulated competition. Another crucial element of the *NPM* agenda for healthcare is the increasing role of private providers of health services (Blank & Burau, 2014).

The table below presents in more detailed way how the key elements of the *New Public Management* reform program are reflected in healthcare systems' transformation. Descriptions of each are accompanied with examples of the European countries where the given element of the *NPM* agenda was implemented. The list of the countries is not exhaustive, yet it aims at showing that *NPM*-driven reforms gained reception in countries representing different models of healthcare system and diverse political and economic conditions.

Table 16.2 Key Elements of the NPM Reflected in Healthcare Systems

Key component of NPM	Forms of application	Examples of application relating to healthcare organizations	Countries
MARKETIZATION	*Outsourcing of public services*	1. Introduction of quasi-markets for health services based on purchaser-provider split and increasing role of private providers contracted by public contracting bodies; 2. Contractual arrangements between public purchaser and providers of health services instead of hierarchical control;	UK, Poland, Finland, Norway, Sweden, Denmark (Flood, 2003; Magnussen et al., 2009; Sześciło, 2014b; Tynkkynen et al., 2013)
	Public-private partnerships	3. PPP contracts for designing, financing, building and operating hospitals;	Sweden, Germany, Portugal (Nikolic & Maikisch, 2006), Spain (Alonso et al., 2015)
	Vouchers for public services	4. Ensuring patients' choice of hospitals and other health services providers from a wide range of service providers contracted by the state authority (money follows patients); 5. GP fundholding scheme—general practitioners have a budget to buy selected health services for their patients; 6. Personal budget scheme—special funding allocated to patients upon assessment of care needs and enabling them to choose treatment options and control costs;	Sweden (Nordgren, 2010), Germany (Richter, 2009), Poland (Sześciło, 2014b), UK (Fisher, 1998), Netherlands (Tarricone & Tsouros, 2008)
	Performance management	7. Pay-for-performance and incentive-based pay arrangements for managers in healthcare institutions and for physicians; 8. Introduction of diagnostic-related groups as a commoditized unit of payment supporting managing performance of health services providers;	Sweden, UK (Saltman, 2015), France (Simonet, 2013)

(Continued)

Table 16.2 (Continued)

Key component of NPM	Forms of application	Examples of application relating to healthcare organizations	Countries
DECENTRALIZATION	*Political decentralization*	9. Transferring responsibilities for managing hospitals to local/regional governments; 10. Transferring responsibilities for financing health services provision to regional governments;	Italy, Spain, Portugal, Sweden, Norway (Bankauskaite & Saltman, 2007; Fredriksson & Winblad, 2008; Magnussen & Martinussen, 2012; Mosca, 2006, 2007; Saltman, 2008)
	Management decentralization	11. Semi-autonomous hospitals compete for public contracts; 12. Autonomy of hospital managers combined with accountability for results;	UK, Norway, Sweden (Axelsson et al., 2007; Saltman, 2015)
DEPUBLICIZATION	*Corporatization of public healthcare institutions*	13. Transformation of legal form of public healthcare organizations—from special public law bodies into commercial companies.	Germany, Belgium, Estonia, Poland, Slovakia, Portugal (IMF [International Monetary Fund], 2003; Maarse et al., 2005; Nemec & Lawson, 2008, Sześciło, 2014b)

NEW PUBLIC MANAGEMENT AS A FAILED PANACEA: OUTCOME OF THE NPM REVOLUTION

More than three decades after the first *New Public Management* reforms were introduced, the dominant trend in the literature and public debate towards the marketization of public services is extremely skeptical. It exposes failed promises regarding benefits of competition and privatization and reveals many adverse effects, i.e., the difficulties in enforcing standards for the services provided by private contractors, high transaction costs, lack of real competition in many markets, steering and accountability problems and concerns about equal access to services (among others; see Bevir, 2009; Carrozza, 2010; Domberger & Jensen, 1997; Flynn, 2012; Mulgan, 2006; Seidenstat, 1996). There is also growing understanding that "public services vary in their suitability for externalization" (Alford & O'Flynn, 2012, p. 29).

Public administration scholars have announced the demise of the *New Public Management* already in the first decade of the 21st century (Drechsler & Randma-Liiv, 2014; Dunleavy et al., 2006). Current, post-crisis reflection on the negative effects of the neo-liberal socio-economic experiment only reinforced the critical judgment on the *NPM*. Previously, the critique of the *NPM* was founded mainly on the lack of conclusive evidence that the *New Public Management* fulfills its most important promises, i.e., providing more and better quality public services at a reduced cost. The literature summarizing the practice of the *NPM* reforms also indicates other adverse and side effects for the integrity of the public service system, as well as the position of the citizen.

First of all, the apologists of the *New Public Management* ignored the shortcomings and failures of market mechanisms that also appear if market logic is applied to the system of public services. Competition in many markets for public services is limited or even nonexistent, because some public services markets are organized as natural monopolies or quasi-monopolies. The only outcome of the marketization and privatization of these services is transformation of a public monopoly into a private one. Second, in the human services (especially in healthcare) the neo-liberal concept of rational choice fails in many cases. The patient or recipient of other social services has very limited capacity to reasonably and fairly assess the quality of services offered. Also, the calculation of prices for services is not based on objective criteria and cannot be verified by the customer because of information asymmetry.

In addition, *NPM* reforms inevitably lead to the fragmentation (disaggregation) of the public sector, because public services are no longer provided by a single, centralized state apparatus but by a network of organizations and institutions, both public and private (Bevir, 2009; Christensen & Laegreid, 2002). It is accompanied by a reduction in the influence of the central government, not only as a result of massive contracting out of the public services to the private sector, but also because of extensive political decentralization and transferring responsibilities to independent local and regional governments. Rhodes (1994, p. 138) described this process as "hollowing out the state" by depriving it of steering and control mechanisms while maintaining its formal accountability. Also, the coordination and control of the standards of services provided by numerous entities independent from the central administration become a challenge. As a reaction to this problem, numerous initiatives have been launched under the label of joined-up government or whole-of-government. They were supposed to develop mechanisms for cross-sector co-operation, especially between the central and local government (Hodges, 2012). Their effectiveness is limited, though, and they create high transaction costs.

Transferring responsibilities for the direct delivery of public services to the private sector has raised the issue of accountability for the availability and quality of these services. The state formally continues to be accountable to the citizen for the actions of private providers, but the state's capacity to influence the actions of private providers is limited. It is restricted to the instruments of contractual liability, whose effectiveness depends on the ability of the administration to formulate contracts with private contractors, the determination of precise standards of services and on the effectiveness of the control and monitoring mechanisms. Experimenting with marketization and privatization of public services can be beneficiary to the citizens and the state only when the administration is strong enough to protect the public interest. It would be naïve to believe that the private provider of publicly funded services, on its own initiative and without constant pressure from the government, would prioritize the highest quality and availability of services rather than the maximization of its own profits. As Savas (2001) noted, in the era of privatization of public services, the state needs more brain cells than muscle.

As mentioned above, the role of the state in the *NPM* model is limited to offering a wide palette of high-quality services to the citizens (the state as a supermarket). This approach ignores the need for tackling socio-economic problems (elimination of social inequalities, the eradication of poverty, etc.) via ensuring equal and cheap access to services. This concept inevitably leads to undermining the core values of public service systems, such as justice, equality and participatory governance (Wu & He, 2009). They are not openly challenged in the doctrine of *NPM*, but stronger emphasis is placed now on performance, efficiency and tailoring services to the individual needs and capacities of the customers. The collective values of a system of public services are not compatible with this approach.

NPM phrases about the citizen as a customer were to express the idea that more attention should be paid to exploring citizens' needs and expectations. However, the *NPM* agenda does not envisage involving citizens in the management of public services, but only enabling them to choose their service providers and to express an opinion on the quality of services

(Ackerman, 2012). Through choice, the customer is to control the process of service provision, not to participate in decision-making. Civic participation in public management is marginalized in the agenda of the *New Public Management* also because it would restrict the autonomy of managers and generate additional costs or delay processes.

The *NPM* did not fulfill its promises for red tape reduction or the elimination of excessively formalized administrative activities. Old bureaucratic tools have been replaced by new *NPM*-based procedures for performance management and evaluation (Bevir, 2009; Goldfinch & Wallis, 2010). Governments started sinking under the weight of more specific indicators and metrics, quality management systems, plans and strategies. Their real impact on raising the effectiveness of public institutions might be questioned in many cases. They also create high transaction costs associated with the need to hire external consultants and experts.

WHAT HAPPENS AFTER THE NPM? SEARCHING FOR THE NEW PARADIGM

As the *NPM* failed in its ambitions to discover the "one best way" for how the state should be organized (Manning, 2001), the debate on the configuration of the public service delivery system received new impetus. The collapse of the *NPM* or, more broadly, the neo-liberal project, triggers the need for a new paradigm of public services or at least for a set of reforms correcting the market model. One of the most popular ideas is the *Neo-Weberian State*, a public management model that focuses on the reaffirmation of the role of the state and public law, while maintaining the elements of the *New Public Management*, which "survived" the test of empirical verification by being put into practice since the 1980s (Drechsler, 2005, 2009). This pragmatic trend of administrative reforms might also inspire theoretical reflection in the area of health policy. However, it requires more detailed conceptualization and adaption to the specific features of healthcare systems.

Another concept present in the debate is the co-production of public services. Co-production focuses on a more active role of the citizen (as a partner and co-producer of public value) in public services planning and delivery combined with more responsibility for outcomes. Co-production refers not only to co-delivery, but also co-planning, co-design and the co-evaluation of public services (OECD, 2011, p. 37). In each area, it may involve a bunch of tools and methods. This includes institutionalized platforms for citizens' participation in decision-making (forums, councils), mechanisms of direct engagement in services delivery and social audit schemes exemplifying the citizens' participation in the evaluation of service delivery. Unlike the market model, co-production is not based on contractual relations, with the state as the principal and private entities as agents. It also opens up cooperation possibilities based on different principles, especially non-commercial ones. Co-production involves active citizen participation in the creation of wealth, rather than treating citizens only as the recipients of services. Co-production is meant not only to improve the quality of services, but also to strengthen civic identity and develop social capital. Co-production is more than communication and consultation between public administration and society; its objective is to build synergy between the two entities. In a number of cases, co-production entails involvement in the production of certain public services of the people who then use these services (Bovaird & Loeffler, 2005; Brandsen & Pestoff, 2006; Fledderus et al., 2014; Jakobsen, 2013; OECD, 2011; Pestoff, 2012).

The spirit of *NPM* continues to influence the management strategies of healthcare organizations. The key issue is not about rejecting a managerial approach and returning to a bureaucratic steering model. This would not be feasible. The real challenge is to establish a "conceptual mix" inspired by various theoretical approaches (bureaucratic, managerial, co-productive), yet based on a shared vision of management values and priorities. Institutional frameworks should contribute to achieving the fundamental objectives of a healthcare system—providing universal (or near-universal) access to health services, equity in sharing the financial burden of illness and good quality of healthcare (Björkman, 2010). *NPM* rhetoric dominated by efficiency, productivity, competition and customers' choice did not openly challenge those values of healthcare system, yet it gradually led to dismantling them. The search for a new paradigm or best "conceptual mix" requires, therefore, the reaffirmation of the values embedded in the healthcare system. All organizational and managerial solutions applied in healthcare organizations require an in-depth examination from this perspective.

NOTE

1   This article was prepared within the framework of the research project "The promises of decentralization in health care" funded by the National Centre of Science under contract no. UMO-2013/11/B/HS5/03896.

REFERENCES

Ackerman, J.M. (2012). From co-production to co-governance. In V. Pestoff, T. Brandsen, & B. Verschuere (Eds.), *New Public Governance, the Third Sector and Co-production*, London: Routledge, pp. 101–126.

Alford, J., & O'Flynn, J. (2012). *Rethinking Public Service Delivery: Managing with External Providers*. Basingstoke, England: Palgrave Macmillan.

Alonso, J.M., Clifton, J., & Diaz-Fuentes, D. (2015). The impact of new public management on efficiency: An analysis of Madrid's hospitals, *Health Policy*, 119 (3), 333–340.

Ashburner, L., Ferlie, E., Fitzgerald, L., & Pettigrew, A. (1996). *The New Public Management in Action*. Oxford, England: Oxford University Press.

Axellson, R., Marchildon, G.P., & Repullo-Labrador, J.R. (2007). Effects of decentralization on managerial dimensions of health systems, In R.B. Saltman, V. Bankauskaite, & K. Vrangbæk (Eds.), *Decentralization in Health Care. Strategies and outcomes*. New York: Open University Press, pp. 141–166.

Bankauskaite, V., & Saltman R.B. (2007). Central issues in the decentralization debate. In R.B. Saltman, V. Bankauskaite, & K. Vrangbaeck (Eds.), *Decentralization in Health Care. Strategies and Outcomes*. New York: Open University Press, pp. 9–21.

Barzelay, M., & Armajani B. (1992). *Breaking through Bureaucracy. A New Vision for Managing in Government*. Oxford, England: University Press.

Bevir, M. (2009). *Key Concepts in Governance*. London: Sage.

Björkman, J.W. (2010). Comparative perspective on health services reform. In J. Nemec, B.G. Peters (Eds.), *State and Administration in a Changing World*. Bratislava, Slovakia: NISPAcee.

Blank, R.H., & Burau V. (2014). *Comparative Health Policy* (4th ed.). Basingstoke, England: Palgrave Macmillan.

Bouckaert, G., Peters, B.G., & Verhoest, K. (2010). *The Coordination of Public Sector Organizations: Shifting Patterns of Public Management*. Basingstoke, England: Palgrave Macmillan.

Bovaird, T., & Loeffler, E. (2005). *Public Management and Governance*. London: Routledge.

Brandsen, T., & Pestoff, V. (2006). Co-production, the third sector and the delivery of public services: An introduction. *Public Management Review*, 8 (4), 493–501.

Carrozza, C. (2010). Privatising local public services: Between industrial legacy and political ambition. *Local Government Studies*, 36 (5), 599–616.

Christensen, T., & Lægreid, P. (2002). New public management: Puzzles of democracy and the influence of citizens. *The Journal of Political Philosophy*, 10 (3), 267–295.

Correia, T. (2011). New public management in the Portuguese health sector: A comprehensive reading. *Sociologia On Line*, 2, 573–598.

Cutler, T., & Waine, B. (1997). *Managing the Welfare State: The Politics of Public Sector Management*. Oxford, England: Berg.

Denhardt J.V., & Denhardt R.B. (2011). *The New Public Service: Serving, Not Steering*. New York: M.E. Sharpe.

Dodds, A. (2013). *Comparative Public Policy*. Basingstoke, England: Palgrave Macmillan.

Domberger, S., & Jensen, P. (1997). Contracting out by the public sector: Theory, evidence, prospects. *Oxford Review of Economic Policy*, 13 (4), 67–78.

Drechsler, W. (2005). The re-emergence of "Weberian" public administration after the fall of new public management: The central and eastern European perspective. *Halduskultuur*, 5, 94–108.

Drechsler, W. (2009). Towards a neo-Weberian European Union? Lisbon agenda and public administration. *Halduskultuur*, 10, 6–21.

Drechsler, W., & Randma-Liiv, T. (2014). *The new public management then and now: Lessons from the transition in central and eastern Europe* (Working Papers in Technology Governance and Economic Dynamics, 57). Retrieved from http://technologygovernance.eu/files/main/2014050506213434.pdf (accessed 1 June 2015).

Dunleavy, P., & Hood, C. (1994). From old public management to new public management. *Public Money & Management*, 5, 9–16.

Dunleavy, P., Margetts, H., Bastow, S., & Tinkler, J. (2006). New public management is dead: Long live digital-era governance. *Journal of Public Administration Research and Theory*, 16 (3), 467–494.

Fábián, A. (2010). New public management and what comes after. *Current Issues of Business and Law*, 5 (1), 41–56. Retrieved from http://www.vta.ttvam.lt/index.php/vta/article/view/34/52 (accessed 31 May 2015).

Fisher, C.M. (1998). *Resource Allocation in the Public Sector: Values, Priorities, and Markets in the Management of Public Services.* London: Routledge.

Fledderus, J., Brandsen, T., & Honingh, M. (2014). Restoring trust through the co-production of public services: A theoretical elaboration. *Public Management Review*, 16 (3), 424–443.

Flood, C. (2003). *International Health Care Reform: A Legal, Economic and Political Analysis.* London: Routledge.

Flynn, N. (2012). *Public Sector Management.* London: Sage.

Fredriksson, M., & Winblad, U. (2008). Consequences of a decentralized healthcare governance model: Measuring regional authority support for patient choice in Sweden. *Social Science and Medicine*, 67 (2), 271–279.

Goldfinch, S., & Wallis, J. (2010). Two myths of convergence in public management reform. *Public Administration*, 88 (4), 1099–1115.

Greve, C. (2010). The global public-private partnerships industry. In G.A. Hodge, C. Greve, & A. Boardman (Eds.), *International Handbook on Public-Private Partnership*, Cheltenham, England: Edward Elgar, pp. 499–509.

Hemerijck A. (2012). *Changing Welfare States.* Oxford, England: Oxford University Press.

Hodges, R. (2012). Joined-up government and the challenges to accounting and accountability researchers. *Financial Accountability & Management*, 28 (1), 26–51.

Hood C. (1991). A public management for all seasons? *Public Administration*, 69 (1), 3–19.

Hood, C., & Peters, G. (2004). The middle aging of new public management: Into the age of paradox? *Journal of Public Administration Research Theory*, 14 (3), 267–282.

International Monetary Fund (IMF). (2003). *Portugal: Report on the Observance of Standards and Codes—Fiscal Transparency Module.* Washington, DC: IMF.

Jakobsen, M. (2013). Can government initiatives increase citizen coproduction? Results of a randomized field experiment. *Journal of Public Administration Research and Theory*, 23 (1), 27–54.

Jones, L.R., & Thompson, F. (2007). *From Bureaucracy to Hyperarchy in Netcentric and Quick Learning Organizations: Exploring Future Public Management Practice.* Charlotte, NC: IAP.

Kamarck, E.C. (2012). Government reform and innovation: A comparative perspective. In G. Tria & G. Valotti (Eds.), *Reforming the Public Sector: How to Achieve Better Transparency, Service and Leadership.* Rome: Brookings Institution Press, pp. 240–259.

Kjaer, A.M. (2004). *Governance: Key Concepts.* Cambridge, England: Wiley.

König K. (1997). Entrepreneurial management or executive administration: The perspective of classical public administration. In W.J.M. Kickert (Ed.), *Public Management and Administrative Reform in Western Europe.* Cheltenham, England: Edward Elgar, pp. 213–232.

Lane J.-E. (2005). *Public Administration and Public Management: The Principal-agent Perspective.* Abingdon, England: Routledge.

Lipsey, R.G., & Lancaster, K. (1956). The general theory of second best. *The Review of Economic Studies*, 24 (1), 11–32.

Maarse, H., Rathwell, T.A., Evetovits, T., Preker A.S., & Jakubowski E. (2005). Responding to purchasing: Provider perspectives. In J. Figueras, R. Robinson & E. Jakubowski (Eds.), *Purchasing to Improve Health Systems Performance.* New York: Open University Press, pp. 265–288.

Magnussen, J., & Martinussen, P.E. (2012). From centralization to decentralization, and back: Norwegian health care in a Nordic perspective. In J. Costa-Font & S.L. Greer (Eds.), *Federalism and Decentralization in European Health and Social Care*. Basingstoke, England: Palgrave Macmillan, pp. 101–121.

Magnussen, J., Vrangbæk, K., & Saltman, R.B. (2009). *Nordic Health Care Systems: Recent Reforms and Current Policy Challenges*. New York: Open University Press.

Manning, N. (2001). The legacy of the new public management in developing countries. *International Review of Administrative Sciences*, **67** (2), 297–312.

Mosca, I. (2006). Is decentralization the real solution? A three country study. *Health Policy*, **77** (1), 113–120.

Mosca, I. (2007). Decentralization as a determinant of health care expenditure: Empirical analysis for OECD countries. *Applied Economics Letters*, **14** (7), 511–515.

Mulgan, R. (2006). Government accountability for outsourced services. *Australian Journal of Public Administration*, **65** (2), 48–58.

Nemec, J., & Lawson, C. (2008). Health care reforms in CEE: Processes, outcomes and selected explanations. *NISPAcee Journal of Public Administration and Policy*, **1** (1), 27–50.

Nikolic, I.A., & Maikisch, H. (2006). *Public-Private Partnerships and Collaboration in the Health Sector. An Overview with Case Studies from Recent European Experience*. Washington: World Bank. Retrieved from http://siteresources.worldbank. org/INTECAREGTOPHEANUT/Resources/HNPDiscussionSeriesPPPPaper .pdf (accessed 1 June 2015).

Nordgren, L. (2010). The healthcare voucher: Emergence, formation and dissemination. *Financial Accountability & Management*, **26** (4), 443–464.

OECD. (2005). *Modernising Govermnent: The Way Forward*. Paris: OECD.

OECD. (2010). *Public Administration after "New Public Management"*. Paris: OECD.

OECD. (2011). *Together for Better Public Services: Partnering with Citizens and Civil Society*. Paris: OECD.

Osborne, D., & Gaebler, T. (1992). *Reinventing Government: How the Entrepreneurial Spirit Is Transforming Government*. Reading, MA: Addison-Wesley.

Pallessen, T. (2010). Privatization. In P. Laegreid & T. Christensen (Eds.), *The Ashgate Research Companion to New Public Management*, Farnham, England: Ashgate, pp. 251–264.

Pestoff, V. (2012). Co-production and third sector social services in Europe: Some concepts and evidence. *Voluntas*, **23** (4), 1102–1118.

Pierre, J. (2009). Why legality matters: The limits of markets and governance reform in public sector. *QoG Working Paper Series*, **5** (5). Retrieved from http://qog.pol.gu.se/digitalAssets/1350/1350709_2009_5_pierre.pdf (accessed 1 June 2015).

Polidano, C. (1999). *The New Public Management in Developing Countries*. Manchester: Institute for Development Policy and Management, University of Manchester. Retrieved from http://unpan1.un.org/intradoc/groups/public/documents/ APCITY/UNPAN014322.pdf (accessed 1 June 2015).

Pollitt, C., & Bouckaert, G. (2004). *Public Management Reform: A Comparative Analysis*. Oxford, England: Oxford University Press.

Pollitt, C., & Dan, S. (2011). *The impacts of the new public management in Europe: A meta-analysis*. COCOPS Work Package 1 —Deliverable 1.1. Retrieved from http://www.cocops.eu/wp-content/uploads/2012/03/ WP1_Deliverable1_Meta-analysis_Final.pdf (accessed 1 June 2015).

Richter, W.F. (2009). *Germany goes ahead with health vouchers* (CESifo DICE report 3), pp. 53–60.

Rhodes, R.A.W. (1994). The hollowing out of the state: The changing nature of the public service in Britain, *The Political Quarterly*, **65** (2), 138–151.

Rondinelli, D.A., & Nellis, J.R. (1986). Assessing decentralization policies in developing countries: A case for cautious optimism. *Development Policy Review*, **4** (1), 3–23.

Rondinelli, D.A., Nellis J.R., & Cheema, G.S. (1983). *Decentralization in developing countries: A review of recent experience* (World Bank Staff Working Papers 581). Retrieved from http://www-wds.worldbank.org/servlet/WDSContentServer/ IW3P/IB/1983/07/01/000009265_3980928162717/Rendered/PDF/multi0page. pdf (accessed 1 June 2015).

Saltman, R.B. (2008). Decentralization, re-centralization and future European health policy. *European Journal of Public Health*, **18** (2), 104–106. Retrieved from http://eurpub.oxfordjournals.org/content/eurpub/18/2/104.full.pdf (accessed 31 May 2015).

Saltman, R.B. (2015). Healthcare policy and innovation. In E. Kuhlmann, R.H. Blank, I.L. Bourgeault & C. Wendt (Eds.), *The Palgrave International Handbook of Healthcare Policy and Governance*. Basingstoke, England: Palgrave Macmillan, pp. 23–36.

Saltman, R.B., Durán, A., & Dubois, H.F.W. (2011). *Governing Public Hospitals Reform Strategies and the Movement Towards Institutional Autonomy*. Copenhagen: WHO Regional Office for Europe. Retrieved from http://www.euro.who. int/__data/assets/pdf_file/0017/154160/e95981.pdf?ua=1 (accessed 1 June 2015).

Savas, E.S. (1982). *Privatizing the Public Sector: How to Shrink Government*. Chatham, NJ: Chatham House.

Savas, E.S. (2001). Privatization and the new public management. *Fordham Urban Law Journal*, **28** (5), 1731–1737.

Seidenstat, P. (1996). Privatization: Trends, interplay of forces and lessons learned. *Policy Studies Journal*, **24** (3), 464–477.

Simonet, D. (2013). New public management and the reform of French public hospitals. *Journal of Public Affairs*, **13** (3), 260–271.

Sześciło D. (2014a). *Rynek—konkurencja—interes publiczny. Wyzwania prawne urynkowienia usług publicznych*. Warsaw: Scholar.

Sześciło, D. (2014b). Nowe zarządzanie publiczne jako wzorzec transformacji systemu ochrony zdrowia w Polsce ze szczególnym uwzględnieniem szpitalnictwa. *Zdrowie Publiczne i Zarządzanie*, **12** (2), 134–143.

Tarricone, R., & Tsouros, A.D. (Eds.). (2008). *Home Care in Europe: The Solid Facts*. Copenhagen: WHO Regional Office Europe. Retrieved from http:// www.euro.who.int/__data/assets/pdf_file/0005/96467/E91884.pdf (accessed 1 June 2015).

Toonen, T.A.J. (2007). Administrative reform: Analytics. In B.G. Peters & J. Pierre (Eds.), *The Handbook of Public Administration*. London: Sage.

Tynkkynen, L.-K., Keskimäkia, I., & Lehtoa J. (2013). Purchaser—provider splits in health care: The case of Finland. *Health Policy*, **111** (3), 221–225.

Wilson, J. (1999). Compulsory competitive tendering and local government financial services: An analysis of the views of local government accountants in the North West of England. *Public Administration*, **77** (3), 541–563.

Wu, X., & He, J. (2009). Paradigm shift in public administration: Implications for teaching in professional training programs. *Public Administration Review*, **69** (S1), s21–s28.

17 Servant Leadership in Healthcare Organizations

Jack McCann

INTRODUCTION

According to Trastek et al. (2014), our current healthcare system is broken, unsustainable and too costly for patients that need and desire the best quality healthcare possible. Furthermore, the current climate in many healthcare organizations is not in alignment with the idea of leadership rooted in the human desire to care for others and improve society. Greenleaf et al. (1996) argued that true leadership is essentially synonymous with service and great leaders are identified by the way they serve others and society.

The US federal government expressed its vision for healthcare in a "triple aim" format: Improving the individual experience of care, improving the health of the populations and reducing the per capita cost of care (Berwick et al., 2008). In the healthcare sector, the creation of value is measured by the outcomes achieved, not the volume of services delivered. Shifting the focus to quality in the healthcare delivery system therefore remains the central challenge. Hence, the most fundamental and critical responsibility for healthcare leaders is to understand their patients and provide the best care possible (Capoccia & Abeles, 2006; Porter, 2010).

This chapter provides the origins, character and purpose of *Servant Leadership*, and describes how *Servant Leadership* works. The chapter also evaluates how *Servant Leadership* may be adapted for use in healthcare organizations along with advantages and disadvantages of *Servant Leadership*. Finally, the chapter examines whether healthcare managers should attempt to be servant leaders and what putting *Servant Leadership* to practice in healthcare may mean.

SERVANT LEADERSHIP: ORIGINS, CHARACTER AND PURPOSE

Servant Leadership is a concept that turns traditional leadership upside down, with the leader serving their followers. The original idea of *Servant*

Leadership as a leadership theory was proposed in an essay written in 1970 by Robert Greenleaf, AT&T's former director of management research and founder of the Robert K. Greenleaf Center for Servant Leadership (Greenleaf, 1970). He originally modeled *Servant Leadership* on Leo, a character in the story *Journey to the East,* written by Herman Hesse. Leo is the servant for a group traveling across the desert and does everything for the group and serves them in any way that they need. Then Leo disappears, and the group realizes that Leo was not their servant, he was their leader, who led by serving them. Greenleaf (1970) carefully considered this paradox and described his leadership philosophy as follows:

> It begins with the natural feeling that one wants to serve, to serve first. Then conscious choice brings one to aspire to lead. The difference manifests itself in the care taken by the servant—first to make sure that other people's highest priority needs are being served. The best test is: Do those served grow as persons; do they, while being served, become healthier, wiser, freer, more autonomous, more likely themselves to become servants? (p. 4)

Greenleaf (1977) refers to this leadership model as one that places serving the needs of others first. The servant leader serves their employees, patients and community. This theory taps into the natural feeling that one desires to serve others first. A conscious choice then brings one to aspire to lead. The true test is whether those served grow as people: Do those being served become healthier, wiser, freer, more autonomous, more likely themselves to become servants?

Barbuto and Wheeler (2006) developed an instrument through which to operationalize and measure five factors derived from characteristics deemed to be indicative of *Servant Leadership.* The *Servant Leadership Questionnaire* measures five factors: Altruistic healing, emotional healing, wisdom, persuasive mapping and organizational stewardship. A description of the subscale, as explained by Barbuto and Wheeler (2006), demonstrates how each determines the extent to which leaders demonstrate their skills in each:

1) Altruistic healing measures the level to which a leader seeks to make a positive impact in the lives of others. From the perspective of *Servant Leadership*, the goal is to serve others; therefore, leaders who are high in this attribute will focus on the interests of others before their own interests and in the process work towards meeting the needs of others. Another significant component of this factor has been described as a generosity of the spirit consistent with a philanthropic purpose in life;
2) Emotional healing assesses the leader's commitment to and skill in developing spiritual recovery from either hardship or trauma. Leaders who score high in this category display such traits as empathy and strong listening skills. Both of these traits serve to facilitate the healing

process by creating an environment that provides a space through which employees feel safe to share personal and professional concerns;

3) Wisdom includes a combination of awareness of one's workplace surroundings and the ability to anticipate consequences within the dynamic of the workplace. A factor in this intuitive skill is the ability to understand organizational dynamics and connect them with reasonable outcomes based upon the environmental cues that they read;

4) Persuasive mapping describes leaders who can influence others. Specifically, this factor encompasses the leader who can use reasoning processes and conceptual frameworks in influencing others. Considered high in the ability to earn buy-in for their organizations' visionary aspirations, these leaders can communicate the reasons that others should support the organizational goals;

5) Organizational stewardship addresses the interconnectedness that an organization has towards other, external bodies in making a positive contribution to society. Founded on the premises of ethics and value orientation, this factor is evidenced by the extent that a leader prepares an organization to be involved in community development, programs and community outreach. Although focused on the work performed in society, this factor also recognizes the importance of developing an internal community spirit workplace through which to engage in societal organizations outside the organization.

Servant leaders create serving relationships with their followers, unlike transformational leaders, who focus on transcending followers' self-interest toward organizational goals (for more information about *Transformational Leadership* and its relevance to healthcare organizations, see Fiery, Chapter 23 in this volume). Netemeyer et al. (2005) discovered that *Servant Leadership* motivates employees to go above and beyond the basic requirements of the job responsibilities in their interaction with customers. Laub (1999) describes *Servant Leadership* as promoting values and developing people, building community and providing leadership for followers and the organization. Walumbwa et al. (2010) state that *Servant Leadership* is conducive to creating positive employee attitudes as well as creating work environments that promote benefits for both individuals and the work group. Studies by Johns (2006) and Ehrhart (2004) further indicate that a strong relationship exists between leaders and followers with the significant benefit of increased organizational effectiveness. In addition, *Servant Leadership* possesses a significant positive correlation with employee satisfaction (85%) and with employee loyalty (79%) (Donghong et al., 2012). Employee satisfaction and organizational commitment are key elements in determining organizational performance and effectiveness.

Boone and Makhani (2012–2013) found that the *Servant Leadership* style has received increased attention in recent years as a powerful approach for leaders. Spears (1995) found that *Servant Leadership* had crossed organizational, occupational and national boundaries and is being utilized by a variety of people working in for-profit businesses, non-profit corporations, churches, universities, healthcare institutions and foundations. *Servant Leadership* has influenced many noted writers, thinkers and leaders. The seeds planted have begun to sprout in many institutions, as well as in the hearts of many who long to improve the human condition. *Servant Leadership* is providing a framework with which many are helping improve how we treat those who do the work in organizations. *Servant Leadership* offers hope and direction for a new era in human relations and potentially the prescription for creating healthy organizations (Spears, 2004).

Mueller (2011) ponders the question, "Is servant leadership the way forward?" It appears that *Servant Leadership* is working in many successful corporations. She discovered that such well-known businesses as TDIndustries, Southwest Airlines Co., Starbucks, ServiceMaster and the Toro Company are each companies that fully and clearly practice the principles of *Servant Leadership*. Furthermore, these companies have performed extremely well when considering financial metrics. *Servant Leadership* is a big part of what makes these organizations into companies that are routinely listed in *Fortune*'s "100 Best Companies to Work For".

Servant Leadership is an approach that can improve organizations, as it advocates a team or group-related approach to analysis and decision-making. This leadership style also focuses the power of persuasion and seeking consensus versus the mechanistic or top-down approach to leadership and may even be comparable to turning the hierarchical pyramid upside down. According to *Servant Leadership*, the purpose of a business should be to create a positive impact on its employees, community and society, rather than have simple profit as the primary business goal.

According to Waterman (2011), *Servant Leadership* is characterized by the mantra of putting other people first. The adoption of this caring, empathic attitude is necessary in healthcare organizations and should not only be displayed towards patients, but it should also be applied in the workplace and surrounding community. Capoccia and Abeles (2006) discovered that there is sufficient evidence of the need to respect and develop the frontline workers. Furthermore, Bodur (2002) discovered through analysis of job satisfaction in healthcare organizations a close correlation between job satisfaction and the quality of healthcare. The nature of *Servant Leadership* may be the perfect vehicle to engage healthcare employees in caring for their customers or patients, as people are placed first and empathy for others is important in this leadership style. Parris and Peachey (2013) found that *Servant Leadership* is not only about creating a trusting, fair, collaborative, helping culture, but also supports and promotes the followers' well-being, whether they are staff members or patients.

Servant Leadership research had its origin in the medical, healthcare and policy fields used primarily to make clinical and policy decisions (Parris & Peachey, 2013). McCann et al. (2014) discovered that *Servant Leadership* exists in today's healthcare organizations and that it provides a unique avenue through which to assess leadership behaviors and the relationship to employee satisfaction and healthcare patient satisfaction measures. Their study determined that leaders in community hospitals were perceived as servant leaders by their employees. They also discovered that *Servant Leadership* is correlated with the level of employee satisfaction in rural community hospitals. Two hundred and nineteen surveys were completed from 10 community hospitals. This research revealed that *Servant Leadership* and employee satisfaction are strongly correlated. In addition, they discovered that *Servant Leadership* has a significant correlation between intrinsic satisfaction and *Hospital Consumer Assessment of Healthcare Providers and Systems* scores.

A survey of physical therapists, occupational therapists and speech language pathologists revealed that intrinsic motivations, rather than extrinsic motivations such as pay, tend to be predictive of career satisfaction and desire to stay on the job (Randolph, 2005). Mohammad et al. (2011) also found that a significant link exists between leadership behavior and job satisfaction. They examined the relationship between *Transformational Leadership* and the job satisfaction of Jordanian registered nurses at private hospitals. The results of the study indicated the statistically strongest significant positive relationship was that existing between intrinsic job satisfaction and the variables of intellectual stimulation and inspirational motivation. Intellectual stimulation was described as the employee's empowerment to solve problems and challenges, whereas inspirational motivation refers to the leaders' commitment and ability to build relationships with their staff to achieve a common vision and set of goals. Intrinsic motivational factors, along with intellectual stimulation and inspirational motivation, are considered significant factors in Greenleaf's *Servant Leadership* style. According to Negussie and Demissie (2013), the intrinsic component of job satisfaction depends on an individual's personal perception and emotional state regarding the work environment, recognition, advancement and responsibility. The extrinsic components are job-related variables that typically include such things as salary, supervision and working conditions.

Things are changing in the practice and application of management in today's healthcare organizations. According to Bateman and Snell (2013), current trends in the field of management are also moving away from the traditional command-and-control approach to management towards leadership that is focused on involvement and participatory work settings with goals intended to rally the knowledge, experience and commitment of all workers. These trends are a commitment to teamwork, with today's organizations designed less vertically and more horizontally in structure. They are driven by teamwork, pooling talents and creative problem solving. There is an increase emphasis on technology and changes in computer and information technology bringing continuous opportunities, since technology keeps changing the ways organizations operate and people work. In addition, new workforce expectations are becoming apparent, with a new generation of workers that is more informal and less tolerant of hierarchy. This new generation tends to value performance merit over status and seniority. Today's organizations are now actively helping people balance work and personal affairs. These trends point to *Servant Leadership*.

Drucker (2001) defined businesses as those organizations that create value for the customer. If businesses did not create value and did not meet a customer's unsatisfied need, they would not exist. Drucker (2001) further stated:

> With respect to the definition of business purpose and business mission, there is only one such focus, one starting point. It is the customer. The customer defines the business. A business is not defined by the company's name, statutes, or articles of incorporation. It is defined by the want the customer satisfies when he or she buys a product or a service. To satisfy the customer is the mission and purpose of every business. The question, 'What is our business?' It can, therefore, be answered only by looking at the business from the outside, from the point of view of customer and market. All the customer is interested in are his or her own values, wants, and reality. For this reason alone, any serious attempt to state, 'what our business is' must start with the customer's realities, his situation, his behavior, his expectations, and his values. (p. 24)

In many of today's organizations, the core value guiding corporate governance has been that of an economic nature and the maximization of stock value, at any cost, has been the driving force (Rodriguez et al., 2002). The core value of organizations should not be of an economic nature, but one based on the sustainable development of the organization based on a dynamic, innovative and sustainable governance and leadership. According to Rodriguez et al. (2002), the ultimate goal of organizations should be to create value for shareholders and society as a whole, through shareholder satisfaction and engagement only when organizations do the right thing for the right reasons.

HOW SERVANT LEADERSHIP WORKS

The premise of the *Servant Leadership* style is that servant leaders want to lead and serve others. Smith et al. (2004) found that *Servant Leadership* is based on serving and growing people. Its adopters in leadership look ahead to the benefit of people. Servant leaders' focus on attending to the needs of all stakeholders and its fundamental principles are ethical and effective. *Servant Leadership* is not just a management style, but also a set of attitudes that needs to be developed by leaders who choose to adopt it.

Smith et al. (2004) assert that the ethical behavior of organizational leaders significantly affects the ethical behavior of their employees. If leaders behave unethically, then it may have a negative impact on the standards, productivity and success of the organization. A great strength of *Servant Leadership* is in its moral foundation and this ethical behavior drives the daily decision-making in organizations. The ethical behavior of servant leaders is embedded in the principles that guide them in their daily decision-making. Since healthcare organizations desire an ethical approach and to improve the performance of organizations, leaders in this industry would then need to model and teach *Servant Leadership* to current and future leaders.

In order to implement this style genuinely and effectively, leaders should be sure that they either possess or can readily adopt certain attitudes that meld with the successful application of *Servant Leadership*. According to Boone and Makhani (2012–2013), key among these attitudes are:

1) Visioning isn't everything, but it's the beginning of everything;
2) Listening is hard work that requires a major investment of personal time and effort—and it is worth every ounce of energy expended;
3) My job involves being a talent scout and committing to my staff's success;
4) It is good to give away my power;
5) I am a community builder. (p. 95)

The focal management idea of *Servant Leadership* is on the core values of "caring" and "serving others", and focuses on the values of trust, appreciation of others and empowerment in the workplace and beyond (Hoveida et al., 2011). The "servant leader" model centers around identifying and addressing the requirements of followers ahead of individual considerations, ultimately leading to the development and growth of the follower as opposed to the needs of the manager or the organization (Jones, 2012a). It is further characterized by the key qualities of being a good listener, self-awareness, empathy and stewardship, which enable the leader to better understand their constituents' needs and maximize their potential, while tailoring their aspirations to the organizational needs and objectives. The servant leader leads by example and, as such, enables and empowers the follower with all the tools necessary to succeed. This practice of leading through genuine caring and authenticity for the needs of others has led to improved organizational effectiveness. The same characteristics lend the *Servant Leadership* model to be considered the most appropriate leadership style for increased organizational performance and enhanced employee satisfaction through improved focus on the customer (Jones, 2012b).

McGee-Cooper et al. (2013) state that the benefits that businesses can gain from the practice of *Servant Leadership* are that servant leaders awaken and engage employee knowledge, build strong interdependence within and beyond the organization's boundaries, meet and exceed the needs of numerous stakeholders, and make wise collective decisions. They described how TDIndustries and Southwest Airlines each created a unique culture based on *Servant Leadership* owing to the founding leader and their beliefs. They stated that any kind of organization can successfully adopt and apply *Servant Leadership*.

ADAPTING SERVANT LEADERSHIP FOR USE IN HEALTHCARE ORGANIZATIONS

There are a number of different leadership styles that managers in healthcare organization may choose to practice, and the context and situation may dictate the use of the particular style that is the best match. Some situations may dictate a more proactive leadership style than *Servant Leadership*, which may on the surface appear to be a more passive style of leadership that implies working behind the scenes and serving others. There are times in healthcare organizations when an authoritative leadership style may be needed, especially in times of emergency and life or death situations that need expertise to lead the situation.

According to Smith et al. (2004), the most popular leadership styles currently identified in research are charismatic, transactional, transformational and *Servant Leadership*. Their use depends on the context and situation. Typically, leadership models do not normally begin with an analysis of the leader's motivation. *Servant Leadership* is unique in this sense. This theory appears to have its foundation in charismatic leadership (as described by Bass, 1998; Conger & Kanungo, 1998). Greenleaf et al. (1996), and is focused on describing the behaviors of servant leaders that define the leadership style and its influence on followers. The difference between many leadership styles and *Servant Leadership* is in its ability to produce a culture that is different due to a foundation that begins with motivation from the leader.

The *Servant Leadership* style exemplifies leaders as servants of their followers. Servant leaders place the interest of their followers before theirs and emphasize personal development and empowerment of followers. The servant leader is a facilitator for followers to achieve a shared vision (Greenleaf, 1977, 1996; Spears, 1998, 2004). The charismatic leader style focuses on extraordinary leadership abilities and skills that may inspire, direct and lead followers through a commitment to a shared vision and the values of the leader (House, 1977; Conger & Kanungo, 1998). Greenleaf (1977) stated that the ultimate goal of the servant leader is to become a servant and to help others become servants, too.

The idea of *Transformational Leadership* expanded on House's (1977) theory of charismatic leadership that compares behaviors of this leadership to personal traits and situational variables. Burns (1978) provided a seminal examination of the theories of *Transformational* and *Transactional Leadership* in politics and among political leaders that framed the differences between these two leadership styles. Burns (1978) defines *Transactional*

Leadership as the exchange of one thing for another in organizations, and *Transformational Leadership* as a way to satisfy the higher needs of followers in terms of Maslow's (1954) needs hierarchy. Burns (1978) added that *Transformational Leadership* emphasizes followers' needs, values and morals.

Bass (1990) lists the characteristics of the transformational leader as charisma, inspiration, intellectual stimulation and individualized consideration. Bass (1990) defines these characteristics as follows:

1) Charisma: Provides vision and sense of mission, instills pride, gains respect and trust;
2) Inspiration: Communicates high expectations, uses symbols to focus efforts and expresses important purposes in simple ways;
3) Intellectual Stimulation: Promotes intelligence, rationality and careful problem solving;
4) Individualized Consideration: Gives personal attention, treats each employee individually, coaches and advises. (p. 22)

Smith et al. (2004) compared *Transformational Leadership* and *Servant Leadership*. They developed a model that compared leader initiatives, resulting cultures and resulting success in environments, along with other factors. Figure 17.1 compares leader initiatives, cultures and environments from that model.

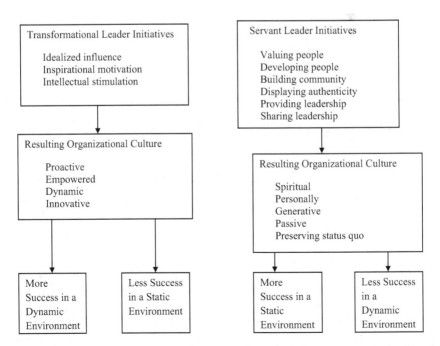

Figure 17.1 Comparison of *Transformational Leadership* to *Servant Leadership*

Smith et al. (2004) found that the *Servant Leadership* will be more effective than *Transformational Leadership* in some contexts, and Figure 17.1 represents these comparisons. A more static environment is considered to be more characteristic of organizations such as not-for-profit, volunteer and religious organizations, which may have employees seeking personal growth, nurturing and healing. On the other hand, *Transformational Leadership* is best for a dynamic external environment where employees are empowered with greater responsibility and the need to innovate, take initiative and risks. A *Transformational Leadership* model focuses on the success of the organization, while the *Servant Leadership* model focuses more on the success of the individual as they reach self-actualization (for more information about *Transformational Leadership* and its relevance to healthcare organizations, see Fiery, Chapter 23 in this volume).

In light of Figure 17.1, a *Servant Leadership* model may be a good fit for the healthcare organization as a whole. Even though healthcare is a dynamic market environment with changes to the policies regarding healthcare, the majority of healthcare organizations operate in a more static environment, where processes and procedures are more valuable than innovation and risk taking.

Healthcare organizations are successfully transforming their organizations through *Servant Leadership*. Kevin Cowan, former CEO of St. Michael's Health Centre in Lethbridge, Alberta, Canada, led an effort that changed this healthcare organization from one that was underperforming and nearly bankrupt into a profitable and innovative organization that set numerous performance standards in Canadian healthcare. Cowan's strategies and belief that the *Servant Leadership* approach is critical had a direct impact on this organization's ability to innovate and form alliances (Vanderpyl, 2012).

When Cowan turned this organization over to his successor in 2008, they had built in CAD 43 million in capital assets, and had a CAD 30 million annual budget, with an annual surplus. It had also built an emerging culture of *Servant Leadership* with amiable management and labor relations. Its workforce was growing in pride about its work. His leadership inspired a new model of senior care that has since become the template for senior facilities in western Canada (Vanderpyl, 2012). This facility's design has been praised by numerous dignitaries and won an award that recognized its artistic contributions and design. His efforts represent a true high-performing servant leader that generates results and the turnaround of organizations not through their charisma or talent, but through their hearts. These strategies and successes can be realized by any servant leader, but require the servant-minded heart first (Vanderpyl, 2012).

Healthcare leadership needs to get the most from its staff. Waterman (2011) suggests that leaders in healthcare can obtain the most from their staff and deliver better services by embracing a more egalitarian model of management. When leaders focus on achieving a higher purpose, they may be able to increase standards and professional integrity. Having a servant heart may not mean offering service at all times in all situations. However, it does mean having a servant mindset when decisions are made.

Healthcare leadership may need to change its focus in order to achieve top performance. Waterman (2011) stated that leadership in healthcare organizations is often focused on meeting organizational targets, goals and mission statements, along with many other challenges. However, many leaders are still able to focus on service, community and organizational vision. Leaders who utilize the principles of *Servant Leadership* can help their organization focus on service and community, and on client care and the quality of services offered. *Servant Leadership* is concerned about providing high-quality services by releasing leaders from the proverbial quality checklists. By doing so, leadership can ensure that clients and other key stakeholders are treated with the respect and compassion that is necessary. Servant leaders provide direction to their staff and support their performance. They also provide ways that employees are able to give their best, and they share their vision with employees to focus them on achieving organizational objectives.

Management and leadership are defined and practiced differently in healthcare organizations. Kotter (1998) differentiated management and leadership through a key element in that leaders establish a vision for the future. Greenleaf (1977) defined foresight and conceptualizing vision in terms of *Servant Leadership*. He indicated that foresight was the primary ethic of leadership and that conceptualizing was the prime leadership talent. Kotter (1998) stated that the function of leadership is to produce change, and setting the direction of that change is leadership. Leaders lead followers through commitment and example. Servant leaders in particular attract followers into commitment and dedication to excellence. They also model and visibly interact with their followers, who they appreciate, value, encourage and care for in pursuit of success (Greenleaf, 1977).

ADVANTAGES AND DISADVANTAGES OF SERVANT LEADERSHIP

The intriguing message of *Servant Leadership* is serving employees and demonstrating commitment to their well-being, growth and self-actualization, along with working toward the long-term success of the organization. Greenleaf (1991) defined the mental model of the servant leader, in that the great leader is a servant because serving others is fundamental to their core personal identity. DePree (2004) emphasized that building relationships with individuals honored the leader's ethical obligation to be a servant to colleagues and employees, and specified that this relationship includes the leader's obligation to define reality in dealing honestly with employees about requirements and about how they align with the needs of the organization. The servant leader serves individuals, the organization and society.

The practice of *Servant Leadership* may be difficult to discern in today's healthcare organization. Russell and Stone (2002) found that the *Servant Leadership* literature is a bit ambiguous and anecdotal, making it difficult to determine the attributes along with the observable behaviors of servant leaders. However, with so many different literature styles reporting on *Servant Leadership*, there is sufficient consistency to describe the characteristics of a servant leader. Spears (1998, 2004) described the following list of characteristics about *Servant Leadership* from Greenleaf's writings:

1) Listening: Servant leaders listen, and including reflection is important for the servant leader;
2) Empathy: Servant leaders seek to understand and empathize with others;
3) Healing: Servant leaders learn how to heal themselves and others, along with difficult situations in organizations;
4) Awareness: Servant leaders are strengthened by being generally aware and are self-aware;
5) Persuasion: Servant leaders focus on convincing versus coercing;
6) Conceptualization: Servant leaders nurture their ability to dream the big dreams;
7) Foresight: Servant leaders foresee the outcome of situations;
8) Stewardship: Servant leaders hold their organization responsible for the overall good of society and seek what is best;
9) Sense of Community: Servant leaders build a sense of community in their organizations and with other stakeholders;
10) Commitment to Growth of Employees: Servant leaders believe that employees have more to offer than just work and seek to develop it.

There are advantages and disadvantages that healthcare managers and their organizations must consider regarding the implementation or utilization of *Servant Leadership*. Waterman (2011) presented a number of advantages and disadvantages of *Servant Leadership* that healthcare management should consider:

Advantages:

1) Values people and treat them as ends rather than means;
2) Enables others to develop and flourish;
3) Shows commitment to the community;
4) Expresses a human face in an often impersonal environment;
5) Puts the concept of caring back into care;
6) Seeks to improve care through encouragement and facilitation, rather than through power and authority;
7) Improves performance by developing and nurturing followers.

Disadvantages:

1) It is similar to *Transformational Leadership* approaches in definition and is hard to discern;
2) A target-fixated system pigeonholes it as a religious leadership style;
3) It disturbs the concept of hierarchy, which many in healthcare organizations may be considered sacrosanct;
4) It can be perceived as a "religious" concept and therefore alien to modern sensitivities;
5) The title of "servant" can be seen as detrimental to administrators, doctors or nurses;
6) Humility can be perceived as a weakness by patients and other employees;
7) Some workers may not respond to this approach and need a more direct approach.

Servant Leadership appears to be proving successful, and it has also gained popularity in healthcare organizations because it is viewed as a promising solution to help leaders become more efficient, principled and employee focused (Waterman, 2011). However, there is little empirical research to prove this is case. The following results from two empirical studies indicate the promise of *Servant Leadership* in today's organizations that can be considered by healthcare organizations.

Leadership influences employees' behavior, and Kool and Dierendonck (2012) set out to gain an understanding of the processes whereby leadership can positively influence commitment to change in a sample of employees in a reintegration company. They discovered the importance of combining a people-oriented and a task-oriented approach. Leaders combining *Servant Leadership* with contingent rewards or a transactional model of leadership are more likely to create an environment that embraces change in a positive way. They summarized that their results are in line with growing evidence that leadership style influences the success or failure of organizational change processes.

Jones (2011) explored conditions to maintain *Servant Leadership* in an organization and the role *Servant Leadership* might play in creating and keeping a participative business culture along with profitability, employee satisfaction and empowerment. The data from this study suggested that *Servant Leadership* may lead to greater organizational productivity and increased fiscal strength, which was revealed through decreased turnover, increased job satisfaction and increased revenues. The participants were all senior leaders in their respective organizations, which comprised revenues from a few hundred thousand dollars to organizations with revenues in the billions. The study sheds light on the conditions that maintain and sustain *Servant Leadership* along with why

Servant Leadership benefits the organization. What stands out from these research findings are the level of drive and determination that leaders had to not just be successful, but to encourage and support others to be a success and to achieve their goals. This compassion for others becomes priceless. Organizations will be able to see the benefits of *Servant Leadership* and determine through the conclusions in this study that they too may be motivated to develop and grow others, thereby contributing to greater organizational success.

Spears (2004) states that *Servant Leadership* is a long-term approach to transform life and work, and it can be a way of life. Leadership in healthcare must reinvigorate awareness in the service aspect of healthcare, and adherence to *Servant Leadership* principles may realign healthcare leadership, so that it can provide increased compassion and understanding to those served. *Servant Leadership* may help healthcare leadership provide better care and ensure a more caring workforce (Waterman, 2011).

SHOULD HEALTHCARE MANAGERS ATTEMPT TO BE SERVANT LEADERS?

Healthcare managers have a choice of the leadership style that is best for them and their organization. Scruggs-Garber et al. (2009) consider Greenleaf's *Servant Leadership* to be the most effective leadership model to address the challenges that face the healthcare industry and one that should be adopted. The healthcare industry by nature serves and cares for people, and in such a capacity, is the ideal platform to adopt and incorporate *Servant Leadership*.

Servant Leadership behaviors appear to be what healthcare organizations may need to effectively lead their organizations in today's challenging times. Organizations are beginning to understand that no part of an organization is insignificant. *Servant Leadership* calls for leading from a level of deep, revolutionary vision. Servant leaders change the organization, invent the new paradigm, clear a space where something new can be, and they accomplish this not so much by doing as by being (Zohar, 1997). *Servant Leadership* can be considered a philosophy of life and leadership dedicated to the growth and development of others. The servant leader is committed to building organizations that are value based and that ultimately contribute to creating organizations that are sustainable, ethical and socially concerned, which can be achieved by practicing *Servant Leadership*. According to Kouzes and Posner (2002), the leader must have an ideal and unique image of the future state. *Servant Leadership* is vision based and something that is needed in all organizations, but it can benefit the healthcare organization in particular. Blanchard (1997) stated that vision is essential for effective leadership and wrote that, "All good leadership starts with a visionary role" (p. 22).

Spears (1995, pp. 1–14) identified and recommended six areas in which managers can practice *Servant Leadership*:

1) Adopt *Servant Leadership* as part of the organization's philosophy. The idea of the leader as a servant must be the framework for the organization's mission and vision;
2) Incorporate servant leadership into the education of the board of directors, leading them to think of trustees or boards as servants. Ask them, "Whom do you serve?";
3) Integrate servant leadership concepts into community leadership organizations, creating a business that serves the community;
4) Use servant leadership in experiential education or learning by utilizing service learning in the organization. Service learning combines classroom instruction with meaningful community service;
5) Offer servant leadership courses for the education and training of management, such as books, films, articles, speakers and possibly attending a symposium at the Greenleaf Center in Indianapolis;
6) Apply servant leadership concepts in personal growth training programs.

Greenleaf (1991, 1996) argued that the task facing the servant leader is to withdraw and orient him/herself, and then a manager must prioritize the important from the less important and attend to the priorities. This may not be unique to *Servant Leadership*, but it is a focus of this leadership style.

All organizations and especially healthcare organizations need vision, and adopting *Servant Leadership* can help them focus on their vision. Bennis and Nanus (1985) stated, "The problem with many organizations, and especially the ones that are failing, is that they have the tendency to be over managed and under led" (p. 21). Leaders are vision, judgment and effectiveness oriented, while managers were more concerned with efficiency and mastering routines or doing things right. Bennis and Nanus (1985) stated that vision brings to life and transforms organization purpose into practical action. They further stated that vision is important when choosing a direction to follow. In addition, they postulate that the leader must first have formulated a mental image of the possible and desired future state of the organization. In their view, vision may be as vague as a dream or as precise as an organizational goal or mission statement. The visioning process can help facilitate organizational change and transformation.

Greenleaf et al. (1996) drew inspiration and reflected about vision by quoting a familiar passage from the "Book of Proverbs": "Where there is no vision, the people perish" (29:18). He believed that vision was primarily about foresight, the ability to see the issues of the past and then learn their realities in the present and to discern their consequences for the future. He used the term "healer" when it came to seeing the purpose or mission, and the value of a person. Healers make whole by helping others see a larger and nobler vision and purpose for the organization and one greater than they would attain for themselves.

According to Bennis and Nanus (1985), vision inspires the best and most effective performance within people. Patterson (2003) found that vision was most often regarded as an organizational attribute identifying the organization's destination or destiny. However, the servant leader must have a faith and vision of what can be and create the ability and belief that individuals can improve, move forward and reach goals. Servant leaders encourage the enrichment of lives and of human beings, and encourage people to become better than they ever thought possible. They encourage employees to believe their work is more than just a job, and servant leaders focus on mission and the mission to serve (Melrose, 1995). Patterson (2003) stated that vision in *Servant Leadership* is about person-centered vision for others and not necessarily organizational vision. However, improving the person should lead to organizational improvements as well, because the leader looks into the future to see the future state for each individual, and then works to assist each one in reaching that goal.

Practicing *Servant Leadership* encompasses three dimensions: Motives, means and ends (or outcomes). *Servant Leadership* further embraces the "triple bottom line" (sustaining people, profits and the planet) and practices moral symmetry to balance the needs of all affected (SanFacon & Spears, 2010). *Servant Leadership* effects are closely linked to employee satisfaction and organizational profits, as various studies have alluded to a direct causal relationship between leadership and customer satisfaction, employee satisfaction and financial performance (Jones, 2012b; Khan, et al., 2012; Obiwuru, 2011).

Irving and Longbotham (2007) found that *Servant Leadership* has also been identified as a significant predictor of team effectiveness as defined by Laub's (1999) *Organizational Leadership Assessment*. This is an important matter in health services, where so much care is delivered through multi-professional teams. Their research utilized a multiple regression model to examine the effectiveness of teams. The essential *Servant Leadership* variables identified were: 1) Providing accountability; 2) Supporting and resourcing; 3) Engaging in honest self-evaluation; 4) Fostering collaboration; 5) Communicating with clarity; 6) Valuing and appreciating (p.110). Organizations who utilize team structures in organizations are advised to gain a better understanding of *Servant Leadership* in general and the six essential *Servant Leadership* themes, if they desire to increase their effectiveness.

PUTTING SERVANT LEADERSHIP IN PRACTICE IN HEALTHCARE

The challenge for healthcare organizations will be implementing this leadership style in practice, even though it appears to be a natural one for healthcare. Scruggs-Garber et al. (2009) consider Greenleaf's *Servant Leadership* to be the most effective leadership model to address the challenges that face the healthcare industry. Healthcare by nature serves and cares for people, and in such a capacity is the ideal platform to adopt and incorporate *Servant Leadership*. The "servant leader" model centers around identifying and addressing the requirements of followers ahead of individual considerations, ultimately leading to the development and growth of the follower as opposed to the needs of the manager or the organization (Jones, 2012a).

Servant leaders should therefore be viewed as trustees of the human capital of an organization. Jones (2012b) investigated the effects of *Servant Leadership* on the leader-follower relationship and the resulting impact on the customer focus within the framework of employee satisfaction, empowerment, organizational culture and performance. The results of his study indicate that employing *Servant Leadership* is conducive to greater organizational productivity and increased fiscal stability. He further concluded that the increased profits occurred as a net effect of *Servant Leadership* as mediated through improved job satisfaction, a reduction in employee turnover and a greater focus on the customer. Mayer et al. (2008) echoed the sentiment that increased employee performance leads to greater customer focus when an employee views their manager as exhibiting *Servant Leadership* skills.

McGee-Cooper et al. (2013) discuss what this means for healthcare managers in normative terms. Servant leaders must listen to their employees without judgment and seek first to understand what they may need and help them accomplish their goals. They must be also be authentic and be willing to admit to their mistakes and be accountable to employees and the organizations. Servant leaders must build community in their workplace by showing appreciation for those they work with and building a culture of trust. They are willing to share power and collaborate with co-workers and those they supervise. Servant leaders must develop people in preparation for openings and promotional opportunities. They also challenge others to be better and hold high expectations for their employees. Servant leaders must co-create with employees a shared vision of where their organization is going.

CONCLUSIONS

Murray (2010) described *Servant Leadership* as meeting the needs of the organization. Servant leaders are typically known to lead by example and display traits of integrity and lead with generosity. *Servant Leadership* is also known as a form of democratic leadership because such leaders favor participatory decision-making. Many believe that servant leaders will often "lead from behind", meaning that they prefer to stay out of the focus and do not accept rewards themselves, but instead let their team accept recognition for success. Many who support *Servant Leadership* suggest that it is a good way to advance in a workplace where values are increasingly important. In this environment, servant leaders can achieve power because of their values, ideals and ethics. *Servant Leadership* can create a positive corporate culture leading to high morale among the organization's members. On the other hand, many believe that in a competitive leadership situation, those who practice *Servant Leadership* will be left behind by leaders using other leadership styles. Murray (2010) found that *Servant Leadership* is known to take time to incorporate, and it may not be a good fit in situations where quick decisions must be made or tight deadlines must be met.

It has been readily observed that *Servant Leadership* is effective in many situations, but it may often be more practical in politics or in organizations and positions where leaders are elected to serve a team, committee, organization or community. *Servant Leadership* is only one style for leading an organization, and it may not for everyone or every organization. However, if *Servant Leadership* is as effective as portrayed in this chapter and the current research, then it should be more prevalent in healthcare organizations.

REFERENCES

Barbuto, J.E. Jr., & Wheeler, D.W. (2006). Scale development and construct clarification of servant leadership. *Group & Organization Management*, **31** (3), 300–326.

Bass, B.M. (1990). *Bass and Stodgill's Handbook of Leadership: Theory, Research, and Managerial Applications* (3rd ed.). New York: Free Press.

Bass, B.M. (1998). *Transformational leadership: Industrial, military, and educational impact*. Mahwah, NJ: Erlbaum.

Bateman, T.S., & Snell, S.A. (2013). *Leading and Collaborating in a Competitive World* (10th ed.). New York: McGraw-Hill/Irwin.

Bennis, W.G., & Nanus, B. (1985). *Leaders: The Strategies for Taking Charge*. New York: Harper and Row.

Berendt, C.J. (2012). Transformational leadership: Lessons in management for today. *International Business Research*, 5 (10), 227–232.

Berwick, D.M., Nolan, T.W., & Whittington, J. (2008). The triple aim: Care, health and cost. *Health Affairs*, 27 (3), 759–769.

Blanchard, K. (1997). Situational leadership. In K. Shelton (Ed.), *A New Paradigm of Leadership: Visions of Excellence for 21st Century Organizations*. Provo, UT: Executive Excellence, pp. 140–153.

Bodur, S. (2002), Job satisfaction of health care staff employed at health centres in Turkey. Occupational Medline, 52 (6), 353–355.

Boone, L.W., & Makhani, S. (2012–2013). Five necessary attitudes of servant leaders. *Review of business*, 33 (1), 83–96. Retrieved from http://www.stjohns.edu/sites/default/files/documents/Tobin/vol33-num1-winter_2012-2013.pdf (accessed 31 May 2015).

Burns, J.M. (1978). *Leadership*. New York: Harper & Row.

Capoccia, V.A., & Abeles, J.C. (2006). A question of leadership: In what ways has the challenge of improving health and health care informed your understanding and practice of leadership? *Leadership in Action*, 26 (1), 12–13.

Conger, J.A., & Kanungo, R.N. (1998). *Charismatic Leadership in Organizations*. Thousand Oaks, CA: Sage.

DePree, M. (2004). *Leadership Is an Art*. New York: Doubleday.

Donghong, D., Lu, H., & Lu, Q. (2012). Relationship of servant leadership and employee loyalty: The mediating role of employee satisfaction. *iBusiness*, 4 (3), 208–215. Retrieved from http://file.scirp.org/Html/23013.html (accessed 31 May 2015).

Drucker, P.F. (2001). *The Essential Drucker: The Best of Sixty Years of Peter Drucker's Essential Writings on Management*. New York: Harper Collins.

Ehrhart, M. (2004). Leadership and procedural justice climate as antecedents of unit-level organizational citizenship behavior. *Personnel Psychology*, 57 (1), 61–94.

Greenleaf, R.K. (1970). *The Servant as Leader*. Indianapolis, IN: Robert K. Greenleaf Center.

Greenleaf, R. K. (1980). "Servant: Retrospect and prospect", in Spears, L.C. (Ed.), *The Power of Servant Leadership*, San Francisco, CA: Berrett-Koehler Publishers, pp 17–60.Greenleaf, R.K. (1991). *The Servant as Leader*. Indianapolis, IN: Greenleaf Center.

Greenleaf, R.K., Frick, D.M., & Spears, L.C. (1996). *On Becoming a Servant Leader*. San Francisco, CA: Jossey-Bass.

House, R.J. (1977). A 1976 theory of charismatic leadership. In J.G. Hunt & L.L. Larson (Eds.), *Leadership: The Cutting Edge*. Carbondale, IL: Southern Illinois University Press, pp. 189–207.

Hoveida, R., Salari, S., & Asemi, A. (2011). A study on the relationship among servant leadership (SL) and the organisational commitment (OC): A case study. *Interdisciplinary Journal of Contemporary Research in Business*, 3 (3), 499–509.

Irving, J.A., & Longbotham, G.J. (2007). How the adoption of team effectiveness and six essential servant leadership themes: A regression model based on items in the Organizational Leadership Assessment. *International Journal of Leadership Studies*, 2 (2), 98–113.

Johns, G. (2006). The essential impact of context on organizational behavior. *Academy of Management Review*, 31 (2), 386–408.

Jones, D. (2011). *The role of servant leadership in establishing a participative business culture focused on profitability, employee satisfaction, and empowerment*. Doctoral dissertation. UMI Dissertation Publishing (UMI 3450515). Retrieved from http://search.proquest.com/docview/864831621 (accessed 31 May 2015).

Jones, D. (2012a). Servant leadership's impact on profit, employee satisfaction and empowerment within the framework for a participative culture in business. *Business Studies Journal*, 4 (1), 35–49.

Jones, D. (2012b). Does servant leadership lead to greater customer focus and employee satisfaction? *Business Studies Journal*, 4 (2), 22–33.

Khan, V.S. (2012). Relationship of leadership styles, employees commitment and organization performance. *European Journal of Economics, Finance and Administration Sciences*, 49 (June) 134–143.

Khan, V., Hafeez M.H., Rizvi, S.M.H., Hasnain, A., & Mariam, A. (2012). Relationship of leadership styles, employees commitment and organization performance. European Journal of Economics, Finance and Administrative Sciences, 49 (June), 133–143.

Kool, M., & Dierendonck, D. (2012). Servant leadership and commitment to change, the mediating role of justice and optimism. *Journal of Organizational Change Management*, 25 (3), 422–433.

Kotter, J.P. (1998). What leaders really do. In J.P. Kotter (Ed.), Harvard Business Review on Leadership. Boston, MA: Harvard Business Review Press, pp. 37–60.

Kouzes, J., & Posner, B. (2002). *The Leadership Challenge* (3rd ed.). San Francisco, CA: Jossey-Bass.

Laub, J. (1999). *Assessing the servant organization: Development of the servant organizational leadership (SOLA) instrument.* Dissertation Abstracts International, 60 02 308 (UMI No. 9921922).

Maslow, A.H. (1954). *Motivation and Personality.* New York: Harper & Row.

Mayer, D.M., Bardes, M., & Piccolo, R.F. (2008). Do servant leaders help satisfy follower needs? An organizational justice perspective. *European Journal of Work and Organizational Psychology*, 17 (2) 180–197.

McCann, J., Graves, D., & Cox, L. (2014). Servant leadership, employee satisfaction, and organizational performance in rural community hospitals. *International Journal of Business and Management*, 9 (10), 28–38.

McGee-Cooper, A., Trammell, D., & Kosec, M. (2013). *The Essentials of Servant Leadership: Principles in Practice.* Dallas, TX: Ann McGee-Cooper. Retrieved from http://amca.com/amca/wp-content/uploads/The-Essentials-of-Servant-Leadership-Final.pdf (accessed 31 May 2015).

Melchar, D.E., & Bosco, S.M. (2010). Achieving high organization performance through servant leadership. *The Journal of Business Inquiry*, 9 (1), 74–88.

Melrose, K. (1995). *Making the Grass Greener on Your Side: A CEO's Journey to Leading by Serving.* San Francisco, CA: Berrett-Koehler.

Mohammad, S., AL-Zeaud, H., & Batayneh, A. (2011). The relationship between transformational leadership and employees' satisfaction at Jordanian private hospitals. *Business & Economic Horizons*, 5 (2), 35–46.

Mueller, C.D. (2011, September–October). Servant leadership: The way forward? *Health Progress*, 21–25. Retrieved from https://www.chausa.org/docs/default-source/health-progress/e1a64799527347b5a002ed1aaff2833a1-pdf.pdf?sfvrsn=4 (accessed 31 May 2015).

Murray, A. (2010). *The Wall Street Journal Essential Guide to Management: Lasting Lessons from the Best Leadership Minds of Our Time.* New York: Harper-Collins.

Negussie, N., & Demissie, A. (2013). Relationship between leadership styles of nurse managers and nurses' job satisfaction in Jimma University specialized hospital. *Ethiopian Journal of Health Sciences*, 23 (1), 49–58.

Netemeyer, R.G., Maxham, J.G., III, & Pullig, C. (2005). Conflicts in the work-family interface: Links to job stress, customer service employee performance, and customer purchase intent. *Journal of Marketing*, 69 (2), 130–143.

Obiwuru, T.C. (2011, October). Effects of leadership style on organizational performance: A survey of selected small scale enterprises in Ikosi-Ketu council development area of Lagos state, Nigeria. *Austrian Journal of Business and Management Research*, 1 (7), 100–111.

Parris, D.L., & Peachey, J. (2013). A systematic literature review of servant leadership theory in organizational contexts. *Journal of Business Ethics*, 113 (3), 377–393.

Patterson, K. (2003). *Servant leadership: A theoretical model.* Dissertation Abstracts International, 64 02 570 (UMI No. 3082719).

Porter, M.E. (2010). What is value in health care? *The New England Journal of Medicine*, 363 (26), 2477–2481. Retrieved from http://www.nejm.org/doi/full/10.1056/NEJMp1011024 (accessed 31 May 2015).

Randolph, D.S. (2005). Predicting the effect of extrinsic and intrinsic job satisfaction factors on the recruitment and retention of rehabilitation professionals. *Journal of Healthcare Management*, 50 (1), 49–60.

Rehman, S.U. (2012, May). Perceived leadership styles and organizational commitment. *Interdisciplinary Journal of Contemporary Research in Business*, 4 (1), 616–622.

Rodriguez, M.A., Ricart, J.E., & Sanchez, P. (2002). Sustainable development and sustainability of competitive advantage: A dynamic and sustainable view of the firm. *Sustainable Development and Competitive Advantage*, **11** (3), 135–146.

Russell, R.F., & Stone, A.G. (2002). A review of servant leadership attributes: Developing a practical model. *Leadership & Organizational Development Journal*, **23** (3), 145–157.

SanFacon, G., & Spears, L.C. (2010). Servant-leaders. *Leadership Excellence*, **27** (2), 17.

Scruggs-Garber, J.M., Madigan, E.A, Click, E.R., & Fitzpatrick, J.J. (2009). Attitudes towards collaboration and servant leadership among nurses, physicians and residents. *Journal of Interprofessional Care*, **23** (4), 331–340.

Smith, B.N., Montagno, R.V., & Kuzmenko, T.N. (2004). Transformational and servant leadership: Content and contextual comparisons. *Journal of Leadership and Organizational Studies*, **10** (4), 80–91.

Spears, L.C. (1995). Servant leadership and the Greenleaf legacy. In L.C. Spears (Ed.), *Reflections on Leadership: How Robert K. Greenleaf's Theory of Servant Leadership Influenced Today's Top Management Thinkers*. New York: John Wiley & Sons, pp. 1–14.

Spears, L.C. (1998). Creating caring leadership for the 21st century. *The Not-For-Profit CEO Monthly Newsletter*, **4** (9), 1–4.

Spears, L.C. (2004). Prescription for organizational health: Servant leadership. *Reflections on Nursing Leadership*, **30** (4), 24–26.

Trastek, V.F., Hamilton, N.W., & Niles, E.E. (2014). Leadership models in healthcare: A case for servant leadership. *Mayo Clinic Proceedings*, **89** (3), 374–381. Retrieved from http://www.mayoclinicproceedings.org/article/S0025–6196(13)00889–6/fulltext (accessed 31 May 2015).

Vanderpyl, T.H. (2012). Servant leadership: A case study of a Canadian health care innovator. *Journal of Healthcare Leadership*, **4**, 9–16. Retrieved from http://www.dovepress.com/servant-leadership-a-case-study-of-a-canadian-health-care-innovator-peer-reviewed-article-JHL (accessed 31 May 2015).

Walumbwa, F.O., Hartnell, C.A, & Oke, A. (2010). Servant leadership, procedural justice climate, service climate, employee attitudes, and organizational citizenship behavior: A cross-level investigation. *Journal of Applied Psychology*, **95** (3), 517–529.

Waterman, H. (2011). Principles of "servant leadership" and how they can enhance practice. *Nursing management*, **17** (9) 24–26.

Zohar, D. (1997). *Rewiring the Corporate Brain: Using the New Science to Rethink How We Structure and Lead Organizations*. San Francisco, CA: Berrett-Koehler.

18 Shared Leadership in Healthcare Organizations

D. David Persaud

INTRODUCTION

Leadership is an influence process whereby an individual engages others to achieve strategic goals aimed at ensuring organizational success (Pearce et al., 2014; Wang et al., 2014). Therefore, effective leadership is critical for enhancing organizational effectiveness and survival (Drescher et al., 2014; Kocolowski, 2010; Liu et al., 2014; Park & Kwon, 2013; Pearce et al., 2013). The aims of this chapter are to develop a framework that describes the concept of *Shared Leadership* and then to demonstrate how it can be successfully adapted to healthcare settings. This will be done by first describing important drivers that have led to the emergence of the concept of *Shared Leadership* in the management literature. This will then be followed by a generic definition of *Shared Leadership* and an examination of its antecedents and outcomes. Next, the importance of teams in healthcare provision will be described and a definition of *Shared Leadership* that is germane to healthcare will be proposed. A model of *Shared Leadership* will then be outlined, and empirical studies will be utilized to outline the barriers and facilitators to successful implementation within healthcare organizations. Finally, a summative description of the factors that must be present for the successful implementation of *Shared Leadership* in healthcare facilities will be presented. Additionally, other types (or concepts) of leadership are considered insofar as they bear upon *Shared Leadership*—e.g., as being elements of *Shared Leadership* or that are consistent with *Shared Leadership*

THE POST-HEROIC LEADERSHIP ERA AND THE EMERGENCE OF SHARED LEADERSHIP

The majority of leadership theories have focused on leadership by an individual and his/her relationships with followers (Crevani et al., 2007; Pearce & Manz, 2005). Furthermore, the relationship between the leader and those being led has generally been perceived through top-down (vertical leadership) influence mechanisms (Pearce & Conger, 2003). However, in the last three decades, alternative models of leadership in which leadership is not limited to the formally appointed leader have garnered increased attention (Hoch et al., 2010; Nicolaides et al., 2014; Wang et al., 2014). This change reflects a shift from individual, heroic models of leadership to a more collaborative or *Shared Leadership* perspective. The reasons for this include factors related to environmental complexity, rapid technological growth, increasing global competition, a rise in consumer expectations, increasingly professional workforces and employee empowerment (Crevani et al., 2007; Pearce & Manz, 2005). All of these factors contribute to rapidly changing environments that are the source of the adaptive challenges faced by organizations. This need to adapt to complex environments has led to concerns of organizational sustainability, which in turn has shifted more accountability and responsibility to teams and increased interdependence among employees while highlighting the necessity for coordination, thereby affecting the division of labor within organizations (Pearce & Manz, 2005; Persaud, 2014).

Therefore, it is impossible for a single person to have all of the necessary information and requisite skills to perform the leadership role alone. This is reinforced by Pearce & Conger (2003, p. 2), who have stated, "[S]enior leaders may not possess sufficient and relevant information to make highly effective decisions in a fast changing and complex world". Because of the totality of these myriad of interacting factors, leadership models that are different from the extant top-down models are better placed to fit these new realities. Such models would avoid the perception of leadership as a formal and hierarchical role bestowed on a single leader, and would instead view leadership as a lateral social and influence process, such as is espoused by *Shared Leadership* (Hoch, 2012; Pearce & Conger, 2003; Scott, 2010; Wang et al., 2014).

The concept of *Shared Leadership* had its beginnings long before scholars began showing more interest in the concept in the 1990s. There were several instances where leadership was spoken of in terms of a plurality (Denis et al., 2012). These include the concept of role differentiation in groups, participative decision-making (Vroom & Yetton, 1973), substitutes for leadership—such as subordinate ability, task type and group cohesion (Kerr & Jermier, 1978), self-managing work teams (Manz & Simms, 1987) and empowerment (Conger & Kanungo, 1988). Also, Gibb (1954) indicated that leadership could be conceived of as a set of functions carried out by a group. Katz and Kahn (1978) felt that when team members voluntarily offered their skills to achieve shared goals and were open to reciprocal influence, this *Shared Leadership* can offer a competitive advantage to organizations through increased commitment.

Nevertheless, in spite of these scholars pointing to the possible utility of *Shared Leadership* in changing environments (Gibb, 1954; Katz & Kahn, 1978), the dominant paradigm of leadership as a situation where a single individual inspires and influences followers to achieve goals has continued to persist unabated (Crevani et al., 2007, 2010; Pearce et al., 2009). Pearce et al. (2009) have said:

> In recent years, however, a few scholars and some practitioners have challenged this conception, arguing that leadership involves roles and activities that can, and should, be shared among members of a team or organization. For example, depending upon the demands of the moment, individuals who are not formally appointed leaders can rise to the occasion to exhibit leadership and then step back when appropriate to allow others to lead. (p. 234)

Therefore, *Shared Leadership* can be thought of as an emergent, shared influence process whereby leadership is laterally distributed among individuals in a way that maximizes both individual and collective efforts aimed at achieving shared organizational goals (Pearce et al., 2009). This means that *Shared Leadership* is demonstrated by the sharing of power and influence among a group of individuals as opposed to the exercise of power being the sole purview of one specific individual. This stands in stark contrast to the general perception of leadership as being a downward influence process on subordinates by a formally elected leader (Pearce et al., 2009). Specifically, the key aspects of *Shared Leadership* pertain to the ideas of emergence, interactive influence processes, lateral influence, upward or downward hierarchical influence, collaborative processes, mutual influence, shared responsibility and goal achievement. Integrating these ideas, a definition of *Shared Leadership* could be expressed as, "a dynamic, emergent interactive influence process among individuals and groups for which the objective is to collaboratively share the responsibility for leading one another in the achievement of agreed upon goals" (Carson et al., 2007; Kocolowski, 2010; Pearce & Conger, 2003; Pearce et al., 2008; Wang et al., 2014).

ANTECEDENTS OF SHARED LEADERSHIP

Several studies have examined the antecedents of *Shared Leadership* (Carson et al., 2007; Houghton et al., 2003). Carson et al. (2007) examined the conditions that lead to the development of *Shared Leadership* and the effect of *Shared Leadership* on team performance. The antecedent domains were comprised of internal team environment factors (shared purpose, social support and voice) and an external environmental factor (coaching provided by an external leader). A regression analysis demonstrated that a team's internal team environment (shared purpose, social support and voice), and coaching by an external leader were important precursors for *Shared Leadership* to emerge. Additionally, *Shared Leadership* was also found to be significantly positively correlated to team performance (Carson et al., 2007).

Self-leadership has been found to be an important enhancer of *Shared Leadership* (Bligh et al., 2006; Houghton et al., 2003; Pearce & Manz, 2005). Similarly, supportive leadership (provides coaching and enhances efficacy beliefs in others about their leadership potential) also helps to enhance *Shared Leadership* by providing the necessary factors that can augment self-leadership (Houghton et al., 2003). Self-leadership has been defined as "a process through which people influence themselves to achieve the self-direction and self-motivation to perform" (Houghton et al., 2003, p. 126). It has been argued that in order to develop the skills of dynamic and reciprocal influence processes that are the hallmarks of *Shared Leadership*, team members must first develop the intermediate behaviors and prerequisites necessary to be a full participant in *Shared Leadership* teams that will result in mutual learning and knowledge creation (Bligh et al., 2006). Bligh et al. (2006) posit that self-leadership leads to these intermediate behaviors at the individual level, which are reflected by individual trust, self-efficacy and individual commitment (Figure 18.1).

OUTCOMES OF SHARED LEADERSHIP

Research has demonstrated that *Shared Leadership* is positively related to improved team attitude outcomes and team performance (Carson et al., 2007; Drescher et al., 2014; Hoch, 2012; Hoch, et al., 2010; Liu et al., 2014; Nicolaides et al., 2014; Park & Kwon, 2013; Pearce & Sims, 2002; Wang et al., 2014). *Shared Leadership* has also been shown to be a better predictor of team effectiveness than vertical (formal, hierarchical) leadership, since it explained more variance than vertical leadership using regression modeling (Pearce & Sims, 2002). Consciously distributing leadership among members of a group (*Shared Leadership*) enhances team effectiveness, thus making *Shared Leadership* a good candidate for incorporation into leadership and teamwork training programs for team members (Pearce & Sims, 2002; Wang et al., 2014).

A strong relationship between *Shared Leadership* and knowledge-based work has been demonstrated (Wang et al., 2014). *Shared Leadership* results in team attitudinal outcomes such as team satisfaction, team cohesion, team trust, team commitment and team coordination. This indicates that by sharing leadership, team members may be more engaged to work toward common goals, thereby enhancing trust, commitment, cooperation and cohesion (Wang et al., 2014). It has also been observed that when task interdependence was high, it produced strong correlations between *Shared Leadership* and performance (Nicolaides et al., 2014; Wang et al., 2014). This demonstrates that when people have to work closely with one another and coordinate and integrate actions, *Shared Leadership* would be well suited to such situations—situations that are ubiquitous in modern healthcare. A positive association between *Shared Leadership* and innovation has also been noted (Hoch, 2012). Since most organizations seek to innovate in order to adapt and survive, the utilization of *Shared Leadership* practices could enhance this imperative (Persaud, 2014). Finally, *Shared Leadership* has been shown to be positively correlated with individual and team learning in teams operating in intense knowledge environments (Liu et al., 2014). Since learning is an important precursor of innovation (Persaud, 2014), these empirical observations further reinforce the utility of *Shared Leadership* in healthcare settings.

THE HEALTHCARE ENVIRONMENT AND THE IMPORTANCE OF TEAMS

Teams are the mainstay of organizational life in healthcare (Fried et al., 2012). The use of teams in healthcare is not optional—it is a necessity (Fried et al., 2012). Clinical and management work requires teams because for all but the simplest treatments, one individual does not have the time, knowledge or skills to do it all. The work performed by healthcare teams is complex, demanding and precise. In addition, there is an expectation of accountability and responsibility in every aspect of the work (Fried et al., 2012). The provision of holistic care to chronic care patients (diabetes, stroke, brain injury) is provided by interdisciplinary teams (Blackmore & Persaud, 2012; Saul et al., 2014; Lingard et al., 2012). The utilization of multiple perspectives in assessing problems and providing innovative solutions depends on the input of different types of professionals who bring their unique training and skills to bear on complex healthcare problems. Quality improvement and performance management practices as well as almost all clinical and managerial innovations are dependent to a large degree on teams and teamwork (Fried et al., 2012; Weiner & Helfrich, 2012). However, in order to benefit from the power of interdisciplinary teams, teams need to work collaboratively in an atmosphere of trust, where team members are empowered and allowed to participate fully in decision-making, are encouraged to develop their self-leadership skills and to voice their opinions and know they are being taken seriously and are held accountable for leading when it is necessary (Fallis & Altimier, 2006; Kunzle et al., 2010; Muethel et al., 2012; Muller-Juge et al., 2014; Rosengren & Bondas, 2010; Rosengren et al., 2010; Spooner et al., 1997; Steinert et al., 2006).

The openness of healthcare organizations to *Shared Leadership* perspectives has also coincided with increased interest in collective leadership, which gained momentum in the 1980s and 1990s (Pearce & Conger, 2003; Porter-O'Grady, 1992; Porter-O'Grady et al., 1997; Scott & Caress, 2005). This reflected a recognition that healthcare is largely provided by well-trained healthcare professionals working in interdisciplinary teams, and healthcare organizations could see the promise of a plural leadership perspective given this reality (Blackmore & Persaud, 2012; Jackson, 2000; Merkens & Spencer, 1998; Miller et al., 2007; Spooner et al., 1997; Steinert et al., 2006). *Shared Leadership* was first practiced within shared governance (partnership, equity, ownership, empowerment and accountability), with the aim of enhancing the provision of effective interdisciplinary care by nurses and other healthcare professionals (Porter-O'Grady, 1992). It has also been promoted as "a nursing management model that supports staff nurses in extending their influence about decisions that affect their practice, work environment, professional development, and self-fulfillment" (Fallis & Altimier, 2006, p. 3).

Empirical studies of the implementation of *Shared Leadership* in different healthcare settings and in different countries indicates that *Shared Leadership* improves team members' ability to speak up when necessary in order to improve patient care and makes them more confident and capable when acting as leaders in their own professional sphere (Jackson, 2000; Miller et al., 2007; Rosengren & Bondas, 2010; Rosengren et al., 2010; Steinert et al., 2006). Miller et al. (2007, p. 36) further observed that "shared leadership interventions have the potential to deliver multi-level benefits to clinical teams, to individuals working within those teams; to service delivery and to patient outcomes". Muethel et al. (2012, p. 526) found that *Shared Leadership* is "particularly effective in task contexts that are intensive, highly interdependent, complex, and dynamic". However, it is very important to bear in mind that *Shared Leadership* does not occur naturally in healthcare organizations (Lingard et al., 2012). This is due to the hierarchical nature of healthcare professions and existing hierarchical governance mechanisms (Lingard et al., 2012; Porter-O'Grady et al., 1997). Nevertheless, this does not mean that *Shared Leadership* should not be implemented in healthcare organizations. This assertion is reinforced by Scott (2010, p. 87), who feels that

> without embracing leadership as a collective action and the redistribution of authority throughout the organization, healthcare delivery will remain burdened by adverse events and randomized care. To address the growing public demand for accountability and improvement, healthcare delivery systems must be founded on complexity science and the principles of shared leadership. (p. 87)

Furthermore, the King's Fund in the UK has urged the National Health Service to adopt the *Shared Leadership* model (Lipley, 2011). Saul et al. (2014) have proposed the adoption of *Shared Leadership* in healthcare in order to advance patient care and reduce errors. Therefore, it is this author's belief that *Shared Leadership* should be adopted by healthcare organizations, but with the caveat that implementers acknowledge the contextual factors (cultural and administrative) inherent in healthcare that must be considered while designing its implementation. Furthermore, there must also be a recognition that there will always be a need for vertical leadership. This would be incongruent with the history, culture and practice of healthcare (Lingard et al., 2012). However, it should be the type of vertical leadership that is supportive (Carson et al., 2007; Houghton et al., 2003; Pearce & Manz, 2005; Wang et al., 2014).

Upon careful assessment of the definition of *Shared Leadership* proposed previously, and the descriptions and empirical assessments of *Shared Leadership* in healthcare, a definition of *Shared Leadership* for healthcare contexts is given as follows: "[A] dynamic interactive influence process among group members who commit to collaborate within an environment that values and reinforces empowerment, accountability, equity, psychological safety, collaboration, and participative decision making while embracing shared responsibility for leading each other toward the achievement of agreed upon goals that ultimately lead to improved patient care". This influence process is based upon horizontal (peer-to-peer) influence that is integrated with vertical (formal, hierarchical) influence.

A MODEL OF SHARED LEADERSHIP RELEVANT TO HEALTHCARE ORGANIZATIONS

Evidence has been presented of the generally positive effect of *Shared Leadership* on the behavioral (individual and team commitment, team satisfaction) and performance (budget performance, mutual learning, knowledge creation and innovation) aspects of team effectiveness (Carson et al., 2007; Drescher et al., 2014; Hoch, 2012; Hoch, et al., 2010; Liu et al., 2014; Muethel et al., 2012; Nicolaides et al., 2014; Park & Kwon, 2013; Pearce & Sims, 2002; Rosengren & Bondas, 2010; Rosengren et al., 2010; Wang et al., 2014). Miller et al. (2007) observed that team members felt that teams should always have a leader. However, team members also indicated that the *Shared Leadership* intervention had enabled each of them "to develop as leaders in their own spheres, had made the team leader more willing to listen to them, and had given them the confidence to put their own ideas forward more" (Miller et al., 2007, p. 34).

Therefore, an important question for healthcare organizations to now consider is: When is leadership most appropriately shared? The extant evidence indicates that *Shared Leadership* may be particularly effective when the following factors exist (Hoch, 2012; Nicolaides et al., 2014; Pearce & Manz, 2005; Pearce et al., 2009; Pintor, 2013; Wang et al., 2014):

1) Complexity—tasks that require knowledge workers, where skills in different areas are needed to ensure goals are achieved, and where the less likely it is that one person can perform them;

2) *Interdependent tasks*—when people have to work closely with each other and coordinate and integrate actions;
3) *Employee commitment is essential*—in situations where the need for team members to go above and beyond the call of duty is an expectation;
4) *Creativity*—when work involves aspects of thinking on one's feet and helping to develop innovative solutions.

These factors are all intrinsic to healthcare and reinforce the utility of *Shared Leadership* in healthcare organizations. Figure 18.1 depicts the *Shared Leadership* framework that emerges from the empirical and theoretical literature of *Shared Leadership* in various organizational settings, including healthcare. There are five elements that must be emphasized at the organizational level (Figure 18.1). These are as follows: The organization's strategic direction makes the implementation and institutionalization of *Shared Leadership* a top priority, with the aim of it becoming an integral aspect of the organization's culture, which is tangibly demonstrated through resource allocation for training in practicing *Shared Leadership*; the implementation of *Shared Leadership* in areas where complex interdependent tasks are utilized to do work; the promotion of teamwork and collaboration throughout the organization; an emphasis on supportive leadership that is integrated with *Shared Leadership* practice; and making a priority the gaining and maintaining of physician commitment to *Shared Leadership* by developing policies that enhance physician involvement in its implementation (Figure 18.1) (Carson et al., 2007; Drescher et al., 2014; Hoch, 2012; Hoch et al., 2010; Liu et al., 2014; Muethel et al., 2012; Nicolaides

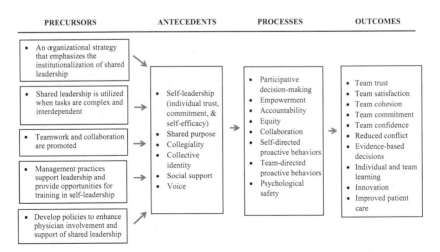

Figure 18.1   Shared Leadership Framework for Healthcare Organizations

et al., 2014; Park & Kwon, 2013; Pearce et al., 2009; Pearce & Manz, 2005; Wang et al., 2014).

The practice of supportive leadership by senior management and the provision of opportunities for training in *Shared Leadership* helps team members to internalize its antecedents such as self-leadership behaviors, which in turn lead to individual trust, commitment and self-efficacy (Figure 18.1) (Bligh et al., 2006; Houghton et al., 2003; Pearce & Manz, 2005). Additionally, the strategic prioritization of *Shared Leadership* by management continuously reinforcing, providing training in and utilizing *Shared Leadership* principles reinforces a shared purpose in teams (Figure 18.1) (Jackson, 2000; Kunzle et al., 2010; Miller et al., 2007). The promotion of teamwork and collaboration and the presence of a shared purpose has been linked to antecedents such as improved collegiality and collective identity, which in turn improves the chances of team members empathizing with each other and recognizing each person's contributions (social support), as well as allowing others to contribute to decisions and airing concerns (voice) (Figure 18.1) (Carson et al., 2007; Hoch, 2012; Jackson, 2000; Miller et al., 2007; Pearce et al., 2014; Spooner et al., 1997).

The processes involved in *Shared Leadership* are seen in Figure 18.1. These include participative (shared) decision-making that is demonstrated by team members being open to other members' perspectives and actively asking for them. Empowerment is exhibited by team members identifying problems and taking the appropriate action, while aspects of accountability include not shifting blame to others and coaching when necessary (Spooner et al., 1997). Self-leadership also contributes to *Shared Leadership* processes such as equity (treating co-workers with respect and fairness as well as recognizing each member's unique contribution) and collaboration (actively soliciting input into decision-making and communicating honestly). Self-directed proactive behaviors by team members are aimed at ensuring that their contribution to the team integrates seamlessly with the work contribution of others. This is done by team members utilizing feedback from other team members to adjust their work process to ensure a fit with the work of others (Muethel et al., 2012). Team-directed proactive behaviors, on the other hand, involve anticipating other members' information needs, assessment of task interdependencies and facilitation of implementation processes (Muethel et al., 2012). Psychological safety (being able to report errors without punishment) is important to the practice of *Shared Leadership* because it encourages the participation of team members who may be reticent to do so.

The last box in Figure 18.1 shows the predicted outcomes of *Shared Leadership*. The observation that *Shared Leadership* leads to these attitudinal outcomes demonstrates that by sharing leadership, team members may be more engaged to work toward common goals, thereby enhancing trust, which leads to team satisfaction, cohesion, commitment, confidence and reduced conflict, and improves the prospect of evidence-based decisions (Drescher et al., 2014; Kunzle et al., 2010; Nicolaides et al., 2014; Wang et al., 2014). Additionally, empirical evidence indicates that individual and team learning as well as innovation are related to collaboration, psychological safety, trust and *Shared Leadership* (Drescher et al., 2014; Hoch, 2012; Liu et al., 2014). This is an important affirmation for the implementation of *Shared Leadership* in healthcare contexts because learning and innovation are key to improved performance and ultimately, improved patient care (Fallis & Altimier, 2006; Kunzle et al., 2010; Liu et al., 2014; Miller et al., 2007; Persaud, 2014). Finally, the observation that there is a stronger relationship between *Shared Leadership* and outcomes when work is knowledge-based, complex and interrelated is further evidence of its utility as a leadership model for healthcare teams (Wang et al., 2014).

IMPLEMENTATION OF SHARED LEADERSHIP BY HEALTHCARE ORGANIZATIONS

The adoption and implementation of *Shared Leadership* by healthcare organizations has to overcome several barriers (Black & Westwood, 2004; Jackson, 2000; Kunzle et al., 2010; Lingard et al., 2012; Miller et al., 2007; Muller-Juge et al., 2014; Rosengren et al., 2010; Scott & Caress, 2005; Steinert et al., 2006; Walker, 2001). These include:

1) Insufficient training to enhance the internalization of *Shared Leadership*;
2) An unwillingness to internalize and therefore utilize the concepts of *Shared Leadership*;
3) The inability of management to provide opportunities for staff to use the concepts of *Shared Leadership* in practical ways;
4) Staff may become discouraged and their involvement may dissipate if senior management does not implement their recommendations;
5) Some staff may not be inclined to participate in *Shared Leadership*;
6) Junior staff may hesitate to engage in *Shared Leadership* because of the perceived risks;
7) The disinclination of some physicians to commit to the model because of a perceived loss of power and concerns about medical liability in teams;
8) The enactment of *Shared Leadership* can be challenging because of the hierarchical nature of healthcare and cause resistance from those who are not inclined to share power;
9) The socialization process of professionals and the medico-legal system can prove insurmountable to the successful implementation of *Shared Leadership*.

On the other hand, facilitators of the implementation and institutionalization of *Shared Leadership* have also been noted (Black & Westwood, 2004; Jackson, 2000; Kunzle et al., 2010; Scott & Caress, 2005; Steinert et al., 2006; Walker, 2001) These include:

1) Internalization of the concepts of *Shared Leadership*;
2) A commitment to the *Shared Leadership* model by senior management modeling it and investing financial and educational resources toward its implementation in clinical and non-clinical areas;
3) The provision of trained facilitators to work with management and teams;
4) Continuous education about *Shared Leadership* concepts;
5) The clear communication of tangible outcomes attributable to *Shared Leadership*;
6) The utilization of processes that make staff feel valued when implementing the model;
7) Physician support and involvement in promoting the model;
8) A cultural assessment to determine congruence with *Shared Leadership* principles and the work needed to improve its acceptance.

The barriers and facilitators associated with the implementation of *Shared Leadership* have emerged from an analysis of the implementation of *Shared Leadership* in a variety of healthcare settings (acute care, mental health, primary care) and in several jurisdictions around the world (Black & Westwood, 2004; Hawken et al., 2012; Jackson, 2000; Miller et al., 2007; Muller-Juge et al., 2014; Rosengren & Bondas, 2010; Scott & Caress, 2005; Steinert et al., 2006; Walker, 2001). Although there were no cases where *Shared Leadership* was completely implemented successfully, the lessons learned from these implementations (as outlined in the barriers and facilitators) can be utilized to describe the vital factors necessary for improving the chances of successful implementation (Miller et al., 2007; Rosengren & Bondas, 2010). However, several caveats must be emphasized before contemplating the implementation of *Shared Leadership* in healthcare facilities.

First, *Shared Leadership* is not a leadership panacea for all areas within healthcare organizations, and there are barriers to successful implementation. Second, there are specific circumstances where this type of leadership is best exercised. These include situations where work is accomplished through the utilization of complex and interdependent tasks that are performed by different types of healthcare professionals working collaboratively in teams (Kunzle et al., 2010; Miller et al., 2007; Nicolaides et al., 2014; Rogers, 2014; Rosengren & Bondas, 2010; Saul et al., 2014; Wang et al., 2014). Third, like all frameworks, *Shared Leadership* cannot be simply adopted or copied verbatim from implementations elsewhere, but must be adapted and modified so as to be congruent with the specific context where implementation is proposed. Centuries of socialization in medical practice will pose serious impediments to the implementation of *Shared Leadership* (Lingard et al., 2012). Therefore, successful implementation is predicated on the healthcare organization's culture eventually being aligned with the tenets of *Shared Leadership* that are developed specifically for the organization (Drescher et al., 2014; Hepp et al., 2014; Jackson, 2000; Kocolowski, 2010; Lipley, 2011; Scott & Caress, 2005).

This section will utilize the barriers and facilitators that have been outlined as well as lessons learned from previous implementations of *Shared Leadership* in healthcare settings to describe processes that can be utilized to improve the chances of the successful implementation of *Shared Leadership* (Jackson, 2000; Kunzle et al., 2010; Miller et al., 2007; Rosengren et al., 2010; Steinert et al., 2006; Walker, 2001). Implementation must begin with consultation and discussions between all levels of management and staff that will be affected by the implementation of *Shared Leadership*. Discussions should center on developing and agreeing upon a definition of *Shared Leadership* that is applicable to that particular organization and how it will be practiced to achieve the outcomes that are anticipated (Figure 18.1). Consultants must work with affected members from all levels and professions within the organization to develop an implementable definition of *Shared Leadership* specific to its context. A definition of *Shared Leadership* for healthcare organizations as outlined in this chapter can be a starting point. Management must also agree to make *Shared Leadership* a strategic imperative of the healthcare organization (Jackson, 2000; Kunzle et al., 2010; Miller et al., 2007). This is further legitimized by senior management modeling the behaviors of *Shared Leadership* and committing the resources necessary for successful implementation. This includes the utilization of experts in *Shared Leadership* to provide ongoing education and guidance to staff involved in practicing *Shared Leadership* (Black & Westwood, 2004). Similar education must also be provided to senior management. These factors and the presence of the other precursors outlined in Figure 18.1 will enhance the successful implementation of *Shared Leadership* (Jackson, 2000; Kunzle et al., 2010; Miller et al., 2007). A cultural assessment must also be performed to determine the level of knowledge and internalization of *Shared Leadership* principles as well as perceptions of efficacy regarding the willingness to practice *Shared Leadership*. This assessment can also be used at various times during implementation to determine the internalization and institutionalization of *Shared Leadership* principles (Black & Westwood, 2004; Hepp et al., 2014).

The institutionalization of *Shared Leadership* is the ultimate aim of its implementation. This eventuality occurs when organization members believe that *Shared Leadership* will fulfill aspects of organizational life that are important to them, such as aspects of job satisfaction and improved patient care (Figure 18.1). To this end, senior management must not only gain the commitment of organization members for practicing *Shared Leadership*, they must maintain commitment so that *Shared Leadership* is institutionalized and becomes an integral part of the fabric of the organization's culture (Narine & Persaud, 2003). This can be enhanced by providing continuous training in shared and self-leadership. The framework displayed in Figure 18.1 will allow implementers to see how their actions can influence the outcomes they expect during the implementation of *Shared Leadership*. The five precursors are foundations of implementation, and without them, it will be difficult to achieve the proximal (processes) and distal outcomes. The promotion of teamwork and collaboration is essential, and all teams must receive training in teamwork as well as in *Shared Leadership* development (Black & Westwood, 2004; Hepp et al., 2014; Hoch, 2012; Jackson, 2000; Miller et al., 2007; Muller-Juge et al., 2014; Scott & Caress, 2005).

Black and Westwood (2004) have described a group-based team leadership development workshop aimed at helping team members to learn and relate interpersonally, to enhance trust and solidarity among group members and to develop skills that prevent misunderstanding and conflict among group members. The authors indicated that all of the objectives of the intervention were achieved and a similar intervention would be useful in preparing staff for the implementation of *Shared Leadership* (Black & Westwood, 2004). Further to this, Jackson (2000) observed that employee internalization of the processes described in Figure 18.1 was important to successful *Shared Leadership* implementation. Therefore, senior management must also endeavor to foster a collaborative, psychologically safe environment, which is believed to enhance the development of the antecedent conditions of shared vision and purpose, social support, voice, collegiality and collective identity (Carson et al., 2007; Jackson, 2000; Miller et al., 2007; Spooner et al., 1997). Additionally, gaining physician support is critical to any innovation that directly affects patient care (Hawken et al., 2012; Hepp et al., 2014; Jackson, 2000; Lingard et al., 2012; Miller et al., 2007; Muller-Juge et al., 2014; Steinert et al., 2006). Physicians must be shown how *Shared Leadership* can benefit them. They must receive leadership training as outlined by Black and Westwood (2004) that is tailored to helping them to understand their roles within a *Shared Leadership* framework. Physicians must also be remunerated for attendance at training and meetings on *Shared Leadership* that cut into their time for practicing medicine (Hepp et al., 2014). Medico-legal barriers such as individual or team responsibility related to liability are a concern and are being addressed in various jurisdictions and should help to improve physician acceptance of *Shared Leadership* (Lingard, et al., 2012).

The importance of supportive leadership cannot be overemphasized (Bligh et al., 2006; Hoch, 2012; Houghton et al., 2003; Pearce & Manz, 2005). As Pearce and Manz (2005) state:

[E]ven in empowered organizations that perform knowledge work (often in teams) there are typically formally designated leadership roles that are recognized as part of the organization structure. Sometimes the individuals in these roles are referred to with titles such as 'team leader', 'coordinator', 'facilitator', or 'coach'. Regardless of the title used, the special challenge for these designated leaders is to foster the self-leadership of individual members as well as the sharing of leadership influence throughout the system. (p. 137)

Therefore, to enhance the adoption of *Shared Leadership*, these leaders should practice supportive leadership by modeling and actively encouraging the practice of self-leadership behaviors (Figure 18.1) that lead to individual trust, individual commitment and self-efficacy (Bligh et al., 2006; Pearce & Manz, 2005). These behaviors are reflected in three self-leadership strategies: Behavior-focused strategies, natural reward strategies and constructive thought pattern strategies (Bligh et al., 2006). Behavior-focused strategies include self-awareness and self-regulation, goal setting and self-correcting feedback; natural reward strategies are related to the intrinsic motivation inherent in performing tasks, and constructive thought patterns reflect the utilization of positive self-talk and mental imagery to enhance performance (Bligh et al., 2006; Houghton et al., 2003). Finally, senior management must also promote and develop a culture of learning from mistakes without punishment (psychological safety). Leaders can be given training and coaching in practicing these skills. The ultimate goal is to eventually create a culture where *Shared Leadership* is the accepted leadership style in healthcare teams. It will take much effort.

REFERENCES

Black, T.G., & Westwood, M.J. (2004). Evaluating the development of a multidisciplinary leadership team in a cancer-center. *Leadership and Organization Development Journal*, 25 (7), 577–591.

Blackmore, G., & Persaud, D. (2012). Diagnosing and improving functioning in interdisciplinary health care teams. *The Health Care Manager*, 31 (3), 195–207.

Bligh, M., Pearce, C., & Kohles, J. (2006). The importance of self- and shared leadership in team based knowledge work: A meso-level model of leadership dynamics. *Journal of Management Psychology*, 21 (4), 296–318.

Carson, J.B., Tesluk, P.E., & Marrone, J.A. (2007). Shared leadership in team: An investigation of antecedent conditions and performance. *Academy of Management Journal*, 50 (5), 1217–1234.

Conger, J.A., & Kanungo, R.K. (1988). The empowerment process: Integrating theory and practice. *The Academy of Management Review*, 13 (3), 471–482.

Crevani, L., Lindgren, M., & Packendorff, J. (2007). Shared leadership: A post-heroic perspective on leadership as a collective construction. *International Journal of Leadership Studies*, 3 (1), 40–67.

Crevani, L., Lindgren, M., & Packendorff, J. (2010). Leadership, not leaders: On the study of leadership as practices and interactions. *Scandinavian Journal of Management*, 26 (1), 77–86.

Denis, J., Langley, A., & Sergi, V. (2012). Leadership in the plural. *The Academy of Management Annals*, 6 (1), 211–283.

Drescher, M.A., Korsgaard, M.A., Welpe, I.M., Picot, A., & Wigand, R.T. (2014). The dynamics of shared leadership: Building trust and enhancing performance. *Applied Psychology*, **99** (5), 771–783.

Fallis, K., & Altimier, L. (2006). Shared leadership: Leading from the bottom up. *Newborn and Infant Nursing Reviews*, **6** (1), 3–6.

Fried, B., Topping, S., & Edmondson, A.C. (2012). Teams and team effectiveness in health services organizations. In L.R. Burns, E.H. Bradley, & B.J. Weiner (Eds.), *Shortell and Kaluzny's Health Care Management: Organization Design and Behavior* (6th ed.), Clifton Park, NY: Delmar, pp. 221–248.

Gibb, C.A. (1954). Leadership. In G. Lindzay (Ed.), *Handbook of Social Psychology*, Reading, MA: Addison-Wesley, pp. 877–917.

Hawken, J., Wright, R., & Walsh, S. (2012). Creating an environment of shared leadership. *British Journal of Healthcare Management*, **18** (8), 426–428.

Hepp, S., Misfeldt, R., Lait, J., Armitage, G.D., & Suter, E. (2014). Organizational factors influencing inter-professional team functioning in primary care networks. *Healthcare Quarterly*, **17** (2), 57–61.

Hoch, J.E. (2012). Shared leadership and innovation: The role of vertical leadership and employee integrity. *Journal of Business Psychology*, **28** (2), 159–174.

Hoch, J.E., Pearce, C.L., & Welzel, L. (2010). Is the most effective team leadership shared? The impact of shared leadership, age diversity, and coordination on team performance. *Journal of Personnel Psychology*, **9** (3), 105–116.

Houghton, T.D., Neck, C.P., & Manz, C.L. (2003). Self-leadership and super leadership. In C.L. Pearce & J.A. Conger (Eds.), *Shared Leadership: Reframing the Hows and Whys of Leadership*, Thousand Oaks, CA: Sage, pp. 123–137.

Jackson, S. (2000). A qualitative evaluation of shared leadership barriers, drivers and recommendations. *Journal of Management in Medicine*, **14** (3–4), 166–178.

Katz, D., & Kahn, R.L. (1978). *The Social Psychology of Organizations* (2nd ed.). New York: Wiley.

Kerr, S., & Jermier, J.M. (1978). Substitutes for leadership: Their meaning and measurement. *Organizational Behavior and Human Performance*, **22** (3), 375–403.

Kocolowski, M.D. (2010). Shared leadership: Is it time for a change? *Emerging Leadership Journeys*, **3** (1), 22–32.

Künzle, B., Zala-Mezö, E., Wacker, J., Kolbe, M., Spahn, R., & Grote, G. (2010). Leadership in anesthesia teams: The most effective leadership is shared. *Quality and Safety in Health Care*, **19** (6), e46. Retrieved from http://qualitysafety.bmj.com/content/19/6/e46.full.pdf+html (accessed 31 May 2015).

Lingard, L., Vanstone, M., Durrant, M., Fleming-Carroll, B., Paeds, N.P., Lowe, M., Rashotte, J., Sinclair, L., & Tallett, S. (2012). Conflicting messages: Examining the dynamics of leadership on interprofessional teams. *Academic Medicine*, **87** (12), 1762–1767.

Lipley, N. (2011). King's fund urges NHS to adopt shared leadership style that involves care staff. *Nursing Management*, **18** (4), 4.

Liu, S., Hu, J., Li, Y., Wanga, Z., & Lin, X. (2014). Examining the cross-level relationship between shared leadership and learning in teams: Evidence from China. *The Leadership Quarterly*, **25** (2), 282–295.

Manz, C.C., & Simms, H.P. (1987). Leading workers to lead themselves: The external leadership of self-managing work teams. *Administrative Science Quarterly*, **32** (1), 106–129.

Merkens, B.J., & Spencer, J.S. (1998). A successful and necessary evolution to shared leadership: A hospital's story. *Leadership in Health Services*, **11** (1), 1–4.

Miller, K., Walmsley, J., & Williams, S. (2007). Shared leadership: An idea whose time has come in healthcare? *International Journal of Leadership in Public Services*, **3** (4), 24–37.

Muethel, M., Gehrlein, S., & Hoegl, M. (2012). Socio-demographic factors and shared leadership behaviors in dispersed teams: Implications for human resource management. *Human Resources Management*, **51** (4), 525–548.

Muller-Juge, V., Cullati, S., Blandon, K.S., Hudelson, P., Maitre, F., Vu, N.V., Savoldelli, G.L., & Nendaz, M.R. (2014). Inter-professional collaboration between residents and nurses in general internal medicine: A qualitative study on behaviors enhancing teamwork quality. *PLoS One*, **9** (4), 1–8.

Narine, L., & Persaud, D. (2003). Gaining and maintaining commitment to large scale change in health care organizations. *Health Services Management Research*, **16** (3), 179–187.

Nicolaides, V., LaPort, K., Chen, T., Tomassetti, A., Weis, E., Zaccaro, S., & Cortina, J. (2014). The shared leadership of teams: A meta-analysis of proximal distal, and moderating relationships. *The Leadership Quarterly*, **25** (5), 923–942.

Park, J.G., & Kwon, B. (2013). Literature review on shared leadership in teams. *Journal of Leadership, Accountability and Ethics*, **10** (3), 28–56.

Pearce, C.L., & Conger, J.A. (2003). All those years ago: The historical underpinnings of shared leadership. In C.L. Pearce & J.A. Conger (Eds.), *Shared Leadership: Reframing the Hows and Whys of Leadership*, Thousand Oaks, CA: Sage, pp. 1–18.

Pearce, C.L., Conger J.A., & Locke E.A. (2008). Shared leadership theory. *The Leadership Quarterly*, **19** (5), 622–628.

Pearce, C.L., & Manz, C.C. (2005). The new silver bullets of leadership: The importance of self- and shared leadership in knowledge work. *Organizational Dynamics*, **34** (2), 130–140.

Pearce, C.L., Manz, C.C., & Akanno, S. (2013). Searching for the holy grail of management development and sustainability: Is shared leadership development the answer? *Journal of Management Development*, **32** (3), 247–257.

Pearce, C.L., Manz, C.C., & Sims, H.R., Jr. (2009). Where do we go from here? Is shared leadership the key to team success? *Organizational Dynamics*, **38** (3), 234–238.

Pearce, C.L., & Sims, H.P. (2002). Vertical versus shared leadership as predictors of the effectiveness of change management teams: An examination of aversive, directive, transactional, transformational, and empowering leader behaviors. *Group Dynamics: Theory, Research, and Practice*, **6** (2), 172–197.

Pearce, C.L., Wassenaar, C.C., & Manz, C.C. (2014). Is shared leadership the key to responsible leadership? *The Academy of Management Perspectives*, **28** (3), 275–288.

Persaud, D. (2014). Enhancing learning, innovation, adaptation, and sustainability in health care organizations: The ELIAS performance management framework. *The Health Care Manager*, **33** (3), 183–204.

Pintor, S. (2013). *When Is Sharing Leadership in Teams Effective? Research Translations*. Irvine, CA: The Paul Merage School of Leadership. Center for Global Leadership, UC Irvine. Retrieved from http://merage.uci.edu/ResearchAndCenters/CLTD/Resources/Documents/[612]Pintor_Sandra__When%20is%20Sharing%20Leadership%20in%20Teams%20Effective_2013.pdf (accessed 31 May 2015).

Porter-O'Grady, T. (1992). *Shared Governance Implementation Manual*. Maryland Heights, MO: Mosby.

Porter-O'Grady, T., Hawkins, M., & Parker, M. (1997). *Whole Systems Shared Governance*. Gaithersburg, MD: Aspen Publications.

Rogers, J.K. (2014). Reinventing shared leadership to support nursing's evolving role in healthcare. *Nurse Leader*, **12** (2), 29–33.

Rosengren, K., & Bondas, T. (2010). Supporting "two-getherness": Assumption for nurse managers working in a shared leadership model. *Intensive and Critical Care Nursing*, **26** (5), 288–295.

Rosengren, K., Bondas, T., Nordholm, L., & Nordstrom, G. (2010). Nurses' views of shared leadership in ICU: A case study. *Intensive and Critical Care Nursing*, **26** (4), 226–223.

Saul, J., Noel, K., & Best, A. (2014). *Advancing the art of healthcare through shared leadership and cultural transformation*. Ghostbusting Series 2 —Synthesis II. Retrieved from www.longwoods.com/content/23770 (accessed 31 May 2015).

Scott, E.S. (2010). Perspectives on healthcare leader and leadership development. *Journal of Healthcare Leadership*, **2**, 83–90.

Scott, L., & Caress, A. (2005). Shared governance and shared leadership: Meeting the challenges of implementation. *Journal of Nursing Management*, **13** (1), 4–12.

Spooner, S.H., Keenan, R., & Card, M. (1997). Determining if shared leadership is being practiced: Evaluation methodology. *Nursing Administration Quarterly*, **22** (1), 47–57.

Steinert, T., Goebel, R., & Rieger, W. (2006). A nurse-physician co-leadership model on psychiatric hospitals: Results of a survey among leading staff members in three sites. *International Journal of Mental Health Nursing*, **15** (4), 251–257.

Vroom, V.H., & Yetton, P.W. (1973). *Leadership and Decision Making*. New York, NY: Wiley.

Walker, J. (2001). Developing a shared leadership model at the unit level. *Journal of Perinatal and Neonatal Nursing*, **15** (1), 26–39.

Wang, D., Waldman, D.A., & Zhang, Z. (2014). A meta-analysis of shared leadership and team effectiveness. *Journal of Applied Psychology*, **99** (2), 181–198.

Weiner, B.J., & Helfrich, C.D. (2012). Complexity, learning, and innovation. In L.R. Burns, E.H. Bradley, & B.J. Weiner (Eds.), *Shortell and Kaluzny's Health Care Management: Organization Design and Behavior* (6th ed.). Clifton Park, NY: Delmar, pp. 221–248.

19 Six Sigma Applicability and Implementation in Healthcare

Jacob Krive

SIX SIGMA: BACKGROUND AND DEFINITION

Six Sigma is a quality improvement and maintenance management concept specifically focused on defect rate reduction through quantitative process analysis, reduction of waste and the iterative development of techniques aimed at producing the highest output at the lowest cost with the lowest number of defects. Originally formulated by Motorola in 1986 (Tennant, 2001), the method incorporates many of the discoveries made by process researchers such Walter Shewhart (statistical methods, including control chart), W. Edwards Deming (the *Total Quality Management* system that was adopted by Toyota for its own process improvement version, called the *Toyota Production System*), Joseph Juran (quality management process focused on the end product), Taiichi Ohno (*Just in Time* system that reduces inventory and waste under a combined *Lean/Six Sigma* concept) and other management concepts. Jack Welch made this method central to the business strategy of General Electric, which was focused on high innovation and low cost. It was subsequently adopted by such technology giants as IBM and Verizon, with the added target of growth in addition to quality management. *Six Sigma* is most closely associated with manufacturing, targeting 99.99966% of all production opportunities to be free of defects when turned into a final product. This translates into 3.4 defects per million opportunities (DPMO). The International Organization for Standardization published its first 13053:2011 *Six Sigma* standard based on the define, measure, analyze, improve, control (*DMAIC*) process in 2011 (ISO, 2011), and a number of other industry and academic variations are in existence.

Mathematically speaking, *Six Sigma* means targeting six standard deviations between the mean and the nearest specification limit in any process regardless of the industry and organizational settings the concept is applied in. In other words, it is statistical distance, or deviation, between the actual performance of the process and its quality target. Experience shows that processes usually do not perform as well over the long term as they do over

Table 19.1   Short- and Long-Term *Six Sigma* Output Specifications

Sigma Level	Sigma (with 1.5σ shift)	DPMO	Percent Defective	Percentage Yield
1	-0.5	691,462	69%	31%
2	0.5	308,538	31%	69%
3	1.5	66,807	6.7%	93.3%
4	2.5	6,210	0.62%	99.38%
5	3.5	233	0.023%	99.977%
6	4.5	3.4	0.00034%	**99.99966%**
7	5.5	0.019	0.0000019%	99.9999981%

the short term (Tennant, 2001). Therefore, the number of sigmas that will fit between the process mean and the nearest output specification limit may drop over time, compared to short-term quality measurement output. To account for this real-life increase in process variation, an empirically based 1.5 sigma shift is introduced into the calculation, so the 3.4 defects figure actually corresponds to a 4.5 sigma once a long-term correction is made to the specification (Harry, 1988). Table 19.1 shows long-term and short-term sigma specifications, and the resulting defective output percentage with actual yields.

One may ask why *Six Sigma* is selected as an ideal target, and not any of the other values in Table 19.1. The actual quantitative target calculation, as well as the measurement instruments to maintain operations in accordance with this target, is an academic exercise showing the impact of defect rates on the quality of the output. Companies will choose their desired and realistic targets based on the real application of the defect measures in their business environments—based on their analysis of the customer base, customer preferences, the industry they operate in and core manufacturing capabilities. Some organizations may consider the target unachievable, while others may consider it unacceptably low. What matters are the methodologies, processes and necessary organizational structures behind *Six Sigma* that drive business transformation to support quality and cost management.

There are two core project management methods behind *Six Sigma*: Recognize, define, measure, analyze, improve, control (*DMAIC* is the standard acronym and will therefore be used in this chapter, although "*RDMAIC*" to include the "recognize" step might be preferable) and define, measure, analyze, design, verify (*DMADV*). *DMAIC* is utilized for projects aimed at improving existing processes, while *DMADV*, also known as *DFSS* (design for *Six Sigma*), is applied to new process designs without the need for business process reengineering (De Feo & Barnard, 2005). Adding an initial row for "recognize", Table 19.2 shows basic *DMAIC* concepts and explains the acronym.

Table 19.3 explains the *DMADV* acronym and its core steps.

Table 19.2 Basic *DMAIC* Concepts

Acronym Letter	Concept	Explanation
R	Recognize	Recognizing that a problem exists is regarded as a core step in the *Six Sigma* journey, and is appended at the beginning of the original *DMAIC* acronym, resulting in *RDMAIC*.
D	Define	Define system, customer requirements and project goals.
M	Measure	Measure key aspects of the current process and collect relevant data to establish a measurement baseline.
A	Analyze	Analyze data to investigate problem cause and effect relationships. Seek root cause after determining what causes current problems. Provide quantitative support to justify proposed corrective actions.
I	Improve	Improve the process based on analysis using various techniques such as design of experiments, behavior shaping, mistake proofing (a.k.a. poka yoke—a testing process that assumes immediate feedback to operator based on alert, shape, color, size, etc.) and introduction of new standard routines.
C	Control	Control the future process to ensure its permanence within the organizational culture and its adaptability to future organizational and process changes.

Table 19.3 Basic *DMADV* Concepts

Acronym Letter	Concept	Explanation
D	Define	Define design goals that are consistent with customer demands.
M	Measure	Measure critical to quality characteristics, product capabilities, production process capability and tasks.
A	Analyze	Analyze potential new processes and product designs to meet specifications.
D	Design	Design new processes and products.
V	Verify	Verify the design, set up pilots, implement permanent process and perform handover to permanent process owner.

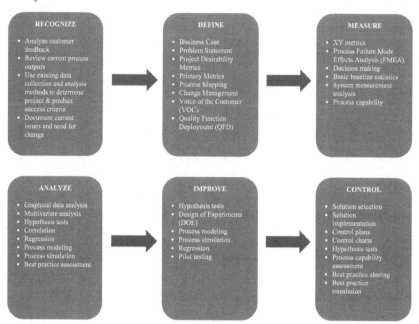

Figure 19.1   Core *DMAIC* Measurement and Implementation Processes

Most healthcare organizations are currently concerned with *RDMAIC* processes aimed at correcting processes within established organizational structures and cultures, although some of the more *Six Sigma*-invested organizations utilize *DMADV* to establish greenfield operations for new facilities and/or clinical teams. Figure 19.1 shows a few more details about core processes commanding each *DMAIC* phase.

SIX SIGMA VERSUS OTHER MANAGEMENT CONCEPTS

While *Six Sigma* was initially created as a single concept aimed at the reduction of defects to improve the core manufacturing capabilities of companies such as Motorola and General Electric, further development and evolution of process modeling created other management ideas that are utilized in conjunction to or in combination with *Six Sigma*. For most non-manufacturing organizations, pure defect reduction focus will not produce a full array of desired outcomes. In the case of healthcare organizations, the reduction of defects would equate to reduction or elimination of medical errors, adverse drug effects, misplaced and/or undelivered equipment and mislabeled lab specimens. This would ultimately lead to a combination of various management concepts for consideration as parts of far-reaching initiatives to reengineer the production of service delivery, processes, operations, workflows, customer service and supply chain management.

Six Sigma would rarely be considered in isolation by healthcare organizations. Instead, it would become one of the core parts of the business and clinical transformation strategies. Although it might be best to adopt a holistic approach to selecting and employing process management methods, the following method selection flowchart could be helpful for organizations considering selective adoption, perhaps to pilot processes and determine effects on operations. Figure 19.2 outlines the basic logic of method selection. *Six Sigma* is perceived as a quantitative concept aimed at a reduction in cycle time and/or the number of defects. While *Lean* could also lead to defect reduction indirectly through process improvement, it is considered to be a process-oriented concept aimed at improving a system's effectiveness and efficiency. The best outcomes would be achieved from combining the strengths of both *Lean* and *Six Sigma*, and without specifically focusing on one of the two management concepts.

An alternative way for determining organizational readiness to undertake serious *Business Process Reengineering* initiatives is by considering a linear introduction of processes upon the completion of each transformation stage (for more information about *Business Process Reengineering* and its relevance to healthcare organizations, see Patwardhan et al., Chapter 6 in this volume). Figure 19.2 shows logical choices among the available methods for a piecemeal solution focused on resolving a specific problem

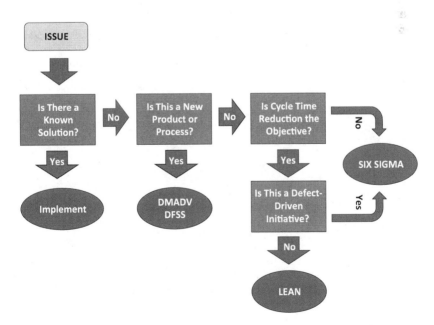

Figure 19.2 Process Improvement Management Concepts Selection Framework

or a set of problems. An organization considering a holistic journey into the overall transformation of its work processes could employ a method of gradual introduction of processes and concepts to its process management structure, from simple changes to quantitatively driven major restructuring. For example, the process could start with a thorough review of the current supplies management practices—a frequent contributor to cost escalation and associated dissatisfaction—using the 5S process management concept. Under this concept, the organization would Sort existing processes and materials, Store by critically reformulating its supply storage and delivery procedures, Shine to delegate some basic organization and cleaning tasks to people who use supplies, Standardize to ensure the uniformity of the new process and Sustain to design and implement a permanent process that is embedded into the operational workflow (Graban, 2012). This process may seem counterproductive to healthcare managers who would question the use of highly compensated human resources on localized materials management tasks, but the process could be viewed through the prism of efficiency: Workers spend less time maintaining well-organized and properly stocked materials management areas, which is when taking charge locally may start making sense.

After 5S and materials management initiatives, organizations could consider adopting the *Kaizen* approach of continuous improvement based on Deming's *Plan-Do-Study-Act* (*PDSA*) iterative cycle of redesigning processes until the desired improvement level is reached (for more information about *Kaizen* and its relevance to healthcare organizations, see Graban, Chapter 11 in this volume). *Kaizen* includes such stages as define, achieve, maintain and improve. The next stage could potentially be a *Lean Management* concept (for more information about *Lean* and its relevance to healthcare organizations, see Poksinska, Chapter 13 in this volume), which assumes comprehensive *Business Process Reengineering* through a thorough review of the existing practices (value stream mapping), waste elimination and new process stabilization. *DMAIC* under the *Six Sigma* management concept for redesigning existing processes could become the next phase to quantitatively review each process for defects, following value stream mapping by the detailed proactive risk review process called *Suppliers-Inputs-Process-Outputs-Customers* and reducing waste. Finally, the next phase after the reorganization of all existing processes under the *Six Sigma DMAIC* method could be testing the sustainability of the new processes by applying the method to greenfield investments and starting new initiatives with *DMADV* from the outset. The latter two processes could also be reversed to first fully implement greenfield investment utilizing *DMADV* and then apply the lessons learned to redesign existing processes using the *DMAIC* approach. Gradual investment in the transformation of work processes is shown in Figure 19.3. The sequence is broken down into manageable steps to invest organizational resources into *Lean* methods, enabling organizations to test their desire to continue, investigate cultural tolerance to new

Six Sigma Methodology Investment Plan

Six Sigma–DMADV
5 – Robustness
- Design for Six Sigma
- Organizational Six Sigma design
- QFD

Six Sigma–RDMAIC
4 – Business Transformation
- SIPOC
- Reduction of variation
- In process control
- Quantitative approaches

Lean
3 – Process Efficiency & Stability
- Process mapping
- Waste elimination
- Process stability

Kaizen
2 – Insight and Continuity
- Continuous improvement culture
- Visual management

5S
1 – Structure
- Work environment
- Processes, procedures, instructions
- Visible process abnormalities

Figure 19.3 Gradual *Six Sigma* Investment and Implementation Plan

processes implementation, hire appropriate subject matter experts and reorganize to adopt new process management philosophies.

Although studies performed in manufacturing settings claim positive effects on performance from the implementation of both *Lean Management* and *Six Sigma* (Bisgaard, 2009; De Menezes et al., 2010; Habidin et al., 2012; Kwak & Anbari, 2004), it is difficult to establish concrete, traceable links between single or multiple/combined performance outcomes and indicators (Harris et al., 2007). In a more complex and fragmented healthcare environment already known for an abundance of processes and procedures, as well as numerous ongoing process-related projects, it would be even more difficult to track the performance of a single method. Some of the studies, such as the one performed by Gowen et al. (2012), found that process-oriented methods have a greater effect on outcomes in healthcare settings than do more quantitative defect reduction measures like *Six Sigma*. In particular, the researchers empirically measured error rate improvements in a comparison of the *Continuous Quality Improvement* (*CQI*), *Lean Management* and *Six Sigma* management concepts. They found that the *CQI* and *Lean Management* outcomes to have a far greater impact on reducing errors, compared to *Six Sigma*.

In reality, the majority of organizations will use a combination of multiple methods, selecting specific process improvement measures that work in their cultures and environments. It is rare to learn of a healthcare organization that commits to a "pure" *Six Sigma* process and culture, or only *Lean Management* or *Kaizen*, etc. There is not a prescriptive formula that works for any type of healthcare environment, and thus one may observe a large variety of methods and combinations applied. Some leaders may have a tendency to select methods that are aimed at the reduction of error rates, such as misrouted radiology reports or mislabeled lab specimens; others may focus on efficiency and cost management, such as the centralization of supply chain operations. Yet others may see their goal in clinician and patient satisfaction, such as a reduction in emergency department or out-patient medical office wait times. As the purposes, expectations and outcome measures of quality improvement initiatives vary, so do the quality management concepts applied to achieve the desired results.

SIX SIGMA APPROACHES TO HEALTHCARE TRANSFORMATION

Organizational Commitment

The most common cause for resistance to *Six Sigma* implementation in healthcare settings is recognition of the fact that the medical decision-making process is largely varied, situational and unpredictable, and can lead to many unforeseen delays and complications. All of the above are true: Embedding prescriptive management processes into the clinical thought process is both a challenging and a dangerous task. The physician-to-patient relationship needs to remain personal and situational. However, what *Six Sigma*, along with other quality and cost management techniques, allows us to do is to focus on processes outside of the physician-to-patient relationship, i.e., putting the clinical decision-making process aside and letting physicians do their work. Literally so: Physicians need their patients to be in the room when they are ready to see them, supplies to be available in the cabinets when they are most needed, lab reports to be in the electronic medical records (EMR) system as soon as possible, radiology results to be provided in the speediest possible manner and so on for all attributes of care that play supporting roles for that physician-to-patient relationship. This is where process, and cost as a dependent variable of an efficient process, is key to making a sizable improvement, reducing cost and increasing both physician and patient satisfaction.

The three main areas targeted by healthcare *Six Sigma* implementations are to: 1) Improve patient satisfaction; 2) Reduce cycle time; 3) Decrease the number of defects, e.g., mislabeled lab specimens (Turney, 2007). As an example, Turney (2007) cites a process implemented by the radiology staff at Mercy St. Anne Hospital in Toledo, Ohio that targeted DXA scan reports delivery to physicians within 24 hours in 95% of the cases. They exceeded the target goals by reaching 100% of the cases figure through the implementation of *Six Sigma* quality improvement strategies. This case represents a targeted *Six Sigma* focus to tackling a specific problem or concern rather than full investment into the *Six Sigma* program and culture, perhaps as an exploratory measure to test and refine methods that can be subsequently extended to other processes and facilities.

The *Six Sigma*-based reengineering process is defined as the fundamental rethinking and radical redesign of business processes to achieve dramatic improvements in critical process performance indicators (Hammer & Champy, 1993). Consequently, Motorola defined *Six Sigma* as the method focused on improvements in all operations within a process, producing the same or better results more rapidly and efficiently (Harry & Schroeder, 2000). *Six Sigma* recognizes that 1) Processes are key to quality outcomes; 2) Many processes are poorly designed; 3) The overall success rates are sensitive to individual sub-process rates; 4) Rapid change requires a review of the entire process, not just its individual components (Benedetto, 2003). Thus, running pilots on specific processes and narrowly targeted improvements is a fine method to test the waters, but an overall rapid success from a *Six Sigma* investment can only come from a full investment in this philosophy, a major project that subsequently targets a full review of all supporting processes in a clinical enterprise in search for efficiency, effectiveness and error (defect) reduction.

Leadership and Human Factors Considerations in Six Sigma Implementations

Leadership is one of the most important *Six Sigma* success factors to recognize. First, a top-down commitment to change and cultural transformation secures the method and protects it from the culture of "optionalism", when individual divisions and teams may choose to deviate from the new operational methods and tools, or decide to forego the transformation process altogether. Second, establishing project championship and leadership, as well as appropriate training programs for "leaders on the ground", ensures that the right people with the right skill sets are in charge of the transformation efforts. And third, there are differences among commitment levels outside of *Six Sigma* that must be recognized in healthcare organizations (Benedetto, 2003). For example, for workers in environmental, food or film services departments, their tasks are merely those that the job requires them to perform. And education/training levels tend to be at the high school level or below.

For the majority of skilled healthcare professionals, their work is a higher calling, meaning that in the *Six Sigma* case, their buy-in likely ensures the appropriate commitment, as well as the ability to grasp key concepts, recognize benefits and champion/support transformation projects. It is also important to recognize that support services departments with less educated workforces tend to be the ones that are critical to the success of the quality programs, given factors such as cost, quality outcomes and size/headcount. A low(er) level of commitment means that strong leadership is necessary to ensure the success of the transformation process there, as well as highly tailored on-the-job training programs.

The last but not least factor to recognize in terms of leadership and commitment is that there will always be differences in point of view among professionals and non-professionals in any healthcare organization. There are non-believers among clinicians who are most concerned about patients, clinical innovation and health outcomes, disregarding process as something they don't need to be concerned with. Convincing these critically important quality improvement project stakeholders is a variable of time and results. As physicians and nurses receive better services that help make sizable differences in their daily routines, their level of commitment to *Six Sigma* and other quality programs rises. Attempting to convince them up front may become an emotionally and politically charged process with a tendency to destroy culture and comfortable work environments that are welcoming and safe for patients and healthcare workers. Depending on an organization's culture and state of readiness for *Six Sigma* implementation, a slower and/ or more gradual progress for transforming work processes could become the preferred method, rather than destroying the culture and making a giant leap while losing committed and dedicated professionals as beneficiaries of the process along the way.

There is no one formula to prescribe for making a change, but recognition of the leadership and commitment factors is the key step in the process of *Six Sigma* consideration and planning. But one *Six Sigma* concept helps to develop an understanding of the big picture: It requires training all employees to act as change agents who work together on quality improvement projects (Summers, 2010). Effective human resources management is reported as one of the most important keys to success in the implementation of *Six Sigma* initiatives (Pocha, 2010). While case studies demonstrate the efficacy of healthcare *Six Sigma* programs in reducing costs and improving quality (Bisgaard, 2009; Dusharme, 2009; De Koning et al., 2006; Kim et al., 2006), a review of 177 studies of *Six Sigma* suggests that the actual degree of quality improvement and cost outcomes is relatively modest (DelliFraine, 2010). A similar study by Glasgow et al. (2010) suggests that 62 percent of the *Six Sigma* initiatives analyzed for outcomes at 47 healthcare organizations did not achieve the desired degree of success. The main reason cited for nearly all of these initiatives is a low level of organizational and stakeholder commitment to *Six Sigma* implementation. In terms of the organizational and stakeholder commitment as the critical success factor in quality program implementation, *Six Sigma* does not stand apart from other methods. For example, Lindsay et al. (2014) state similar factors in a study focused on *Lean* implementation and the human factors necessary in the process.

It is also important to note that employee satisfaction and human outcomes in general are not the targets of quality programs. While human factors are critical in the success of such quality programs' planning and implementation, the goals are operational efficiency, error reduction and organizational effectiveness (Stanton et al., 2014). Associate and patient satisfaction may be secondary outcomes of quality programs implementation, but these are not the initial targeted outcomes emphasized by *Six Sigma*, *Lean* and other process improvement methods.

SIX SIGMA: PUTTING IT ALL TOGETHER

Why Should I Consider Six Sigma or Any Other Prescriptive Management Concept?

There is no one single method that is guaranteed to work for any single healthcare organization. Moreover, some of the most complex healthcare organizations, such as integrated healthcare delivery networks consisting of entities that include hospitals, outpatient offices, home health services, skilled nursing facilities and other types of patient care centers, may need to use a wide variety of process/quality improvement techniques or a combination of several methods. It is also true that healthcare environments are vastly different organizational structures compared to manufacturing facilities, where process automation is the key to efficiency and the reduction of variability is the key to effectiveness. However, *Six Sigma*, *Lean* and other management ideas provide useful frameworks for not only individual process improvement initiatives, but also the ones that have proven their ability to work in a systematic way. In other words, adopting existing/proven methods could be a better idea than reinventing the wheel. And applicability depends on organizational goals and metrics for targeted outcomes.

Let's remember that *Six Sigma* and most other manufacturing management concepts are aimed at operational process improvement and defect reduction, not modification of a clinical process or inventing new patient care methods. So by implementing *Six Sigma* in healthcare, the target is operational efficiency, or in other words, support services excellence, aimed at the reduction of waste and increased opportunities for better services to clinicians and patients. Recognition and communication of this fact alone could lead to greater buy-in among many clinical professionals who would eagerly support operational improvements to healthcare support services and know their pains firsthand.

Due to the recognized, critical needs on the part of healthcare organizations to improve quality, increase patient satisfaction, reduce the number of errors and cut costs, there are often multiple initiatives happening at the same time. Hospitals and medical groups have often invested as heavily in EMR and computerized physician order entry systems, which are associated with quality improvement, as in management concepts such as *Six Sigma*. Complexity is high. For example, rapid improvement events that represent

Six Sigma terminology as full-cycle quality improvement processes often include clinically oriented quality improvement protocols such as the timely administration of drugs, early disease/side effects prevention programs, patient condition surveillance, complications management, chronic disease management and others. The basis for the implementation of these protocols lies within the boundaries of clinical committee reviews and health information technology implementation, but *Six Sigma* operational process improvements may interchangeably include or rely on protocols outside of the *Six Sigma* realm.

A number of cases where clinical and operational factors have been employed collectively were reported in the past decade, such as the ones reported by Bandyopadhyay and Coppens (2005) in the USA or the Institute for Innovation and Improvement (2013) in the UK. These cases represent tremendous success in applying operational and clinical quality improvement protocols, yet major emphasis remains on patient services, patient throughput, timely drug administration, proper clinical protocols execution, hospital bed management and supply chain effectiveness. These are operational elements that rely on the clinical innovations embedded in processes outside of the *Six Sigma* or other management ideas domains. In summary, intermixing operational and clinical effectiveness programs is not a bad idea, with proven success scenarios reported from several countries, but the best and most common application of *Six Sigma* is operational—within areas supporting clinicians and empowering them to perform in the most effective and efficient ways.

Are There Organizational Risks to Implementing Six Sigma in Healthcare Organizations?

The healthcare sector is already in a desperate experimentation mode for new methods that lead to greater operating efficiency and improved effectiveness of quality management programs. Attempting the introduction of a new method would be just like embarking on yet another program to introduce more/better cost savings and error reduction initiatives. So there is little harm from the perspective of introducing new operating methods. However, there are specific risks associated with the *Six Sigma* method. First, it represents a greater investment compared to a more targeted and narrowly focused departmental or single process-based quality improvement project, because *Six Sigma* works best when the entire organization commits to the new culture of *Business Process Reengineering* from the top down. This means the reorganization of some departments in charge of quality management and operational effectiveness, as well as supply chain and clinical operations. Second, it requires training and/or retraining many staff members in key positions in clinical and business operations departments, as well as project champions, trainers, coaches and other leaders. *Lean* and *Six Sigma* rely on a hierarchical structure that resembles certain martial arts: Introductory-level professionals in charge of smaller, focused projects are called green belts, and the color designations are upgraded to black and master black belts as responsibility and level of training increase. Certifications require time away from office/patient care and practical project assignments. Third, the risk of failure is higher, because getting off the *Six Sigma* bandwagon would require another reorganization and culture shift.

Fourth, there is a perception that *Six Sigma, Lean* and other quality improvement methods initially designed for highly predictive and mechanical manufacturing environments have the flip side of negatively affecting innovation as organizations become set and fixed in their operating ways. In other words, strong process orientation causes inflexibility and organizational inertia. A number of popular business trade publications investigated the innovation effects of *Six Sigma, Lean, 5S, Kaizen* and *CQI* by interviewing leaders from companies of various sizes and representing different industries and tracking these companies' stock performances. The outcomes are controversial and highly variable, unlike the variability reduction prescription at the heart of *Six Sigma* quality management.

After General Electric was able to gain several operating margin percentage points a few years after implementing *Six Sigma*, about a quarter of the Fortune 200 companies followed suit (Morris, 2006). Yet, according to *Fortune* magazine, 91% of the closely tracked 58 Fortune 200 firms trailed the S&P 500 US stock index since implementing their quality management programs. Among the reasons cited by the article are negative impacts on innovation and flexibility from the introduction of process management, process predictability and zero variation that turn organizations into highly predictable entities operating fixed processes that poorly support change, nimbleness and flexibility. While the majority of the healthcare organizations are not for-profit business entities tracking their stock market performance, business market outcomes are potentially good barometers of the success of quality improvement mechanisms that were created and initially tested in industries outside of healthcare. The commonality between industry and healthcare services is a high reliance on innovation and room for flexibility in innovation-dependent areas. Therefore, comparisons of the impact on such areas between the non-healthcare and healthcare sectors are valid instruments of process performance analysis. Smith (2014) noted that cultures built on a lack of variation are poorly designed for growth and innovation. However, the same publication argued in a different article that innovation and continuous quality improvement and management processes can coexist, given the proper focus on production process review in light of the organizational goals and culture, as opposed to managing fixed variability elimination processes (Ashkenas, 2013).

Impact on innovation is a definite concern for healthcare organizations that tend to adopt the latest and greatest clinical developments to improve the lives of their patients and increase the satisfaction of their healthcare workers by supporting their effectiveness via research and development. But at the same time, these organizations experience high levels of inefficiency due to a lack of procedures to constantly and consistently review operations for quality improvement and cost reduction opportunities. If *Six Sigma* is understood with all its strengths and weaknesses, healthcare organizations can wisely apply that method to operational improvements in areas that can benefit from variability reduction and waste elimination, while avoiding negative innovation effects on research and clinical innovation teams. Drawing the line in terms of self-imposed cultural limitations in the *Six Sigma* journey could help organizations improve efficiency, reduce cost and eliminate waste and errors, while retaining the most precious human resources on board with changes that do not affect areas that should be excluded from prescriptive process methods implementation.

Can Six Sigma Be Effective in Healthcare Organizations?

Operational efficiency projects and cultures can be successful if they are: 1) Applied in appropriate areas that can benefit from a sound production process without crippling innovation; 2) Not too prescriptive and are modified to match organizational goals and operating mechanics; 3) Combined with other appropriate concepts and not stuck with "purist" implementations of "by the book" *Six Sigma, Lean, CQI,* etc. methods; 4) Appropriately communicated to all stakeholders to ensure their buy-in. It is also important to note that massive implementation of too many superficial projects may be one reason why healthcare currently suffers from inefficiency, instead of helping increase the efficiency of healthcare provider organizations. Clinicians are concerned about too many operational and business-oriented projects affecting their practices and workflows at once, frequently competing with each other and for clinicians' time. Diving too far and too deep into quality management diverts healthcare organizations from their primary mission of delivering care to patients. Too many projects also generate large queues that cripple operating efficiency, so getting too excited about quality and cost management projects may defeat their purpose. It is all about figuring out the right operating medicine at the right time in the right places.

Let's review an example of how one innovative healthcare organization in the USA approached a gradual cultural transformation to *Lean, Six Sigma* and *Total Quality Management* by starting with greenfield implementations at its new outpatient facilities, labs and hospital expansions. Not only is starting new operations with quality and cost management philosophies in mind an easier way to manage pilot projects, but it is also a safe way to test custom methods before applying them to risky culture transformation projects within current/existing units of the organization.

The company began by identifying general areas of impact: Supplies, operations, clinical, non-clinical and indexed metrics targeting specific problems typical of the type of facility where the *Six Sigma* method is applied. The latter category is the one to be most frequently manipulated to meet ongoing quality demands and targets of each unit; i.e., once objectives/tasks are met, new ones would replace them as continuous quality review and improvement measures. This category shows the production process' ability to be flexible and address the most pressing needs of the organization, rather than become a permanent fixture that slows change and becomes a dinosaur that few staff members eventually pay attention to.

Each category was broken down into smaller and more targeted goals. A baseline was established, followed by quantitative targets and time frames to reach the target. This enabled managers to focus on very specific objectives, craft plans for targeting these objectives, communicate the goals to project stakeholders and associates, measure progress and track outcomes. The approach left little ambiguity open for questioning, set specific timelines on all projects and eased tensions between project participants and everyone affected by the initiatives. Table 19.4 outlines an example of the quality management initiatives represented by a dashboard.

The first year of implementation at the pilot facilities was successful, with safety ratings up to 95% compared to the 42% average among medical groups in the area, patient process time decreased from 60+ minutes to just above 40 minutes and indexed measures rising from 20% to 85% rate at the end of the patient's visit. As is evident from Table 19.4, there are specific measures being targeted and tracked via the above dashboard that address operating efficiency, quality and patient satisfaction measures—without affecting areas of clinical content and innovation. These measures are clearly displayed, and successes and challenges can be easily communicated to stakeholders and staff at affected facilities. The latter is important for transparency, buy-in and associate satisfaction based on the measures they are asked to work on.

Being specific about operating efficiency measures introduces clarity, removes ambiguity and helps ensure buy-in without politically costly problems. While the items outlined in Table 19.4 are grounded in extensive *Lean Six Sigma* research, it is not necessary to educate staff on all the methods that led up to the operating efficiency measures presented to them. These are already translated into the more familiar clinical and non-clinical outcomes language that resonates well with those involved with tracking, changing and evaluating progress. Therefore, healthcare organizations can afford to focus only on certain designated individuals' acquisition of deep *Six Sigma* knowledge and skills, while others can continue going about their normal work routines. *Six Sigma* innovation for healthcare comes down to research, clinical innovation, organizational culture, communication and common sense.

Table 19.4 *Lean/Six Sigma* Progress Dashboard at an Outpatient Facility

	Indicator	Status	Baseline	Target	Current	Description	Unit of Measure
Supplies	Medical supplies	★				Products in exam rooms for primary care, OB/GYN, sports medicine, cardiology	Number of products
	Pharmacy items	★				Pharmacy products for primary care, OB/GYN, sports medicine, cardiology	Number of products
	Days on hand for medical supplies	★				Supply days on hand across the clinic	Number of days
	Stockouts					Part levels are constantly being monitored and adjusted accordingly	Number of stockouts
Operations	Patient total process time (primary care)					Number of minutes from patient check-in to discharge	Minutes
	Percent of patients seen within first 15 minutes of appointment time					Percent of patients seen by their provider within 15 minutes of check-in	Percentage
Clinical	Percent of patients left with clinical summary (care coordi-nation)					Percent of patients who leave with their clinical summary	Percentage
	Percent of clinical index measures completed by end of appointment					Percent of patients who had their clinical integration measures completed by the end of their visit	Percentage

	Measure	Unit
Non-Clinical	Percent of arrived patients asked to join portal	Percent of patients who have been asked to join the portal	Percentage
	Percent of portal invitations sent	Percent of patients who have had portal invitations sent to them	Percentage
Indexed Measures	Urgent patient messages not opened one hour after generation	Messages received with an urgent priority that have not been closed or marked as in progress within one hour	Number of EMR tasks
	Patient messages not opened one hour after visit	Messages received before clinician's last appointment that have not been opened	Number of EMR tasks
	Patient messages not closed 24 hours after generation	Messages received that have not been closed within 24 hours	Number of EMR tasks
	Ancillary results not verified one hour after last visit	Results received before clinician's last appointment that have not been verified	Number of EMR tasks
	Clinician notes not closed 24 hours after generation	Notes generated before clinician's last appointment that have not been signed	Number of EMR tasks
	Pharmacy renewals not complete one hour after last visit	Pharmacy renewal requests received before clinician's last appointment that have not been completed	Number of EMR tasks

REFERENCES

Ashkenas, R. (2013). Why continuous improvement may need to be discontinued. *Forbes*, July 24. Retrieved from http://www.forbes.com/sites/ronashkenas/2013/07/24/why-continuous-improvement-may-need-to-be-discontinued/ (accessed 32 May 2015).

Bandyopadhyay, J.K., & Coppens, K. (2005). The use of six sigma in healthcare. *International Journal of Quality and Productivity Management*, 5 (1), v1–v12.

Benedetto, A.R. (2003). Adapting manufacturing-based six sigma methodology to the service environment of a radiology film library. *Journal of Healthcare Management*, 48 (4), 263–280.

Bisgaard, S. (2009). *Solutions to the Healthcare Quality Crisis: Cases and Examples of Lean Six Sigma in Healthcare*. Milwaukee, WI: ASQ Quality Press.

De Feo, B., & Barnard, W. (2005). *Juran Institute's Six Sigma Breakthrough and Beyond: Quality Performance Breakthrough Methods*. New York, NY: McGraw-Hill Global Education.

De Koning, H., Verver, J.P.S., van den Heuvel, J., Bisgaard, S., & Does, R.J.M. (2006). Lean six sigma in healthcare. *Journal for Healthcare Quality*, 28 (2), 4–11.

De Menezes, I., Wood, S., & Gelade, G. (2010). The integration of human resource and operation management practices: A longitudinal case study. *Journal of Operations Management*, 28 (6), 455–471.

DelliFraine, J.L., Langabeer, J.R., & Nembhard, I.M. (2010). Assessing the evidence of six sigma and lean in the health care industry. *Quality Management in Health Care*, 19 (3), 211–225.

Dusharme, D. (2009). Six sigma in healthcare: We're leaving money on the table. *Quality Digest*. Retrieved from http://www.qualitydigest.com/print/9083 (accessed 18 April 2015).

Glasgow, J.M., Scott-Caziewell, J.R., & Kaboli, P.J. (2010). Guiding inpatient quality improvement: A systematic review of lean and six sigma. *The Joint Commission Journal on Quality and Patient Safety*, 36 (12), 533–540.

Gowen, C.R., McFadden, K.L., & Settaluri, S. (2012). Contrasting continuous quality improvement, six sigma, and lean management for enhanced outcomes in US hospitals. *American Journal of Business*, 27 (2), 133–153.

Graban, M. (2012). *Lean Hospitals*. Boca Raton, FL: CRC Press.

Habidin, N.F., Yusof, S.M., Zulkifli, C.M.C.O., Mohamad, S.I.S., Janudin, S.E., & Omar, B. (2012). Lean six sigma initiative: Business engineering practices and performance in Malaysian automotive industry. *IOSR Journal of Engineering*, 2 (7), 13–18.

Hammer, M., & Champy, J. (1993). *Reengineering the Corporation: A Manifesto for Business Revolution*. New York: Harper Business (a Division of Harper Collins Publishers).

Harris, C., Cortvriend, P., & Hyde, P. (2007). Human resource management and performance in healthcare organizations. *Journal of Health Organization and Management*, 21 (4/5), 448–459.

Harry, M.J. (1988). *The Nature of Six Sigma Quality*. Rolling Meadows, IL: Motorola University Press.

Harry, M.J., & Schroeder, R. (2000). *Six Sigma: The Breakthrough Management Strategy Revolutionizing the World's Top Corporations*. New York: Doubleday.

Institute for Innovation and Improvement. (2013). *Quality and value: Improving care and efficiency in clinical pathways*. National Health Service, Case study documents. Retrieved from http://www.institute.nhs.uk/quality_and_value/introduction/case_studies.html (accessed 16 May 2015).

International Organization for Standardization (ISO). (2011). *ISO publishes six sigma performance improvement methodology.* Retrieved from http://www.iso.org/iso/home/news_index/news_archive/news.htm?refid=Ref1461 (accessed 18 April 2015).

Kim, C.S., Spahlinger, D.A., Kin, J.M., & Billi, J.E. (2006). Lean health care: What can hospitals learn from a world-class automaker? *Journal of Hospital Medicine*, 1 (3), 191–199.

Kwak, Y.H., & Anbari, F.T. (2004). Benefits, obstacles, and future of six sigma approach. *Technovation*, 26 (5–6), 708–715.

Lindsay, C., Commander, J., Findlay, P., Bennie, M., Dunlop Corcoran, E., & van der Meer, R. (2014). Lean, new technologies and employment in public health services: Employees' experiences in the National Health Service. *The International Journal of Human Resource Management*, 25 (21), 2941–2956.

Morris, B. (2006). New rule: Look out, not in. Old rule: Be lean and mean. *Fortune*, July 10. Retrieved from http://archive.fortune.com/2006/07/10/magazines/fortune/rule4.fortune/index.htm (accessed 31 May 2015).

Pocha, C. (2010). Lean six sigma in healthcare and the challenge of implementation of six sigma methodologies at a veterans affairs medical center. *Quality Management in Healthcare*, 19 (4), 312–318.

Smith, R. (2014). Is six sigma killing your company's future? *Forbes*, June 11. Retrieved from http://www.forbes.com/sites/ricksmith/2014/06/11/is-six-sigma-killing-your-companys-future/ (accessed 31 May 2015).

Stanton, P., Gough, R., Ballardie, R., Bartram, T., Bamber, G.J., & Sohal, A. (2014). Implementing lean management/six sigma in hospitals: Beyond empowerment or work intensification? *The International Journal of Human Resource Management*, 25 (21), 2926–2940.

Summers, D.C. (2010). *Lean Six Sigma: Process Improvement Tools and Techniques.* Upper Saddle River, NJ: Prentice-Hall.

Tennant, G. (2001). *Six Sigma: SPC and TQM in Manufacturing and Services.* Surrey, England: Gower.

Turney, J. (2007). Six sigma and lean six sigma. *Radiologic Technology*, 79 (2), 191–192.

20 Sustainability in Healthcare Organizations

Tony Huzzard, Andreas Hellström and Svante Lifvergren

INTRODUCTION

Sustainability has become an increasingly central topic in the study of organizations over the last decade or so (Blackburn, 2007; Docherty et al., 2002; Epstein, 2008; Laszlo, 2008; Mohrman & Shani, 2011). There is clear evidence too that the diffusion of ideas associated with *Sustainability* has also been reflected in organizational practices (Docherty et al., 2009; Mohrman & Shani, 2011). The increasing amount of literature on the topic attests to a growing realization by business and non-profit organizations that the problems faced by humanity require new solutions in the face of the challenges posed by climate change, degradation of the environment, population migration, economic growth and resource shortages.[1] Underpinning these concerns is a belief that the planet and the global economy are reaching a limit in terms of what can be delivered and guaranteed in terms of infrastructure, services and other activities that secure basic human needs. This insight can be traced back at least to the work of E. F. Schumacher (1973), and was also noted nearly two decades ago when the UN set up the World Commission on Environment and Development, usually referred to as the Brundtland Commission (Brundtland, 1987). The report of the Commission proposed the now widely understood definition of sustainable development as that which "meets the needs of the present without compromising the ability of future generations to meet their own needs".

The challenges identified in the Brundtland Report appear to have had resonance in a wide variety of contexts in terms of markets, communities, ecosystems, sectors and societies. One particular area where sustainable solutions have been seen as being particularly pertinent is healthcare. In the words of Mohrman et al. (2012b):

> By all measures, as currently conceived and practiced, it [healthcare] is not sustainable. A myriad of demographic, cost, and health trends are pushing organizations, governments and societies to rethink and substantially change how health care is designed and what it is designed to do. (p. xi)

As we write, the USA has been grappling with healthcare reform following the controversial introduction of the Affordable Care Act by the Obama administration, and many healthcare systems in Europe and elsewhere have been experimenting with new organizational ideas for some time. These ideas, such as internal markets, greater involvement by the private sector, *Lean* healthcare (for more information about *Lean healthcare* and its relevance to healthcare organizations, see Poksinska, Chapter 13 in this volume) and business process-based approaches (for more information about *Business Process and Reengineering* and its relevance to healthcare organizations, see Patwardhan et al., Chapter 6 in this volume), can all be seen as attempts to respond to the pressures of increased demand without concomitant increases in resources, not least in a period characterized by increasing austerity. The healthcare sector has proved to be a particularly receptive context for the ideas of *Sustainability*, as they hold out both the prospect of a more balanced approach to the consumption and regeneration of resources and the securing of permanent change.

The purpose of this chapter is to explore and evaluate the diffusion of *Sustainability* as a diverse set of innovative ideas and practices in healthcare. We will pose and attempt to answer the question, "How relevant is *Sustainability* to healthcare?" Our argument is that *Sustainability*, as a body of ideas for innovation, is relevant and thereby applicable in the context, although there is a requirement for adaptation. A standard and well-cited model for *Sustainability* is the so-called triple bottom line, whereby financial, environmental and social effectiveness should all be prioritized in equal measure (Elkington, 1997). We also propose that in healthcare, this idea needs to be augmented to include a fourth bottom line—namely, clinical effectiveness (Kira & Lifvergren, 2013). We propose a broad conceptualization of *Sustainability* that includes sustainable production processes and practices as well as sustainable outcomes.

We see *Sustainability* in dynamic or, to be more precise, developmental terms rather than as a static template or snapshot of off-the-peg practices. What we conceptualize as a sustainable health system is best understood as a vocabulary or set of concepts for animating dialogue about and in development processes. In various formats and roles, each of us has been involved in action research projects in the sector over many years and it is from these experiences of developing healthcare through conducting research with practitioners (Hughes, 2008; Lifvergren et al., 2015) that we see potentialities for the discourse of *Sustainability* in the sector (see, e.g., Huzzard et al., 2014). In terms of defining the term "healthcare provider" organization in the chapter, we see this in systems terms; that is, healthcare is best seen as primary care (local health centers or general practitioners), secondary care (typically a focal hospital) and social care (rehabilitation activities, which in the Swedish context are organized by local authorities) all being seen as an integrated whole or holistic system, perhaps falling under the aegis of a regional health authority or trust.

WHAT IS A SUSTAINABLE HEALTH SYSTEM?

Irrespective of the national context or governance regime in place, health systems globally are facing similar challenges. Resources are being increasingly stretched through a lethal combination of factors that are radically changing the basis on which care is delivered. Demographic change is resulting in populations living longer. Technological change, although opening up new possibilities for care and cure, nevertheless commonly entails more costly treatments. Economic change has also been discernible, not least since the financial crash of 2008 and the subsequent ushering in of ongoing austerity measures, notably in Europe. There is also change in the nature of health itself, as aging populations are leading to increasing incidences of chronic diseases. Together, these challenges have led authors to conclude that healthcare systems, as currently designed, are unsustainable (Mohrman et al., 2012a). There is, accordingly, a need for such systems to be redesigned so that they can deliver more from less.

A literature search on the Thomson Reuters Web of Science showed that the discourse about sustainable healthcare is quite young, and has rapidly increased over the last 10 years (see Figures 20.1 and 20.2). At the same time, or maybe due to the novelty of the discourse, there is considerable critique to the effect that the discourse is both vague and contested. Jeanneret

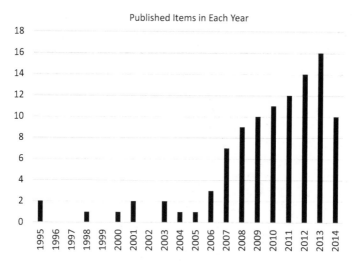

Figure 20.1   Published items in each year on the Web of Science for the last 20 years. Search terms used: "Sustainable Health Care" (57 publications) OR "Sustainable Healthcare" (47 publications).[i]

[i] Literature search conducted by the authors on January 10th, 2015. The search terms "sustainable development" AND "healthcare" gave 42 publications and showed almost an identical distribution, as seen in the graphs shown.

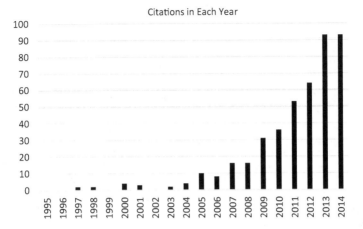

Figure 20.2 Citations in each year on the Web of Science for the last 20 years. Search terms used: "Sustainable Health Care" OR "Sustainable Healthcare".

(2008) argues, for example, that the expression "sustainable development" is both hegemonic and semantically vague and can easily be disregarded as some kind of magic phrase without real substance.

The multifarious nature of the challenges facing the sector has led to a similarly multifarious response. Most notably, scholars and practitioners have increasingly drawn on Elkington's concept of the "triple bottom line" as the starting point for developing new frameworks of developing, implementing and evaluating improvement initiatives (Elkington, 1997). *Sustainability*, in terms of this framework, entails the pursuit of effective outcomes in terms of social objectives, economic objectives and ecological objectives, or, alternately, the 3Ps of people, prosperity and planet (Wals & Schwarzin, 2012). The early definition of *Sustainability* proposed in the Brundtland Report (see introduction) has subsequently been amended to reflect triple bottom line considerations. A recent example of this is offered by Smith and Scharicz (2011, pp. 73–74), who see *Sustainability* as "the result of the activities of an organization, voluntary or governed by law, that demonstrate the ability of the organization to maintain viable its business operations (including viability as appropriate) whilst not negatively impacting any social or ecological systems". In other words, managing the present to secure the future requires a balance between the three elements of the triple bottom line, or at least an absence of conflict between them. A common visualization of the different dimensions of sustainable development is a model in which economic, social and environmental factors overlap. This creates a system that is sustainable in that it is socially bearable,[2] economically equitable and environmentally viable (Adams, 2006) (see Figure 20.3).

However, as well as the triumvirate of social *Sustainability*, economic *Sustainability* and ecological *Sustainability*, we also see the need in healthcare

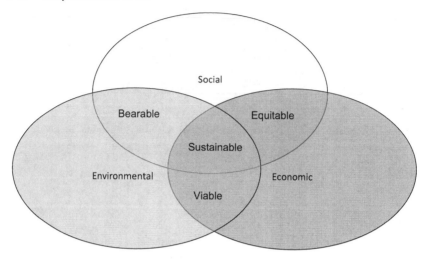

Figure 20.3   The Three Dimensions of Sustainable Development and Their Overlap (adapted from: Adams, 2006 and Wikipedia, 2015)

for a further element—that of clinical *Sustainability*, as health outcomes are of course a central objective or even raison d'être of health systems. Together, these elements of *Sustainability* suggest that in healthcare, *Sustainability* in fact entails a quadruple bottom line, whereby social, economic, ecological and clinical objectives are closely intertwined and no single objective is pursued at the expense of the others (Kira & Lifvergren, 2013). A useful working definition of *Sustainability* in healthcare to reflect this basic idea is proposed by Mohrman et al. (2012a). In their view, a healthcare system is sustainable if:

> The eco-system for the provision of health care services and outcomes operates to continually increase health, societal, and ecological value, functions with a viable economic model, and conserves resources for future generations. (p. 4[3])

Underpinning this definition and the quadruple bottom line it depicts is the idea that the 4Ps need to be in balance: People, prosperity, planet and patients. The disciplinary origins or inspirations here are ecology and environmental science.

The idea of the triple bottom line (or quadruple bottom line, in the healthcare context) sees *Sustainability* in effect as "systemic equilibrium", that is, when the consumption and regeneration of the components of the system's four sub-systems are in balance. It is a seductive view—after all, who could be against outcomes that promote the interests of people, prosperity, planet and patients all at the same time? Yet despite the appeal of the framework, it has been difficult to translate it into sets of concrete practices. Its formulation generally remains at a very abstract level. Perhaps for this reason, some researchers and practitioners in the field have preferred instead to see *Sustainability* in terms of permanent improvements in healthcare organizations rather than the sustainable outcomes of the quadruple bottom line. To be more precise, this preferred approach, what we might call "lasting change", sees *Sustainability* in terms of improvement initiatives or development programs leading to fundamental and irreversible change (e.g., Buchanan et al., 2005; Greenhalgh et al., 2012, Higuchi et al., 2012, Lifvergren et al., 2009). Here, the disciplinary origins are in change management and implementation science. The problem in focus here is the apparent consensus amongst change management researchers that the majority of change management initiatives fail (Beer & Nohria, 2000), or at least that learning outcomes from projects do not result in any permanent change. An illustrative definition of this approach to *Sustainability* is offered by Higuchi et al. (2012):

> Sustainability refers to the process of changing organizational goals and procedures that are maintained beyond the initial introductory period. (p. 1708)

As we see it, this latter view sees *Sustainability* in terms of processes (and perhaps practices), whereas the former view sees *Sustainability* in terms of various outcomes and how effectively they are achieved. The latter view has clearly been the approach that has been more easily transferable to practice as evidenced by, for example, the National Health Service's (NHS) Sustainability Model in the UK (Maher et al., 2010).

HEALTH AND HEALTH PROMOTION

An important goal for sustainable healthcare is, of course, good health and health promotion. However, contemporary approaches to organizing healthcare have been criticized for their emphasis on acute care and the marginalization of prevention and public health—an imbalance between approaches that has been called "sick care" instead of "health care" (Marvasti & Stafford, 2012). Clearly, the implication here is that the latter implies *Sustainability*, whereas the former does not. But what does the latter entail more concretely?

One area where *Sustainability* can be assessed is the health status of disadvantaged groups and its change over time. This is frequently regarded as an indicator for social progress and quality of life. Health here includes physical, mental and social well-being, and is a resource of the individual (WHO, 1998). Health is influenced by a variety of factors at different levels around the individual. An interesting, and relevant, model of health when discussing sustainable development in healthcare is presented by Dahlgren and Whitehead (2007). They argue that health can be thought of as a series of layers. On an overall societal level, we find the major structural environment of socio-economic, cultural and environmental factors. Somewhat closer to the individual are factors that affect the social and material conditions that we live and work in. These concern the workplace, education, agriculture, unemployment, access to water and wastewater treatment plants, healthcare and housing conditions. Next come the factors affecting social networking, family, friends and the local community. Then there are factors that affect the individual's lifestyle and habits, such as what an individual eats, drinks and how s/he exercises. There are also factors within the individual, such as sex, age and genetic inheritance, but these are fixed factors over which we have little control (Dahlgren & Whitehead, 2007).

Another interesting aspect of sustainable development in healthcare is the authors' suggestion that these four layers of influence of health can be translated into four levels of policy interventions. They differentiate between long-term structural changes that usually require political actions on Level 1. Policies on Level 2 are aimed at improving living and working conditions through healthy public and/or business strategies. On Level 3, we find policies aimed at strengthening social and community support to individuals and families to join together against health hazards. Policies on Level 4 are aimed at influencing individual lifestyles and attitudes.

CONCEPTUALIZING SUSTAINABLE HEALTH SYSTEMS: A PROPOSAL

As stated, there are two quite distinct approaches to *Sustainability* in the literature. It is either seen as lasting change or as systemic equilibrium. Unfortunately, there is a tendency to conflate or confuse these (Scheirer & Dearing, 2011; Yang et al., 2010). Moreover, there is also an inconsistency and apparent dissensus in the literature on whether *Sustainability* is fundamentally concerned with efficiency or effectiveness. It is, given this background, a key objective of this chapter to argue that more conceptual precision is required. Accordingly, we propose here a model of a sustainable health system that is attentive to the clear distinction between sustainable production processes or practices on the one hand and sustainable outcomes on the other (see also Øvretveit, 2011; Scheirer & Dearing, 2011). However, the model we propose combines the two in a way that might move the field forward and circumvent some of the confusion and contestation that has beset the field.

We propose the concept of a sustainable ecosystem here to combine two system components that together capture the key systems elements of sustainable processes. Our overall model depicted in Figure 20.4 integrates the various elements discussed here. Firstly, we see such systems as having a set of capacities. Such capacities entail quality improvement practices (Berwick,

2008), ambidexterity, i.e., both must be innovative and make efficient use of knowledge that already exists (Gibson & Birkinshaw, 2004; Tushman & O'Reilly, 1996), inter-professional collaboration across all levels of care (Ekman-Philips et al., 2004) and "upstream thinking", i.e., an emphasis on health promotion and disease prevention. Each of these has been a persistent theme in the more normatively oriented literature on integrated care, although no systematic studies have been undertaken, to our knowledge, of any interaction effects between them. Moreover, the list of system capacities proposed here is unlikely to be exhaustive. In identifying them and locating them in the model, we are using them tentatively as a set of propositions for future empirical exploration.

Secondly, we see sustainable ecosystems as consisting of a set of developmental principles. Such principles are proposed as guiding the implementation of change processes and have been empirically derived from our ongoing action research endeavors that have had the ambition of systems-wide change in cancer care in a regional health authority (Huzzard et al., 2014). Five principles have underpinned such efforts. First, we have usefully seen them as being profession-led (in our case, by senior cancer physicians) (Abbott, 1988). Secondly, such efforts are learning driven, whereby individual and group learning extends to learning at the systems level (Crossan et al., 1999). Thirdly, they are aligned with positive organizational scholarship, being typically informed by action research methods such as appreciative inquiry (Cooperrider & Srivastva, 1987). Fourthly, they entail holistic systems thinking that seeks to integrate the disparate parts of the system (Glouberman & Mintzberg, 2001a,b), such that healthcare systems also

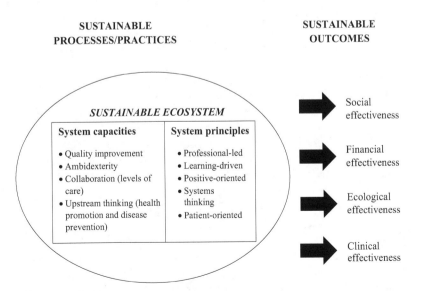

Figure 20.4 Conceptualizing a Sustainable Health System

interact with other actors and stakeholders in society in the pursuit of optimal health for all. Finally, there is an explicit patient orientation, not least in the pursuit of cure and care that are both safe and equitable (Stewart, 2001), since when the patient becomes part of the care team and interacts according a jointly agreed care plan, there is potential for person-centered care, better adherence to the agree-upon treatment and efficient use of resources.

As to sustainable outcomes, we see these in terms of the quadruple bottom line, as already discussed. The first of these emphasizes social *Sustainability*, or what in the literature has been termed sustainable work systems (Docherty et al., 2002, 2009). Such systems, which constantly evolve and are dynamic in nature, entail multiple organizational or system stakeholders. Fundamentally, such systems aim for personal and professional resources to be regenerated rather than consumed. The development of one type of human resource does not exploit the other types, and no one actor seeks gains at the expense of others. In the words of Kira and van Eijnatten (2009), the

> . . . various skills, pieces of knowledge, mental models, beliefs, and other diverse resources of a sustainable employee [grow to be] unique and valuable, and are integrated into a well-functioning whole, into a person and a self. A sustainable employee is thus a highly complex being with rich integrated resources. (p. 235)

A key issue here is that healthcare employees can conduct their work in such a way that is meaningful, developmental and consistent with maintaining their own health and at fair levels of material reward. The evidence, however, suggests that healthcare employees have seen an increase in work intensity over the last decade or so, a phenomenon matched by turnover increases, higher sickness levels and higher early retirement rates (Mohrman et al., 2012a, p. 19).

The second outcome is financial effectiveness. This is usually understood and expressed in monetary terms as the maintenance of capital or at least keeping it intact (Roman, 2009). Arguably, the dominant ideology throughout Western capitalism in the contemporary era is that of shareholder value, whereby shareholders are seen as having a privileged claim on economic surpluses and all operations should be geared towards such a goal (Lazonick & O'Sullivan, 2000). In some cases, healthcare organizations have become subject to such a doctrine, as parts or perhaps even wholes of healthcare systems have been outsourced or sold to private interests and thereby operate according to a commercial logic. Moreover, in for-profit, insurance-based systems, such as those that dominate in US healthcare, such logics or doctrines have always been a central feature. However, even in non-market models of healthcare, such as those that are more prevalent in Europe, healthcare organizations have been increasingly subjected to strict financial controls through centralized budgets that reflect political priorities in times of austerity. Either way, the maintenance or even accumulation of capital[4] have been in the forefront of the objectives of healthcare organizations such that economic effectiveness has often prevailed over the other components of the quadruple bottom line.

The third component of the quadruple bottom line is ecological effectiveness. Here, the ambition is that of ensuring that natural resources, like human and economic resources, are regenerated rather than consumed. Yet although healthcare is commonly seen as a means of curing human ills, its activities also contribute negatively to the natural environment. Hospitals are producers of greenhouse gases, air pollutants and toxic waste from used medical supplies such as drugs. They also consume water and land in significant quantities (Turley et al., 2011), and are invariably polluters whose waste disposal has a negative impact on the environment in terms of the air, drinking water, sewage and soil. Moreover, such waste can also contribute negatively to the physical work environment of healthcare employees. This is often worsened by the fact that older hospital buildings may frequently be composed of dangerous materials such as paint, particle boards, carpets and ventilation systems (Mohrman et al., 2012a). Health Care Without Harm (2015) is an interesting example of a global coalition of more than 500 members in 53 countries that focuses on ecological challenges and aims to develop a shared vision to create a healthcare system that contributes both to better health and a better environment.

Finally, as stated, we believe in the healthcare context that a fourth bottom line can be usefully added to Elkington's original formulation, namely, clinical effectiveness (Kira & Lifvergren, 2013). This necessarily emphasizes disease prevention and health promotion as means to minimize the need for healthcare. As an outcome, this is clearly linked to the system principle of upstream thinking. Also significant here are the twin issues of patient education and empowerment, and typical outcome indicators are metrics that assess reductions in disease progression, the successful pre-empting of complications as well as improvements in the coordination of care through greater patient involvement in his/her own condition. Other aspects of clinical effectiveness include targeted, evidence-based use of investigations, as well as effective IT support in both referral and interventions to reduce duplication and unnecessary travel. Moreover, although considerable amounts are invested in developing health technologies, these are often ineffective against many multiple diseases, including various cancers. Once again, the links between *Sustainability* and preventive medicine are obviously relevant here.

The quadruple bottom line is seen in terms of outcomes, i.e., the various dimensions of effectiveness of the system, and the system capacities and system principles, seen together as a sustainable ecosystem, are seen in terms of production processes and practices. However, it is important to understand how we see the purpose and applicability of this model. *Sustainability* can be seen in both normative and descriptive terms. The difficulty is that much

Financial (Prosperity)	Ecological (Planet)
• Reduce cost of poor quality • Always 'Upstream' • Care practices/safety • Enhance flow and reduce unwanted variation	• Reduce negative environmental impact • Responsible use of natural resources
Social (People)	**Clinical (Patient)**
• Dialogues at all levels in the organization • Participation • Well-being	• Always 'Upstream' • Care practices/safety • Enhance flow and reduce unwanted variation

Figure 20.5 The Four Components of the Quadruple Bottom Line, Inspired by Kira and Lifvergren (2013)

of the conceptual work in the area has been highly abstract and difficult to translate into concrete organizational practices. One exception to this is the NHS Sustainability Model, which proposes a set of explicit instruments relating to process, staff and organizational issues (Maher et al., 2010). However, this model limits itself to the permanency of change initiatives and is silent on outcomes relating to the quadruple bottom line. Operationalizing the quadruple bottom line seems elusive. Accordingly, we present the model here not as a basis for normative guidance on concrete, off-the-peg practices but, rather, as a means for animating dialogue in participative system-wide development or innovation processes (Bushe & Marshak, 2009). In terms of the four components of the quadruple bottom line, Kira and Lifvergren (2013) have proposed a number of themes for such dialogue, as set out in Figure 20.5.

CASE ILLUSTRATION: REGIONAL CANCER CENTRE WEST

One example of developing healthcare where the discourse of *Sustainability* has been significant is the recent work we have been engaged in, that is, effecting system-wide change in cancer care in the Swedish region of Västra Götaland (see Huzzard et al., 2014 for a more detailed discussion). This has been an action research intervention undertaken with the leadership of the Regional Cancer Centre West (RCC West) based at the Sahlgrenska

Hospital in Gothenburg. Prompted by a national cancer strategy formulated by the central government that argued that cancer care in Sweden was in effect unsustainable without major reform, the intervention sought to engage leading cancer physicians as regional process owners in developing quality measures, making transparent their respective care pathways and implementing quality improvements along them.

The system principles proposed in Figure 20.4 have been directly derived from the case. A central aspect of the regional cancer strategy has been to create a coherent set of regional care pathways in all 23 domains of cancer care and a number of support processes. Central here was a decision to mobilize the top cancer physicians as production process owners and build a network or platform around their knowledge and commitment. Secondly, the framing of the project was explicitly and necessarily "patient focused", not least in the pursuit of cure and care that was safe and equitable. To this end, patient representatives were invited to the various discussions within the network (as a platform) and beyond, including to various dialogic events. Thirdly, the importance of learning was recognized as central by the platform, which consisted of the 34 process owners, the RCC West leadership and ourselves. This platform has become a permanent arena for both formal and informal learning. Fourthly, the intervention has significantly drawn on the ideas of appreciative enquiry (Cooperrider & Srivastva, 1987). This approach downplays perceived problems or shortcomings in the system and foregrounds instead ideas from practice that are seen as beneficial and work well, thereby accentuating the positive. Finally, the intervention has sought to encourage systems thinking in the change effort by arranging large network meetings for the diverse stakeholders involved in the regional cancer care, inspired in many cases by appreciative enquiry. This in effect is about acknowledging divergent stakeholder perspectives, including those of healthcare administrators and regional politicians, and facilitating a voice for them.

As to system capacities, the intervention has sought to introduce improvements such as reduced wait times, more transparent feedback on diagnoses and clearer lines of responsibility for x-rays and laboratory tests. The emphasis on learning has also sought to balance the exploitation of knowledge derived from evidence-based medicine with the exploration of new knowledge through experimental approaches to pathway redesign. Broadly, the new structures, processes and relationships entailed a means of institutionalizing ambidexterity, whereby both learning through exploitation and learning through exploration could be in balance (Tushman & O'Reilly, 1996). Collaboration between professionals along the pathways has been key here, as indeed has collaboration across pathways through the opportunities for knowledge sharing and learning via the platform. Finally, many of the sub-projects within the overall intervention have emphasized what can be understood as upstream thinking, that is, looking for ways to promote and support preventive care, such as early testing for breast cancer.

Although this can add to costs in the short term, it can prevent greater outlays in the long run.

Much of the discussion on the learning platform, and indeed among the professional teams organized around the pathways, has been on the various innovations and outcomes of the quadruple bottom line. With researcher support, evaluative studies have been presented and discussed on employee health issues (social *Sustainability*), costs associated with improvement efforts (economic *Sustainability*), the environmental impacts of such efforts (ecological *Sustainability*) as well as the effectiveness of new medical interventions (clinical *Sustainability*).

DISCUSSION

We claim that most of the problems with healthcare today are largely organizational. The elderly population is increasing, as is the incidence of patients with multiple and complex diseases. Effective treatment of such diseases, however, is often badly matched to the current way of organizing healthcare. Moreover, high-quality care that is in line with patients' expectations requires new methods for organizing healthcare systems (Swedish Ministry of Finance, 2005). The demands are high, but the resources are not infinite. If too much focus is directed towards new and better alternatives to deliver treatments, costs might skyrocket. On the other hand, too much pressure on cost cutting may lead to unacceptable service and quality levels (Institute of Medicine, 2001). Consequently, in order to meet future challenges and be sustainable in the system equilibrium sense, healthcare systems must be capable of both improving and innovating—simultaneously, and in balance.

Accordingly, we suggest a dynamic or developmental perspective on sustainable healthcare where organizational learning and change are the focal issues. These fields attempt to understand the processes that lead to changes in organizational knowledge and subsequent changes in organizational behavior, shared conceptions and outcomes. As stated above, it's critical for organizations to be able to pursue exploration (innovations) and exploitation (better use of already exiting knowledge) simultaneously. Literatures on organizational learning and change have argued that organizations with the capabilities of pursuing exploration and exploitation simultaneously and in balance obtain superior performance and enhance their long-term survival. Correspondingly, sustainable organizations need to be ambidextrous (i.e., they are able to do two different things at the same time) and efficient at managing today's demands, while also being adaptable to changes in the environment (Gibson & Birkinshaw, 2004; Tushman & O'Reilly, 1996).

This tension between exploration and exploitation was first observed by Abernathy (1978), who suggested that an organization's focus on productivity gains inhibited its flexibility and ability to innovate. Now, more than 30 years later, the pressures for organizations to meet multiple, often inconsistent, contextual demands have escalated (e.g., Christensen, 1998; Tushman & O'Reilly, 1997), not least within the healthcare sector and its demands to be both innovative (Institute of Medicine, 2001) and efficient (OECD, 2010) in order to face future challenges.

Limited literature is available from the healthcare sector. Some of the previous research involves the in-house learning laboratory for patient-centered innovations at the Mayo Clinic (Armburster et al., 2009), ICT-driven innovations (Corso & Gastaldi, 2010) and Alegent Health's development journey in striving to be both agile and sustainable (Worley, 2012). However, it's easy to translate the thinking above into a healthcare setting where too much focus on new and better alternatives for delivering treatments might cause costs to skyrocket. On the other hand, too much pressure on cost cutting may lead to unacceptable service and quality levels (Institute of Medicine, 2001).

The long-term success of a healthcare system is dependent on the system's ability to capture the needs of every individual patient as well as the population as a whole. It is therefore important to develop the healthcare system in collaboration with the patients. All the results and the value for the organization are created in situations where patients, professionals and support systems interact in daily operations. This has been defined as the clinical microsystem (Nelson et al., 2002). The clinical microsystem is made up of the operationally oriented units that provide care to the majority of patients/users, and it includes the places and locations where patients, their next of kin and healthcare professionals interact. Nelson et al. (2002) and Donaldson and Mohr (2000) propose the following definition of a clinical microsystem in a healthcare context:

> A clinical microsystem is a small group of people who work together on a regular basis to provide care to discrete subpopulations of patients. It has clinical and business aims, linked processes, and a shared information environment, and it produces performance outcomes. Microsystems evolve over time and are often embedded in larger organizations. They are complex adaptive systems, and as such they must do the primary work associated with core aims, meet the needs of internal staff, and maintain themselves over time as clinical units. (Nelson et al., 2002, p. 7)

According to clinical microsystem theory, the system's quality of care can never exceed the synthesis of care quality delivered by each individual microsystem (Nelson et al., 2002). Moreover, successful microsystems often share a culture of respect and common values, providing an inviting community to new employees. A patient focus is equally important, where the patient and his/her relatives can be regarded as parts of the clinical microsystem (Nelson et al., 2002). The microsystem theory points to the importance of studying how the mesosystem (major divisions of a healthcare system, e.g., a clinical department or a women's health program) and the macrosystem (the whole of the actual healthcare organization) coordinate and collaborate to support the frontline microsystems. It is also equally important to link and coordinate the microsystems along the patient process (Nelson et al., 2007).

Healthcare is deeply rooted in the epistemological traditions of the natural sciences and proven experience and evidence, which have been important for the development of safe and good care for patients. Consequently, healthcare has been organized based on different clinical disciplines and organs, which has led to a fragmented and sometimes badly integrated system (Glouberman & Mintzberg, 2001a). A holistic view from the patient's perspective is lacking; care interventions along a patient's journey often occur separated in time and space, and an upstream perspective on the care provided is often missing. This is not least evident for patients with multiple diseases who are passed around between different clinics and physicians, since no proper coordination takes place based on the patient's needs. It seems fair to conclude from this that the organizational design of healthcare is often inappropriate. Or, we can ask, as Richard Bohmer (2010) provocatively proposes, whether healthcare organizations really are "designed" at all. Accordingly, it is important to consider how healthcare delivers value to its patients and other stakeholders and to search for new organizational innovations on how to design healthcare delivery around the patient. On a higher level, this trend can be seen as a shift in the power division between the "user" and "provider" organization in the healthcare sector. It can also be seen as a shift in design away from healthcare organized primarily around the doctor's office and hospital toward much broader criteria for the design of the ecosystem for healthcare.

Healthcare systems have long been under significant pressure to become more patient-oriented and to allow patients to become more involved and empowered, not just in day-to-day practices, but also in the actual development of the system. Although the voice of medical professionals has been historically dominant in healthcare, there are grounds for believing that technology and consumer pressures are beginning to disrupt traditional care delivery processes, such that the sector is becoming a "buyer's" rather than a "seller's" market. This pressure has also been reflected in various political decisions, such as steps toward the deregulation of the healthcare sector in many European countries, the legal and regulatory changes associated with Obamacare in the USA, and in the activities of various patient care advocacy groups.

Empowering individuals to take more responsibility for their own healthcare is also seen by many as integral to healthcare *Sustainability*. However, it has been difficult for many managers and employees within healthcare to bring this rhetoric to realization. Political decisions regarding user involvement to improve the quality of healthcare largely deal with these issues in principle only. For the most part, policy makers have not considered how change in everyday healthcare practices, where the value-creating care for patients is carried out, could occur (Donaldson & Mohr, 2000). Still, an expanding proportion of studies show that it is only through changes in daily practices that decisive improvements can be expected (Ekman et al., 2007; Nelson et al., 2007).

Previous research has exemplified many different roles that the users of healthcare services can play in a more sustainable "patient-centered" system. Greenhalgh et al. (2010) provide the following examples:

1) Co-designer—the user actively participates in the development of care services;
2) Co-producer—the users themselves take responsibility for parts of their own care, perhaps in conjunction with patient-owned insurers such as Group Health in the USA and, nominally, some of the German sick funds;
3) Co-leadership and mutual learning—the user gets involved in leadership activities, actively taking part in evaluating the quality of the provided care as well as getting involved in the education and training of healthcare personnel.

Healthcare innovations have been developed by inspiration from design thinking, human-centered design, and service research. Drawing from these approaches, improvements in the patients' healthcare journey should primarily be based on listening to the experiences that patients, their next of kin and healthcare professionals have of the care that has actually been provided. One such model for user involvement is experience-based co-design (Bate & Robert, 2006). By focusing on user capabilities, it will also connect user involvement with how we can design appropriate organizational innovations for improving the healthcare system on different system levels.

CONCLUSION

In this chapter, we have shown that the discourse of *Sustainability* has become increasingly prevalent in healthcare. However, a closer examination has revealed that the concept is both complex and contested. Two quite distinct ideas about *Sustainability* are discernible, namely those that see the term as lasting change, and those that see it as system equilibrium. In order to move the field forward, we have proposed a model that fruitfully combines both views into a single conceptualization that sees a sustainable health system as consisting of both sustainable production processes/practices that are new and durable and sustainable outcomes defined by a quadruple bottom line that seeks effective outcomes for people, prosperity, planet and patient. Our discussion has been largely conceptual and tentative, and the model we have proposed requires considerable empirical exploration and development. For example, it asks what types of factors help or prevent healthcare organizations from achieving the quadruple bottom line objectives. It also begs the question of whether and how the components of the quadruple bottom line are mutually compatible in practice.

We believe that the emphasis in tomorrow's healthcare should be on the system's overall ability, competence and availability, rather than on the separate healthcare professions. Better health for all requires balancing expectations, needs and resources, both from a national and global perspective. Healthcare professionals have a responsibility to contribute to the healthcare system's priorities and put them in a larger context that includes global threats to health. A guiding principle in medical ethics is, "First do no harm", something that may be given a wider meaning in the context of sustainable healthcare. That healthcare is supposed to cure people and make them well is a fact that unfortunately does not always work in practice when the healthcare sector accounts for a significant environmental impact, which ultimately impacts negatively on human health.

To conclude, there is undoubtedly an increasingly influential discourse on sustainable healthcare, and diverse stakeholders are increasingly calling for actions and redesigns of healthcare systems in order to make them sustainable. However, a recent review of health performance frameworks showed that *Sustainability* was one of the least common performance dimensions (Arah et al., 2006). Nevertheless, we believe that the notion does have practical relevance in debates on the future of healthcare. It challenges politicians and healthcare leaders to think through the implications of our decisions from economic, societal and environmental perspectives, since it links health values with *Sustainability* drivers and in this sense has potential impact as a discourse beyond the immediate locus of healthcare itself. On the other hand, many of the ideas on *Sustainability* to date remain rather abstract. Accordingly, while we certainly see *Sustainability* as an overarching set of ideas for innovation that are undeniably adaptable to healthcare settings, such ideas are best seen as tools for animating dialogue in innovation processes rather than as concrete, off-the-peg practices for roll-out by healthcare professionals and managers.

NOTES

1   As we shall see, however, the concept of *Sustainability* is complex and contested (Faber et al., 2005).
2   Social bearability implies social behavior that is compatible with a sustainable environment.
3   This definition has emerged from discussions within an ongoing international network of researchers and healthcare practitioners for learning and knowledge sharing on the topic of sustainable healthcare.
4   This, of course, takes two different forms—the balance depending on the type of health system. In the USA especially (but also Germany and Switzerland to some degree), corporations provide the more profitable types of healthcare,

hence accumulating capital directly from healthcare. However, policy makers often see public spending on healthcare as a "cost" for business, and hence have indirectly supported capital accumulation outside the health sector by controlling these "costs".

REFERENCES

Abbott, A. (1988). *The System of Professions: An Essay on the Expert Division of Labour*. Chicago, IL: Chicago University Press.

Abernathy, W.J. (1978). *The Productivity Dilemma*. Baltimore, MD: Johns Hopkins University Press.

Adams, W.M. (2006). *The future of sustainability: Re-thinking environment and development in the twenty-first century*. IUCN The World Conservation Union. Report of the IUCN Renowned Thinkers Meeting, 29–31 January 2006.

Arah, O.A., Westert, G.P., Hurst, J., & Klazinga, N.S. (2006). A conceptual framework for the OECD health care quality indicators project. *International Journal for Quality in Health Care*, 18 (S1), 5–13.

Armburster, R., Begun, J., & Alan, D. (2009). An in-house learning laboratory for patient-centered innovation. *Journal for Healthcare Quality*, 31 (1), 10–17.

Bate, P., & Robert, G. (2006). Experience-based design: From redesigning the system around the patient to co-designing services with the patient', *Quality and Safety in Healthcare*, 15 (5), 307–310.

Beer, M., & Nohria, N. (2000). Cracking the code of change. *Harvard Business Review*, 78 (3), 133–141.

Berwick, D.M. (2008). The science of improvement. *JAMA: The Journal of the American Medical Association*, 299 (10), 1182–1184.

Blackburn, W.R. (2007). *The Sustainability Handbook*. London: Earthscan.

Bohmer, R.M.J. (2010). Fixing health care on the front lines. *Harvard Business Review*, 88 (4), 62–69.

Brundtland, G. (1987). *Our Common Future: The World Commission on Environment and Development*. Oxford, England: Oxford University Press.

Buchanan, D., Fitzgerald, L., Ketley, D., Gollop, R., Jones, J.L., Saint Lamont, S., Neath, A., & Whitby, E. (2005). No going back: A review of the literature on sustaining organizational change. *International Journal of Management Reviews*, 7 (3), 189–205.

Bushe, G.R., & Marshak, R. (2009). Revisioning organization development: Diagnostic and dialogic premises and patterns of practice. *Journal of Applied Behavioral Science*, 45 (3), 348–368.

Christensen, C.M. (1998). *The Innovator's Dilemma: When New Technologies Cause Great Firms to Fail*. Boston, MA: Harvard Business School Press.

Cooperrider, D.L., & Srivastva, S. (1987). Appreciative enquiry in organizational life. In W.A. Pasmore & R.W. Woodman (Eds.), *Research in Organizational Change and Development* (Vol. 1). Greenwich, CT: JAI Press, pp. 129–169.

Corso M., & Gastaldi, L. (2010). *Managing ICT-driven innovations to overcome the exploitation-exploration: A collaborative research methodology in the Italian health care industry 11th intern*. Paper presented at the CINet Conference: Practicing Innovation in Times of Discontinuity, Zürich (CH), September 5–7.

Crossan M.M., Lane, H.W., & White, R.E (1999). An organizational learning framework: From intuition to institution. *Academy of Management Review*, 24 (3), 522–537.

Dahlgren, G., & Whitehead, M. (2007). *Policies and Strategies to Promote Social Equity in Health*. Stockholm: Institutet för framtidsstudier. Arbetsrapport 2007:14.

Docherty, P., Forslin, J., & Shani, A.B. (Eds.) (2002). *Creating Sustainable Work Systems: Emerging Perspectives and Practice*. London: Routledge.

Docherty, P., Kira, M., & Shani, A.B. (Eds.) (2009). Creating Sustainable Work Systems: Developing Social Sustainability (2nd ed.). London: Routledge.

Donaldson, M.S., & Mohr, J. (2000). *Exploring innovation and quality improvement in health care micro-systems: A cross-case analysis*. A Technical Report for the Institute of Medicine Committee on the Quality of Health Care in America, Institute of Medicine, Washington DC.

Ekman Philips, M., Ahlberg, B.M., & Huzzard, T. (2004). Planning from without or developing from within? Collaboration across the frontiers of health care. In W. Fricke & P. Totterdill (Eds.), *Regional Development Processes as the Context for Action Research*. Amsterdam: John Benjamin, pp. 103–126.

Ekman Philips, M., Ahlberg, B., Huzzard, T., & Ek, E. (2007). *Innovationer i Vårdens Vardag: De Små Stegens Väg till Förändring*. Lund, Sweden: Studentlitteratur.

Elkington, J. (1997). *Cannibals with Forks*. Oxford, England: Capstone.

Epstein, M.J. (2008). *Making Sustainability Work: Best Practices in Managing and Measuring Corporate, Social, Environmental and Economic Impacts*. San Francisco, CA: Greenleaf and Berret-Koehler.

Faber, N.R., Jorna, R.J., & van Engelen, J.M.L. (2005). The sustainability of "sustainabil-ity": A study into the conceptual foundations of the notion of "sustainability". *Journal of Environmental Assessment Policy and Management*, 7 (1), 1–33.

Gibson, C.B., & Birkinshaw, J. (2004). The antecedents, consequences, and mediating: Role of organizational ambidexterity. *Academy of Management Journal*, 47 (2), 209–226.

Glouberman, S., & Mintzberg, H. (2001a). Managing the care of health and the cure of disease—part I: Differentiation. *Health Care Management Review*, 26 (1), 56–69.

Glouberman, S., & Mintzberg, H. (2001b). Managing the care of health and the cure of disease—part II: Integration. *Health Care Management Review*, 26 (1), 69–84.

Greenhalgh, T., Humphrey, C., & Woodard, F. (2010). *User Involvement in Health Care*. Chichester, UK: Wiley-Blackwell Publishing.

Greenhalgh, T., MacFarlane, F., Barton-Sweeney, C., & Woodard, F. (2012). If we build it, will it stay? A case study of whole-system change in London. *The Millbank Quarterly*, 90 (3), 516–547.

Health Care Without Harm. (2015). Retrieved from www.noharm-global.org (accessed 8 June 2015).

Higuchi, K.S., Downey, A., Davies, B., Bajnok, I., & Waggott, M. (2012). Using the NHS sustainability framework to understand the activities and resource implications of Canadian nursing guideline early adopters. *Journal of Clinical Nursing*, 22 (11–12), 1707–1716.

Hughes, I. (2008). Action research in healthcare. In P. Reason & H. Bradbury (Eds.), *The Sage Handbook of Action Research: Participative Enquiry and Practice* (2nd ed.). London: Sage, pp. 381–393.

Huzzard, T., Hellström, A., Lifvergren, S., & Conradi, N. (2014). A physician-led, and learning driven approach to regional development of 23 cancer pathways in Sweden. In S.A. Mohrman & A.B. Shani (Eds.), *Reconfiguring the Eco-System for Sustainable Healthcare*. Bingley, England: Emerald, pp. 101–132.Institute of Medicine. (2001). *Crossing the Quality Chasm: A New Health Care System for the 21st Century*. Washington, DC: National Academy Press.

Jeanneret, Y. (2008). The epistemic jumble of sustainable development. In D. Cheng, M. Claessens, N.R.J. Gascoigne, J. Metcalfe, B. Schiele & S. Shi (Eds),

Communicating Science in Social Contexts: New Models, New Practices, Courtesy of the European Commission: Springer Science/Business Media B.V, pp. 243–257.

Kira, M., & Lifvergren, S. (2013). Sowing seeds for sustainability in work systems. In I. Ehnert, W. Harry & K.J. Zink (Eds.), *Sustainability and Human Resource Management: Developing Sustainable Business Organizations*. Heidelberg: Springer, pp. 57–82.

Kira, M., & van Eijnatten, F.M. (2009). Sustained by work: Individual and social sustainability in work organizations. In P. Docherty, M. Kira, & A.B. Shani (Eds.), Creating Sustainable Work Systems: Developing Social Sustainability. London: Routledge, pp. 233–246.

Laszlo, C. (2008). *Sustainable Value: How the World's Leading Companies are Doing Well by Doing Good*. Stanford, CA: Stanford University Press.

Lazonick, W., & O'Sullivan, M. (2000). Maximizing shareholder value: A new ideology for corporate governance. *Economy and Society*, 29 (1), 13–35.

Lifvergren, S., Huzzard, T., & Docherty, P. (2009). A development coalition for sustainability in health care. In P. Docherty, M. Kira, & A.B. Shani (Eds.), Creating Sustainable Work Systems: Developing Social Sustainability. London: Routledge, pp. 167–185.

Lifvergren, S., Huzzard, T., & Hellström, A. (2015). After a decade of action research: Impactful systems improvement in Swedish healthcare. In H. Bradbury (Ed.), *The Sage Handbook of Action Research* (3rd ed.). London: Sage.

Maher, L., Gustafson, D., & Evans, A. (2010). *Sustainability Model for Innovation and Improvement*. Coventry, England: NHS Institute for Innovation and Improvement.

Marvasti, F., & Stafford, R. (2012). From sick care to health care: Reengineering prevention into the U.S. System. *The New England Journal of Medicine*, 367 (10), 889–891.

Mohrman, S.A., & Shani, A.B. (2011). Organizing for sustainable effectiveness: Taking stock and moving forward. In A.B. Shani & S.A. Mohrman (Eds.), *Organizing for Sustainability*. Bingley, England: Emerald, pp. 1–40.

Mohrman, S.A., Shani, A.B., & McCracken, A. (2012a). Organizing for sustainable health care: The emerging global challenge. In A.B. Shani & S.A. Mohrman (Eds.), *Organizing for Sustainable Health Care* (Vol. 2). Bingley, England: Emerald, pp. 1–40.

Mohrman, S.A., Shani, A.B., & Worley, C. (2012b). Organizing for sustainable health care: Introduction to volume 2. In A.B. Shani & S.A. Mohrman (Eds.), *Organizing for Sustainable Health Care* (Vol. 2). Bingley, England: Emerald, pp. xi–xiv.

Nelson, E.C., Batalden, P.B., & Godfrey, M.M. (2007). *Quality by Design: A Clinical Microsystems Approach*. San Francisco, CA: Jossey Bass.

Nelson, E., Batalden, P., Huber, T., Mohr, J., Godfrey, M., Headrick, L., & Wasson, J. (2002). Microsystems in health care: Part 1. Learning from high-performing front-line clinical units. *The Joint Commission Journal on Quality and Patient Safety*, 28 (9), 472–493.

OECD. (2010), *Health Care Systems: Efficiency and Policy Settings*. Paris: OECD. Retrieved from http://dx.doi.org/10.1787/9789264094901-en (accessed 29 January 2015).

Øvretveit, J. (2011). Implementing, spreading and sustaining quality improvement. In S. Berman (Ed.), *From Front Office to Front Line: Essential Issues for Health Care Leaders*. Oak Brooke, IL: Joint Commission Resources, pp. 159–176.

Roman, M. (2009). Labelling and sustainability: The case of speciality coffee. In P. Docherty, M. Kira, & A.B. Shani (Eds.), Creating Sustainable Work Systems: Developing Social Sustainability. London: Routledge, pp. 202–216.

Scheirer, M.A., & Dearing, J.W. (2011). An agenda for research on the sustainability outcomes of health programs. *American Journal of Public Health*, **101** (11), 2059–2067.

Schumacher, E.F. (1973). *Small Is Beautiful: A Study of Economics As If People Mattered*. London: Blond & Briggs.

Smith, P.A.C., & Scharicz, C. (2011). The shift needed for sustainability. *The Learning Organization*, **18** (1), 73–86.

Stewart, M. (2001). Towards a global definition of patient centred care. *British Medical Journal*, **322** (7284), 444–445.

Swedish Ministry of Finance. (2005). *Iaktagelser om landsting*. (in Swedish) DS 2005:7, Stockholm, Finansdepartementet, Regeringskansliet.

Turley, M., Porter, C., Garrido, T., Gerwig, K., Young, S., Radler, L., & Shaber, R. (2011). Use of electronic health records can improve the health care industry's environmental footprint. *Health Affairs*, **30** (5), 938–946.

Tushman, M.L., & O'Reilly, C.A. (1996). Ambidextrous organizations: Managing evolutionary and revolutionary change. *California Management Review*, **38** (4), 8–30.

Tushman, M.L., & O'Reilly, C.A. (1997). *Winning through Innovation*. Boston, MA: Harvard Business School Press.

Wals, A.E.J., & Schwarzin, L. (2012). Fostering organizational sustainability through dialogic interaction. *The Learning Organization*, **19** (1), 11–27.

WHO. (1998). *The World Health Report 1998—Life in the 21st Century: A Vision for All*. Geneva: World Health Organization.

Wikipedia. (2015). Retrieved from https://en.wikipedia.org/?title=Sustainability (accessed 26 June 2015).

Worley, C. (2012). Organizing for agile and sustainable health care: The alegent health case. In S.A. Mohrman & A.B. Shani (Eds.), *Organizing for Sustainable Health Care*. Bingley, England: Emerald, pp. 41–75.

Yang, A., Farmer, P.E., & McGahan, A.M. (2010). "Sustainability" in global health. *Global Public Health*, **5** (2), 129–135.

21 Teamwork in Healthcare Organizations[1]

Jan Schmutz, Annalena Welp and Michaela Kolbe

In 2014, the most widespread epidemic of the Ebola virus in history was ongoing in several West African countries (Team, 2014). Ebola is an infectious and highly lethal virus. Although a widespread dissemination in other continents was unlikely (Frieden et al., 2014), healthcare organizations needed to prepare for the worst. In this sudden crisis emerging within only a few weeks, hospitals managed to build or rebuild entire units to be prepared for possible Ebola patients. Ebola isolation units include separate rooms for putting on and taking off protective equipment, pressure rooms and specialized laboratories for blood examination. Quickly building Ebola isolation units in hospitals is only possible via flawless cooperation and coordination among specialists in the field.

Teamwork, like in the Ebola management example, includes experts from different domains with different backgrounds coming together and acting in a coordinated manner towards a common goal. Architects design the rooms in collaboration with physicians and nurses in mind, infection control specialists outline the safety procedures for putting on safety clothing and taking it off and organize—with training specialists—training to prevent the contamination and infection of staff, and paramedics prepare the transportation of an Ebola patient to the unit. The communication department prepares the communication of a potential emergency within and outside the hospital, and the hospital management supervises the whole process, ensuring that it meets local and national regulations.

Such Ebola management arrangements can only be achieved with outstanding *Teamwork*. A group of experts with different backgrounds comes together, shares their experience and coordinates their actions to achieve the shared goal: Being ready for an Ebola emergency. But what mechanisms or processes are critical for good *Teamwork*, and how is *Teamwork* defined? What is the particular importance of effective *Teamwork* in healthcare? This chapter will address these questions in three parts. First, we will provide an overview about *Teamwork* concepts in the management literature. We will apply these concepts to healthcare—with a focus on acute care—and expand them to fit the specific characteristics of healthcare teams. We will have a special focus on *learning* as an important team process. In the second part, we will discuss the specific challenges (i.e., context, structure and learning challenges) of teams working in a healthcare setting compared to traditional teams in companies (e.g., project teams). Finally, in the third part, we provide recommendations (i.e., debriefings) to improve *Teamwork* in healthcare organizations (HCOs) and describe how existing theoretical models need to be adapted to fit the needs of teams in HCOs.

BACKGROUND

Originally, the study of groups was predominantly located in social psychology, with researchers investigating phenomena like de-individuation in groups (Diener et al., 1976), conformity to the majority opinion within a group (Asch, 1955) and groupthink (Janis, 1972). When Levine and Moreland (1990) later reviewed team research, they concluded that "teams are alive, but living elsewhere" (p. 620). What they meant was that research about teams had begun to decline in the field of social psychology, but was increasing in journals devoted to management and industrial and organizational psychology due to the fact that working in teams got more and more relevant in different industries. Authors started to differentiate between groups and teams, using the term "team" specifically for a group in a work context (e.g., project teams, surgical teams). Salas et al. (2007) defined teams as identifiable work units consisting of two or more people with several characteristics, including dynamic social interactions, with meaningful interdependencies, valued and shared goals, a particular lifespan, distributed expertise and clearly assigned roles and responsibilities. The team can be seen as a complex, adaptive and dynamic system (Arrow et al., 2000).

Guzzo and Shea (1992) use the metaphor of a cloud to illustrate the dynamics within a team as well as how it interacts with its environment. This idea is based on a discussion about social systems by Popper (1972), who distinguishes between systems that function like clockwork and systems that function like clouds. Unlike clockwork, which is regular and rigid, clouds change form and size and are strongly affected by environmental conditions. It is almost impossible to predict precisely the movements of the molecules in a cloud. Guzzo and Shea (1992) argue that work teams are similar to clouds: Although they have some regularity, like clouds, they are disorderly and highly responsive to environmental influences. Thus, knowledge of one individual does not give us an understanding of the entire group, and the behavior of one group member only tenuously predicts the behavior of others. Furthermore, the behavior of a team is not regular and predictable like clockwork; rather, variation is the norm.

TEAMWORK MODELS

One of the most-cited models of *Teamwork* in the management literature is the temporally based framework and taxonomy of team processes[2] from Marks et al. (2001). They distinguish between *Teamwork* and taskwork. Taskwork is defined as the teams' interaction with tasks, tools, machines and systems. *Teamwork*, or a *Teamwork Process*, is described as interdependent team activities that orchestrate taskwork in the employees' pursuit of goals (Bowers et al., 1997; Marks et al., 2001). The model is based on the classic Input-Process-Output (IPO) model (McGrath, 1984).

Input typically refers to the things team members bring to the group, including status, personality attributes, level of experience, demographic attributes and others. These inputs are often referred to as team characteristics. Other inputs are the characteristics of the task, like the type of task (e.g., routine vs. non-routine) or the resources a specific task brings with it (Guzzo & Shea, 1992). The *process* or *Teamwork* refers to the interactions among team members that transform inputs into outputs (e.g., exchange of information, distribution of tasks). Finally, *output* refers to the product resulting from the team's work. This product can include ideas, decisions, a finished project or the successful treatment of a patient, but also includes the well-being of the team members. Coming back to the Ebola case, examples for *inputs* are the different areas of expertise, such as architecture or infectiology, resources such as space, time and money and individual attributes, such as communication styles. *Processes* include communication, such as ensuring that team members have a shared understanding about the goal, distribution of expertise within the team (who knows what?) and clarification of roles (who is responsible for what?). Processes also include the coordination of tasks, such as giving orders or delegating subtasks to team members. *Outputs* are a fully equipped Ebola isolation unit, including a specialized ward team, but also team member satisfaction and acquisition of new skills after working on the Ebola task force.

Team Performance Episodes and Action and Transition Phases

More recent adaptations of the IPO model emphasize the dynamic nature of teams (Hackman, 1987; Ilgen et al., 2005; Marks et al., 2001; Morgeson et al., 2010), proposing that a team passes through *episodes* in which IPO cycles run sequentially and simultaneously and in which each output serves as input for the next cycles (Figure 21.1). Episodes can be identified by goals and goal accomplishment. Over time, team performance is best seen as a series of IPO cycles attached to these episodes rather than one IPO sequence constituting a team's life cycle. Episodes consist of two consecutive *phases* that are passed through by the team until the goal is reached: The action phase, during which teams engage in acts that contribute to accomplishing

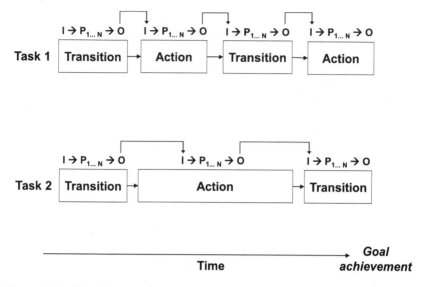

Figure 21.1   Two Team Performance Episodes, Including IPO Cycles of Two Different Tasks Based on McGrath (1984) and Marks et al. (2001).

a goal, and the transition phase, during which teams primarily focus on evaluating and/or planning activities.

The duration of every episode varies and is defined by the nature of the task, the technology and the manner in which the members choose to complete the work. Depending on the episode, a team performs different kinds of teamwork processes. Figure 21.1 illustrates the dynamic nature of team task achievement and describes two episodes of two different tasks. Task 1 describes a fast episode with cyclical transition and action phases (e.g., several inductions of general anesthesia followed by short debriefings with the resident, or repeated simulations of putting protective clothing on and taking it off within a team with respective team briefings and debriefings). Task 2 consists of just one, much longer action phase until the task is completed (e.g., a short briefing, long surgical operation, short debriefing; or planning, building and evaluation of the furnishings of an Ebola treatment room).

The time component in Figure 21.1 needs to be interpreted as much shorter for teams in an acute care HCO than for teams in other healthcare settings. As teams in acute care are often more short-lived than in other organizations, performance episodes are shorter as well. For teams managing long-term illness, episodes might be longer. However, team episodes in healthcare tend to be generally shorter than in other industries: The project team in a software company might work on one project (task) over several weeks until it is completed, whereas teams in an HCO often work together in the same composition only for a few hours—the duration of a shift or an operation.

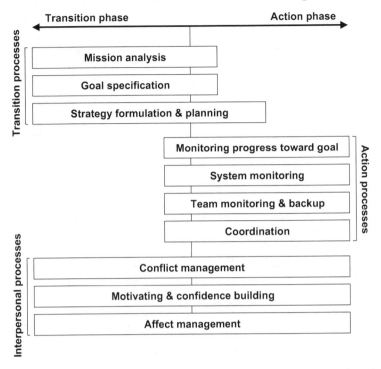

Figure 21.2 Teamwork Processes That Can Occur in Transition and/or Action Phases (Marks et al., 2001)

The *processes* during an action or a transition phase change as teams move back and forth between these two phases. Marks et al. (2001) define three types of *Teamwork* processes that can occur within an action and/or a transition phase: Transition processes, action processes and interpersonal processes. Figure 21.2 provides an overview of specific *Teamwork* processes that can either occur in an action or transition phase or both. The processes are derived from the literature (Marks et al., 2001), but Figure 21.2 does not claim to be exhaustive.

Teamwork Processes

Transition processes occur most likely but not exclusively in transition phases aiming at understanding the larger work environment, developing appropriate strategies and plans to deal with the task and specifying goals. The transition processes investigated in the literature include mission analysis formulation and planning (Prince & Salas, 1993), goal specification (DeShon et al., 2004; Pearsall & Venkataramani, 2014) and strategy formulation (Cannon-Bowers et al., 1995).

Action processes include the monitoring of progress (Cannon-Bowers et al., 1995), system monitoring (Fleishman & Zaccaro, 1992), team monitoring and backup behavior (Kolbe et al., 2014; Salas et al., 2005) and coordination (Fernandez Castelao et al., 2013; Rico et al., 2008). In the action phase, a team is engaged in the acts that contribute directly to goal accomplishment (i.e., the taskwork). The nature of these acts is defined by team and task type. Due to the dependence of *Teamwork* processes on task as well as on team characteristics, there is no general action process that ensures effective *Teamwork* in all kind of teams. A software team is developing new software and an acute care team is providing immediate treatment to a patient. However the literature does provide strong evidence that certain processes are highly linked with the performance of teams in healthcare organizations (Fernandez Castelao et al., 2013; Schmutz & Manser, 2013).

Interpersonal processes occur in transition phases and action phases alike and typically lay the foundation for the effectiveness of other processes. The purpose of these processes is to govern interpersonal activities, and these processes include conflict management, motivation and confidence building and affect management within the team. For instance, conflict may occur and needs to be managed if team members have different expectations about how a specific problem needs to be solved. Unsolved conflicts can have a negative effect on other team processes (e.g., communication) and thus can result in errors (Baldwin & Daugherty, 2008).

LEARNING AS A TEAMWORK PROCESS

As we outline in more detail below, many teams in healthcare do not follow traditional team structures: They are dynamic, nested in dynamic, multi-team systems, with members being part of multiple teams (Edmondson, 2012; Ishak & Ballard, 2011; Tannenbaum et al., 2012). Consequently, their team processes must allow for *teaming*, that is, quickly setting the stage for working well in any team (Edmondson, 2012). A fundamental process of teaming is *reflection*, that is, the explicit discussion of processes based on observation, allowing for team learning (Argyris & Schön, 1974; Edmondson, 2012). The integration of reflection into the current theoretical models of teamwork is just beginning to occur. Related processes such as providing feedback and training have only recently been integrated into models of team transition phases (Morgeson et al., 2010). We propose that *learning*—the acquisition or modification of knowledge, skills and attitudes—should be added as the fourth type of *Teamwork* processes contributing to overall team effectiveness. *Learning* includes observation, feedback and reflection (Gabelica et al., 2012; Gabelica, et al., 2014; Gurtner et al., 2007; West, 2004). Learning through observation can occur in the action phase by observing own as well as other team members' actions and the performance outcomes. This is the basis for feedback, which can occur in the action phase (e.g., an experienced physician provides feedback on the performance of a specific procedure) as well as during the transition phase (e.g., giving feedback on performing a certain surgical operation). Reflection can take place during the action phase (e.g., taking a 10-second time-out during an emergency procedure; Rall et al., 2008) as well as during the transition phase (e.g., holding a structured team debriefing after a resuscitation). We propose that team learning via observation, feedback and regular reflection allows teams in HCOs to face their particular challenges and to transfer knowledge, skills and attitudes across team boundaries. For example, an authoritative member of the Ebola management team may *observe* communication styles used by fellow team members and thus adapt a less authoritarian communication style that results in more effective team processes. She might also receive *feedback* on her own communication style. This may cause her to *reflect* on her role within the Ebola management and other teams, thereby changing the interpersonal processes, which form the foundation of action and transition processes. Team members learning the correct use of protective Ebola equipment may first *observe*, then receive immediate *feedback*—for instance, after a particularly good performance—during the procedure or via a debriefing afterwards. This may cause them to *reflect* on hygiene behaviors within their regular ward and to point out potential infection risks to fellow team members. A resident may be more successful at dealing with unforeseeable circumstances in a newly composed team after having observed a senior surgeon or received feedback himself.

In this section, we have introduced the concept of *Teamwork* as a dynamic phenomenon consisting of episodes, phases (action and transition) and *Teamwork* processes (action, transition, interpersonal and learning processes). In the next section, we will highlight the specifics of HCOs with respect to the importance of *Teamwork* and learning as a special team process.

CHALLENGES OF TEAMS WORKING IN HCOS

Teamwork occurs everywhere in healthcare organizations: Operating room teams performing surgical procedures, acute care teams treating critically ill patients, nurses and physicians working together in daily ward rounds. The administrative and housekeeping staff members are organized in teams as well. Delivering healthcare is inherently based on *Teamwork*—it is impossible to provide quality care within the expertise of just one profession. This is especially true for the secondary and tertiary care settings, where surgeons, anesthetists, nurses, radiologists, physical therapists and many more specialists work together to improve the patient's health. Even in primary care, *Teamwork* is becoming increasingly important, with more physicians working in group practices and an aging population whose multi-morbidity requires clinicians of various specializations to work together. Thus, the question is not whether *Teamwork* has been adopted in healthcare organizations, but whether its potential is fully utilized and its possible downsides are being managed. In our view, the healthcare setting poses several challenges that set it apart from other industries and that might keep it from fully using the potential of *Teamwork* and team training.

Team Context Challenges

The realization that a "team of experts does not make an expert team" (Burke et al., 2004, p. i97), i.e., that medical skills and knowledge are not sufficient to provide quality care as a team and that *Teamwork* requires training and management, has been adopted in healthcare much later than in other high-risk organizations, such as aviation (Ramanujam & Rousseau, 2006). Even though healthcare workers agree that *Teamwork* is an integral part of their job, members of various healthcare professions differ in their perceptions of its quality (Flin et al., 2003; Sexton et al., 2001; Wauben et al., 2011). *Teamwork* skills are not sufficiently taught at medical and nursing schools. As a consequence, clinicians may underestimate the contribution of *Teamwork* to high-quality patient care (Pronovost, 2013). Even though healthcare workers work in a team, they may be unaware of negative team processes that are detrimental to the team's performance and may lack the skills and routine to perceive and change it. Related to this may be the fact that professional hierarchies and power differences—which are necessary and useful to complete urgent tasks—can manifest themselves at the interpersonal level in the form of a disrespectful, dismissive and disruptive atmosphere (Rosenstein & O'Daniel, 2005; Tjia et al., 2009). This notion is illustrated with concepts such as psychological safety, which is defined as the belief that a team is safe for interpersonal risk taking (Edmondson, 1999). It is the prerequisite of teaming processes such as *speaking up* when team members have safety concerns, and it is associated with increased clinical performance (Edmondson, 2004; Edmondson, 2012; Kolbe et al., 2012). Furthermore, team members working in teams with a positive interpersonal climate are less vulnerable to stress-induced outcomes such as burnout (Laposa et al., 2003; Sutinen et al., 2005; Van Bogaert et al., 2010). However, members of different healthcare professions disagree about the level of psychological safety depending on their status (Nembhard & Edmondson, 2006). Encouraging positive interpersonal team processes is important, as they form the foundation of action and transition *Teamwork* processes (Marks et al., 2001).

Team Structure Challenges

Teams in healthcare organizations are rather short-lived. In acute care, ad hoc action teams, which come together for a specific, time-constrained task such as resuscitation and then dissolve, are the predominant form of work organization. In ordinary wards, teams work together somewhat longer, but may also dissolve after the end of the shift. Although team members may be familiar with each other when they start working in a team, and may work together as a team in the future, they are nevertheless required to *team* in changing constellations (Edmondson, 2012; West & Lyubovnikova, 2013).

Multiple teams contribute to the healthcare of a single patient, and a single healthcare employee is a member of many different teams. This multiple team membership can occur simultaneously, such as being a member of a team of physicians and being a member of a team in a ward, or of an Ebola management team, or consecutively, such as being a member of successive trauma teams. Although multiple teams contributing to an overall goal exist in other industries as well, such as automobile building (Ramanujam & Rousseau, 2006), the situation in healthcare differs, because the environment is considered to be much less predictable than in other industries (Begun & Kaissi, 2004; Plsek & Greenhalgh, 2001).

The so-called continuum of care (Ramanujam & Rousseau, 2006), with multiple (short-lived) teams contributing to a global goal, highlights the importance of coordination between teams for transferring knowledge and the skills of individual team members as well as of providing high-quality healthcare. This does not only include inter-team coordination, but also coordination between several teams in one hospital, such as handovers during shift changes or from the recovery room to the ward as well as between different healthcare organizations, for instance, from the primary care physician to the secondary care hospital (Hesselink et al., 2012).

Team Learning Challenge

The fluid and temporally unstable team structure in acute care can pose a challenge for teams and management aiming to improve *Teamwork* because it is not clear how and to what extent the acquired skills can be transferred to a new team in a new situation. Team training based on the IPO model may be insufficient to account for the dynamic nature of teams in healthcare organizations. Several authors have argued that team learning, and, in turn, team performance, occurs through repetitive cycles of joint action and reflection of team members in the transition phase (Edmondson, 1999; Marks et al., 2001; Vashdi et al., 2013). These cycles help generate shared knowledge, such as team mental models (a shared understanding of how to perform a certain task (Mathieu et al., 2000) or transactive memory systems, which is the knowledge of the distribution of expertise across the team (Zhang et al., 2007). These processes function more efficiently in temporally (and interpersonally) stable teams, which may develop routines for repeatedly taking action and reflecting on the results (van der Vegt et al., 2010; Vashdi et al., 2013). Since many teams in HCOs are not temporally stable, their possibilities for joint reflections are limited.

In this section, we discussed the importance of teams in healthcare settings, the specific challenges they face and the importance of learning to ensure team effectiveness. As we outline below, team debriefings, also called after-action reviews, can provide a suitable learning infrastructure for teams in HCOs.

RECOMMENDATIONS FOR ENHANCING TEAM LEARNING IN HCOS

Due to the particular challenges facing HCO teams (outlined above) and the focus on production pressure in many HCOs (Hollnagel, 2014), learning from success and failure and identifying and closing factual performance gaps is difficult, but crucial. Without deliberate learning, failures cannot be reduced and problems are likely to be treated on a superficial, short-term basis rather in a long-term, sustainable fashion (Tucker & Edmondson, 2003). Team learning processes are rarely established and the usual team training approaches will not suffice due to the ad hoc nature of many HCO teams. To facilitate cross-team learning in temporally unstable teams, it could be helpful to widen (or narrow) the focus from the team to the individual. It may seem counterintuitive to switch from a team to an individual approach in order to facilitate team learning. The criticism can, however, be made that traditional team training—targeting stable teams—based on a singular input-process-output loop may not be realistic because of the underlying assumption that team members are able to transfer what they have learned within a stable team without repetition to a new team and situation (Vashdi et al., 2013). In fact, empirical evidence shows that the effectiveness of team training may be greatly reduced if the training is not carried out appropriately (McCulloch et al., 2011; Salas et al., 2008; Vashdi et al., 2013). To approach this transferability problem, Edmondson (1999) and Vashdi et al. (2013) argue that it might be feasible to switch and expand from a within-team to an across-team learning approach. This approach focuses on training each individual team member—ideally in the team setting—by giving them opportunities to reflect on their learning experiences and to learn how to quickly and efficiently engage in any team (Edmondson, 2012). To enable the individual to transfer these learning experiences to new teams and situations, they need to be tailored to the role the individual occupies within teams (i.e., not tied to personal behaviors), and they need to be numerous and consistent (Vashdi et al., 2013). In line with this is the adoption of the idea that team learning and team training is an ongoing process that should and can be integrated into the clinical routine. By doing so, the restriction of temporally unstable teams without repetitive reflective cycles can be overcome (Vashdi et al., 2013). This approach may seem time intensive; however, Vashdi et al. (2013) showed that team effectiveness could be increased through the transfer of knowledge of single team members from previous team learning experiences.

If we think back to the model previously described, this means that the IPO cycles and episodes of one team can influence the cycles and episodes of future teams through the learning process of individual team members instead of the entire team. For example, a resident may be involved in a major complication during a surgical procedure in team A. This experience may influence her work (as an input) in team B a few weeks later when a similar complication occurs.

TEAM DEBRIEFINGS AS A MEANS FOR TEAM LEARNING

The usefulness of team debriefings for team learning is being more and more recognized (Kolbe et al., 2013; Raemer et al., 2011; Rudolph et al., 2008; Salas et al., 2008; Tannenbaum & Cerasoli, 2013). Designed to promote learning from experience, debriefings are guided conversations that facilitate the understanding of the relationship among events, actions, thought and feeling processes and performance outcomes (Rudolph et al., 2007). They can provide a structure allowing for reflection and self-explanation, data verification and feedback, understanding the relationship between *Teamwork* and taskwork, uncovering and closing knowledge gaps and gaps in shared cognition, structured information sharing, goal setting and action planning, as well as changes in attitudes, motivation and self and collective efficacy, and for shifting from automatic/habitual to more conscious/deliberate information processing (DeRue et al., 2012; Eddy et al., 2013; Ellis & Davidi, 2005; Rudolph et al., 2007, 2008; Tannenbaum & Cerasoli, 2013; Tannenbaum & Goldhaber-Fiebert, 2013).

Being a conversation, they allow for double-loop learning because they rely on identifying and changing those mental models that have driven the action (Argyris, 1997; Rudolph et al., 2007). Analyzing the respective literature, Tannenbaum and Cerasoli (2013) found in a recent meta-analysis that debriefings improved performance by 20 to 25 percent on average. The actual use of debriefings in clinical practice is still sparse (Ahmed et al., 2013; Ahmed et al., 2012; Tannenbaum & Cerasoli, 2013); a debriefing culture still needs to be established in most HCOs and should be used in everyday practice to foster on-the-job learning. Debriefings require not only explicit initiation, but also a structure that has been thought through, because teams are not only reluctant to engage in reflection about *Teamwork* but would also—due to ineffective natural information processing tendencies—not talk about many "important issues" (e.g., talking about taskwork only instead of how task- and *Teamwork* contributed to each other) (Eddy et al., 2013, p. 4; Hackman & Morris, 1975).

With regard to the content of these debriefings, *Teamwork* should be addressed as early as possible, particularly with respect to the interaction patterns among team members and their meanings (Kolbe et al., 2013, 2014; Salas et al., 2008; Tannenbaum & Cerasoli, 2013) and the interplay of cognition, clinical and *Teamwork* behaviors, as well as the clinical and behavioral outcomes (Kolbe et al., 2013; Rudolph et al., 2008; Salas et al., 2008). That is, rather than focusing only on taskwork and action processes (e.g., coordination, monitoring, backup behavior), transition processes (e.g., planning, strategy formulation) as well as interpersonal processes (e.g., conflict management) should also be covered. In particular, reflecting on the individual team members' role behavior within the team and its importance for other teams should be part of the debriefing (Vashdi et al., 2013). Tannenbaum and Cerasoli (2013) define four essential elements for a successful debriefing: Active self-learning, developmental intent, specific events and multiple information sources. Active self-learning means that the participants engage in concrete experience and self-discovery and do not just passively receive feedback from a coach. This can be achieved by actively seeking the team members' points of view with respect to a concrete action (Rudolph et al., 2007). A debriefing should focus on learning and development, not on punishing, and should rather be based on reflection on specific events and performance episodes than on general performance or competencies. The success of a debriefing can be increased with the use of inputs from all team members or an external source such as an observer or video recording. It is helpful to explore both positive as well as negative performance outcomes (Smith-Jentsch et al., 2008).

CONCLUSION

Teams are the foundation on which medical knowledge, skills and attitudes are executed to perform healthcare tasks. Effective teamwork is therefore essential to provide safe, high-quality care (Pronovost, 2013). Knowledge of team processes is important for healthcare managers to provide structures that enable teams to function effectively.

In this chapter, we provided an overview of *Teamwork* concepts in the literature. The temporally based framework of Marks et al. (2001) provides a comprehensive definition of *Teamwork Processes* that can and should be adopted in research and practice. However, the framework does not explicitly address the specific challenges that most teams in HCOs face. Ad hoc teams, which come together just for a specific task and then dissolve, are the predominant form. This fact and the possibility for teams in HCOs to influence, through individual learning, future episodes in teams with a different team constellation needs to be integrated into the model. provides an adapted version of the Marks et al. (2001) representation of episodes and phases, including different team constellations (teams A and B) and the transfer of previous team outputs that can influence future team processes and outputs through individual learning (dashed arrow in Figure 21.3).

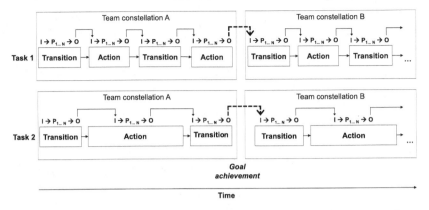

Figure 21.3 Adapted Representation of Episodes and Action and Transition Phases, Including Different Team Constellations

As *Teamwork Processes* are highly dependent on task and team characteristics, there is no generally valid panacea of *Teamwork* that is effective for every team. Research provides some overarching concepts (e.g., shared mental models, backup behavior) that ensure good *Teamwork* (Salas et al., 2005), but when it comes to specific processes in the team, this cannot be addressed without a basic understanding of the task characteristics as well as the team conditions (Schmutz et al., 2015). Explicit coordination might be effective in a team that comes together for the first time, but a team that has worked together many times before might be more effective, coordinating implicitly in the exact same situation due to a shared understanding of how to perform the task together (Burtscher & Manser, 2012).

The question is not whether *Teamwork* has been adopted in HCOs, but if its potential is fully utilized. We state in this chapter that to date, the possibilities of teams in HCOs have not yet been fully taken advantage of due to the specific challenges that teams in healthcare organizations face, especially in acute care. To overcome these challenges, we suggest *learning* (i.e., observation, feedback and reflection) as an important fourth process dimension that facilitates good *Teamwork* and the transfer of knowledge and skills across healthcare teams (Figure 21.4). Future studies as well as *Teamwork* training should pay more attention to learning processes like observation, feedback and reflection. Stimulating learning with debriefings is most likely useful in everyday practice; only via learning can team members develop good *Teamwork* skills and create safer environments for the patients.

Of course, *learning* is an important process for teams in all industries, and teams vary across different healthcare settings, but the described challenges of teams in HCOs make it more difficult for them to explicitly focus on the *learning* process, and imply other strategies than in other teams. HCOs are challenged to maintain a balance of high performance and safety standards,

Figure 21.4 Teamwork Processes, Including *Learning Processes* as a Fourth Dimension

adhering to policies and protocols while allowing teams enough leverage to respond to often swiftly changing circumstances (Amalberti et al., 2006). Learning may provide teams with the necessary resources to respond to unexpected events while maintaining safe practice.

Concluding with the Ebola case: In a very short time period, experts came together and formed teams and sub-teams to achieve a common goal, i.e., building a fully operational ward to treat Ebola patients. The overarching process of building the ward was influenced by inputs such as the knowledge and experiences of every team member, regulation of the hospital and government, state-of-the-art guidelines on how to treat an Ebola patient and many more. The success of this project (episode) was only possible with an alternating course of transition and action phases. A regular meeting of the key actors in a specific field (e.g., laboratory, patient environment, prehospital care) for aligning actions and reflecting about the process was indispensable for success. These transition episodes were used not only to coordinate actions, but also to reflect on the *Teamwork* process per se, especially when there were setbacks in the process. This structure made *learning* possible, and every individual as well as the team as a whole gained valuable knowledge and skills for how to deal with such a crisis, which will help to manage future crises.

NOTES

1 Correspondence about this book chapter should be addressed to Jan Schmutz, Department of Management, Technology, and Economics, ETH Zurich, Weinbergstr. 56/58, 8092 Zurich, Switzerland, jschmutz@ethz.ch, Telephone: +41 44 632 78 40.
2 Teamwork, teamwork processes and team processes are used interchangeably.

REFERENCES

Ahmed, M., Arora, S., Russ, S., Darzi, A., Vincent, C., & Sevdalis, N. (2013). Operation debrief: A SHARP improvement in performance feedback in the operating room. *Annals of surgery*, **258** (6), 958–963.

Ahmed, M., Sevdalis, N., Paige, J., Paragi-Gururaja, R., Nestel, D., & Arora, S. (2012). Identifying best practice guidelines for debriefing in surgery: A tri-continental study. *The American Journal of Surgery*, **203** (4), 523–529.

Amalberti, R., Vincent, C., Auroy, Y., & de Saint Maurice, G. (2006). Violations and migrations in health care: A framework for understanding and management. *Quality and Safety in Health Care*, 15 (S1), i66–i71.

Argyris, C. (1977). Double loop learning in organizations. *Harvard Business Review*, 55 (5), 115–125.

Argyris, C., & Schön, D. (1974). *Theory in Practice: Increasing Professional Effectiveness* (1st ed.). San Francisco, CA: Jossey-Bass.

Arrow, H., McGrath, J.E., & Berdahl, J.L. (2000). *Small Groups as Complex Systems: Formation, Coordination, Development, and Adaptation*. Thousand Oaks, CA: Sage.

Asch, S.E. (1955). Opinions and social pressure. *Scientific American*, **193**, 35–35.

Baldwin, D.C., Jr., & Daugherty, S.R. (2008). Interprofessional conflict and medical errors: Results of a national multi-specialty survey of hospital residents in the US. *Journal of Interprofessional Care*, **22** (6), 573–586.

Begun, J.W., & Kaissi, A.A. (2004). Uncertainty in health care environments: Myth or reality? *Health Care Management Review*, **29** (1), 31–39.

Bowers, C.A., Braun, C.C., & Morgan, B. (1997). Team workload: Its meaning and measurement. In M.T. Brannick, E. Salas, & C. Prince (Eds.), *Team Performance Assessment and Measurement: Theory, Methods, and Applications*. Mahwah, NJ: Lawrence Erlbaum, pp. 85–108.

Burke, C.S., Salas, E., Wilson-Donnelly, K., & Priest, H. (2004). How to turn a team of experts into an expert medical team: Guidance from the aviation and military communities. *Quality and Safety in Health Care*, 13 (S1), i96–i104.

Burtscher, M.J., & Manser, T. (2012). Team mental models and their potential to improve teamwork and safety: A review and implications for future research in healthcare. *Safety Science*, **50** (5), 1344–1354.

Cannon-Bowers, J.A., Tannenbaum, S.I., Salas, E., & Volpe, C.E. (1995). Defining competencies and establishing team training requirements. In R.A. Guzzo & E. Salas (Eds.), *Team Effectiveness and Decision Making in Organizations*. San Francisco, CA: Jossey-Bass, pp. 333–381.

DeRue, D.S., Nahrgang, J.D., Hollenbeck, J.R., & Workman, K. (2012). A quasi-experimental study of after-event reviews and leadership development. *Journal of Applied Psychology*, **97** (5), 997–1015.

DeShon, R.P., Kozlowski, S.W., Schmidt, A.M., Milner, K.R., & Wiechmann, D. (2004). A multiple-goal, multilevel model of feedback effects on the regulation of individual and team performance. *Journal of Applied Psychology*, **89** (6), 1035–1056.

Diener, E., Fraser, S.C., Beaman, A.L., & Kelem, R.T. (1976). Effects of deindividuation variables on stealing among Halloween trick-or-treaters. *Journal of Personality and Social Psychology*, **33** (2), 178–183.

Eddy, E.R., Tannenbaum, S.I., & Mathieu, J.E. (2013). Helping teams to help themselves: Comparing two team-led debriefing methods. *Personnel Psychology*, **66** (4), 975–1008.

Edmondson, A. (1999). Psychological safety and learning behavior in work teams. *Administrative Science Quarterly*, **44** (2), 350–383.

Edmondson, A.C. (2003). Speaking up in the operating room: How team leaders promote learning in interdisciplinary action teams. *Journal of Management Studies*, **40** (6), 1419–1452.

Edmondson, A.C. (2004). Learning from mistakes is easier said than done: Group and organizational influences on the detection and correction of human error. *Journal of Applied Behavioral Science*, **40** (1), 66–90.

Edmondson, A.C. (2012). *Teaming: How Organizations Learn, Innovate, and Compete in the Knowledge Economy*. San Francisco, CA: Jossey-Bass.

Ellis, S., & Davidi, I. (2005). After-event reviews: Drawing lessons from successful and failed experience. *Journal of Applied Psychology*, **90** (5), 857–871.

Fernandez Castelao, E., Russo, S.G., Riethmüller, M., & Boos, M. (2013). Effects of team coordination during cardiopulmonary resuscitation: A systematic review of the literature. *Journal of Critical Care*, **28** (4), 504–521.

Fleishman, E.A., & Zaccaro, S.J. (1992). Toward a taxonomy of team performance functions. In R.W. Swezey & E. Salas (Eds.), *Teams: Their Training and Performance*. Norwood, NJ: Ablex, pp. 31–56.

Flin, R., Fletcher, G., McGeorge, P., Sutherland, A., & Patey, R. (2003). Anaesthetists' attitudes to teamwork and safety. *Anaesthesia*, **58** (3), 233–242.

Frieden, T.R., Damon, I., Bell, B.P., Kenyon, T., & Nichol, S. (2014). Ebola 2014: New challenges, new global response and responsibility. *New England Journal of Medicine*, **371** (13), 1177–1180.

Gabelica, C., Van den Bossche, P., Segers, M., & Gijselaers, W. (2012). Feedback, a powerful lever in teams: A review. *Educational Research Review*, **7** (2), 123–144.

Gabelica, C., Van den Bossche, P., Segers, M., & Gijselaers, W. (2014). Dynamics of team reflexivity after feedback. *Frontline Learning Research*, **2** (3), 64–91.

Gurtner, A., Tschan, F., Semmer, N.K., & Naegele, C. (2007). Getting groups to develop good strategies: Effects of reflexivity interventions on team process, team performance, and shared mental models. *Organizational Behavior and Human Decision Processes*, **102** (2), 127–142.

Guzzo, R.A., & Shea, G.P. (1992). Group performance and intergroup relations in organizations. In M.D. Dunnette & L.M. Hough (Eds.), *Handbook of Industrial and Organizational Psychology* (Vol. 3). Palo Alto, CA: Consulting Psychology Press, pp. 269–313.

Hackman, J.R. (1987). The design of work teams. In J.W. Lorsch (Ed.), *Handbook of Organizational Behavior*. Englewood Cliffs, NJ: Prentice-Hall, pp. 315–342.

Hackman, J.R., & Morris, C.G. (1975). Group tasks, group interaction process, and group performance effectiveness: A review and proposed integration. In L. Berkowitz (Ed.), *Advances in Experimental Social Psychology* (Vol. 8). New York: Academic Press, pp. 45–99.

Hesselink, G., Schoonhoven, L., Barach, P., Spijker, A., Gademan, P., Kalkman, C., Liefers, J., Vernooij-Dassen, M., & Wollersheim, H. (2012). Improving patient handovers from hospital to primary care: A systematic review. *Annals of Internal Medicine*, **157** (6), 417–428.

Hollnagel, E. (2014). *Safety-I and Safety-II: The Past and Future of Safety Management*. Farnham, England: Ashgate.

Ilgen, D.R., Hollenbeck, J.R., Johnson, M., & Jundt, D. (2005). Teams in organizations: From input-process-output models to IMOI models. *Annual Review of Psychology*, **56**, 517–543.

Ishak, A.W., & Ballard, D.I. (2011). Time to re-group: A typology and nested phase model for action teams. *Small Group Research*, **43** (1), 3–27.

Janis, I.L. (1972). *Victims of Groupthink: A Psychological Study of Foreign-Policy Decisions and Fiascoes*. Boston, MA: Houghton Mifflin.

Kolbe, M., Burtscher, M.J., Wacker, J., Grande, B., Nohynkova, R., Manser, T., Spahn, D.R., & Grote, G. (2012). Speaking-up is related to better team performance in simulated anesthesia inductions: An observational study. *Anesthesia and Analgesia*, **115** (5), 1099–1108.

Kolbe, M., Grande, B., & Spahn, D.R. (2015). Briefing and debriefing during simulation-based training and beyond: Content, structure, attitude, and setting. *Best Practice & Research: Clinical Anaesthesiology*, **29** (1), 87–96.

Kolbe, M., Grote, G., Waller, M.J., Wacker, J., Grande, B., Burtscher, M.J., & Spahn, D.R. (2014). Monitoring and talking to the room: Autochthonous coordination patterns in team interaction and performance. *Journal of Applied Psychology*, **99** (6), 1254–1267.

Kolbe, M., Weiss, M., Grote, G., Knauth, A., Dambach, M., Spahn, D.R., & Grunde, B. (2013). TeamGAINS: A tool for structured debriefings for simulation-based team trainings. *BMJ Quality & Safety*, **22** (7), 541–553.

Laposa, J.M., Alden, L.E., & Fullerton, L.M. (2003). Work stress and posttraumatic stress disorder in ED nurses/personnel. *Journal of Emergency Nursing*, **29** (1), 23–28.

Levine, J.M., & Moreland, R.L. (1990). Progress in small group research. *Annual Review of Psychology*, **41** (1), 585–634.

Manser, T. (2009). Teamwork and patient safety in dynamic domains of healthcare: A review of the literature. *Acta Anaesthesiologica Scandinavica*, **53** (2), 143–151.

Marks, M.A., Mathieu, J.E., & Zaccaro, S.J. (2001). A temporally based framework and taxonomy of team processes. *The Academy of Management Review*, **26** (3), 356–376.

Mathieu, J.E., Heffner, T.S., Goodwin, G.F., Salas, E., & Cannon-Bowers, J.A. (2000). The influence of shared mental models on team process and performance. *Journal of Applied Psychology*, **85** (2), 273–283.

McCulloch, P., Rathbone, J., & Catchpole, K. (2011). Interventions to improve teamwork and communications among healthcare staff. *British Journal of Surgery*, **98** (4), 469–479.

McGrath, J.E. (1984). *Groups: Interaction and Performance* (Vol. 14). Englewood Cliffs, NJ: Prentice-Hall.

Morgeson, F.P., DeRue, D.S., & Karam, E.P. (2010). Leadership in teams: A functional approach to understanding leadership structures and processes. *Journal of Management*, **36** (1), 5–39.

Nembhard, I.M., & Edmondson, A.C. (2006). Making it safe: The effects of leader inclusiveness and professional status on psychological safety and improvement efforts in health care teams. *Journal of Organizational Behavior*, **27** (7), 941–966.

Pearsall, M.J., & Venkataramani, V. (2014). Overcoming asymmetric goals in teams: The interactive roles of team learning orientation and team identification. *Journal of Applied Psychology*, 100 (3), 735–748.

Plsek, P.E., & Greenhalgh, T. (2001). The challenge of complexity in health care. *BMJ: British Medical Journal*, 323 (7313), 625–628.

Popper, K.R. (1972). *Objective Knowledge: An Evolutionary Approach*. Oxford, England: Clarendon Press Oxford.

Prince, C., & Salas, E. (1993). Training and research for teamwork in the military aircrew. In E.L. Wiener, B.G. Kanki, & R.L. Helmreich (Eds.), *Cockpit Resource Management*, Orlando, FL: Academic Press, pp. 337–366.

Pronovost, P. (2013). Teamwork matters. In E. Salas, S.I. Tannenbaum, D. Cohen, & G. Latham (Eds.), *Developing and Enhancing Teamwork in Organizations: Evidence-based Best Practices and Guidelines*. San Francisco, CA: Jossey-Bass, pp. 11–12.

Raemer, D., Anderson, M., Cheng, A., Fanning, R., Nadkarni, V., & Savoldelli, G. (2011). Research regarding debriefing as part of the learning process. *Simulation in Healthcare*, 6 (7), S52–S57.

Rall, M., Glavin, R., & Flin, R. (2008). The "10-seconds-for-10-minutes principle": Why things go wrong and stopping them getting worse. *Bulletin of the Royal College of Anaesthetists*, 51, 2614–2616.

Ramanujam, R., & Rousseau, D.M. (2006). The challenges are organizational not just clinical. *Journal of Organizational Behavior*, 27 (7), 811–827.

Rico, R., Sanchez-Manzanares, M., Gil, F., & Gibson, C. (2008). Team implicit coordination processes: A team knowledge-based approach. *The Academy of Management Review*, 33 (1), 163–184.

Rosenstein, A.H., & O'Daniel, M. (2005). Disruptive behavior & clinical outcomes: Perceptions of nurses & physicians. *American Journal of Nursing*, 105 (1), 54–64.

Rudolph, J.W., Simon, F.B., Raemer, D.B., & Eppich, W.J. (2008). Debriefing as formative assessment: Closing performance gaps in medical education. *Academic Emergency Medicine*, 15 (11), 1010–1016.

Rudolph, J.W., Simon, R., Rivard, P., Dufresne, R.L., & Raemer, D.B. (2007). Debriefing with good judgment: Combining rigorous feedback with genuine inquiry. *Anesthesiology Clinics*, 25 (2), 361–376.

Salas, E., DiazGranados, D., Weaver, S.J., & King, H. (2008). Does team training work? Principles for health care. *Academic Emergency Medicine*, 15 (11), 1002–1009.

Salas, E., Klein, C., King, H., Salisbury, M., Augenstein, J.S., Birnbach, D.J., Robinson, D.W., & Upshaw, C. (2008). Debriefing medical teams: 12 evidence-based best practices and tips. *The Joint Commission Journal on Quality and Patient Safety*, 34 (9), 518–527.

Salas, E., Rosen, M.A., & King, H. (2007). Managing teams managing crises: Principles of teamwork to improve patient safety in the emergency room and beyond. *Theoretical Issues in Ergonomics Science*, 8 (5), 381–394.

Salas, E., Sims, D.E., & Burke, C.S. (2005). Is there a "Big Five" in teamwork? *Small Group Research*, 36 (5), 555–599.

Schmutz, J., Hoffmann, F., Heimberg, E., & Manser, T. (2015). Effective coordination in medical emergency teams: The moderating role of task type. *European Journal of Work and Organizational Psychology*, Published online ahead of print.

Schmutz, J., & Manser, T. (2013). Do team processes really have an effect on clinical performance? A systematic literature review. *British Journal of Anaesthesia*, 110 (4), 529–544.

Sexton, J., Thomas, E.J., & Helmreich, R.L. (2001). Error, stress, and teamwork in medicine and aviation: Cross sectional surveys. *Journal of Human Performance in Extreme Environments*, 6 (1), 6–11.

Smith-Jentsch, K.A., Cannon-Bowers, J.A., Tannenbaum, S., & Salas, E. (2008). Guided team self-correction: Impacts on team mental models, processes, and effectiveness. *Small Group Research*, 39 (3), 303–329.

Sutinen, R., Kivimaki, M., Elovainio, M., & Forma, P. (2005). Associations between stress at work and attitudes towards retirement in hospital physicians. *Work and Stress*, 19 (2), 177–185.

Tannenbaum, S.I., & Cerasoli, C.P. (2013). Do team and individual debriefs enhance performance? A meta-analysis. *Human Factors*, 55 (1), 231–245.

Tannenbaum, S.I., & Goldhaber-Fiebert, S. (2013). Medical team debriefs: Simple, powerful, underutilized. In E. Salas & K. Frush (Eds.), *Improving Patient Safety through Teamwork and Team Training*. New York, NY: Oxford University Press, pp. 249–256.

Tannenbaum, S.I., Mathieu, J.E., Salas, E., & Cohen, D. (2012). Teams are changing: Are research and practice evolving fast enough? *Industrial and Organizational Psychology*, 5 (1), 2–24.

Team, W.E.R. (2014). Ebola virus disease in West Africa: The first 9 months of the epidemic and forward projections. *New England Journal of Medicine*, 371 (16), 1481–1495.

Tjia, J., Mazor, K.M., Field, T., Meterko, V., Spenard, A., & Gurwitz, J.H. (2009). Nurse-physician communication in the long-term care setting: Perceived barriers and impact on patient safety. *Journal of Patient Safety*, 5 (3), 145–152.

Tucker, A.L., & Edmondson, A.C. (2003). Why hospitals don't learn from failures. *California Management Review*, 45 (2), 55–72.

Van Bogaert, P., Clarke, S., Roelant, E., Meulemans, H., & Van de Heyning, P. (2010). Impacts of unit-level nurse practice environment and burnout on nurse-reported outcomes: A multilevel modelling approach. *Journal of Clinical Nursing*, 19 (11–12), 1664–1674.

van der Vegt, G.S., Bunderson, S., & Kuipers, B. (2010). Why turnover matters in self-managing work teams: Learning, social integration, and task flexibility. *Journal of Management*, 36 (5), 1168–1191.

Vashdi, D.R., Bamberger, P.A., & Erez, M. (2013). Can surgical teams ever learn? The role of coordination, complexity, and transitivity in action team learning. *Academy of Management Journal*, 56 (4), 945–971.

Wauben, L.S.G.L., Doorn, C.M., van Wijngaarden, J.D.H., Goossens, R.H.M., Huijsman, R., Klein, J., & Lange, J.F. (2011). Discrepant perceptions of communication, teamwork and situation awareness among surgical team members. *International Journal for Quality in Health Care*, 23 (2), 159–166.

West, M.A. (2004). *Effective Teamwork: Practical Lessons from Organizational Research* (2nd ed.). Oxford, England: BPS Blackwell.

West, M.A., & Lyubovnikova, J. (2013). Illusions of team working in health care. *Journal of Health Organization and Management*, 27 (1), 134–142.

Zhang, Z.X., Hempel, P.S., Han, Y.L., & Tjosvold, D. (2007). Transactive memory system links work team characteristics and performance. *Journal of Applied Psychology*, 92 (6), 1722–1730.

22 Total Quality Management in Healthcare

*Ali Mohammad Mosadeghrad
and Ewan Ferlie*

INTRODUCTION

Healthcare organizations face a number of challenges, particularly concerning quality, efficiency and equity. Healthcare managers using quality management strategies can improve healthcare systems and procedures to achieve optimum outcomes, i.e., high-quality services, patient satisfaction and better performance. *Total Quality Management (TQM)* aims to improve the competitiveness of an organization through employee participation, customer-driven quality and continuous quality improvement. The term *TQM* was first used in 1985 by the Naval Air Systems Command to express the Japanese management style focused on quality control (Bemowski, 1992).

The origin of *TQM* is ascribed to Japan's desperate search for quality improvements of its products after World War II. In the 1950s, the Japanese Union of Scientists and Engineers invited Edward Deming, an American management theorist, to help them improve their economy. Deming shifted their focus from profit to quality. He encouraged them to improve continuously the production processes based on customers' needs and expectations.

By the 1970s, the challenge of Japanese high-quality and competitively priced products led to the adoption of quality management initiatives within the USA (The Economist, 1992). The quality management movement then hit Europe with the founding of the European Foundation for Quality Management (EFQM) in 1988 to improve the position of European industries in the world markets.

Total Quality Management was adopted in the health sector during the 1980s. The *TQM* success in industry encouraged many managers to examine whether it could also work in the health sector. As a result, in the last 35 years, many healthcare managers increasingly implemented *TQM* principles to improve the quality of outcomes, reduce medical errors and increase the efficiency of health service delivery. However, many organizations are experiencing dissatisfaction with their *TQM* program (Huq & Martin, 2000).

TQM has to be tailored to the special needs of the organization. The success of *TQM* depends on various variables, which are specific to the organization's environment, structures, cultures, processes and procedures. There is no "one-size-fits-all" approach that can be applied to the healthcare environment. The approach and speed of *TQM* implementation should be unique to each organization. The purpose of this chapter is to introduce a *TQM* model to assist healthcare managers and practitioners to improve the quality of services and sustain a competitive advantage.

DEFINITION OF TQM

In the term *"Total Quality Management"*, **Total** means that everyone associated with the company (i.e., managers, employees, customers and suppliers) should be involved in quality improvement. It is concerned with all work processes and inputs, and applies to every aspect of activities in a business, from identifying customer needs to evaluating whether the customer is satisfied. **Quality** means conformance to requirements or meeting and exceeding customers' requirements. **Management** means developing the organizational capabilities to constantly improve the quality of products and services.

The concept of *TQM* has evolved over the years and is still changing. Feigenbaum (1991, p. 6) defined *TQM* as "an effective system for integrating the quality-development, quality-maintenance, and quality-improvement efforts of the various groups in a firm so as to enable marketing, engineering, production, and service at the most economical levels which allow for full customer satisfaction". Juran and Gryna (1993, p. 12) described the term as "a system of activities directed at achieving delighted customers, empowered employees, higher revenues and lower costs". According to Steingard and Fitzgibbons (1993, p. 27), *TQM* is "a set of techniques and procedures used to reduce or eliminate variation from a production process or service-delivery system in order to improve efficiency, reliability and quality".

Joss and Kogan (1995) believe that *TQM* is "an integrated, corporately led program of organizational change designed to create and sustain a culture of continuous improvement based on customer-oriented definitions of quality" (p. 13). Mosadeghrad (2014) defined *TQM* as a management strategy to enhance customer satisfaction and organizational performance by providing high-quality products and services through the collaboration of all stakeholders, teamwork, customer-driven quality and continuously improving the performance of inputs and processes by applying quality management techniques and tools (p. 320).

From the above definitions, two aspects that comprise *TQM* can be identified: Management values and principles (e.g., customer focus, teamwork and continuous improvement), and management techniques and tools (e.g., statistical process control tools). The application of appropriate *TQM* techniques and tools supports the implementation of *TQM* core values and basic principles in an organization.

PRACTICAL MODELS OF TQM

Nowadays, three major quality management frameworks—standards-based approaches (e.g., the International Organization for Standardization: *ISO 9000* standard), quality award models and *TQM* frameworks developed by quality management gurus and consultants—are accepted as guides to *TQM* implementation.

The *ISO 9000* series are internationally recognized quality assurance standards issued by the International Organization for Standardization. *ISO 9001* seeks to standardize and control procedures and document quality activities within an organization. An *ISO 9001* certification demonstrates that an organization meets the minimum standards for a quality management system and there is confidence in the conformance of its products to the established requirements. The standards are generic and are applicable to all organizations. Up to the end of December 2013, at least 1,129,446 *ISO 9001* certificates were issued in 187 countries (ISO, 2013). The *ISO 9001* standard is increasingly being considered for implementation in the healthcare sector (Staines, 2000; van den Heuvel et al., 2005).

Quality award models provide a framework of essential quality management practices for organizations to implement the *TQM* program, benchmark best practices and perform self-assessments against established criteria to identify their strengths and weaknesses. There are many quality award models all over the world. Some of them are regional awards, (e.g., the Minnesota Quality Award), others national (e.g., the Malcolm Baldrige National Quality Award) or international (e.g., the European Foundation Quality Management Award in Europe).

Many *TQM* frameworks and models have been presented by quality scholars around the world (Ahire et al., 1996; Black & Porter, 1996; Mann & Kehoe, 1995; Tamimi, 1995). All of these researchers developed their *TQM* models based on their own research.

TQM AND ORGANIZATIONAL PERFORMANCE

Implementing an appropriate model of *TQM* appropriately results in increased employee motivation and teamwork, reduced employee absenteeism and turnover (Karia & Asaari, 2006), improved quality of products and services and increased customer satisfaction and loyalty (Agus, 2002). Other benefits of successful *TQM* implementation include reduced rework and waste, improved operational performance (Lagrosen & Lagrosen, 2005), increased profit and market share (Rahman, 2001) and enhanced business competitiveness (Lakhal et al., 2006).

TQM enables healthcare organizations to identify patients' requirements, to benchmark for best practices and improve working processes to reduce the frequency and severity of medical errors and deliver appropriate care. Successfully implementing *TQM* will lead to better employee morale, improved interdisciplinary working relationships (Sommer & Merritt, 1994), higher-quality patient care, reduced patient complaints, improved patient satisfaction (Macinati, 2008) and increased productivity and profitability (Alexander et al., 2006).

OBSTACLES TO TQM SUCCESS IN HEALTHCARE ORGANIZATIONS

While *TQM* has been suggested in theory to be effective for improving performance, its application in practice involves many difficulties. Healthcare organizations are inherently difficult to change due to their complexity, occupational subcultures and clinical professionals' resistance (Ferlie et al., 2005). Although some *TQM* projects have been shown to be effective (Francois et al., 2003; Lagrosen, 2000), most of these have been limited to a small number of departments or to a narrow aspect of departmental performance.

The literature provides little evidence of the effectiveness of *TQM* in healthcare. Bigelow and Arndt (1995) and Counte and Meurer (2001) questioned the effectiveness of *TQM* in the health sector. Øvretveit (2000) concluded that there is no evidence to prove that *TQM* works in European healthcare institutions. Huq and Martin (2000) reported high failure rates (60–67%) among implementations of *TQM* in the health sector. Kivimäki and colleagues (1997) in a study of a *TQM* prize-winning hospital concluded that *TQM* implementation did not change employees' quality of working life and well-being very much.

There are both theoretical problems and practical difficulties in applying *TQM* in healthcare organizations. A clear understanding of *TQM* is crucial for its effective implementation. While *TQM* is widely practiced, there is little agreement on what it is and what its essential features are. *TQM* is a diffuse concept and an abstract term, with many vague descriptions, and no generally accepted definition or agreed-upon content. Mosadeghrad (2014) found 73 definitions of *TQM* when conducting an intensive literature review. *TQM* has been variously defined as an "approach" (Flynn et al., 1994), a "culture" (Kanji & Yui, 1997), a "philosophy" (Joyce et al., 2006), a "system" (Hellsten & Klefsjö, 2000), a "strategy" (Harvey & Brown, 2001), a "programme" (James, 1996), a "process" (Almaraz, 1994), a "technology" (Camison, 1996) and a "technique" (Wong et al., 2010). Consequently, *TQM* is used interchangeably with other terms, such as continuous quality improvement, *Quality Assurance* and *Total Quality Control*. There is no agreement among TQM gurus about TQM basic principles and critical success factors. Various quality gurus and consultants have included different principles in their TQM frameworks. Consequently, different TQM models may result in different outcomes.

The theory of TQM has partially developed over the last 35 years. Some complementary management theories must be combined with TQM to achieve a competitive advantage. Due knowledge of sociology, psychology and change management helps one develop an effective TQM model (Singh & Smith, 2006).

Difficulties also arise when an attempt is made to implement TQM. Many of the failures of TQM are attributed to the methods of implementation. Although many quality management gurus and consultants have contributed to the evolution of TQM, few offered practical methods for its implementation to achieve good outcomes. According to Zairi and Matthew (1995), the "ends" have been defined, but not the "means". TQM offers a vision of organizational change without providing clear techniques and tools for implementing such a change. This is left to the interpretation of quality practitioners. Consequently, the same TQM program may have different outcomes in different organizations.

The complexity of healthcare processes and the prevalent culture and practices in healthcare can hinder efforts to improve performance. The case of Japanese healthcare reinforces this point. Despite being a leader in industrial quality management, the health sector in Japan did not undergo a similar quality revolution (Øvretveit, 2001). The reasons for this are rooted in the institutional characteristics of the Japanese health sector. A physician-oriented healthcare system, resistance of clinical professionals, lack of professional management and lack of customer focus are obstacles to implementing TQM effectively in Japanese healthcare (Takahashi, 1997).

The very complexity of the health system, its highly departmentalized and hierarchical organizational structures, strong occupational subcultures, professional autonomy and the difficulty involved in evaluating healthcare delivery processes and outcomes can pose significant obstacles to the implementation of TQM and decrease its effectiveness (Adinolfi, 2003; Nembhard et al., 2009). Other obstacles to TQM success in healthcare include a lack of consistent top management leadership, resistance of clinical professionals to change, lack of customer focus and unrealistic expectations (Mosadeghrad, 2014).

Delivery of healthcare services is based on a complex collection of diagnostic, therapeutic and logistic processes, all of which must be highly coordinated to ensure the delivery of quality care. Unlike manufacturing companies, it is difficult to define, measure and control outcomes in healthcare. Distinct healthcare service characteristics, such as intangibility, heterogeneity, simultaneity and inseparability, make it difficult to define and measure healthcare quality.

Healthcare problems are complex and require a high degree of customized solutions. A simple task requires the communication and cooperation of various departments and employees. Every situation and every patient are different. Patients cannot be treated like manufactured products. This aspect of healthcare is in contradiction with the concept of standardization and variation control in *TQM*. Besides, customers are powerless to change healthcare providers' behavior through market transactions (Zabada et al., 1998). Socio-demographic factors (e.g., age and gender), severity of illness and psychosocial factors (e.g., patient fears and dependence on healthcare providers) affect the expression of dissatisfaction.

The success of *TQM* depends on its fit with the organization's structure. Organic structures with low centralization and formalization are more conducive to the success of *TQM* implementation. Mechanistic, bureaucratic and authoritative structures, risk aversion and complexity impede successful *TQM* implementation (Jabnoun, 2005). McLaughlin and Kaluzny (1990) argue that a complex, bureaucratic and highly departmentalized structure and multiple layers of authority are the most difficult barriers to *TQM* implementation in the health sector. The hierarchical structure of healthcare organizations exemplifies bureaucratic and authoritative cultures that are not conducive for employee empowerment, which is crucial to successful *TQM* implementation (Zabada et al., 1998). Healthcare organizations are structured in departments that are defined by occupation and with significant autonomy of action, which further enhances their ability to resist change (McNulty & Ferlie, 2002).

There are various powerful groups, such as physicians, nurses and paramedics, who have their own definition of quality and follow specific ways to achieve it. Their interests and functional orientations do not facilitate a systems approach to quality promotion and create a situation where management has little control over the most strategic areas where *TQM* could yield the greatest results (Natarajan, 2006). This also makes it difficult to satisfy the needs of all those people who are involved in healthcare service delivery.

Clinical professionals are practicing according to rigid plans (gold standards of care) and pre-programmed activities. Therefore, they demand the professional autonomy and authority to define, measure and assure the quality of care (quality assurance). However, the *TQM* philosophy is based on ongoing, flexible plans. *TQM* highlights the importance of administrative authority and accountability (continuous quality improvement).

The workforce is fragmented in healthcare organizations. Professional autonomy and specialized accountability segment the work processes. As a result, efforts to improve the quality of care take place within occupational "silos". Physicians take responsibility for one aspect, nurses for another and managers for still another. No single group is held accountable for the total process (Kaluzny et al., 1992). *TQM* takes a systemic and participatory approach and asks managers to get key stakeholders, including clinical professionals, involved in quality improvement activities (managerial leadership), rather than leaving it up to clinicians to solve quality problems (clinical leadership). *TQM* looks for collective responsibility, while the dominant healthcare culture is based on individual responsibility.

A TQM MODEL FOR HEALTHCARE ORGANIZATIONS

Many of the *TQM* models are general guidelines and do not specifically address all areas relevant to the healthcare system. Therefore, there is a need for an empirical, concise, comprehensive and holistic model for implementing *TQM* successfully in the health sector. A research-based model of *TQM* was developed using the literature review and quality management experts' opinions. From each study, a list of constructs of *TQM* was created. The opinions of quality management experts were used in completing this list. The fifteen most common constructs of *TQM* were chosen for inclusion in the model, of which ten are enablers and five are results. Enablers direct and drive the results. Consequently, a framework for *TQM* implementation is proposed (see Figure 22.1).

The proposed model starts from the logical point of leadership and management and ends with overall organizational results. It assumes that "excellent results with respect to organizational performance, customer, employee, supplier and society are achieved through leadership and management, strategic quality planning, quality culture, education and training, and management of employees, customers, suppliers, resources, information and working processes" (Mosadeghrad, 2012, p. 100).

A strong and committed leadership is necessary for successful *TQM* implementation. The success of *TQM* depends largely on management's

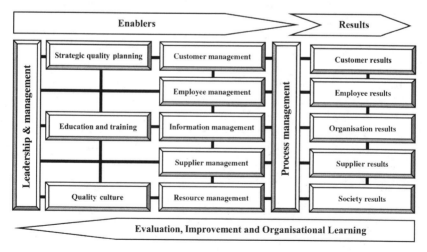

Figure 22.1   A Conceptual Framework of *TQM* for Healthcare Organizations

ability to create a vision, plan for and lead the organizational change required for *TQM* success. Shortell and colleagues (1995) argue that leadership styles based on command and control are a major obstacle to the application of *TQM* in healthcare organizations. Changing managerial behavior from command-and-control approaches to more participatory ones accelerates *TQM* progress. A top-down, authoritative leadership style must be replaced with a more charismatic, supportive, democratic and participative style that allows employees' involvement in the *TQM* program to improve their performance.

Many of the obstacles found to hinder *TQM* efforts, such as lack of a vision, lack of a strategic plan, poor organizational culture, poor communication, lack of employee empowerment, inadequate resources and employee resistance to change are linked to how effectively the quality transformation is managed. Top managers must create a clear quality vision for employees and inspire them to continuously improve the quality of their outcomes.

Low management commitment and involvement can lead to *TQM* failure in as many as 80% of firms (Jaehn, 2000). Juran and Gryna (1993) attribute the failure of the quality management initiatives in the West in the 1970s and 1980s to the lack of top manager involvement in quality management. They related the quality excellence of Japanese companies to the commitment of senior managers to quality. A lack of *TQM* knowledge, mobility of management, risk aversion and ineffective communication between managers and employees are the main reasons for the low manager commitment to *TQM* (Psychogios & Priporas, 2007; Soltani et al., 2005). Knights and McCabe (1997) believe that managers often do not understand the basic philosophy of *TQM*. Subsequently, they adopt contradictory approaches, such as attempting to control employees and costs while emphasizing the needs of a trust-based culture and customer importance.

Newall and Dale (1991) concluded that the lack of detailed planning prior to the introduction of *TQM* was a key reason for its future difficulties in eight UK-based companies. Many *TQM* implementation problems can be overcome by proper planning. A well-defined plan for *TQM* implementation (time frame, resources, training and supportive organizational structure) is important. Quality should be recognized as an organization's strategic goal and should be reflected in the organization's corporate vision and mission. Quality efforts will fail if they are not incorporated into the organization's strategies (Lawrence & Early, 1992).

Poor education and training are also obstacles to the development and implementation of a *TQM* program (Huq & Martin, 2000). Education and training help develop employees' capabilities on a continuous basis. Managers and supervisors should be trained in leading quality improvement teams. Employees should be trained in continuous quality improvement. Education and training improve employees' job-related skills and facilitate behavioral change towards continuous quality improvement. Training and education have an important role in securing commitment and behavioral change toward continuous quality improvement. Education and training should also be provided for patients and suppliers in healthcare organizations.

Organizational culture is one of the most important influencing factors in *TQM* implementation in the health sector. Cultural variables are responsible for more than 50% of the variance in *TQM* implementation (Mosadeghrad, 2006; Wakefield et al., 2001). *TQM* initiatives will not succeed unless they are rooted in a supportive organizational culture. According to Anjard (1995), cultural change is the most-often ignored component of *TQM* change. Changing organizational culture and creating a supportive culture are the most difficult obstacles to *TQM* implementation in the healthcare sector (Mandal et al., 2000).

TQM requires changes in language, behavior and managers' priorities and changes in employees' behavior to focus on continuous improvement (Anjard, 1995). A collaborative culture characterized by transparency, honesty, respect, trust, empowerment, teamwork, social responsibility and public accountability, and a culture that is conducive to learning, risk taking and creativity is necessary to promote *TQM* implementation efforts (Mosadeghrad, 2006; Wardhani et al., 2009). Transforming a corporate culture to a genuine quality culture requires visionary leadership, strategic planning, training, commitment and explicit focus on internal and external customers. Continuous and widespread education and training provide a good foundation for the cultural change required for *TQM* implementation. However, it needs to be supplemented by the appropriate systems. Leadership has a key role in changing the organizational culture. Changing employees' knowledge, attitudes and behavior requires political and diplomatic skills (Harrington & Williams, 2004).

TQM models usually assume that every employee is responsible for quality, and hence, that employees should implement a *TQM* program. Their empowerment, commitment and involvement are key factors in successful *TQM* implementation. Everyone in the organization must adopt *TQM* principles as integral parts of their work and embrace a philosophy that quality is not extra work. Many *TQM* program fail because too little attention is paid to the human factor. The implementation of *TQM* will result in more demands on employees and more work pressure. This is often caused by the organizational changes, new relationships and the responsibilities involved (Walston et al., 2000). Human resource systems must support the *TQM* program through the development of the necessary motivation, attitudes and competencies.

Clinical professionals, particularly physicians, have remained separated from management. They believe that *TQM* is used mainly for cost control and can be applied only in administrative and support departments (Zabada et al., 1998). They do not feel that *TQM* activities are part of their tasks. Physicians are not likely to be distracted from their patients in a fee-for-service payment system towards a *TQM* system that expects them to be more transparent, more responsible, more customer-oriented and to follow managerial rules and standards.

Lack of time is the main barrier for their involvement in *TQM*. They perceive a conflict between allocating time for treating patients and performing *TQM* activities (Valenstein et al., 2004). Perceived loss of autonomy is another reason for the high resistance among physicians (McLaughlin & Kaluzny, 1990). They think the standardization concept in *TQM* may limit their freedom to diagnose and treat patients freely. Their relative inexperience in teamwork and unwillingness to work as team members also contribute to their indifference to *TQM* (Zabada et al., 1998).

Physicians' negative attitudes toward *TQM* are a threat for sustaining its implementation. Managers must get physicians involved from the initial stages of *TQM* and develop systems to encourage and reward their commitment and participation though training and financial incentives. It is not necessary to include all physicians in all *TQM* activities. It is better to involve those interested physicians who are both respected by their colleagues and clinically knowledgeable about the patient care areas selected for improvement. They can serve as models, mentors and motivators for others. As a result, other physicians will gradually join the *TQM* program.

TQM can be a source of fear and anxiety. The reasons for employees' resistance to *TQM* change may include fear of losing jobs and related benefits, personal uncertainty, group pressure, the reluctance of individuals to leave perceived secure situations, perceived loss of control, the lack of knowledge of the nature and impact of the proposed change, communication difficulties and the lack of adequate planning (Carter, 2008; Self & Schraeder, 2009). Managers must minimize the sense of ambiguity among employees using effective communication and planning. Managers must clarify the future state for employees and let them know what would happen and how they would be affected by the *TQM* change program. Managers should create the belief among employees that the appropriate training and education will be provided. Consequently, employees will be able to perform well and take advantage of opportunities that may arise from the implementation of the change initiative.

Customer focus is the foundation of the quality management philosophy. Organizations should identify customer needs and meet them. Lack of knowledge of customers' requirements results in serious problems in *TQM* implementation. Peters and Waterman (1982) recognized learning customers' preferences and meeting their needs as crucial success factors differentiating "excellent" companies from those that were not. Customer focus in *TQM* requires that customers are identifiable and can define and recognize quality. However, it is difficult to identify customers and satisfy their needs in the health sector. Unlike in most other industries, purchasing decisions, payment and receipt of healthcare services are separate. The patient is not necessarily the ultimate "external" customer in healthcare. Other external groups, such as the government, employers and third-party payers affect patient expectations, and this makes it difficult to anticipate patient needs. Patients, in general, lack the ability to judge the technical aspects of healthcare services (Cheng et al., 2002). Many patients do not even know their own healthcare needs (Berwick et al., 1992). Therefore, various healthcare stakeholders' perspectives, desires and priorities must be considered in any effort to define, measure and improve the quality of healthcare. The paternalistic attitude among many clinical professionals that only they can define quality attributes limits the application of customer-driven *TQM* initiatives (Milakovich, 2005).

Allocating and optimizing resources are essential for any *TQM* program to be continued effectively. Failure to provide adequate resources is another cause for the failure of *TQM*. Several studies reported that a lack of resources required for quality improvement projects negatively influences the success of *TQM* (Alexander et al., 2007; Withanachchi et al., 2007). Managers should allocate the necessary resources to quality improvement projects. According to Besterfield (1994), on an average, 40 percent of production cost is due to purchased materials. Therefore, supplier management is an extremely important aspect of *TQM*. Companies must develop long-term relationship with their suppliers. An effective supplier relationship management system reduces procurement costs, enhances the quality of purchased products and services and provides differentiated and customized services for companies (Rao et al., 1999).

Several studies reported that the lack of a good information system and information required influenced the success of *TQM* (Lee et al., 2002; Moeller, 2001). Collecting timely, reliable and relevant data and information from both inside and outside the organization is fundamental for assessment and improvement purposes (Joss & Kogan, 1995). Such information is necessary for effective resource utilization, identification of customer requirements, evaluating the productivity of the operations and determining the causes of quality problems. *TQM* requires an effective information system to facilitate the implementation of quality management techniques and to support healthcare research and knowledge.

TQM focuses on improving working processes continuously. Process management involves defining and optimizing the production process. The complexity of healthcare processes, bureaucracy and difficulties in defining and measuring healthcare quality are major procedural problems that healthcare organizations may encounter during *TQM* implementation (Buciuniene et al., 2006; Huq, 2005; Mosadeghrad, 2005). A number of issues resulting from traditional organizational design and management practices, as well as the characteristics of healthcare professionals, pose significant challenges to *TQM* implementation. The challenges to adopting *TQM* in healthcare organizations suggest that managers should take a cautious and an incremental approach in its implementation, rather than implement it in one step. A radical transformation of production processes has been found to have negative and detrimental effects on many organizations (Singh & Smith, 2006).

Total Quality Management does deliver better performance when an appropriate *TQM* model is appropriately implemented in a supportive environment (i.e., supportive infrastructure, appropriate leadership and quality culture). This can be shown as the following equation:

Effective TQM model + Effective implementation method + Supportive environment = Improved quality of products and services

A well-designed, robust, wisely adapted and well-implemented *TQM* program can be a powerful vehicle by which healthcare organizations can achieve excellence in their overall performance. A successful *TQM* program requires an effective quality management system to be established for planning and executing *TQM* practices, and monitoring and improving the quality of healthcare services. The proposed *TQM* model as a systematic quality management system advocates an integrated approach in order to support the transition from a traditional organization to a total quality organization. The proposed *TQM* model provides a comprehensive triad of conceptual, implementation and assessment models. Its conceptual model represents a set of core values and principles that focus on continuous quality improvement as a driving force in all functional areas and at all levels of the organization.

The proposed *TQM* implementation model represents the approach and sequence needed for the implementation of *TQM* principles and practices. The approach to applying *TQM* involves structural, cultural and procedural changes. Changing structure and culture helps accelerate total quality improvement through procedural changes. Procedural changes may have little effect if there are incompatibilities between the organization's structure and culture and the principles and core values of the *TQM* initiative. The logic of structural, contextual and procedural changes seems to be the best *TQM* implementation sequence for reaching the maximum result. Such a change provides lasting and significant positive results.

While the conventional *TQM* models involve quality improvement teams choosing the topics of improvement after listing and prioritizing all the department's problems, in the proposed *TQM* model, the emphasis is to standardize healthcare delivery processes, determine reasonable and achievable objectives for processes and improve them continually and continuously until the objectives are achieved. Employees using the proposed *TQM* model plan for the desired situation and change the organization accordingly. They would be more motivated and committed.

While the conventional *TQM* models place too much emphasis on customers and fail to address the needs of other stakeholders, the proposed *TQM* model places balanced emphasis on the needs and legitimate expectations of various stakeholders. Collaboration and cooperation among employees, customers and suppliers are crucial in a system as complex as healthcare.

TQM must be results-oriented for employees to believe in it. The proposed *TQM* model is more results-oriented than the other *TQM* models. It looks at the impact of a production process improvement on overall organizational performance. This includes performance related to employees, customers, suppliers, society and the organization. The proposed *TQM* model highlights the importance of supplier results, which are missing from the EFQM and the Malcolm Baldrige National Quality Award models.

The proposed *TQM* assessment model evaluates the approach, the implementation and the results of *TQM* concepts and principles. Conducting assessments and using benchmarks allow organizations to assess their performance, determine the areas in need of improvement and continually improve the quality of their services.

Figure 22.2 shows how a *TQM* model could be successful. A number of factors at the individual, organizational and environmental levels influence the continuity of *TQM* over the longer term. Constancy of purpose, strong management and clinical leadership, visible support from top management,

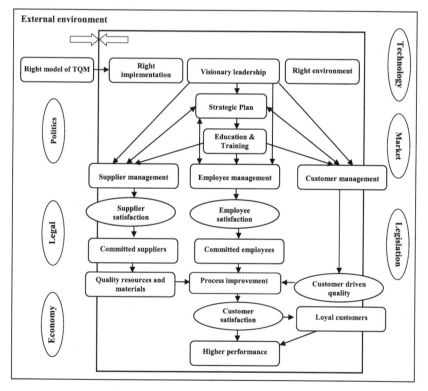

Figure 22.2 Factors Affecting the Successful Implementation of *TQM*

management skills in change management, the quality structure and integrating quality into the strategic plan are the major factors affecting the success of implementing *TQM* in healthcare organizations. In addition, experienced and well-trained employees, their willingness to change and belief in quality and their involvement in quality management activities, teamwork, resource availability, clear and well-defined processes, regular audits and performance measurement and customer orientation are also critical for successful *TQM* implementation.

TQM does not offer quick answers to all organizational problems. *TQM* implementation in the health sector is a complex and long process. It can take an organization years to put the fundamental quality management principles, procedures and systems into place, create an organizational structure and culture that is conducive to continuous improvement and change the values and attitudes of its people to adopt the new behavior as a consistent way of working (Dale et al., 1997). The longer organizations work at *TQM* practice, the more successful they will be. Therefore, consistency and constancy of purpose should be guaranteed. Managers and practitioners should be patient and persistent in continuous quality improvement using the *TQM* program. Managers choosing a *TQM* model should remember that the model itself does not bring about improvement. Institutionalizing a *TQM* program requires commitment, effort and resources. The *TQM* model will not succeed unless a receptive context and supportive environment (supportive leadership, culture and structure) are created.

CONCLUSION

Healthcare organizations are increasingly using quality management programs in order to improve the quality of outcomes and efficiency of healthcare service delivery. There is controversy surrounding the effectiveness of *TQM* programs. While some studies showed improvements in healthcare services due to *TQM* implementation, other researchers reported a high rate of failure. There are both theoretical and practical difficulties in applying *TQM* in organizations.

Contemporary industrial quality management practices and techniques can be adopted, adapted and successfully applied within professional healthcare organizations to achieve excellence. A well-developed and well-implemented *TQM* program offers significant benefits to healthcare organizations. *TQM* should be customized to the unique needs and capabilities of healthcare organizations. In addition, cultural factors may have an impact on implementing *TQM* practices. Top management commitment to lead the *TQM* initiative, strategic quality planning, management and clinical leadership, developing a quality culture, education and training, both internal and external customers' involvement in *TQM* activities, partnership with suppliers, continuous improvement and the monitoring and evaluation of quality are necessary for *TQM* to be successful.

A theoretical *TQM* framework was introduced for healthcare organizations. The proposed model can overcome many of the pitfalls encountered in the implementation of *TQM*. The proposed *TQM* model offers a holistic and integrated approach that can be applied to healthcare organizations to sustain their quality improvement efforts. Integrating *TQM* principles into the organization's strategies and plans is the best way to ensure that *TQM* will be a way of life and an ongoing process. The incremental and evolutionary nature of the change in the proposed *TQM* model is suitable for healthcare organizations with complex production processes and structures and powerful political sub-cultures, and gives organizations enough time to adopt and adapt the *TQM* model and gradually and continuously improve the processes. It nurtures a quality culture by changing the dominant cultural variables and power relations within the organization.

REFERENCES

Adinolfi, P. (2003). Total quality management in public healthcare: A study of Italian and Irish hospitals. *Total Quality Management*, **14** (1), 141–150.

Agus, A. (2002). TQM as a focus for improving overall service performance and customer satisfaction: An empirical study on a public service sector in Malaysia. *Total Quality Management*, **15** (5–6), 615–628.

Ahire, S.L., Golhar, D.Y., & Waller, M.A. (1996). Development and validation of TQM implementation constructs. *Decision Sciences*, **27** (1), 23–56.

Alexander, J.A., Weiner, B.J., & Griffith, J. (2006). Quality improvement and hospital financial performance. *Journal of Organisational Behaviour*, **27** (7), 1003–1029.

Alexander, J.A., Weiner, B.J., Shortell, S.M., & Baker, L.C. (2007). Does quality improvement implementation affect hospital quality of care? *Hospital Topics*, **85** (2), 3–12.

Almaraz, J. (1994). Quality management and the process of change. *Journal of Organisational Change Management*, **7** (2), 6–15.

Anjard, R.P. (1995). Keys to successful TQM training and Implementation. *Training for Quality*, **3** (1), 14–22.

Bemowski, K. (1992). The quality glossary. *Quality Progress*, **25** (2), 18–29.

Berwick, D., Enthoven, A., & Bunker, J.P. (1992). Quality Management in the NHS: The doctor's role. *BMJ: British Medical Journal*, **304** (6821), 235–239.

Besterfield, D. (1994). *Quality Control* (4th ed.). Englewood Cliffs, NJ: Prentice Hall.

Bigelow, B., & Arndt, M. (1995). Total quality management: Field of dreams. *Health Care Management Review*, **20** (4), 15–25.

Black, S.A., & Porter, L.J. (1996). Identification of the critical factors of TQM. *Decision Sciences*, **27** (1), 1–21.

Buciuniene, I., Malciankina, S., Lydeka, Z., & Kazlauskaite, R. (2006). Managerial attitude to the implementation of quality management systems in Lithuanian support treatment and nursing hospitals. *BMC Health Services Research*, **6** (120). Retrieved from http://www.biomedcentral.com/content/pdf/1472-6963-6-120.pdf (accessed 6 June 2015).

Camison, C. (1996). Total quality management in hospitality: An application of the EFQM model. *Tourism Management*, 17 (3), 191–201.

Carter, E. (2008). Successful change requires more than change management. *The Journal for Quality and Participation*, 31 (1), 20–23.

Cheng, S., Ho, Y., & Chung, K. (2002). Hospital quality information for patients in Taiwan: Can they understand it? *International Journal for Quality in Health Care*, 14 (2), 155–160.

Counte, M.A., & Meurer, S. (2001). Issues in the assessment of continuous quality improvement implementation in health care organizations. *International Journal for Quality in Health Care*, 13 (3), 197–207.

Dale, B., Boaden, R., Willcox, M., & McQuater, R. (1997). Sustaining total quality management: What are the key issues? *The TQM Magazine*, 9 (5), 372–380.

The Economist. (1992). The cracks in quality. April 18, pp. 67–68.

Feigenbaum, A.V. (1991). *Total Quality Control* (3rd ed.). New York: McGraw Hill.

Ferlie, E., Fitzgerald, L., Wood, M., & Hawkins, C. (2005). The non-spread of innovations: The mediating role of professionals. *Academy of Management Journal*, 48 (1), 117–134.

Flynn, B.B., Schroeder, R.G., & Sakakibara S. (1994). A framework for quality management research and an associated measurement instrument. *Journal of Operations Management*, 11 (4), 339–366.

Francois, P., Peyrin, J.C., & Touboul, M. (2003). Evaluating implementation of quality management system in a teaching hospital's clinical department. *International Journal for Quality in Health Care*, 15 (1), 47–55.

Harrington, D., & Williams, B. (2004). Moving the quality effort forward: The emerging role of the middle manager. *Managing Service Quality*, 14 (4), 297–306.

Harvey, D., & Brown, D. (2001). *An Experiential Approach to Organization Development* (6th ed.). Upper Saddle River, NJ: Prentice-Hall.

Hellsten, U., & Klefsjö, B. (2000). TQM as a management system consisting values, techniques and tools. *Journal of Quality & Reliability Management*, 18 (3), 289–306.

Huq, Z. (2005). Managing change: A barrier to TQM implementation in service industries. *Managing Service Quality*, 15 (5), 452–469.

Huq, Z., & Martin, T.N. (2000). Workforce cultural factors in TQM/CQI implementation in hospitals. *Healthcare Management Review*, 25 (3), 80–93.

International Organization for Standardization (ISO). (2013). *The ISO Survey of Management System Standard Certifications—2013*. Retrieved from http://www.iso.org/iso/iso_survey_executive-summary.pdf?v2013 (accessed 25 May 2015).

Jabnoun, N. (2005). Organizational structure for customer-oriented TQM: An empirical investigation. *The TQM Magazine*, 17 (3), 226–236.

Jaehn, A.H. (2000). Requirements for total quality leadership. *Intercom*, 47 (10), 38–39.

James, P.T.J. (1996). *Total Quality Management*. London: Prentice-Hall.

Joss, R., & Kogan, M. (1995). *Advancing Quality: Total Quality Management in the National Health Service*. Buckingham, England: Open University Press.

Joyce, J., Green, R., & Winch, G. (2006). A new construct for visualizing and designing e-fulfilment systems for quality healthcare delivery. *The TQM Magazine*, 18 (6), 638–651.

Juran, J.M., & Gryna, F.M. (1993). *Quality Planning and Analysis* (3rd ed.). New York, NY: McGraw-Hill.

Kaluzny, A.D., McLaughlin, C.P., & Simpson, K. (1992). Applying total quality management concepts to public health organisations. *Public Health Reports*, 107 (3), 257–264.

Kanji, G.K., & Yui, H. (1997). Total quality culture. *Total Quality Management*, 8 (6), 417–428.

Karia, N., & Asaari, M.H. (2006). The effects of total quality management practices on employees' work-related attitudes. *The TQM Magazine*, 18 (1), 30–43.

Kivimäki, M., Mäki, E., & Lindström, K. (1997). Does the implementation of total quality management (TQM) change the wellbeing and work-related attitudes of health care personnel? Study of a TQM prize-winning surgical clinic. *Journal of Organizational Change Management*, 10 (6), 456–470.

Knights, D., & McCabe, D. (1997). How would you measure something like that? Quality in a retail bank. *Journal of Management Studies*, 34 (3), 371–388.

Lagrosen, S. (2000). Born with quality: TQM in a maternity clinic. *The International Journal of Public Sector Management*, 13 (5), 467–475.

Lagrosen, Y., & Lagrosen, S. (2005). The effects of quality management: A survey of Swedish quality professionals. *International Journal of Operations & Production Management*, 25 (9–10), 940–952.

Lakhal, L., Pasin, F., & Limam, M. (2006). Quality management practices and their impact on performance. *International Journal of Quality and Reliability Management*, 23 (6), 625–646.

Lawrence, D.M., & Early, J.F. (1992). Strategic leadership for quality in healthcare. *Quality Progress*, 25 (4), 45–48.

Lee, S., Choi, K.S., Kang, H.Y., & Chae, Y.M. (2002). Assessing the factors influencing continuous quality improvement implementation: Experience in Korean hospitals. *International Journal for Quality in Health Care*, 14 (5), 383–391.

Macinati, M.S. (2008). The relationship between quality management systems and organisational performance in the Italian National Health Service. *Health Policy*, 85 (2), 228–241.

Mandal, P., Love, P.E., Sohal, A.S., & Bhadury, B. (2000). The propagation of quality management concepts in the Indian manufacturing industry: Some empirical observations. *The TQM Magazine*, 12 (3), 205–211.

Mann, R.S., & Kehoe, D.F. (1995). Factors affecting the implementation and success of TQM. *International Journal of Quality & Reliability Management*, 12 (1), 11–23.

McLaughlin, C.P., & Kaluzny, A.D. (1990). Total quality management in health: Making it work. *Health Care Management Review*, 15 (3), 7–14.

McNulty, T., & Ferlie, E. (2002). *Reengineering Health Care: The Complexities of Organisational Transformation*. Oxford, England: Oxford University Press.

Milakovich, M.E. (2005). *Improving Service Quality in the Global Economy: Achieving High Performance in Public and Private Sectors*. Boca Raton: CRC Press.

Moeller, J. (2001). The EFQM excellence model: German experiences with the EFQM approach in health care. *International Journal for Quality in Health Care*, 13 (1), 45–49.

Mosadeghrad, A.M. (2005). A survey of total quality management in Iran: Barriers to successful implementation in health care organisations. *Leadership in Health Services*, 18 (3), 12–34.

Mosadeghrad, A.M. (2006). The impact of organisational culture on the successful implementation of total quality management. *The TQM Magazine*, 18 (6), 606–625.

Mosadeghrad, A.M. (2012). Towards a theory of quality management: An integration of strategic management, quality management and project management. *International Journal of Modelling in Operations Management*, 2 (1), 89–118.

Mosadeghrad, A.M. (2014). Why TQM does not work in healthcare organisations. *International Journal of Health Care Quality Assurance*, 27 (4), 320–335.

Natarajan, R.N. (2006). Transferring best practices to healthcare: Opportunities and challenges. *The TQM Magazine*, 18 (6), 572–582.

Nembhard, I.M., Alexander, J.A., Hoff, T.J., & Ramanujam, R. (2009). Why does the quality of health care continue to lag? Insights from management research. *Academy of Management Perspectives*, **23** (1), 24–42.

Newall, D., & Dale, B.G. (1991). The introduction and development of a quality improvement process: A study. *International Journal of Production Research*, **29** (9), 1747–1760.

Øvretveit, J. (2000). Total quality management in European health care. *International Journal of Health Care Quality Assurance*, **13** (2), 74–79.

Øvretveit, J. (2001). Japanese healthcare quality improvement. *International Journal of Health Care Quality Assurance*, **14** (4), 164–167.

Peters, T., & Waterman, R. (1982). *In Search of Excellence: Lessons from America's Best Run Companies*. New York: Harper and Rowe.

Psychogios, A.G., & Priporas, C.V. (2007). Understanding total quality management in context: Qualitative research on managers' awareness of TQM aspects in the Greek service industry. *The Qualitative Report*, **12** (1), 40–66.

Rahman, S. (2001). A comparative study of TQM practice and organisational performance with and without ISO 9000 certification. *International Journal of Quality & Reliability Management*, **18** (1), 35–49.

Rao, S.S., Solis, L.E., & Raghunathan, T.S. (1999). A framework for international quality management research: Development and validation of a measurement instrument. *Total Quality management*, **10** (7), 1047–1075.

Self, D.R., & Schraeder, M. (2009). Enhancing the success of organizational change: Matching readiness strategies with sources of resistance. *Leadership & Organization Development Journal*, **30** (2), 167–182.

Shortell, S.M., O'Brien, J.L., Carman, J.M., Foster, R.W., Hughes, E.F., Boerstler, H., & O'Connor, E.J. (1995). Assessing the impact of continuous quality improvement/total quality management: Concept versus implementation. *Health Services Research*, **30** (2), 377–401.

Singh, P.J., & Smith, A. (2006). Uncovering the faultiness in quality management. *Total Quality Management*, **17** (3), 395–407.

Soltani, E., Lai, P., & Gharneh, N.S. (2005). Breaking through barriers to TQM effectiveness: Lack of commitment of upper-level management. *Total Quality Management*, **16** (8–9), 1009–1021.

Sommer, S.M., & Merritt, D.E. (1994). The impact of a TQM intervention on workplace attitudes in a health care organization. *Journal of Organizational Change Management*, **7** (2), 53–62.

Staines, A. (2000). Benefits of an ISO 9001 certification: The case of a Swiss regional hospital. *International Journal of Health Care Quality Assurance*, **13** (1), 27–33.

Steingard, D.S., & Fitzgibbons, D.E. (1993). A postmodern deconstruction of total quality management. *Journal of Organisational Change Management*, **6** (5), 27–42.

Takahashi, T. (1997). The paradox of Japan: What about CQI in health care? *The Joint Commission Journal of Quality Improvement*, **23** (1), 60–64.

Tamimi, N. (1995). An empirical investigation of critical TQM factors using exploratory factor analysis. *International Journal of Production Research*, **33** (11), 3041–3051.

Valenstein, M., Mitchinson, A., Ronis, D.L., Alexander, J.A., Duffy, S.A, Craig, T.J., & Lawton Barry, K. (2004). Quality indicators and monitoring of mental health services: What do front-line providers think? *Journal of Psychiatry*, **161** (1), 146–154.

Van den Heuvel, J., Koning, L., Bogers, A.J., Berg, M., & van Dijen, M. (2005). An ISO 9001 quality management system in a hospital: Bureaucracy or just benefits? *International Journal of Health Care Quality Assurance*, **18** (5), 361–369.

Wakefield, B.J., Blegen, M.A., Uden Holman, T., Vaughn, T., Chrischilles, E., & Wakefield, D.S. (2001). Organizational culture, continuous quality improvement, and medication administration error reporting. *American Journal of Medical Quality*, **16** (4), 128–134.

Walston, S.L., Burton, L.R., & Kimberley, J.R. (2000). Does engineering really work? An examination of the context and outcomes of hospital reengineering initiatives. *Health Services Research*, **34** (6), 1363–1388.

Wardhani, V., Utarini, A., van Dijk, J., Post, D., & Groothoff, J. (2009). Determinants of quality management systems implementation in hospitals. *Health Policy*, **89** (3), 239–251.

Withanachchi, N., Handa, Y., & Karandagoda, K.K. (2007). TQM emphasizing 5-S principles: A breakthrough for chronic managerial constraints at public hospitals in developing countries. *International Journal of Public Sector Management*, **20** (3), 168–177.

Wong, C.H., Sim, J.J., Lam, C.H., Loke, S.-P., & Darmawan, N. (2010). A linear structural equation modeling of TQM principles and its influence on quality performance. *International Journal of Modeling in Operations Management*, **1** (1), 107–124.

Zabada, C.P., Rivers, A., & Munchus, G. (1998). Obstacles to the application of total quality management in health care organisations. *Total Quality Management*, **9** (1), 57–66.

Zairi, M., & Matthew, A. (1995). An evaluation of TQM in primary care: In search of best practice. *International Journal of Health Care Quality Assurance*, **8** (6), 4–13.

23 Transformational Leadership in Healthcare Organizations

Bettina Fiery

INTRODUCTION

Transformational Leadership requires essential building blocks to create successful healthcare organizations. These building blocks break down even further the characteristics described by previous authors known for transformational theory. These essential ingredients are not only critical for leader effectiveness, but also for those he or she leads. This chapter outlines these additional skills and abilities as the building blocks of *Transformational Leadership*, skills that may aid leaders to confront contexts affecting healthcare organizations today and into the future. *Transformational Leadership* is architectural; it builds and develops both people and organizations.

Transformational leaders emerge during particular times, such as when organizations restructure, when organizations are needing a renewed vision or when the context requires a significant transformation (Conger, 1999; Smith et al., 2004). *Transformational Leadership* received considerable attention because of its ability to transform organizations and followers in times of change (Avolio et al., 2004; Bass, 1999; Oshagbemi & Gill, 2004). With rapid changes and multiple challenges occurring in the healthcare industry, the practice of a transformational style of leadership assisted leaders with what Rost (1993) deemed a post-industrial paradigm shift. Leadership in the 21st century is largely about dealing with change (Donley, 2005; Higgs & Rowland, 2005). *Transformational Leadership* is not the same as *Transactional Leadership*. Many healthcare organizations have the misfortune of *Transactional Leadership* within their architecture.

We live in a new age, the Age of Technology, with instant communication and information everything. Think back to just twenty years ago—before we had personal computers on our desks, before mobile phones, before the Internet became a major resource, before iPhones and iPads. . . The computer chip may have single-handedly altered the human experience forever. Among other things, technology changed the very foundations of social life by connecting people in a new way. Further, we now live with the knowledge that everything is linked. We may see more change in the next 25 years than we saw in the last 100 years.

As we leave the Industrial Age and enter the Age of Technology, the leader's challenge is to adapt to all that is new while leading others. Changes occur at a rapid-fire pace and can be overwhelming even to the most efficient. In order to survive, leadership cannot be the same as it was even 10 years ago. The infrastructure of society is becoming less institutional and more informational. The architecture of our places of work, service and business has changed dramatically.

All over the world, people are being overwhelmed by endless changes in contexts: The work, the pace of change and the limitations on their time. Healthcare is in an ever-changing world and by its very nature, disequilibrium exists. Those who try to maintain the status quo will be knocked off balance. Futurologist Ilya Prigiogine's work on complexity demonstrated that disequilibrium is the necessary ingredient for system growth (Prigiogine & Nicolis, 1977). Any change brings new relationships with new ideas and new people, and new processes develop. Healthcare seems to be experiencing severely increased demands and severely constrained resources; more patients with comorbid conditions, fewer physicians and longer wait times, just to name a few. The rate of change and apparent uncertainty caused many healthcare leaders to leave the field. In the 21st century, the healthcare industry is in the midst of multiple transformations. Small hospitals can no longer afford to be freestanding, and many are merging with other, larger hospital systems. Customer service carries just as much significance as the quality of care and medical outcomes. Additionally, US healthcare leaders need to manage initiatives such as the Affordable Care Act, and in most health systems, pay for performance and population management as well as meeting the needs of a diverse workforce. Now is the time for leaders with a transformational leader framework to lead people through these multitudes of change.

The healthcare industry is laced with leaders, from physician office managers and their physicians, to various layers of management in freestanding medical centers, to the multiple layers and a sundry of departments within large hospital centers. The executive suite within healthcare organizations often places physicians among CEOs, CFOs, CIOs and CHROs. Many of these executives have a greater length of service within the healthcare organization and/or MBAs, yet few receive education in leadership development. Transformational leaders in the healthcare industry not only have to work within these confines, but also across functions and work along those regulatory agencies such as the government, insurance companies and non-profit agencies.

Transformational Leadership

In his Pulitzer Prize-winning book, *Leadership*, Burns (1978) distinguished between *Transactional Leadership*, which is management required to run a business, and *Transformational Leadership*, which is changing people through higher levels of moral values and personal expectations. *Transformational Leadership* offers employees and the organization the cultivation and continuous reinforcement of core values, off the wall plaque and into the attitudes and behavior of every employee.

The potent force-shaping behavior in organizations is the combination of expressed expectations of purpose, intent and values. Behaviors do not change just by announcing organizational values. Leaders move gradually into being able to act congruently with those values. These ideas speak with a simple clarity to issues of effective leadership. The leader's task is first to embody these principles, and then help the organization become this standard. Leaders with integrity have truly learned there is no choice but to *walk the talk* and thus lead organizations to success.

Healthcare leaders could benefit from applying the tenets of *Transformational Leadership*. According to Burns, transformational leaders sought to satisfy needs, which resulted in a mutual affiliation between leaders and followers, with a merging of roles between leaders and followers where both benefited. Burns believed the leader's power was inseparable from the followers' needs (Northouse, 2004). Years later, Bass (1999) indicated that people sought transformational leaders as the ideal role model whom people wanted to emulate. Transformational leader behaviors, such as placing value on specified and idealized goals, motivated followers to do more by raising followers' levels of consciousness of these goals. Bass listed the *Transformational Leadership* components as: 1) Idealized influence or charisma; 2) Inspirational motivation; 3) Intellectual stimulation; 4) Individualized consideration. "Idealized influence" describes leaders as strong role models with whom followers identified and who they wanted to emulate. These leaders usually have high standards of moral conduct and receive respect from followers who place high trust in them. Idealized influence also involves providing followers with a vision and sense of purpose. Inspirational motivation involves the ability to communicate high expectations to followers and inspire these followers through motivation to commit to accomplishing the organizational vision. Leaders accomplish innovation through intellectual stimulation. Finally, leaders who use individualized consideration create a supportive environment, meeting the needs of each of the followers through active listening and appropriate coaching, and assist followers in achieving actualization.

Transactional Leadership

According to Burns (1978), *Transactional Leadership* was about exchange. Leaders used rewards such as praise and recognition, money, promotions or some honor in exchange for effort (McGuire & Kennerly, 2006). These rewards were given or withheld according to employee performance. According to McGuire and Kennerly (2006), "The outcome for such contingent reward behavior was role clarity, job satisfaction, and improved performance" (p. 182). Transactional leaders worked within their self-interest to meet their immediate needs or the needs of the organization (Bass, 1990; Bennis & Nanus, 1985).

Rost (1993) interpreted Burns's *Transactional Leadership* style as a managing style. The distinction between management and leadership was the "fundamental differences in assessing orientations toward goals, work, human relations, and their selves" (Rost, 1993, p. 131). Managers sought to fulfill obligations by using contingent rewards, not out of followership, but of subordination. Transactional leaders set goals, directed and used rewards to reinforce behavior. Transactional leaders or managers differed from transformational leaders in that these leaders did not meet the needs of subordinates or attempt to improve their personal growth, and did not seek to satisfy the followers' higher needs. Conversely, transformational leaders' behaviors raised both leaders and followers to become higher "moral agents" (Bass, 1990, p. 23). Transformational focuses on the *top line* and is principle centered. *Transactional Leadership* focuses on the *bottom line* and is *event centered*. Obviously, both are necessary. But *Transformational Leadership* must be the parent, as it provides the strategic boundaries within which transactions take place. The goal of *Transformational Leadership* is literally to "transform" people and organizations—to change both in mind and heart, enlarge vision, insight, and understanding, clarify purposes, make behavior congruent with beliefs, principles or values and bring about changes that are permanent, self-perpetuating and momentum building. People gain confidence that "this place is run by principles" and everyone, including the top people, are accountable to those values, as well as to each other.

Table 23.1 shows further distinctions between *Transformational* and *Transactional Leadership*:

ORGANIZATIONAL CONTEXTS

When first learning about *Transformational Leadership*, one might think practicing this form of leadership is not complicated. However, further understanding of leadership theory suggests that the practice of *Transformational Leadership* is not *easy*. Kouzes and Posner (2003) wrote in *The Leadership Challenge* that "all people have the ability to lead" (p. 386), yet not all people want to learn and practice the necessary behaviors for effective and efficient leadership. Having knowledge and skill are only secondary to the behaviors needed to successfully lead people toward both personal and professional success. Leadership theories, models and practices remain relatively constant; dealing with changing contexts is a driving force behind the ability to effectively lead.

Unseen influences exist, like it or not. Leaders cannot see what fills the space, but they can feel it. To learn what is in the space, they need to look

Table 23.1 Differences Between *Transformational* and *Transactional* Leadership

Transformational Leadership	Transactional Leadership
Builds on man's need for meaning	Builds on man's need to get a job done and to make a living
Is concerned with purposes, values, morals, ethics	Is preoccupied with power, position, politics, perks
Transcends daily affairs	Is mired in daily affairs
Is oriented toward meeting long-term goals without compromising human values	Is short term and hard-data oriented
Identifies and develops new talent	Focuses on tactical issues
Makes full use of human resources	Focuses on tactical issues
Releases human potential	Focuses on tactical issues
Designs job roles to make them meaningful and challenging	Follows and fulfills role expectations by striving to work effectively within current systems
Aligns internal structures and systems to reinforce overarching objectives, values, goals	Supports structures and systems that reinforce the bottom line, maximize efficiency
Is proactive, catalytic, patient	Confuses causes and symptoms and concerns are more with treatment than prevention
Recognizes and rewards significant contributions	Involves contingent reinforcement

and listen to the employees. When that space is filled with divergent messages, only contradictions float through the ether, and there are more arguments, complaining, power plays, dissonance and fear. Leaders are the ones who must fill the space with congruence by living in word and deed the organization's values. Then, others automatically follow suit. After all, the leader is on the stage.

According to Conger (1999), only certain organizations can effectively practice *Transformational Leadership*. These organizations have contexts, including trusted and innovative climates, along with an educated workforce. Pawar and Eastman (1997) were among the first authors to recognize the effects of contextual influences on *Transformational Leadership*. They focused on top-level leaders in organizations and the influence of "organizational emphasis on efficiency and adaptation orientation, relative dominance of technical core and boundary-spanning units in organizational task system, organizational structure, and mode of governance" (1997, p. 89). Modes of governance include clan, market or bureaucratic governance and reflect how leaders administer communication, projects, initiatives, etc. An organization's structure reflects the number of managerial layers. Pawar and Eastman proposed that organizations would be more receptive to *Transformational Leadership* if these organizations adapted to change, expanded, had simple structures and implemented a clan mode of governance.

Pawar and Eastman's (1997) propositions illustrated an organization's potential lack of receptivity to *Transformational Leadership*. Hospitals and healthcare organizations may need to adapt to change and continually expand in services, but a hospital's *structure is not simple* and not all hospitals use a *clan mode of governance*. However, a new appreciation for the element of complexity created a paradigm shift.

According to Gardner (1990), "The impulse of most leaders is much the same as it was a thousand years ago: accept the system as it is and lead it" (p. 122). Gardner indicated that institutions unable to adapt to the pace of change could not compete. Leaders needed to transform organizations through renewal. The main leadership task, then, is not so much to manage function or work, but rather to coordinate the workers and facilitate their relationships at every organizational level. Leaders must maintain a panoramic view of the organizational world to see the intersections, relationships and themes.

In the organizational world, everything is interconnected like a vast network of patterns; "things" change form and properties as they respond to one another. In organizations, people are at the edge of this unpredictable new world of relationships. Our understanding of the value of work has undergone a change. In the past, the focus was on process, and the existence of a good work process was taken to be a sufficient condition of good service. We now recognize that a process gets its value from the purpose toward which it is directed (the desired outcome). In other words, work becomes meaningful and adds value when it fulfills an important purpose. Increasingly, healthcare is measured by its outcomes.

Leadership is now recognized as an art, something to be learned over time. In today's healthcare, leaders must lead differently than in the past if the best outcomes are to be achieved. Who could have predicted even 10 years ago the changes we now live with in healthcare? Then, we were concerned with the impact of "managed care". Leadership is more tribal than scientific, more a weaving of relationships with the amassing of information. One of the key tasks for transformational leaders is to build relationships with staff and others throughout the organization, know the pulse and then lead staff through the changes. Researchers and theorists confirm that leadership is best thought of as a behavior, not a role.

To live in such a world, to weave here and there with ease and grace, we need to become savvy about how to foster relationships, how to nurture growth and development. Transformational leaders use the *four I's* to be better at listening and respecting one another's uniqueness; these abilities

Table 23.2 Distinctions Between Leadership and Management

Leadership	Management
Deals with direction	Deals with speed
Deals with vision, effectiveness, results	Deals with establishing structure and systems to get those results
Focuses on top line	Focuses on bottom line
Derives its power from values and correct principles	Organizes resources to serve selected objectives to produce bottom line
Is the highest component of management	Is hierarchical
Involves vision, direction, values, purpose, inspiration, motivating people to work together with common purpose	Hires, fires, plans, controls
Fosters mutual respect	Top-down decision making
Builds a complementary team where each strength is made productive	Uses leverage to multiply the work and role of the producer
Identifies strengths and weaknesses of self and others	Identifies staff changes needed to secure a bottom line
Asks: What difference did it make?	Asks: What have you done?

are essential for strong relationships. The era of the rugged individual has been replaced by the era of the team player. However, this phenomenon is only the beginning; the concept that we are unconnected individuals is long discredited (Wheatley, 1996). Transformational leaders notice the significant role of the human being in accomplishing organizational goals and objectives. To be a transformational leader, one must not set aside the management skills necessary to function in the role. Management is a job description. It is something you do. Leadership is a life decision. It is who you are. If you decide to be a transformational leader, then set about learning what you need to know and develop the skills you need to have. It is a wonderful and exciting journey. Both roles are critical to be a successful leader.

Power in an organization is the capacity generated by relationships. When transformational leaders share power in such workplace redesigns, power shows up as significant increases in productivity and personal satisfaction (Weber, 2011).

In some workplaces, leaders attempt to force better results through coercion and competition; sometimes, these leaders may exhibit flagrant disregard for people and their abilities. In such organizations, a high level of energy is also created, but it is an entirely negative one. People use their creativity to work against their leaders, or in spite of them.

ORGANIZATIONAL STRUCTURE

The structure of an organization could be defined as "the sum total of the ways in which it divides its labor into distinct tasks and then achieves coordination among them" (Mintzberg, 1979, p. 2). Mintzberg discussed five types of organizational structures: 1) Simple; 2) Machine; 3) Professional; 4) Divisionalized form; 5) Adhocracy. Hospitals have been referred to as professional bureaucracies that hire trained professionals and provide these professionals with control over their work (Vandenberghe, 1999).

Mintzberg referred to healthcare organizations as professional bureaucracies, "relying on the skills and knowledge of professionals to function; producing standard services" (p. 349), but professional bureaucracies had parallel machine bureaucracies for their support staff. Professional bureaucracies provided for skills standardization, machine bureaucracies provided for standardizing work processes. Professional bureaucracies also had multiple layers of management and were, therefore, hierarchical in structure (Pawar & Eastman, 1997). Weber (1946) described the following characteristics of a bureaucracy: 1) Hierarchy of authority; 2) Impersonality; 3) Written rules of conduct; 4) Promotion based on achievement; 5) Specialized division of labor; 6) Efficiency. These characteristics represented the means to achieve the organization's goals proficiently. According to Weber (1946), "Bureaucracies were goal-oriented organizations designed according to rational principles in order to efficiently attain their goals" (p. 197). Information flows up the chain of command in hierarchical order through ranked offices, with directives flowing down. Furthermore, according to Weber, "Operations of the organizations were characterized by impersonal rules that explicitly stated duties, responsibilities, standardized procedures and conduct of office holders" (1946, p. 198).

However, bureaucratic organizations "can inhibit an empowering environment, disseminating information, or communicating a vision" (Brazier, 2005, p. 128). Vandenberghe (1999) found hospitals to be bureaucratic organizations in that "hospitals are traditionally characterized by a lack of vision creation and implementation because professionals (nurses and physicians) are weakly committed to the organization" (p. 30). Information structures function horizontally, whereas most business structures function vertically; yet, healthcare is a business. Leading in this horizontal work culture is radically different than leading in a predominately vertical work culture.

What is meant by all this? People no longer work in a "Mother may I" world in which leaders provide all the details of projects and assignments. One of the most significant factors affecting life in today's organization is the rising expectation of personal power. People naturally expect to voice their opinions, be heard, be treated well and have the opportunity to participate in decisions affecting their work and workplace. Bureaucratic organizations can be restricted by mechanistic requirements, such as predictability and stability with no competition (Shivers-Blackwell, 2006). Healthcare may be referred to as bureaucratic; issues occurring in the 21st century may be creating a context for the industry to face unpredictability, instability and intense competition.

Using Mintzberg's (1979) typology of organizational structure, Pawar and Eastman (1997) compared each organizational structure to the conditions required for transformational responsiveness. Pawar and Eastman proposed that *Transformational Leadership* would not be accepted in professional, machine or divisional forms of bureaucracies. According to Mintzberg (1979), the machine bureaucracy uses standardized work processes and tasks to coordinate the work of individuals. It generates the work standards for the operations of the organization and relies on the authority of the hierarchical professional bureaucracy. Skill standardization used by trained professionals is the means of ensuring the coordination of services in a professional bureaucracy. In professional bureaucracies, professionals have power but lack organizational commitment (Mintzberg). The divisional bureaucracy focuses on outcomes and controls worker performance by providing objectives and goals to achieve greater outcomes.

In the past, organizations were built on the Weberian principles of mechanistic functioning, compartmentalization and vertical control. The dominant theme of this type of thinking is that the organization is simply one vast machine. Almost all organizational, and in particular, leadership, theories of the late 19th century and the first half of the 20th century were modeled on, or purported to imitate, Weberian concepts.

In the Industrial Age, leaders were concerned most of all with function and operation. Compartmentalized work focused on the activities of the individual employee. The employee's work life was regulated by a set of job obligations, and the employee was evaluated on the quality of the work, not on whether the work made a difference to other employees or the organization as a whole. Many of the elements of traditional leadership theories reflected a mechanical, Newtonian framework, especially those focusing on hierarchical control and compartmentalization in order to manage people and productivity, and the structures of their organizations reflected this tendency.

A world based on machine images is a world described by boundaries. In a machine, every piece knows its place. Organizations are broken into chunks. Hence, silos are built around common work experiences. Healthcare leaders must learn to lead through all this constant change in a world that is round with networks of connections: Not of hierarchies, but of encircling partnerships.

ORGANIZATIONAL CULTURE

Organizational culture guides and shapes employee behavior. A culture consisting of trust, empowerment (for more information about *Empowerment* and its relevance to healthcare organizations, see Oranye and Ahmad, Chapter 10 in this volume) and transparent communication have an association with effective leadership (Avolio et al., 2004; Brazier, 2005; Chaffee & Arthur, 2002; Kleinman, 2004; Thyer, 2003; Upenieks, 2003, 2005). Many of today's healthcare organizations may still be seen as bureaucracies with a more business-like culture. Within many healthcare organizations, leaders still take a mechanistic approach, wanting control and limiting the vitality of healthy relationships. Yet, one person can be a catalyst of change; a "transformer" is the yeast that can leaven the whole loaf. Some ingredients of a catalyst include: Vision, patience, respect, persistence, courage and faith to be a transforming leader.

Defined by shared meanings evolving over time, organizational culture serves to manage and shape employee behavior in organizations (Owens, 2004; Shivers-Blackwell, 2006). According to Owens (2004), behavioral norms and assumptions define an organization's culture. Norms or standards are ideas about what members within the organization should do (Owens, 2004). Norms, based on assumptions, "dealt with what people in the organization accepted as true, sensible, and possible . . . norms were tacit and nonnegotiable" (Owens, 2004, p. 185). Culture is a determinant of performance because of its influence on behavior and decision-making patterns, and values and beliefs are the core of culture (Cakar et al., 2004; Mele, 2003). Culture influences the ethical behavior of people in organizations (Sims & Binkerman, 2002); leadership defines and sets an organization's culture.

"Character is Destiny", said Heraclitus. What determines character? In a word, values. In organizations, culture is destiny, since culture is to the organization what character and attitude are to the individual. Culture, over time, becomes a reflection of the collective character and behavior of the people who work there, and vice versa. Plato said that a society cultivates whatever is honored there. The organization's values are its lifeblood. The most important determinant of long-term success for any organization is its culture. Culture is defined by the values manifested in the attitudes and behaviors of the people who make up that organization. Leaders who treat their employees with respect and provide a culture of support for personal and collaborative innovation will achieve greater results in the coming years. Doing more with less, through organizational efficiency, has become an audible mantra over the past decade. Shared meanings and embracing the organization's culture raises individual and group performance and satisfaction, which provide advantages from a mere survival tool to one that is a substantial competitive edge. Other organizations may copy a product or service, but organizations cannot copy a culture.

We can learn how leaders treat their employees by noticing how these employees treat patients. An organization's values determine the type of people it recruits and retains and how effectively those people manage both success and adversity. The attitude leaders bring to work is one of the most important choices made on a daily basis. This choice defines the excellence with which leaders work, the personal and career goals the leader sets and the level of happiness and work fulfillment, or whether workers are chronically stressed out, burned out and put out.

Values disappear in a sea of trivial memos and impertinent reports without effective communication that is actively practiced. There may be no single thing more important in our efforts to achieve meaningful work and fulfilling relationships than to learn and practice the art of communication.

Aligning the behaviors of leaders and employees with the organization's mission helps lead to organizational success. A leader's ability links to organizational capability. Organizational capability includes an operational arrangement and practice that enables performance, provides sufficient resources and organizational support, enables environment and culture and aligns abilities and experience with organizational direction (Armitage et al., 2006).

Healthcare leaders cannot share their vision unless this vision is clearly articulated to their followers. Healthcare workers cannot trust a leader who does not communicate (Casimer et al., 2006). "Trust is framed by one person's perception of the other, and this perception grows when individuals have exchanges on a regular basis that involve communication of ideas, feelings, and vulnerabilities" (Szumanski, 2004, p. 89). Vision is the organizational clarity of purpose and direction, or creating a destination for the organization. The impact of vision, values and culture occupies a great deal of attention. And while many healthcare organizations remain bureaucratic in nature and maintain transactional management approaches, some leaders choose to adapt leadership styles and implement new behavioral practices to improve organizational performance.

TEAM PERFORMANCE

A leader has the responsibility to create the right conditions for employees to learn and grow. In fact, one of the main purposes of leadership is ensuring that members develop and become what they must in order to thrive in shifting circumstances. In this era of revolution, changing work is not only occurring, the very workplace is also changing: The conditions, elements and technologies of work. Leaders must help workers understand that innovation is a way of life and enable them to develop the skills to live in this transformed world. To apply new thinking by rote or through using a "straight line" approach is nearly impossible. Talented people must be gathered together and supported. The outcomes of ideas are often unpredictable; therefore, ideas must be tried and possibly modified. This process means allowing members of the organization to take risks. A strong, innovative leader will encourage everyone to challenge the status quo, challenge each other's thoughts and experiment with alternative approaches. Moreover, this type of leader will strive to ensure the environment supports such attitudes and behaviors.

Healthcare organization work in teams, communicating with those they work beside, making decisions without constantly checking with the supervisor. Amy Edmondson (2012) introduces the term *teaming* as a verb denoting team-based activities whereby increased collaboration and insight increases better outcomes, especially in industries such as healthcare. Leaders with a transformational philosophy could incorporate this practice into their repertoire of tools and resources due to teaming and learning conjointly. Unfortunately, according to Edmondson, top-heavy bureaucracies offer low psychological safety (through leadership) and accountability, and hence have a high level of apathy. However, transformational leaders create change, and could create *Learning Organizations*—where teaming is about learning and "learning from the work is part of the work" (Edmondson, 2012, p. 284). Thus, leaders create a new culture through the by-product of practicing this new teaming effort and as a result, generate greater organizational performance.

ORGANIZATIONAL PERFORMANCE

A multitude of authors (Bennis, 2009; Gardner, 1990; Kouzes & Posner, 2002) argue the positive effects of *Transformational Leadership* on organizational performance, and these same authors indicate that people would rather be led than managed (refer to Table 23.2 earlier in the chapter for the distinctions). The *Transformational Leadership* theory is simple: Provide employees with the organization's vision, share and involve employees how to achieve this vision, provide tools and resources (or remove barriers) in order to achieve the vision, set milestones and be aware of your employees' needs as everyone travels together to achieve the final destination. An even simpler tone to this theory: See it! Believe it! Walk it! Talk it! Teach it!

The transformational leader's role is not just to make sure people know what to do and when to do it, but to ensure purpose and meaning for the employee's role in the organization and provide growth and development. The results of effective *Transformational Leadership* appear in higher employee engagement, low employee turnover, increased productivity, high patient satisfaction and high-quality outcomes (Dionne et al., 2004; Hargis et al., 2011; Kleinman, 2004; Upenieks, 2005).

In today's post-modern era, conducting business that provides better and less costly service is critical to an organization's growth and even to its survival. Achieving organizational growth requires strategic planning. Transformational leaders use the strategic plan as a map to achieve their vision. Goals are the bricks in the foundation of the leader's palace. Goals are the stepping stones that help lead from the current reality to the desired future. Part of the responsibility of having a mission is figuring out how to support it, which means leaders must have a plan with measurable goals. The scaffolding holding all these factors in place is a coherent business strategy.

SUMMARY

The leadership theory is not complicated; however, the contexts around the ability to practice *Transformational Leadership* theory are complicated. While everyone may have the ability to be a leader, not everyone chooses to be a transformational leader, and not every organization has the capability to practice *Transformational Leadership*. The healthcare industry faces a myriad of changes. What better time than now to embrace *Transformational Leadership* and implement new practices, behaviors and concepts to improve the lives of employees and patient care outcomes?

If understanding new ideas and changes are real forces in an organization, then they must be communicated clearly. Transformational leaders must seek a much deeper level of integrity in words and acts than ever before. Leaders need to make certain everyone has access to the necessary information, tools and resources. Leaders must give time to allow changes to assimilate and for adjustments to become routine. A leader's role is to lead everyone through the chaos into this new environment using constant communication to encourage and reassure all who are involved. Without *Transformational Leadership*, the chaos becomes negative and filled with fear, doubt, discontent, complaining and a rampant grapevine.

Is *Transformational Leadership* the panacea of leader theory for healthcare? Absolutely not. Leadership development is an ongoing journey. Few people have the tenacity and perseverance for both personal growth and development and organizational transformation simultaneously. Is *Transformational Leadership* possible in healthcare organizations? . . . Absolutely! This chapter provided the reader with information about the necessary ingredients required to confront the contexts that may affect the ability to practice *Transformational Leadership* (i.e., organizational structure, mode of governance and receptivity to change).

Transformational leaders need courage, tenacity and perseverance to work with multiple layers of management, boards and professionals to make changes within healthcare. These leaders need all the building blocks and the essential ingredients known as the *four I's*: 1) Idealized influence or charisma; 2) Inspirational motivation; 3) Intellectual stimulation; 4) Individualized consideration to confront the barriers existing in healthcare organizations. Not everyone can be a leader, not everyone can be transformational, but the journey is worth the effort.

REFERENCES

Avolio, B.J., Zhu, W., Koh, W., & Bhatia, P. (2004). Transformational leadership and organizational commitment: Mediating role of psychological empowerment and moderating role of structural distance. *Journal of Organizational Behavior*, 25 (8), 951–968.

Armitage, J.W., Brooks, N.A., Carlen, M.C., & Schulz, S.P. (2006). Remodeling leadership. *Performance and Improvement*, 45 (2), 40–48.

Bass, B.M. (1990). *Bass & Stogdill's Handbook of Leadership: Theory, Research, & Managerial Applications* (3rd ed.). New York: Free Press.

Bass, B.M. (1999). Two decades of research and development in transformational leadership. *European Journal of Work and Organizational Psychology*, 8 (1), 9–32.

Bennis, W. (2009). *On Becoming a Leader*. Philadelphia, PA: Perseus Books Group.

Bennis, W.G., & Nanus, B. (1985). *Leaders: The Strategies for Taking Charge*. New York: Harper & Row.

Brazier, D.K. (2005). Influence of contextual factors on health-care leadership. *Leadership & Organizational Development*, 26 (2), 128–141.

Burns, J.M. (1978). *Leadership*. New York: Harper & Row.

Cakar, N.D., Ergun, E., Altintas, O.C., & Bulut, C. (2004). The effects of charismatic leadership and collective behavior of follower performance. *Economic Studies*. Retrieved from http://www.eastweststudies.org/makale_detail.php (accessed 17 June 2006).

Casimer, G., Waldman, D.A., Bartram, T., & Yang, S. (2006). Trust and the relationship between leadership and follower performance: Opening the black box in Australia and China. *Journal of Leadership & Organizational Studies*, 12 (3), 68–84.

Chaffee, M.W., & Arthur, D.C. (2002). Failure: Lessons for health care leaders. *Nursing Economics*, 20 (5), 225–231.

Conger, J.A. (1999). Charismatic and transformational leadership in organizations: An insider's perspective on these developing streams of research. *The Leadership Quarterly*, 10 (2), 145–170.

Dionne, S.D., Yammarino, F.J., Atwater, L.E., & Spangler, W.D. (2004). Transformational leadership and team performance. *Journal of Organizational Change Management*, 17 (2), 177–193.

Donley, R. (2005). Challenges for nursing in the 21st century. *Nursing Economics*, 23 (6), 312–319.

Edmondson, A.C. (2012). *Teaming*. San Francisco, CA: Jossey-Bass.

Gardner, J.W. (1990). *On Leadership*. New York: Simon & Schuster.

Hargis, M.B., Watt, J.D., & Piotrowski, C. (2011). Developing leaders: Examining the role of transactional and transformational leadership across business contexts. *Organization Development Journal*, 29 (3), 51–68.

Higgs, M., & Rowland, D. (2005). All changes great and small: Exploring approaches to change and its leadership. *Journal of Change Management*, 5 (2), 121–154.

Kleinman, C. (2004). The relationship between managerial leadership behaviors and staff nurse retention. *Hospital Topics*, 82 (4), 2–10.

Kouzes, J.M., & Posner, B.Z. (2002). *The Leadership Challenge* (3rd ed.). San Francisco, CA: Jossey-Bass.

McGuire, E., & Kennerly, S.M. (2006). Nurse managers as transformational and transactional leaders. *Nursing Economics*, 24 (4), 179–185.

Mele, D. (2003). Organizational humanizing cultures: Do they generate social capital. *Journal of Business Ethics*, 45 (1–2), 3–14.

Mintzberg, H. (1979). *The Structuring of Organizations*. Englewood Cliffs, NJ: Prentice Hall.

Northouse, P.G. (2004). *Leadership: Theory and Practice* (3rd ed.). Thousand Oaks, CA: Sage.

Oshagbemi, T., & Gill, R. (2004). Differences in leadership styles and behavior across hierarchical levels in UK organisations. *Leadership & Organizational Development Journal*, 25 (1), 93–106.

Owens, R.G. (2004). *Organizational Behavior in Education: Adaptive Leadership and School Reform* (8th ed.). Boston, MA: Allyn & Bacon.

Pawar, B.S., & Eastman, K.K. (1997). The nature and implications of contextual influences on transformational leadership: A conceptual examination. *Academy of Management*, **22** (1), 80–109.

Prigogine, I., & Nicolis, G. (1977). *Self-Organization in Non-Equilibrium Systems*. San Francisco, CA: Wiley.

Rost, J.C. (1993). *Leadership for the Twenty-first Century*. Westport, CT: Praeger.

Shivers-Blackwell, S. (2006). The influence of perceptions of organizational structure & culture on leaders. *Journal of Leadership & Organizational Studies*, **12** (4), 27–49.

Sims, R.R., & Binkerman, J. (2002). Leaders as moral role models. *Journal of Business Ethics*, **35** (4), 327–339.

Smith, B.N., Montagno, R.V., & Kuzmenko, T.N. (2004). Transformational and servant leadership: Content and contextual comparisons. *Journal of Leadership and Organizational Comparisons*, **10** (4), 80–92.

Szumanski, K. (2004). Share your vision, voice. *Nursing Management*, **35** (9), 88–89.

Thyer, G.L. (2003). Dare to be different: Transformational leadership may hold the key to reducing the nursing shortage. *Journal of Nursing Management*, **11** (2), 73–79.

Upenieks, V. (2003). Nurse leaders' perceptions of what compromises successful leadership in today's acute inpatient environment. *Nursing Administration Quarterly*, **27** (2), 140–153.

Upenieks, V. (2005). Recruitment and retention strategies: A magnet hospital prevention model. *Medical Surgical Nursing*, Supplement, April, 21–27.

Vandenberghe, C. (1999). Transactional vs. transformational leadership: Suggestions for future research. *European Journal of Work and Organizational Psychology*, **8** (1), 9–32.

Weber, L. (2011). *Something Needs to Change around Here: The Five Strategies to Leveraging Your Leadership*. Hagerstown, MD: RidgeRunner.

Weber, M. (1946). *Essays in Sociology* (H.H. Gerth & C.W. Mills, Trans.). New York: Oxford Press.

Wheatley, M.J. (1996). The unplanned organization: Learning from nature's emergent creativity. *Noetic Sciences Review*, **37** (spring). Retrieved from http://www.margaretwheatley.com/articles/unplannedorganization.html (accessed 27 April 2015).

24 Value-Based Healthcare
Utopian Vision or Fit for Purpose?

Thomas Garavan and Gerri Matthews-Smith

INTRODUCTION

Healthcare organizations worldwide are under major pressure to demonstrate that what they do adds value. Healthcare costs continue to rise at a rate that outpaces national economic growth and household incomes (Griner & Hampton, 2013). Increasing costs place major burdens on the capacity of healthcare organizations to maintain the quality of care delivered to patients (Brook et al., 2000; Strite & Stuart, 2005). Therefore, commentators have called for a major paradigm shift and transformation of healthcare organizations. Michael Porter (2010) has characterized this paradigm shift and transformation as a move from a volume-based to a *Value-Based Healthcare* system.

Michael Porter and Elizabeth Teisberg proposed the concept of *Value-Based Healthcare* (*VBHC*) in their book *Redefining Healthcare: Creating Value-Based Competition on Results* (2006). They argued that the goal of *VBHC* is not to minimize costs, but to maximize "value". They defined value as patient outcomes divided by costs. To realize *VBHC*, Porter and Teisberg (2006) argued that providers and payers should strive to identify, codify and promote treatment protocols to enhance patient well-being through more cost-effective care.

The challenges facing healthcare organizations are very significant and, some would argue, intractable. Porter and Teisberg (2006) and Larson et al. (2010) outline some of these challenges. They include: 1) Significant restrictions or reductions in service that fall below the recommended standard of care; 2) Escalating costs that continue to rise; 3) Major evidence of both over- and under-use of care; 4) Major preventable errors in diagnosis and treatment; 5) Major variations in the quality of healthcare and cost differences across providers and countries; 6) Poor uptake of best practices by healthcare organizations and in-built resistance to major innovation; 7) Major changes in the cost dynamics of healthcare driven by people living longer and major increases in chronic illness and infectious diseases.

VBHC is viewed by some commentators as the great panacea to the problems inherent in healthcare organizations. Others are quick to dismiss it as unfit for purpose due to the lack of timely and reliable data (Solomons & Spross, 2011), too many stakeholders with divergent rather than convergent interests (Karash, 2013; Robinson, 2008) and an aversion of healthcare organizations to undertake major transformation and change (Bigelow & Arndt, 2005). Strite and Stuart (2005) articulate both the opportunities and challenges inherent in *VBHC* when they argue that it:

> [r]equires a systematic review and synthesis of the evidence regarding benefits, harms, risks, costs, alternatives and uncertainties of healthcare interventions as well as an assessment of the tradeoffs between effectiveness, cost, the patient perspective and the organization's priorities. (p. 6)

Given the complexity of what this statement suggests, *VBHC* may be impossible to orchestrate or realize in the real world. There are many unanswered questions concerning the effectiveness and realizability of *VBHC*. Examples include: Is it a good fit to the healthcare context? What are the challenges in adopting value as a primary goal in healthcare? How is the concept of value defined in a healthcare context? What are the challenges involved in measuring value? What are the complexities in producing an evidence base to measure value? We address these issues in this chapter and highlight the significant efforts required to make *VBHC* a reality in healthcare organizations. This chapter addresses these questions about *VBHC*. We first outline some of the major problems that pervade healthcare worldwide. We then consider the key dimensions of *VBHC*, and we critically evaluate the complexities and challenges inherent in the concept. Finally, we consider the implementation issues.

Why Focus on VBHC?

It is generally assumed that the current cost burden within healthcare worldwide is unsustainable. Larson et al. (2010) argued that rising costs would be a serious problem irrespective of whether improvements in healthcare quality could keep pace. The reality is that healthcare quality has not kept pace, but in fact has fallen behind in many countries. The most difficult situation is to be found in the USA. Healthcare policy in the USA is financed through a combination of private insurance and government benefits, and provided through a mixture of care delivery through public and private institutions (Watson, 2010). Healthcare expenditures doubled between 1994–2005; however, the quality of care measured using multiple criteria such as patient safety, timelines, patient centeredness and effectiveness improved by a third. The World Health Statistics (2010) reveal that the USA spends more on healthcare than any other country; however, Americans have fewer healthy life years than do citizens in other developed countries.

Europe is in a similar, if less acute, situation. In the majority of European countries, healthcare is paid for out of taxes. The World Bank (Economist Intelligence Unit, 2011) has estimated that expenditure on healthcare in the EU will grow from an average of 8% of GDP in 2000 to 14% in 2030. In Japan, public expenditure grew more slowly, from 6.29% in 2000 to 6.7% of GDP in 2009 (World DataBank, 2012). The Organisation for Economic Co-operation and Development's (OECD) Health Data (2009) show that the gaps between the rates of growth of healthcare costs, GDP and wages is greatest for the UK, Spain, the USA and France. Both Germany and Sweden record the smallest gaps for developed countries.

The USA is considered an outlier in terms of healthcare costs and affordability. A study by Thomson and his colleagues on the Commonwealth Fund (http://www.commonwealthfund.org/publications/in-brief/2013/apr/value-based-cost-sharing-in-the-united-states) found that the USA spends €8,508 per person on healthcare whereas Norway, the second highest spender, spends €5,450 per person. Europe spends 10% of its GDP on public and private funding of healthcare, whereas the USA spends 18% of its GDP. A common trend across all developed and developing countries is that rising costs are considered unaffordable and unsustainable. The Commonwealth Fund study found for example, that 23% of US adults, 13% of adults in France and lower percentages in other countries experienced significant problems in paying medical bills or were simply unable to pay. The most intricate problem of all is that higher costs of healthcare are not strongly correlated even in developed countries with better results or higher-quality care. In order to respond to spiraling costs, numerous countries have implemented a variety of cost containment measures. These include: 1) Prescription drug price cuts and controls; 2) Evidence-based medicine; 3) New physician incentive models. There is an increased emphasis on encouraging greater use of generic drugs, and many countries, such as India, China and Brazil, are mandating prices.

A number of important trends are fueling the increase in healthcare costs: An aging population, an increase in chronic disease, access to care and the cost of new technology (Deloitte, 2014a).

The Aging Population

Populations worldwide are aging due to falling birthrates and increased life expectancy (Greenberg et al., 2011). UN data reveals the global population aged 60 or above has tripled in a period of 50 years and it is expected to more than triple again during the next half century. The forecast for 2050 is that two billion of the world's population will be 60 or over in 2050. This compares to only 10% for Africa. Mexico has the youngest population in the world; however, 7.5% of its population will be 65 or older by 2017. Cancer and heart disease are major killers in many countries. Diabetes and cardiovascular illness are major problems in Latin America and China (Deloitte, 2013). These changes in population will fuel a major increased demand for healthcare. In particular, great strain will be placed on governments that offer national health benefits and pensions (Andreason, 2011). As a result, governments have begun to scale back benefits, increase the age of retirement and raise additional taxes to cope with the aging population.

Chronic Illness

Chronic diseases are the leading cause of morality worldwide, accounting for 64% of all deaths (WHO, 2011). There is a major increase in chronic illnesses, the majority of which are lifestyle related. The World Health Organization (2011) has estimated that chronic illnesses such as cancer, diabetes, and asthma are increasing at a rapid rate worldwide. By 2020, for example, it is estimated that 157 million Americans will have at least one chronic condition, and 80% of all healthcare expenditure will be on chronic conditions (Wu & Green, 2000). The situation in low-income nations is equally intractable. In China, India and the nations of Africa, cardiovascular disease is a major problem (Greenberg et al., 2011). The OECD (2010) has estimated that half of the EU population and two thirds of Americans are overweight and obese. In developing countries, approximately 3.5 million children are classified as overweight (WHO, 2011). The developing world accounts for almost 56% of cancer cases and 64% of deaths due to cancer (Jemal et al., 2011). In developed countries, morality rates due to cancer have stabilized (Eheman et al., 2012).

Access to Care

The majority of countries worldwide have major problems around access to care. These access problems are primarily due to staff shortages, infrastructure problems, patient locations and cost restrictions. In the UK, for example, in 2012, the healthcare system had a shortage of 40,000 nurses (Buchan & Seccombe, 2012). The European Commission has estimated that across the continent of Europe, there is a shortage of 230,000 doctors (Glinos, 2012). In Africa, for example, the scarcity of doctors is so intractable that these countries are unable to deliver the most basic healthcare services. In Asia, the situation is extremely variable. In Singapore, Japan, Taiwan and South Korea, for example, they offer an excellent healthcare system, whereas in Vietnam, India, China and Indonesia, they struggle to deliver the most basic healthcare (Deloitte, 2015).

New Technology

There is increased pressure to implement new technology and develop new drugs. The Economic Intelligence Unit (2011) estimated that the cost of bringing a new drug to market in 2006 was on average €1.3 billion. This represented a ten-fold increase since 1979. Deloitte (2014b) estimated the cost to be $2.9 billion. There is major investment in biomedical research and innovations in biotechnology, e-health and imaging technology. Public awareness of the role of technology has increased, and there is an expectation that healthcare organizations will have the most advanced technology and provide the best quality of care.

These challenges have forced many healthcare organizations worldwide to consider a value-driven model. In Europe, both the UK and Germany have been at the forefront in introducing aspects of *VBHC*. These innovations include cost-benefit assessment of health technology and evidence-based protocols for individual diseases. Germany, for example, through the *Arzneimittelmarkt-Neuordnungsgesetz* (AMNOG: Pharmaceutical Market Reform Law) of 2010 has implemented a scoring system that identifies the incremental benefit of newly approved drugs. In both the UK and Ireland, there exists a value-based pricing system for branded drugs purchased through the National Health Service and Health Service Executive, respectively. Sweden and the Netherlands were also early adopters of *VBHC*. The Netherlands, for example, has benefited from a collegial and well-integrated community of healthcare providers. In France, Italy and Spain, the situation is significantly different. There are initiatives taken by individual institutions or at the regional level. However, the overall implementation of *VBHC* is very fragmented.

The USA enacted the Patient Protection and Affordable Care Act in 2010, which has had major implications for the healthcare market. The world's largest health insurance program, Medicare, has implemented a value-based purchasing initiative and payment for performance (Cortese et al., 2012).

Defining the Scope of VBHC

Porter (2010), a major proponent of *VBHC*, has argued the following in the *New England Journal of Medicine*:

> Since value depends on results, not inputs, value in healthcare is measured by the outcomes achieved, not the volume of services delivered and shifting focus from volume to value is the central challenge. (p. 6)

The overarching strategic goal that underpins *VBHC* is the desire to achieve the best outcomes for patients at the lowest costs. Porter (2010) proposed that it is composed of six interdependent and mutually reinforcing components (Figure 24.1).

The six components are: 1) The organization and interaction of care into practice units rather than around specialties and departments; 2) The measurement of outcomes and costs for every patient rather than an emphasis on measures of process, compliance and changes; 3) A movement to bundled prices for case cycles rather than fee-for-service based on the "volume of services delivered" approach; 4) The integration of care delivery systems rather than each hospital or practice offering a full range of services; 5) Expansion of geographic reach rather than the limitation of service provision to an immediate geographic area; 6) The development of an enabled IT platform rather than the use of siloed 1T systems (i.e., IT systems divided up into separate IT "silos" for each organization, department or even profession). *VBHC* is premised on a multidisciplinary approach at all levels of the healthcare system. The outcomes derived for the patient are the result of collaboration and teamwork (Pollock & Godden, 2008; Dunbar-Rees & McGough, 2013). There is joint responsibility for both outcomes and costs.

Porter and Teisberg (2006) articulated a number of underlying principles that should drive a value-based approach. This formulation is frequently called "the value proposition for healthcare delivery" (Feeley et al., 2010). The first principle argues that the goal of healthcare should be value for patients and not simply a focus on lowering costs, access, equity or convenience. The second principle proposes that quality improvement is essential to contain costs and demonstrate value improvement. Porter argues that the typical scenario is that quality metrics have focused on processes due to the relative simplicity of measurement. The third principle is that there should be unrestricted competition based on results and that care should be organized around medical conditions over the full cycle of care. The fourth principle asserts that learning at the level of the medical condition drives value improvement. This will contribute to the learning and experience of the provider and lead to improved outcomes. This principle is not practiced to the degree desired, and the healthcare system is not effective in directing patients with particular conditions to high-volume providers (Gruen et al., 2009). The fifth principle advocates the integration of care across geographies and facilities, thus leading to reduced duplication of services within stand-alone units. The notion of the regionalization of care is highly controversial and politically sensitive. Therefore, it has not developed at the rate desired, and costs have not been reduced or value to the patient enhanced. Principle six states that providers need to report both outcomes and costs for every medical condition. Porter envisages that the reporting of outcomes will drive competition and

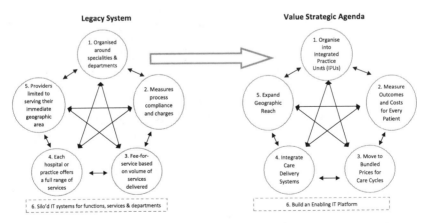

Figure 24.1   The *VBHC* Model (adapted from VBHCD Intensive Seminar, by M.E. Porter & E. Teisberg, 2014)

lead to better results. The seventh principle proposes that reimbursement must be aligned to value. This alignment must be coupled to the treatment provided at the level of the condition and not to the services provided.

These seven principles represent a tidy formulation of the essence of *VBHC*. However, not all agree that it is a very practical or realistic solution. Reinhardt (2006) calls it a utopian vision and questions the ease with which it is possible to define medical conditions and other dimensions of the seven principles. Porter (2010) is very clear on what is the essence of "value". He enumerates a number of its key features:

1) It is a customer (patient) -centric concept. Patient health outcomes are achieved relative to the costs of care. He considers value for the patient as the essence of *VBHC*, not value for other stakeholders;
2) Value is conceptualized as an outcome rather than an input. The outcomes of relevance are patient health outcomes—not the volume of services that are delivered to a patient;
3) Value includes both measures of effectiveness and efficiency;
4) Outcomes are actual outcomes of care defined in terms of patient health. The full spectrum of outcomes will constitute the quality of care received by a patient;
5) Costs refer to the total costs incurred over the full cycle of care for a patient;
6) Costs, if they are to be calculated correctly, should include the full set of resources involved in a care episode or intervention;
7) Outcomes and costs should be measured separately and they should not be confused with each other.

The reality is that a universal definition of what constitutes "value" is almost impossible to achieve. It will depend in reality on who is doing the evaluation. Patient outcomes may be assessed in terms of quality-adjusted life years. However, the assessment will need some adjustment for different patient groups or populations, or it may simply be ignored for rare diseases. In the case of some stakeholders, such as pharma and medical device companies, the patient is not the only consideration. Likewise, clinicians may assess a drug by whether it is easy to administer or a medical device by whether it is easy to use, besides its effectiveness. Value may therefore be in the eyes of the beholder. Important questions that arise in the context of defining value include:

1) Are outcomes focused on survival, quality-adjusted life years, the patient experience, patient centeredness or the wider economic and social benefits?
2) What are the issues to be included in costs? Does it, for example, include the price of treatment, total care costs and/or patients' own costs?

3) Are there any exceptions? For example, are end-of-life care, rare diseases, age groups or societal priorities excluded from the definitions of value?

Porter is very clear that the most appropriate unit for measuring value should incorporate all activities and services that are fundamental to meeting a set of patient needs. The unit of measurement must be over the cycle of care, in contrast to the "one point in time" approach. It should involve a sequence of interventions involving different types of care. Value to the patient will accrue only over time. Therefore, outcomes and costs will need to be measured longitudinally. Kaplan and Porter (2011) propose a chain of causality (Figure 24.2). The chain begins with a set of initial or pre-existing conditions. This leads to processes of care. These processes of care are influenced by a variety of structures or factors that enable them. The third stage of the chain involves health indicators. These are patient-level biological measures that predict health outcomes. The causal chain also includes patient adherence or compliance with the care system and with treatments, rehabilitation and disease prevention measures. The demonstrated effectiveness of this causal chain is premised on a number of systems that provide evidence. For example, does the organization have significantly robust data on outcomes? Does the organization have robust cost data? Are the comparators used the correct ones? To what extent is different evidence required in different markets, for different conditions, etc.?

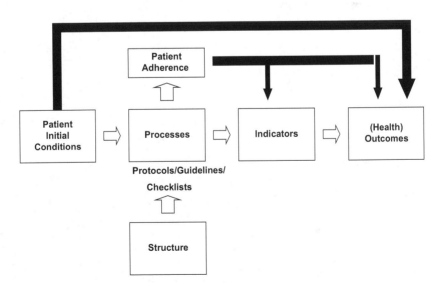

Figure 24.2 The "Causal Chain of Outcomes" (adapted from Kaplan & Porter, 2014, p. 5)

VBHC: UTOPIAN VISION OR FIT FOR PURPOSE?

Value-Based Healthcare is considered by some commentators (Porter & Teisberg, 2006; Porter & Guth, 2012) as the great panacea to all the ills that exist within healthcare. Others are more cautious (Muir-Gray, 2005; Reinhardt, 2006), and highlight the complex context that is the healthcare sector and its traditional resistance to innovation and transformational change. In Table 24.1, we summarize the normative best-practice guidelines found in the literature.

Table 24.1 Normative Best-Practice Suggestions to Implement *VBHC*: A Multiple Stakeholder Approach (adapted from Muir Gray, 2005; Porter, 2010)

Healthcare Providers
- Articulate and communicate goals that focus on superior patient value.
- Develop a culture that is patient centered and reinforce its implementation through rewards and sanctions.
- Emphasize uniqueness, excellence and results as core elements of culture.
- Structure the organization around medical conditions.
- Strategically select the range of services that the organization will provide.
- Design the organization to have medically integrated practice units and develop an explicit strategy for each unit.
- Be innovative on pricing approaches and move to single bills.

Healthcare Payers
- Create incentives to ensure that providers deliver high quality rather than volume-based care.
- Utilize a novel mix of payment schemes, including capitation, diagnosis-related groups and bundled payment approaches.
- Develop measures and generate results information on providers and treatments.
- Provide to all members a broad range of disease management prevention services irrespective of condition.
- Partner with providers, share information and reward excellence in generating patient value.

Employers
- Employers should implement an approach that focuses on enhancing employee health rather than minimizing health benefit costs.
- Ensure continuity for employees on health plans.
- Support employees in making good healthcare choices.
- Encourage employees to take responsibility for their health.
- Develop measures that emphasize the health value received by the organization.

Suppliers to Healthcare
- Manage R&D pipelines with a focus on value for the patient.
- Use value assessment and modeling processes at the early stages of R&D.
- Ensure that there is effective integration between R&D and commercial teams within pharma and medical devices organizations.

- Focus investments on drugs that are likely to succeed.
- Be informed and up to date on developments that may affect new product value.
- Ensure that clinical trials' post-marketing surveillance is undertaken as cost effectively as possible.
- Partner with payers and health technology assessment(HTA) agencies to identify their information requirements.
- Partner with providers to ensure enhanced real-world patient outcomes.
- Design incentives that include risk sharing and pilot programs.

Physicians
- Involves physicians as a key group in any innovation to deliver patient value.
- Develop and espouse a mindset that emphasizes patient value.
- Continuously champion innovation, rationalization, integration and relocation where it enhances patient value.
- Develop networks and social capital to effectively leverage healthcare across locations and geographies.
- Be a champion for the implementation of work practices that deliver value.
- Utilize multidisciplinary teams to maximize value to the patient.

Patients
- Patients should take personal responsibility for their health.
- Patients should engage in a rational way with health services.
- Champions of value-based healthcare should educate patients in health service delivery to eliminate under- and overuse.

National Governments
- Implement policy initiatives that enhance the process of care, integrate it and make it less complex.
- Promote certification and best practice standards around care cycle coverage, care management and multidisciplinary teams.
- Develop and implement a national framework of medical condition outcome registries.
- Make explicit links between reimbursement policies and practices and the reporting of outcomes.
- Develop national accounting standards that objectively and accurately measure resource utilization by patient condition.
- Encourage and develop bundled pricing frameworks.

These guidelines are universal rather than contingent in their focus. They emphasize the multi-stakeholder approach required to make *VBHC* a reality. They primarily focus on education, changes in work practices, cultural changes and reward systems and sanctions to embed such an approach to healthcare. They do, however, give limited recognition to the complexity of healthcare organizations and their structural and cultural characteristics. These contextual issues make the implementation of aspects of *VBHC* challenging. We focus on five contextual issues: 1) The complexities of transformational change and innovation in healthcare; 2) The politicized environment of healthcare; 3) The management-professional interface; 4) Organizational culture and leadership in healthcare; 5) The fragmentation of the healthcare system.

Complexities of Transformational Change and Innovation in Healthcare

Christensen and Remler (2009) argued that only disruptive innovation would transform the healthcare industry to being value focused. *VBHC* would represent a major transformation of how things are currently done in healthcare organizations. Transformational change is both radical and discontinuous. *VBHC* requires a significant dissociation from current practice and a radical rethinking of it. Its intent is to transform healthcare and disrupt the status quo within the sector. The ideas proposed by the *VBHC* concept demand frame-breaking change within a highly complex organizational context.

VBHC assumes linearity, separability and simple causation, and therefore, it may find difficulty in gaining a foothold in complex organizations. Many public policy initiatives fail because they do not acknowledge conditions of growing complexity or the need to take a more holistic perspective and tolerate complexity, uncertainty and ambiguity (Pfeiffer & Chapman, 2010). Healthcare organizations are already responding to pressures to deliver better or increased value. These include:

1) Organizing to ensure the integration of teams of specialists to deal with complex conditions (Cosgrove, 2011);
2) Measuring outcomes and increased reporting of outcomes to facilitate continuous improvement (Swensen et al., 2011);
3) Measuring and reporting costs and the use of activity-based cost accounting systems (Kaplan & Porter, 2011);
4) The use of electronic medical records systems to facilitate better decision-making around value (Sperl-Hillen et al., 2010).

These represent important changes. However, they have not transformed the healthcare sector into a value-based entity due to the inertia built into institutional structures and the self-interest of key players. Important challenges in the context of *VBHC* concern the definition of value and its measurement. These are challenging innovations for healthcare organizations. Established organizations find it difficult to change their business models because they are tied to old ways and to patients and stakeholders who want the status quo. Therefore, *VBHC* may work better where it is an emergent rather than an imposed process. *VBHC* involves many thorny and complex implementation questions, such as: Is it necessary to rethink the care pathways within health sector organizations? How should organizations manage multiple stakeholders with divergent interests? How does the concept affect provider-supplier relationships? How will providers and suppliers be paid? Does *VBHC* represent a new frontier of innovation, and how will it affect new treatments being developed or marketed? Therefore, while it is tempting to argue that *VBHC* will help deliver enhanced patient outcomes, the reality is much more complex and messy.

The Politicized Environment of Healthcare

Healthcare organizations are highly politicized. It is a highly regulated sector shaped by a variety of political forces and ideologies. Healthcare is politicized because some social groups gain more from it than others. It is amenable to political interventions and therefore dependent on political action or inaction. It is also political due to the complexity of the worldwide factors and issues that contribute to ill health. Changes in healthcare practices are slow to emerge because they happen through political processes, where the numerous stakeholders argue for their preferred courses of action. Health stakeholders typically have very different ideologies and priorities that make agreement difficult and the pace of change slow. The pessimists suggest that very little actually changes in the healthcare sector (Bambra, et al., 2003). This suggests that the wholesale implementation of *VBHC* will be difficult due to an inherently highly politicized environment. This includes both the macro- and micro-political dynamics found at the national and organizational levels.

The Management-Professional Interface

The healthcare sector is characterized by an inherent tension between managerial and professional values. Edwards et al. (2002) have argued that there is a mismatch between what doctors are trained to do and what they are required to do. They increasingly spend more time on management, communication and financial issues. Degeling et al. (2001) acknowledges the difficulties of getting professionals to engage with business processes and the need for reform. Arndt and Bigelow (2000), for example, argued that managers are required to manage in a hostile, turbulent environment where they have little or no control over much of what happens in an organization and where patients and customers are vulnerable and idiosyncratic in how they respond to what the organization does. *VBHC* therefore challenges both professionals and managers to pursue a path that balances professional autonomy with accountability, participate in value-based processes that enhance value for the patient and acknowledge the linkages between the clinical and value dimensions of care. *VBHC* initiatives that are imposed are doomed to failure. For change to happen, it is necessary to develop a common sense of purpose and develop a set of core values that are shared by both groups.

Organizational Culture and Leadership

VBHC has as its core principles ideas that challenge well-established cultural values in healthcare organizations. What works is essentially contingent on the context in which it is implemented (Mannion et al., 2005). The adoption of a "one-size-fits-all" value-based approach and encouragement of the adoption of new value-focused approaches is unlikely to be successful. This suggests that the introduction of VBHC is a long haul rather than a quick fix. Initiatives that are at odds with the core cultural values of an organization will take time and may require unexpected shifts and changes in direction. Therefore, it is important to be cognizant of contextual factors and the need for flexibility. Variations in cultural context also highlight the need to be aware of localism. Organization-wide transformational change initiatives such as VBHC may be viewed with suspicion in some parts of the system. Implementation therefore requires a more subtle approach.

Fragmentation of the Healthcare System

The healthcare system is highly fragmented. It has traditionally been organized around specialized medical disciplines, with corresponding organizational silos, and has not practiced in a wide-scale way multidisciplinary or coordinated-treatment approaches. Patients are often kept in the dark about what is happening, they often have to coordinate their own care and each encounter with healthcare professionals is essentially a new starting point. Bohmer (2009) suggested that fragmentation is particularly detrimental to the treatment of patients with acute and serious illness or illnesses that are poorly understood. He suggested that the patients are treated sequentially and in a very uncoordinated fashion. In many health systems, fragmentation is also inherent in how providers are paid. The focus on episodes of care rather than outcomes is deep seated and it produces fragmentation rather than integration. VBHC therefore faces a very major challenge simply to reverse this cycle and set of behaviors. Kaplan and Porter (2011) expressed the view that the healthcare sector has great potential to enhance value. However, fragmentation leads to sub-optimal outcomes and creates inertia and a preference for the status quo, suggesting that the potential may exist but that there is not necessarily the will to change. Swensen et al. (2010) suggested that individualized care plans and treatment approaches work against a value-based approach whose focus is on integration, standardization and quality with the goal of increased value.

CONCLUSION

Value-Based Healthcare is put forward as the great panacea to address the burgeoning cost structure of healthcare worldwide. Important principles and processes are proposed to enhance patient value. However, these principles, which on the face of it are sound, are essentially normative in nature and do not account for the role of context and the complexities of implementation in healthcare organizations. *VBHC* represents an innovation that requires the adoption of new principles, new strategies, business and operating models and, most important of all, fundamental changes in the relationships between stakeholders in the complex healthcare sector. It is best realized through an emergent approach that facilitates a value-based approach to thrive. Therefore, proponents of *VBHC* need to take more cognizance of the complexity of implementation and that one size will not fit all. Given the complexities and politicized nature of the healthcare system, implementation is a marathon rather than a short sprint.

REFERENCES

AMNOG Health Reform. (2010). Retrieved from http://www.aicgs.org/issue/health-care-reform-in-germany-2011-reform/ (accessed 19 June 2015).

Andreason, A. (2011). Will the EU survive its demographic deficit? *Yale Economic Review*, 7 (1), 19–23.

Arndt, M., & Bigelow, B. (2000). Presenting structural innovation in an institutional environment: Hospitals' use of impression management. *Administrative Science Quarterly*, 45 (3), 494–522.

Bambra, C., Fox, D., & Scott-Samuel, A. (2003). *A new politics of health*. Politics of health group, Liverpool. Retrieved from http://www.liv.ac.uk/PublicHealth/Publications/publications01.html (accessed 7 August 2004).

Bigelow, B., & Arndt, M. (2005). Transformational change in health care: Changing the question. *Hospital Topics*, 83 (2), 19–26.

Bohmer, R.M. (2009). *Designing Care: Aligning the Nature and Management of Health Care*. Cambridge, MA: Harvard Business Press.

Brook, R.H., McGlynn, E.A., & Shekelle, P.G. (2000). Defining and measuring quality of care: A perspective from US researchers. *International Journal for Quality in Health Care*, 12 (4), 281–295.

Buchan, J., & Seccombe, I. (2012). *Overstretched. Under resourced. The UK nursing labour market review 2012*. Retrieved from https://www.rcn.org.uk/__data/assets/pdf_file/0016/482200/004332.pdf (accessed 30 June).

Christensen, M.C., & Remler, D. (2009). Information and communications technology in US health care: Why is adoption so slow and is slower better? *Journal of Health Politics, Policy and Law*, 34 (6), 1011–1034.

Cortese, D., Landman, N., & Smoldt, K. (2012). *The First Step Towards Value Based Healthcare*. New York: Institute of Medicine.

Cosgrove, D.M. (2011). A healthcare model for the 21st century: Patient-centered, integrated delivery systems. *Group Practice Journal*, 60 (3), 11–15.

Degeling, P., Hunter, D., & Dowdeswell, B. (2001) Changing health care systems. *Journal of Integrated Pathways*, 5 (2), 64–69.

Deloitte. (2013). *2013 Global life sciences outlook*. Retrieved from http://www2.deloitte.com/ie/en/pages/life-sciences-and-healthcare/articles/2013-global-ls-outlook.html (accessed 19 June 2015).

Deloitte. (2014a). *2014 Global Healthcare Outlook: Shared Challenges, Shared Opportunities*. London: Deloitte Zouche.

Deloitte. (2014b). *State of the industry report*. Retrieved from http://www2. deloitte.com/us/en/pages/public-sector/articles/translational-medicine-state-of-the-industry-report.html (accessed 19 June 2015).

Deloitte. (2015). *Global healthcare outlook, common goals, competing priorities*. Retrieved from https://www2.deloitte.com/content/dam/Deloitte/global/Documents/Life-Sciences-Health-Care/gx-lshc-2015-health-care-outlook-global.pdf (accessed 19 June 2015).

Dunbar-Rees, R., & McGough, R. (2013). Team Effort: Communicating through alliance contracts. *The Health Service Journal*, **123** (6376), 26.

Economist Intelligence Unit. (2011). *The future of healthcare in Europe*. Retrieved from http://www.eufutureofhealthcare.com/sites/default/files/EIU-Janssen%20 Healthcare_Web%20version.pdf (accessed 19 June 2015).

Edwards, N., Kornaki, M., & Silversin, J. (2002). Unhappy doctors: What are the causes and what can be done? *BMJ: British Medical Journal*, **324** (7341), 835.

Eheman, C., Henley, S.J., Ballard-Barbash, R., Jacobs, E.J., Schymura, M.J., Noone, A.M., Pan, L., Anderson, R.N., Fulton, J.E., Kohler, B.A., Jemal, A., Ward, E., Plescia, M., Ries, L.A.G., & Edwards, B.K. (2012). Annual report to the nation on the status of cancer, 1975–2008, featuring cancers associated with excess weight and lack of sufficient physical activity. *Cancer* (published online first before inclusion in issue). Retrieved from http://onlinelibrary.wiley.com/doi/10.1002/cncr.27514/pdf (accessed 19 June 2015).

Feeley, T., Albright, H., & Burke, T. (2010). A method for redefining value in healthcare using cancer care as a model. *Journal of Healthcare Management*, **55** (6), 399–411.

Glinos, I. (2012). Worrying about the wrong thing: Patient mobility versus mobility of health care professionals. *Journal of Health Services Research & Policy*, **17**(4), 254–256.

Greenberg, H., Raymond, S.U., & Leeder, S.R. (2011). The prevention of global chronic disease: Academic public health's new frontier. *American Journal of Public Health*, **101** (8), 1386–1391.

Griner, B., & Hampton, T. (2013). *Navigating the New World of Value-based Healthcare Global Trends and Regulatory Reforms that Will Shape the Future of Healthcare*. New York: Quintiles.

Gruen, R., Putts, V., Green, A., Parkhall, D., Campbell, D., & Jolley, D. (2009). The effects of provider health care volume on cancer mortality: Systematic review and meta-analysis. *CA: A Cancer Journal for Clinicians*, **59**, 192–211.

Jemal, A., Bray, F., Center, M.M., Ferlay, J., Ward, E., & Forman, D. (2011). Global cancer statistics. *CA: A Cancer Journal for Clinicians*, **61**(2), 69–90.

Kaplan, R.S., & Porter, M.E. (2011). How to solve the cost crisis in health care. *Harvard Business Review*, **89** (9), 46–52.

Kaplan, R.S., & Porter, M.E. (2014). *Defining, measuring, and improving healthcare value*. Lancet commission of global surgery, 18 January, Harvard Business School. Retrieved from http://www.globalsurgery.info/wp-content/uploads/2014/01/Kaplan.pdf (accessed 30 June 2015).

Karash, J. (2013), Investing in value-based healthcare. *Hospitals & Health Networks*, **87** (5), 54–58.

Larson, S., Lawyer, R., & Silverson, M.B. (2010). *From Concept to Reality, Putting Value-based Healthcare into Practice in Sweden*. New York: Boston Consulting Group.

Mannion, R., Davies, H., & Marshall, M. (2005). *Cultures for Performance in Health Care*. Maidenhead: Open University Press.

Muir-Gray, J.A. (2005) Evidence based and value based healthcare. *Evidence Based Healthcare and Public Health*, **9** (5), 317–318.

OECD Health data. (2009). Retrieved from http://www.oecd.org/els/health-systems/health-data.htm (accessed 19 June 2015).

Organization for Economic Co-operation and Development (OECD). (2010). *Education at a glance*. Retrieved from http://www.oecd.org/education/skills-beyond-school/educationataglance2010oecdindicators.htm (accessed 19 June 2015).

Pfeiffer, J., & Chapman, R. (2010). Anthropological perspectives on structural adjustment and public health. *Annual Review of Anthropology*, 39, 149–165.

Pollock, A.M., & Godden, S. (2008). Independent sector treatment centres: Evidence so far. *BMJ: British Medical Journal*, 336 (7641), 421.

Porter, M. (2010) What is value in healthcare? *New England Journal of Medicine*, 363 (26), 2477–2481.

Porter, M.E., & Guth, C. (2012). *Redefining German Health Care: Moving to a Value-based System*. New York: Springer Science & Business Media.

Porter, M.E., & Teisberg, E. (2006) *Redefining Healthcare: Creating Value-based Competition on Results*. Cambridge, MA: Harvard Business Press.

Porter, M.E., & Teisberg, E. (2014). *VBHCD intensive seminar*. Harvard Business School. Retrieved from http://www.isc.hbs.edu/resources/courses/health-care-courses/Pages/vbhcd-intensive-seminars.aspx (accessed 30 June).

Reinhardt, U. (2006). *Health reform Porter and Teisbergs Utopian vision*. Retrieved from http://healthaffairs.org/blog/2006/10/10/health-reform-porter-and-teisbergs-utopian-vision/ (accessed 19 June 2015).

Robinson, J.C. (2008) Slouching towards value-based healthcare. *Health Affairs*, 27 (1), 11–12.

Solomons, N.M., & Spross, J.A. (2011). Evidence based practice barriers and facilitators from a continuous quality improvement perspective: An integrative review. *Journal of Nursing Management*, 19 (1), 109–120.

Sperl-Hillen, J.M., O'Connor, P.J., Rush, W.A., Johnson, P.E., Gilmer, T., Biltz, G., Asche, M., & Ekstrom, H.L. (2010). Simulated physician learning program improves glucose control in adults with diabetes. *Diabetes Care*, 33 (8), 1727–1733.

Strite, S., & Stuart, M. (2005). What is an evidence-based, value-based health care system? Part 1. *The Physician Executive*, 31(1), 50–54.

Swensen, S.J., Kaplan, G.S., Meyer, G.S., Nelson, E.C., Hunt, G.C., Pryor, D.B., & Chassin, M.R. (2011). Controlling healthcare costs by removing waste: What American doctors can do now. *BMJ Quality & Safety*, 20, 534–537.

Swensen, S.J., Meyer, G.S., Nelson, E.C., Hunt G.C., Jr., Pryor, D.B., Weissberg, J.I., Kaplan, G., Daley, J., Yakes, C., Chassin, M., James, B., & Berwick, D.M. (2010). Cottage industry to postindustrial care—the revolution in health care delivery. *New England Journal of Medicine*, 362 (5), e12.

Thomson, S., Osborn, R., Squires, D., & Jun, M. (2013). *International Profiles of Health Care Systems*. New York: Commonwealth Fund.

Watson, T. (2010). *Health Care Reform: Looming Fears Mask Unprecedented Employer Opportunities to Mitigate Costs, Risks and Reset Total Rewards*. New York, NY: Towers Watson.

World Databank. (2012). *World development indicators and global development finance*. Retrieved from http://databank.worldbank.org/data/home.aspx (accessed 19 June 2015).

World Health Organization. (2011). *Obesity and overweight*. Bulletin no. 311. Retrieved from http://www.who.int/mediacentre/factsheets/fs311/en/ (accessed 19 June 2015).

World Health Statistics. (2010). *World health organisation*. Retrieved from http://www.who.int/whosis/whostat/2010/en/ (accessed 19 June 2015).

Wu, S.Y., & Green, A. (2000). *Projection of Chronic Illness Prevalence and Cost Inflation*. Santa Monica, CA: RAND Health.

Part III

Conclusions and Future Research

25 Should Healthcare Organizations Adopt, Abandon or Adapt Management Innovations?

Carina Abrahamson Löfström, Anders Örtenblad and Rod Sheaff

In this book, the aim has been to explore the relevance of a fairly comprehensive collection of management innovations for healthcare organizations. Starting with an overview of healthcare organizations from an international perspective and a general definition of healthcare organization, the different chapters have dealt with the appropriateness of these various management innovations. In order to test the relevance, the authors have discussed which parts of the focal management innovation are relevant and if they concluded that there was a need, they also suggested adapted versions that would better fit healthcare organizations.

We have now reached the final chapter of the book, where some conclusions will be outlined based on the previous chapters. We will thus return to the question of whether, and if so, in what way, the various management innovations considered in the book could be appropriate for healthcare organizations. Thereafter, on the basis of the experiences gained from this book, we discuss how further studies aiming at relevance-testing management innovations for healthcare organizations ideally could be conducted. In the final section of the chapter, we outline a few theoretical contributions of the book.

ON THE RELEVANCE OF MANAGEMENT INNOVATIONS FOR HEALTHCARE ORGANIZATIONS: CONTRIBUTIONS FROM CHAPTERS 3 TO 24

It can be concluded that the management innovations examined in the present book have many similarities with each other. For instance, none of them (plausibly with the exception of *Value-Base Healthcare*) were in the first place developed for healthcare organizations. Rather, most of them (such as *Business Process Reengineering, Lean, Total Quality Management*) were created to better manage manufacturing companies, that is, to reduce waste, improve efficiency and enhance quality and profitability. However, some of the management innovations in the book evolved in other types of organizations (as, for example, *360-Degree Feedback* in the military) or initially had another purpose (such as *Empowerment*, with roots in the Civil Rights Movement, and *Sustainability*, focusing on the survival of the planet).

Furthermore, it can be noted that most of the management innovations in the book have several overlapping parts (as, for example, the focus on the reduction of defects in *Kaizen*, *Lean* and *Six Sigma* or the focus on the restructuring of work processes in *Business Process Reengineering* and *Total Quality Management*). The fact that some of the management innovations also have been addressed in more than one chapter but at the same time been interpreted in somewhat different ways shows their vague and/or ambiguous character (as discussed in Chapter 1 in this volume). For instance, when *Transformational Leadership* is compared to *Servant Leadership* (see McCann, Chapter 17 in this volume) it is in some parts differently interpreted than when *Transformational Leadership* is compared to *Transactional Leadership* (see Fiery, Chapter 23 in this volume).

Another similarity between the management innovations is that they all tend to accentuate continuous improvement and change rather than leading to one final result. Moreover, as mentioned in Part I of the book, the various management innovations can be categorized in different ways. Some of them deal with leadership (such as *360-Degree Feedback*, *Management by Objectives*, *Servant Leadership*, *Shared Leadership* and *Transformational Leadership*), while others deal with decision-making (such as *Consensus* and *Empowerment*). There are also management ideas on knowledge and learning (*Knowledge Management* and *Learning Organization*), marketization, corporatization and decentralization (*New Public Management* and *Decentralization*) and collaboration (*Teamwork*), and yet some others deal with quality improvement (such as *Accreditation*, *Balanced Scorecard*, *Business Process Reengineering*, *Kaizen*, *Lean*, *Six Sigma*, *Total Quality Management* and *Value-Based Healthcare*). A few of them also include the ecosystem (*Corporate Social Responsibility* and *Sustainability*). However, all the management innovations deal with more than one aspect that can be found in the other management innovations as well. For example, teamwork, which is specifically discussed in Chapter 21, which focuses on *Teamwork* as a management innovation, is taken up as an important aspect in several other chapters.

Nevertheless, several common themes can be observed between the chapters that will be presented below in three main categories: The complexity in healthcare organizations, hindrances and enablers for implementation and the human factor.

The Complexity in Healthcare Organizations

According to the contributors to the book (and also discussed in Chapter 2 in this volume), there is no doubt that healthcare organizations are far more complex than manufacturing companies (which is a statement that can be confirmed by a numerous other studies, for example, Plsek & Greenhalgh,

2001; Scott et al., 2000; Sheaff et al., 2004; Southon et al., 2005). As will be shown in this section, the contributors describe healthcare organizations as multifaceted, complicated and sometimes also unpredictable. In their examinations of whether their management innovations are appropriate, all of the chapters discuss the specific characteristics of healthcare organizations. For example, Poksinska (Chapter 13 in this volume) argues that:

> The adoption of *Lean* in healthcare can certainly contribute to several dimensions of quality care. Having said that, we must acknowledge that adopting a production system designed for car manufacturing to an advanced service system such as healthcare cannot meet all the development needs of healthcare.

Due to the fact that healthcare organizations are human intense, and people are different, for example, in abilities, past experiences, age, pain thresholds or in the need for a hand to hold, the work content for every healthcare worker becomes inevitably more or less variable in each situation. In addition, every patient may need service and support from a number of departments and professions simultaneously. Mosadeghrad and Ferlie (Chapter 22 in this volume), describe the complexity like this:

> A simple task requires the communication and cooperation of various departments and employees. Every situation and every patient are different. Patients cannot be treated like manufactured products.

Specifically, the authors of the book address the bureaucratic, legally and ethically regulated and hierarchical structures that are typical of healthcare organizations. Nevertheless, corporations in other sectors, and other parts of the public sector, are mostly also hierarchical. What differentiates healthcare hierarchies is their often professionally based vertical structures (the "silos") and the "semi-detached" character of the medical sub-hierarchy (Mintzberg, 1979), such that several somewhat autonomous professional groups and individual clinicians are expected to cooperate. The authors of the earlier chapters also consider the embedded tensions between professional autonomy and bureaucratic control (as, for instance, described by Mintzberg, 1979, in his configuration "professional bureaucracy"). Persaud (Chapter 18 in this volume), for instance, says that:

> . . .it is very important to bear in mind that *Shared Leadership* does not occur naturally in healthcare organizations [. . .] due to the hierarchical nature of healthcare professions and existing hierarchical governance mechanisms.

Another feature specific for healthcare organizations, and very different from manufacturing companies, is the matter of life and death in many decisions. For example, McCann (Chapter 17 in this volume) points to the fact that certain circumstances like acute incidents may need customized solutions:

> There are times in healthcare organizations when an authoritative leadership style may be needed, especially in times of emergency and life or death situations that need expertise to lead the situation.

This complexity in healthcare organizations affirmed by the contributors and other authors thus reveals a context in which "the clockwork universe" and "linear models" are not very applicable (Plsek & Greenhalgh, 2001, p. 628). The term "ambidextrous", as suggested by Huzzard et al. (Chapter 20 in this volume), may instead be useful to describe what is needed in healthcare organizations:

> . . .sustainable organizations need to be ambidextrous (i.e., they are able to do two different things at the same time) and efficient at managing today's demands, while also being adaptable to changes in the environment.

We conclude that the larger amount of complexity in healthcare, compared to other industries and sectors, which the contributors to the book note, points towards an answer to the question: Should management innovations be adopted as is, outright abandoned or adapted (before being adopted). Management innovations might well be needed, but they first need to go through modifications (i.e., they need to be adapted before being adopted).

Hindrances and Enablers for Implementation

The second main category that can be noted from the chapters concerns various hindrances and enablers for implementing the management innovations. Given the complex context in healthcare organizations, the contributors have discussed many themes commonly analyzed within organizational change research (e.g., Abrahamson, 2004; Czarniawska & Sevón, 1996; Greenwood & Hinings, 1996; Scott et al., 2000) and implementation research (e.g., Fixsen et al., 2005; Greenhalgh et al., 2004; Hill & Hupe, 2005; Sabatier, 1986).

When examining how their management innovation could be used in healthcare organizations, many of the authors recommend that it has to be modified according to the specific context (see Table 25.1). And this does not only mean the complexity in healthcare organizations in general, but also that the context must be reflected upon in each specific organization. It

Table 25.1 An Overview of Chapters 3 to 24 and Their Recommendations for Healthcare Organizations as to Whether the Certain Management Innovations Considered Should Be Adopted (as is), Abandoned or Adapted

Chapter No., Management Innovation & Author(s)	Relevant For Hcos?	What Do They Have To Do? How?	Forms Of Adaptation/Adoption
3. *360-Degree Feedback* Joan F. Miller	Yes, but . . .	. . . modification of methods of assessment to reduce time and communication concerns	Subtraction
4. *Accreditation* Marie-Pascale Pomey	Yes, but . . . (it varies between different external evaluations)	. . . integrate with continuous quality improvement processes	Minor alteration
5. *Balanced Scorecard* Elin Funck	Yes, but . . .	. . . modify according to the recipients' and inventors' knowledge and needs (bottom up)	Minor alteration
6. *Business Process Reengineering* Anjali Patwardhan, Dhruv Patwardhan and Prakash Patwardhan	Yes, but so far the failure rate is above 70 %, and. . .	. . . add the human aspect (patients, professionals) and ethical awareness	Adding
7. *Consensus* Marie Carney	Yes, but also needs other concepts and dimensions and. . .	. . . add the concepts of strategic involvement and organizational commitment, as well as a strong organizational culture	Adding
8. *Corporate Social Responsibility* Sherif Tehemar	Yes, but. . .	. . . use TQM as a catalyst for proper implementation	Adding
9. *Decentralization* Mark Exworthy and Martin Powell	Yes, but . . .	. . . context is vital to understand implementation and impact. Different types of decentralization may fit better with different systems and policy goals.	Minor alteration

(*Continued*)

Table 25.1 (Continued)

Chapter No., Management Innovation & Author(s)	Relevant For Hcos?	What Do They Have To Do? How?	Forms Of Adaptation/ Adoption
10. *Empowerment* Nelson Ositadimma Oranye and Nora Ahmad	Yes, but . . .	. . .modify according to different work group environments and gender, race, minority groups, certification status. Should thus be based on contingency and a dynamic application of models	Minor alteration
11. *Kaizen* Mark Graban	Yes, even better than for manufacturing	Leaders have to trust their employees	Adoption
12. *Knowledge Management* Nilmini Wickramasinghe and Raj Gururajan	Yes, but . . .	. . .also focus on non-technical success factors	Adoption
13. *Lean* Bozena Poksinska	Yes, but . . .	. . .better incorporate the patient's perspective	Adding
14. *Learning Organization* Rod Sheaff	Yes, but . . .	. . .should reflect its easier application to clinical than managerial practice	Minor alteration
15. *Management by Objectives* Grigorios L. Kyriakopoulos	Yes, but fits best with the nursing profession, and. . .	. . .managers should adopt a management style that could cope with the assets and the philosophy of the organization	Adopting
16. *New Public Management* Dawid Szescilo	Not much	Establish a "conceptual mix" that fits the specific features of healthcare systems	Major alteration
17. *Servant Leadership* Jack McCann	Yes, but not in situations where quick decisions must be made or tight deadlines must be met, and. . .	. . .use depends on context and situation	Minor alteration

18. *Shared Leadership* D. David Persaud	Yes, but fits best when complexity, interdependent tasks, employee commitment and creativity exists and. . .	. . .consider contextual factors	Minor alteration
19. *Six Sigma* Jacob Krive	Yes, but if applied in appropriate areas, and. . .	. . .modify to match organizational goals and operating mechanisms, combine with other concepts and communicate with all stakeholders	Addition
20. *Sustainability* Tony Huzzard, Andreas Hellström and Svante Lifvergren	Yes, but better seen as tools for animating dialogue in development processes, and. . .	. . .include a fourth bottom line: Clinical effectiveness	Addition
21. *Teamwork* Jan Schmutz, Annalena Welp and Michaela Kolbe	Yes, but . . .	. . .include a fourth process dimension: Learning	Addition
22. *Total Quality Management* Ali Mohammad Mosadeghrad and Ewan Ferlie	Yes, but . . .	. . .modify according to context and create supportive leadership, culture and structure	Minor alteration
23. *Transformational Leadership* Bettina Fiery	Yes, but . . .	. . .modify according to context with focus on organizational structure, mode of governance and receptivity to change	Minor alteration
24. *Value-Based Healthcare* Thomas Garavan and Gerri Matthews-Smith	Yes, but . . .	. . .modify according to context and complexities of implementation	Minor alteration

may, according to the contributors, vary between organizations and groups as well as countries:

> What is effective in one country or group may not be effective in another. (Oranye and Ahmad, Chapter 10 in this volume)

> There is not a prescriptive formula that works for any type of health-care environment, and thus one may observe a large variety of methodologies and combinations applied. (Krive, Chapter 19 in this volume)

Thus, one theme discussed by many of the authors is that there are no quick-fix-solutions for all healthcare organizations. Instead, implementation takes time and needs in-depth examinations of each organizational culture. For example, Garavan and Matthews-Smith (Chapter 24 in this volume), argue that:

> Initiatives that are at odds with the core values of an organization will take time and may require unexpected shifts and changes in direction. Therefore, it is important to be cognizant of contextual factors and the need for flexibility. Variations in cultural context also highlight the need to be aware of localism.

In addition, even if thorough examinations have been made it is, as discussed by Patwardhan et al. (Chapter 6 in this volume), hard to change organizational cultures:

> In practice, changing an organizational culture takes years, if not decades [. . .] Consultants engaged in *BPR* may aim to improve timelines, lead time and dollars' worth of savings, but the old cultural constraints can make the whole effort fail.

Therefore, as Sześcilo (Chapter 16 in this volume) states, if management innovations (in his case, *New Public Management*) are to be implemented in healthcare systems, it requires adaptations more fitting for that specific context:

> The search for new paradigm or best "conceptual mix" requires, therefore, the reaffirmation of the values embedded in the healthcare system. All organizational and managerial solutions applied in healthcare organizations require an in-depth examination from this perspective.

In conclusion, and on the basis of the above discussion, we believe that it would be fair to claim here that management innovations definitely should be considered, but in doing so, should take both the hindrances and the enablers for implementing them into account. None of the hindrances dealt with in earlier chapters seem to be totally insurmountable, and for this reason, the answer to whether management innovations should be adopted, abandoned or adapted is, on the basis of the above discussion, that they should be either adopted as is or should first be adapted and then adopted.

The Human Factor

The third main category that can be observed in the various chapters in the book is what we call "the human factor". The themes discussed in this category could be placed within the other two categories as well, since it might be perceived both as a part of the complexity in healthcare organizations and as an implementation hindrance or enabler. However, given that "the human factor" also is the very core of healthcare organizations, it has specifically been emphasized by several authors. This is also the main difference from manufacturing companies. Despite heavy investments in new technology and equipment, there is always the bedside work where people (various professionals) are taking care of (sick) people. So when it comes to the people who work in healthcare organizations, for instance, Patwardhan et al. (Chapter 6 in this volume) argue that:

> It is easy to manage a change in the equipment, structure or process, but not in the humans, who cannot be programmed like machines to work differently.

Graban (Chapter 11 in this volume) discusses the same idea when he points to the fact that the employees need to be listened to:

> It's easy for leaders to label employees as being "resistant to change" when the problem is leaders not engaging employees in developing changes and improvements from the start.

Regarding the people taken care of, the patients, some of the contributors have also emphasized their unique situation during that period when they actually are patients. Under other circumstances, they may very well be strong and able to make well-grounded choices. But when they are patients, they might not have the same strengths and capabilities, and thus might not be able to act like a customer or co-producer. Poksinska (Chapter 13 in this volume) describes it like this:

> In healthcare, the customers are people who are often fragile, vulnerable and scared, and they are unable to define the product or service they need, or explain how this would help them get better.

The fact that healthcare involves the human factor to such a high extent than perhaps no other industry or sector does indicates that the answer to the question of whether healthcare organizations should adopt, abandon or adapt management innovations is rather that they should abandon them, because most of them are developed for industries and sectors that are much less focused on the human factor. At the least, management innovations may need to go through a critical examination and adaptation before being adopted in healthcare organizations.

Conclusions

So, can it be concluded that the management innovations examined in this book are relevant for healthcare organizations? Yes, according to the contributors, they are (see Table 25.1). A few of them (Graban on *Kaizen* in Chapter 11, Kyriakopoulos on *Management by Objectives* in Chapter 15 and Wickramasinghe and Gururajan on *Knowledge Management* in Chapter 12, all in this volume) argue that certain management innovations can be adopted without modifications and recommend only changes within the healthcare organization (in terms of, first changing the managers' attitudes towards the management innovation, and, second, changing practices in accordance with what the certain management innovation prescribes). But all the other contributors suggest modifications, major or minor, of the management innovation, that is, that it needs to be adapted to be appropriate. "Adaptation" is also the most reasonable answer gained from our thematic review above; the conditions in healthcare organizations are definitely special and different from many other industries and sectors, but like any other industry or sector, there is space in healthcare organizations for improvements.

In Table 25.1, we have used a somewhat modified version of Røvik's (2011) concepts of different types of adaptation (or "translation", which is the concept that Røvik uses), which were described in Chapter 1. In addition to the concepts of "adding", meaning that some elements are added to the management innovation, and "subtraction", meaning that some elements are removed from the management innovation, which both are Røvik's original concepts, we have divided "alteration" into "major alteration", meaning that the management innovation is radically changed, and "minor alteration", meaning that the management innovation is changed to a lesser extent (than is the case in "major alteration"). We categorize suggested adaptations as either a minor or major alteration when neither of the terms adding or subtraction does it justice, and nor does simultaneous adding and subtraction. Thus, "alteration", rather signifies a transformation from one shape to another, a transformation that cannot be reduced to adding or subtraction (think, for instance, of ice turning into water turning into steam). It can be confirmed that some of the authors (Carney on *Consensus Management* in Chapter 7, Huzzard et al. on *Sustainability* in Chapter 20, Krive on *Six Sigma* in Chapter 19, Patwardhan et al. on *Business Process Reengineering* in Chapter 6, Poksinska on *Lean* in Chapter 13, Schmutz et al. on *Teamwork* in Chapter 21 and Tehemar on *Corporate*

Social Responsibility in Chapter 8, all in this volume) propose adding elements to the management innovation (see Table 25.1). It may, for example, be to "better incorporate the patient's perspective" (Poksinska, Chapter 13 in this volume) or "combine with other concepts" (Krive, Chapter 19 in this volume). In one case only—*360-Degree Feedback* (Miller, Chapter 3 in this volume)—does the author suggest that some elements need to be subtracted from the original version of the management innovation before it fully makes sense for healthcare organizations. One of the contributors (Sześcilo on *New Public Management* in Chapter 16 in this volume) puts forward that the management innovation discussed would need major changes to be relevant for healthcare organizations. But most authors suggest slight modifications, more specifically, so that the certain management innovation would be a better fit to the local complex context. It could, for example, involve adjustments according to different groups or specific cultures.

However, by concluding that the adopted or adapted versions of management innovations can be relevant for healthcare organizations, what does that mean in practice? Are they relevant for the same reasons as the initial aims of the management innovations in other sectors? The contributors have mostly discussed the benefits from the managerial (organization) perspective, which values such benefits as efficiency, quality of care and reducing waste. But, it might be that the substantive criteria of success in achieving these aims sometimes are defined differently in healthcare organizations than in other organizations. One might also ask why the management innovations are alleged to be appropriate to healthcare when most of them, according to the authors, require modifications for that setting.

For example, as Patwardhan et al. report in Chapter 6, the failure rate of *Business Process Reengineering* projects in healthcare organizations has so far been about 70%. Why should it then be implemented? The answer to that question, and what the contributors in the book have emphasized as well, might be that there are both pros and cons to any management innovation (also discussed in Chapter 1 in this volume). Instead of abandoning it completely, it seems there can be elements in every management innovation worth to at least considering. On the other hand, it also seems clear that most management innovations, at least those examined within the book, have to be adapted to be relevant for healthcare organizations, which will need to investigate thoroughly what purpose a given innovation might serve for them.

We believe that there is reason to be cautious when it comes to generalizing the conclusions from the individual chapters to every healthcare organization in the world. As we mentioned in Chapter 2 (see especially Table 2.1), some chapters focus on healthcare organizations in general, but the lion's share consider hospitals specifically. A few also discuss particular types of care, like nursing, acute care, hospital pharmacy and mental health. Some of them mention primary care and social care. The chapters also span several countries and continents, but mainly they concern American, Canadian or

European healthcare organizations. What may be true for hospitals in Australia may not be as self-evident or helpful for, e.g., primary care units in the Bahamas. At least, we cannot be sure that the kinds of healthcare settings and kinds of studies presented in the preceding chapters have not slanted our conclusions. We do dare to claim, though, that the conclusions we have drawn do appear relevant for most types of healthcare organizations in a variety of health systems. There is likely *something* of value for healthcare organizations in each and every management innovation, but most likely not *everything* is of value. The recommendations in each of the chapters in this book can definitely be used as guidelines, but each individual healthcare organization still has to make its own analysis as to what elements exactly of a given management innovation are relevant for that particular organization. Factors such as type of healthcare organization, its particular history and objectives, the national culture, etc. should be taken into account in such analyses (see Örtenblad, forthcoming). Another aspect to take into account, not only for particular organizations but also in further research, is a *stakeholder-based perspective*, which will be dealt with in the following section.

FURTHER EXPLORING THE RELEVANCE OF MANAGEMENT INNOVATIONS FOR HEALTHCARE ORGANIZATIONS

As a matter of fact, one or more stakeholder perspectives are almost always taken in studies where the relevance of certain management innovations for organizations in certain industries or sectors is tested. Our review of Chapters 3 to 24 (see Table 25.2) shows that most of the contributors take on a managerial perspective or that of the whole healthcare "organization" (which in practice, comes to much the same thing). Yet considering the professionals' perspective is also quite common. Some of the contributors consider the patient perspective and a few chapters that of society.

While the stakeholder perspective is implicit in almost all of the chapters in this book (an exception, though, is Tehemar's examination of *Corporate Social Responsibility*, Chapter 8 in this volume), the chapters contain explicit rationales for the managerial innovations. A comparison of opening paragraphs across Chapters 3 to 24 reveals certain recurrent themes. Most of the following chapters justify their respective managerial innovation as helping to achieve one or more of the following aims:

1) Raise the quality of products or services in terms of physical consistency, reliability and safety, or conversely, defect reduction;
2) Increase the speed of production or service, i.e., reducing production times and wait times, including (indirectly) the lead time for innovations to be implemented;

Table 25.2   Stakeholder Perspective(s) Taken in Chapters 3 to 24

Chapter No., Management Innovation & Author(s)	Stakeholder Perspective
3. *360-Degree Feedback* Joan F. Miller	-Different professionals (physicians, nurses) -Leaders -Patients
4. *Accreditation* Marie-Pascale Pomey	-The healthcare organization
5. *Balanced Scorecard* Elin Funck	-The healthcare organization (the managers) -Different medical professionals
6. *Business Process Reengineering* Anjali Patwardhan, Dhruv Patwardhan and Prakash Patwardhan	-The healthcare organization -Patients -Employees
7. *Consensus* Marie Carney	-Nurses/health professionals
8. *Corporate Social Responsibility* Sherif Tehemar	-The healthcare organization
9. *Decentralization* Mark Exworthy and Martin Powell	-Society -Government -Health managers
10. *Empowerment* Nelson Ositadimma Oranye and Nora Ahmad	-Healthcare workers -Healthcare organizations -Patients -Society
11. *Kaizen* Mark Graban	-Healthcare professionals -Healthcare organizations -Patients
12. *Knowledge Management* Nilmini Wickramasinghe and Raj Gururajan	-Healthcare organizations
13. *Lean* Bozena Poksinska	-Patients -The healthcare organization
14. *Learning Organization* Rod Sheaff	-The healthcare organization -Doctors
15. *Management by Objectives* Grigorios L. Kyriakopoulos	-The healthcare organization (the managers) -Nursing
16. *New Public Management* Dawid Szeście	-Society -The state
17. *Servant Leadership* Jack McCann	-The employees

(*Continued*)

Table 25.2   (Continued)

Chapter No., Management Innovation & Author(s)	Stakeholder Perspective
18. *Shared Leadership* D. David Persaud	-The healthcare organization
19. *Six Sigma* Jacob Krive	-The healthcare organization
20. *Sustainability* Tony Huzzard, Andreas Hellström and Svante Lifvergren	-Patients
21. *Teamwork* Jan Schmutz, Annalena Welp and Michaela Kolbe	-The healthcare organization
22. *Total Quality Management* Ali Mohammad Mosadeghrad and Ewan Ferlie	-The healthcare organization (the managers)
23. *Transformational Leadership* Bettina Fiery	-The healthcare organization (the managers)
24. *Value-Based Healthcare* Thomas Garavan and Gerri Matthews-Smith	-The healthcare organization

3) Increase customer satisfaction, hence loyalty, hence the "return of customer";

4) Coordinate care more closely across professions, teams and organizations;

5) Adapt to technological changes outside the organization (implicitly, other organizations', perhaps competitors or substitutes, increasing technological sophistication). Often the technology in question is IT as much as clinical, diagnostic, pharmaceutical or other production technologies;

6) Increase the organization's competitiveness, or (viewed another way) market share. A pessimistic formulation speaks of organizational "sustainability" in the sense of financial survival, an optimistic one about "economic leadership". Either way, this rationale can be combined with the previous one to focus on the assumption that consumers have increased power because they can increasingly choose between alternative providers and goods and services;

7) Raise job satisfaction, worker morale and commitment to or "engagement" with the "organization", or, more modestly, reduce absenteeism or staff turnover. (If the "organization" is seen as distinct from its workers, the term "organization" must mean "management" or "owners");

8) Reduce, or at least not compromise, cost control and profitability;
9) Increase "organizational performance" or "goal attainment". What this means depends on what kind of organization, and hence what goals, are in question. It might mean any or all the above, or "added value", return on investment (profitability) and share value (sometimes expressed in terms of whether the price of shares in the corporation adopts a given innovation, thereby keeping pace with stock market indices);
10) Adapt to a more complex or unstable external environment. Besides technical and competitive changes (see above), this catch-all category might also include changing legal and regulatory requirements. Insofar as consumerism goes beyond consumer choice between providers, these conditions might also include "consumerism" in the sense of consumers becoming better informed, more skeptical and more "resistant" to marketing.

These rationales for managerial innovations fall into two broad classes: Those that are narrowly relevant just to the process of healthcare production itself, and therefore the patient's immediate experience of it, and those relevant to a wider range of stakeholders and social relationships.

Into the narrower category of rationales, those narrowly relevant to the care production process, fall aims 1 to 5 above, i.e., those of maintaining service quality and safety, reducing wait times for treatment, increasing patient satisfaction, exploiting new clinical, diagnostic, pharmaceutical and IT developments and improving inter-organizational care coordination. These aims are obviously relevant to all healthcare systems, but in different ways to different kinds of provider organizations and clinicians. Different health systems institutionalize them in different ways.

Besides being relevant to the processes of care production (and therefore especially relevant to patients and clinicians), the other, wider-ranging rationales (aims 6 to 10 above) also involve not only additional stakeholders, but stakeholders whose interests are more likely to conflict at times. That makes the rationale for those managerial innovations more problematic in healthcare. In healthcare, it would be irrational—at least, from the patient's standpoint—to adopt a management (or any other) innovation to promote repeat business. Indeed, the number of patients returning to the hospital within a month of discharge for re-treatment of the same condition is becoming, despite some criticisms (Roland et al., 2005; Weissman et al., 1999), an internationally recognized proxy indicator for poor-quality hospital care (Van Walraven et al., 2011). At most, one might for healthcare purposes replace this aim with that of providing a good "relational continuity" of care between patients and clinicians (see above) so that these caregivers come to know the patient's medical history and personal circumstances in the round (Baker et al., 2007; Mercer et al., 2007) (but that is essentially different from the "return of the customer"). Competitive advantage is only relevant to those parts of healthcare systems where the supply of services exceeds the demand (or, differently, need—see Sheaff, 1996) for services, and patients can choose where they obtain their healthcare, and is most obviously for privately funded and corporate-provided health services. In healthcare, terms such as "organizational performance" or "goal attainment" have usually to be re-interpreted in terms of clinical outcomes (e.g., five-year survival rates, for cancers), patient safety (e.g., hospital-acquired infection rates) or epidemiological or behavioral terms (e.g., unplanned pregnancy rates, prevalence of obesity). Rather than being a means to financial ends, cost reduction is, in most health systems, a means to release funds for investment in new technologies or other service developments.

So healthcare organizations, as we have defined them above, do not always have the aims upon which many of the management innovations were initially predicated in their economic sectors of origin. Even when they do have verbally similar aims (e.g., to enhance organizational "performance" or "effectiveness"), the substantive criteria of success in achieving these aims may at times be defined differently in healthcare than elsewhere. Neither, therefore, do the stakeholders in healthcare organizations necessarily always have the same aims as can be attributed to, say, customers for other (non-distress) consumer goods and services.

A further problem, as anyone who has ever worked as a health manager is likely to tell you, is that in practice, different stakeholders' interests do not always align. Disputes about professional jurisdictions and demarcations (Ferlie et al., 2005), resistance to managerial decisions, haggling or sometimes "zero-sum" negotiations with payers (Forder & Allan, 2011), policy disagreements (Lister, 2009), labor disputes, the "gaming" of information systems and even disputes about technical questions are as much a part of everyday healthcare management life as teamwork, collaboration, "relationality" and mutual learning are. In addition to the above factors that a healthcare organization might consider, in deciding whether to adopt and how to adapt a management innovation, is its own internal micro-political climate. In particular, it might consider how each different stakeholder is liable to answer the question: "Cui bono?" or, "Who benefits from this innovation, at whose expense?" Depending on the case, one managerial innovation (e.g., the introduction of charges to patients) might prove highly contested, while another (e.g., case management) appears to benefit all concerned.

What we would like to suggest for future studies of the relevance of any certain management innovation for healthcare organizations is that stakeholder perspectives are explicitly included as an important factor. We believe that openness regarding different stakeholders' perspectives would make the conclusions about the likely effects and means of implementing a given management innovation more reliable. It can at the least be assumed that the recommendations for a healthcare organization may differ when different stakeholder perspectives are taken.

One other extension to the study of managerial innovations in healthcare is also needed. The reader will have noticed that the contributors to this book (and its editors) have focused their attention mainly on Europe, North America, Canada, Australia and New Zealand. Far less attention was given to South America, Africa and Asia, although the range of health systems and organizations, social and economic settings (in particular the range of middle- and low-income countries) is far wider, and perhaps also the range of managerial innovations there. Whatever managerial innovations may be relevant to health services in these settings, it appears reasonable to expect that they will be a somewhat different selection of management innovations to most of those discussed in this book, due to the frequent presence of (at least) the following circumstances:

1) Poor material conditions of life for large parts of the population of many of these countries, necessitating a healthcare focus on infant mortality, infectious disease, public health and nutrition, rather than upon the "medical arms race", such as between specialized doctors and hospitals (Berenson et al., 2006), for dealing with the degenerative diseases of old age;

2) Limited healthcare infrastructure and resources, necessitating a technical focus not so much on the reliability and quality management of high-technology interventions as upon the basics of maintaining physical infrastructure, hygiene and safety, the supply of basic materials (pharmaceuticals, disposables, cleaning materials, food for patients) and staff safety and payment in the healthcare provider organizations;

3) Low ratios of qualified health workers to population, and the loss of many of the most skilled to Europe and North America (Ahmad, 2005);

4) Variable, sometimes low, levels of education among patients, especially women; female literacy is an important predictor of women's and children's health status (Gokhale et al., 2004; Kickbusch, 2001; McTavish et al., 2010), and sometimes among health workers too;

5) Health systems sharply divided between high-cost, high-quality "Western" style healthcare for a minority of the population, with limited healthcare resources for the rest.

Not all health systems in middle- and low-income countries, however, succumb to these difficulties. A celebrated, if controversial, example is the Cuban health system (De Vos, 2005). Health systems and healthcare organizations that have already made progress in tackling the above problems, rather than European or North American corporations, business schools or international trade organizations, may be the source of the managerial innovations of the greatest practical relevance to other health systems in much of Africa, Asia and South America.

THEORETICAL CONTRIBUTIONS

There are two main theoretical contributions that we want to offer. Both contribute to the study of management innovations and of how their relevance for organizations in specific industries or sectors could best be tested. In particular, both apply to the relevance testing of management innovations for healthcare organizations.

The Six A's of Relevance-Testing Management Innovations

We started this book by asking whether management innovations could be adopted outright, or whether there is reason to adapt management innovations before adopting them, or whether they should be abandoned outright. We concluded that most or all of the management innovations dealt with in this book seem relevant for healthcare organizations, but after first being adapted so that they fit healthcare organizations better. But we also concluded that each individual healthcare organization still needs to make its own analysis of the relevance of each management innovation for that individual organization, with its particular characteristics and needs. The work presented in this book suggests that any relevance testing of management innovations for organizations in any specific industry or sector, or for any particular individual organization, would benefit from making an Analysis—the fourth A—open enough to have any of the three first A's—Adopt, Abandon and Adapt—as plausible outcomes.

We have also suggested that a stakeholder perspective be openly chosen and taken as the basis for relevance testing. At the end of the day, it all comes down to values—whether a certain management innovation is relevant or not is not only a question of "science", but also of rational reflections and choices. Even more, it is a matter of values, which can, for instance, be expressed in terms of various stakeholders' perspectives. Management innovations cannot be characterized only as neutral knowledge, but rather as ideologies (Furusten, 1999), in that they come with certain views and values regarding things such as what people are, why and how much we should work, and how efficient production processes ought to be (to name just a few). To continue with the A's, a fifth A would thus be the Angle that is taken when examining the relevance of a certain management innovation for any particular individual organization or organizations in a specific industry or sector. Tightly connected to this concept of Angle is the Aim (or Aims) that the chosen stakeholder prioritizes, some of which we discussed in the previous section.

Thus, the "six A's of relevance-testing management innovations"—which, we believe, would make a good start for such relevance-testing projects—involve an Analysis where Adoption, Abandonment and Adaptation all are possible outcomes, an Analysis that is based upon an explicit Angle and certain Aims.

A Terminology for Various Types of Adaptation of Management Innovations

Another contribution originating from this book is a small rethinking of Røvik's (2011) valuable concepts about the adaptation of management ideas (or the "translation" of management ideas, as Røvik [2011] originally expressed it). As stated above, we believe that there are occasions where neither "adding", "subtraction" nor "alteration" are terms that sufficiently describe the extent of the modifications required for making a given management innovation fully relevant for the organization where it is to be used. By "alteration", Røvik meant that the management innovation is radically changed, so extensively and in such a manner—we assume—that to describe the changes even as major adding and/or subtraction is not valid. When interpreting the contributors' suggestions for the adaptations of the various management innovations for healthcare organizations' use, we found occasions when the suggested modifications could not be described only in terms of subtraction and/or adding, although the modifications were still relatively minor. For this reason, we suggest that alteration as a way of adapting management innovations be divided into a major and a minor variant—major alteration and minor alteration.

REFERENCES

Abrahamson, E. (2004). *Change without Pain*. Boston, MA: Harvard Business School Press.

Ahmad, O.B. (2005). Managing medical migration from poor countries. *British Medical Journal*, **331** (7507), 43–45.

Baker, R., Boulton, M., Windridge, K., Adair, C., Bankart, J., & Freeman, G. (2007). Interpersonal continuity of care: A cross-sectional survey of primary care patients' preferences and their experiences. *British Journal of General Practice*, **57** (537), 283–289.

Berenson, R.A., Bodenheimer, T., & Pham, H.H. (2006). Specialty-service lines: Salvos in the new medical arms race. *Health Affairs*, **25** (5), w337–w343.

Czarniawska, B., & Sevón, G. (1996). *Translating Organizational Change*. Berlin, Germany: Walter de Gruyter.

De Vos, P. (2005). "No one left abandoned": Cuba's national health system since the 1959 revolution. *International Journal of Health Services*, **35** (1), 189–207.

Ferlie, E., Fitzgerald, L., Wood, M., & Hawkins, C. (2005). The nonspread of innovations: The mediating role of professionals. *Academy of Management Journal*, **48** (1), 117–134.

Fixsen, D.L., Naom, S.F., Blake, K.A., Friedman, R.M., & Wallace, F. (2005). *Implementation Research: A Synthesis of the Literature*. Tampa, FL: University of South Florida, Louis de la Parte Florida Mental Health Institute, The National Implementation Research Network.

Forder, J., & Allan, S. (2011). *Competition in the Care Homes Market*. London: OHE.

Furusten, S. (1999). *Popular Management Books: How They Are Made and What They Mean for Organisations*. London: Routledge.

Gokhale, M.K., Kanade, A.N., Rao, S., Kelkar, R.S., Joshi, S.B., & Girigosavi, S.T. (2004). Female literacy: The multifactorial influence on child health in India. *Ecology of Food and Nutrition*, **43** (4), 257–278.

Greenhalgh, T., Robert, G., MacFarlane, F., Bate, P., & Kyriakidou, O. (2004). Diffusion of innovations in service organizations: Systematic review and recommendations. *The Milbank Quarterly*, **82** (4), 581–629.

Greenwood, R., & Hinings, C.R. (1996). Understanding radical organizational change: Bridging together the old and the new institutional. *Academy of Management Review*, **21** (4), 1022–1054.

Hill, M., & Hupe, P. (2005). *Implementing Public Policy*. London: Sage.

Kickbusch, I.S. (2001). Health literacy: Addressing the health and education divide. *Health Promotion International*, **16** (3), 289–297.

Lister, J. (2009). *London's NHS: On the Brink*. London: BMA London Region.

McTavish, S., Moore, S., Harper, S., & Lynch, J. (2010). National female literacy, individual socio-economic status, and maternal health care use in sub-Saharan Africa. *Social Science & Medicine*, **71** (11), 1958–1963.

Mercer, S., Cawston, P., & Bikker, A. (2007). Quality in general practice consultations: A qualitative study of the views of patients living in an area of high socio-economic deprivation in Scotland. *BMC Family Practice*, **8** (1), 22.

Mintzberg, H. (1979). *The Structuring of Organizations*. Englewood Cliffs, NJ: Prentice-Hall.

Örtenblad, A. (forthcoming). Researcher intervention in the process of contextualizing fashionable management ideas: Some previous experiences. In A. Örtenblad (Ed.), *Handbook of Research on Management Ideas and Panaceas: Adaptation and Context*. Cheltenham, England: Edward Elgar.

Örtenblad, A., Hsu, S.-W., & Lamb, P. (forthcoming). A stakeholder approach to advising on the relevance of management ideas and panaceas. In A. Örtenblad (Ed.), *Handbook of Research on Management Ideas and Panaceas: Adaptation and Context*. Cheltenham, England: Edward Elgar.

Plsek, P.E., & Greenhalgh, T. (2001). The challenge of complexity in health care. *BMJ: British Medical Journal*, **323** (September), 625–628.

Roland, M., Dusheiko, M., Gravelle, H., & Parker, S. (2005). Follow up of people aged 65 and over with a history of emergency admissions: Analysis of routine admission data. *British Medical Journal*, **330** (7486), 289–292.

Røvik, K.A. (2011). From fashion to virus: An alternative theory of organizations' handling of management ideas. *Organization Studies*, **32** (5), 631–653.

Sabatier, P.A. (1986). Top-down and bottom-up approaches to implementation research: A critical analysis and suggested synthesis. *Journal of Public Policy*, **6** (1), 21–48.

Scott, W.R., Ruef, M., Mendel, P.J., & Caronna, C.A. (2000). *Institutional Change and Healthcare Organizations. From Professional Dominance to Managed Care*. Chicago: University of Chicago Press.

Sheaff, R. (1996). *The Need for Health Care*. London: Routledge.

Sheaff, R., Schofield, J., Mannion, R., Dowling, B., Marshall, M., & McNally, R. (2004). *Organisational Factors and Performance. A Scoping Exercise*. London: NIHR-SDO. Retrieved from http://www.nets.nihr.ac.uk/projects/hsdr/081318055 (accessed 30 June 2015).

Southon, G., Perkings, R., & Galler, D. (2005). Networks: A key to the future of health services. *Australian Health Review*, **29** (3), 317–326.

Van Walraven, C., Bennet, C., Jennings, A., Austin, P.C., & Forster, A.J. (2011). Proportion of hospital readmissions deemed avoidable: A systematic review. *Canadian Medical Association Journal*, **183** (7), E391–E402.

Weissman, J.S., Ayanian, J.Z., Chasan-Taber, S., Sherwood, M.J., Roth, C., & Epstein, A.M. (1999). Hospital readmissions and quality of care. *Medical Care*, **37** (5), 490–501.

Index